brand
management
Principles and Practices

KIRTI DUTTA

Assistant Professor (Marketing)
Bhartiya Vidya Bhavan's
Usha & Lakshmi Mittal Institute of Management
New Delhi

OXFORD
UNIVERSITY PRESS

Oxford University Press is a department of the University of Oxford.
It furthers the University's objective of excellence in research, scholarship,
and education by publishing worldwide. Oxford is a registered trademark of
Oxford University Press in the UK and in certain other countries.

Published in India by
Oxford University Press
YMCA Library Building, 1 Jai Singh Road, New Delhi 110001, India

ISBN-13: 978-0-19-806986-7
ISBN-10: 0-19-806986-3

Typeset in Garamond
by Anvi Composers, New Delhi 110 063
Printed in India by Adage Printers (P) Ltd., Noida 201301 U.P.

To my inspiration and motivation

*my husband, **Anil Dutta**, and*

*my daughters, **Yoshita** and **Ridhima***

Foreword

Several decades ago, people lugged home from local *kirana* shops unremarkable bags made from the previous month's newspaper. These contained raw kitchen consumables such as rice, sugar, flour, lentils—even *masalas*. Since everyone was buying this way there was nothing unusual. No one complained and life went on.

But there was an unarticulated problem. When the rice from the gunny bag from which the paper bag was filled was exhausted, the next gunny bag had a different quality of product. In this way, month after month consumers paid full value for their purchase but ended up buying inconsistent quality.

The reason for this variable quality was simple. The gunny bag was nameless. So even if the quality was poor, there was no one who could be held responsible. The kirana shop was simply a conduit for smuggling in dubious quality that had been sourced from a huge godown, which in turn was piled high with more nameless bags. This was the era of the commodity.

The market changed when someone raised his hand and said, 'I will guarantee excellence.' He did that by placing a name and an emblem on a plastic bag and then working to ensure that each contained quality as promised. The story of branded goods begins here.

Over the years, consumers realised that the gentleman who had promised to supply guaranteed quality had, indeed, lived by his word. And the gentleman in turn realised that the name and emblem was now being recognised as a symbol of assurance. People could blindly reach out for it and feel a sense of comfort. So for the first time, there was a value that began to be attached to the name; this was simply the premium people were now willing to pay—and, interestingly, without demur—for peace of mind.

As more consumers accepted the fact that brands offered great value, more entrepreneurs raised their hands with the promise of at least equal quality. But equal quality did not provide an edge in the marketplace and a search for a product plus began. In this way consumers became more demanding and brands more powerful.

The race for a share-of-pocket led to a highly complex market. In this volatile environment, battle-scarred category leaders were born. They were modern-day pied-pipers and they did everything right.

They researched the market, learnt to read the data that it threw up, developed products that consumers sought, created demand where none existed, crafted marketing and advertising strategies to reach an increasingly restless audience, and battled to protect hard-fought gains.

This book, *Brand Management—Principles and Practices* by Kirti Dutta, is an exceptional treatise on what makes a brand tick, what powerful doctrines come into play, the challenges that brand development faces, how brands can survive in a volatile market, why they need to be re-energised, how marketing and communications strategies are developed... in fact, everything an ardent student or a curious reader wants to know about brands is out here in this exceptional commentary of real brands, real people, and real markets.

Anmol Dar
Managing Director
Superbrands India Private Limited

Preface

A brand is not a name or an accessory added at the end of the production process. It is a value that needs to be considered at each and every step of the creation of the product. Branding is that differentiating factor that ensures the success of an organization in a highly competitive and product-cluttered world. A brand is a perceptual reality for the consumers. Consumers draw strength from the superior value associated with the perceptual entity of the brand. The brand perspective thus decides the fate of the firm in the marketplace. This is further reiterated by the fact that even though new brands are being launched, the success ratio for new brand launch is just 5 per cent. The growing importance of brand equity can be gauged by the fact that the focus of corporate mergers over the last decade has been more about the brand equity or the intangible assets of the brand rather than the existing focus on synergies to gain economies of scale.

A brand can be delineated at three levels: organizational (through its vision), internal stakeholders (through internal branding), and external stakeholders (through brand identity and image). When these three move together in unison like a wheel, it ensures that the brand will go places. Brand is therefore a powerful force that binds the consumers with the organization and provides value to both the external and internal stakeholders. Brilliant execution of a brand provides innumerable opportunities in terms of brand extensions, and successful brands can be used to endorse new brand launches, which can lead to a portfolio of strong brands.

Building a strong brand also requires an understanding of the brand in terms of product, pricing, promotion, and distribution. The Internet is an important growing media tool and is necessary both for communicating about the brand and for selling the brand. Building resilient brands requires an understanding of the brand architecture and branding strategies like brand extension and stretching. These then need to be managed over time for a profitable innings. Brands can consistently create excitement and buzz (with the help of various strategies) in the marketplace and be ageless and young forever. A brand can cash in on its effort by going global and also enhance its brand equity in the process.

ABOUT THE BOOK

Brand Management—Principles and Practices is specially designed to meet the needs of management students, faculty, and practitioners by presenting a comprehensive overview of creating, understanding, managing, and building brands. The book provides a complete understanding of brand management: from the steps that can be followed to create a brand to how the brands can be sustained for longevity and growth of the organization. It tries to demystify and simplify the concept of creation, execution, and management of successful brands for current and future brand managers. The book is an attempt to understand how to build and manage a successful brand, so that the benefits can be reaped by the organization in monetary and non-monetary terms. It explores key topics such as brand identity, brand personality, brand image-building, researching and managing brand equity, organization culture, consumer behaviour towards a brand, and positioning of the brand.

PEDAGOGICAL FEATURES

The book provides a comprehensive understanding of a brand from both the consumer and brand management perspectives. The key concepts are explored with the help of global iconic brands, with a special focus on successful and resilient Indian brands like Amul, Life Insurance Corporation (LIC) of India, Godrej, Tata, Aditya Birla Group, Boroline, etc.

Every chapter starts with outlining the scope of the chapter and concludes with key definitions and summary for better assimilation of the content. The text in each chapter is full of rich images and corporate examples and includes boxed exhibits for better understanding of the theoretical concepts explored. The critical review questions and Internet exercises help in applying the concepts studied to real-life situations. Each chapter is followed by a case study that helps in providing an understanding of the concepts studied. The case studies are contemporary and help in enhancing the analytical skills of the students. Each chapter has a link with the accompanying CD for better understanding of the concept and also CD exercise(s), wherein the student can think beyond the concepts discussed in the chapter through the videos and presentations that have been provided in the CD.

KEY FEATURES

The key highlights of the book are:

- Looks at the concepts and pioneering research works of various practitioners and authors, and provides a holistic and broader learning
- Provides rich insights into successful brands and includes exhibits with marketing insights from industry
- Includes unique topics like creating a brand, understanding organizational culture for successful branding, consumer behaviour and brand buying decisions, and e-branding
- Has been written in Indian context and numerous examples and case studies of Indian brands such as Kingfisher, Maggi, Airtel, Aircel, Micromax, ITC, and LIC have been discussed, which provide rich learning from their brand practices
- Discusses practices of global and Indian companies such as Singapore Airlines, Lux, Amul, Tata Group, Aditya Birla Group, and so on
- Explains concepts through tables, exhibits, images, figures, and case studies
- Provides Internet exercises for each chapter to practice the concept studied

The key highlights of the CD are:

- Links each chapter with the CD and provides an understanding of key concept of the chapter and includes exercise(s) for enhancing decision-making abilities
- Includes insights about renowned brands by their brand managers through video case studies, television commercials (TVCs), and presentations of iconic brands such as Aditya Birla Group, Amul, Yamaha Motors, Vodafone, McDonald's, Max New York Life Insurance (MNYL), and Adani Wilmar Group
- Includes a video on the making of Zoozoos, the popular Vodafone characters, which help in understanding the creative side of branding

COVERAGE AND STRUCTURE

The book is divided into five parts containing fifteen chapters, along with a multimedia CD. Various aspects of branding have been explored to provide a complete overview of brand management.

Part I, Overview of Brand Management, consists of three chapters.

Chapter 1, Introduction to Branding, explores the concepts of brand and branding. The history of branding, need for building strong brands, and the various challenges and opportunities that exist are explained. Chapter 2, Creating a Brand, explores the process of creation of a brand, starting from the vision and mission of the organization, the brand vision, and the creation of the brand identity to growing and sustaining brands over time. Chapter 3, Understanding Organizational Culture for Successful Brand Management, delves into the importance of aligning the staff with the brand value and performance, so that integrated welcoming experiences are delivered.

Part II, Understanding and Measuring Brand Equity, consists of three chapters.

Chapter 4, Brand Equity, gives an understanding of the concept of brand equity from consumer perspective and business customer perspective and discusses various factors contributing to brand equity. Chapter 5, Researching for Brand Equity, explains the various qualitative and quantitative measures that help track a brand and also understand the impact of various brand-building tools. Chapter 6, Measuring Brand Equity, explores the various ways by which brand equity can be measured, from the financial and consumer-based brand measures.

Part III, Understanding Consumers and Markets, consists of two chapters.

Chapter 7, Consumer Behaviour and Brand Buying Decisions, draws on the integrated approach of the main theories of consumer behaviour, how the customer decides about a purchase, and various factors affecting consumer behaviour vis-à-vis branding. Chapter 8, Brand Positioning, discusses the ways in which a brand can be positioned, so as to build a favourable perception for the brand in the target market.

Part IV, Managing Brands, consists of three chapters.

Chapter 9, Branding and the Marketing Programme, discusses the strategy to be adopted for the product, pricing, and distribution aspects of the brand and how all these strategies should provide a consistent brand image to the consumer. Chapter 10, E-branding—Building the

Brand Online, recognizes online media as an attractive tool to reach the audience and explores its use to build a brand.

Chapter 11, Branding and Marketing Communications, discusses the management of the different channels of marketing communications from the perspective of building a brand and maintaining and enhancing brand equity.

Part V, Building Resilient Brands, consists of four chapters.

Chapter 12, Brand Strategies, gives a perspective on leveraging an established brand in the market through brand extensions and various branding and naming strategies. Chapter 13, Managing Brand Architecture, provides insights into how to manage brands successfully and how the brand portfolio can be rationalized to maintain a bouquet of successful brands. Chapter 14, Brands Over Time, discuses a number of strategies leading to brand longevity and strategies that can help the brand stage a comeback and be successful. Chapter 15, Brands in a Borderless World, provides an understanding of the various challenges and opportunities that a brand must address while going global. Localization and standardization strategies have been discussed along with the brand strategy that can be followed for global brand success.

IN THE CD

The CD content is closely linked to the main text. A CD icon in the left margin of the text indicates digital support. This content, which would be very useful for classroom sessions, is divided into the following two modules.

Understanding the Text This module contains 24 videos, 5 presentations, 6 e-cards, and 12 wallpapers. Each chapter has a link with the CD for better understanding of the concepts through the accompanying material.

CD Exercises This module contains 15 videos. Through these, the student can think beyond the concepts discussed in the chapter.

System Requirements

- Operating System: Windows 2000 and higher
- Flash Player: Version 9 and higher
- Processor Speed: 500Mhz
- Sound card and speakers

Note: For security reasons, this CD is copy-protected. Users working on a LAN may need administrative rights to run the CD the first time.

CD Content

The CD content is divided in the following way:

Chapter	Understanding the Text	CD Exercises
1. Introduction to Branding	• Amul Corporate Ad	• Aditya Birla Corporate Ad – The Chase
2. Creating a Brand	• Presentation on Creating the Aditya Birla Brand	• Adani Wilmar Corporate Ad

Chapter	Understanding the Text	CD Exercises
3. Understanding Organizational Culture for Successful Brand Management	• Presentation on Organizational Culture at Aditya Birla	–
4. Brand Equity	• Fortune 5 ka Ashirwaad TVC • Fortune Kachi Ghani Oil TVC • Fortune Saina Nehwal TVC	• Idea Date TVC • Idea Glory TVC
5. Researching for Brand Equity	• Presentation on Aditya Birla Brand Research	–
6. Measuring Brand Equity	–	–
7. Consumer Behaviour and Brand Buying Decisions	• Presentation on MNYL Shiksha Plus • MNYL Actor TVC • MNYL Painter TVC • MNYL Cricketer TVC	• MNYL Pension Plan TVC
8. Brand Positioning	• Background Music Vodafone Zoozoo TVC • Beauty Alert Vodafone Zoozoo TVC • Busy Message Vodafone Zoozoo TVC • Call Filter Vodafone Zoozoo TVC • Prayers Vodafone Zoozoo TVC • TVC of Idea 3G Gym	• MNYL Karo Zyaada ka Irada TVC • MNYL Your Partner for Life TVC
9. Branding and the Marketing Programme	• TVC of India Yamaha Motors	• Idea Language TVC
10. E-branding— Building the Brand Online	• Six Vodafone Zoozoos e-cards • Twelve Vodafone Zoozoo Wallpapers	–
11. Branding and Marketing Communications	• Video on the Making of Vodafone Zoozoos	• TV Interview of Mrs Rajashree Birla • Fortune Refined Oil TVC
12. Brand Strategies	• Fortune Kachi Ghani TVC • Fortune Soya Oil TVC • Fortune Sunflower Oil TVC (Tamil)	• Corporate Ad of Amul • MNYL Life Insurance TVC • MNYL College Plan TVC • MNYL Pension Plan TVC
13. Managing Brand Architecture	• Fortune Kachi Ghani TVC • Fortune Soyabean TVC • Fortune Refined Oil TVC	• Idea TVC
14. Brands Over Time	• Presentation of Various Topical Print Ads of Amul	
15. Brands in a Borderless World	• Presentation on McDonald's • European McDonald's TVC • Indian McDonald's TVC	• Aditya Birla TVC—Taking India to the World

Acknowledgements

I would like to express my heartfelt gratitude to a number of individuals without whose support and encouragement I would have not been able to complete this work.

The heavenly blessings of my parents-in-law, Late Mrs Krishna Dutta and Mr Manohar Lal Dutta, have always been a source of divine inspiration in the accomplishment of my meaningful endeavours.

The role of my parents, Mrs Sudesh Mehta and Mr K.K.M. Mehta, in making me what I am today is unfathomable.

I would like to commend my husband, Mr Anil Dutta, for always standing by me and cheering me on. His constant encouragement has had a big influence on my research agenda and work. My daughters—Yoshita and Ridhima—have been a constant source of inspiration and energy. Without them, this book would never have been possible.

I would like to thank Bharatiya Vidya Bhavan, Shri Ashok Pradhan (currently heading the Bhavan's Delhi Kendra and former Secretary, Government of India), Bhavan's Usha & Lakshmi Mittal Institute of Management (BULMIM), and Dr Rattan Sharma (Director, BULMIM) for the motivation and support provided.

My heart-felt gratitude and thanks to Mr Anmol Dar, Managing Director, Superbrands India Pvt. Ltd for his continued and invaluable support through the development of the text and for taking crucial time out and writing the foreword for the book.

The effort of Dr (Mrs) Pragnya Ram, Group Executive President – Corporate Communications and CSR of the Aditya Birla Group in penning down a case study and three presentations for the book is something I cherish. In spite of her busy schedule, she managed to give a compelling inside view of one of the iconic corporate brands of India. The wealth of information provided would otherwise not have been possible for me to develop as an outsider.

I would also like to thank Mr Anil Katyal, Vodafone, for providing the invaluable inside perspective on the making of the Zoozoo phenomenon, which provides rich creative learning experience, where the user can witness firsthand the development of the concept of building a brand character and its successful implementation.

I would like to express deep thanks to the following individuals and institutions, which have been very supportive in sharing their resources for this publication. The vivid images of the print ads and the insights into various iconic brands that have been an added resource for our exhibits and have provided a crisp perspective to the discussion were possible courtesy Superbrands India. My sincere thanks to Mr Anmol Dar and the team for putting special efforts into arranging the same, especially when their own edition was going into print. The videos and presentations in the CD were possible due to the efforts of Dr (Mrs) Pragnya Ram (for Aditya Birla corporate ads, presentations, and Idea ads); Mr R.S. Sodhi and his team (for brand Amul ads); Ms Monica Mudgal, Ms Anisha Motwani, Mr Sumit Sehgal and their team (for ads and presentation for MNYL); Ms Abha Mary Xess and Vikas Raheja (for brand Yamaha ad); Mr Angshu Mallick and his team (for the various Adani Wilmar and Fortune ads); Mr Anil

Katyal and his team (for the Vodafone ads and the making of the Zoozoo phenomenon); and Mr Rameet Arora and Ms Amrita Pai (for the presentation and ads on McDonald's).

I would also like to express my thanks to *Economic Times* and *Business Standard* for coming out with excellent readings and articles, which provided current information in the world of brands and which I have woven into the fabric of the text.

I would like to express my heartfelt thanks to my brother-in-law Vijay Bali and sister Neelam, the caring Ankita and the confident and charming Tarun, brothers Dalip, Ramesh, Yash, sister-in-law Archana, sister Jaya, brother-in-law Rishi Kinger, my angels Mahima, Devya, Catherine, Palak, Divya, Abhijat and Varun, who have always been on my side and provided the motivation to progress in my professional career.

The role of Prof. H.G. Parsa and Mr Ajay Jaitly for all their motivation and support for my research endeavours is something I really cherish. The presence of friends such as Anjali Tuteja, Dr Urvashi Makkar, Usha, Meena, Dr Swati Singh, Pankaj, and Kirti Madan has always encouraged me.

The contributions of Sanjay Sharma, Amit Bhargava, Akansha Lamba, and Tanya Seth and their constant support has been a source of great strength. A special word of thanks to dear Sandeep Kumar Dash and Vaibhav Agarwal who provided technical support for developing the CD accompanying the book. Their timely support is much appreciated and I would remember their contribution forever.

I would like to thank the entire team of Oxford University Press for the standards laid by them and for in motivating me to improve the earlier drafts. The painstaking efforts of the editorial team and their constructive feedback are indeed commendable and have always encouraged me. I thank them for orchestrating the entire work.

I would like to thank all my students for developing my perspective over the years. Their inquisitive minds have always challenged the limits and helped me explore and expand the learning curve.

Kirti Dutta

Features of the Book

Creating a Brand

Understanding Organizational Culture for Successful Brand Management

E-branding—Building the Brand Online

Consumer Behaviour and Brand Buying Decisions

Managing Brand Architecture

Exclusive Chapters

Includes exclusive chapters that help in better understanding brand management

Learning Objectives

Includes the main objectives/concepts that would be discussed in the chapter

LEARNING OBJECTIVES

After reading this chapter, you will be able to understand the following:

- Concept of branding
- Significance of branding
- How branding evolved
- Need to build strong brands
- Key issues in branding

ABOUT THE CHAPTER

In this book, we begin the journey of learning about branding by first exploring the concepts behind brands and branding. This chapter introduces the idea of a brand. It begins by tracing the history of branding, so as to give an idea of how branding has evolved over time and where it stands today. The chapter then builds a case for the need to build strong brands, and discusses the various challenges and opportunities that exist, which can be leveraged by organizations to create perceptual differentiation in the minds of the customers. Organizational success in the twenty-first century is defined by 'what' the organization does (i.e., what products or services it offers) and most importantly 'who' the organization is (i.e., the corporate brand) (Keller and Aaker 1998; Keller and Richey 2006). This highlights the importance of building a successful brand in a highly competitive and maturing market scenario.

Chapter Introduction

Provides the scope of each chapter

CD Links

Includes CD links that aid in better understanding of the concepts discussed in the book

 See how Amul is providing functional benefits to its consumers through the use of its moppet as a symbol.

Brand–customer relationships This includes the relationship the brand develops with its customers, and consumers can associate the brand as their party companion, friend, adviser, etc. For example, Titan launched its Raga series targeted at women with the 'ek khoobsorat rishta' (a beautiful relationship) ad featuring Rani Mukherjee. The ad showed Rani waiting for her man with the watch as her companion.

 See how Amul is providing functional benefits to its consumers by providing brand/customer relationship.

Exhibits

Includes a number of exhibits on Indian and global brands

Exhibit 1.4   Branding Eggs

The approximate consumption of eggs in India stands at 360 crore per month, and out of this around 60 lakh eggs are from the branded category. This segment is catching up in the metros with a growth rate of 20 per cent. Suguna group, Vangili Feeds, Keggs, and SKM are some of the key players in this segment that have differentiated their eggs on the basis of protein, less fat content, herbal features, odourless eggs, etc.

These eggs ensure quality and convenience to the customers, are hygienic, and have a premium look. Modern retail has given a fillip to retailing of branded eggs with stores such as Nilgiris, Easy Day stores, Spencers, More, etc. storing these branded eggs. The eggs are priced higher than the normal eggs, and if a pack of six normal eggs cost ₹18, the same number of branded eggs may cost up to ₹45 (Sujatha 2010).

Images

Includes various print advertisements, screenshots, and colour plates

Figures

Includes numerous of figures for easy comprehension

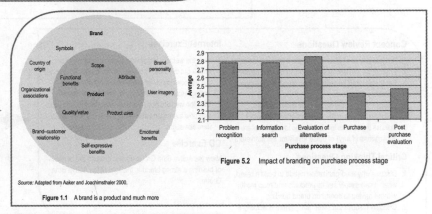

Source: Adapted from Aaker and Joachimsthaler 2000.

Figure 1.1   A brand is a product and much more

Figure 5.2   Impact of branding on purchase process stage

Tables

Includes numerous tables that supplement the concepts discussed

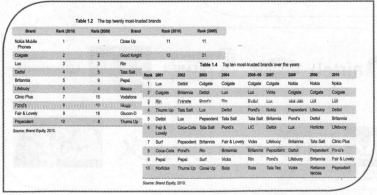

Table 1.2   The top twenty most-trusted brands

Brand	Rank (2010)	Rank (2009)	Brand	Rank (2010)	Rank (2009)
Nokia Mobile Phones	1	1	Close Up	11	11
Colgate	2	2	Good Knight	12	21
Lux	3	3	Rin		
Dettol	4	5	Tata Salt		
Britannia	5	9	Pepsi		
Lifebuoy	6	4	Maaza		
Clinic Plus	7	15	Vodafone		
Pond's	8	10	Mugu		
Fair & Lovely	9	18	Glucon-D		
Pepsodent	10	8	Thums Up		

Source: Brand Equity, 2010.

Table 1.4   Top ten most-trusted brands over the years

Rank	2001	2002	2003	2004	2005–06	2007	2008	2009	2010
1	Lux	Dettol	Colgate	Colgate	Colgate	Colgate	Nokia	Nokia	Nokia
2	Colgate	Britannia	Dettol	Lux	Lux	Vicks	Colgate	Colgate	Colgate
3	Rin	Colgate	Pond's	Rin	Dettol	Lux	Tata Salt	Lux	Lux
4	Thums Up	Tata Salt	Lux	Dettol	Pond's	Nokia	Pepsodent	Lifebuoy	Dettol
5	Dettol	Lux	Pepsodent	Tata Salt	Tata Salt	Britannia	Pond's	Dettol	Britannia
6	Fair & Lovely	Coca-Cola	Tata Salt	Pond's	LIC	Dettol	Lux	Horlicks	Lifebuoy
7	Surf	Pepsodent	Britannia	Fair & Lovely	Vicks	Lifebuoy	Britannia	Tata Salt	Clinic Plus
8	Coca-Cola	Pond's	Rin	Britannia	Britannia	Pepsodent	Dettol	Pepsodent	Pond's
9	Pepsi	Pepsi	Surf	Vicks	Rin	Pond's	Lifebuoy	Britannia	Fair & Lovely
10	Horlicks	Thums Up	Close Up	Bata	Bata	Tata Tea	Vicks	Reliance Mobile	Pepsodent

Source: Brand Equity, 2010.

SUMMARY

Measuring brand equity is important for an organization as it provides feedback about its branding activities. The measured equity is a report card of the organization and provides a backdrop for taking necessary action, so that the brand maintains its differentiation and lead in the market. The financial perspectives provide monetary value for brand equity and are important for mergers and amalgamations, whereas the customer perspectives provide a sound basis for the strategic and tactical marketing strategies of an organization.

The various ways by which both can be measured are discussed and the methods that may be used by the organization, keeping in mind the nature of the organization, are outlined. The ways in which brand value or the financial value can be measured are cost-based valuation, market-based valuation, the royalty-relief method and the economic use method. Brand strength or the customer-based measures that can be adopted by an organization are: The Brand Asset Valuator Model and the Aaker Model.

The Brand Asset Valuator Model developed by Young and Rubicam measures brands on the basis of differentiation, relevance, energy, esteem and knowledge. On the basis of the brand's performance along these parameters they are then categorized into four quadrants—unfocused/new, niche/unrealized potential, leadership declining and eroding. The Aaker Model consists of loyalty measures, perceived quality, awareness, differentiation measures and market-behaviour measures. These two measures can also be combined to measure the performance of an organization like in the example of Millward Brown discussed in the chapter.

Summary

Includes chapter-end summary that aids in recapitulation of the concepts discussed

Key Terms

Includes the main terms discussed in the chapter, along with brief definitions

KEY TERMS

Brand associations   Anything and everything that is linked to a brand in the memory of the consumer.
Brand attribute   The tangible and intangible features along with the physical characteristics of the brand.
Brand essence   It is the brand identity that is meant to energize the internal audience of an organization.
Brand gap   The gap caused due to the difference between the brand identity established by the company and the brand image perceived by the customers.

Brand identity   A set of associations that the brand strategist seeks to create or maintain.
Brand image   A set of beliefs held about a particular brand by consumers.
Brand personality   A set of human characteristics associated with the brand.
Brand tagline   It is the brand positioning that is communicated to the external audience.

Concept Review Questions

1. What is a brand? How is it different from a product?
2. Enumerate five benefits of branding for the customers.
3. Enumerate four benefits of branding from the organization's perspective.
4. Discuss the various issues in branding. Which, according to you is the most important and why?
5. Discuss the various levels of brand loyalty. What are the implications (if any) of these levels for the marketers?

Critical Thinking Questions

1. Discuss why an organization needs to build a brand, when it can simply sell its products and reap profits without having to spend on brand building.
2. Critically discuss the statement, 'There is actually a difference between a product and a brand'.

Internet Exercises

1. Visit the website http://www.sugunapoultry.com and check out the various brands of this group. Enumerate the various brands of value-added eggs they are selling. How have they tried to brand these eggs?
2. Visit the website http://www.dhampuresugar.com and see how the organization has branded a commodity item like sugar.

CD Exercise

View the Aditya Birla Group ad and discuss the benefits of building a strong brand in the light of the Aditya Birla Group.

Exercises

Includes a variety of chapter-end exercises that help in applying the concepts studied to real-life situations

Case Studies

Includes cases of various Indian and global brands (with discussion questions), which help in providing an understanding of the concepts studied

About the CD

Each chapter has links with the accompanying CD for better understanding of the concepts and also includes CD exercises, wherein the student can think beyond the concepts discussed in the chapter. The CD includes videos and presentations of the following brands.

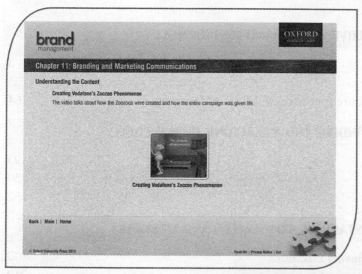

Understanding the Content

Includes videos and PPTs and key learnings that aid in better understanding and application of the concepts discussed in the book

CD Exercises

Includes videos and presentations that help the students think beyond the concepts discussed in the book and enhances their decision-making abilities

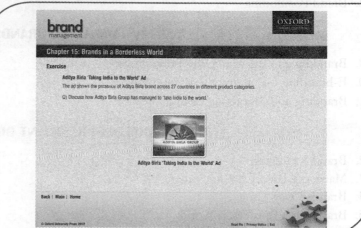

Brief Contents

Contents

PART II   UNDERSTANDING AND MEASURING BRAND EQUITY

PART III   UNDERSTANDING CONSUMERS AND MARKETS

PART V   BUILDING RESILIENT BRANDS

List of Colour Plates

Part I
OVERVIEW OF BRAND MANAGEMENT

Introduction to Branding 1

LEARNING OBJECTIVES

After reading this chapter, you will be able to understand the following:

- Concept of branding
- Significance of branding
- How branding evolved
- Need to build strong brands
- Key issues in branding

ABOUT THE CHAPTER

In this book, we begin the journey of learning about branding by first exploring the concepts behind brands and branding. This chapter introduces the idea of a brand. It begins by tracing the history of branding, so as to give an idea of how branding has evolved over time and where it stands today. The chapter then builds a case for the need to build strong brands, and discusses the various challenges and opportunities that exist, which can be leveraged by organizations to create perceptual differentiation in the minds of the customers. Organizational success in the twenty-first century is defined by 'what' the organization does (i.e., what products or services it offers) and most importantly 'who' the organization is (i.e., the corporate brand) (Keller and Aaker 1998; Keller and Richey 2006). This highlights the importance of building a successful brand in a highly competitive and maturing market scenario.

SIGNIFICANCE OF BRANDING

Branding is one of the key issues and biggest challenges in corporate and marketing strategies (Opoku, Abratt, and Pitt 2006). A product that is not branded is a commodity, such as sugar, rice, etc., and while purchasing a commodity, one only considers its physical attributes and benefits. A brand, on the other hand, is a 'lens through which the consumers view the product and the firm' (Blythe 2007). It is basically a product with added dimensions that make it different in one way or another from other products that satisfy similar needs (Keller 2004). For the consumers, a brand is a product, and the brand identifies the maker or the seller and the promise of consistently delivering the features/benefits that the consumers desire from the brand (Kotler and Keller 2005). Exhibit 1.1 shows an instance of a brand delivering on the promise of style.

Brand association represents some product quality in the mind of the customers. (*Superbrands,* 2009) For instance, when a customer purchases Nike footwear, some assurance of quality comes with it and the subsequent confidence that the product is going to be of specific standards (Jauhari and Dutta 2010). This highlights the fact that a brand name, apart from identification, also provides a differential advantage, i.e., how the brand is different from

Exhibit 1.1   The Status Dilemma

Courtesy: Superbrands.

Image 1.1a   Tupperware's high level of association with style; also see Plate 1

Neha is a working woman, and she needs a lunch box to carry to office. She remembers her father leaving for work every morning clutching his colourless stainless steel lunch box. But Neha shudders at the thought of the look on her colleagues' faces if she walks into office with such a lunch box. Neha has a number of options available in the market to choose from, but what she needs are bright trendy containers that can keep food fresh for longer periods of time.

Neha found exactly what she was looking for when her friend Meena brought her lunch box to office one day. Meena told her about Tupperware—a global brand, recognized the world over. Tupperware products are excellently designed (see Image 1.1a) and have won prestigious awards like the Red Dot Award in 2009 (an award for excellence in product design instituted by Design Zentrum Nordrhein Westfalen in Essen, Germany), and the company has also featured in Forbes.com Platinum 400—America's Best Big Companies List—for the sixth time in a row in 2009. Tupperware has 'a range of high quality, lightweight, rust- and break-proof, colourful, airtight, stylish containers, which keeps food fresh for longer, thus avoiding waste' (*Superbrands,* 2009) (See Image 1.1b). They are leak-proof as well, which means that Neha can carry and store curry and gravy items.

Image 1.1b   Brand to the rescue

other products satisfying the same needs and wants of the consumer. This is why branding is gaining importance, and more and more products are being branded (Datta 2003), from commodity items such as salt (Tata Salt) and sugar (Dhampure Sugar) to technical gadgets such as the iPad and the Kindle. In spite of the cost involved, one hardly finds anything that is unbranded, as branding has a number of advantages and marketers look to tap these via their brands.

HISTORICAL PERSPECTIVE OF BRANDING

How did branding come into being? What functions does it perform? Has there been a change in its functions over time? Has the concept of branding changed at all? These are some of the questions that come to mind when we discuss the concept of branding. Let us now develop an understanding of the same.

Studies show that brands and branding are not a recent phenomena. In fact, branding has existed for ages and can be traced back to the time when human civilizations originated. Early language was developed to convey information about two things—religion and business transactions. Business transactions ('who' is involved, 'what' was transacted, and 'how' much) were recorded using symbols. These symbols were pictorial in nature (also known as brand marks, logotypes, or icons) and were sometimes accompanied by some text and the use of colour. These 'early brands' can be called 'proto-brands' and their elements—i.e., the use of a logo, text, and colour—are important for brands even today (Moore and Reid 2008). Take, for example, the logo of Anchor Electricals. It includes a pictorial symbol, some text, and a red and white colour combination, which denotes stability and dependability (*Superbrands,* 2009) (see Image 1.2 for a black-and-white representation).

Image 1.2 Logo of Anchor Electricals

A look at the history of the Harappan or Indus Valley Civilization, which existed in 2250–2000 BCE, shows the prevalence of branding in the form of seals. Craftsmen in Harrapan cities crafted stone and bronze seals, which were sold to merchants. These seals were attached to goods were used for dispatching information and for trademarking goods. The seals were used to identify the sender of the merchandise and the markings were used for storing information useful for trading—for manufacturers, re-sellers, and the government. According to Moore and Reid (2008), information helped in performing various functions of marketing like 'sorting, storage, and transportation'. The use of Lord Shiva on the seals denotes the secondary use of seals to transfer some imagery to potential buyers or users. These seals are 'the earliest known examples of branding', and were used by merchants to 'brand their wares'. The seals are called 'proto-brands or early type of brands, as they perform the function of modern-day brands by giving information regarding the quality and origin of the brand, and help in logistical functions as well.'

Until the Iron Age (825–336 BCE), temples and palaces controlled the socio-economic activities. The Iron Age saw the rise of the entrepreneurial culture, which was market-oriented. This lead to market competition and gave an impetus to branding, as various entrepreneurs started branding their wares both for labelling and for use of imagery. Potters started branding their works as early as the seventh century BCE and Sophilos was the first Athenian potter to identify his work. This was done primarily to denote pride in the work and to elicit further orders. Mottos and slogans were used on Greek pottery to convey elaborate information or to provide 'an image to the potential buyer'. A motto on a cup imported into Italy from Rhodes may be history's first recorded commercial advertisement: 'Nestor (a hero from Greek mythology) had a most drinkworthy cup, but whoever drinks of mine will straightaway be smitten with desire for the fair-crowned Aphrodite.' This is an early example of using sex to sell wares, as Aphrodite is the goddess of beauty, sex, and love.

The Greek market revolution around the 6th century BCE had lead to an entrepreneurial culture, and a look at the pottery industry of that time reveals the fact that in Greece, potters were making wares targetted at specific markets. Some potters were designing artistic wares and branding them to guarantee the content and also to market an image of value, power, etc. There were also those who produced less artistic wares, which targeted the mass markets. These potters, however, had to create persuasive packaging and attractive images to beat the competition at the retail level. The competition was intense, as the layout of the marketplace was such that the sellers were segregated on the basis of the products category of. Therefore, various brands of pottery were side by side. This shows a gradual transition of a brand from 'transactional to transformational' (Moore and Reid 2008). The transactional function was utilitarian and provided information regarding the quality and the origin of the wares, which helped reduce risks and uncertainty at the time of purchase. The transformational function was fulfilled by building an image for the brand and included 'status/power, inherent value, and finally, the development of a brand personality. These brand characteristics, through substantial efforts by marketers, connect well to the consumer side of the equation, relating to consumers' cognitive representation of a brand or 'brand knowledge' as information (awareness, attributes, benefits) and image (images, thoughts, feelings, attitudes, and experiences)'.

Moore and Reid (2008) state that while evidence from early societies proves that logos have been used 'for as long as the record allows us to identify them the use of the term 'brand' only appears as such much later on in history. The term 'brand' became extended to 'branding' as an act wherein humans were stamped with embers or hot irons (also known as 'pyroglyphics') to identify harlots or wrongdoers, or for the identification of animals.' The various characteristics of a brand from the early Bronze Age to the current times are highlighted in Table 1.1.

The concept of branding evolved further in the twentieth century and the concept of brand personality gradually came into being. Brand personality is 'the set of human characteristics associated with a brand' (Aaker 1997). Brand personality enables consumers to express themselves through a brand. Aaker segregated five different dimensions that people associate with brands—sincerity, excitement, competence, sophistication, and ruggedness. Brand personality is not static, but evolves with the customers over time. We see a gradual transition of a brand from the utilitarian—where it provided information regarding logistics and origins in order to reduce a sense of risk and uncertainty (and thereby enhanced perceived quality) at

Table 1.1 Evolution of brand characteristics

Brand characteristics	Early Bronze IV (2250–2000 BCE) The Indus Valley	Middle Bronze Age (2000–1500 BCE) Shang China	Late Bronze Age (1500–1000 BCE) Cyprus	The Iron Age revolution (1000–500 BCE) Tyre	The Iron Age (825–336 BCE) Greece	Modern times
Information logistics	√					
Information origin	√	√	√	√	√	√
Information quality	√	√	√	√	√	√
Image power	√		√	√	√	√
Image value			√	√	√	√
Image personality						√

Source: Adapted from Moore and Reid 2008.

the time of purchase—to the addition of complex characteristics like image building (including status, power, value), and finally brand personality. Thus, over the years, there was a transition from the transactional (information-related) purpose of the brand to the transformational (image-related) purpose, where the brand personality helped in lending an image to the brand. Since consumption is culture and time-specific, 'the ultimate role of the brand is to carry and communicate cultural meaning that is transactional (information-related) as well as transformational (image-related) in character' (Moore and Reid 2008).

BRAND DEFINED

According to the American Marketing Association, a brand is 'a name, term, sign, symbol, or design, or a combination of these, intended to identify the goods or services of one seller or group of sellers and to differentiate them from competitors'. This definition answers the what, why, and how aspects of a brand. The 'what' aspect of a brand is answered by 'a name, term, sign, symbol, or design, or a combination of them', the 'why' aspect is answered by 'to identify the goods or services or a seller or group of sellers', and the 'how' aspect by 'differentiating them from competitors'. Exhibit 1.2 gives some facts of the Bata Shoe Organization—an iconic brand that has stood the test of time.

Exhibit 1.2 What You Didn't Know about Bata

- The Bata Shoe Organization (BSO) was founded by Tomas Bata on 24 August 1894 in Zlin (a town in former Czechoslovakia and now in the Czech Republic).

- Over the years, Bata has established itself globally and operates more than 4600 retail stores in over 50 countries.

Contd

Exhibit 1.2 *contd*

- Bata is estimated to serve one million customers each day and employs more than 40,000 people.
- It has sold more than 15 billion pairs of shoes— more than the number of people who have walked the earth during this time. If all the shoes sold by Bata are laid end to end, they would extend to 12 million kilometres—more than 30 times the distance between the earth and the moon.

- The Bata pricing is not a sales ploy and has nothing to do with psychological pricing as is widely believed. The numeral 9 is used because the founder, Tomas Bata, was a ninth generation shoemaker.

Source: Superbrands 2009.

A product becomes a brand when some dimensions are added to it to differentiate the product in some way from other similar products. The dimensions can be rational, functional, and/or tangible, or they can be emotional, symbolic, and/or intangible. In the former case, the dimensions can be related to the performance of the brand and in the latter case, 'related to what the brand represents' (Kotler and Keller 2005). Thus, a brand can also be defined as 'a product that provides functional benefits plus added values that some consumers value enough to buy' (Jones 1998). At the operational level, the function of the brand is to convey the identity of the brand, that it 'embodies a specific set of unique features, benefits, and services' to the consumers (Mascarenhas, Kesavan, and Bernacchi 2006). The top twenty brands of the year 2010 are given in Tables 1.2 (most-trusted brands) and 1.3 (most-trusted service brands).

Table 1.2 The top twenty most-trusted brands

Brand	Rank (2010)	Rank (2009)	Brand	Rank (2010)	Rank (2009)
Nokia Mobile Phones	1	1	Close Up	11	11
Colgate	2	2	Good Knight	12	21
Lux	3	3	Rin	13	43
Dettol	4	5	Tata Salt	14	7
Britannia	5	9	Pepsi	15	26
Lifebuoy	6	4	Maaza	16	46
Clinic Plus	7	15	Vodafone	17	30
Pond's	8	16	Maggi	18	35
Fair & Lovely	9	18	Glucon-D	19	14
Pepsodent	10	8	Thums Up	20	39

Source: Brand Equity, 2010.

Table 1.3   The top twenty most-trusted service brands, 2010

Brand	Rank	Brand	Rank
Vodafone	1	Canara Bank	11
BSNL	2	Tata Docomo	12
State Bank of India	3	Punjab National Bank	13
LIC	4	Central Bank of India	14
Tata Indicom	5	Idea Cellular	15
Big Bazaar	6	HDFC Bank	16
ICICI Bank	7	Indian Bank	17
Bank of India	8	Reliance Fresh	18
Hindustan Petroleum	9	Aircel	19
Bharti Airtel	10	Pizza Hut	20

Source: Brand Equity, 2010.

These brand rankings are the result of a survey conducted by *Brand Equity* and The Nielsen Company, and represent the brands that consumers are most familiar with and which provide 'quality and reassurance' to the consumers. The brand attributes considered for this measurement are given in Exhibit 1.3 (for a detail of the methodology, please refer to the chapter on measuring brand equity).

Table 1.4 shows that we can brand both a product and a service. But is that all we can brand? Branding can be applied virtually to anything or anywhere. For example, in India, branding has also been applied to commodities such as salt (Tata Salt, Captain Cook Salt, etc.), sugar (Dhampure Sugar), eggs (see Exhibit 1.4: Branding Eggs), etc. It is possible to brand the following (Kotler and Keller 2005):

- A service—for example, Life Insurance Corporation, State Bank of India
- A product—for example, Nokia mobiles, Lux soaps, Knorr soups
- A store—for example, Big Bazaar, Shoppers Stop

Exhibit 1.3   Brand attributes for measuring the most-trusted brands

1. Always maintains a high level of quality
2. Is worth the price it commands
3. Is a brand I would surely consider if I have to buy the product
4. Has been a popular brand for many years
5. Has something that no other brand has
6. Evokes a feeling of confidence and pride among its users
7. Is a very special brand with unique feelings associated with it

Source: Brand Equity, 2010.

Table 1.4 Top ten most-trusted brands over the years

Rank	2001	2002	2003	2004	2005–06	2007	2008	2009	2010
1	Lux	Dettol	Colgate	Colgate	Colgate	Colgate	Nokia	Nokia	Nokia
2	Colgate	Britannia	Dettol	Lux	Lux	Vicks	Colgate	Colgate	Colgate
3	Rin	Colgate	Pond's	Rin	Dettol	Lux	Tata Salt	Lux	Lux
4	Thums Up	Tata Salt	Lux	Dettol	Pond's	Nokia	Pepsodent	Lifebuoy	Dettol
5	Dettol	Lux	Pepsodent	Tata Salt	Tata Salt	Britannia	Pond's	Dettol	Britannia
6	Fair & Lovely	Coca-Cola	Tata Salt	Pond's	LIC	Dettol	Lux	Horlicks	Lifebuoy
7	Surf	Pepsodent	Britannia	Fair & Lovely	Vicks	Lifebuoy	Britannia	Tata Salt	Clinic Plus
8	Coca-Cola	Pond's	Rin	Britannia	Britannia	Pepsodent	Dettol	Pepsodent	Pond's
9	Pepsi	Pepsi	Surf	Vicks	Rin	Pond's	Lifebuoy	Britannia	Fair & Lovely
10	Horlicks	Thums Up	Close Up	Bata	Bata	Tata Tea	Vicks	Reliance Mobile	Pepsodent

Source: Brand Equity, 2010.

- A place/geographic location—for example, Taj Mahal, India (the Incredible India! campaign)
- A person—for example, Aamir Khan, Amitabh Bachchan
- An idea—for example, Worldwide Fund for Nature
- An online organization—for example, Amazon, MakeMyTrip
- An organization—for example, UNICEF

Branding in itself does not denote success. Brands need to be managed over time, and brand managers need to constantly ensure the success of their brands, otherwise once successful brands can ride into oblivion (see Exhibit 1.5: 'Hamara Bajaj').

Exhibit 1.4 Branding Eggs

The approximate consumption of eggs in India stands at 360 crore per month, and out of this around 60 lakh eggs are from the branded category. This segment is catching up in the metros with a growth rate of 20 per cent. Suguna group, Vangili Feeds, Keggs, and SKM are some of the key players in this segment that have differentiated their eggs on the basis of protein, less fat content, herbal features, odourless eggs, etc. These eggs ensure quality and convenience to the customers, are hygienic, and have a premium look. Modern retail has given a fillip to retailing of branded eggs with stores such as Nilgiris, Easy Day stores, Spencers, More, etc. storing these branded eggs. The eggs are priced higher than the normal eggs, and if a pack of six normal eggs cost ₹18, the same number of branded eggs may cost up to ₹45 (Sujatha 2010).

Exhibit 1.5 'Hamara Bajaj'—Fall of the Icon

The year 2009 was a watershed moment in the history of the scooter market in India. An iconic scooter brand that once symbolized an 'Indian trying to survive, to maximize his resources, and who wanted to be mobile' (Bhagat 2010), the Hamara Bajaj scooter was on its way out. Once the 'strong symbol' of 'strong India', the Bajaj scooter was to shut shop. Chetak, once the world's largest selling scooter, had stopped production in 2006–07. Its Kristal brand was losing market share and the sales were dropping in spite of the 15 per cent growth in the domestic scooter market (Chauhan 2009).

Compare this to the 1980s, when consumers had to wait for their deliveries (with the waiting period extending to years), when it was a sought after wedding gift and strings were pulled for speedy allotments. A parallel lucrative industry grew around the waiting period and those who took a delivery, resold the scooters at a premium equal to the original cost of the scooter. Rivals LML scooters collected more than ₹120 crore just by booking scooters at ₹500 per scooter—though half of them were never delivered and the company went out of business after the motorcycle surge (Doval 2009).

Post liberalization, the entry of Hero Honda into the market was the game-changer. The 'Fill it, forget it' positioning of Hero Honda immediately tilted the market in favour of the motorcycle. The sleek designs, fuel efficiency, and hi-tech features drove the final nails into the coffin. Bajaj felt the need to innovate and reinvent—scooters were on their way out and motorcycles were in.

Bajaj tied up with Kawasaki to regain market confidence by selling over half a million motorcycles in a single year. The Caliber and Pulsar models followed and were an instant hit with the customers (Money Control 2006). Bajaj Auto wants to focus on the road ahead and become the motorcycle specialist by stepping on its iconic scooter brand.

DIFFERENCE BETWEEN A PRODUCT AND A BRAND

A product is the core focus of a firm, around which the activities of the firm revolve. It is what the organization produces or offers to the market for consumption, and what consumers purchase to satisfy their needs and wants. All the marketing activities revolve around the product and the product forms the thread that links all the activities and functions of the organization that revolve around the 'offering' to the market. If this 'offering' does not satisfy the customers' needs and wants in any way, all the activities of the organization would have been in vain.

'A product can be a tangible object, an intangible service, or an idea, which a marketer has to offer to satisfy the needs and wants of the consumers' (Jauhari and Dutta 2010). According to Kotler, Armstrong, Agnihotri, and Haque (2010), a product can be thought of at different levels, as discussed below. (Also see Exhibit 1.6.)

Core product The core product is the most fundamental product sought by customers to satisfy their needs and wants. For instance, when customers want to print something they can purchase a printer, in order to reproduce a document they can buy a scanner or a photocopier, to listen to music they can purchase an MP3 player, when they want to move from one city to another they can purchase an airline ticket, when they want to communicate they can purchase a mobile phone or a landline phone, and when they are hungry they can order a pizza, etc.

Actual product This second stage occurs when the core benefit that the manufacturer or service provider wants to supply in the market is transformed into an actual product with various attributes. These attributes are the features, design, brand name, packaging, and the

Exhibit 1.6 Tupperware—The Different Levels of the Product

The core product that Neha was looking for was a product that could store food. The actual product (Tupperware products) was developed by Earl Tupper in 1946 and continues to be made from 100 per cent food-grade, virgin plastic, which is free of the plastic odour otherwise common in such type of containers. The Tupperware products are stylish, lightweight, and at the same time airtight and leak-proof. Tupperware is an augmented product because it also comes with a lifetime guarantee. If the product is returned it is 'recycled and reused to make non-food items like plant pots, pipes, etc. Thus, no plastic is dumped and the company contributes to a greener and cleaner environment' (*Superbrands* 2009).

quality level offered by the manufacturer or the service provider. Thus, an HP deskjet printer with a scanner and a photocopier attached provides consumers with a complete solution for copying and printing.

Augmented product   When a product is accompanied by additional benefits and services, it leads to the third stage of the augmented product. These can be the delivery and credit facilities, warranty, after-sales service, and product support services. Thus, when customers purchase an HP deskjet printer, they will get a manual with the complete information, warranty on the parts, a toll-free number and website details to have queries answered or any problems resolved.

A product should be designed carefully and its features should be considered in detail, as it is these features that provide the ultimate consumer experience that brings consumers back to purchase the product again and again. The product should be reviewed from time to time as the environment is dynamic and technology is continuously opening up new avenues that provide immense opportunities to organizations for innovation. All products include the following (Aaker and Joachimsthaler 2000).

Scope   This includes the extent of the product a company plans to cover. For example, MDH makes spices, Atlas manufactures cycles, etc.

Attributes   The features and qualities of the product. Colgate toothpaste, for instance, contains clove oil, Dove contains moisturizer that keeps the skin soft and nourished, etc.

Uses   The various ways in which the product can be used. For example, mobile phones can be used for communication, Internet applications, as a camera, etc.

Quality/value   For example, there are many quality products from the house of Tatas, such as Tata Salt, Tata Indica (car), Tata Consultancy Services (IT services, business solutions), etc.

Functional benefits   The function that is performed by the product is important. For example, Big Bazaar performs the function of offering extra value.

An organization that invests time and money in developing a product and making it unique in the market needs to reap the benefits as well (see Exhibit 1.7). All the benefits of the product can be milked for a longer period of time, if the product is uniquely identified in the minds of the customers. This can be done with the help of a brand name. This name helps in uniquely identifying the product and along with it the following (also see Figure 1.1).

Exhibit 1.7   Tupperware—The Brand

Brand Tupperware is not just about selling products, but about providing solutions that benefit customers. Health being the biggest concern for Indians, Tupperware has positioned itself on the health and wellness platform. It holds the 'wealth of wellness' programmes in schools to educate children about the health benefits of using Tupperware (Image 1.3). That it cares for the Indian consumers is reflected in the range of products it has designed especially for the needs of the 'Indian housewife, her Indian kitchen, and Indian food'. Thus, it has products like the spice box, idli maker, heat-resistant serving spoons, refrigerator bottles, lunch boxes to ensure that dry and wet foods stay segregated, etc.

These specially designed products that offer solutions have instilled confidence in the Indian housewife, and changed her kitchen from the 'traditional rasoi' to the 'modern kitchen' (*Superbrands* 2009), while providing self-expressive and emotional benefits.

Courtesy: Superbrands.

Image 1.3   Brand positioning of Tupperware

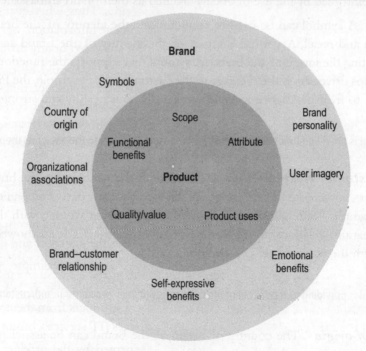

Source: Adapted from Aaker and Joachimsthaler 2000.

Figure 1.1   A brand is a product and much more

Functional benefits   This includes the various functional aspects of the brand, which can be aided by user imagery, organizational associations, brand personality, symbols, brand-customer relationships, and country of origin.

User imagery   User imagery aims at creating a certain image of the person using a particular brand. Lifestyle brands use this to create an exclusive image for the customers purchasing their brands. For example, people who wear Armani clothes, Bvlgari watches, etc. are perceived as belonging to an elite section of society.

Organizational associations   This links the characteristics of the company to the brand, which creates an aura around it. For example, Tata products are associated with innovation and quality ('from the house of Tata'). This is especially relevant for services, durable goods, and high-tech brands.

 See how Amul in providing functional benefits to its consumers by providing organizational association.

Brand personality   The personality of a brand makes it memorable and interesting for customers. Brand personality helps in increasing brand awareness and 'developing a relationship with the customers'. It adds the dimension of youthfulness and energy to the brand. For example, Thums Up projects an outgoing and adventurous brand personality and is further reinforced by the use of Akshay Kumar as their brand ambassador.

Symbols   A symbol can be used to communicate the identity of the brand with a quicker recognition and recall. A symbol is a part of the identity of the brand and plays a strategic role in creating the image of the brand. A symbol that supports the functional benefits of the product helps drive across the message to the customers. For example, the Pillsbury doughboy who relates to fresh and light food, the Amul girl who is healthy and strong, etc.

 See how Amul is providing functional benefits to its consumers through the use of its moppet as a symbol.

Brand–customer relationships   This includes the relationship the brand develops with its customers, and consumers can associate the brand as their party companion, friend, adviser, etc. For example, Titan launched its Raga series targeted at women with the 'ek khoobsorat rishta' (a beautiful relationship) ad featuring Rani Mukherjee. The ad showed Rani waiting for her man with the watch as her companion.

 See how Amul is providing functional benefits to its consumers by providing brand/customer relationship.

Country of origin   The country of origin of the brand can be associated with the brand to add value to the product attributes. For example, watches from Switzerland, electronic products from Japan, etc.

Self-expressive benefits   Brands allow people to express themselves to others.

Emotional benefits   A consumer can derive emotional pleasure, such as pride, joy, thrill, etc. while consuming a brand. Emotional benefits such as entertainment, belongingness, and brand community can be created and it is these emotional benefits that are difficult to duplicate (Mascarenhas, Kesavan, and Bernacchi 2006).

See how Amul is providing emotional benefits to its consumers.

The brand name benefits as perceived by customers depend, to a large extent, on the benefits of the product (Rio, Vazquez, and Iglesias 2001). A product serves to fulfil a functional need of the customer. A brand, on the other hand, includes both functional benefits and something extra in the form of added values and emotional experiences. The functional experiences can be duplicated, but it is the emotional bonds that are difficult for competitors to duplicate or break (Mascarenhas, Kesavan, and Bernacchi 2006). It can thus be said that all brands are products as they provide a functional benefit, but not all products are brands (Jones 1998). This is also true because it is extremely difficult to differentiate the many products and provide value at the same time.

 See how generic products like milk and butter were transformed into brand Amul.

RATIONALE FOR BUILDING A BRAND

We have studied what a brand is and the difference between a product and a brand. But, why do organizations need to invest time and money in building brands when they already have a product that can be offered to the market? Also, given that the transaction of a brand is between an organization and the consumers, the second question that comes to mind is, are the benefits of building strong brands restricted to organizations alone, or do the consumers benefit too? Let us see the various reasons and benefits of building a strong brand.

Benefits of Building Strong Brands—Organizational Perspective

A strong brand is an asset for any organization. It can help the firm by acting as:

An identifier A brand name identifies the maker of the brand and helps in assigning responsibility during the distribution stage whether it be for storing, sorting, selling, or after-sales service (Kotler and Keller 2005; Moore and Reid 2008).

A shorthand for information A brand name helps consumers store information related to the brand and thus helps them cope with the 'deluge of marketing information' provided to them (de Chernatony 2008). The quality of information stored for a brand is therefore important and guides the behaviour of consumers towards a brand. Brand extensions try to build on the brands in the hope that association with an existing brand will make it easier for consumers to accept the new extension. This is known as the 'shorthand' concept.

Legal protection A brand name uniquely identifies the brand and its unique features and aspects, thereby providing legal protection for the branded product through trademarks, patents, and copyrights (Jones 1998; Kotler and Keller 2005). Organizations invest a lot of time and money in building a brand, therefore legal ownership and protection helps a company protect and enforce its ownership. For example, as a brand strategy, Absolut Vodka continually monitors competitors' activities to stop any organization from 'adopting the name or bottle design' (de Chernatony 2008).

Differential advantage Branding also helps in differentiating a product from other products in the product category (Jones 1998; Rio, Vazquez, and Iglesias 2001).

Unique associations The mention of a brand name evolves a number of different thoughts and feelings in the minds of consumers. These associations are a result of the different feelings and images a brand creates in the minds of the consumers (Kotler, Armstrong, Agnihotri, and Haque 2010).

Price premiums By building a strong brand and loyal customers, an organization can demand a higher price for its product (Kotler and Keller 2005).

Enhancing customer loyalty Brand equity and trust are the most influential factors that lead to brand loyalty among the consumers (Taylor, Celuch, and Goodwin 2004).

Higher market share A high positive customer perception about the brand leads to increased earnings and translates into a higher market share for the organization (Rio, Vazquez, and Iglesias 2001).

Inelastic response to price increase A strong brand inculcates brand loyalty, and brand loyal customers are not easily swayed by price increases (Rio, Vazquez, and Iglesias 2001).

As a barrier to the entry of other brands A strong brand can act as a barrier to the entry of other brands into the market, as brand loyal customers will take a longer time to switch to another brand (Kotler and Keller 2005).

Can be bought and sold as an asset Brands can be measured in financial terms and can be found on the asset side in a balance sheet. Strong and successful brands can be bought and sold by organizations, and can also be at the centre of hostile takeover bids. For example, the Cadbury brand was bought over by Kraft Foods Inc.

 See the Amul video to understand the organizational perspective of building a brand.

Benefits of Building Strong Brands—Customer Perspective

For the consumers, branding is all of the following.

Source of identification Brand name identifies the source or the manufacturer of the product or service, thus helping consumers in the allocation of responsibility.

Heuristic or proxy for quality The brand name acts as a symbol of quality for consumers. The brand name is also found to impact purchase decisions, when information about the quality of the product is not available to facilitate a customer's decision-making (Jiang 2004). A brand name guarantees homogeneity of the products and instils confidence in consumers by denoting quality products (Jones 1998).

Source of evaluation Consumers can evaluate different products on the basis of their brand attributes (Kotler and Keller 2005). It is easier to collect information about known brands, and therefore strong brands reduce the search cost for consumers.

A tool to simplify decision-making On the basis of their experience with a brand (either through a search for information or through the use of the brand), consumers can easily decide which brand to purchase (Kotler and Keller 2005).

Risk reducer   The brand, through its brand image builds confidence and trust in consumers and reduces the risk involved in making a purchase (Kotler and Keller 2005). The various risks that a consumer can perceive at the time of purchase are as follows.

Financial risk   Customers are concerned about value for money and feel that a brand may/may not deliver good value for money.

Performance risk   Customers are concerned about the performance of the brand and whether it will deliver according to the functional specifications.

Time risk   Consumers are concerned about the amount of time they will spend on the collection of and information the pre-purchase stage. Also post-purchase, if the brand does not fulfil its promise, then how much time would they have wasted.

Social risk   Consumers are concerned about how their peers will perceive them if they use a particular brand. Will the use of the brand add to their self-image?

Psychological risk   Consumers should be satisfied with the brand, and it should match their self-image.

The brand, by constantly delivering quality over a period of time and through its reputation and image, can act as a cue for the customers. It can remove or reduce the various risks involved and promote brand consumption.

Tool to express self-image   Customers consume brands to express their self-image, either an actual image or an ideal one, or both through the brand image (Ataman and Ulengin 2003). Thus, consumers purchase brands that they feel best express their actual self or ideal self, or both and make a statement about themselves in society.

TYPES OF BRANDS

Brands can represent different value propositions, and thus the type of value provided can be categorized into (Tybout and Carpenter 2006; Ramaswamy and Namakumari 2009) the following.

Functional brands   When the functional value of a brand is highlighted along with the product features and efficient performance, the brand can be categorized as a functional brand. For example, the Nano car provides the functional benefit of transportation for the entire family at an affordable price, and Nirma offers a clean wash also at an affordable price.

Image brands   To differentiate itself from other brands and add value for customers, a brand can also build on its brand image and emphasize the image value. This image can be built by using celebrities like film actors, sports personalities, etc. The idea is that by using a particular brand, customers will feel as if they also belong to the same class or league. For example, the Scooty ads show Priyanka Chopra using the two-wheeler; Parker Pens show Amitabh Bachchan using the pen. Customers will want to purchase these brands to be in the same league as their favourite celebrities.

Experience brands   A brand can project the unique experience customers will have on using it in order to create value. Service brands particularly use this to highlight the experience that the customers would get. For example, Kingfisher Airlines states 'Fly the good times', which customers perceive and interpret as 'Fly five star' (see Image 1.4). The ad highlights the experience of an 'exclusive lounge and bar on board' (*Superbrands*, 2009).

BRANDING CHALLENGES

The Indian market saw a deluge of new brands between February 2009 and July 2010; the period witnessed 1500 brand launches. New brands were launched in sectors like telecom, retail, automotive, FMCG (fast moving consumer goods), apparels, etc. There were approximately three brands being launched in a day, but only 5 per cent of these survived. Some brands like Marico suspended the test run of its brand Saffola Zest (in the healthy snack category) due to poor market response (Pinto 2010) (see Exhibit 1.8: Brand Survival).

The best in business.
Served by the best in the business.

Courtesy: Superbrands.

Image 1.4 Kingfisher ad; also see Plate 1

There are a number of challenges that brand managers have to overcome to see their product succeed. Brand managers have to understand these challenges well if they are to make effective branding decisions. Some of the key challenges are as follows.

Exhibit 1.8   Brand Survival

The market for organized products is growing, and brands have not yet penetrated the entire Indian market. New brands are being launched but the success ratio is only 5 per cent. All the same, this is better than the markets in the West according to Santosh Desai, CEO, Future Brands (cited in Pinto 2010) where the black-eye ratio is applicable. According to this, if 10 brands are launched in a year, only two survive and do well in twenty-four months and this comes down to one brand in seventy months. India still displays a huge gap between organized and unorganized trade in many categories. Modern trade, still in its infancy in the country, holds a lot of promise for organized products. According to Technopak, organized retail, which currently is at 5 per cent, will reach 25 per cent in the next ten years and will make launching brands easier (Pinto 2010).

A lot of companies have launched new brands, but have had to pull them out because the desired results were not there. For example, since its entry into India in 1998, Hyundai has withdrawn the Elantra Sedan and Terracan SUV from the market and is now ready to phase out its Getz model, which was introduced in the year 2004 at a price of ₹4.5 lakh. The car was meant for people who wished to upgrade from entry-level hatchbacks like Alto, Maruti 800, and its own Santro. Maruti Swift in the same segment (at a price tag of ₹4 lakh) launched in the year 2005 is still going strong and is the fourth largest selling car currently (Chauhan 2010).

Exhibit 1.9 Future Group Is Kellogg's 'Cereal Killer'

Future Group is a prominent player in the organized retail sector, and Kellogg's is a global player that commands a whopping share of more than 70 per cent of the Rs 400 crore breakfast cereal market in India. When Future Group demanded a 15–16 per cent margin as against the existing 12 per cent on the sales of Kellogg's products at its outlets, the cereal maker refused to budge. An angry Future Group decided to ban the sale of Kellogg's products at its retail outlets.

A year prior to boycotting Kellogg's, Future Group had boycotted Cadbury also on the issue of margins. A series of conflicts have been brewing between modern retailers and FMCG companies with retailers demanding higher margins on the sales of products and manufacturers accusing retailers of pushing their own brands. In fact, Future Group replaced Kellogg's with their own brand of 'Tasty Treat' cereals (Vijayraghavan and Bhushan 2009).

Intelligent and educated customers These days consumers are well-educated about the brands available in the market and also about what to do and whom to complain to if the brand promise is not met. Internet has brought a wealth of information at the click of a mouse, and these well-informed customers choose intelligently.

Growth of private labels With organized retail catching up in India, we now find a number of private labels being sold at Big Bazaar, 98.4 Pharmacy, etc., which are giving the manufacturer brands a run for their money (see Exhibit 1.9: Future Group Is Kellogg's 'Cereal Killer').

Brand proliferation There are a number of brands vying for consumers' attention, leading to increased competition and difficulty in differentiation of brands from competitor's brands. Globalization has lead to brands being sold across geographical boundaries and this has further lead to brand proliferation (see Exhibit 1.10: Superbikes in India).

Increasing trade power The power of retailers and wholesalers is increasing and organizations have to engage in a number of below-the-line activities to motivate retailers and wholesalers to sell their brands.

Media fragmentation and the rise of the new media The growth in the number of television channels, radio channels, and magazines has resulted in the target audience

---

Exhibit 1.10 Superbikes in India

Rising income, increasing aspiration, and declining average age of bike owners from 39 to 32 has led to a demand for superbikes in India. India has the world's second largest two-wheeler market. There is an upswing in the demand for superbikes since 2007 when Yamaha launched its twin superbikes YZR R1 and

MT-01. The other players in this segment in India are Honda's 1000 RR Fireblade and CBR 1000 R, Suzuki's 1348 cc Hayabusa, Ducati, and Harley Davidson. BMW is also retailing its S 1000 RR and the R and K series models in India (*The Economic Times*, 2010) which has further heated up the competition in this segment.

being distributed across these channels. This has added to the woes of the marketers, as the advertising budget has to be spread over a number of media, leading to increased costs and uncertainty regarding the attention of the audiences.

Increasing cost of product introduction and support To cut above the clutter and establish themselves, products need a lot of marketing support initially. Customers have a number of brands to choose from, and to catch their eye is a huge task for marketers. For example, Raymond Limited is scrapping its non-performing brands. It shut its home accessories brand 'Be: Home' two years after it was launched, and the kids wear brand Zapp! was closed four years after its launch.

Increasing job turnover A brand is built over time and it requires consistent delivery of the brand promise by a team of dedicated employees. Money has to be spent on training and educating there employees about the brand and motivating them to deliver the brand promise. In such a scenario, job turnover is an issue that needs to be dealt with strategically.

OVERCOMING THE CHALLENGES

With markets maturing, brands can overcome the challenges in the market by creating a strong brand equity and building customer loyalty. It needs to be clarified that brand equity is different from brand loyalty. Brand equity is the favourable response (in case of positive brand equity) or the less favourable response (in case of negative brand equity) of customers towards a brand and the way it is marketed. One of the characteristics of firms that possess strong brand equity is 'stronger brand loyalty' (Keller 2004). It is said that 'brand loyalty is both a dimension and an outcome of brand equity' (Taylor, Celuch, and Goodwin 2004). Here we discuss these two constructs in detail.

Brand equity A brand name has a differential effect on customers, and this influences the customer's response towards a brand. This response of the customer is termed as brand equity (Keller 2004). Brand equity is defined as 'a set of brand assets and liabilities linked to a brand, its name, and symbol that adds value to or subtracts from the value provided by a product or service to a firm and/or to that firm's customers.' (Aaker 1991). It is this biased behaviour towards the brand that motivates organizations to spend time and money in building a brand. This is further discussed in detail in the chapters on brand equity and measuring brand equity.

 See the Amul video to understand how through the years, Amul has built a strong brand with high brand equity.

Brand loyalty Customer loyalty is often associated with a brand (Mascarenhas, Kesavan, and Bernacchi 2006). The market is cluttered with a number of brands, be it a manufacturer's brand or the retailer's own labels. A slight change in the market share has a significant financial implication, and it is the brand loyal customers that ensure sales in such a competitive scenario (Datta 2003). A 5 per cent increase in customer loyalty can enhance the profitability of a company by 40–95 per cent (Kim, Morris, and Swait 2008) depending on the type of industry.

Brand loyalty is a measure of how attached the consumer is to a brand. Brand loyalty tells one how likely a consumer is to shift to a newly launched brand or to an existing brand that is in some way upgraded (Aaker 1991). Loyalty is defined as 'the biased (i.e., non-random) behavioural response (i.e., purchase), expressed over time by some decision-making unit, with respect to one or more alternative brands out of a set of such brands, and is a function of psychological (decision-making, evaluative) processes' (Sheth, Mittal, and Newman 1999). Loyalty is both behavioural and attitudinal and can be expressed at the following five levels (Aaker 1991) (see Figure 1.2).

Brand switchers These consumers form the lowest level of the brand loyalty ladder and are indifferent to the brand name. Their buying decisions are based on price, availability, etc., and they do not attach any importance to the brand.

Habitual buyers Such types of customers are satisfied with a brand and are characterized by the absence of any kind of dissatisfaction with the brand. They are habitual buyers, but can also switch over to another brand when provided with proper stimuli by competitors. All the same, it is quite a task to reach out to such customers as they have no reason to be on the lookout for alternatives.

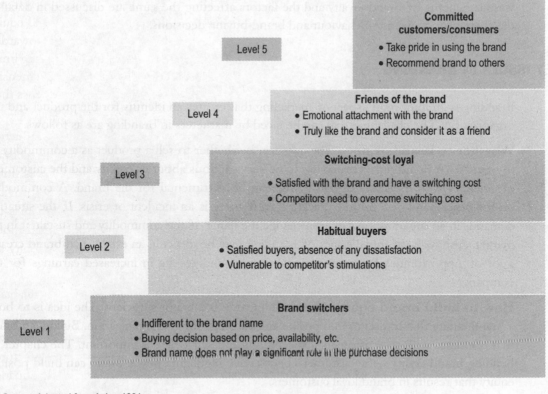

Committed customers/consumers
- Take pride in using the brand
- Recommend brand to others

Level 5

Friends of the brand
- Emotional attachment with the brand
- Truly like the brand and consider it as a friend

Level 4

Switching-cost loyal
- Satisfied with the brand and have a switching cost
- Competitors need to overcome switching cost

Level 3

Habitual buyers
- Satisfied buyers, absence of any dissatisfaction
- Vulnerable to competitor's stimulations

Level 2

Brand switchers
- Indifferent to the brand name
- Buying decision based on price, availability, etc.
- Brand name does not play a significant role in the purchase decisions

Level 1

Source: Adapted from Aaker 1991.

Figure 1.2   Customer brand loyalty levels

Switching-cost loyals   These customers are similar to habitual buyers, as they are also satisfied with a particular brand. They are different from habitual buyers in that they have a switching cost as well, which can be in the form of 'time, money, or performance risk associated with the switching.' These customers can be induced to switch over to a new brand by offering them a benefit that is large enough to compensate the risks involved.

Friends of the brand   These consumers really like a brand and consider it a friend. They prefer the brand, have a liking for the brand, and are emotionally attached to the brand.

Committed customers   These customers form the top rung of the brand loyalty ladder. They are committed towards the brand and feel that the brand helps them in expressing themselves, or that the functional use of the brand is extremely important to them. They take pride in the brand and even recommend it to others.

These five levels are indicative and there can be overlaps and combinations of levels. For example, there can be customers who like the brand and have a switching cost as well. There can also be other exceptions, for example, there may be customers who are dissatisfied with a brand, but continue to use it because of the non-availability of alternatives (for instance, earlier in the Indian aviation sector, even dissatisfied fliers had to fly Indian Airlines or Air India in the absence of any competing airlines), or because the switching cost is high, etc. The various benefits of brand loyalty and the factors affecting the same are discussed in detail in the chapter on consumer behaviour and brand-buying decisions.

KEY ISSUES IN BRANDING

Branding is an important aspect of marketing that creates an identity for the product and the organization. The challenges that can be faced by marketers in branding are as follows.

Whether to brand or not   The question is whether to sell a product as a commodity or to brand it? A brand once created has to be very cautious about its quality and the customer's experiences with it, as any negative issue can be detrimental for the brand. A commodity, on the other hand, will not die quickly even if there is an incident or crisis. If the situation demands it, an organization can even change the name of the commodity and sustain it in the market. Although the initial stages of branding may be difficult, an established brand creates a lot of opportunities for organizational success and results in increased earnings for the company.

How to build brand equity   Just building a brand is not sufficient. The idea is to build a brand equity that translates into profits and earnings for the organization. Building a brand that resonates with the customers' expectations and self-belief is important. The chapter on building brand equity—the customer's perspective highlights how a brand can build positive equity that results in brand loyal customers.

How to measure brand equity   Brand equity needs to be measured from time to time, so that strategies can be guided by the feedback from the market and the customers. There are various ways by which brand equity can be measured. These are broadly divided into brand value, which consists of the financial parameters, and brand strength, which consists of customer-based measures. As an organization, it is important to decide how the company intends to measure its brand equity—either through the financial parameters or customer-based measures, or a mix of both. The chapter on measuring brand equity looks at this issue in detail.

Understanding customers and how they purchase a brand   An understanding of the customers' perceptions and attitudes towards a brand is important. It helps marketers decide on their branding and product mix strategies. An understanding of the customers is also imperative, as the marketers have to try and influence this behaviour in such a way that it is favourable to their brand.

How to position the brand   Once an organization understands the consumers' attitudes and the way how to influence them, it can position the brands in such a manner so that this perception fits in well with what is important to the consumers at the time of purchase. Organizations need to inculcate the brand values that the customers are looking for and clearly communicate the same to them so that their brand achieves a top of the mind recall among the customers. The various ways by which a brand can be positioned are discussed in the chapter on brand positioning.

Which marketing mix strategies to choose   Once the brand characteristics and attributes have been decided, the next steps for the organization are to design the product, price it, package it, and deliver it to the customers. It then has to communicate this to the customers to build awareness, recognition, and recall for the brand. Previous studies on marketing show that for each mix, there are a number of strategies and that an organization must choose from them to build a brand. The idea is to build an integrated brand image and since all the elements of the marketing mix communicate, they should be chosen with great care, so that they all add to the brand equity. Online marketing is also on the rise, and with more and more customers going online, organizations could ignore this tool only at their own peril. Since online marketing is relatively inexpensive and has a wide reach, it is an attractive strategy in branding. However, marketers should take care while building their brands through this media because any miscommunication could cost the brand dearly. The chapters on branding and marketing programmes and branding and marketing communications deal with the same.

How to design branding strategies   The task of a brand manager is not over even after a brand has been established. Managers have to design their brand architecture and the number of brands they need to keep in their portfolio in the different product categories that they intend to cater to. A major task is to choose whether to opt for brand extensions or to own different brands. If brand managers opt for brand extensions, they can leverage their brand using the existing brand equity of the established brand. On the other hand, establishing different brands gives the opportunity to own well-recognized brands in different product categories, which can then be extended further. This is discussed in detail in the chapter on brand strategies.

How to manage brands over time The world is getting hypercompetitive and consumer trends are evolving. A brand that is stagnant and does not adapt to the changing times is bound to die a natural death. Brand managers, therefore, need to track the changes in the external environment and help grow and sustain their brand over a long period of time, so that the coming generation adopts the brand with the same alacrity as the generation before them. This is a challenge for marketers; all great brands have stood the test of time and have reinvented themselves in order to continue to be relevant to customers even today. This is discussed in further detail in the chapter on managing brands over time.

How to manage brands across geographical boundaries The world is a global village, and brand managers need to market their brands across geographical boundaries to remain competitive and enhance profitability. While marketing a brand beyond existing borders, an organization has to consider a number of issues before adopting a branding strategy. The chapter on brands in a borderless world takes a detailed look at these issues.

SUMMARY

Branding is a key issue and a challenge that can define the life of a product and hence of the organization in the marketplace. For the consumers, a brand is a product but for the organization, it is a mammoth task to convert a product into a brand.

A brand is different from a product. To be successful in a highly competitive market, a brand must provide some differential advantage. The benefits are successful legal protection, price premiums, and customer loyalty. Benefits to the customer are a proxy for quality, help in decision-making, and reduction in purchase risk.

There are three types of brands: functional brands, image brands, and experience brands. Challenges to creating a successful brand are better-informed consumers; the growing number of private labels; competition from local, national, and global brands; fragmented media; and large employee turnover. Brand equity and brand loyalty can help marketers, the key issue then is how to build and measure brand equity. An in-depth understanding of the consumers' purchase decision-making process and subsequent appropriate positioning and developing of the marketing mix, the branding strategies, and the management of brands over time is becomes important.

KEY TERMS

Brand A name, term, sign, symbol, design, or a combination of them, intended to identify the goods or services of one seller or group of sellers and to differentiate them from competitors.

Brand equity Brand equity is the added value (positive or negative) that a product or a service is endowed with due to a perception of the customers towards the brand.

Brand loyalty Brand loyalty is having a particular brand as the primary choice while making a purchase.

Proto-brands Early brands that existed since the origin of civilizations. Their brand elements were logo, text, and colour.

EXERCISES

Concept Review Questions

1. What is a brand? How is it different from a product?
2. Enumerate five benefits of branding for the customers.
3. Enumerate four benefits of branding from the organization's perspective.
4. Discuss the various issues in branding. Which, according to you is the most important and why?
5. Discuss the various levels of brand loyalty. What are the implications (if any) of these levels for the marketers?

Critical Thinking Questions

1. Discuss why an organization needs to build a brand, when it can simply sell its products and reap profits without having to spend on brand building.
2. Critically discuss the statement, 'There is actually a difference between a product and a brand'.

3. How are brand equity and brand loyalty different when both are responsible for the increased sales of an organization's brands?

Internet Exercises

1. Visit the website http://www.sugunapoultry.com and check out the various brands of this group. Enumerate the various brands of value-added eggs they are selling. How have they tried to brand these eggs?
2. Visit the website http://www.dhampuresugar.com and see how the organization has branded a commodity item like sugar.

CD Exercise

View the Aditya Birla Group ad and discuss the benefits of building a strong brand in the light of the Aditya Birla Group.

REFERENCES

'BMW to ride in superbikes in Dec — German luxury carmaker to launch Motorrad at ₹18 lakh onwards', *The Economic Times*, 29 October 2010, p. 4.

'Superbrands: An Insight into India's Strongest Consumer Brands', Vol. 3, 2009, Superbrands India Private Limited, Gurgaon.

'Ten Years of Trust', *Brand Equity, The Economic Times*, New Delhi, 1 September 2010, pp. 1–14.

Aaker, D.A. (1991), Chapter 2, *Managing Brand Equity*, The Free Press, New York.

Aaker, J.L., 'Dimensions of Brand Personality', *Journal of Marketing Research*, Vol. 34, Issue 3, 1997, pp. 347–356.

Ataman, B. and B. Ulengin, 'A Note on the Effect of Brand Image on Sales', *Journal of Product and Brand Management*, Vol. 12, Issue 4, 2003, pp. 237–250.

Bhagat, A., 'Human Factor Analysis: Aspiration and Change', http://www.businessworld.in/bw/2010_03_23_Human_Factor_Analysis_Aspiration_And_Change.html, accessed on 31 August 2010.

Blythe, J., 'Advertising Creatives and Brand Personality—A Grounded Theory Perspective', *Journal of Brand Management*, Vol. 14, Issue 4, 2007, pp. 284–294.

Chauhan, C.P. 'Bajaj to stop scooter production, focus on motorcycles', http://www.economictimes.indiatimes.com/articleshow/5320461.cms, accessed on 30 August 2010.

Chauhan, C.P., 'Getz ready or phaseout—Hyundai to end production of hatchback on poor sales, focus on high–selling i20', *The Economic Times*, 25 June 2010, p. 4.

Datta, P.R., 'The Determinants of Brand Loyalty', *The Journal of American Academy of Business*, Cambridge, Vol. 3, Issue ½, 2003, pp. 138–144.

Doval, P. 'End of the road for Bajaj scooters', http://timesofindia.indiatimes.com/business/india–business/end–of–the–road–for–bajaj–scooters/articleshow/5320432.cms#ixzz0x4bJUtSG, accessed on 30 August 2010.

http://www.retailangle.com/newsdetail.asp?newsid=3300&newstitle=Raymond_shuts_down_kidswear_brand_Zapp!, accessed on 06 November 2010

Jauhari, V. and K. Dutta (2009), *Services Marketing Management and Operations*, Oxford University Press, New Delhi.

Jiang, P., 'The role of brand name in customization decisions —A search vs experience perspective', *The Journal of Product and Brand Management*, Vol. 13, Issue 2, 2004, pp. 73–83.

Jones, J.P. (1998), Chapter 2, *What's in a brand? Building Brand Equity through Advertising*, Tata McGraw Hill Publishing Company Limited, New Delhi.

Keller, K.L. (2004), *Strategic Brand Management: Building, Measuring and Managing Brand Equity*, Prentice-Hall of India Private Limited, New Delhi.

Keller, K.L. and K. Richey, 'The Importance of Corporate Brand Personality Traits to a Successful 21st Century Business', *Journal of Brand Management*, Vol. 14, Issue ½, 2006, pp. 74–81.

Keller, K.L., and D.A. Aaker, 'Corporate level marketing: the impact of credibility on a company's brand extensions', *Corporate Reputation Review*, Vol. 1, Issue 4, 1998, pp. 356–378.

Kim, J., J.D. Morris, and J. Swait, 'Antecedents of true brand loyalty', *Journal of Advertising*, Vol. 3, Issue 2, 2008, pp. 99–117.

Kotler, P. and K.L. Keller (2005), *Marketing Management*, 12th edition, Prentice–Hall of India New Delhi.

Kotler, P., G. Armstrong, P.Y. Agnihotri, and Ehsan ul Haque (2010), *Principles of Marketing: A South Asian Perspective*, 13th edition, Prentice-Hall of India, Delhi.

Mascarenhas, O.A., R. Kesavan, and M. Bernacchi, 'Lasting Customer Loyalty—A total Customer Experience Approach', *Journal of Consumer Marketing*, Vol. 23, Issue 7, 2006, pp. 397–405.

Money Control (2006), 'How hamara Bajaj became a sign of independent India', http://www.moneycontrol.com/news/management/how–hamara–bajaj–becamesignindependent–india_230375–2.html, accessed on 31 August 2010.

Moore, K. and S. Reid, 'The Birth of Brand—4000 years of Branding', *Business History*, Vol. 50, Issue 4, 2008, pp. 419–432.

Opoku, R., R. Abratt, and L. Pitt, 'Communicating brand personality— Are the websites doing the talking for the top South African Business Schools?' *Journal of Brand Management*, Vol. 14, Issue 1/2, 2006, pp. 20–39.

Pinto, V.S., 'India sees three brand launches a day, but only 5 per cent survive', *Business Standard*, 17 July 2010, p. 1.

Ramaswamy, V.S. and S. Namakumari (2009), *Marketing Management*, MacMillan, New Delhi.

Rio, A.B. Del, R. Vazquez, and V. Iglesias, 'The role of the Brand Name in Obtaining Differential Advantage', *Journal of Product and Brand Management*, Vol. 10, Issue 7, 2001, pp. 452–465.

Sheth, J.N., B. Mittal, and B.I. Newman (1999), *Consumer Behavior*, Orlando, Dryden.

Sujatha, S., 'Ande ka Funda: Poultry Farms Hatch Branded Dreams—Vangili Feeds, Suguna Goup and SKM eggs offer branded, value–added eggs to woo health–conscious people', *The Economic Times*, 29 June 2010, p. 4.

Taylor, S.A., K. Celuch, and S. Goodwin, 'The Importance of Brand Equity to Consumer Loyalty', *Journal of Product and Brand Management*, Vol. 13, Issue 4, 2004, pp. 217–227.

Tybout, A.M. and G.S. Carpenter (2006), 'Creating and Managing Brands' in Kellogg on Marketing, Wiley India, New Delhi.

Vijayraghavan, K. and R. Bhushan, 'Scorn Flake— Biyani not to have Kellogg's for Breakfast: Big Bazaar, Food Bazaar boycott breakfast cereal maker over margin row', *The Economic Times*, 12 November 2009, p. 4.

CASE STUDY

Cooking Up Maggi Noodles*

Maggi Noodles was launched in 1982 by Nestlé India Limited as Maggi 2-Minute Instant Noodles under the prepared dishes category. Nestlé is a Swiss company, whose link with India goes back to 1912, when it was well known as 'Nestlé Anglo-Swiss Condensed Milk Company (Export) Limited'. Since then, Nestlé has stood its ground firmly in India, by setting its foundation as a well-known brand, offering solutions to customers' wants in different segments. The brand still commands an envious market share of more than 90 per cent and has successfully launched sauces, pastas, and soups (Chamikutty 2010a). Maggi Noodles is one of those brand names for whom

*Amit Bhargava (Management Executive – Marketing, Global Agrisystem Pvt. Ltd) and Akansha Lamba (Management Executive – Consultancy and Projects, Global Agrisystem Pvt. Ltd).

the quote, 'I came, I saw, and I conquered' is apt. The brand replaced favourite Indian *desi* snacks such as *samosas* and *kachoris* with a hot bowl of Maggi Noodles (Viswanath 2002). Over the years, the success of the brand has been commendable, especially considering the fact that it had the added task of creating the category as well (Das 2010).

'Fast to Cook ... Good to Eat Maggi 2-Minute Noodles'

Maggi used the tagline of 'fast to cook, good to eat' to woo the Indian audience in the early 1980s. Maggi understood the consumers' inertia and apathy to try new things (Chamikutty 2010b). Indian consumers, at that time, were evincing interest in Chinese noodles and Maggi launched its noodles to take advantage of this craze (Das 2007). It offered convenience to the housewife and at the same time did not undermine her involvement with the kids (Sharma 2010). The housewife could be creative and add her own variations to the recipe by adding different vegetables to the noodles. Maggi blended itself with the Indian culture, which is known as the land of masalas and curries. It launched the masala flavour in the introductory stages, which was instrumental in making the brand a success in the industry. The masala flavour made its way in to the heart of the consumers, and Maggi found a place in the monthly budget plan of a household (Das 2010).

An uphill task

The task for Maggi Noodles at the time of its launch was twofold—first to promote the concept of noodles and second to establish the brand and educate consumers about the advantages of the brand. The use of brand elements like its tagline 'Fast to cook and good to eat' and its catchy jingle 'mummy bhook lagi hai' (Mummy I am hungry) helped in brand recall. The brand targeted mothers with the convenience plank and children with the fun element. The advertising campaign was followed by promotional activities to encourage consumers. Free samples were given away in metros and small towns to introduce the brand to consumers. Promotional trial packs were distributed in schools as well (Sharma 2010). The other promotional activity that helped in attracting the target market was the introduction of schemes offering 'gifts such as toys and utensils in return for empty noodle

packs'. This promotional stint not only helped the brand identify its potential consumers, but also helped it create a new market segment—the segment of the 'instant noodles', which greatly attracted the Indian consumers. Maggi never looked back. With time, everybody wanted a hot bowl of Maggi Noodles, which became a trustworthy companion for breakfast, lunch, and dinner (and occasionally the in-between meals). Moreover, if you did not feel like cooking or the end-of-the-month budgetary constraints did not allow eating out, Maggi was always a good substitute. Soon, Maggi became as synonymous to noodles as Xerox to photocopiers.

Wastage of 2 minutes

In the years of the 1990s, Maggi saw a phase of downfall— unimaginable for a brand that had built and ruled the category. This undreamt-of-situation occurred when Indo-Nissin came in with Top Ramen Noodles, a product relatively similar to Maggi, but with a twist in the taste category (see Image 1.5). Top Ramen was not alone in entering the market in that era (Sharma 2010). Another brand was the Nepal-based company Wai Wai. Both these brands instantly took charge of the market, as there was a difference in their flavours as compared to Maggi. Image 1.6 shows what Wai Wai had on offer.

In 1997, Maggi tried innovating itself to add excitement to the market. Its noodles got thinner and there was the addition of a new flavouring agent named 'tastemaker'. This new variation instead of taking the brand to a new high dampened the consumer's enthusiasm and damaged its brand image. Maggi Noodles touched its lowest point in the entire 15 years of its existence in the country. On seeing the negligible impact of the new flavouring, Maggi Noodles Masala was completely phased out, instead new variants were tried, and Maggi Macaroni was brought in. The macaroni did no good to save the Maggi Noodles brand and therefore was phased out as well, two years after its launch.

For two years, Maggi experimented with its noodles. It finally understood that the path to recovery was the original flavour. To heal its deteriorating brand image, it re-introduced the Maggi Noodles Masala in 1999. Nestlé brought back the much loved Masala Noodles, but this time keeping in mind the market trend, they gave it a twist of

Source: http://www.nissinfoods.com/topramen/.

Image 1.5 Flavours offered by Top Ramen Noodles

being 'healthier' and 'tastier'. This proposition did wonders for them and within a year, it went back to becoming the market leader. Indo-Nissin had become complacent and was taken by surprise at this comeback. Maggi not only recovered lost ground, but also wiped out the competition. The recall power of Maggi was so strong that eliminating the competition became easy for Maggi (Sharma 2010). 'In July 2001, Maggi replaced Nescafé (Nestlé's coffee brand) as the company's core brand. Nescafé had been NIL's core brand since 1998.'

The health plank

The turn of the century saw Nestlé shifting to 'healthy' products. Consumers too were becoming greatly health conscious. Thus, Maggi repositioned itself on the health platform with its tagline 'Taste bhi. Health bhi' (i.e., it is both tasty and healthy). In 2005, it launched a number of 'healthy' products to attract the health conscious consumers. There was the Maggi Atta Noodles (vegetable

atta noodles) made of whole wheat flour and vegetables, which is healthier compared to the refined flour variety. Maggi Dal Atta Noodles was also launched (containing whole wheat flour and pulses), which had to be phased out again as it did not go down well with the consumers' palate. This was followed by rice noodles and the range consisted of shahi pulao, lemon masala, and chilly chow. The traditional range was enriched with calcium and protein, so that the children (their target market) got up to 20 per cent of the required intake from Maggi (Das 2007).

Bonding with consumers

Maggi has launched many commercial campaigns in order to connect itself with the Indian customers, and instead of using big Bollywood stars, they have used common people or used models who appeal to the common man (see Image 1.7). It had used Preity Zinta to build awareness about its ₹5 pack, and she has the distinction of being the only celebrity to endorse this iconic brand.

Source: http://cgfmcg.com/white_noodles.php.

Image 1.6   Instant noodles by Wai Wai

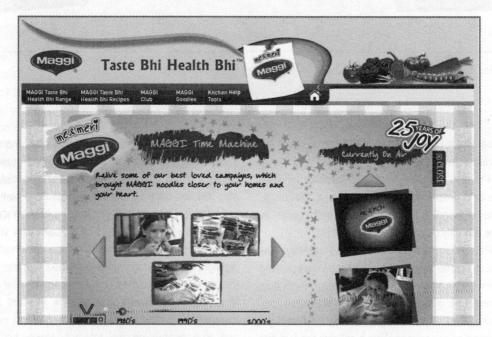

Source: http://www.maggi.in/merimaggitvc.aspx.

Image 1.7   Maggi's 'Aam Aadmi' packaging

Image 1.8 Me and Meri Maggi

The use of the common man in the commercials led to a relevant linkage between the customer and Maggi Noodles. Pradeep Kumar, CA, says, 'Whenever I missed my mother or *gharwala khana,* I always used to eat Maggi.' A consumer of Maggi relates to it strongly and it generally goes in the monthly buying list of a household.

Shaili Patnaik, another consumer, states that Maggi has become such an integral part of her life that while travelling abroad, she tends to carry packets of Maggi depending on the time-frame of her journey, trying different recipes and flavours as add-ons, ending up having a different yet similar comforting experience. This highlights the fact that there exists a strong integration and foundation of the brand in the minds of the consumers.

On completing 25 years in the Indian market and having a whole generation of consumers who had grown up on Maggi, it made sure that it did something special. People who had first tasted the brand as kids were now running households. Seeking to strengthen this association, Maggi initiated the 'Me and Meri Maggi' campaign (Bhandari 2009). (See Image 1.8.) The campaign was an attempt to highlight the happy occasions the consumers had had with the brand and relive their best experiences—their 'Maggi Moments'. The chosen entries were enacted in a TV commercial, printed on Maggi's packs or in newspapers, and also posted on the Internet. Maggi had people participating from all over India, illustrating the fact that Maggi was not just a snack for them, but had become their companion and soul mate. The identity of the brand was still very strong and the company understood this after the response it received in relation to this campaign.

Manaya Garg from Delhi says Maggi has held an essential place in her life. From her childhood days, to her school, college, office, and marriage, Maggi has always been there for her. Consumers like Paremal state that every time the Indian cricket team wins a match, they celebrate it with a hot bowl of Maggi. Maggi is not just an integral part of Indian consumers, but also of the Indians living in different parts of the world. Neelam Sean, a native of Canada, states that it was splendid seeing Maggi in Canada, and also that it is the only snack that her 9-year-old can cook; hence it has made a special place in her life. Consumers connect with the brand and the relationship they have developed with the brand over the years has resulted in a high brand equity that is unrivalled. Its reliability, convenience, and health platform has resulted in it being a part of the Indian kitchen with high recall in anytime snacking category.

Conclusion

A market size of ₹1000 crore, along with a CAGR of more than 20 per cent, has attracted a number of players to the Indian market. Unilever's Knorr Soupy Noodles, GSK's Foodles, Wai Wai, Top Ramen, Big Bazaar's Tasty Treat, etc., are some of the brands that are vying for their share of the pie. Knorr has Kajol explaining to kids 'thoda khao, thoda piyo' and the soupy part adds value making it healthy and adding fun at the same time. Foodles used the nutrition plank to differentiate themselves and were able to capture 5 per cent of the market share within three months of their launch in the South. Though a number of players are entering the market, Ajay Gupta, CEO of Capital Foods believes that with a CAGR of 20 per cent, there is room for everyone. However, it is Maggi that is credited with teaching the unwilling and unadventurous consumers of the 1980s to eat instant noodles out of the pack. In a country like India, where language changes every four kilometres and food habits change every 200 kilometres (Chamikutty 2010a), Maggi has successfully broken this barrier and is a brand to reckon with. Its success lies in its ability to refresh its brand portfolio at regular intervals of time according to the tastes and preferences of the consumer and maintain the ever-important connection with the consumers. Thus, Maggi as a brand is resilient, and over the ages manages to be young for the consumers.

Discussion Questions

1. How did Maggi climb the ladder of success through its branding activities in its initial years?
2. Child: 'Mummy Bhuk Lagi Hai', Mummy: 'Bas 2 Minutes'. This became a household phenomenon instantly. What was the major reason for Maggi to pick-up an Indian line for branding itself?
3. Comment on the branding strategies of Maggi over the years. What further recommendations can you suggest to Maggi to enhance its brand equity?

Case References

Bhandari, Bhupesh (2009), 'Maggi @25', http://www.business-standard.com/india/news/maggi@25/354948/, accessed on 7 March 2011.

Chamikutty, P. (2010a), 'Storm in a Bowl', *Brand Equity*, The *Economic Times*, dated 23 June 2010, p. 1.

Chamikutty, P. (2010b), 'Instant noodles: Rivals turn the heat on Nestlé's Maggi', http://economictimes.indiatimes.com/articleshow/6079650.cms, accessed on 21 August 2010.

Das, D. (2007), Nestlé's Maggi matters, http://www.thehindubusinessline.com/catalyst/2007/12/06/stories/2007120650010100.htm, accessed on 22 August 2010.

Das, D. (2010), 'My strategy is to develop Indian concepts', http://www.thehindubusinessline.com/catalyst/2010/04/15/stories/2010041550030100 htm, accessed on 22 August 2010.

Sharma, R. (2010), 'Maggie more than a 2-minute campaign', http://www.financialexpress.com/news/Maggi-More-than-a-2minute-campaign/616926/, accessed on 22 August 2010.

Viswanath, V. (2002), 'The brand way to success', http://www.thehindubusinessline.com/life/2002/09/23/stories/2002092300100400.htm, accessed on 21 August 2010.

Web resources

http://cgfmcg.com/white_noodles.php, accessed on 23 August 2010.

http://www.exchange4media.com/e4m/news/fullstory. asp?section_id=1&news_id=11985&tag=6718&pict=, accessed on 7 March 2011.

http://www.icmrindia.org/casestudies/catalogue/Marketing/MKTG021.htm, accessed on 23 August 2010.

http://www.icmrindia.org/casestudies/catalogue/Marketing/MKTG144.htm, accessed on 21 August, 2010.

http://www.indiantelevision.com/mam/headlines/y2k9/apr/aprmam29.php, accessed on 23 August 2010.

http://www.maggi.in/merimaggistories.aspx, accessed on 22 August 2010.

http://www.maggi.in/merimaggitvc.aspx, accessed on 23 August 2010.

http://www.Nestlé.in/AnOverview.aspx?nesindia=1, accessed on 21 August 2010.

http://www.Nestlé.in/Nestlé_india_landing.aspx, accessed on 21 August 2010.

http://www.Nestlé.in/PresenceAcrossIndia.aspx?nesindia=2, accessed on 21 August 2010.

http://www.nissinfoods.com/topramen/, accessed on 23 August 2010.

Creating a Brand

2

LEARNING OBJECTIVES

After reading this chapter, you will be able to understand the following:

- Building a brand
- Brand identity
- Brand meaning
- Brand personality
- Brand image

ABOUT THE CHAPTER

The previous chapter highlighted the need for branding. It showed that a brand is a physical entity (a tangible aspect), which has something extra (an intangible aspect) to offer. This chapter provides an understanding of how a brand can be successfully created and how the right combination of both the tangible and intangible attributes results in creating brand loyal customers. It highlights the fact that though a brand is a physical reality, for the customer it is more to do with perception. It is this perceptual entity that decides the customer's response towards the brand and results in creating brand loyal customers (Kotler and Keller 2005), who act as a barrier to the entry of other brands. A brand is not a name or an accessory added at the end of the production process. It is a value that needs to be considered at each and every step of the creation of the product (Kapferer 2009). Any commodity can be transformed into a brand by adding value to it. The value can be in the form of some set of differentiation added to the product. The product can be imbibed with images and this along with values added, form the brand halo. A brand is not what we create in factories, but as Alvin Achenbaum (marketing guru) observed, 'Ultimately, a brand resides in the minds of the consumers' (Parameswaran 2010).

INTRODUCTION

Branding continues to be a strong force in the marketing of an organization's products—be it a physical product or a service. 'A brand is more than a name. It is a relationship based

Exhibit 2.1   Unilever's Brand Imprint

Unilever has incorporated the sustainability agenda and the 'brand imprint' process into its brand innovations and development programme. This enables it to develop brands according to the social and environmental considerations of the consumers. For example, Lifebuoy soap, which for long had positioned itself on the 'germ kill' plank, now goes a step further to creating a healthy nation by keeping people free from diseases. Such campaigns help Unilever connect with its consumers at an emotional level and build loyalty 'on parameters that are beyond the immediate brand use and brand promise'. Surf Excel Quick Wash is another example of an innovation based on customers' concerns of water shortage. By educating customers that Quick Wash saves two buckets of water per wash, it has endeared itself to customers who face water shortage problems and also to customers who are environmentally conscious (Paranjpe 2010).

on an assurance, a promise, and trust. Successful brands deliver these timeless values, build on them, and resonate not just with the immediate needs of the consumers, but also with their larger aspirations.' This helps organizations deliver their brand promise and at the same time build a long-term brand relationship with the customers (Paranjpe 2010). For consumer goods, business branding is one of the best ways to 'deliver long-term profitability, and see real increases in business and shareholder value' (Ataman and Ulengia 2003).

A brand is successful when consumers are convinced that a particular brand is significantly different from the other brands in the same product category. A brand consists of tangible attributes and some intangible benefits. The differences can therefore take the form of either product attributes or of images created around the product (Kotler and Keller 2005). For example, Micromax launched its clamshell mobile phone, Bling, decked with Swarovski crystals on Valentine's Day. This differentiation was compelling enough, and attracted women consumers making it one of Micromax's most successful selling products (Mukerjee and Sengupta 2010).

Exhibit 2.1 shows that designing a product and a brand are activities that go hand in hand. While designing a product, both brand identity and brand personality need to be considered at each step, so that a brand gap does not occur between the two. The question that comes to mind is—how can an organization develop products and build strong brands that are consistent in their brand value and image in order to attract loyal customers? For a layperson, a brand is basically a product (a product is a brand and a brand is a product), but although a product can be copied, a brand cannot. Strong brands endure in the mind of consumers (Briggs 2004) and their benefits can be reaped over a long period of time. So, when and how does a product become a brand? The subsequent sections discuss the same.

STRATEGIC PLANNING FOR THE BRAND—CREATING A BRAND

One of the key determinants of a consumer's relationship with a brand is how the consumer perceives the brand (Fournier 1998). Thus, for marketers it is extremely important to build a strong perception about their brand (Morris 1996). Brands are built over a period of time, and it is a complex phenomenon involving consumers' interactions with the brands, both direct (i.e., by consuming the brand, interacting with the brand, perceiving information about the brand, etc.) and indirect (observing the interactions of family and friends with the brand, through word of mouth, etc.). Thus, both brand identity and brand image are equally important.

Brand identity is 'a set of associations that the brand strategist seeks to create or maintain' (Aaker and Joaschimsthaler 2000). Brand identity is different from brand image, as it is aspirational. Brand image includes the current associations attached to the brand. Brand identity implies that this image can be changed. Thus, brand image is what a brand currently is and brand identity is what a brand should ideally stand for. To create a successful brand identity, organizations need to strategically manage their brands. The brand manager needs to understand that consumers play a dynamic role in building a brand. Consumers are not mere recipients of brand-building activities, they evaluate the brand and form their own perceptions based on various touch points with the brand. The brand-building process, therefore, needs to be understood in its entirety, so that managers can understand customers' perspectives as well. These perspectives need to be built into brand-building activities for a holistic and realistic development of brand equity. This can be done by implementing the strategic brand-building and management process, discussed below and illustrated in Figure 2.1.

Conducting Strategic Analysis

Effective management of a brand starts with a strategic analysis of the internal as well as the external environment of the brand building organization (see Exhibit 2.2). The internal and external analyses can be performed as follows.

Internal company analysis   The brand that is to be built should be as per the 'soul' of the organization. It should flow from the vision and mission of the organization and should be able to capture the strengths of the organization. The competitive advantage of the organization needs to be uncovered and understood along with its weaknesses, so as to frame a realistic brand strategy. Organizational culture is another important aspect that needs to be considered while performing the internal analysis. An organizational culture that directs employees towards providing a consistent brand experience at various levels of interaction should be encouraged. The organization, thus, needs to look at the strengths of the employees as a whole. It then needs to decide how it can leverage this and create a unique brand experience for the customers. More about organizational culture is discussed in the chapter on understanding organizational culture for successful brand management. Brand heritage or how the brand came into being and the current image of the brand need to be understood for building brand identity.

External audit   External audit consists of understanding the external environment of the organization. This understanding is crucial, as this is an uncontrolled variable, which needs constant monitoring for the long-term success of a brand. PESTE analysis gives an understanding of the politico-social environment of the county. This is explained below.

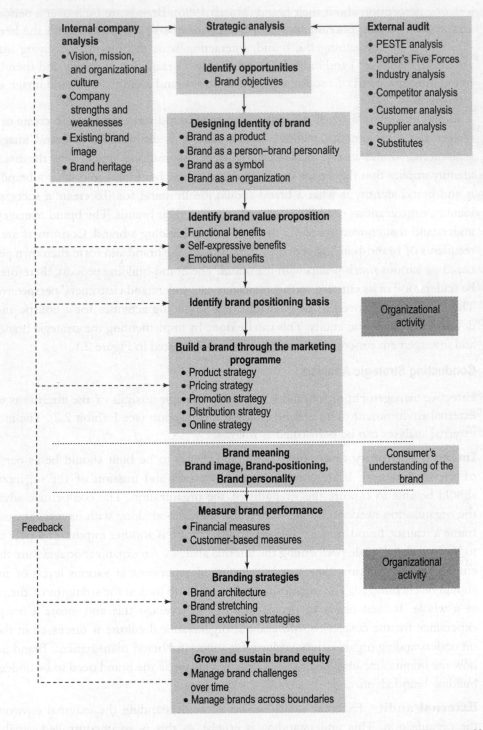

Source: Aaker and Joachimsthaler 2000, Keller 2004, de Chernatony 2001, Jevons, Gabbot, and de Chernatony 2005.

Figure 2.1 Strategic brand-building and management process

Exhibit 2.2   Building the Cera Sanitaryware Brand

The company   Cera Sanitaryware Limited is the third- largest sanitaryware company in India. It commands a market share of '20 per cent in the ₹1000 crore organized market'.

The start   The company was started in 1979, when a split in the family business, Hindustan Sanitaryware Industries Limited (HSIL), led Vikram Somany (Chairman and Managing Director of CSL) to venture out. Being comfortable with sanitaryware, he chose this product category. 'Vikram started doing the rounds of the state government offices in Ahmedabad. He was promised land in Kadi and natural gas from an isolated field.'

Focus on quality   Cera, right from the beginning, focused on one aspect—quality. The conscious use of natural gas in the kiln was a means to this end. Natural gas helped provide a differentiated product and made CSL products superior. (Coal or other fuel left specs on the ceramics.) It took the competition 12–13 years to switch to natural gas as the preferred fuel.

Consumer's demand   Cera understood the need and demand for coloured sanitaryware at the time of its launch (in 1979). It offered consumers a range of 30 colours. Cera's designs were refreshingly different and a 'break from the past'. The 'younger and more youthful' customers lapped up these products. In later years, the 'emerging tastes and preferences of consumers was towards more expensive items with contemporary styling and designs. The market gravitated towards two main colours—ivory and white.' Keeping this in mind, Cera launched 'Whitest White' range of products retailing them at the exclusive company outlets, 'Cera Bath Studios', and through premium retail showrooms in the year 2009.

Current scenario   CSL is currently retailing through 500 distributors and 5000 retail outlets. It has expanded its production capacity, which will soon reach 28 lakh pieces a year. ₹15–20 crore have been set aside for ad campaigns across TV, print, and outdoor media. 'To consolidate its position in the premium segment', Cera launched Novellini, an Italian wellness brand, in the bathroomware segment. This includes shower enclosures and hydro massage bath cubicles. 'The company is betting big on the mid-to-premium segments of the market.' It has set a sales target of ₹500 crore for the next 2–3 years (Mazumdar 2010).

Politico-legal environment   The laws, the various government agencies, and their rules prevailing in an area are important considerations for any organization as they provide a framework of rules and regulations within which a business has to function. A constant monitoring of the political environment helps corporates frame strategies, which are compliant with the legal norms.

Economic environment   This consists of factors affecting the purchasing and spending patterns of consumers. The economic environment is an important indicator of whether it will be worthwhile for an organization to sell its brands in a particular area. The increasing number of affluent customers in India's rural markets is influencing organizations to innovate and sell their brands in these markets.

Socio-cultural environment   The culture and the society of an area impacts the consumption habits and buying behaviours of people.

Technological environment   Technology provides an important platform for organizations to innovate, be it in the way their products are made or the manner in which they are delivered by the organizations or consumed by consumers. The adoption of technology provides a number of opportunities for the brands to update the product and provide current options for consumers.

Environment A concern for the environment and protection of the same is rising not only among consumers, but also among the corporates and the governments. There are a number of rules being framed to ensure environmental protection that organizations have to abide by (for example, the emission norms in vehicles, effluent discharge norms, etc.). Under corporate social responsibility (CSR) programmes, organizations are undertaking activities to help society prosper, whether it is by taking care of the less-privileged sections of society or the environment.

Porter's Five Forces Analysis helps in understanding the competitive environment and the opportunities in the market. The five forces are as follows.

Industry analysis This shows the present trends of growth within an industry and its future projected growth rate. The analysis helps in understanding the attractiveness of the industry and the feasibility of launching a brand within this industry.

Competitor analysis This helps understand the various competitors in the product category, their strategies regarding the marketing mix, and the gap in the market, which the organization can help to fill with its own brand offering.

Supplier analysis Supplier analysis helps identify the bargaining power of the suppliers and ensures the smooth availability of inputs required in manufacturing the brand.

Customer analysis Customer analysis is crucial and helps in identifying potential consumer segments that the organization can target profitably.

Substitutes The various substitutes for a given product category help identify the indirect competition against a brand.

Identifying Opportunities

Once the internal and external analyses are done, the organization needs to do a SWOT (strengths, weaknesses, opportunities, and threats) analysis to identify the opportunities that exist for it in the market. The alignment of the environment opportunities with the company's strengths identifies the niche area that the company can effectively target. This helps in further identification of the objectives of the brand that the organization is planning to offer.

Designing the Identity of the Brand

Brand identity is 'a vision of how the brand should be perceived by its target audience. It is a vehicle that guides and inspires the brand-building programme. If the brand identity is confused or ambiguous, there is little chance that effective brand building will occur' (Aaker and Joaschimsthaler 2000). Brand identity is discussed in detail in the subsequent section. To broaden the scope of identity conceptualization, the framework provided by Aaker (1996) can be considered. This framework helps conceptualize the brand from the following perspectives.

Brand-as-product While formulating the brand identity, the most important aspect for an organization is to consider the brand as a product. This is because a product is directly linked with a brand, and for the consumer the brand and the product are the same thing. Thus, if the product is good it will be among the preferred buying choices of the consumer and will impact user experience. If a consumer has to consider a product as excellent, an organization has to consider the aspects given below.

Scope of the product A brand is always associated with a product. For example, 'Nokia' brings to our minds a range of mobile phones, whereas 'Tata' means cars, FMCG (fast moving consumer goods) products, hotels, etc. A higher product scope leads to a higher brand recall.

Attributes of the product Attributes translate into the features and benefits of a brand, which impact the consumption of the brand by the consumer. A brand that has a higher number of attributes and features, strengthens the identity of the brand.

Country of origin The country from where the brand has originated can be highlighted to strengthen brand identity. For example, German cars, Japanese electronic products, etc.

Quality The quality of the product can be highlighted as its core identity, and organizations can leverage this to strengthen the brand identity. For example, Gillette's tagline says, 'The best a man can get', highlighting that the product has the best quality that is being offered by none other.

Brand-as-organization According to this perspective, organizational attributes can also be highlighted to enhance a brand. Organizational factors, such as innovation and trust can be highlighted to strengthen brand identity.

Brand-as-person This includes the brand personality dimension. Brand personality is 'a set of human characteristics that can be associated with a brand, such as gender and age, and personality traits such as warmth, honesty, integrity, etc.'

Brand-as-symbol Considering the brand as a symbol is helpful in 'giving strength and structure to brand identity.' It is also beneficial in aiding customers to have high recognition and recall about the brand. Brands can be symbolized through visual imagery or by highlighting the brand heritage.

A brand can choose any one or a combination of these to create an identity. A company need not focus on all these aspects to build their brand identity, but should consider only those that effectively communicate what the organization wants to say about the brand or what the organization wants consumers to remember or think about the brand. Exhibit 2.3 shows how an effective brand identity can be designed.

Exhibit 2.3   Designing an Effective Brand Identity—Points to Remember

Brand perspective The brand perspective should not be limited. A brand mantra captures its identity in three or four words, but it should not be a limiting or the only factor for developing brand identity. A brand is much more than what can be captured in a simple phrase. Thus, Big Bazaar is more than just 'value for money'. It also stands for a variety and range of merchandise under one roof. To develop a broader brand perspective, all the elements of branding as discussed in Chapter 1 should be kept in mind.

Functional benefits Compelling functional benefits of the brand should be highlighted wherever possible. The bunny of the Energizer batteries brings to mind that the batteries that have a long life and 'keep going',

Contd

Exhibit 2.3 *contd*

Pantene shampoo advertisements highlight the functional benefit of strong and healthy hair, etc.

Brand constructs Brand constructs that are helpful in creating a positive identity should alone be used. Identity constructs like brand as a product, organization, person, and symbol have been discussed in the text. Apart from this, there are the functional, emotional, and self-expressive benefits. For an organization, highlighting all the constructs is not possible or relevant. The constructs that create a strong, believable, relevant, differentiated image that resonates with the customers and energizes the employees are important and should be used.

Consumer insight It is important to develop an understanding of the consumer. The factors that impact consumers while making a purchase decision are important to understand, so that brand managers can better influence them by developing relevant brand identities.

Competitors For an organization it is easy to focus on their core competencies and what the consumers are looking for. However, another major force that impacts customers is the availability of competing brands. It is therefore imperative to understand what the competitors are doing and how they have positioned their brands. This also helps in developing a brand with unique differential advantage for the organization.

Brand identity The identity of the brand creates an impact on the customers and needs to be managed well. To avoid ambiguity and to cater to the needs of the customers with global exposure, brands should have an identity that is uniform across geographical boundaries. For example, Pantene always focuses on healthy hair and in every country uses the visual image of beautiful strong hair to drive across the message. However, a brand that caters to multiple segments of customers with different needs requires multiple brand identities. For example, multiple brand identities are important for Hewlett Packard, which sells to business professionals, engineers, home users, etc.

Execution Brand identity should be the prime consideration while designing and executing the brand strategy. Various forms of business communication, their product design, their positioning strategies should all be in line with the brand identity and should reinforce same. A company that involves agencies to design brand communication should be particular about the communication being in line with brand identity.

Elaboration The elaboration of brand identity is important to ensure clarity of the same for the employees and various stakeholders. Reducing the brand identity to a few words can lead to perceptual differences and will not effectively communicate what the brand stands for to all the employees. Effective translation of the same to business decisions will not be uniform across the organization, thus leading to faulty execution.

Sources: Aaker and Joaschimsthaler 2000.

Brand identity structure consists of the following (Aaker and Joaschimsthaler 2000).

Core identity of the brand This consists of two to four dimensions that are the most vital elements of brand identity. Typically, brands are represented by 6–12 dimensions that adequately describe the brand identity. Since this large set of dimensions is difficult to manage and communicate to customers, the core elements, which provide a focus to the organization, are identified. The core identity remains constant even when the brand is extended to other product categories or across geographical boundaries. The core elements reflect the values of the organization and its strategy. At least one of these elements should provide the brand with differentiation, so that the band resonates with the customers. A brand is successful when its core identity is clearly understood and perceived by the customers.

Table 2.1 Differences between brand essence and tagline

Brand essence	Brand tagline
Represents brand identity	Represents brand positioning
Meant to energize the internal audience of an organization (primarily the employees of the organization)	Meant to communicate about the brand to external audiences (primarily customers and consumers)
It is expected to be relevant for a long period of time	Has a limited life
Relevant across products and markets for the same brand	Tagline is relevant in a confined area and may vary from product to product and market to market

Extended identity of the brand   A brand cannot be represented by a few core elements alone. Other elements which are important for the brand and which represent the brand form the extended brand identity. The extended brand identity is helpful in providing a perspective to strategy formulators and removes ambiguity, which the core elements may not be able to due to the nature of their brief descriptions. Examples of extended brand identity include brand personality, symbols, etc.

Brand essence   Brand essence is 'a single thought that captures the soul of the brand' and provides the organization with a focus. Just putting together the core brand elements in a sentence is not brand essence. Apart from providing value and differentiation from the competition, brand essence inspires employees, and communicates with and energizes the various partners of the organization. For example, the brand essence of Tata is trust, Fevicol is bonding, Dettol is protection against germs, etc.

Brand essence should consistently be delivered upon and should be scalable, that is brand extensions should be possible. It should not limit the brand, but allow it to grow in other categories as well. Thus, we have Tata, which is represented across a number of product categories—from salt to software. Brand essence is different from a brand's tagline. Brand essence can be used as a tagline, but not all taglines are brand essences. See Table 2.1 for the differences between brand essence and brand tagline.

Identifying Brand Value Proposition

Brand essence provides a value proposition and a differentiation for the customers. This value proposition shows how a brand is unique from its competitors. Brand essence and subsequently the value proposition can be based on functional benefits, self-expressive and/or emotional benefits of the brand. Functional benefits focus on the product attribute, and they can provide a significant sustainable advantage. The disadvantage of using functional benefits, however, is that it limits the brand to one product and brand extensions become difficult. To overcome this, brand essence can be based on the emotional or self-expressive benefit. Emotional benefit is the feeling the customer gets on purchasing or using a brand. Strong identities are built around the emotional aspect. For example, glamour for Lux (Sridhar 2009), 'It's the way you make me feel' for Monte Carlo, etc. Self-expressive benefits allow consumers to express some aspect of their image through the use of the brand. For example, Saffola is 'the healthy oil for healthy people'. Thus, housewives who are concerned about the health of their family would like to use Saffola oil. Another organization that has been successful in identifying its beand value proposition is Castrol (see Exhibit 2.4).

Exhibit 2.4   Castrol Brand Values

Castrol celebrated one hundred years in India in the year 2009. It has been able to ink a success story during these years based on the four pillars of a strong brand, continuous innovation, enduring relationships, and passion of its employees.

It is widely recognized as the leading provider of specialist lubricants. The company remains committed to its core brand values. According to *Superbrands* (2009), 'it is passionate about the customer's success, it is driven by performance but respects the environment, it has confidence that comes from experience from around the world and it challenges the status quo and it always gets things done.' (See Image 2.1.)

Courtesy: Superbrands.

Image 2.1   Castrol ad; also see Plate I

Identifying brand value proposition is important so that a personal relationship can be built with the customer. Thus, a brand can be an enabler (Scooty Pep Plus is a scooter that allows girls to have fun), a friend, etc.

Identifying Brand Positioning Basis

Once the value proposition has been identified, the next step is to communicate the same to the customers, and position the brand in the minds of the customers. Positioning is not something that is done to the brand, but is something that is targeted towards the minds of the consumers. It is what the customers think about a brand vis-à-vis other brands available in the same product category in the market. Positioning is effective when customers think and feel about the brand in a manner similar to the core identity/essence of the brand.

Building a Brand through the Marketing Programmes

Once the positioning is set, it needs to be backed by other strategies of the organization, which are in line with the positioning statement. The strategies that need to be aligned with the brand are the product strategy, pricing strategy, promotion strategy, distribution strategy, and online strategy. All these strategies are discussed in detail in the chapters on branding and marketing programme and branding and marketing communications. A product has to be the best and as per the needs and wants of the customer. It should satisfy some need and want of the customer, and be backed by a high perceived value. An organization that spends time and money in building a brand does not want consumers to develop a negative perception about the brand due to a poorly designed product or due to a product that lacks in the attributes the consumers are looking for.

Building Brand Meaning

Brand managers design a brand and market it. Through their various marketing cues, they communicate with the customers. The consumers also form an understanding of the brand on the basis of their interaction with and usage of the brand. All these inputs result in the consumers forming their own perception about the brand (Jevons et al 2005). This brand meaning can be studied through brand image, brand positioning by the consumers, and brand personality.

Brand image   The consumers, through various interactions and 'moments of truth' with the brand develop a perception about that brand. All the brand associations that consumers hold in their memories help in forming the perception that is known as the brand image (Keller 2004). Brand association is any information that is linked to a brand in the memory of the consumer (Aaker 1991). These associations can denote a physical attribute, functional benefit of a brand, or a symbolic aspect of the brand (Kressmann et al 2006). For marketers, these brand associations differentiate the brand. Developing a positive feeling about the brand and a favourable attitude towards the brand is done by highlighting the benefits of consuming a brand. This further helps in positioning and extending the brand. For consumers, brand associations help organize bits of information together to form a definite perception, and help to retrieve this information at the time of the purchase. For an organization, brand associations can be multi-dimensional (Aaker 1991), and an understanding of the various brand elements is necessary. Brand image is discussed in further detail in the subsequent section.

Brand positioning Identifying the basis on which a brand has to be positioned is an organizational activity. When this positioning is communicated to the consumers, there is no guarantee that consumers will perceive the brand as the organization wants them to. Consumers can form their own perception about the brand and decode brand positioning in an entirely different context. It is, therefore, important for brand managers to develop an understanding of how the consumers have positioned the brand in their minds vis-à-vis the competitors' brands.

Measuring brand personality An organization while designing its brand identity delineates how it wants the consumers to perceive its brand. The consumers can, however, interpret and associate the brand with characteristics that reflect themselves (Fournier 1998). The discussion of brand personality in deriving brand meaning focuses on how brand personality can be measured in order to understand how the consumers personify the brand. A detailed discussion on the measurement of brand personality follows in the brand personality section of brand identity.

Measuring Brand Performance

An established brand has some customer following and recognition. But a brand's true standing in the market can only be identified by measuring its financial performance vis-à-vis the projected performance. The financial performance of a brand can be compared with the financial performances of the other brands in the market to see how well a brand is performing. However, an understanding of the financial measures alone is not sufficient to gauge the performance of a brand. The financial understanding has to be backed by an understanding of customer loyalty and the perception of the customers towards a brand. A brand with a loyal customer base and with a brand image consistent with its brand identity is bound to be successful sooner or later. This understanding is important, as it can help during further revisions of brand strategies.

Strategic Branding

An organization, over a period of time, can launch different brands in the marketplace. This necessitates an understanding of brand architecture or how the brands of an organization are organized or structured in the brand portfolio. Brand portfolio highlights the relationship between brands and 'between different product-market contexts'. This helps provide clarity as to which brand is meant for which segment of the market, leads to optimum offering by an organization, and also avoids confusion in the minds of the customers. It also allows an organization to focus on its brands better and avoid wastage of resources by adding new brands unnecessarily. A successful brand can support the launch of other brands through brand stretching and brand extension strategies. The equity of the established brand will give momentum to a new brand being launched. Brand extension can be done in the following ways.

Endorsers An established brand can endorse a new brand, or in other words lend credibility to a new brand-offering. Consumers who recognize the established brand will feel reassured about the new offering and will be comfortable in purchasing the new brand. For instance, Emami, a long-established brand in the Indian cosmetic industry (established in 1974) used this equity to launch the Emami Fair and Handsome cream targeting the male segment of the market.

Sub-brands These are 'brands connected to a master or parent brand that augment or modify the associations of the master brand.' These brands help the master brand to extend into a meaningful and profitable new market segment. Thus, Himani Navratan Oil, Himani Navratan Cool Talc, etc. are all sub-brands with the master brand name Himani Navratan. Descriptive sub-brands simply describe the offering. For example, there is the Himani Boroplus Antiseptic Cream and the Himani Boroplus Prickly Heat Powder, where the antiseptic cream and the prickly heat powder describe the offering.

Driver roles   The driver role is the extent to which a brand influences the consumer's purchase decision and use of a brand. For instance, if we ask a consumer which brand of car he bought and the answer is 'Nano' rather than Tata Nano, it means that Nano is primarily driving the sales of the brand and not 'Tata', or if the answer is 'Indica', instead of Tata Indica, it signifies that Indica rather than Tata is the primary driver of the sales. Although Tata as a brand is important in increasing the sales of its cars, it is Indica or Nano that are the primary drivers.

This understanding of brand extensions helps an organization to create a brand architecture strategy for the organization, and it can position itself anywhere on the spectrum between a 'branded house' and a 'house of brands'. Further details on this are given in the chapter on managing brand architecture.

Growing and Sustaining Brand Equity

Brand equity needs to be grown and sustained over time. A brand needs to reinvent itself and stay young, so that subsequent generations do not feel that the brand is dated and that is not meant for them. For growing and sustaining brand equity, brand challenges also need to be met over time. All this has been discussed in the chapter on brands over time.

The feedback from brand equity over time forms an input for the strategic analysis stage and also towards designing identity of the brand, identifying value proposition, positioning base, marketing programmes, and branding strategies. This helps the brand grow and stay relevant for the consumers.

Brands need to expand their horizons across geographical boundaries as well. This will help the brand not only to cash-in on but also to grow its brand equity. This has been discussed in further detail in the chapter on brands in a borderless world.

 See how the Aditya Birla Group has strategically built its brand.

STRATEGIC FIT

Figure 2.1 includes a mix of organizational activity and the consumer's perception or understanding of the brand. It is important that there be a strategic fit between the consumers' perception of a brand and the organization's activities (see Figure 2.2), i.e., the identity of the brand designed by the organization should be clearly and readily perceived by the customers. The organization first decides on a brand identity and creates a brand. Then marketing mixes are built around the brand and offered to the consumers. The consumers purchase the brand and consume it. They then evaluate the brand on the basis of the marketing mixes of product design and features, communication regarding the brand with the consumers, price, place from where the brand was purchased (can be a physical or a virtual store), the social responsibility endeavour of the brand, and last but not the least the perceived self-image of the consumers.

A brand perceived to fit the self-image of the consumer has a higher probability of being chosen and consumed. Brand image gains importance in the maturity stage of the product life cycle. At this stage, the image of the brand helps create a competitive advantage and drives the sales of the brand (Ataman and Ulengin 2003).

The customer, after evaluating the brand, forms a perception or image of the brand. This brand image maybe similar or dissimilar to the brand identity created by the organization. If the image is similar to the identity, then the brand meets the customer's expectations, the customer is satisfied and the brand becomes a preferred brand leading to the creation of a strong brand. If on the other hand, the brand image is not as per the brand identity, it creates a brand gap, and the customers will be left confused as the brand promise has not been met. Take the instance of Reliance Telecommunications, when a few years ago, the Dhirubhai Ambani scheme was launched. The brand promised to be affordable, but the consumers on using the plan, realized that there were a number of hidden costs and the offer was not as lucrative as was being communicated by the organization.

 See how the Aditya Birla Group has achieved strategic fit over the years.

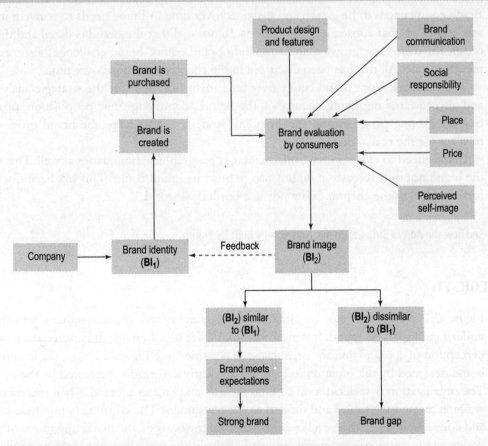

Source: Kapferer 2009, Ataman and Ulengin 2003, Briggs 2004, Christiansen et al. 2009.

Figure 2.2 Fit between brand identity and brand image

DESIGNING BRAND IDENTITY—KAPFERER'S IDENTITY PRISM

Kapferer (2009) categorized brand identity into six dimensions, which may be represented by the six faces of a 'hexagonal prism'. The six facets are broadly categorized under two perspectives—internal and external (see Figure 2.3). The prism helps in providing an understanding of the essence of the brand. The two sides of the prism are discussed as follows.

Left side   The left side projects the brand outward, i.e., the faces on this side are the social faces of the brand and help in expressing the brand. As these faces are visible they result in externalization of the brand. The left side consists of the physique of the brand, the relationship, and the reflection.

Right side   The right side of the prism results in internalization of the brand, i.e., the faces on this side of the prism are incorporated into the spirit of the brand. The right side of the prism consists of the personality of the brand, culture, and self-image.

These six facets are interrelated, help to identify the brand, and set the boundaries within which the brand can be developed. Let us understand the facets of the prism one by one.

Physique of the brand   The physique or the physical features of the brand consist of the external attributes, colours, and forms. The physique is the backbone and defines the brand; what it looks like, what the brand does, and how it can add value to the consumers. Its physique will help differentiate the brand. Marketers can also take the help of packaging to differentiate their brands, for example, the black and yellow packaging of Kodak, the classic bottle of Coca-Cola, etc. For Savlon the physique is described in Figure 2.3.

Brand is a relationship   Brands forge a relationship with their customers, which form the basis of transactions between the brand and the customer. This relationship also helps bind the customers and facilitates the exchange process. Thus, Apple conveys a relationship of friendliness, Punjab National Bank denotes a relationship of trust and reliability, Bank of India talks about relationship beyond banking, etc.

Brand as a reflection of the customer   A brand is a reflection, as over a period of time it reflects the image of the buyer using the brand. For instance, people who consume Pepsi will consider themselves 'young', whereas those who consume Thums Up will consider themselves 'adventurous'. Brands, therefore, need to position themselves not as per the segment they have chosen to market their products in, but according to how their consumers feel or think about themselves. Thums Up is an adventurous brand targeted towards the young. Children consume this brand, as they aspire to be adventurous when they grow up and teenagers and young people drink it because they feel it represents their way of life.

Personality of the brand   Brand personality is an important element of branding, as it helps differentiate one brand from competing brands in the same category. It is defined as 'the set of human characteristics associated with a brand' (Aaker 1997). Brand personality helps in building a sustainable competitive advantage (Ang and Lim 2006). The personality of a brand can drive consumer preference and usage. For example, McDonald has differentiated

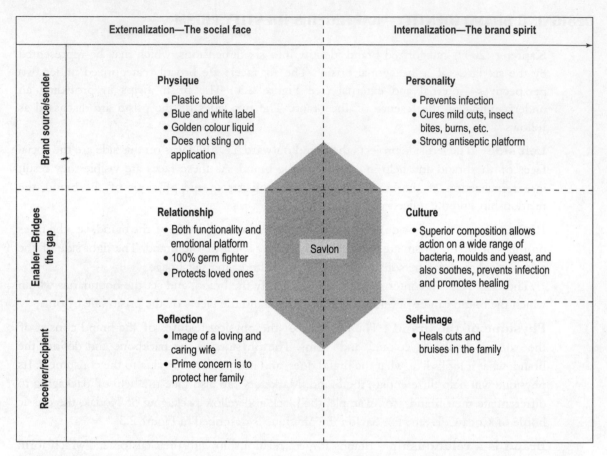

	Externalization—The social face	Internalization—The brand spirit
Brand source/sender	**Physique** • Plastic bottle • Blue and white label • Golden colour liquid • Does not sting on application	**Personality** • Prevents infection • Cures mild cuts, insect bites, burns, etc. • Strong antiseptic platform
Enabler—Bridges the gap	**Relationship** • Both functionality and emotional platform • 100% germ fighter • Protects loved ones	**Culture** • Superior composition allows action on a wide range of bacteria, moulds and yeast, and also soothes, prevents infection and promotes healing
Receiver/recipient	**Reflection** • Image of a loving and caring wife • Prime concern is to protect her family	**Self-image** • Heals cuts and bruises in the family

Savlon

Source: Kapferer 2009, http://www.super branda-brands.com/brand_salvon.htm, Azoulay and Kapferer 2003, Jaiswal, Srivastav, and Kothari 2009.

Figure 2.3　Identity prism for the brand Savlon

itself as a 'child-friendly place' by providing happy meals, by partnering with kids' movies, by using Ronald McDonald as a mascot, etc. (Knutson 2000). For an organization retailing brands across cultural boundaries, the personality of the brand is an important aspect for marketing their brand. Celebrity endorsements help in creating a brand personality, as the celebrity's characteristics rub off onto the brand, helping consumers to relate to the personality of a brand. Thus, Catch brand has taken the help of Juhi Chawla to build their brand and Panasonic has got Ranbir Kapoor to portray their brand personality (*Superbrands*, 2009) (see Images 2.2 and 2.3).

Brand personality can be built in many ways. An organization can build a brand using one or more of the following ways.

User imagery　This consists of a person using a brand. The use of celebrities as endorsers of brands helps in this aspect. Consumers easily relate to their celebrity icons, and this helps them in developing a personality of the brand.

Courtesy: Superbrands.

Image 2.2   Juhi Chawla endorsing Catch; also see Plate 2

Courtesy: Superbrands.

Image 2.3   Ranbir Kapoor endorsing Panasonic; also see Plate 2

Symbols   Organizations can use symbols to develop their brand personality. Amul has built the personality of its brand around the 'Amul girl'. By using the girl in their topical ads, Amul carved out a personality that is friendly, fun-loving, and contemporary. Companies can also change their symbols over time to keep abreast of their changing strategies. For example, Bajaj changed its symbol when it moved from manufacturing scooters to manufacturing motorcycles. The hexagonal symbol with Bajaj Auto embedded was replaced with the open 'Flying B' form to denote dynamism and vibrancy.

Country of origin   Organizations can also use their country of origin to create a personality for their brands. For example, Foster's identifying itself as an Australian beer, Slice of Italy leveraging the Italian expertise for its pizzas, etc.

Sponsorships   Brands through their sponsorship decisions try to build a personality for their brands. For example, Bournvita, a health drink for children, sponsors quiz contests to reflect a personality of intelligent consumers.

Brand is a culture   Brand culture consists of the values that inspire the brand and are the major drivers of the brand. Every brand has its specific culture, which is communicated by the product, and through the message of the brand that is carried by the media. The culture can be communicated through the country of origin, by using the organization brand name. For example, Coca-Cola embodies the American culture, Tata named its first small car—Tata Indica—to denote both the culture of Tata and to communicate the identity of a completely Indian car. The culture of the brand is the key to understanding the differences between competing brands in the same product category.

Brand speaks to the customer's self-image   The consumers form for themselves an image of the brand, which is central to their relationship with the brand. This, therefore, reflects the dimensions of brand identity and delineates the aspects that can be developed further (i.e., favourable dimensions) or changed (unfavourable dimensions). According to the prism concept, a brand should communicate a message and should 'speak for itself'. Consumers purchase brands that closely represent their own characteristic traits.

Self-image is the internal mirror of the consumers. It shows how the consumers feel about themselves. Reflection, on the other hand, is the external mirror or how the consumers want to be perceived by others. A brand identity needs to look at both these aspects and build a relationship with the customer.

Brands can create identity prisms for themselves, and the characteristics of a strong prism are that each facet has a different world and they all contribute towards building a strong identity for the brand, which in turn will make the brand stand out. The importance of this prism can be understood in the context of luxury brands. A luxury brand is an expression of taste and creative identity, and should tell its own story. Today, luxury brands are getting more fashionable and attractive, and they can be successfully marketed by applying the concept of brand identity (Kapferer and Bastien 2009).

Measuring Brand Personality

An important aspect that needs to be discussed is how is brand personality is measured. This has not been discussed within the brand identity prism, because the focus in brand identity is on the internal—the personality that the organization wants its brand(s) to possess. When we talk about measuring brand personality, the focus is external, i.e., how the consumer perceives the brand or what the personality of the brand is according to the consumers.

Aaker (1997) created a scale to measure brand personality. Azoulay and Kapferer (2003), though argue that this personality scale only measures the traits of the brand. But, the five dimensions delineated by Aaker (1997) help in reliable, multi-dimensional measurement of a brand's personality. Aaker was able to identify five major dimensions from a study of 114 personality traits, which are highlighted in Figure 2.4 and Table 2.2.

Brand personality helps in attaching a face to the brand. Companies identify their brands with a personality, but the consumers form their own personality of the brand. As brand managers, it is interesting to learn whether a gap exists between the organizational personality

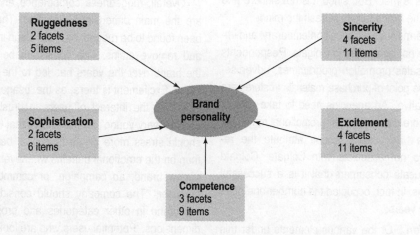

Figure 2.4 Aaker's (1997) brand personality framework

Table 2.2 Aaker's brand personality traits

Sincerity	Excitement	Competence	Sophistication	Ruggedness
1. **Down to earth**	1. **Daring**	1. **Reliable**	1. **Upper class**	1. **Outdoorsy**
Down to earth	Daring	Reliable	Upper class	Outdoorsy
Family oriented	Trendy	Hard-working	Glamorous	Masculine
Small town	Exciting	Secure	Good-looking	Western
2. **Honest**	2. **Spirited**	2. **Intelligent**	2. **Charming**	2. **Tough**
Honest	Spirited	Intelligent	Charming	Tough
Sincere	Cool	Technical	Feminine	Rugged
Real	Young	Corporate	Smooth	
3. **Wholesome**	3. **Imaginative**	3. **Successful**		
Wholesome	Imaginative	Successful		
Original	Unique	Leader		
4. **Cheerful**	4. **Up-to-date**	Confident		
Cheerful	Up-to-date			
Sentimental	Independent			
Friendly	Contemporary			

Exhibit 2.5 Brand Personality for Colgate

Thomas and Sekar (2008) applied Aaker's brand personality framework to study the personality of brand Colgate in Tamil Nadu (India). Let us look at the dimensions one by one:

Sincerity The other dimensions—'realistic, sentimental, down-to-earth'—are more relevant, because the brand is meant for cleaning teeth. Also, the benefits highlighted (white and strong teeth) are based on facts. Thus, the 'physical satisfaction based on functional benefits is met'. But, since it is not sincere and wholesome, the brand fails to refresh the mind.

Exciting Terms such as 'cool, contemporary, and imaginative' are not applicable to Colgate. Respondents felt that the sales promotion programmes, advertisements, and the point-of-purchase materials in stores are not 'very creative'. Ad agencies need to take note of this and be more creative in their promotional materials.

Competence Successful is one attribute the respondents do not associate with Colgate. Colgate needs to educate consumers that it is a successful brand and has, in fact, occupied the number one position for many years.

Sophistication Of the various elements under this dimension, 'charming, smooth, and glamorous' are the most relevant for Colgate. By using the brand, consumers feel physically attractive, and the chances of being admired by relatives and friends are higher. Thus, the concept of 'Colgate users being admired by friends and relatives can be highlighted in their promotional programmes.'

Ruggedness Although the respondents feel that the brand is rugged and tough, it is still not masculine enough. Consumers also do not consider the brand feminine, therefore, it is wise for Colgate not to highlight its gender specific characteristics.

Overall, 'ruggedness, competence, and excitement' are the main dimensions identified. The brand has been found to be rugged, as it can clean irregular teeth and remove stains. The consistent performance of the brand over the years has led to the competence factor. Excitement is there, as the 'usage of the brand increases the interest of users in brushing, making one feel very young'. All this shows that 'the company should stress more on its functional benefits, rather than on the emotional benefits whenever it introduces a new brand, ad campaign, or communicates with the user.' 'The company should consider extending the brand in other categories and projecting these dimensions. 'Potential users who are looking for these dimensions among oral care brands' will be attracted to using the brand once these attributes form the basis of brand communication (Thomas and Sekar 2008).

and the consumer's perceived personality (see Exhibit 2.5). Brand personality can be used by consumers to express themselves or their ideal selves; therefore brand personality will affect their choice of brand (see Figure 2.5).

Actual self Consumers consume a brand on the basis of what they are. For example, people going to work daily will choose the brand of clothing they wish to wear depending on what they think of themselves.

Aspirational self Consumers also consume a brand on the basis of what they aspire to be. For example, a young graduate may choose to wear a particular brand to an interview.

Situational self Consumers may consume a brand depending on the situation they are in. For example, in Japan, Kit Kat (known as Kittu Katsu in Japan) launched a new blue packaging (to symbolize the heavens) instead of the traditional red package. Parents now gift Kit Kat

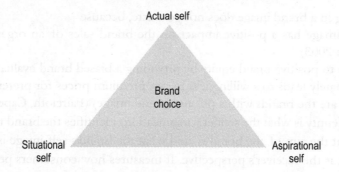

Figure 2.5 Brand choice and brand personality

to their children during exams as a token of good luck, as *kittu katsu* in Japanese closely translates into good luck.

According to de Chernatony (2008), a consumer's choice of brand depends on certain factors. Consumers consume brands on the basis of their self-image and reject brands that do not match their self-image. Thus, while communicating the emotional aspect of brand personality, marketers should keep in mind the emotional role the brand is supposed to play for the potential consumers. The friendly Amul girl, the Pillsbury doughboy, Gattu of Asian Paints, etc. all contribute to building their respective brand personalities.

Brand personality is important because (Sagar, Singh, Agarwal, and Gupta 2009, Aaker 1996):

1. It is a vehicle for the customers to express their identity. For example Scooty Pep Plus advertisements show actor Priyanka Chopra expressing her identity through the use of the brand
2. It forms the basis of the relationship between the brand and the customer. Banks, for instance, focus on providing friendly help and building relationships as key attributes of their personality, in order to attract consumers.
3. It performs a functional benefit by effectively communicating the key product attributes. For example, the Michelin Man represents the strong and sturdy tyres of the Michelin Company, the muscleman of MRF tyres denotes the strength of the tyres, etc.
4. It contributes to building customer preference and brand equity. For example, the use of famous personalities like Sachin Tendulkar, Amitabh Bachchan etc. as brand personalities helps in building customer preference for the brand.

BRAND IMAGE

Brand image is 'the set of beliefs held about a particular brand' (Kotler and Keller 2005) by the consumer. This image is formed by an understanding of all the brand associations (Faircloth, Capella, and Alford 2001). Brand associations are developed from all the 'signals emitted by the brand' (Kapferer 2009), and through the consumer's use of the brand (Keller 2004). Brand image gives an understanding of how consumers choose a particular brand over the others.

Investing in a brand image does not go waste, because

- Brand image has a positive impact on the brand sales of an organization (Ataman and Ulengia 2003).
- It leads to positive brand equity by providing a biased brand evaluation (Krishnan 1996).
- It ultimately leads to a willingness to pay premium prices for preferred brands (preferred brands are the brands with a positive brand image) (Faircloth, Capella, and Alford 2001).

Brand identity is what the sender (organization) identifies the brand to be—what the brand means, what the aim of the brand is, and what the brand's self-image is. Brand image, on the other hand, is the receiver's perspective. It measures how consumers perceive the brand.

Brand image is defined as, 'the perceptions about a brand as reflected by the brand associations held in the consumer's memory.' Brand associations are 'anything linked to the memory of a brand'. The association can be with the brand's attribute, benefit, or attitude (Keller 1993, 2001). 'Brand attributes are the tangible and intangible features and the physical characteristics of the brand.' Thus, even though they are based on objective criteria they actually become perceptual. This is due to the fact that the way in which the consumers perceive an attribute determines the worth of that attribute (Faircloth, Capella and Alford, 2001).

A brand benefit is the significance and meaning attached to a brand attribute by the consumer. Research shows that consumers rely heavily on their past experiences as an important source of information regarding a brand. Organizations should, therefore, focus on the experience of the customers and try to be more innovative, in order to create a memorable impact on the customers through their brand benefits. Organizations should study the perception of brand benefits on part of the customers, as these individuals also constitute the reference set for other potential customers (Dutta 2009). This has been further discussed in the chapter on consumer behaviour. Brand image should be 'strong, favourable, and unique' and can be developed on the basis of any, or all, or a combination of the following attributes (Keller 1993).

Product Product attributes are related to the physical composition of the product and vary according to the product category. For example, the attributes necessary in a TV would be different from those sought for in vacuum cleaners or mobile phones. When evaluating the TV category, consumers look for picture quality, sound quality, colour composition, etc.

Price Price is an important consideration when consumers are evaluating products. They tend to organize their product category knowledge on the basis of price tiers of different brands.

Packaging This has also been considered an important part of the purchase and consumption process. It influences brand equity, both directly (as a brand element) and indirectly (by impacting the brand image). Packaging has been discussed in detail in the section on brand element.

User imagery This relates to the type of person using the product. Demographic factors, psychographic factors, etc., will affect user imagery.

Usage imagery This relates to the type of situations in which the product is used. The time of the day, week, or year, type of activity, etc., contribute to forming usage imagery.

Both, the user and usage imagery could either be the result of the consumer's own experience with the brand or be based on the marketing communications of the organization. Together, they produce the brand personality attributes, which 'reflect the feelings evoked by the brand.'

Brand attitude is the 'overall evaluation of the brand', which may be good or bad (Mitchell and Olson 1981).

To help develop the image of the brand in the mind of consumers, organizations can use metaphors. Examples of organizations using metaphors are Rin (is white—'Safedi ki chamkar'), Zatak (it's very, very sexy), etc. Metaphors help us measure brand associations. Brand meanings can be studied by adopting any of the following measures.

Free association   What are the first three words that come to mind when thinking of the brand?

Picture interpretation   Respondents are asked to interpret a picture that is given to them. The picture will allow the respondents to express their real feelings, however awkward they may be.

Brand as a person   If the brand was a person, would it be friendly, cheerful, and honest? Peter England shirts through their communications strategy tried to express that their brand was an honest person.

Brand as an animal/magazine   If the brand were an animal/magazine, what kind of animal or magazine would it be? Why? What characteristics of the animal, flower, etc., remind you of the brand? And so on.

Use experience   Brand managers can discuss with consumers, their past experiences with the brand. This helps in creating a picture of the brand that has not been summarized.

Decision process   A study of how consumers decide about a brand can help identify the meanings consumers associate with the brand.

Brand user   This aspect looks at and identifies the brand users rather than the brand use. It highlights 'how do the needs and motivations of the users of the two brands differ?'

Differential perception   This includes perception of the brand by the customers and how the brand is different from competing brands. This helps in understanding whether the customers think differently about brands or not.

Personal values that drive choice   An understanding of the personal values of the customers highlights the end state of the customers. For example, feeling of importance, self-esteem, happiness, etc. The desired ends can be met by benefits like 'saves money', 'miles per litre', etc., which can then be used as key brand associations.

SUMMARY

Organizations invest time, money, and effort in building a product and establishing a reputation in the market. To get maximum returns on the investment and to increase marketability, organizations use branding.

Creating a brand is a sequential task and starts with the strategic analysis of the external and internal environment. From this analysis, the opportunities are highlighted and brand objective is delineated. The next step is to design the personality of the brand, which can be done by denoting the brand as a product, person, symbol, or organization. The brand value proposition is then drawn along the lines of functional, self-expressive, or emotional benefits. The brand positioning basis and the marketing strategies of the organization related to the product, price, promotion, place, and online strategies are drawn up next. After its creation, the brand needs to be monitored constantly.

All the communication with a customer regarding a brand leads to the creation of brand image and brand personality. Brand managers, therefore, need to be very sure of their product, of the communications with customers, and of the various interactions the customers have had with the brand. These various inputs result in the creation of a brand identity.

The customers' understanding of the brand in terms of positioning, personality, and brand image is then studied and the performance of the brand is measured both in financial and customer-based terms. A successful brand so created can then offer opportunities to the organization in terms of extension and stretching strategies, and hence brand architecture is important for the successful management of different brands.

Brand extensions can take the form of endorsers, sub-brands and driver-roles. Kapferer's brand identity prism provides an understanding of how brand identity can be designed. The left side is external and consists of physique, relationship, and reflection, and the right side is internal and consists of personality, culture, and self-image. Aaker's brand personality traits help in measuring the personality of the brand and consist of sincerity, excitement, competence, sophistication, and ruggedness.

All the signals of the brand result in the formation of a brand image which impacts brand equity, sales, and willingness to pay a premium for the brand. A positive image can be developed on the basis of product, price, packaging, user and usage imagery.

KEY TERMS

Brand associations   Anything and everything that is linked to a brand in the memory of the consumer.

Brand attribute   The tangible and intangible features along with the physical characteristics of the brand.

Brand essence   It is the brand identity that is meant to energize the internal audience of an organization.

Brand gap   The gap caused due to the difference between the brand identity established by the company and the brand image perceived by the customers.

Brand identity   A set of associations that the brand strategist seeks to create or maintain.

Brand image   A set of beliefs held about a particular brand by consumers.

Brand personality   A set of human characteristics associated with the brand.

Brand tagline   It is the brand positioning that is communicated to the external audience.

EXERCISES

Concept Review Questions

1. Discuss how an organization can undertake strategic analysis for the identification of brand opportunities.
2. Discuss the strategic brand building process.

3. Differentiate between the following:
   (a) Brand essence and brand tagline
   (b) Brand value proposition and brand positioning basis
   (c) Core identity and extended identity

(d) Externalization and internalization from the brand identity prism

4. What is brand identity? How is it different from brand image?

5. Discuss any three ways in which an organization can build its brand image. Why do you think these ways are important?

Critical Thinking Questions

1. Apply external audit to evaluate the market opportunities for a firm that plans to enter the market with a brand of cheese in the processed food category.
2. Critically discuss how the identity of a brand can be designed.
3. Which of the various PESTE (political, economic, social, technological, environmental) factors can be identified for CSL (refer Exhibit 2.2)?
4. Critically discuss the strategic fit. Can you identify situations when brands actually faced the issue of a strategic fit?

Internet Exercises

1. Visit the website of Micromax at http://www.micromaxinfo.com/. Discuss how the organization is trying to build its brand identity. How is this different from/in line with the brand image you and your friends have about the brand?
2. Visit the Thai Airways website at http://www.thaiairways.co.in/. Which of Aaker's brand personality traits can you identify for the organization? Give reasons.
3. Visit the website of Samsung at http://www.samsung.com/in/. What brand image can you form for the organization by looking at the website? Is there a brand gap between the image you have and the image the organization is trying to build through the website? Discuss possible solutions.

CD Exercise

View the Adani Wilmar ad and discuss the various measures taken by the company to create the Fortune brand.

REFERENCES

Aaker, D. (1991), *Managing Brand Equity—Capitalizing on the value of a brand name,* The Free Press, New York.

Aaker, D. (1996), *Building Strong Brands*, The Free Press, New York.

Aaker, D.A., and E. Joachimsthaler (2000), *Brand Leadership*, The Free Press, New York.

Aaker, J.L. (1997), 'Dimensions of Brand Personality', *Journal of Marketing Research*, Vol. 34, Issue 3, pp. 347–56.

Ataman, B. and B. Ulengin ((2003), 'A note on the effect of brand image on sales', *Journal of Product and Brand Management*, Vol. 12, Issue 4, pp. 237–250.

Azoulay, A. and J.N. Kapferer (2003), 'Do brand personality scales really measure brand personality?' *Journal of Brand Management*, Vol. 11, No. 2, pp. 143–155.

Briggs, H. (2004), 'The value of integrating the brand experience into the product development process', http://www.pdma.org/vision/oct04/product development-practices.html, accessed on 25 December 2009.

Christiansen, J., C.J. Varnes, B. Hollensen, and B.C. Blomberg (2009), 'Co-constructing the brand and the product',

International Journal of Innovation Management, Vol. 13, Issue 3, pp. 319–348.

Dutta, Kirti (2009), 'Consumer information sources and Effectiveness of Advertising Media—An analysis of India, Turkey, and New Zealand' presented at the 4th International Conference on Services Management held at Barceló Hotel, Oxford, organized by the Oxford Brookes University, Pennsylvania State University, USA and IIMT between 8 and 9 May 2009.

Faircloth, J. B., L.M. Capella, and B.L. Alford 2001, 'The effect of brand attitude and brand image on brand equity', *Journal of Marketing Theory and Practice*, Vol. 9, Issue 3, pp. 61–75.

Fournier, S. (1998), 'Consumers and their brands—Developing relationship theory in consumer research', *Journal of Consumer Research*, Vol. 24, Issue no. 4, pp. 343–373.

http://www.superbrands-brands.com/brand_salvon.htm; Savlon, accessed on 25 December, 2010

Jaiswal, A. K., A. Srivastava, and D. Kothari (2009), 'Dettol—Managing brand extensions', *Asian Case Research Journal*, Vol. 13, Issue 1, pp. 105–143.

Jevons, C., M, Gabbon, and L. de Chernatony (2005), 'Customer and brand manager perspectives on brand relationships—A conceptual framework', *Journal of Product and Brand Management*, Vol. 14, Issue 4/5, pp. 300–309.

Kapferer, J. N. (2008), *The New Strategic Brand Management*, 4th Edition, Kogan Page, New Delhi.

Kapferer, J. N. and V. Bastien (2009), 'The specificity of luxury management—turning marketing upside down', *Journal of Brand Management*, Vol. 16, Issue 5/6, pp. 311–322.

Keller, K. L. (1993), 'Conceptualizing, Measuring and Managing Customer-based brand equity', *Journal of Marketing*, Vol. 57, Issue no. 1, pp. 1–22.

Keller, K. L. (2001), 'Building customer-based brand equity—Creating brand resonance required carefully sequenced brand-building efforts', *Marketing Management*, Vol. 10, Issue 2, pp. 14–16.

Keller, K. L. (2004), *Strategic Brand Management—Building, Measuring and Managing Brand Equity*, Prentice-Hall of India Private Limited, New Delhi.

Knutson, B. J. (2000), 'College students and fast food—how students perceive restaurant brands', *Cornell Hotel and Restaurant Administration Quarterly*, Vol. 41, Issue 3, pp. 68–74.

Kotler, P. and K.L. Keller (2005), *Marketing Management*, 12th Edition, Prentice-Hall of India, New Delhi.

Kressmann, F., M.J. Sirgy, A. Hermann, F. Huber, S. Huber, and D.J. Lee (2006), 'Direct and indirect effects of self-image congruence on brand loyalty', *Journal of Business Research*, Vol. 59, Issue no. 6, pp. 955–964.

Krishnan (1996), 'Characteristics of memory associations—a consumer-based brand equity perspective', *International Journal of Research in Marketing*, Vol. 13, Issue no.4, pp. 389–405.

Mazumdar, R. (2010), 'After 30 years, it's Que Cera Cera', *The Economic Times*, dated 16 June 2010, pp. 4.

Mitchell, A. A. and J.C. Olson (1981), 'Are product attribute beliefs the only mediator of advertising effects on brand attitude?' *Journal of Marketing Research*, Vol. 18, Issue no. 3, pp. 318–332.

Morris, B. (1996), 'The brand's the thing', *Fortune*, Vol. 133, Issue 4, pp. 28–38.

Mukerjee, W. and D. Sengupta, 'Desi mobile brands ringing in smart tunes', *The Economic Times*, New Delhi, dated 28 July 2010, pp. 4.

Parameswaran, A. M. G., 'You can make a brand out of any commodity', *The Economic Times*, New Delhi, dated 22 November 2010, pp. 4.

Paranjpe, N. 'Great expectations—Looking at brands as citizens', *Brand Equity, The Economic Times*, New Delhi, dated 1 September 2010, pp. 4.

Sridhar, R. (2009), 'Bending the global brand', http://www.thehindubusinessline.com/catalyst/2009/12/03/stories/2009120350040200.htm accessed on 26th December, 2010

Superbrands 2009, 'Superbrands—An insight into India's strongest consumer brands', Vol. 3, Superbrands India Private Limited, Gurgaon.

Thomas, B. J. and P.C. Sekar (2008), 'Measurement and validity of Jennifer Aaker's brand personality scale for Colgate brand', *Vikalpa*, Vol. 33, Issue 3, pp. 49–61.

CASE STUDY

LUX—Symbolizing Beauty*

Lux is an established brand of Hindustan Unilever Limited (HUL), renowned to be one of the giant players in the fast moving consumer goods (FMCG) segment. Over the course of time, HUL has diversified its portfolio and has marked its presence across twenty different categories, such as food brands (Annapurna, Knorr, Taaza, etc.), homecare brands (Vim, Surf Excel, Active Wheel, etc.), personal care brands (Axe, Ponds, Sunsilk, etc.), and Pure-it water purifier to reach the pinnacle of success.

Lux continues to be a star performer in Unilever's brand portfolio and this case explores how Lux has successfully overcome the challenge of appealing to all consumers, young and old, from Sec A to Sec E across the length and breadth of a huge country like India.

The product glitterati of the soaps

Lux was launched as a toilet soap by Unilever's Lever Brothers in the year 1925 and in a span of three years,

*Amit Bhargava (Management Executive – Marketing, Global Agrisystem Pvt. Ltd) and Akansha Lamba (Management Executive – Consultancy and Projects, Global Agrisystem Pvt. Ltd).

it was introduced in the UK market as a product 'offering people a chance to pamper themselves for a modest price'. In the year 1929, Lux expanded its international customer base by introducing itself in India. The brand name, 'Lux', has been derived from the word 'luxury', but the word in Latin symbolizes 'light'. Unilever blended both these elements and portrayed Lux in sync with stardom and the luxurious lifestyle of Bollywood celebrities, well-known among the Indian audiences. Its journey continued to enlighten women about the power of beauty bestowed them. The various variants in its portfolio, lend Lux a certain charm (see Table 2.3).

Table 2.3 Lux variants

Soft Kiss	Made from strawberries and moisturizing whipped cream for soft and kissable skin.
Velvet Touch	Made with peach and moisturizing whipped cream for velvety and kissable skin.
Silk Caress	Made with rich macadamia and moisturizing whipped cream for nourished and kissable skin.
White Glamour	For fair and admired skin with vitamin B3, Rose oil, and white tea oxidant.
Wake Me Up	For recharged and fresh skin with refreshing mineral salts and seaweed.
Magic Spell	For soft and fragranced skin with fine aromatic oils and lotus essence.

Source: HUL—Reveal Your Star Appeal, 2010.

Apart from these, in its eighty years of experience in the market, Lux has also launched other variants, which include Lux Strawberry and Cream, Lux Peach and Cream, Lux Festive Glow with Honey, Lux Cream White, Chocolate Seduction, Sandalwood+Honey, Purple Aromatic Glow, etc. All these variations have made it a sensuous brand, which focuses on caressing a woman's body with gentleness to give it a glow and also develop a fragrance to mesmerize her partner.

Brand strategy

Bollywood beauties through the ages

Right from its launch in 1929, Lux has roped in reigning beauties of the silver screen to endorse the brand. The foremost beauty brand ambassador being Leela Chitnis

(Srinivasan and Shashidhar 2007), and following this tradition was Madhubala in the era of the 50s; Waheeda Rehman, Saira Banu, Parveen Babi, and Simi Grewal during the 60s and 70s; and Hema Malini, Zeenat Aman, Poonam Dhillon, Rati Agnihotri heading the generation of the 80s (Mitra 2010). Marking the change in generations and to maintain the market dynamics, Sridevi endorsed it in the 80s, and the 90s were ruled by Juhi Chawla (Chatterjee 2005), Karisma Kapoor, Rani Mukherji, and Madhuri Dixit (Mitra 2010). The other leading ladies associated with the brand have been Kareena Kapoor, Priyanka Chopra, and Aishwarya Rai, the latest additions to this bandwagon being Katrina Kaif (Chatterjee 2010) and Asin. (Image 2.4 shows Katrina Kaif endorsing Lux.)

All these beauties from Bollywood joined the Lux fraternity at the very peak of their careers, which resulted in the belief that by joining the Lux fraternity, a star is born. Jayalalitha who endorsed the brand during the 70s, has distinguished herself in the field of politics along with mastering the key to success in cinema (Mitra 2010). All this has helped the brand in mounting strong relationships with customers from all sections, ranging from SEC A to E (Chatterjee 2005). Lux cashed in on the consumer's secret desire of being a Bollywood celebrity someday and the aspiration to be at the top spot in whichever field they choose to enter. This helped in establishing an assured linkage between the consumers and the brand. The beauty soap manufacturer has continued to establish its relationship with every generation, and continues to innovate its product and packaging by using young and vibrant colours and celebrities who are in sync with the latest styles.

On the eve of its 75th platinum jubilee, there was a complete transformation in its branding strategy when reigning superstar Shah Rukh Khan was seen promoting the brand along with the Bollywood beauties who had endorsed the brand in the past. He 'portrayed the metro-sexual male with a soft touch' and 'a soft guy who is in touch with his emotions'. This unique transition was adopted as he has been a great favourite with women of all ages (Chatterjee 2005) and 'the usage of the brand actually showed a gender split' (Mitra 2010).

Promotional offers

A promotional offer of Lux that has enjoyed immense popularity is the Lux Gold Star offer, 'in which consumers

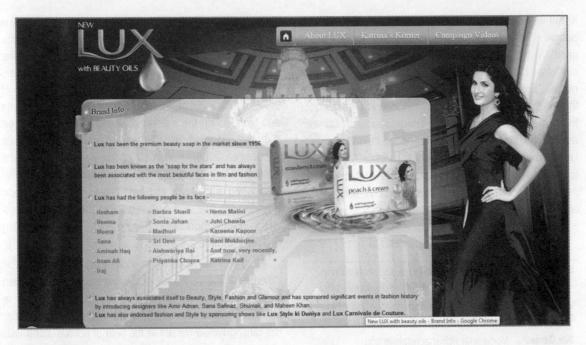

Source: http://www.lux.com.pk/brand_info.html, accessed 22 August 2010.

Image 2.4   Lux and Katrina Kaif; also see Plate 3

had the chance of finding a gold coin inside their Lux soap'. This was initially offered in the year 2000 and in the succeeding year it was themed 'Chance Hai', where the winner of the gold coin had an additional opportunity to win an extra thirty grams of gold by calling the advertised telephone number. The first ten callers each week were given the additional 30 grams of gold. 'The offer was valid on 100 grams (pink, white, and black) and 150 grams (pink and black) Lux toilet soaps, bearing the specially designed gold star logo on the wrapper. The 100 grams soap bar contained a 3 grams gold coin and the 150 grams soap bar contained a 5 grams gold coin.' Actress Raveena Tandon who was roped in for the 2001 endorsement travelled 'across select cities and made surprise visits to several homes, rewarding those having Lux gold star wrappers with more gold stars'.

The year 2009 saw a decline in sales of the brand, especially in small towns where the housewife was falling out of love with Lux. 'Post research, a key insight emerged—the small town housewife wants to look beautiful for her husband and wishes to recapture the magic of her early days of marriage, but without being too obvious

about her 'seducing' efforts, as societal pressures did not permit her to be too bold.' To meet this need, 'Bollywood's real-life star couple, Abhishek Bachchan and Aishwarya Rai Bachchan' were roped in. (Image 2.5 shows a still from the Abhi-Aish ad campaign for Lux.) 'Aishwarya, had been a longstanding brand endorser for Lux (for more than a decade) and roping in her husband seemed to be the logical thing to do', to portray couple play. This was helped by the fact that there was a lot of curiosity surrounding Bollywood's ideal romantic couple post their marriage. 'The commercial showed Aishwarya enjoying a luxurious bath using the new Lux with beauty oils, and deciding to spring a surprise on her husband. When Abhishek comes home from work, she blindfolds him and he has to find her by her new-found scent. A playful sensual game of 'catch me if you can' ensues, with Abhishek unable to catch his wife as his hands glide off her smooth skin. Finally, when he thinks he has her, he removes his blindfold, only to see that he is hugging his cleaning lady instead, as Aishwarya laughs on. A music track composed by trio Shankar-Ehsaan-Loy lent a rustic, Sufi-esque feel to the film. The ad was unveiled on a reality show about marriage,

Source: http//www, luxindia.in/, accessed 23 August 2010.

Image 2.5   Lux promotion; also see Plate 3

called Lux Perfect Bride (on Star Plus), with an in-serial placement for the brand's skin softening elements, as well as a blindfold game akin to the one in the commercial being played out by the contestants. The campaign was extended to another quick promotional one featuring the couple talking about 'good news'—a double meaning quip—about the Lux gold coin offer. The Sufi-esque track, *Sone se bhi sona lagey*, became a popular download item (as ringtones and others) with thousands of downloads over the Internet' (Joshi 2010).

The couple endorsed the 'Lux soap rich with beauty oils for soft skin like never before'. The new variant, along with offering a lavish bathing experience offers 'softer skin and a new you' (Lad 2009). Abhishek's ad was much appreciated, as it had a woman's beauty being cherished. Further, Lux capitalized by portraying Aishwarya Rai's 'noticeably softer skin to disarm even the most unflappable of men' (Lad 2009). This reflects Lux's old tradition of remaining a beautifying symbol for Indian women (Kashyup 2009).

Events and contests such as '22 carat gold star offer' were hosted to relate to customers' feelings of becoming a star. In another campaign, Lux also promised customers a chance to meet brand endorsers—Abhi-Ash—in London (Chatterjee 2010).

This activity helped the brand gel with the consumer. The consumer got an opportunity to rub shoulders with real-life stars in London, and the company managed to showcase the fact that when it says Lux is a soap for the stars, it means it!

All that glitters did turn out to be gold for Lux

In more than eight decades of its existence, Lux has consistently proved itself to be the beauty soap for the stars.

Lux during its existence has remained persistent in grabbing the number one slot in the personal care segment (2010). Following its line of success, it won the title of the 'most trusted brand' by grabbing the third position (2010a). Lux has gained immense popularity amongst different stratam of customers during its journey, be it the housewife, the young male, or the adult female (*Brand Equity*, 2010b). The star endorsers over the years have felt that endorsing Lux has added to their stature as well. According to Hema Malini, 'One of the turning points of my career was when I was signed up by Lux. It was then that I knew that I had made my mark in Indian cinema. To be a Lux star is a much sought-after honour among leading ladies and it truly means a lot to me.' Juhi Chawla had once said, 'I do believe that a significant recognition I received other than winning the Miss India crown was being named a Lux star.' Thus, it is not only Lux that has gained from the endorsers, but being an endorser for the brand is a matter of honour and a stamp of achievement.

Conclusion

Lux has successfully forged a link between the usage of the brand and consumers becoming stars and following in the footsteps of the leading ladies of the silver screen of their times. Lux has continued its romance with the consumers over the years (Shukla 2008). The perspective of having customers relate to their favourite Bollywood star from generation to generation is a tough nut to crack. This reflects the brand's competitive edge, even as it continues to link itself to the 'beauty', 'style', 'fashion', and 'glamour' of the Bollywood beauties endorsing the product. The brand has grown from strength to strength and with the help of a long star-studded heritage has sustained customers' interest and its reputation in the market.

Discussion Questions

1. Using the Kapferer model, elaborate the long and star-studded journey of Lux.
2. Discuss the strategy of using film stars to promote the product.

Case References

'Category Rank', *The Economic Times—Brand Equity*, Wednesday, 1 September 2010, pp. 9–12.

'100 most trusted brands', *The Economic Times—Brand Equity*, Wednesday, 1 September 2010a, pp. 1–4.

'Demographic Dashboard', *The Economic Times—Brand Equity*, Wednesday, 1 September 2010b, pp. 5–8.

Chatterjee, P. 2005, 'Coup Lux Khan', http://www.thehindubusinessline.com/catalyst/2005/09/29/stories/2005092900160300.htm, accessed on 22 August 2010.

Chatterjee, P. 2010, 'HUL Renewed Soap Saga' http://www.thehindubusinessline.com/catalyst/2010/07/22/stories/2010072250020100.htm, accessed on 22 August 2010.

Joshi, D. 2010, 'Effies 2010—Lux and Abhi-Ash magic', http://www.afaqs.com/news/story.html?sid=28988, accessed on 8 March 2011.

Kashyup, P. 2009, 'Brand Yatra—Bolloywood queens' beauty in a bar', http://www.exchange4media.com/brandspeak/brandspeak_FS.asp?Section_id=42&News_id=35241&Tag=30849, accessed on 23 August 2010.

Lad, M. 2009, 'Abhishek Bachchan, Aishwarya Rai feature in Lux's latest campaign', http://www.campaignindia.in/news/2009/11/02/abhishek-bachchan-aishwarya-rai-feature-in-lux-s-latest-campaign, accessed on 22 August 2010.

Mitra, M. 2010, 'Scent of the Women', *The Economic Times—Brand Equity*, Wednesday, September,1, pp. 13–16.

Shukla, A. 2008, 'In Consumer Custody', http://www.livemint.com/2008/06/08234444/In-consumer-custody.html, accessed on 23 August 2010.

Srinivasan, S. and A. Shashidhar 2007, 'Survival of the focused', http://business.outlookindia.com/article.aspx?100117, accessed on 22 August 2010.

Web resources

http://www.businesswireindia.com/pressrelease.asp?b2mid=193, accessed on 23 August 2010.

http://www.hul.co.in/aboutus/introductiontohul/HULataglance/?WT.LHNAV=HUL_at_a_glance, accessed on 21 August 2010.

http://www.hul.co.in/brands/personalcarebrands/, accessed on 22 August 2010.

http://www.hul.co.in/brands/personalcarebrands/Lux.aspx, accessed on 22 August 2010.

http://www.hul.co.in/mediacentre/pressreleases/2010/HULJuneQuarterResults2010.aspx, accessed on 21 August 2010.

http://www.icmrindia.org/casestudies/catalogue/Marketing1/MKTA022.htm, accessed on 21 August 2010.

http://www.indiaglitz.com/channels/hindi/article/16713.html, accessed on 21 August 2010.

http://www.indiantelevision.com/mam/headlines/y2k5/sep/sepmam25.htm, accessed on 22 August 2010.

http://www.luxindia.in/, accessed on 23 August 2010.

http://www.luxindia.in/, accessed on 8 March 2011.

http://www.unilever.co.uk/brands/personalcarebrands/lux.aspx, accessed on 21 August 2010.

http://www.unilever.com.my/brands/personalcarebrands/lux.aspx, accessed on 22 August 2010.

Understanding Organizational Culture for Successful Brand Management

3

LEARNING OBJECTIVES

After reading this chapter, you will be able to understand the following:

- Organizational culture
- The strategic brand wheel
- Brand mantras
- Internal branding
- Aligning staff with brand performance

ABOUT THE CHAPTER

The previous chapter discussed how a brand is created. As shown in Figure 2.1, creating a brand is largely an organization dominated activity. This chapter further explores the role of an organization in creating a brand. It brings to light how organizational culture can influence the building of a brand and the delivery of a brand experience to the customer. The corporate brand vision needs to be translated and woven into the organizational culture. The employees need to have an understanding of the brand, so that at each stage of customer interaction the brand promise can be fulfilled.

INTRODUCTION

The corporate strategy of any organization is designed by its top management. The top management provides a strategic framework, which 'takes the brand from its current value to its potential value'. 'In an increasingly competitive environment with continuous pressures of quarterly performance, the operating team is forced to focus on the short-term objectives of meeting sales and customer acquisitions. This approach is myopic and completely overlooks the long-term potential of the brand to the business' (Unnikrishnan 2010). The top management needs to carefully delineate the core brand values and design a brand identity based on their corporate vision. This brand identity, through an internal branding process, is clarified to the employees. The employees of the organization, in turn, build the brand and deliver the brand experience to the customers. The customers interpret the brand values according to their experiences with the brand. This results in what is called the brand image—the customers' perception of the brand identity. Organizations, through various feedback and market research methods, gain an understanding of the brand image. How customers interpret a brand is reflected in the confidence they place in the brand and in the number of times they purchase and consume it. This act of the consumers influences and helps the senior management in designing their brand strategies. This is a continuous process and highlights the crucial link between brand managers or the organization's employees and their customers (see Exhibit 3.1 and Figure 3.1) and forms the brand value delivery.

Organizations are recognizing the importance of their staff in delivering brand experiences and providing a competitive advantage. The organizations create the brand and provide what

Exhibit 3.1 Apollo Hospitals Brand Value

The Apollo Hospitals Group was founded by Padma Bhushan Dr Pratap C. Reddy. Dr Reddy 'shaped and nurtured the ethos of Apollo Hospitals with his vision and inspiring leadership. Recognized as the architect of India's healthcare revolution, Dr Reddy made Apollo Hospitals a centre for medical excellence, innovation, and a catalyst of positive change.' What started in 1983 with a team of twenty-five members has now spread across Asia with 46 hospitals, 8000 beds, and over 60,000 team members. It is Asia's largest and most trusted healthcare group and has achieved international recognition. How does it manage to consistently deliver the high levels of service quality standards?

The employees of Apollo are 'enjoined to follow rigorously the Florence Nightingale approach of "tender loving care". All efforts are made to ensure that every patient who comes to Apollo is put at ease instantly.

It's not just the quality of the diagnosis, the equipment, the medical staff, or the exceptional success rates at Apollo that have made it the leading healthcare provider in the region, it is largely the emotional bond that the hospital creates with the patient that makes Apollo so special' (*Superbrands,* 2009) (see Image 3.1).

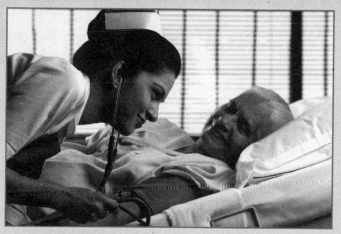

Courtesy: Superbrands.

Image 3.1 Apollo Hospitals; also see Plate 3

the customers need (i.e. functional values), and the staff influences the manner in which the brand experience is delivered to the customers (i.e. emotional values) (i.e. de Chernatony 2001). Organizations, through their marketing communications and brand promise, motivate customers to purchase their brand. If this brand promise is not delivered, customers will not be satisfied and will defect to other brands. The focus of the organization should be not only to communicate the brand promise to the customers, but also to orchestrate the staff towards delivering this promise (de Chernatony 2002, de Chernatony and Segal-Horn 2003).

Exhibit 3.1 highlights the fact that although it was Dr Reddy's vision that resulted in the creation of brand Apollo, it is its 60,000 employees who are consistently delivering on this brand's value to create a bond with the patients. Thus, while vision and continued support by the top management towards building a brand is what drives the brand, it needs to be replicated in the day-to-day motivation for the employees. According to Mr T.S. Vijayan, Chairman, Life Insurance Corporation of India (LIC), one of the factors that can be attributed to the success of LIC is the fact that it 'consistently reinforces its mission to its employees. They are reminded of the motto, *Yogakshema Vahamyaham,* which means 'your welfare is my responsibility', day in and day out', so that they deliver on this brand promise. 'The (LIC) logo shows that it offers protection to the people and is the trusty of their money' (Vijayan 2011).

It can be said that the success of a brand depends on the employees and the extent to which they are able to interpret and implement the brand values and deliver the brand promise. The customer's interpretation and appreciation of these brand values is equally important. While the rest of the chapters in the book are dedicated to the customer, this chapter will focus on the employees, along with the other internal stakeholders. Internal stakeholders create the brand and they need to mirror the brand values laid down by the senior management. Thus, an understanding of how we can motivate and influence the internal stakeholders is crucial to developing successful brands.

 See how the Aditya Birla Group specified the core brand value for its employees.

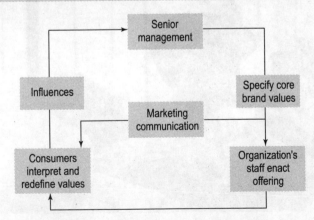

Source: Adapted from de Chernatony 2002, de Chernatony and Segal-Horn 2003.

Figure 3.1 Brand value delivery

Exhibit 3.2 What You Didn't Know about Apollo Hospitals

- Apollo Hospitals was named after the first spacecraft that landed on the moon, reflecting the promoter's vision of the hospital being the first and the foremost in all its chosen fields.
- Nearly 50,000 patients from fifty-five countries seek treatment at Apollo Hospitals every year.
- India's first CyberKnife (world's most advanced robotic radiosurgery system) was installed at Apollo Speciality Cancer Hospital in Chennai.
- Apollo became the first hospital in India to perform liver, multi-organ, and cord-blood transplants, and orthopaedic procedures like hip and knee replacements and Birmingham hip resurfacing.
- Apollo Hospitals, Chennai, became the first hospital in Asia to receive the JCI International (gold standard for excellence in healthcare the world over) accreditation.
- The 'Save a Child's Heart' (SACH) project was established in 2003 by the Apollo Hospitals Group to reach out to underprivileged children afflicted with heart diseases. It is the largest voluntary organization in Asia that provides care and treatment for underprivileged children suffering from paediatric heart diseases.
- To address the growing need for healthcare talent, the group is developing the Apollo Health Knowledge City, a state-of-the-art centre that expects to develop 25,000 skilled healthcare workers each year.

Source: Superbrands 2009.

The concept of brands has evolved over time and so has the concept of brand management. The classic brand management model was tactical, whereas the model that has evolved (the 'brand leadership model') is strategic. It focuses on building brand equity rather than brand image (see Exhibit 3.2).

These days, one organization is managing a number of brands, and the brand architecture is getting complex. Every organization's perspective is also shifting towards the global market rather than limiting itself to the country of origin. To build a brand at the global level, which has a high brand equity, the communication focus needs to be internal as well as external (Aaker and Joachimsthaler 2000). That is, for the organization to have brand leadership (rather than be involved in the mere management of the brand), it needs to communicate with its internal audience too. An organization, through its culture, communicates with and influences the manner in which employees behave in an organization. Let us now understand what this organizational culture is.

DEFINING ORGANIZATIONAL CULTURE

Organizational culture is defined as the 'company's overall philosophy, a set of values, and beliefs that shape the way people think and behave' (Hankinson and Hankinson 1999). It is 'an amalgamation of values, which gives rise to behaviour' (de Chernatony and Cottam 2008). Thus, we can define organizational culture as 'the values of the organization that give rise to and influence the behaviour of employees.' This definition highlights the fact that the way people behave in an organization is largely influenced by the organization itself. (See Exhibit 3.3.) This chapter explores how the organization can induce the employees and the other internal stakeholders to behave in line with the organization's brand vision.

Exhibit 3.3 Tata's Organizational Values and Culture

The Tata group was 'established by Jamshetji Tata in the second half of the 19th century' (Tata 2010). Jamshetji ventured into the hospitality business when he was insulted in one of the British hotels and not allowed to stay. The iconic Taj brand currently boasts of sixty-six hotels in forty-two locations across India and sixteen international properties (Taj 2010). The Tata culture is prevalent here, and employees are always told that 'customers and guests are their top priority'.

They also emphasize to their employees 'to think and act first as a citizen' (H.N. Shrinivas, HR Head of the Taj Group of Hotels cited in Rao 2010). Like the other Tata organizations, its hotels too are evaluated on the basis of the 'Tata Leadership programme and the Tata Business Excellence model'. The model focuses on the values of integrity, understanding, excellence, unity, and responsibility (Rao 2010).

 See how the Aditya Birla Group defined organizational culture for motivating its employees.

ORGANIZATIONAL CULTURE AND BRAND PERFORMANCE

Organizational culture is the invisible guiding force of an organization. It helps the employees in an organization work towards a common goal. Organizational culture is 'the pattern of shared values and beliefs,' which helps individuals in gaining an understanding of how the organization functions. This understanding further provides them 'norms for behaviour in the organization' (Deshpande and Webster 1989). This means that the workings of the employees in organizations are uniquely influenced by the prevailing culture of the organization. The values and beliefs (i.e., culture) thus drive the way the employees interact with the customers.

This experience influences the perception of the customers and provides substance to the brand (Bitner et al. 1990). This discussion leads to the belief that the employees influence the customer's experience of the brand. An aspect like this gains importance in a services brand, where employees are part of the seven Ps of the marketing mix. Here, the employees form a part of the product and thus directly influence the manner in which the product is delivered to the customers. It is, therefore, all the more important that employees reflect the brand attributes and provide a holistic brand experience to the customers. For the employees to 'live the brand' (Schultz 2003), employees need to be supported by an appropriate organizational culture. Organizations need to build a culture that revolves around the core brand values. This will influence the employees to perform their duties in line with the brand identity that the organization has delineated (see Exhibit 3.4).

Apart from the employees, there are other people like the suppliers and vendors who play an integral part in the co-creation of a brand. The organizational culture influences, and in turn is influenced by these stakeholders too. All the internal and external stakeholders (involved in the creation of a brand) need to understand the brand vision and work towards the same while creating the brand. Organizations can influence these internal stakeholders through internal brand building activities. This results in these stakeholders appreciating the brand value that

Exhibit 3.4 Taj Employees' Acid Test

The Taj Mahal Palace Hotel at Mumbai was set up in 1903. A century later, Taj employees are still delivering on the organizational values as was amply evident during the 26/11 terror attack (in 2008) at Taj Mumbai. The Taj staff at all levels—directors, captains, waiters, janitors, artisans—demonstrated exemplary courage in providing selfless service to the customers. As many as 80 employees were hurt—some fatally—but their heroic acts of saving other lives rather than their own stunned a number of people. 'The employees knew all the back exits and could have easily fled the building, but they all stayed at their posts during the attacks, jeopardising their safety in order to save the hotel guests' (PTI 2011).

The widow of Thomas George (a captain who escorted fifty-four guests from a backdoor staircase, and was later shot dead by the terrorists) said that she was not aware that 'the man she had lived with for twenty-five years was so courageous.' A management trainee protected and took out all the Unilever guests (who had come to attend a Unilever event at the hotel) through the kitchen. She was not instructed by any supervisor and just took three minutes to perform her duty.

There were over 500 emails from various guests who thanked the staff for saving their lives while narrating their heroic deeds. 'The sense of duty and service among the employees was unprecedented' (Rao 2010).

the organization wants to deliver. The overall impact is that all the internal stakeholders now work towards providing a similar brand experience to the customers and all the energies are synchronized towards a common brand goal.

A brand interacts at the following three major levels (see Figure 3.2):

1. With the organization through the organizational vision.
2. With the internal stakeholders through the organizational culture.
3. With the external stakeholders through the identity of the brand, which it portrays through its communications and the image the consumers develop upon consumption of the brand.

The organizational vision is the major guiding force for the brand. It guides and shapes the identity of the brand. The major input of what the brand is and should be is derived from the organization. Brand vision is 'the future environment a brand wishes to bring about, its purpose, and its core values' (de Chernatony 2002). Brand vision, thus, is indicative of what the brand experience will be like. Once the organization decides on what the brand is all about, the second level of interaction begins with the employees as the internal stakeholders while the brand is being created. These internal stakeholders translate the vision and mission of the organization into a tangible (product) or an intangible (service product) offering for the consumers and customers. The vision of the organization needs to be translated into concrete objectives that can be followed by the staff. This further encourages a series of coherent activities spread across the company. As a result, there is a holistic development of the brand. At the third level, the customers come in. They purchase the brand and through their brand experiences form their own images of the brand. Besides the customers, there are other stakeholders that are interested in the brand. These are the shareholders, suppliers, etc., and together they form the external stakeholders. Apart from interacting at the brand level, the three stakeholders (the organization, internal, and external stakeholders) also interact through direct communication.

The organization, through internal branding, influences the internal stakeholders. Through external brand-building measures, such as marketing communication including advertising, and public relations, the organization communicates with the external stakeholders. Apart from the organization, the internal stakeholders—especially the employees—also interact with the external stakeholders. The degree of interaction of the various employees may vary, as the front-staff employees interact more with customers than the back-end staff. These employees influence the manner in which the brand experience is delivered to the customers.

Source: Adapted from Hatch and Schultz 2001, de Chernatony 2001.

Figure 3.2 Strategic brand wheel

 See how the Aditya Birla Group promoted talent to motivate employees for brand performance.

STRATEGIC BRAND WHEEL AND GAPS

The three aspects of the brand interaction model can be visualized through the hub and spoke model (refer Figure 3.2). Here, the brand lies at the hub of the model. The three aspects, i.e., the organization, the internal stakeholders, and the external stakeholders, form the periphery of the circle. The brand, through its spokes of vision, culture, and identity/image, communicates with these three aspects. If any of the spokes are lacking in any way, the three aspects will not coincide with the attributes lying on the periphery of the circle. To form a perfect circle, the organization's internal branding (see Table 3.1), external branding, and brand delivery should be in agreement. Since the late 1990s, the focus has shifted from internal marketing to internal branding or from orientation and motivation of the customer-contact employees to a 'common value-based work ethos' (Mosley 2007). Internal branding takes off from internal marketing and the differences between the two are given in Table 3.1.

Table 3.1 Differences between internal marketing and internal branding

	Internal marketing	Internal branding
Perspective	To 'orient and motivate its customer-contact employees and supporting service people to work as a team in order to provide customer satisfaction' (Kotler et al. 2010)	To 'develop and reinforce a common value-based ethos, typically attached to some form of corporate mission or vision' (Mosley 2007)
Scope	Only the customer-contact employees	All the employees in the organization
Employee role	Employees are used as a tool to deliver the brand	Employees are strategically involved in creating the brand
Employee status	Channel to market	Employees 'live the brand'
Focus	Narrow. Just focus on customer-brand experience	'Broader range of brand-led corporate goals and objectives'
Approach	'Outside-in' approach as 'focus on communicating the customer brand promise, and the attitudes and behaviours expected from employees to deliver on that promise'	'Inside-out' value-based approach

Source: Adapted from Gapp and Merrilees 2006; Mosley 2007; Kotler et al. 2010.

 See how the Aditya Birla Group as an organization managed its employees to create strong brand equity among its customers.

A brand can gain leadership when this circle rotates freely and in unison. The vision of the organization is reflected in the culture of the brand and in the image of the brand. The culture, in turn, reflects the vision and the image/identity of the brand, and the identity/image is the same as the culture and vision of the brand. When this occurs, the brand is in unison with all the players it interacts with and results in the creation of both involvement and value to the customers. When both involvement and value are high, it catapults the brand to the 'brand is a religion' status (Kunde 2000 cited in de Chernatony 2008), where the brand becomes the preferred choice for the customers (see Exhibit 3.5: The Cat's Meow Turns into a Roar).

However, if the circle is not moving in unison, then it is due to the occurrence of any/some/all of these gaps:

1. Vision-culture gap—This gap occurs when the vision of the organization is not truly and accurately reflected in the culture of the organization. The implication is that the internal stakeholders are not in line with what the management wants for or thinks about the brand. As a result, the employees might not behave in a manner that reflects the true brand spirit, and thus dilute the brand experience for the customers. As the culture of the organization influences employee behaviour, the vision-culture gap will lead to a second gap, i.e., the vision-identity gap, and to a third, vision-image gap.

Exhibit 3.5 The Cat's Meow Turns into a Roar

The Hello Kitty brand is a 'cartoon character of a small cat that looks kind and cute with a button nose, two black eyes, six whiskers, and a ribbon or flower in her hair' (branding asia.com). The cat has no mouth and helps in projecting many different feelings on the cat—happy, sad, thoughtful, etc. The brand was founded in '1960 by Shintaro Tsuji (Chairman of Sanrio Co, a stationery producer) to manufacture branded gift products' (Rusch 2001). Though more than half a century old, the brand is perpetually young. It has extended over the years from candy, stationery, and school supplies to clothing, cell phone skins, and even motorcycles. These products are available not only in Tokyo, where the company is headquartered, but throughout Asia, Europe, and the Americas.

'To say that Asians are mad for Sanrio products is to understate the near fanatical devotion to the cartoon character. Sanrio has its own theme park in Tokyo, which is a huge success among the Japanese, Chinese, and Taiwanese. What's more, Hello Kitty products are collectibles and have built up quite a value over the last couple of decades. Some items are valued at thousands of dollars. And Sanrio is clever in its marketing efforts. There is always a new must-have product. "Old" items are moved off the shelf every six months or so and replaced with new products to keep the public interested and the pressure on the purchaser to add to the collection.' The brand is a religion for children who have grown up on the character, and on becoming adults, they continue to buy the adult-oriented objects the brand has extended itself to (Rusch 2001).

2. Vision-delivery or culture-image gap—This gap occurs when the vision of the organization does not match the manner in which the brand experience is being delivered to the customers. Thus, the resultant brand experience leaves something to be desired for by the customers. Thus, though the involvement of the customers with the brand was there, they did not get the complete value. There can be instances when the vision is appropriately translated into culture, but still the vision-delivery gap occurs. This ultimately leads to the third gap—the vision-image gap.

3. Vision-image gap or the identity-image gap—This gap occurs when the vision of the organization and the image that the consumers have about the brand are not in unison. The implication is that the organization designed a brand and had a particular identity in mind; however, the consumers' perception of the brand was different. This results in an image that is different from the one the organization was trying to portray.

The identity-image gap is not always the result of first two gaps. This gap can also exist because of faulty external brand building measures or variability aspect of service delivery. To overcome these gaps, there should be complete harmony between the organizational vision, culture, and brand image. Also, the external brand building measures should be monitored carefully and the brand should be appropriately positioned. Powerful brands have clear visions, appropriate cultures, and a staff that is aligned with the values of the brand. 'The integration of these elements makes it hard for competitors to surpass the position of the strong brands' (Ind 2001 cited in de Chernatony 2002).

BRAND MANTRAS AND INTERNAL BRANDING FOR A SUCCESSFUL BRAND

The brand wheel highlights the need for 'operationalizing' the brand, i.e., integrating the brand with all aspects of the business. This is also referred to as internal branding. Internal branding is composed of the following:

1. Communicating the brand to the employees in an effective manner
2. Convincing the employees that the brand is relevant and worth the effort
3. Successfully linking all the job profiles in the organization, so that the brand essence is delivered to the customers.

This provides clarity to the employees working in the different departments of a large organization by influencing their behaviour. It also unifies the functioning of the different departments and companies in the portfolio of the organization. It directly influences the 'extent to which employees perform their role in relation to the brand promise. It also influences the attitude that the employees have towards the brand, which in turn affects employee performance' (Punjaisri and Wilson 2007). Internal branding also makes the employees more productive in their contribution towards building the brand equity (Bergstrom, Blumenthal, and Crothers 2002). The model for implementing internal branding (see Figure 3.3) can help the organization align the on-brand behaviour of the employees with the brand identity. The on-brand behaviour includes all the actions of the employees while performing brand-related activities. The internal branding process is broadly divided into three stages as discussed below.

Planning

In the planning stage, the organization decides what they need to communicate to the customers on the basis of their organizational vision. The leadership needs to decide the key attributes of the brand character, which form the brand identity. These are then translated into visual symbols and language that become the 'face' and 'voice' of the brand, respectively. For effective implementation, the identity should be 'relevant, believable, desirable, and liveable' (Bergstrom et al. 2002) by the employees. A brand mantra is very helpful in this regard. It is a 'three to five word phrase that captures the irrefutable essence or spirit of the brand'. It represents the aspects that are most important to the company and to the consumers and forms the core brand association. The brand mantra is also called the 'brand essence' (or 'core brand promise') (Keller 2004).

Once the organization has decided on the brand identity, they need to go on to the next level, the execution of the brand identity which has been prepared by the top management. Successful leaders 'consistently and repeatedly' communicate the brand identity and commitment to live up to the brand's promise (Vallaster and de Chernatony 2006).

Execution

For an appropriate execution of the brand identity, the following steps should be kept in mind.

Communication and commitment The first step is communication of the identity to the internal audience. This identity needs to be communicated, so that the organization can build a consensus. This is helpful as the employees willingly adopt, enact, and build upon the brand identity, i.e., there is commitment to the brand. Through communication, the employees

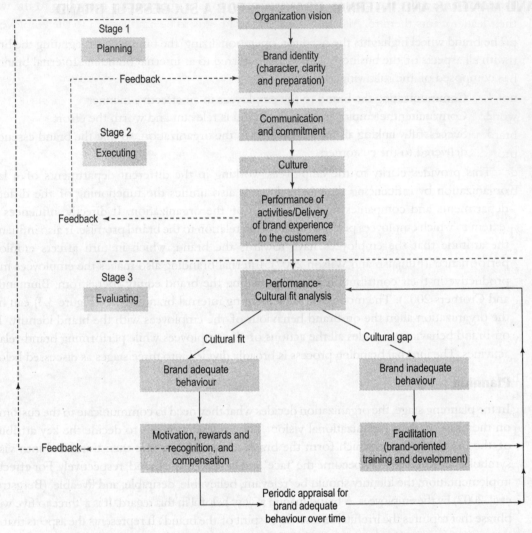

Source: Adapted from Bergstrom; Blumenthal; and Crothers 2002; Grace and O'Cass 2002; Vallaster and de Chernatony 2006; Alwi and Da Silva 2007; Mahnert and Torres 2007; Mosley 2007; Punjaisri and Wilson 2007; Steen 2010.

Figure 3.3 Internal branding process

are educated about what the brand is (the brand mantra) and the relationship between the employees and the brand. Research shows that many brand-building efforts fail to be internalized by the staff due to a lack of communication (Vallaster and de Chernatony 2006). This highlights the need for proper communication of the brand mantra to the employees.

 See the internal branding process at the Aditya Birla Group.

One way in which employees can be made to listen is by making the organizational leader the brand communicator. For the employees, his/her voice is the most important one and they listen and internalize the message. They are bound to take note and act according to the way their leader wants them to. Also, the brand mantra needs to be emphasized to the employees time and again, in order to consistently deliver on the brand parameters. This can be done through a number of channels like appropriate messages in brand fact sheets, through e-mails, brochures, company reference manuals, videos, reports, etc. Apart from these verbal cues, non-verbal ones like the dress code of the employees, the manner of addressing employees, working environment, etc. also communicate and motivate the employees to deliver on the brand promise. Through all these activities, the management facilitates the individuals and provides a framework that 'encourages brand-supporting employee behaviour' (Vallaster and de Chernatony 2006). The framework is important considering the fact that building an internal brand is an ongoing process and employees should not feel that it is just a one-time affair.

Culture   The culture of an organization is 'how things are done around here (the organization)' (Bergstrom et al. 2002), and through culture, stories about valued behaviour by the employees are spread. As discussed earlier in this chapter, the culture of an organization has an influence on the type and manner in which employees perform their tasks. Two important dimensions of culture are cultural strength and cultural content. Cultural strength is 'the degree to which beliefs and attitudes are shared'. The content aspect of culture is 'what these people believe and value.' Both, the strength and the content influence the firm's performance (Steen 2010). When an organization is new, it is easy to decide the content through the core brand attributes and build the organizational culture around the same. Things are difficult when the organization has to change its existing culture to suit the brand. This can be done when the organization feels that its culture is not in line with the brand and also during times of repositioning, when brand identity is changed and the employees need to know the new on-brand behaviour. The level of difficulty in changing an existing culture is directly proportionate to the cultural strength, and higher the degree of sharing of beliefs and attitudes, the more difficult it is to change the culture.

Performance of activities   The employees perform their activities, and the experience of the brand (a services brand or a product brand) is delivered to the customers. Appropriate performance of activities (keeping in mind the brand mantra) is essential for delivering the brand experience. Faulty execution can harm the brand and result in contradiction of brand values (see Exhibit 3.6).

Exhibit 3.6   PricewaterhouseCoopers Contradicts Its Brand Values

The year 2009 did not go well for Pricewaterhouse-Coopers (PwC). It was in the limelight for all the wrong reasons. PwC that was famous for advising clients on how to manage businesses, itself behaved in an off-brand manner. The Satyam scam brought to fore, the organization's inability to deliver on its brand values of 'teamwork, excellence, and leadership.' It was unable to 'spot a seven-year, ten-figure super fraud' at Satyam, where 'several senior managers forged invoices and bank statements to the tune of

Contd

Exhibit 3.6 *contd*

more than $1 billion.' On being questioned by the authorities, PwC admitted that due to the problem of understaffing, it could not audit Satyam's accounts. It had outsourced this work to a local firm of accountants, who had shared their Bengaluru office. Despite the claim that 'it's very special kind of leadership demands "courage, vision, and integrity"', it still signed off the undeclared outsourced work of accounts each year. By not delivering on the brand values, PwC's brand image was damaged globally during the ten months of media outrage that followed the scandal.

In the same year, PwC faltered again, this time in the United States. 'A day before a critical vote in the Senate committee on healthcare insurance reform, PwC released a report warning of increased family premiums and a rise in healthcare costs if the legislation was passed. The report that was paid for by the industry trade group America's Health Insurance Plans (AHIP) was attacked by the Democrats and healthcare experts as being factually misleading. A day later, PwC admitted that AHIP had instructed it to focus on some features of the bill without taking into account other major provisions such as the effect of subsidies for those buying insurance.' Being the most valuable brand of 'the big four' audit firms, PwC has 'much to lose from these debacles' (Ritson 2009).

Evaluation

Based on their experiences, customers form their perception about the brand. This perception results in an image of the brand in the minds of the customers and is referred to as the brand image (see Chapter 2). Over a period of time, the organization gets to know the customers perception through various kinds of feedback from the customers (either directly or through their frontline employees). This perception is then compared with the brand identity and corrective measures (if necessary) are to be taken. The employees also need to be evaluated in order to check whether their performance behaviour is in line with the organizational culture. This can lead to either of the two situations discussed below.

Cultural fit The employees who understand the brand identity and have values similar to the brand are found to be culturally fit. Such employees' performances are found to be as per the expectations of the organization. Their acts result in the delivery of the brand experience that is positively aligned with the brand identity. According to Mr Nitin Paranjpe, CEO and Managing Director, Hindustan Unilever Ltd., when they recruit employees, the selected candidates 'have to have a cultural fit with what the brand stands for' (Paranjpe 2011). The employees need to be positively motivated through rewards and recognition (see Exhibit 3.7; see Exhibit 3.8 to know more about Taj). Over a period of time, their activities need to be evaluated, monitored, and again reinforced, so that employees deliver consistently on the brand values. Employees need to understand that the brand's consistent behaviour is not a one-off activity.

Cultural gap Alternately, employees can also be at the other end of the spectrum, where they do not understand the brand culture. This results in a gap, as the employee behaviour is not in accordance with the expected behaviour for the brand. This brand inadequate behaviour

---

Exhibit 3.7   Tata Takes Care of Its Employees at Taj

The heroism that was displayed by the staff during the 26/11 terrorist attack 'is often attributed to values such as making customers and guests their first priority'. These acts of service did not go unnoticed. Ratan Tata (Chairman of Tata Sons—the Tata promoter company) personally visited the families of all the eighty employees who were injured or killed. He asked the family and dependants what they wanted him to do. 'Settlement for every deceased member ranged from 36–85 lakh, in addition to a number of benefits like full last salary for life for the family and dependants, complete responsibility for the education of the children anywhere in the world, full medical facility for the whole family and dependants for the rest of their lives, waiver of all loans and advances irrespective of the amounts; provision of a counsellor for life for each person. All categories of employees (even those who had only completed a single day as casuals) were treated as on duty during the time the hotel was closed for renovation. All the salaries were sent by money order' (Rao 2010). In many more ways, Mr Ratan Tata ensured that each and every employee and their family and dependants were taken care of well.

---

translates into a customer perception, which is less than the customer's expectations and hence there is dissatisfaction on part of the customer. To overcome this inadequate behaviour, employees need to be educated about the brand. Brand-oriented training and development activities need to be organized for such employees, so that the gap can be filled and they have an appropriate understanding of the brand values and brand identity. The employees should then be monitored to see if the cultural gap continues to exist. The employees who perform as per the brand culture need to be motivated further. Employees, who are consistently not performing in accordance with brand attributes, need to be evaluated for consistent non-performance. The reason(s) for this non-performance should then be ascertained and appropriate action should be taken, so that the culture is reinforced. It has been studied that the only way strong brands are built is to offer payback for those employees who deliver on the brand promise (Bergstrom et al. 2002). The payback can include various monetary and non-monetary methods that motivate the employees.

Feedback

In the model on the internal branding process, feedback is very important. It can be taken at the stage of delivery of services to customers and at a later stage, when employees are motivated and their performances are recorded. In the first instance, an interaction with the customers, helps the organization in getting feedback from their target audience. The customer's perception of the business results in the brand image. Their satisfaction and loyalty to the brand will result in profits for the organization and long-term success for the brand (Alwi and Da Silva 2007). The image that they develop needs to be studied vis-à-vis the brand identity and the gaps need to be identified and addressed. Employees should be empowered to take the necessary corrective action(s) when the identity and image do not match. This helps in the evolution of brand identity (Kapferer 2008). The organization's vision and the resultant culture needs to incorporate and document this feedback for better employee performance.

The ability to adapt, reflect the brand identity, and what the brand stands for is imperative to the success of brands over time.

At the second stage, feedback is also important for further revision of strategies. Once the particular behaviour is incorporated by a majority of the employees, this should shift to being a part of their job description. New benchmarks now need to be created, so that the level of delivery of the brand experience can be built further. Thus, over time, culture is built and brand delivery is enhanced, leading to increased customer satisfaction and loyalty.

ALIGNING STAFF WITH THE BRAND

Organizations are increasingly recognizing the importance of their staff as their brand builders (de Chernatony 2001). 'A brand consistent behaviour supports the development of a coherent

Exhibit 3.8   What You Didn't Know about the Taj

- The Taj group is India's flagship brand and has been felicitated at a number of national and international forums.
- The Taj group with its hotels, resorts, and palaces is the largest hotel brand in South Asia.
- The Taj group has been recognized as the sixth best employer in India during 2009 by Hewitt Associates and Outlook Business.

- The Taj Mahal Palace, Mumbai, which stands opposite the Gateway of India (see Image 3.2), was constructed much before the Gateway of India itself.
- Taj hotel symbolizes the best of Indian hospitality and is the foremost Indian luxury hotel. The multitude of awards to its name only supports the claim.

Courtesy: Superbrands.

Image 3.2   Taj Mahal Palace, opposite the Gateway of India; also see Plate 4

brand image, and is considered one of the critical success factors in brand management' (Vallaster and de Chernatony 2006). However, the different members of staff in an organization may have various different motivations for working. This influences their interpretation of the brand and reflects in their behaviour. This, in turn, hampers the development of an integrated brand strategy. For successful internal branding, where the staff are completely aligned with the brand, the following factors (Mahnert and Torres 2007) need to be kept in mind.

1. Organizational culture should support and encourage the staff to be a part of the branding process. An alignment of the employees with brand values helps them find their 'own meaning at work' (de Chernatony 2002). This helps them creatively find new ways by which they can increase and add to the brand value.

2. Strong corporate brands like Tata, Reliance, Virgin, Walt Disney, etc. have had entrepreneurs who have had a brand philosophy and recruited staff who shared similar values. Together they have managed to create a culture that enshrines the core values and has resulted in consistent staff behaviour. It would be easier for employees to deliver a brand experience in line with the vision of the organization, when their values are found to be aligned with the brand's value. Given that each individual is unique, it is highly unlikely that everyone's values will be in line with the brand's values. It is, therefore, important that there be an alignment between the values of the organization and the individual employees. This can be done by the following

   • During recruitment—At the time of recruitment, individuals are often asked about their values through in-depth interviews, psychometric tests, etc., so that individuals whose values concur with the values of the brand can be hired (de Chernatony 2008).

   • By appreciation of role—Employees who have values in common with the brand need to appreciate the role they will play in the delivery of the brand. To appreciate what the values mean in terms of behaviour and how they will impact the customer's brand experience, it is important to align the employees' values and their behaviour.

   • Over a length of time—Over a length of time, managers may be asked to express their perception about the brand's values. This is important considering the fact that as time goes by, the values of an organization may change according to the change in consumer trends. Thus, it is important that these changing values be accurately perceived by the managers and be reflected in the performance of their brand-related acts.

3. Apart from the employees, the top management should also be quizzed about what they feel are the values of the brand over a given length of time (de Chernatony 2002). This helps in delineating fresh values, which may have become relevant or which the management thinks are important. This is especially true for repositioning a brand and goes a long way in keeping the brand fresh and young.

4. Consistent employee behaviour results in a consistent perception among stakeholders and ensures repeat brand buying. The confidence of the consumers signals the appropriateness of the values, which in turn reinforces brand culture. The newly recruited staff learns from the existing culture and adds to brand building. Less successful brands are indicative

of an environment, where the employees are uncertain of the brand vision and culture, which then causes organizations to lose their core values over a period of time. Such employees are not able to demonstrate any consistency behaviour with the customers, and this results in customers who do not remain loyal to their brands (Kotter and Heskett 1992 cited in de Chernatony 2008).

5. Employees should also be surveyed to assess their perceptions about what they feel the external stakeholders think about their brand's values. This helps in aligning the employees with the external perception or the perception of the consumers (Chernatony 2002).

6. Branding programs should not be perceived by the staff to be a one-off activity. The management should consistently motivate the staff to perform acceptable 'on-brand' behaviour (de Chernatony 2002). The achievements of the staff should be linked to the brand values, so that the strategic brand wheel comes into play.

7. Individual employees should be shown how their job description and responsibilities map on a 'brand building chart' (de Chernatony 2002). This helps the employees in understanding how their activities are going to impact the brand value and they fully realize the gravity of their actions.

8. The management needs to consistently measure and communicate the various brand gaps to the employees. This helps in sensitizing employees towards activities that the consumers feel are important for the success of a brand.

A consistent delivery of the brand experience helps in building brand equity. Employees are the most important part of any organization and they are directly (through direct interaction) or indirectly (by being involved in the creation of a brand or brand experience at the back-end) responsible for the consumer's brand experience. This brand experience forms the crux of the decision-making process for the customers and contributes to the forming of brand associations. To help the employees and the organizations further, it is necessary to understand what is important for the customers and how brand equity can be built among them. All this is discussed in the next chapter on brand equity.

SUMMARY

This chapter looks at the organizational culture as a strategic tool for the effective and consistent delivery of brand experience. The power to build a successful brand lies in the hands of the management. The management needs to move from internal marketing to internal branding in order to create a uniform brand experience for its employees. This uniform experience needs to be consistent and thus helps in enhancing brand equity.

The strategic brand wheel is a tool that ensures uniformity in brand experience. The brand can gain a following of consumers if it avoids the three gaps: the vision-culture gap, vision-delivery or culture-image gap, and vision-image gap or identity-image gap. The internal brand management process further provides guidelines to managers for effective planning, execution and evaluation of the same.

Employees need to be seen as a strategic input in the entire process of the creation of a brand experience rather than as tools for the delivery of brand values. Thus, an alignment of the employees with the brand is crucial to the success of a brand.

KEY TERMS

Brand mantra   It is a three to five word phrase that captures the essence or the spirit of the brand.

Brand vision   This is by the future environment a brand wishes to bring about, its purpose, and its core values.

Cultural fit   The employees who understand the brand identity and have values similar to the brand are found to be culturally fit.

Internal branding   This is developing and reinforcing a common value-based ethos, typically attached to some form of corporate mission or vision.

Internal marketing   This is the orientation and motivation of the customer contact employees and supporting service people to work as a team in order to provide customer satisfaction.

Organizational culture   These are the values of an organization that give rise to and influence the behaviour of its employees.

Strategic brand wheel   The three aspects of the brand interaction model (organization, employees, and customers) can be visualized through the hub and spoke model, where the brand lies at the hub and is connected through the spokes of vision, identity/image, and culture.

Vision-culture gap   The gap that occurs when the vision of the organization is not truly and accurately reflected in the culture of the organization.

Vision-delivery or culture-image gap   It is the gap that occurs when the vision of the organization does not match with the manner in which the brand experience is being delivered to the customers.

Vision-image gap or the identity-image gap   This gap occurs when the vision of the organization and the image the consumers have about the brand are not in unison.

EXERCISES

Concept Review Questions

1. What is organizational culture? How can organizational culture impact the brand?
2. What is internal branding? Evaluate its impact on brand equity.
3. Discuss the internal branding process.
4. Discuss the term 'cultural fit'. Why is it important for the organization and the brand?

Critical Thinking Questions

1. 'Cultural fit is important for the delivery of the brand promise'. Critically discuss this statement. Is it not possible to deliver the brand values otherwise?
2. 'Staff is just a tool for the delivery of the brand experience. A successful brand is all an organization needs.' Give your reasons for or against this statement.
3. Critically evaluate the role of organizational culture in the success of a brand. Through effective communi-

cation, the management can tell the employees about the brand, is there then a need for internal branding?
4. Critically discuss the strategic brand wheel.

Internet Exercises

1. Visit the website http://www.tata.com/ and study the Tata Code of Conduct. What does this tell you about its organizational culture and organizational vision?
2. Visit the website http://www.maxhealthcare.in/aboutus. Go through the different information given there. What inference can you make about the organizational culture and brand values?

CD Exercise

Visit an organization and look at their brand mantra, internal branding, and how they have aligned their staff to deliver the brand promise.

REFERENCES

Aaker, D.A. and E. Joachimsthaler (2000), *Brand Leadership*, The Free Press, New York.

Alwi, S.F. and R.V. Da Silva (2007), 'Online and offline corporate brand images—do they differ?' *Corporate Reputation Review*, Vol. 10, Issue 4, pp. 217–244.

Bergstrom, A., Blumenthal, D. and Crothers, S. (2002), 'Why internal branding matters—The case of Saab', *Corporate Reputation Review*, Vol. 5, Issue 2/3, pp. 133–142.

Bitner, M.J., Booms, B.H. and Tetreault, M.S. (1990), 'The service encounter—diagnosing favourable and unfavourable incidents', *Journal of Marketing*, Vol. 54, Issue no. 1, pp. 71–84.

de Chernatony, L. (2001), 'A model for strategically building brands', *Journal of Brand Management*, Vol. 9, Issue 1, pp. 32–44.

de Chernatony, L. (2002), 'Would a brand smell any sweeter by a corporate name?' *Corporate Reputation Review*, Vol. 5, Issue 2/3, pp. 114–132.

de Chernatony, L. (2008), *From Brand Vision to Brand Evaluation*, Second Edition, Elsevier, New Delhi.

de Chernatony, L. and Cottam, S. (2008), 'Interactions between organizational cultures and corporate brands', *Journal of Product and Brand Management*, Vol. 17, Issue 1, pp. 13–24.

de Chernatony, L. and Segal–Horn, S. (2003), 'The criteria for successful services brands', *European Journal of Marketing*, Vol. 37, Issue 7/8, pp. 1095–1118.

Deshpande, R. and Webster, F. E. Jr. (1989), 'Organizational culture and marketing—defining the research agenda', *Journal of Marketing*, Vol. 53, Issue 1, pp. 3–15.

Gapp, R. and Merrilees, B. (2006), 'Important factors to consider when using internal branding as a management strategy—a healthcare case study', *Journal of Brand Management*, Vol. 14, Issue 1 and 2, pp. 162–176.

Grace, D. and O'Cass, A. (2002), 'Brand associations—looking through the eye of the beholder', *Qualitative Market Research*, Vol. 5, Issue 2, pp. 96–111.

Hankinson, P. and Hankinson, G. (1999), 'Managing successful brands—an empirical study which compares the corporate cultures of companies managing the world's top 100 brands with those managing outside brands', *Journal of Marketing Management*, Vol. 15, Issue 1, pp. 135–155.

Hatch, M.J. and Schultz, M. (2001), 'Are the strategic stars aligned for your corporate brand', *Harvard Business Review*, Volume 79, Issue 2, pp. 128–135.

Ind, N. (2001), *Living the Brand*, Kogan Page, London.

Kapferer, J. N. (2008), *The New Strategic Brand Management*, 4th Edition, Kogan Page, New Delhi.

Keller, K. L. (2004), *Strategic Brand Management—Building, Measuring and Managing Brand Equity*, Prentice–Hall of India Private Limited, New Delhi.

Kotler, P., G. Armstrong, Agnihotri, P.Y. and Haque, E. ul (2010), *Principles of Marketing—A South Asian Perspective*, 13th Edition, Prentice Hall, Delhi.

Kunde, J. (2000), *Corporate Religion*, Pearson Education, London.

Mahnert, K.F. and Torres, A.M. (2007), 'The brand inside—the factors of failure and success in internal branding', *Irish Marketing Review*, Vol. 19, Issue 1 & 2, pp. 54–63.

Mosley, R.W. (2007), 'Customer experience, organizational culture and the employer brand', *Journal of Brand Management*, Vol. 15, Issue 2, pp. 123–134.

Paranjpe, N. (2011), 'Power of marketing—changing lives', at AIMA World Marketing Congress, held on 4–5 February 2011 at Hotel Lalit, New Delhi.

PTI, '26/11 response by Taj staff a case study at Harvard', *Business Standard*, New Delhi, 28 January 2011, pp. 20.

Punjaisri, K. and Wilson, A. (2007), 'The role of internal branding in the delivery of employee brand promise', *Journal of Brand Management*, Vol. 15, Issue 1, pp. 57–70.

Rao, T.V. (2010), Book extract 'Managers who make a difference—Sharpening your management skills' cited in 'Nurturing Organizational Values', *The Strategist, Business Standard*, New Delhi, 22 November 2010, p 2.

Ritson, M., 'When a firm pays price for brand contradiction—scandals involving PwC in India and the US could well harm its global brand', *The Economic Times*, New Delhi, 3 November 2009, p 4.

Rusch, R. D., 'Sanrio—The cat's meow', http://www.brandchannel.com/features_profile.asp?pr_id=9, accessed on 24 January 2011.

Schultz, D.E. (2003), 'Live the brand', *Marketing Management*, Vol. 12, Issue 4, pp. 8–9.

Steen, Eric Van den (2010), 'On the origin of shared beliefs (and corporate culture)', *Rand Journal of Economics*, Vol. 41, Issue 4, pp. 617–648.

Superbrands (2009), Superbrands—An insight into India's strongest consumer brands, Volume III, Superbrands India Private Limited, Gurgaon.

Unnikrishnan, 'Brand valuation a key tool', *The Economic Times*, New Delhi, 15 June 2010, p 4.

Vallaster, C. and de Chernatony, L. (2006), 'Internal brand building and structuration—the role of leadership', *European Journal of Marketing*, Vol. 40, Issue 7/8, pp. 761–784.

Vijayan, T.S., 'Growing by leaps and bounds' at AIMA World Marketing Congress, held on 4–5 February 2011 at Hotel Lalit, New Delhi.

Web resources

http://www.brandingasia.com/cases/case7.htm, accessed on 25 January 2011.

http://www.tajhotels.com/AboutTaj/CompanyInformation/default.htm, accessed on 25 December 2010.

http://www.tata.com/aboutus/sub_index.aspx?sectid=uZJCH0l2iwA=, accessed on 25 December 2010.

CASE STUDY

Delivering Kingfisher First's Brand Promise

Introduction

The United Breweries (UB) Group is one of India's largest conglomerates with annual sales of over US$4 billion and a market capitalization of approximately US$12 billion. The group has diverse interests in brewing, distilling, real estate, engineering, fertilizers, biotechnology, information technology, and aviation. It is also the largest Indian manufacturer of beverage alcohol (beer and spirits). The group already owned the brand Kingfisher—its flagship brand for beer—which was extended to launch the Kingfisher Airlines in 2005. Kingfisher Airlines Limited (KAL) is a wholly-owned subsidiary of United Breweries Holdings Ltd—the investments holding company of the UB group. 'KAL offers the maximum number of flights by any single airline network in India. It flies to 60 cities in India and 8 international destinations, and has more than 330 daily departures with a fleet of 66 aircraft.' It is a full service airline that caters to a number of destinations both regional and international. KAL is one of the six airlines in the world to receive a five-star rating from Skytrax (a UK-based specialist global air transport advisor). Skytrax awards provide the most prestigious recognition of outstanding quality excellence for product and customer service delivery across today's world airline industry.

The Kingfisher promise

The Kingfisher promise of an excellent in-flight experience starts from its logo, which says 'Fly five star' (*Superbrands*, 2009) (see bottom right of Image 3.3 for the logo).

Courtesy: Superbrands.

Image 3.3　Kingfisher 'Fly five star'; also see Plate 4

Kingfisher promises a flight experience through its vision and values. The vision is: 'The Kingfisher Airlines family will consistently deliver a safe, value-based, and enjoyable travel experience to all our guests.'

And the values of Kingfisher are discussed below.

Safety

This is our overriding value. In our line of business, there is no compromise.

Service

We are all in the hospitality business; we must always seek to serve our guests and gain their trust, goodwill, and loyalty.

Happiness

We seek to build an organization with people who choose to be happy, and will endeavour to influence our guests and co-workers to be happy too.

Teamwork

We will succeed or fail as a team. Each one of us must respect our colleagues regardless of their rank, and we must work together to ensure our mutual success.

Accountability

Each one of us will be held accountable for the successful execution of our duties, commitments, and obligations, and we will strive to lead by example.

Apart from its vision and values, customer experience and expectations are built up right from the moment customers log on to the Kingfisher website (see Image 3.4). Here, feedback about the customer's experience is solicited and it reassures the customers, who are referred to as guests, that the organization is focused on customer satisfaction. In the 'About Us' and the 'Guest Commitment' statement (see Image 3.5), the guest is reassured of the

safety and performance of the aircraft and the personalized entertainment awaiting them.

Kingfisher culture

Various cues can be taken from the vision and values, regarding how the employees are supposed to perform. The vision statement, guides the employees to deliver an experience that is 'safe, value-based, and enjoyable.' By emphasizing on safety in its values, Kingfisher shows that it is not going to compromise on this aspect, and therefore, employees need to keep this in mind. Happiness and teamwork drive the employees to respect each other and 'be happy and keep the co-workers and guests happy', and this is one of the key values of the company. The accountability aspect drives home the fact that each 'role holder' (employee) is accountable for the successful execution of his/her own duties. Through the monthly house magazine of UB group—*Pegasus*—the employees are updated about the events and activities of the UB group's companies. Dr Vijay Mallya (Chairman, UB Group and KAL) personally takes an interest in all the recruitment activities at KAL.

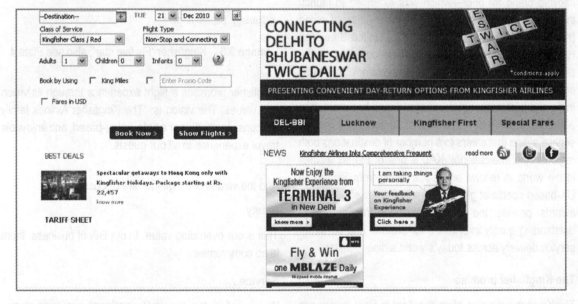

Source: http://www.flykingfisher.com.

Image 3.4　Kingfisher feedback

ABOUT US

Chairman's Message | Vision & Values | Achievements | Our Fleet | Guest Testimonials

"Welcome to a world without passengers"

Welcome aboard Kingfisher Airlines, where you are made to feel like an honoured guest and not just a passenger. At Kingfisher, a flight is not a journey between two airports but an experience of a lifetime.

As our esteemed guest you can experience Kingfisher Airlines in three unique classes of service - Kingfisher First (Business class) Kingfisher Class (Premium economy) and Kingfisher Red (Low fare). Kingfisher First and Kingfisher Class is available on our international routes too.

As Kingfisher takes off into the international skies, you can expect a world-class experience. Every Kingfisher aircraft meets the global standards that I have set in terms of safety and performance. Our brand-new fleet incorporates the latest technology and each aircraft is fitted with a personalized in-flight entertainment system and top quality programming content from around the world for your viewing and listening pleasure, and to create an environment that you will truly cherish.

Aboard our flights, you will be delighted by the various sensory experiences on offer – from tantalizing aromas of world cuisine to the magic touch of your personal therapeutic massage seat - we really have thought about every little thing that will exhilarate you.

▸ Chairman's Message
▸ Vision & Values
▸ Achievements
▸ Our Fleet
▸ Guest Testimonials

Source: http://www.flykingfisher.com/about-us.aspx.

Image 3.5 About Kingfisher

The service offerings at Kingfisher Airlines

'Kingfisher Airlines caters to all segments of air travel, ranging from low-fare service—Kingfisher Red, to the premium economy service—Kingfisher Class, to the luxurious Kingfisher First.' Let us now take a look at the Kingfisher first service offerings.

Brand promise at Kingfisher First

Dr Mallya refers to KAL as the 'Harrods of the sky'. It offers a fleet of all-new aircraft and is the first Indian airline to order the impressive Airbus A 380. The guest experience on an international flight includes 'personal valets at airports for baggage handling and boarding, exclusive lounges with private space, refreshments and music, audio and video on-demand with extra-wide personalized screens in the aircraft, sleeperette seats with extendable footrests and three-course gourmet cuisine. The gourmet meals feature six different vegetarian and non-vegetarian menu options for breakfast, lunch, and dinner with rotation of meals through every day of the week. Jain meals are also offered' (Superbrands 2009). The in-flight entertainment (which includes live TV), stand-up bar, and lounge (see Image 3.6), and the good-looking hostesses all add to the experience.

Courtesy: Superbrands.

Image 3.6 The Kingfisher experience; also see Plate 4

Dr Mallya is involved in all the recruitments. He looks for height, figure, command over English, manner, and style of speaking in a prospective candidate. The selected candidates then have a psychometric test to delve a bit deeper into their inner psyche to see if they are service-oriented, if service comes naturally to them' (Osborne 2008). This prompts the claim that the guests are served by the best in business (see Image 1.4).

Kingfisher promises and delivers a five star experience in the skies. According to Dr Mallya, 'Aboard every Kingfisher Airlines flight, you will meet your crew .... They have been instructed to treat you in the same way as if you were a guest in my own home.' This claim is backed by the number of national and international best service awards received by the airline over the years (see Exhibit 3.9). KAL received the Skytrax award for the third time in a row in 2010, highlighting the organization's commitment to its product and the services being rendered.

Exhibit 3.9   Some of the Awards that Kingfisher Airlines Has Received

- Best Airline in India and Central Asia', 'Best Economy Class Seats' and 'Staff Service Excellence Award for airlines in India and Central Asia' at the World Airline Awards, 2010
- '5-STAR AIRLINE' award by Skytrax for 3rd consecutive year, 2010
- 'India's Favourite Airline' in HT MARS Consumer Satisfaction Survey, 2009
- 'Best Airline in India and Central Asia', 'Best Cabin Crew-Central Asia' for Kingfisher Airlines and 'Best Low-Cost Airlines in India and Central Asia' for Kingfisher Red services in Skytrax World Airline Awards, 2009
- 'Bonus Promotion' (Japan, Pacific, Asia, Australia) and 'Best Customer Service' (Japan, Pacific, Asia, Australia) in Freddie Award, 2009
- Kingfisher Airlines frequent-flyer programme, King Club has won Top Honours at the 21st Annual Freddie Awards 2008 in the Japan, Pacific, Asia, and Australia region.

  King Club has won the Freddie Awards 2008 in the following categories:

  Best Bonus Promotion

  Best Customer Service

  Best Member Communications*

  Best Award Redemption*

  Best Elite Level**

  Best Website**

Program of the Year**

- Kingfisher Airlines has received three global awards at the SKYTRAX World Airline Awards in 2010
  Named Best Airline in India/Central Asia; Best Cabin Crew—Central Asia
  Kingfisher RED named Best Low-Cost Airline in India/Central Asia
- NDTV Profit 'Business Leadership Award for Aviation' awarded to Kingfisher Airlines by NDTV twice in two years
- 'India's only 5 Star airline', rated by Skytrax and '6th airline in the world' to be certified as 5 star airline by Skytrax
- Rated India's 'Second Buzziest Brand 2008' by afaqs! and The Brand Reporter
- Ranked amongst India's 'Top Service Brands of 2008' in a ranking by Pitch magazine
- Voted as 'India's Favourite Airline' in a survey conducted by an independent research firm with 46% votes compared to Jet Airways' 23%
- Rated as Asia Pacific's 'Top Airline Brand' in a survey conducted by TNS on 'Asia Pacific's Top 1,000 Brands' for 2008
- 'Brand Leadership Award' in the service and hospitality segment against several acclaimed hotels, leading banks, and other airlines
- Economic Times Avaya Award 2006 for Excellence in 'Customer Responsiveness'

Contd

Exhibit 3.9 *contd*

This prestigious award is presented by the highly acclaimed business daily, *The Economic Times*

- 'India's No. 1 Airline in customer satisfaction' *Business World*
- 'Rated amongst India's most respected companies' in 2007, *Business World*
- 'Rated amongst India's 25 Innovative Companies' in a survey conducted by Planman Media in 2006
- 'The Best Airline' and 'India's Favourite Carrier' in a Survey conducted by IMB for *The Times of India*
- 'Best New Domestic Airline for Excellent Services and Cuisine' Pacific Area Travel Writers Association (PATWA)—the biggest travel writers' organisation, representing members from 70 countries across the globe, that conducts independent annual surveys across various industries related with Travel and Tourism in order to select the best in each category
- 'Service Excellence 2005-2006 for a New Airline' by Skytrax

- 'Ranked Third in the survey on India's Most Successful Brand launch of 2005' under the Brand Derby Survey conducted by India's leading business daily, *The Business Standard*
- 'Buzziest Brands of 2005' ranked amongst the Top Ten buzziest brands of 2005 and 2006 across product categories, in the survey conducted by agency faqs and The Brand Reporter
- Rated amongst the Top Ten Internet Advertisers Yahoo! India
- Rated amongst 'the top ten in the Best Television Commercial Jingles' NDTV
- 'Best New Airline of the Year' Award for 2005 Centre for Asia Pacific Aviation (CAPA) Award in the Asia-Pacific and the Middle-East region

Source: http://www.flykingfisher.com/about-us/achievements.aspx.

Note:
* First runner-up
** Second runner-up

The other unique services being provided on its first class section are steam-ironing of jackets, spectacle cleaning, and special stationery. The Airline has won the 'Staff Service Excellence Award for airlines in India and Central Asia' at the World Airline Awards, 2010'.

This reinforces the excellent services being provided by the employees of Kingfisher Airlines. A number of testimonials of satisfied customers can be traced on the official website, some of which are given in Exhibit 3.10.

Exhibit 3.10   Testimonials by Satisfied Customers of Kingfisher Airlines

I was a guest in your own home

Many thanks for the treatment onboard my Kingfisher flights last week during our wine launch, in combination with the UB Group. As per your instructions, your crew treated me, 'As if I was a guest in your own home'! A cricket career spanning 16 years takes you around the world a few times, so I can comfortably say that my Kingfisher flights in India were by far the most *welcoming domestic journeys I have ever undertaken at 30,000 feet!*

— Jonty Rhodes
South African Cricket Legend

Thank you for a wonderful experience!

I wanted to thank you for a wonderful experience of flying Kingfisher Airlines. I flew from Indore to Bombay on 26 November 2007 at 8 pm.

Contd

Exhibit 3.10 *contd*

My job involves a lot of travelling and on an average I fly about 1,00,000 miles a year. I have flown almost all US airlines and a couple of international ones and I must say that the Kingfisher experience was the best.

Couple of points

1. *Attendant helping with the luggage refused a tip of ₹10. (Never heard or seen that before.)*
2. *Attendants at the ticketing counter were friendly and smiling.*
3. *Excellent food.*

4. *Complete entertainment for 1 hr. Did not get a chance to get bored.*
5. *Help at the baggage claim. This was most helpful and least expected.*

Thanks again and it would be wonderful if you can start international service soon.

– Anonymous

Source: http://www.flykingfisher.com/about-us/guest-testimonials.aspx.

Conclusion

'Kingfisher Airlines prides itself as India's youthful, premium superbrand that has created a following of fans and not just loyalists. It has consistently kept pace with the changing times and evolving consumer aspirations. The brand values emanate from a heady combination of lifestyle, sport, and fashion' (Superbrands 2009). Kingfisher is an example of an organization, where the chairman is extensively involved in the creation and delivery of the brand values. He maintains touch points with the employees and the customers. His constant endeavour to meet and exceed the expectations of the customer is reflected in the personal feedback that is encouraged from the guests on the website and also on board the airlines.

Discussion Questions

1. Discuss the vision of the Kingfisher organization.
2. What conclusions can you draw about the culture of the organization?
3. Perform a quick image survey of the Kingfisher brand and discuss your findings vis-à-vis their vision and organizational culture.
4. Apply the 'strategic brand wheel' for KAL. Can you highlight any brand gaps? Discuss these. What solutions and further suggestions can you delineate for the organization?

Case References

Osborne, A. 2008, 'Vijay Mallya aims to leave Kingfisher's rivals in his vapour trail', http://www.telegraph.co.uk/finance/newsbysector/transport/2795745/Vijay-Mallya-aims-to-leave-Kingfishers-rivals-in-his-vapour-trail.html >, accessed on 15 December 2010.

Superbrands 2009, Superbrands—An insight into India's strongest consumer brands, Volume III, Superbrands India Private Limited, Gurgaon.

Web resources

http://economictimes.indiatimes.com/news/news-by-industry/transportation/airlines-/-aviation/Kingfisher-is-best-in-India-Central-Asia-Skytrax/articleshow/5991180.cms >, accessed on 18 December 2010.

http://www.airlinequality.com/main/Qlty-awds.htm, accessed on 15 December 2010.

http://www.businessworld.in/index.php/Surveys/Index-Page_Survey.html, accessed on 28 January 2011.

http://www.domain-b.com/companies/companies_k/kingfisher_airlines/20050509_takes-off.html, accessed on 18 March 2010.

http://www.finchannel.com/news_flash/Travel_Biz_News/72168_Kingfisher_Airlines_Launches_Direct_Flights_From_Bengaluru_to_Mysore, accessed on 29 January 2011.

http://www.flykingfisher.com, accessed on 18 December 2010.

http://www.flykingfisher.com/about-us.aspx, accessed on 18 December 2010.

http://www.flykingfisher.com/about-us.aspx>, accessed on 18 December 2010.

http://www.flykingfisher.com/about-us/achievements.aspx, accessed on 18 December 2010.

http://www.flykingfisher.com/about-us/guest-testimonials.aspx, accessed on 28 January 2011.

http://www.theubgroup.com/group_information.aspx, accessed on 19 January 2011.

Part II

UNDERSTANDING AND MEASURING BRAND EQUITY

Brand Equity

4

LEARNING OBJECTIVES

After reading this chapter, you will be able to understand the following:

- The concept of brand equity
- Steps in building a brand
- Sources of brand equity

ABOUT THE CHAPTER

The need to build a brand arises as the product or service provider needs to differentiate its offering from those of the competitors. This differentiation provides the competitive advantage to firms and helps in building strong brands. If a brand is successful in creating an image in the minds of the consumers and develops a certain following among the target audience, because of the awareness, perceived quality, etc., that it managed to create, then the customers do not mind paying a higher price for the brand and companies can avoid price competitions. The growing importance of brand equity can be gauged by the fact that the focus of corporate mergers over the last decade has been more on brand equity or intangible assets of the brand rather than on synergies to gain economies of scale (Myers 2003).

INTRODUCTION—WHAT IS BRAND EQUITY?

Building brands is an important aspect of marketing for the long-term sustenance of a firm. A brand name not only imparts recognition to a product but gives it an identity. In the same product class, products of different firms can have different meanings for consumers. Thus, in the same product class, the product of one firm can mean quality, of another, value for money, yet another company's product can mean fun and good times, etc. The question is how do consumers associate these different meanings with different brands? This is because a brand name adds value to a product beyond the brand elements and the value added depends on customer perception and hence different customers associate different meanings with the various brands (see Exhibit 4.1). This value added to the product is brand equity and how this equity is built by customers is important, since it is the customers' evaluation of the brand that influences by this understanding. For example, even before the recent launch of the Apple iPad, the product generated a lot of interest among people, and there was speculation as to the type of product being launched. This was due to the interest and excitement generated in the new product by consumers who associated the brand with 'a great experience' and 'innovation in design' (Sadagopan 2010; *The Economic Times* 2010). Thus, even though Apple launched products that were only additions to the existing markets (example, Apple Mac computer was another personal computer, and neither iPod nor iPad were the first products in their categories), all its products managed to stand out and capture the attention of the customers (Sadagopan 2010).

BRAND EQUITY DEFINED

Brands, if managed well, add value to a product, like the value added to Apple products by the brand name—Apple. The value, as perceived by customers, is important as it impacts the customer's evaluation of the brand. Some of the definitions of brand equity as delineated by eminent authors and researchers are as follows.

'Brand equity is the set of associations and behaviours on the part of a brand's customers, channel members, and parent corporation that permits the brand to earn greater volume or greater margins than it could without the brand name, and that gives the brand a strong, sustainable, and differential advantage over competitors' (Marketing Science Institute 1988, cited in Chay 1991).

'Brand equity can be thought of as the additional cash flow achieved by associating a brand with the underlying product or service' (Biel 1992).

'Brand equity is a set of brand assets and liabilities linked to a brand, its name, and symbol, that adds value to or subtracts from the value provided by a product or service to a firm and/or to that firm's customers' (Aaker 1991).

Keller (2004) defines brand equity from the customer's perspective as 'the differential effect the brand knowledge has on consumer response to the marketing of that brand'. For consumer-based brand equity, therefore, it is said that the knowledge of a brand has a differential effect on the response that the customer shows towards that brand, but it is different from customer loyalty. According to Keller (2004), if a consumer shows a less favourable reaction towards a brand compared to an unbranded product, it leads to negative consumer-based brand equity. On the other hand, if a customer shows a more favourable reaction towards a brand as compared to an unnamed product, it leads to positive customer-based brand equity. If customers do not respond at all to the brand name, then the brand can be equated to a commodity or generic product and the competition is based on price only. It is the knowledge that the customer has about the brand that affects this differential behaviour. This can lead to an improved perception of product performance, enhanced loyalty, diminish the competitors' marketing actions, and reduce the effects of a marketing crisis. Marketers can charge a higher profit, as there is an inelastic response to price hikes and a more elastic response to price decreases. The middlemen tend to support and provide greater trade cooperation

Exhibit 4.1   Boroline Survives Extinction

From a humble beginning in a house in 1929 to a superbrand marks the eventful journey of the brand, Boroline. Its insistence on growth in 'strength rather than growth in volumes' has helped the brand keep in good stead. The brand faced some tough times in 1990s 'due to stagnant pricing following a statutory order from the authorities'. Due to this order, every tube of Boroline sold meant a loss for the company.

The production was brought down to a minimum and the tube 'disappeared unceremoniously from the retail shelves' for as long as two years. What was surprising was that after these two years when the brand returned to the counters, it was welcomed with open arms. The emotion was the same that would be accorded to a long lost friend. Sales doubled and the brand's goodwill helped it survive extinction (*Superbrands* 2004).

to established brands. Highly recognized brand names also have increased possibilities of licensing and brand extension opportunities. A brand name, which provides high equity, can be used to launch another product (brand extension), as people are bound to associate it with the brand they like, leading to a greater acceptance of the new product launched.

This understanding of brand equity can be summarized as the added value (positive or negative) endowed on a product or service by the customers' perception of a brand. Brand equity has been defined as 'the biased behaviour a consumer has towards a branded product versus an unbranded equivalent' (Faircloth, Capella, and Alford 2001). For the customer, the value of a brand extends beyond its performance on the basis of functional features. It is an intrapersonal construct and moderates the impact of marketing activities (Raggio and Leone 2009). A positive added value can lead to differential behaviour of consumers towards the branded product or service, providing an advantage to the brand owner, which the brand owner can cash in on, in a number of ways. Exhibit 4.1 suggests that consumers welcomed back the green tube of Boroline like a long lost friend, since they had strong positive brand values that they associated with that brand.

NEED FOR BUILDING BRAND EQUITY

The study of brands has been an active area of study for marketing researchers for many years, but the 1990s saw a shift towards how strong brands can be formed and cultivated (Faircloth, Capella and Alford 2001). A strong brand helps the organization connect with customers and elicits a differential response from them. When customers develop a positive attitude towards a brand it leads to brand equity (Farquhar 1989). It is also possible that customers develop a negative attitude towards a brand; such a brand then leads to a decrease in the value endowed on a product. A brand that has a negative equity will not only that succeed, it will not have the option of brand extensions either. This highlights the importance of managing brands to build a positive equity and providing leverage to the product with the brand name. Research also shows that brand equity, along with trust, consistently appears as the most influential factor in cultivating both behavioural and attitudinal loyalty (Taylor, Celuch, and Goodwin 2004). 'More and more companies are realizing that brand equity is one of their most valuable intangible assets' (Liaogang, Chongyan, and Zi'an 2007). The benefits of building strong brand equity are as follows:

1. Brand equity has a positive influence on market power (Farquhar 1989).
2. It positively impacts consumers' willingness to pay price premiums (Keller 1993).
3. It leads to 'higher efficiency and effectiveness of their marketing programs' (Bernick 2005, Keller 2001).
4. It positively impacts the company's market share (Baldauf et al. 2003).
5. It results in improved future profits and long-term cash flow (Srivastava and Shocker 1991, cited in Zeugner-Roth et al. 2008).
6. It can build brand loyalty, which in turn reduces marketing costs (Kayaman and Arsali 2007).
7. It can deliver emotional safety, prestige, or other benefits that are important to consumers (Raggio and Leone 2007).
8. It reduces the anticipated risk, enhances anticipated confidence in the brand purchase decision, and increases satisfaction with the brand (Broyles et al. 2009).
9. It leads to a sustainable competitive advantage (Bharadwaj et al. 1993).
10. It ultimately leads to marketing success for the brand (Ching and Ellis 2006).
11. Strong brand equity can help in achieving success for new products launched as brand extensions (Pitta and Katsanis 1995).

An understanding of brand equity and the sources of brand equity is a must for marketers, so that they can enhance their brand equity relative to the competitor's brands (Myers 2003).

STEPS IN BUILDING A BRAND—BRAND RESONANCE PYRAMID

The definition of brand equity talks about the added value endowed on a product or service. The catch here is that customers should have a positive perception of the brand, which in turn depends on their knowledge of the brand. This knowledge can again vary from customer to customer on the basis of marketing communication, their perception of marketing communication, and their individual experiences with the brand, i.e., their moments of truth with the brand. As far as the tangible attributes are concerned, marketers can hope to educate the customers, but what about the intangible attributes? Do the marketers create intangible attributes via positioning and promotions, or are they ascribed to the consumers? Research shows that the answer lies in between, i.e., the consumer opinion about the brand depends on the 'conversation' with the brand promoters, history of the brand, market conditions, and communication from the competing brands (Myers 2005). How then can we build the brand so that the consumers develop a positive perception of the brand?

Consumer-based Brand Equity

Keller (1993, 2001, 2004), developed the brand resonance pyramid model, wherein a series of four steps, further sub-divided into six brand-building blocks, which lead to a strong brand were identified. These four steps are:
 (a) Craft a proper brand identity
 (b) Create appropriate brand meaning

(c) Obtain required brand responses

(d) Form appropriate brand relationships with customers

The brand resonance pyramid is divided into four levels as follows (see Figure 4.1.):

(a) Brand identity

(b) Brand meaning

(c) Brand response

(d) Brand relationships

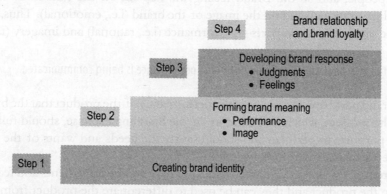

Source: Keller 2004.

Figure 4.1 Building brand equity

According to Keller (2004), these are the building blocks for establishing a strong brand, which he represented with the help of a pyramid, wherein instituting a proper brand identity forms the first step and the base of the pyramid. This step is followed by crafting a suitable brand meaning, bringing forth the right brand response from the customers, which leads to creating the right brand relationships at the top of the pyramid. This brand building process is as follows.

(a) Brand identity—This responds to the customer's question, 'Who is the brand'? As has been discussed earlier in this section, for the customers, brand awareness is an important construct of identifying a brand, i.e., brand salience. How often the customer recalls or recognizes a brand under different situations of purchase or consumption is important. The cues necessary to remind the consumers about the brand help build a ubiquitous brand. The idea is to create 'deep, broad brand awareness', where depth relates to how easily the brand is recalled and breadth relates to the range of consumption situations which bring the brand to mind. Thus, if we want to purchase a mobile phone, then the ease with which a Nokia/Samsung/Sony Ericsson comes to mind is the depth of brand awareness. If we want to purchase an MP3 player for listening to music, or if we want to purchase a camera, and the 'mobile phone brand name' still comes to mind, then that is the breadth of brand awareness. To increase the breadth of brand awareness, Nestlé's Kit-Kat came out with a series of advertisements showing people consuming Kit-Kat in different situations saying 'Kit-Kat break banta hai' (i.e., you deserve a Kit-Kat break now).

(b) Brand meaning—Brand awareness brings the brand to mind whenever a consumer wants to consume, but is this the only criteria on the basis of which purchases are made? For a consumer, in different situations the meaning or image of the brand is also important. This aspect, thus, denotes what the brand is about. For example, one may consume soft drinks in different situations and mostly a cola drink may come to mind. However, when a consumer has the problem of acidity or is not feeling particularly well, then he/she would like to consume a Limca rather than any other soft drink. This brand image can be formed by the consumers' direct association with the brand, or indirectly by observing others (parents, grandparents, friends, etc.), or through organization-influenced sources like advertisements, sales people, and so on. Brand feeling will depend on the functional attributes of the brand (i.e., rational) and on the image of the brand (i.e., emotional). Thus, brand meaning can be divided into two parts—performance (i.e., rational) and imagery (i.e., emotional).

 See the Fortune Kachi Ghani ad and how the brand performance is being communicated.

(i) Brand performance relates to the performance of the product that the brand represents. The product, which is at the core of the branding exercise, should fulfil the functions it purports to perform and should satisfy the needs and wants of the customers. The performance, therefore, includes:

- Product features and characteristics—These are the ingredients and features that make up the product and they can be used to differentiate the product from its competitors (for details see the chapter on brand positioning).
- Product performance—How the product performs can be measured in terms of reliability (consistent performance over a period of time), durability (the duration for which the product is expected to have an economic life), and serviceability (ease of getting the product repaired if needed).
- Service delivery—How service has been delivered during customer interactions—be it the speed of service, effectiveness in terms of customer satisfaction, or service empathy (service employees were seen as trusting, caring, and focused on safeguarding the interest of the customers), etc.
- Product design—The aesthetic aspects of the product, such as the colour, shape, feel, look, smell, etc., also influence customers.
- Product price—The price of the brand in relation to other brands in the product category, and the frequency with which discounts are offered is also an important consideration.

(ii) Brand image: As discussed, this is the emotional aspect of the brand or how the brand meets the 'consumers' psychological or social needs.' It is the intangible aspect that deals with feelings rather than the actual tangible performance of the brand. The four categories of brand imagery identified are as follows:

- User profiles—Demographic profiles like age, gender, income, etc. can be used to create an image of the type of people who use the brand or the aspirational users.

 See the Fortune '5 ka Aashirwad' ad and how it builds on the brand image by highlighting the user profile.

- Purchase and usage situations—The purchase association relates to the type of channel (for example, *kirana* store, organized retail outlet, Internet, etc.), ease of purchase, and other benefits while making a purchase. Organized retailers in India have been facing competition from the friendly neighbourhood mom and pop stores. To provide purchase benefits, Reliance Mart—Reliance Retail's biggest hypermarket in Faridabad (National Capital Region)—gives loyalty bonuses and also provides free home delivery. Usage situations are the myriad situations where the brand can be used, like a specific time, day, week, location of use, etc. For example, LM 365 retail stores are open from 6 a.m. to 11 p.m. every day to capture the working class in India (moneycontrol.com, 2008).

- Personality and values—Brands, like people can take on personality traits like honesty, cheerfulness, reliability, and others. For example, Peter England shirts (for men) were positioned as the 'honest' shirts, i.e., they were available at honest-to-goodness (genuine) prices. The brand talked about being honest and instantly connected with people who considered honesty a virtue. It has been studied that people purchase those brands that they feel would match their personalities, whether this is their concept of the self or a desired self-image they would like to exhibit.

- History, hierarchy, and experiences—Brands may highlight significant events of the past or build associations with history, heritage, and experiences. This can also help build the brand image. Take the example of State Bank of India, which in 2009 released a series of advertisements showing eminent personalities like Rabindranath Tagore (first Indian Nobel laureate), Dadabhai Naoroji (the grand old man of India), Jagdish Chandra Bose (eminent scientist), etc., along with the tagline, 'The banker to *this* Indian' and the 'The Banker to every Indian'. MDH tries to highlight its heritage by saying 'real spices since 1919' (see Image 4.1).

Source: http://mdhspices.com/, accessed on 23 February 2010.

Image 4.1   MDH—Spices with a heritage

Brand meaning should be able to create 'strong, favourable, and unique' brand associations with the customers. Associations should be strong so that customers recall the same and link it to the brand; these strong associations should be flattering in order to elicit a favourable response from the customers, and they should be unique when compared to other brands. This is important, as it results in eliciting brand responses from customers.

(iii) Brand response: As the word suggests, it relates to how customers respond to the marketing activities of a brand, and the brand meaning they derive from it. It depicts how customers think (i.e., brand judgement, which is a rational aspect) or feel (i.e., brand feelings, which are an emotional aspect) about the brand. These are discussed as below:

- Judgements—The various company-influenced marketing activities, experiences of customers, and their own sources of information, cause the customers to develop certain associations with the brand. Based on these associations formed, customers can draw different conclusions for the brand. These can be on the basis of the quality of the brand, credibility of the brand, consumers' consideration in purchasing the brand, which will happen when they feel the brand is appropriate and meaningful for them, and the superiority of the brand to the other brands in the category.

- Feelings—Brands can evoke different feelings in customers, which can be that of warmth, fun, excitement, security, social approval, and/or self-respect. Customers can feel warm-hearted, cheerful, and excited when they experience the brand. On the other hand, they can privately think that the brand adds security and comfort to their lives, gets them approval from society, and adds to their feeling of self-respect and accomplishment.

These brand responses whether rational or emotional can influence customers when they are reinforced and come to mind every time customers experience/encounter the brand. It is crucial for the marketers to derive favourable brand-responses from the customers, as these brand responses lead to the development of customers' relationships with the brand.

(iv) Brand resonance: Brand resonance is developed when customers form relationships with the brand and feel 'in sync' with the brand. This is directly proportional to the depth of the psychological bond the customers have built and the level of activity generated due to this. An example of this are the Harley-Davidson brand owners who take pride in their HOG (Harley Owners Group) activities, and according to Nicholas Westons's 'Tattooed Brands Global Survey' 2009, it was found that Harley-Davidson was the most popular brand tattooed on the body. Favourable brand relationships result in loyal customers and this is reflected in their repeat purchases. Customers develop an attachment to the brand, to take pride and pleasure in owning and consuming the brand, as well as develop a sense of community (see HOG example). The company builds an active engagement with the customers, which results in consumers spending extra resources (time, money, etc.) on the brand than when actually purchasing and consuming the brand. These consumers then become brand ambassadors who help in communicating and reinforcing the brand ties of other consumers as well. Thus, brand relationship involves the intensity of attachment and activity to engage not only in purchase but also to communicate about the brand to others.

Keller (1993, 2001, 2004) concluded that the 'strongest brands excel in all the brand-building blocks.' Brand resonance occurs when all the other brand-building blocks synchronize with the needs and wants of the customers and the brand and customer are in complete harmony. Brand resonance leads to the customers sharing a positive relationship with the brand, and this subsequently has a positive influence on brand extensions and the intention to repurchase (Wang, Wei and Yu 2008). This provides a framework to marketers for building strong brands and also in assessing their brand building efforts.

Brand Equity in a Business-to-Business Context

The equity of a brand in a business-to-business environment is different from a business to consumer setting. Organizational buyers are different in the types of products purchased and in the decision-making process (Wilson and Woodside 2001). Kuhn, Alpert, and Pope 2008, have applied Keller's brand equity model to the business concept. The four levels of the brand resonance pyramid can be modified for a B2B context as follows:

(a) Brand identity—Manufacturer's brand salience
(b) Brand meaning—Includes performance and reputation
(c) Brand response—Includes judgements and sales force relationships
(d) Brand relationships—Partnership solutions

Thus, in the organizational context, the four levels of the brand resonance pyramid are the same, but the differences exist in the sub-dimensions of these blocks as follows.

Brand identity   In brand identity, it was found that the manufacturer's corporate brand name played an important role rather than individual product brands.

Brand meaning   Brand meaning included the performance of the product rather than brand elements like brand name and slogans. The user profiles and the purchase and usage situations have special relevance in brand imagery, as corporates are interested in knowing, which reputed organizations are using the products they are about to purchase. Few sub-points of brand imagery like personality, values and history, and hierarchy were found to be of least importance.

Brand response   In a B2B context, brand response is dominated by the relationship the business houses have with the company representatives rather than by the feelings towards the brand product. The purchase process in organizations is rational rather than emotional. In judgements, credibility and technology are the most important of the various parameters of consumer-based equity.

Brand relationships   Organizational members usually fail to demonstrate loyalty, attachment, a sense of community or engagement with a brand as per the fourth level. Thus, organizations do not demonstrate brand resonance. They look at the interaction with the company representatives and the after-sales service as well as the support provided, rather than the interaction between the consumer and the brand as in a consumer environment. Organizations look for solutions and if the suppliers can form partnerships to provide relevant solutions, loyalty can result as an outcome.

In an organization, an individual member's perception is overtaken by the collective perception of the deciding members of the purchasing committee. Thus, the brand perception of all the members is important rather than the of just a single individual. It can be concluded that in an organization the company manufacturing the product is more important than the brand name. The members of the purchasing committee are detached and do not let feelings influence their decision. Active engagements are not possible, as organizations tend to switch quality, price, terms and conditions of use, technology, etc.

Sources of Brand Equity

Brand equity can be built by 'creating the right brand knowledge structures with the right consumers.' All the brand related contacts (whether personal or marketer-initiated) act as building blocks (Kotler and Keller 2005). As marketers how do we influence customers in such a way that they seek the brand whenever they need to make a purchase in that category and across categories too? (See Exhibit 4.2.) This can be answered by building a strong brand that positively influences customers and by understanding the sources of brand equity for the customers. A review of literature highlights the various factors that lead to building brand equity (see Figure 4.2).

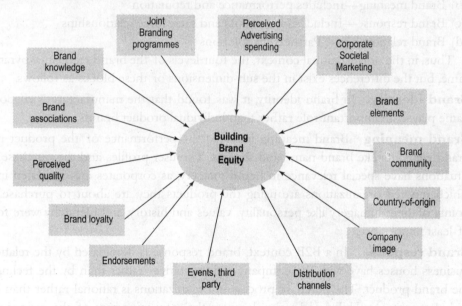

Source: Aaker 1991, Keller 1993, Aaker 1996, Keller 2001, Aaker and Joachimsthaler 2000, Yoo and Donthu 2001, Berthon, Holbrook, and Hulbert 2003.

Figure 4.2   Factors affecting brand equity

Exhibit 4.2   Establishing Boroline's Brand Identity

To establish the brand identity of Boroline, 'the logo was developed carefully. For all Indians, and especially the merchant class, the Elephant God—or Ganesha (see Image 4.2 top left)—has an auspicious significance. The elephant signifies steadiness and strength. It is also synonymous with success or "siddhi". Keeping

Contd

Exhibit 4.2 *contd*

these in mind, Gourmohan Dutta (founder of the brand) chose the elephant as Boroline's logo hoping that it would bestow luck and spell success for what was considered a reckless venture in 1929. The logo caught on immediately. In the rural heartland and for the millions who cannot read, Boroline is still known as the "hathiwala cream" (cream with the elephant logo)' (*Superbrands,* 2004; *Superbrands,* 2009).

Source: http://www.boroline.com/boroline.php.

Image 4.2 Boroline's logo—The 'hathiwala cream'

Brand Knowledge

Brand knowledge is the understanding that consumers have about a brand. Brand knowledge can be understood on the basis of two components—brand awareness and brand image (Keller 1993, 2001).

Brand Awareness

Aaker (1991) has talked about brand awareness as an important dimension of brand equity from a customer's perspective. He describes brand awareness as the ability of consumers to recognize or recall the brand as a member of a particular product class category. Keller (1993), on the other hand, simply puts it as the ability of customers to identify the brand under different conditions. Recognizing the brand under different conditions, thus, highlights the importance of two parameters—brand recognition and brand recall. People are said to have high brand awareness when they are able to recognize the brand even by clues given about the brand (i.e. brand recognition) and are able to recall the brand when needs related to the product category are to be fulfilled (i.e. brand recall). Aaker (1996) further describes six levels of brand awareness (see Figure 4.3), namely recognition (they have heard of the brand), recall (brand names they can recall), top-of-the mind (first-mentioned brand), brand dominance supremacy (the only brand recalled), brand knowledge (consumers understand what the brand stands for), and brand opinion (when consumers have an opinion about a brand, which is in accordance with the brand image). Awareness is the most important building-block, as the subsequent brand-based decisions are influenced by it (Keller 1993, 2001). Brand awareness is also important as people like what they are familiar with. Consumers generally ascribe all the good attributes to the items they are familiar with (Aaker and Joachimsthaler 2000).

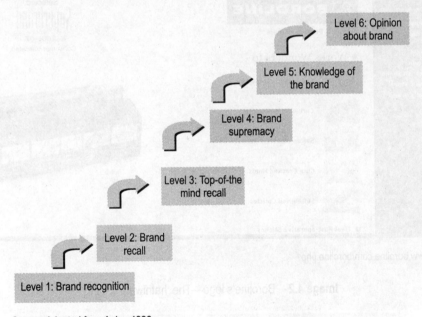

Source: Adapted from Aaker 1996.

Figure 4.3 Levels of brand awareness

Brand Image

This is broadly the perception that consumers have about a brand. These perceptions lead to the development of a representation of a brand in the minds of the consumers. Over a period of time, people can have more than one perception of the brand and this leads to the formation of a brand image. The brand image and attitude are to be created first in order to achieve brand equity (Faircloth, Capella, and Alford 2001).

See the Fortune '5 ka Aashirwad' ad and how fortune builds its brand knowledge.

Brand Associations

These are 'anything that connects the consumers to the brand' (Aaker 1991, Aaker and Joachimsthaler 2000). People can have more than one connection and these connections act as the building blocks that lead to developing brand equity. Thus, if we talk about Big Bazaar, associations like 'value for money', 'variety of products', 'fashion trends for the youth', etc. come to mind. Apart from user imagery and product attributes discussed in brand image, the situations in which the brands are used, the symbols (discussed under brand elements), and brand personality (discussed in Chapter 1) all add to the brand associations (Aaker and Joachimsthaler 2000).

Perceived Quality

According to Aaker (1991), the quality of the brand as perceived by the consumers also leads to brand equity, which he defined as, the 'customer's perception of the overall quality or superiority of a product or service with respect to its intended purpose relative to alternatives'. This is also kind of brand association, but its relative importance has led to its elevation as a separate dimension of brand equity. If the perceived quality is high it will lead to 'price premiums, price elasticites, and brand usage' and it will be applicable across product classes though the importance may vary (Aaker 1996). The extent to which the product fulfils the basic function is an important factor signalling quality (Anselmsson, Johansson, and Persson 2007). The year 2010 saw a number of product recalls by established players in the automobile sector. For example, Nissan's Titan pickup trucks, Armada and Infiniti QX56 special utility vehicles, and Quest minivans, and Maruti Suzuki's A-star to name a few. The question is, how does this impact the consumers' perceived quality? According to Koshy (2010), such product recalls signal the willingness of the brand to improve product quality, which reinforces the brand's quality standards and leads to a favourable perceived quality by the customers.

Brand Loyalty

The importance of brand loyalty as a construct of brand equity has been delineated by Aaker (1991), who treated it as a behavioural dimension. However, brand loyalty as an attitudinal dimension has also been identified and defined as 'the tendency to be loyal to a focal brand, which is demonstrated by the intention to buy the brand as a primary choice' (Yoo and Donthu 2001). Thus, if consumers have a tendency to buy the brand again and again it will lead to brand equity. The advantages of brand loyalists are that they 'represent barriers to entry for competitors, are a basis for a price premium, time to respond to competitor innovations, and a barricade against deleterious price competition. Loyalty is of sufficient importance that other measures, such as perceived quality and associations, can be evaluated based on their ability to influence it' (Aaker 1996). Three levels of loyalty (Gremler and Brown 1996) have been identified—behavioural loyalty (purchase repeatedly), attitudinal loyalty (customer feels some devotion to the brand and prefers the brand), and cognitive loyalty (brand name comes as top-of-the mind recall, and is the consumer's first choice whenever a purchase decision arises).

Company Image

Keller (2003, 2005) identified the image of the company as an influencer of brand equity. The image, the organization has in the mind of the consumers, is bound to impact the brands launched by the organization due to the halo effect. Using halo marketing, firms can increase their overall positive image so that consumers recognize their positive attributes and discount the negative attributes. This results in an increase of sales and positively impacts brand equity (Ross-Wooldridge, Brown, and Minsky 2004). The relationship the company has with customers, the various programmes pursued by the organization (including corporate social responsibility), their mission, values, and the credibility that they have in the market all impact the brand that is currently being reviewed by the customers (Ross-Wooldridge et al. 2004; Keller 2005). The market performance of the company also affects brand equity. This includes factors like corporate performance including revenue and growth-rate and corporate innovation, (Wang et al. 2008). Organizations can use the company image to leverage the brands by corporate branding (like Tata Salt, Tata Motors, etc.), or by using sub-brand strategy (e.g. Maggi Sauce, Maggi Pickles, Maggi Noodles, etc.).

Brand Community

This includes the people associated with the brand, such as users or representatives of the firm marketing the brand (Berthon, Holbrook, and Hulbert 2003). In customer-based brand equity, we focus on the community formed by the customers and its impact on brand equity. By building such consumer-based brand community, organizations can interact with customers rather than just communicate with them. The Internet is acting as a great enabler for organizations. Canon, LG, Samsung, and others, are busy creating their brand communities online. Canon boasts of 80,000 users who are a part of its online community (in India), Samsung mobile has 3 million users in India. Brand communities help in building brand salience, and the online communities also act as a platform for cross-selling products. Apart from this, companies can also track consumer behaviour, especially in an industry like telecom, where tariffs are changing every day. Keeping this in mind, Tata Teleservices is using online communities to track the behaviour of consumers for its three brands—Tata Indicom, Tata Photon, and Tata Docomo (Mukherjee 2010).

Brand Elements

Brands can be identified and differentiated with the help of small brand identities that can be trademarked. These brand equity drivers are called brand elements. Brand elements need to be strategically chosen, so that they are easily remembered and invoked for the product class. They should reinforce the positioning of the brand, be transferable to a variety of products so that brand extension is possible, and meaning should be able to transcend geographic boundaries. Take the example of Puma. The company has incorporated the leaping panther in its logo and even though it manufactures high-end athletic shoes and sportswear, the logo is broad and can be used to represent other products as well like fragrances, which they sell under the same brand name. The brand elements should be legally and competitively protectable. However, it is difficult for a brand element to satisfy all these criteria. The major brand elements as discussed by Keller (2005) are as follows.

Brand Name

In the process of brand development, brand name selection should be one of the most important and well-thought out of activities, since the brand name is most closely associated with the success of a product. A distinctive and memorable brand name can lead to triumph on the shelf (at the stores) and is the major contributor to the product's longevity (Bernick 2005). Brand name is the central theme or key association of the product. It should be simple so that even a small child can remember it. Take the example of Alpenliebe. When it was launched in 1995 by Perfetti Van Melle (India), analysts were sceptical, as they believed no one would be able to learn and remember a name like 'Alpenliebe'. The company was not deterred and in an advertisement in the first campaign, the entire duration (30 seconds) was spent in pronouncing the name five times. To ensure that the target audience remembered the name and pronounced it properly, a jingle was used 'Jee lalchaye, raha na jaye, Alpenliebe', where the name was broken down into four distinct phonetics, 'al', 'pen', 'lie', 'be'. The result was that people not only learnt the name but many years down the line, it is still a success (Sagar, Singh, Agrawal, and Gupta 2009). Thus, with the help of a brand name, an organization can register and position the brand in the mind of the customers within a few minutes. Renaming a product or changing the brand name involves a lot of effort and money. Take the case of the UTI bank, which after thirteen years had to change its brand name to Axis Bank (for details see Exhibit 4.3: Changing the brand name from UTI Bank to Axis Bank).

Deciding on a brand name is both a science and an art. Landor Associates (cited in Keller 2004) gave the following brand name taxonomy that can be used while selecting a brand name:

- Descriptive—When the brand name describes the function of the brand literally. For example, Singapore Airlines describes itself as the airline for travel to Singapore.

Exhibit 4.3 Changing the Brand Name from UTI Bank to Axis Bank

Axis Bank, India, was the first bank to begin operations as a private bank in 1994 post liberalization. It was jointly promoted by Unit Trust of India (UTI-I), Life Insurance Corporation of India (LIC) and General Insurance Corporation Ltd, and four other PSU insurance companies—National Insurance Company Ltd, The New India Assurance Company Ltd, The Oriental Insurance Company Ltd, and United India Insurance Company Ltd (India Finance and Investment guide 2010, Axis Bank 2010). At the time of its incorporation, it was named UTI Bank. However, thirteen years later it had to change its brand name to Axis Bank due to the split in the erstwhile UTI. The need for a brand name change arose when the board felt that the 'existence of several shareholder-unrelated entities using the UTI brand' led to subsequent brand confusion. According to Mr P.J. Nayak, chairman and CEO, Axis Bank, the new name was chosen considering the bank's pan-Indian as well as international presence. The bank hired the advertising firm O&M to help create awareness about the new brand across the country, as the bank had a customer base of six million. The logo and colour of the logo were all changed and the bank spent around ₹50 crore (₹500 million) on the re-branding exercise.

Source: http://www.financialexpress.com/news/uti-bank-is-now-axic-bank/207000/, http://www.axisbank.com/aboutus/aboutaxisbank/About-Axis-Bank.asp, http://www.domain-b.com/finance/banks/uti_bank/20070430_axis_bank.html, http://finance.indiamart.com/investment_in_india/uti_bank.html, http://www.rediff.com/money/2007/apr/30uti.htm, all accessed on 24 February 2010.

- Suggestive—Suggests function or benefit. For example, Fair and Lovely fairness cream for women, Fair and Handsome fairness cream for men, etc.
- Compounds—Combinations of two or more, often, unexpected words, e.g. Red Bull energy drink.
- Classical—When Latin, Greek, Sanskrit words are used. For example, Maruti cars (the word Maruti is the Sanskrit name of the Indian deity Hanuman.)
- Arbitrary—Real words with no obvious tie-in to the company. For example, Apple computers, Kingfisher, etc.
- Fanciful—Coined words with no obvious meaning. For example, Xerox, Nirma (Karsanbhai Patel, the founder of the brand derived the word Nirma from the name of his daughter 'Nirupama', Limbdiwala 2009.).

The brand name should be such that it adds to the awareness of people and is easy to pronounce. Simple brand names that can be easily recalled and are familiar, yet distinctive and unusual, are preferred. Apart from the ease of remembering, brand names can also be used to transfer some feeling, for example, Splendour bike, Passion bike, Spark car, Mr Muscle kitchen cleaner, etc. All these brand names, though easy to remember, transfer some meaning also (brand association). The first three are emotion-laden and the last focuses on performance just like Close-up toothpaste and Head and Shoulders shampoo.

 See how Fortune is building on its brand name through its various ads.

URLs

According to Internet World Stats 2010, Internet penetration in the top twenty countries (with the highest number of Internet users) is approximately 76 per cent. In India there are eighty-one million Internet users, and in the last nine years (2000–2009), users have grown by 1520 per cent. Even though Internet penetration is 7 per cent, Indian users form 9.8 per cent of the total users in Asia. The current Internet population globally is approximately 1.97 billion and accounts for a penetration level of just approximately 29 per cent (Internet World Stats, 2010). This highlights the fact that the Internet can be used to reach out to a vast population and in times to come, this opportunity will be limitless. A look at the domain counts and Internet statistics 2010 shows that there are 115 million domain names registered already, and there were 111,687 new registers on a single day (28 February 2010). This means that with so many domain names already registered, it will be increasingly difficult for new entrants to get simple domain names. Therefore, it will be the coined or fanciful brand names, which will be registered on the net. Companies also have to constantly monitor the web to ensure that their brand names are not being used by common people or groups, as this creates confusion in the minds of the consumers, especially if they are not aware of the fact that the site is not owned by the organization itself.

Logos and Symbols

Logos are used to visually represent 'origin, ownership, or association' (Keller 2004). The advantage is that they are easily recognized and an important means to identifying products. Logos, if abstract, can be used over a range of products, i.e., over brand extensions to endorse the sub-brands. They can also be easily updated over time and generally transfer well across cultural boundaries (see Exhibit 4.4: The New Logo of HUL). Logos can be in the form of word-marks, pictorial (non-word) marks, or a combination of both (Keller 2004). For example, the logos of Adidas and Puma have both word-mark (their respective names) and pictorial mark (three stripes for the former and a leaping puma or panther for the latter). Word-marks are corporate names written in a distinct form or style, such as Kit-Kat, Cadbury's, Yahoo, etc. Non-word mark logos are also called symbols and are abstract logos that are unrelated to the corporate name, like Nike's swoosh. Over time, the logo, the symbol, and the brand 'may become inseparable and increase memorability, aid recall, and help sales'. Due to this fact, organizations have to be very careful while selecting a logo. Also, in India and across other countries, which have to deal with issues such as 'illiteracy, cultural diversity, multiple languages– pictorial logos can cut across all these and convey the same meaning' (Ramaswamy and Namakumari 2009).

Characters

'These are brand symbols that take on a human or real-life characteristic' (Keller 2004). They can be animated like the 'Tiger for Britannia biscuits', 'Tony the Tiger and Coco the monkey of Kellogg's', or live figure forms like Ronald McDonald (of McDonald's), the Devil (of Onida), Colonel Saunders (of Kentucky Fried Chicken), etc. Such characters also help in building a strong brand identity. For example, Asian Paints and its character—Gattu ('the impish little boy with a paintbrush in one hand and a dripping can of paint in the other') almost became synonymous with each other, especially in rural markets, where it was even referred to as 'bacha chaap paint' (the kid's paint) (Ramaswamy and Namakumari 2009). Characters can also be updated over time, for example, Colonel Saunders (of KFC) got an updated image in a red cook's apron (instead of the earlier white jacket) against a red background, and since 1957 (when it was sold in buckets for the first time), Colonel Saunders' character has been updated four times (KFC 2010).

Exhibit 4.4   The New Logo of HUL (Hindustan Unilever Limited)

Hindustan Unilever Limited (HUL) celebrated its seventy-fifth year of existence in India in 2007. On 25 June 2007, Hindustan Lever Limited was renamed as Hindustan Unilever Limited and a new logo was unveiled (see Image 4.3). The company known as Lever Brothers India Limited was incorporated on 17 October 1933. However, the company's journey in India started much before that in 1888 with Sunlight soap. This was soon followed by Lifebuoy in 1895 and other famous brands like Pears, Lux, and Vim.

'The Company believes that the new name provides optimum balance between maintaining the heritage of the company and the synergies of global alignment with the corporate name of Unilever. Most importantly, the name retains 'Hindustan' as the first word in its name to reflect the company's continued commitment to the local economy, consumers, partners, and employees. The new logo is symbolic of the company's mission of 'Adding vitality to life'. It comprises of twenty-five different icons representing the organization, its brands, and the idea of Vitality. For example:

'The Sun is our primary natural resource. All life begins with the sun—the ultimate symbol of vitality. The Heart represents love, care, and health—feeling

Contd

Exhibit 4.4 *contd*

good. The shirt represents fresh laundry—looking good. A bird is a symbol of freedom, relief from daily chores—getting more out of life, etc.'

Mr Doug Baillie, CEO, Hindustan Lever Limited, said, 'The identity symbolizes the benefits we bring to our consumers and the communities we work in. Our mission is full of promise for the future, opening up exciting opportunities, where we have competitive advantage for developing our business, and our new identity will help us confidently position ourselves in every aspect of our business.'

'The new name and the new logo will leverage the positioning, scale, and synergy that comes with being part of Unilever globally. It positions our organization on a global scale and … retaining "Hindustan" in the name, brings the very best of local and global to the forefront.

For us, this is really an opportunity, collectively as an organization, to renew and strengthen our commitment to continue our endeavour to earn the love and respect of India, by making a real difference to every Indian,' Mr Baillie added.

Source: http://www.rediff.com/money/2005/feb/26hll.htm.

Image 4.3   Unilever's new logo

Slogans

Research suggests that slogans of brands are effective keystones in building brand equity (Mathur and Mathur 1995). These are short phrases used to position the organization's offering. They can communicate information about the brand (about how they provide the benefit in a particular product class, or how they are different, or both) to persuade consumers. Slogans lead to increased product differentiation and brand recall (Law 2002). They also lead to improved brand evaluations and product beliefs (Pryor and Bodie 1998). Slogans work as carriers of brand equity and remind consumers of their liking for the brand (Dahlen and Rosengren 2005). By incorporating the brand name, slogans also help in building brand awareness. Slogans and brand name, logo, symbol, character all go hand in hand and should be reinforcing each other to send an integrated message to the consumers. For example, LG Electronics uses the logo LG in grey and stylized smiling face in red colour with the matching slogan, 'Life's Good' (see Image 4.4 of LG). Some other examples of slogans are, 'King of Good Times' (Kingfisher), 'Connecting People' (Nokia), 'Bond with the Best' (Reid and Taylor), 'You Are Worth It' (L'Oreal), etc. These form an important part of marketing communications, and can also be used on the packaging and on the websites.

 See the use of the slogan 'Ab bas toot pado' by Fortune.

Jingles

These are musical messages of the brand and are used for advertising purposes to communicate the benefits of the brand (Keller 2004). They are different from slogans as they are musical.

Source: http://www.in.lge.com/, accessed on 5 March 2010.

Image 4.4 LG's slogan—Life's good with LG

Like slogans, they are also used to communicate about the brand and add to the brand equity. Due to their catchy nature, people tend to hum them, and therefore, remember them for a longer time. By building the brand name into a jingle, the awareness of the brand can be enhanced. For example, Hutch, now Vodafone, endeared a lot of people with the help of its jingle, 'You and I in this beautiful world'. Nirma is another example of a brand that has used its jingle of 'Washing powder Nirma, Doodh si safedi…' to successfully position itself in the minds of the consumers. The latest ad uses this same old jingle to reach out to the consumers. Corporates are also setting their jingles as their call-back tunes for their employees. For example, ICICI's 'Hum hai na' (We are there) jingle is set as the call-back tune for all its employees (*Financial Express* 2005).

 See Fortune's 'Paanch Ka Aashirwad' ad to understand the use of jingles in building brand equity.

Packaging

Packaging includes wrappers or containers in which the product is sold. It does not directly contribute to the product performance, but characterizes the product. It facilitates in transportation, storage of the product at the retailer's outlet, acts as a silent salesman on the shelves, carries a lot of information, aids in the consumption process, can be used as an in-home storage for the product, and after the product has been consumed, as a storage for other items (if it is reusable). The functional importance of packaging can be explained by referring to Cadbury's worm crisis in 2003. In October 2003, a month before the festival of Diwali, consumers in Mumbai complained about finding worms in Cadbury's Dairy Milk chocolates. Maharashtra's Food and Drug Administration (FDA) was quick to respond and seized the stocks at the Pune plant. Cadbury's said that the infestation had occurred at the storage site and not at the manufacturing site, which brought forward the issue of packaging. Cadbury's responded by investing ₹150 crore on importing machinery, and its packaging now came to include an aluminium foil heat-sealed for complete protection from all sides and further enclosed in a poly-flow pack. An integrated marketing communications strategy was also undertaken to build the lost customer confidence in the brand (Rediff News 2006). Apart from the functional aspect, consumers are found to develop an emotional connect with the packaging. The need to pay attention to packaging design is highlighted by Exhibit 4.5: Packaging Lessons from Tropicana.

Exhibit 4.5   Packaging Lessons from Tropicana

The packaging of Tropicana's Pure Premium orange juice was changed in January 2009. The new cartons attempted to modernize the image with a depiction of fresh-squeezed juice, instead of the long time brand symbol of an orange with a straw protruding from it (see Image 4.5). The deep emotional bond of the loyal customers with the original packaging came as a surprise when there was a lot of public outcry against the new packaging.

Old packaging   New (rejected) packaging

Source: http://www.nytimes.com/2009/02/23/business/media/23adcol.html accessed on 10 February 2010.

Image 4.5   Tropicana's old and new packaging

PepsiCo received feedback on the design via letters, phone calls, and e-mails. The new packaging was also the most blogged topic in the week of 23–27 February 2009, and was next only to the 'machinations of President Obama's new administration'. Consumers described the new packaging as 'ugly', 'stupid', and resembling 'a generic bargain brand' or a 'store brand.' People were confused and passed right by the new Tropicana cartons on the store shelves mistaking them for private-label offerings. One e-mail message read, 'Do any of these package-design people actually shop for orange juice? Because I do, and the new cartons stink.'

According to Neil Campbell, President, Tropicana North America, it was not the volume of complaints that jolted them, but the fact that it was a group of loyal customers who were complaining. Their research (on the basis of which the packaging-change decision was taken) had shown that people had not necessarily had a huge connection with the original packaging. However, the research failed to take into account the passion of the very loyal small group of consumers.

Two months and a reported US$ 35 million later, PepsiCo bowed to public demand and reverted to the original Tropicana packaging. The only remnants of the US$ 35 million experiment—the cute, orange-shaped plastic caps, were retained on cartons of low-calorie Trop50.

Source: Elliott 2009 and Gidman 2009.

Corporate Societal Marketing

When organizations use their resources to undertake at least one marketing initiative that has a non-economic objective, it is called corporate societal marketing. Corporate societal marketing came into being because consumers' perception of the company and its role in society can significantly affect brand equity (Hoeffler and Keller 2002). 'Consumers believe that corporate philanthropy should be the norm and not the exception for companies'. Tangible aids and donations or the creation of social programmes are found to impact the most. It was also studied that consumers are willing to pay more for a product if it is associated with a cause they care for (Simon 1995). For example, Aircel has associated itself with the Save the Tigers campaign and garnered brand promotion at the same time (see Images 4.6 and 4.7) (Thomson, Sharma, and Dhall 2010); similarly, the Aditya Birla Group has associated itself with CSR activities (see Image 4.8).

Source: http://www.aircel.com/AircelPortal/aircel.portal.

Image 4.6   Positioning by Aircel

Companies like Usha Martin and Bhushan Steel are reaping rich dividends by investing in corporate social responsibility initiatives in the mining belts of Jharkhand, Orissa, etc. They feel that local people connect well with companies following such practices and once their trust is gained, the local people are then more ready to sell their lands for new plants (Mazumdar 2010).

Perceived Advertising Spending

Any potential encounter with the brand impacts the awareness and image of the brand in the minds of consumers (Keller 1993). This encounter can be marketing initiated or personal to

Source: http://saveourtigers.com/.

Image 4.7   Aircel 'Save our tigers'

the consumer. The marketing communications of the firm affect the awareness of the brand, impact the perceived quality, brand loyalty, and brand image. It was studied that the more the resources allocated to advertising a brand, higher the awareness, perceived quality, and brand equity (Villarejo-Ramos and Sanchez-Franco 2005). A synergistic and effective marketing communication programme results in high brand equity (Madhavaram, Badrinarayanan and McDonald, 2005). For example, Coke and Pepsi are perceived to be spending more on advertising and are high on brand equity.

Joint Branding Programmes

An organization can tie up with another brand (either its own or some other organization's) to leverage its brand. It has been studied that companies can create, communicate, or deliver value in a better manner when they partner with other companies. When companies undertook joint-branding they were perceived to be innovative and progressive, and this added to their brand equity (Lebar et al. 2005). According to Keller (2003, 2004, 2005), this can be done in the following ways.

Forming Alliances

Alliances can be formed between two brands to leverage the launch of a new product. This can be done either by co-branding or licensing.

The Aditya Birla Group
Transcending business

A US$ 30 billion corporation, the Aditya Birla Group is in the League of Fortune 500. It is anchored by an extraordinary force of 131,000 employees, belonging to 42 nationalities. The Group operates in 28 countries. Over 60 per cent of its revenues flow from its overseas operations.

Beyond Business -
The Aditya Birla Group is:

■ Working in 3,000 villages. Reaching out to 7 million people annually through the Aditya Birla Centre for Community Initiatives and Rural Development, spearheaded by Mrs. Rajashree Birla.

■ Focusing on: Health Care, Education. Sustainable Livelihood, Women Empowerment Projects, Infrastructure and espousing social causes.

Highlights 2010

■ Over a million patients treated at 3,000 Medical Camps and its 18 hospitals. More than 800 children learnt to smile again as they underwent cleft lip surgery. We helped immunise 6 million children against polio.

■ At our 42 Schools across India we provide quality education to 45,000 children. Of these 18,000 students receive free education. Merit Scholarships are given to an additional 8,000 children from the interiors.

■ Our Vocational Training Centres and the Aditya Birla Rural Technology Park accord training in sustainable livelihood projects to 27,000 people.

■ Our 4,000 Self-Help Groups have led to the empowerment of 38,000 women.

■ Working closely with Habitat for Humanity, we have so far built more than 350 houses as part of our community outreach programme, besides supporting the building of an additional 1,550 houses.

■ We are also engaged in creating model villages in rural India. We have chosen 300 villages for this transformation - whereby in a five year time frame the villages would be self-reliant in every aspect, moving out of the "below the poverty line" status. So far more than 80 villages in India's hinterland have already reached the level of model villages.

■ To embed CSR as a way of life in organizations, we have set up the FICCI - Aditya Birla CSR Centre for Excellence, in Delhi.

■ In line with our commitment to sustainable development, we have partnered the Columbia University in establishing the Columbia Global Centre's Earth Institute in Mumbai.

Transcending the conventional barriers of business because we believe it is our duty.

ADITYA BIRLA GROUP

www.adityabirla.com

Courtesy: Aditya Birla Group.

Image 4.8 Aditya Birla Group ad; also see Plate 5

Co-branding A company can bundle its new brand with an existing brand of the same organization (i.e., the parent brand) or the existing brand of another organization to leverage the brand (Keller, 2004). For example, Kit Kat is sold as Nestlé's Kit Kat, where Nestlé is highlighted prominently on the packaging. This is known as same company co-branding. Other types of co-branding are joint venture co-branding (Panda, n.d.) wherein both the brands are represented, for example, Bharti Wal-Mart in India and multiple-sponsor co-branding wherein all the sponsors are represented. Ingredient co-branding is discussed below.

Licensing Organizations can also get a license from an established branded organization to market their products. This license can be for a brand name, logo, etc., which is already well-established and has a brand equity of its own. The licensee, by paying a fee to the licensor, can get to market their products under the same brand name and leverage their products by cashing in on the brand equity of the established brand. Disney generally licenses its characters to different players in different geographic areas.

Ingredient Branding

The ingredients used in the manufacturing of a brand can be employed to highlight the brand's unique differentiation from other products in a similar category that satisfy the same need. For example, when Proctor and Gamble launched Ariel detergent in the 1990s, they positioned it on the basis of 'Micro systems', i.e., an enzyme-based detergent to combat stains. Garnier Fructis '2-in-1 Shampoo with Oil' has been introduced in the market, in which the three fruit oil ingredients provide nourishment to the hair and the shampoo cleanses the hair. Ingredient branding is a type of co-branding and ingredient branding is done on the basis of the prominent ingredient used in the brand, which is from a supplier (unless the organization goes for backward integration).

Distribution Channels

The channel of distribution or where the brand is being sold also transfers value to a brand. Different retail outlets are perceived differently by consumers, and this gets rubbed on to the brand retailed at the outlets (Keller 2003, 2005) (see Exhibit 4.6: Maruti Suzuki's Distribution Strategy). Organized retailers in India like Big Bazaar and the Emporio Mall, according to the product assortments they keep and the pricing strategies at their stores, transfer an image to the brands that are showcased in their outlets. Thus, if a brand is retailed at Big Bazaar, it would be value for money and if it is retailed at the Emporio Mall, it would be a lifestyle product at a premium price.

Exhibit 4.6   Maruti Suzuki's Distribution Strategy

Maruti Suzuki revolutionized the market in the 1980s with the launch of the people's car—Maruti 800. Indian consumers have come a long way and so has Maruti Suzuki. A number of brands in different price ranges have been added to its portfolio. However, with increased competition in the market, the market share of Maruti has been dwindling. The company launched a sedan—Kizashi—on 2nd February 2011.

Contd

Exhibit 4.6 *contd*

Kizashi will be in the price range of ₹16.5–17.5 lakh (ex-showroom Delhi) (Maruti Suzuki, 2011) and will compete with superior brands like Honda Civic, Toyota Corolla, and Skoda Laura. To upgrade its image as that of a big sedan player, and to create a perception in the minds of the customers that is in line with this brand image, Maruti Suzuki has bought prime properties in Mumbai, Delhi, etc., 'to build upmarket showrooms and capture footfalls of cash-rich customers. It spent ₹50–60 crore each to buy properties in posh locations like Lokhandwala (a shopping hot spot with glitzy malls and luxury car showrooms) in Mumbai's Andheri and Indraprastha in central Delhi.' The plush outlets built on five of its own properties were handed over to dealers—a deviation from the traditional model of outsourcing distribution to private franchisees. 'Maruti Suzuki's lifestyle products such as apparel, sports products, car miniatures, baggage, and other branded stuff are also being displayed in the showrooms to provide a premium look' (Chauhan 2011).

Country-of-Origin Effect

The world has become a global village, and increasingly products from other countries are fighting for shelf-space with the local brands. The country of origin stands for 'the country in which the product is made, and the consumer's perception of the product or the assessment of the product on the basis of this is called the 'country of origin effect' (Samiee 1994). The country of origin's impact on brand equity is well-researched and documented (Thakor and Katsanis 1997, Keller 1993, Aaker 1991). It leads to a generation of secondary associations with the brand (Aaker 1991, Keller 1993, 2003, 2005) A foreign sounding name too has an effect on brand equity (Leclerc, Schmitt, and Dube 1994). The country of origin is found to affect product quality, perceived risk, likelihood of purchase (Elango and Sethi 2007), brand awareness, brand association, and brand loyalty (Pappu, Quester, and Cooksey 2006), thus, it should be given due importance when marketing communication strategies are being formulated by the marketers. Multinational firms who are shifting production bases to other countries due to availability of cheap labour also need to study the perception of that country by the consumers related to the product category. For example, Sony VCR suffered erosion in its brand image when it was manufactured in countries like Poland, Hungary and the former USSR. It is important to understand that brand equity is product-category specific, and so an organization with presence in different product categories needs to monitor customer-based brand equity for each product category. High brand equity in one product category does not necessarily mean high brand equity in the other product categories for the organization (Pappu, Quester, and Cooksey 2006). For consumer durables, it has been found that the image of the country is one of the factors influencing purchase decision. Consequently, products from countries with a good image can capitalize on this by their brand-naming strategy (Yassin, Noor, and Mohammad 2007).

People Endorsements

When well-known people and celebrities associate themselves with the brand to promote it, it is called an endorsement (Keller 2003, 2005). These celebrities can be famous personalities in different fields, acclaimed sportspersons, actors, etc. Choosing a celebrity who is well-known and who has a rich set of potentially useful associations, which match with the brand image, is important. For example, Godfrey Philips India's initiative of the blood donation drive with the Rotary Club was an astounding success and in the words of Nita Kapoor, Executive Vice-president, Marketing and Corporate Affairs, 'The reason we were able to collect so many blood units was…the celebrity endorsement by actor Preity Zinta who helped us in spreading the message to participate in the drive and donate,' (Saxena 2008). Aamir Khan has signed an endorsement deal for a United Arab Emirates based telecommunications service provider for ₹35 crore. The company feels that as Aamir 'is very particular about his own image and the image of the product he endorses', people are bound to associate the firm's product as being genuine and best in the class (Iyer 2010). However, there is also a risk involved when celebrities are used to endorse brands as was seen in the cases of Gillette, Nike, Accenture, etc., all of who had used Tiger Woods to endorse their brands. Once the scandal involving Tiger Woods surfaced, the companies had to distance themselves from his behaviour. The reverse is also true for brands that have inappropriate antecedents and a celebrity is used to endorse this brand. This was recently the case when Shah Rukh Khan (owner of KKR— Kolkata Knight Riders) signed a deal with Lux Cozi for KKR's apparel merchandise and to be their brand ambassador. This was immediately followed by a public outcry, as there was a criminal case against the owner of the brand and the deal was cancelled (Banerjee 2010, Times of India 2010). The brand endorsement sector being a ₹1000-crore industry, industry experts feel that brand endorsers need to manage themselves (see Exhibit 4.7: Celebrity Endorsement Management and Exhibit 4.8: Celebrity Endorsements).

 View the Fortune Plus ad of Saina Nehwal to know how celebrity endorsements build brand knowledge and images.

Exhibit 4.7　Celebrity Endorsement Management

Globally, celebrity endorsement has come a long way since Queen Victoria endorsed Cadbury's Cocoa in the 19th century. India too stands witness to this change, and the last five years have seen celebrity endorsements emerge as a favourite tool for Indian marketers. This has caused celebrity endorsements, appearances, and performances to turn into a ₹1000-crore business (Economic Times 2010). 'Remember the time when you looked at a Palmolive shaving cream and immediately thought of Kapil Dev and his Palmolive *da jawab nahin*? That was a true brand ambassador. Today, stars endorse so many products

that it is difficult to distinguish one from another' (Kher 2004). The top fifty celebrities account for more than 80 per cent of the endorsement money (Economic Times 2010).

In spite of the spurt in celebrity endorsements, industry experts still feel that endorsement management is in its infancy. Celebrity endorsers fall into the following three categories:

(a) Money-seekers—This set of celebrities are in it for money, and so will endorse 'almost any decent brand if the price is right'. For example, Shah Rukh Khan, Amitabh Bachchan, Shahid Kapoor, Akshay Kumar,

Contd

Exhibit 4.7 *contd*

etc. So, concepts like brand fit do not bother them, as brand managers force-fit their image attributes to what suits their products or revel in statements, such as 'but his appeal cuts across all segments, geographies, age-groups'. Stars get a disproportionately high amount of money to endorse brands—anywhere between ₹1-1.5 crore per day and even during the recent recession, the amount did not stand corrected, but actually showed a positive growth.

(b) Image fits brand seekers—These celebrities are true to their image attribute and usually work only with those brands whose traits suit their image. These endorsers also make a deep contribution towards the endorsement decisions. This category includes stars such as Aamir Khan, John Abraham, and Ranbir Kapoor. Till February 2010, Ranbir had reportedly refused to endorse ICICI Bank, Minto, Coca-Cola, and Chevrolet.

(c) Interchangeables—This set of celebrities includes the small stars who don't generally have a positioning

of their own and hence can be used interchangeably. For example, Neil Nitin Mukesh, Zaheer Khan, Irfan Khan, etc.

'While the smaller stars work with various celebrity management agencies, biggies like Shah Rukh Khan, Aamir Khan, Amitabh Bachchan, and Ranbir Kapoor work independently. While most agencies proclaim they will only take endorsement deals that fit well with their stars' image, if you observe closely, each star's portfolio is a mish-mash of brands. But, some science is creeping in with research studies such as Percept and Hansa Research's CelebTrack and media monitoring agencies like TAM Media starting separate divisions to track celebrity endorsements. The celebrity manager is thus moving from being the gatekeeper to the consultant who helps brands find celebrities with the right fit.'

Source: Kher 2004, Economic Times 2010.

Exhibit 4.8   Celebrity Endorsement

Celebrity endorsers like Priyanka Chopra, Aishwarya Rai Bachchan, Sonam, Kajol, Shah Rukh Khan, Sachin Tendulkar can be seen in the advertisements of a number of brands. Mahendra Singh Dhoni overtook all other endorsers in the January to June 2010 period. While Dhoni endorsed brands of 24 companies, Shah Rukh and Sachin respectively endorsed brands of 16 and 15 firms on TV. Further, Dhoni has signed a ₹26-

crore endorsement contract with the UB group and has renegotiated his contract with Maxx Mobiles for ₹29 crore that was initially valued at ₹10 crore. The sports endorsement market is estimated to be approximately ₹200 crore, which can grow by leaps and bounds in the year 2011 due to 'big ticket sporting events like ICC World Cup 2011 and the fourth edition of the Indian Premier League' (Mukherjee 2011).

Things

Events, third party: Things like events, causes, and third-party sources can also be used to build brand equity (Keller 2003, 2004, 2005). Events like sporting, cultural events, etc., can be used to increase brand awareness. Red and white cigarettes (a brand of Godfrey Philips India), through events like the Red and White bravery awards, was able to establish a brand identity for itself. This annual bravery award was started in 1990 and helped in generating awareness about the brand by promoting and rewarding the culture of selfless action among Indians (Saxena 2008).

SUMMARY

Strong brands help the organization connect with customers and elicit a differential response from them. Brands, if managed well, add value to a product. Value as perceived by customers is important as it impacts the customer's evaluation of the brand. This highlights the fact that it is an intrapersonal construct and an understanding of how consumers perceive the brand is important. A positive added value can lead to differential behaviour of consumers towards the branded product or service and provide an advantage to the brand owner which can be cashed in on, in a number of ways.

Building strong brands has a number of advantages as far as market share, consumer response, and the financial activities of the firm are concerned. The brand resonance pyramid discusses how strong brands can be built by following the four levels of brand identity, brand meaning, brand response leading to brand relationship. With the help of brand identity, we can establish brand awareness in the mind of consumers. Brand meaning has both rational and emotional aspects in the form of performance of the brand and the image formed for the brand.

The next level, i.e., brand response is also grouped into rational and emotional—judgement on the basis of interaction with the brand and the feelings experienced upon the consumption of the brand. When all these steps are favourable it will lead to formation of strong relationships with the brand on part of the customers and they then become brand ambassadors.

To assist in all these steps, it is necessary to understand from where and how the customers take cues about the brand that act as building blocks in developing brand equity. Fourteen factors (for example brand knowledge, brand elements, endorsements, events, joint branding programmes etc.) have been delineated and they all towards contribute brand equity if the organization uses them effectively. Organizations need to effectively manage all the factors that lead to building strong equity for sustainable competitive advantage and success over a period of time.

KEY TERMS

Brand associations The various cues/factors that connect the consumers to the brand.

Brand awareness It is the ability of a consumer to recognize or recall a brand as a member of a particular product class category.

Brand elements These are brand identities that are used to identify and differentiate a brand.

Brand equity Brand equity is the added value (positive or negative) endowed on a product or service due to the customers' perception of the brand.

Brand identity This is a deep, broad awareness of the brand and what the brand stands for.

Brand image This is the perception that the consumers have about a brand.

Brand knowledge Brand knowledge is the understanding that the consumers have about a brand and is constituted by brand awareness and brand image.

Brand loyalty It is the repeated tendency to buy a particular brand as a primary choice.

Brand meaning This is what a brand stands for in the minds of the customers and the meaning associated with a brand by the customers. The meaning can be derived from the function performed by the brand and/or by the image of the brand in the minds of the customers.

Brand resonance pyramid model A series of steps that are sequential, which if loyally followed till the last step will lead to the establishment of strong brands.

Brand resonance   Brand resonance is developed when customers form relationships with the brand and feel 'in sync' with the brand.

Brand response   This is the customer's response to the marketing activities and the brand meaning that they have developed.

Co-branding   It is the bundling of a brand with an existing brand of the same organization (i.e., parent brand) or the existing brand of another organization to leverage the brand.

EXERCISES

Concept Review Questions

1. Critically evaluate the importance of brand equity.
2. How can organizations build strong brands?
3. Out of the various factors that influence brand equity, delineate any four, and discuss them critically.
4. Evaluate the country-of-origin effect on building brand equity. How can organizations use this to leverage their brands?

Critical Thinking Questions

1. Pick a brand of your choice and delineate the various factors that have contributed towards building its brand equity.
2. Consider the factors important for building brand equity for mobile phones and TV sets. Will they be the same/different and why? How will this vary for soaps and MP3 players?

3. Identify a brand that has been in the marketplace for more than two decades. Delineate how the brand elements have been used by the organization. Have they changed their brand elements over a period of time? If yes, discuss the level of effectiveness of the new elements versus the old.

Internet Exercises

1. Visit the websites of LG and Samsung. Discuss how they have been building brand communities online. Compare and contrast the two.
2. Visit websites of two banking service providers. Discuss how they are using their Internet website to build brand equity. How is it similar or dissimilar to their offline activities?

CD Exercise

View Idea ads and discuss the various sources of brand equity.

REFERENCES

Aaker, D.A. (1991), *Managing Brand Equity*, Free Press, New York.

Aaker, D.A. and Joachimsthaler, E. (2000), *Brand Leadership*, Free Press, New York.

Aaker, D.A., 'Measuring brand equity across products and markets', *California Management Review*, Vol. 38, Issue no. 3, 1996, pp. 102–120.

Anselmsson, J., Johansson, U. and Persson, N. 'Understanding price premium for grocery products—a conceptual model of customer-based brand equity', *Journal of Product and Brand Management*, Vol. 16, Issue no. 3, 2007, pp. 401–414.

Baldauf, A., Cravens, K.S. and Binder, G. 'Performance consequences of brand equity management—evidence from organization in the value chain', *Journal of Product and Brand Management*, Vol. 12, Issue no. 4, 2003, pp. 220–236.

Banerjee, R., 'In the woods', *Brand Equity, The Economic Times*, New Delhi, 3 March 2010, p 4.

Bernick, Carol L. (2005), 'Finding the right brand name', in *Kellogg on Branding* edited by Tybout, A. M. and Calkins, Tim, John Wiley, and Sons, New Jersey, pp. 289–297.

Berthon, P., Holbrook, M.B. and Hulbert, J.M. 'Understanding and managing the brand space', *Sloan Management Review*, Vol. 44, Issue no. 2, 2003, pp. 49–54.

Bhardwaj, S.G., Varadarajan, P.R. and Fahy, J. 'Sustainable competitive advantage in service industries—a conceptual model and research proposition', *Journal of Marketing*, Vol. 57, Issue no. 4, 1993, pp. 83–99.

Biel, A. L., 'How brand image drives brand equity', *Journal of Advertising Research*, Vol. 32, Issue no. 6, 1992, pp. 6–12.

Broyles, S. A., Schumann, D. W. and Leingpibul, T. 'Examining brand equity antecedent/consequence relationships', *Journal of Marketing Theory and Practice*, Vol. 17, Issue no. 2, 2009, pp. 145–161.

Chauhan, C. P., 'Maruti to build upmarket showrooms—Ahead of Kizashi launch, co-buys prime properties in Mumbai, Delhi to lure the rich', *The Economic Times*, New Delhi, 17 January 2011, pp. 6.

Chay, R. F., 'How marketing researchers can harness the power of brand equity', *Marketing Research—A Magazine of Management and Applications*, Vol. 9, 1991, June, pp. 30–37.

Ching, H. L. and Ellis, P. 'Does relationship marketing exist in cyberspace', *Management International Review*, Vol. 46, Issue no. 5, 2006, pp. 557–572.

Dahlen, M. and Rosengren, S. 'Brands affect slogans affect brands? Competitive interference, brand equity and the brand-slogan link', *Brand Management*, Vol. 12, Issue no. 3, 2005, pp151–164.

Dutta, Kirti, 'Consumer information sources and effectiveness of advertising media—an analysis of India, Turkey, and New Zealand' presented at the 4th International Conference on Services Management held at Barceló Hotel, Oxford organized by Oxford Brookes University, Pennsylvania State University, USA and IIMT, 8–9 May 2009.

'Apple to unveil a "major new product" today', *The Economic Times*, New Delhi, 27 January 2010.

Elango, B. and Sethi, S.P. 'An exploration of the relationship between country of origin (COE) and the internationalization-performance paradigm', *Management International Review*, Vol. 47, Issue no. 3, 2007, pp. 369–392.

Elliott, S. (2009), 'Tropicana discovers some buyers are passionate about packaging', *New York Times*, http://www.nytimes.com/2009/02/23/business/media/23adcol.html?pagewanted=all

Faircloth, J. B., Capella, L.M. and Alford, B.L. 'The effect of brand attitude and brand image on brand equity', *Journal of Marketing Theory and Practice*, Vol. 9, Issue no. 3, 2001, pp. 61–75.

Farquhar, P. (1989), 'Managing Brand Equity', *Marketing Research*, Volume 1, Issue 3, pp. 24–33.

Gidman, J. (2009), 'Packaging—Lessons from Tropicana's Fruitless Design', http://brandchannel.com/features_effect.asp?pf_id=469 accessed on 9 March 2010.

Gremler, D. D. and Brown, S.W. 'The loyalty ripple effect—appreciating the full value of customers', *International Journal of Service Industry Management*, Vol. 10, Issue no. 3, 1996, pp. 271–293.

Hoeffler, S. and Keller, K.L. 'Building brand equity through corporate societal marketing', *Journal of Public Policy and Marketing*, Vol. 21, Issue no. 1, 2002, pp. 78–89.

Internet World Stats (2010) 'Usage and population statistics' http://www.internetworldstats.com/stats.htm accessed on 3 May 2011

Iyer, Meena, 'Aamir bags record ₹35 cr ad deal', *Times of India*, New Delhi, 5 March 2010, p 1.

Kayaman, Ruchan and Arsali, Huseyin 'Customer-based brand equity—evidence from the hotel industry', *Managing Service Quality*, Vol. 17, Issue no. 1, 2007, pp. 92–109.

Keller, K. L. (2004), *Strategic Brand Management—Building, Measuring and Managing Brand Equity*, Prentice Hall of India Private Limited, New Delhi.

Keller, K. L., 'Brand synthesis—the multidimensionality of brand knowledge', *Journal of Consumer Research*, Vol. 29, Issue no. 4, 2003, pp. 595–600.

Keller, K. L., 'Building customer-based brand equity—Creating brand resonance required carefully sequenced brand-building efforts', *Marketing Management*, Vol. 10, Issue no. 2, 2001, pp. 14–16.

Keller, K. L., 'Choosing the right brand elements and leveraging secondary associations will help marketers build band equity', *Marketing Management*, September–October, 2005, pp. 18–23.

Keller, K. L., 'Conceptualizing, Measuring and Managing Customer-based brand equity', *Journal of Marketing*, Vol. 57, Issue no. 1, 1993, pp. 1–22.

Kher, Anuradha (2004), 'Million star endorsements on TV today, do you buy them?' http://timesofindia.indiatimes.com/city/pune-times/Million-star-endorsements-on-TV-today-do-you-buy-them/articleshow/788790.cms, accessed on 1 March 2010.

Koshy, A. (2010), 'Brands must constantly track quality', *The Economic Times*, New Delhi, 5 March 2010, p 4.

Kotler, P. and Keller, K.L. *Marketing Management*, 12th Edition, Prentice-Hall of India, New Delhi, pp. 280–283.

Kuhn, K. A. L., Alpert, F. and Pope, N. K. L. 'An application of Keller's brand equity model in a B2B context',

Qualitative Market Research—An International Journal, Vol. 11, Issue no. 1, 2008, pp. 40–58.

Law, S., 'Can repeating a brand claim lead to memory confusion? The effects of claim similarity and concurrent repetition', *Journal of Marketing Research*, Vol. 39, Issue 3, 2002, pp. 366–378.

Lebar, E., Buehler, P., Keller, K.L., Sawicka, M., Aksehirli, Z. and Richey, K. 'Brand equity implications of joint branding programs', *Journal of Advertising Research*, Vol. 45, Issue no. 4, 2005, pp. 413–425.

Leclerc, F., Schimtt, B.H. and Dubc, L. 'Foreign branding and its effect on product perceptions and attitudes', *Journal of Marketing Research*, Vol. 31, Issue no. 2, 1994, pp. 263–270.

Liaogang, Hao, Chongyan, Gao and Zi'an, Liu 'Customer-based brand equity and improvement strategy or mobile phone brands—Foreign versus Local in the Chinese Market', *International Management Review*, Vol. 3, Issue no. 3, 2007, pp. 76–106.

Limbdiwala, Tasneem (2009) http://www.exchange4media.com/brandspeak/brandspeak_FS.asp?section_id=42&news_id=35840&tag=31646 accessed on 21 February 2010.

Madhavaram, S., Badrinarayanan, V. and McDonald, R.E. 'Integrated marketing communication (IMC) and brand identity as critical components of brand equity strategy', *Journal of Advertising*, Vol. 34, Issue no. 4, 2005, pp. 69–80.

Maruti Suzuki (2011) "Maruti Suzuki unveils its luxurious sporty sedan Kizashi" http://www.marutisuzuki.com/Maruti-Suzuki-unveils-its-luxurious-sporty-sedan-Kizashi.aspx accessed on 3 May 2011

Mathur, L. K. and Mathur, I. 'The effect of slogan changes on the market values of firms', *Journal of Advertising Research*, Vol. 35, Issue no. 1, 1995, pp. 59–65.

Mazumdar, R. (2010), 'Companies reap rich from sowing CSR in mining belt—education, training initiatives help firms earn trust of villagers', *The Economic Times*, New Delhi, 19 February 2010, p 1

Mukherjee, S. (2011), 'Brand Sachin, Dhoni on a new high—The two stars' endorsement rates may go up 40–50 per cent', *Business Standard*, New Delhi, 24 January 2011, p 14.

Mukherjee, W. (2010), 'Brand-New game—Canon, LG, Samsung among companies creating online communities to connect with consumers', *The Economic Times*, New Delhi, 5 March 2010, p 4.

Myers, Chris A., 'Managing brand equity—a look at the impact of attributes', *The Journal of Product and Brand Management*, Vol. 12, Issue no. 1, 2003, pp. 39–51.

Panda, T. K (n.d.) "Strategic advantage through successful co-branding" http://dspace.iimk.ac.in/bitstream/2259/203/1/Strategic+Advantage+through+Successful+CoBranding.pdf accessed on 3 May 2011

Pappu, Ravi, Quester, P. G. and Cooksey, R. W. 'Consumer-based brand equity and country-of-origin relationships—some empirical evidence', *European Journal of Marketing*, Vol. 40, Issue no. 5–6, 2006, pp. 696–717.

Pitta, D. A. and Katsanis, L. P. 'Understanding brand equity for successful brand extension', *The Journal of Consumer Marketing*, Vol. 12, Issue no. 4, 1995, pp. 51–64.

Pryor, K. and Brodie, R. J. 'How advertising slogans can prime evaluations of brand extensions—further empirical results', *Journal of Product and Brand Management*, Vol. 7, Issue no. 6, 1998, pp. 497–508.

Raggio, R. D. and Leone, R. P. 'Chasing brand value—fully leveraging brand equity to maximize brand value' *Brand Management*, Vol. 16, Issue no. 4, 2009, pp. 248–263.

Raggio, R. D. and Leone, R.P. 'The theoretical separation of brand equity and brand value—managerial implications for strategic planning', *Brand Management*, Vol. 14, Issue no. 5, 2007, pp. 380–395.

Ramaswamy, V. S. and Namakumari, S. (2009), *Marketing Management Global Perspective Indian Context*, Macmillan, New Delhi.

Ross-Wooldridge, B., Brown, M. P. and Minsky, B. D. 'The role of company image as brand equity', *Corporate Communications*, Vol. 9, Issue no. 2, 2004, pp. 159–167.

Sadagopan, S. (2010), 'Will Apple iPad also be a game changer?' *The Economic Times*, http://economictimes.indiatimes.com/Infotech/Hardware/Will-Apple-iPad-also-be-a-game-changer/articleshow/5511289.cms?curpg=2, accessed on 24 February 2010.

Sagar, M., Singh, D., Agrawal, D. P. and Gupta, A. (2009), *Brand Management*, Ane Books Pvt. Ltd, New Delhi.

Samiee, S., 'Customer evaluation of products in global market', *Journal of International Business Studies*, Vol. 25, Issue no. 3, 1994, pp. 579–604.

Saxena, Ruchita (2008), 'Godfrey Phillips lends a helping hand', http://www.business-standard.com/india/news/godfrey-phillips-lendshelping-hand/313423/ accessed on 3 March 2010.

Simon, F. L., 'Global corporate philanthropy—a strategic framework', *International Marketing Review*, Vol. 12, Issue no. 4, 1995, pp. 20–37.

Superbrands (2009), 'Superbrands—An insight into India's strongest consumer brands' Volume III, 2009, Superbrands India Private Limited, Gurgaon.

Taylor, Steven A., Celuch, Kevin and Goodwin, Stephen 'The importance of brand equity to customer loyalty', *The Journal of Product and Brand Management*, Vol. 13, Issue no. 4, 2005, pp. 217–227.

Thakor, M. V. and Katsanis, L. P. 'A model of brand and country effects on quality dimensions—issues and implications', *Journal of International Consumer Marketing*, Vol. 9, Issue no. 3, 1997, pp. 79–100.

Thomson, L. M., Sharma, R.T. and Dhall, A. (2010), 'Save Our Tigers campaign gives India Inc's CSR drive a new twist', *The Economic Times* http://economictimes.indiatimes.com/news/news-by-industry/services/advertising/save-our-tigers-campaign-gives-india-incs-csr-drive-a-new-twist/articleshow/5598281.cms, accessed on 25 February 2010.

Times of India, 'KKR puts on hold tie-up with Lux Cozi' http://timesofindia.indiatimes.com/sports/cricket/ipl/top-stories/KKR-puts-on-hold-tie-up-with-Lux-Cozi/articleshow/5604100.cms, accessed on 22 February 2010.

Villarejo-Ramos, A. F. and Sanchez-Franco, M. J. 'The impact of marketing communication and price promotion on brand equity', *Brand Management*, Vol. 12, Issue no. 6, 2005, pp. 431–444.

Wang, H., Wei, Y. and Yu, C. 'Global brand equity model—combining customer-based with product-market outcome approaches', *Journal of Product and Brand Management*, Vol. 17, Issue no. 5, 2008, pp. 305–316.

Wilson, E. J. and Woodside, A.G. 'Executive and consumer decision processes—increasing useful sensemaking by identifying similarities and departures', *Journal of Business and Industrial Marketing*, Vol. 16, Issue no. 5, 2001, pp. 401–414.

Yassin, N. M., Noor, M. N. and Mohamad, O. 'Does image of country-of-origin matter to brand equity?', *Journal of Product and Brand Management*, Vol. 16, Issue no. 1, 2007, pp. 38–48.

Yoo, B. and Donthu, N. 'Developing and validating a multidimensional consumer-based brand equity scale', *Journal of Business Research*, Vol. 52, Issue no. 1, 2001, pp. 1–14.

Zeungner-Roth, K. P., Diamantopoulos, A. and Montesinos, M. A. 'Home country image, country brand equity and consumers product preferences—an empirical study', *Management International Review*, Vol. 48, Issue no. 5, 2008, pp. 577–601.

Web resources

http://economictimes.indiatimes.com/features/brand-equity/Celebrity-management-is-still-evolving-in-India/articleshow/5529633.cms, accessed on 1 March 2010.

http://economictimes.indiatimes.com/news/news-by-industry/services/advertising/Dhoni-tops-list-of-celebrity-endorsements-on-TV-in-Jan-June/articleshow/6507411.cms, accessed on 1 February 2011.

http://finance.indiamart.com/investment_in_india/uti_bank.html, accessed on 24 February 2010.

http://india.gov.in/sectors/consumer_affairs/weight.php, accessed on 19 January 2011.

http://mdhspices.com/, accessed on 23 February 2010.

http://www.australiantrademarkslawblog.com/2009/05/articles/miscellaneous-intellectual-pro/annual-nicholas-weston-tattooed-brands-global-survey-2009-results/, accessed on 23 February 2010.

http://www.axisbank.com/aboutus/aboutaxisbank/About-Axis-Bank.asp, accessed on 24 February 2010.

http://www.boroline.com/boroline.php, accessed on 6 January 2011.

http://www.domain-b.com/finance/banks/uti_bank/20070430_axis_bank.html, accessed on 24 February 2010.

http://www.domaintools.com/internet-statistics/, accessed on 28 February 2010.

http://www.financialexpress.com/news/uti-bank-is-now-axis-bank/207688/, accessed on 24 February 2010.

http://www.financialexpress.com/printer/news/155669/, accessed on 6 March 2010.

http://www.in.lge.com/, accessed on 5 March 2010.

http://www.internetworldstats.com/stats3.htm, accessed on 27 February 2010.

http://www.kfc.com/about/history.asp, accessed on 2 March 2010.

http://www.moneycontrol.com/news/business/lalmahal-group-forays-into-retail_327987.html, accessed on 22 February 2010.

http://www.nytimes.com/2009/02/23/business/media/23adcol.html, accessed on 10 February, 2010

http://www.rediff.com/money/2006/dec/24cad.htm, accessed on 7 March 2010.

http://www.rediff.com/money/2007/apr/30uti.htm, accessed on 24 February 2010.

http://www.retail.co.in/?p=47, accessed on 27 February 2010.

http://www.saveourtigers.com/, accessed on 25 February 2010.

http://www.superbrandsindia.com/images/brand_pdf/consumer_1st_edition_2004/boroline/index.htm, accessed on 6 January 2011.

http://www.hul.co.in/mediacentre/pressreleases/2007/HLLAnnouncesNewCorporateIdentity.aspx.

http://www.rediff.com/money/2005/feb/26hll.htm.

http://www.hul.co.in/mediacentre/pressreleases/2007/HUCelebrates75YrsInIndia.aspx.

CASE STUDY

Aircel—Building Brand Equity

Introduction to Aircel

The Aircel group is a joint venture between 'Maxis Communications, Berhad, Malaysia and Sindya Securities & Investments Private Limited, whose current shareholders are the Reddy family of the Apollo Hospitals Group of India, with Maxis Communications holding a majority stake of 74 per cent.' Aircel started its operations in 1999 in Tamil Nadu and became the leading mobile operator in that state in eighteen months. In December 2003, it entered Chennai and established itself as a market leader. The success story repeated itself in the other places such as the Northeastern states, Orissa, Bihar, Jammu and Kashmir, Himachal Pradesh, West Bengal, Kolkata, Kerala, Andhra Pradesh, Karnataka, Delhi, Uttar Pradesh (West and East), Maharashtra, especially Mumbai, and Goa. The company got a fillip when it was allocated a spectrum for thirteen new circles across India by the Department of Telecom. With over twenty-five million people as a customer base, Aircel is a national operator now.

Establishing brand Aircel

Aircel Cellular started off as a niche player in South India. It has been in India for eleven years now, but is one of the newest pan-India telecom operators. In spite of strong competition from established biggies like Airtel and Vodafone, Aircel has been able to draw attention to itself across the country. Aircel has invested heavily in building their infrastructure. They have installed their own towers, and their network equipment deal is with top-notch players like Ericsson, Nokia, Huawei, etc. Its IT infrastructure is managed by Wipro. In the product category, they are adding exciting offers like the recharge dhamaka

in Uttar Pradesh, local calls at ten paisa in Tamil Nadu and Chennai, unlimited night calling and sms packs in West Bengal, double talk time on prepaid recharges in Mumbai, ABCD prepaid in Kerala, etc. Their 'Unlimited DialerTunes' has been short-listed for Best Mobile Music Service, while its most popular Airce PocketInternet ($14 and $98) had been short-listed for the Best Mobile Internet Service for the Global Mobile Awards 2010 held at Barcelona. This highlights Aircel's 'efforts to offer a refreshing experience to customers to cut over the clutter. Their innovative customized products are specially designed keeping the need of various segments in mind, such as the youth, migrants, professionals, dependants, etc. Their services are loaded with value-added applications. It is also working with content aggregators like Yahoo and MakeMyTrip to position itself in the VAS (value added services) space. As an organization, they encourage innovation and new out-of-the-box ideas (Ghosh 2009).

The core values of the Aircel brand are simplicity, creativity, and trust (*Financial Express* 2009). A lot of time was spent on developing the positioning strategy. A country wide research was carried out to find out what people think of Aircel as a brand. The study was conducted across India so as to develop a national brand (Jagannathan 2006). Aircel focuses on the future of telephony, i.e., data play, to position itself. The brand positions itself with the tag line, 'Explore your world of possibilities', focusing on VAS, and going beyond voice.

Measures taken to build brand equity

The company has invested heavily in promotional activities to build brand awareness and brand equity. In May 2009, when its services were launched in Delhi, the mobile services company spent over ₹35 crore (₹350 million) buying space in newspapers, magazines, and television channels to promote its products.

Aircel has also actively involved the out-of-home (OOH) media to build brand awareness. 'Their "Just arrived" boxes at the Mumbai airport; the projection of the logo on the landmark Gateway of India; the IPL Scoreboard put up at the Mahim Causeway in Mumbai, created a lot of buzz for Aircel. Aircel branded airport placards had names of celebrities, such as Tom Cruise, which immediately grabbed people's attention. A number of these innovations were useful. The IPL scoreboard, for instance, helped commuters keep track of the latest score.

Another of their exercises that created a lot of buzz and won them appreciation was the inflated raft that they anchored at the Milan Subway in Mumbai. The idea emerged when 'there was news that Mumbai will witness the highest tides in the last 50 years and the Met Department's subsequent admission that Mumbai will flood and that they can do nothing about it, given the city's infrastructure. Aircel

decided to provide a solution in the form of a inflated raft to be stationed at the Milan Subway, which sees a lot of flooding every year with a message that simply said, "In case of emergency, cut rope". The raft actually came in handy on 13 and 14 July, when heavy rains lashed the city. People stranded at the subway used the raft to move around and men in Aircel branded T-shirts were also available to help commuters.'

On 1 February 2010, Aircel launched its initiative 'Save our Tiger' in partnership with Dentsu Communications and WWF India (i.e., co-branding). The campaign highlight the fact that the tiger population was alarmingly low (1411) and that action should be taken to protect them. 'Aircel had launched a website, www.saveourtigers.com (see Image 4.9) for propagating and disseminating information about the same. They encouraged people not only to make donations but also to join the movement and spread the news. Participants could blog and write about the urgency of the situation and the importance of supporting this cause. People with a social networking profile could

Image 4.9   Save our tigers

update their status with this social message. They even encouraged people to act if they saw or knew of any one in their village hurting tigers, be it for whatever reason. They could educate them and if possible bring them to the law.'

'The Aircel advertising campaign portrayed the world as it is seen through the eyes of a six-month old tiger cub named Stripey by Dentsu Communications. He is shown to be waiting for his mother who will never return' (Media Asia 2010). Although tigers are portrayed as majestic and dangerous animals in many documentaries and films, in reality these majestic animals are vulnerable and confused.

The campaign called on the support of prominent Indian sportspersons, such as Mahendra Singh Dhoni and Baichung Bhutia and actors Suriya, Kabir Bedi, and Shernaz Patel. All efforts were supported through the website www.saveourtigers.com as well as executions on Facebook, Twitter, and YouTube (see Image 4.10). People could join a fun pledging section on saveourtigers.com called 'Join the Roar'. Participants could pick from a series of tiger pictures, choose a square in a mosaic grid, and enter their contact details to fill the piece and complete the photo.' So far, 1,88,678 people have already participated in this pledge (cited on 9 March 2010).

Aircel has also sponsored the Professional Golf Tour of India 2010; information regarding which is displayed on its website (see Image 4.11). Aircel decided to partner with PGTI (Professional Golf Tour of India) to increase the number of golf professionals representing the country and to promote the sport. 'Golf, as the best networking business sport, provides Aircel a perfect value-based platform to communicate with the Indian corporate fraternity, which shares a close affinity with the sport, not only from a viewer's, but also from a player's point of view.' It has tried to build a golf lovers' community online by providing a golf tip of the day, a golf bank, fun strokes, event gallery, etc. (see Image 4.12).

Conclusion

Graduating from a niche player (South India) to a national player (pan-India), Aircel has come a long way and is still growing. It is the fifth largest telecom player (on the basis of the number of customers) and has successfully taken on biggies like Airtel and Vodafone. With its innovative strategies and out-of-the-box thinking, they have been able to generate a lot of buzz in their target market. The innovative use of the OOH media and the use of the 'Save

Source: http://saveourtigers.com/.

Image 4.10 Join the roar

Image 4.11 PGTI 2010

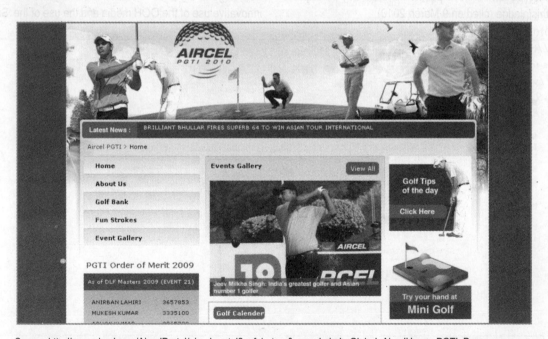

Image 4.12 Golfing tips

the Tiger' campaign in its television advertising has helped Aircel cut above the clutter. The effective use of online media has also helped them generate brand awareness and create a brand identity that is specific and unique. Aircel has effectively used a number of brand equity measures to build its brand equity.

Discussion Questions

1. What do you think about Aircel as a brand?

2. With the help of theoretical inputs, delineate the various factors that have been used by Aircel to build its brand equity.

3. Comment on how Aircel, despite being a late entrant, has still been able to create a brand identity and brand knowledge in the target market.

4. What further suggestions can you give Aircel to build its brand equity?

Case References

Ghosh, Durba 2009, 'Our strategy is driven by data', http://economictimes.indiatimes.com/opinion/interviews/Our-strategy-is-driven-by-data/articleshow/4835889.cms, accessed on 7 March 2010.

Jagannathan, K. T. 2006, 'Aircel's plans to roll out national brand', http://www.thehindu.com/2006/11/03/stories/2006110301311800.htm, accessed on 8 March 2010.

Web resources

http://saveourtigers.com/, accessed on 9 March 2010.

http://telecomtalk.info/category/aircel/, accessed on 8 March 2010.

http://thetelecomnews.com/aircel-partners-with-wwf-india-to-save-our-tigers/, accessed on 9 March 2010.

http://www.aircel.com/AircelPortal/aircel.portal, accessed on 9 March 2010.

http://www.aircel.com/AircelPortal/aircel.portal?_nfpb=true&_pageLabel=Global_AircelHome_AboutUs_Pages_about_us_page, accessed on 8 March 2010.

http://www.aircel.com/AircelPortal/aircel.portal?_nfpb=true&_pageLabel=Global_AircelHome_PGTI_Pages_PGTIAboutUs_page, accessed on 9 March 2010.

http://www.financialexpress.com/news/aircel-bags-cmai-infocom-national-telecom-award-2009-for-excellence-in-marketing-of-new-telecom-service/494616/, accessed on 9 March 2010.

http://www.managementparadise.com/forums/effective-methods-communication-ec/137457-aircel-innovative-marketing-campaign.html, accessed on 9 March 2010.

http://www.media.asia/searcharticle/2010_02/Aircel--Save-Our-Tiger-Initiative--India/38737, accessed on 9 March 2010.

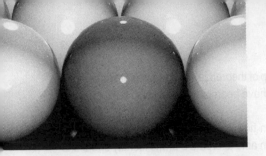

Researching for Brand Equity

LEARNING OBJECTIVES

After reading this chapter, you will be able to understand the following:

- Rationale for tracking a brand
- Qualitative techniques to track a brand
- Quantitative techniques to track a band

ABOUT THE CHAPTER

This chapter explores the areas of researching for and tracking the performance of a brand over a period of time. In the previous chapter we have seen what brand equity is and how we can build the equity of a brand through various brand associations. An organization then needs to understand the impact of these brand-building measures, so that it can take necessary action. Let us now learn about the ways and means by which the various aspects of a brand can be tracked.

TRACKING A BRAND

Tracking a brand involves collecting information about the brand from customers at regular intervals of time. Let us see why we need to track a brand.

Need to Track a Brand

The process of tracking a brand involves soliciting customer feedback on the various dimensions of the brand. These dimensions can be related to the brand personality, brand image, marketing activities undertaken by the organization, etc. Managers can also undertake a brand audit to delineate the factors that they need to track about the brand. A brand audit is 'a consumer-focused exercise that involves a series of procedures to assess the health of the brand, uncover its sources of brand equity, and suggest ways to improve and leverage its equity' (Kotler and Keller 2005). Brand audits can help organizations highlight the brand gaps discussed in Chapter 3. They can also help find the gap between brand identity and brand image, or the gap between what the organizations envision the brand to be and how the

Exhibit 5.1   Dainik Bhaskar's Survey for Success

The first edition of *Dainik Bhaskar* was launched on 13 August 1958 in Bhopal. However, it was only in 1983 that it ventured out of its hometown and embarked on an ambitious journey to become the largest read newspaper in India by launching its Indore edition. Within a few months, *Dainik Bhaskar* became the market leader and then there was no stopping it. First came Raipur and Bilaspur, and then by 1995, it was the number one newspaper in Madhya Pradesh (MP) and the fastest growing daily. Outside MP, the first market it entered was Chandigarh. This was a challenging task since it was about launching a Hindi newspaper in a region primarily perceived to be dominated by English newspapers. To cater to the Chandigarh audience, a pre-launch survey was carried out. The findings revealed that people preferred a mix of an Indian language and English, and that the English newspapers were perceived to be of better quality. *Dainik Bhaskar* immediately got down to work on its design and used a blend of Indian language and English to launch its Chandigarh edition. The same year saw 'Dainik Bhaskar emerge as the largest newspaper of Chandigarh city with a significant lead of approx 2.5 times over its closest English newspaper rival'.

Source: Dainik Bhaskar Group 2009; *Superbrands*, 2009.

consumers perceive the same. Brand strategies can be formulated and revised so as to maintain the relevance of the brand for the consumers (see Exhibit 5.1). This involves qualitative techniques to explore the thoughts and sentiments of the consumers, which can then be tested quantitatively (see further discussion in the section on research techniques). The audits have strategic implications and provide valuable inputs into the organizational activities revolving around the designing of a brand personality and identity, and the marketing strategies.

 See how the Aditya Birla Group found the need to track its brand.

What to Track?

Brand audits highlight consumer sentiments and delineate factors that need to be tracked. However, there are other aspects also that need to be tracked. In the first chapter, we have studied the process of building a brand. The second chapter highlighted the organization's role in delivering brand experience to the customers through its organizational culture and employee behaviour. This understanding takes into account the broad activities involved in brand creation and its delivery as highlighted in Figure 5.1. As an organization, it then becomes important to track all these aspects.

Organizational Vision and Culture

The organizational vision decides the direction of the organization. The most senior and influential person of the organization or the top management decides what it wants the brand to be. The top management provides the strategic orientation towards a brand and delineates brand values. Over time, the staff also comes to be involved in the building of the brand vision, as it helps to solicit their commitment towards the appropriate delivery of the brand experience. Organizational culture influences employees and their action in an organization (as discussed in Chapter 3). The culture, therefore, needs to embody the brand vision, so that the same can be achieved. The following parameters (de Chernatony 2008) can be researched to assess brand visions:

- Leadership provided by the top management or the senior-most influential person
- Commitment of the top management towards brand vision
- Level of inspiration provided by the top management
- The degree to which organizational culture supports brand vision
- Involvement of the staff
- Awareness among the staff about the vision of the brand
- Commitment of the staff towards brand values
- The extent to which the brand values and employees' values match
- The relevance of the brand values for consumers and external stakeholders in general
- The degree of appreciation for brand values by the various stakeholders, etc.

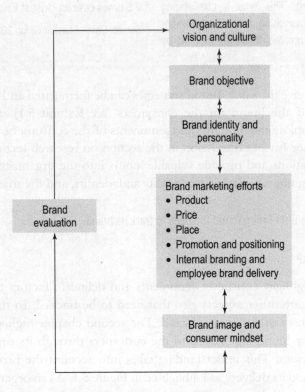

Source: Aaker and Joachimsthaler 2000; Keller 2004, de Chernatony 2001, Bergstrom, Blumenthal, and Crothers 2002; Grace and O'Cass 2002; Jevons, Gabbot, and de Chernatony 2005; Vallaster and de Chernatony 2006; Alwi and Da Silva 2007; Mahnert and Torres 2007; Mosley 2007; Punjaisri and Wilson 2007; de Chernatony 2008; Steen 2010.

Figure 5.1   The brand chain

Brand Objectives

The vision of the organization is translated into brand objective. This delineates the boundary of the brand and provides an understanding of the market offering. The objectives can be further classified into long-term and short-term. The long-term objectives are the objectives

RESEARCHING FOR BRAND EQUITY ■ 133

that the staff wish to achieve over a period of time (say five years or more). The short-term objectives are the objectives that are to be achieved in the near or immediate future, say within six months or a year. The following parameters (de Chernatony 2008) about brand objectives can be researched

- The extent to which the brand objectives can be stretched.
- How the objectives can be achieved 'differently'?
- Awareness levels of the staff about both the long-term and short-term objectives.
- Commitment levels of the staff in achieving the objectives.
- The extent to which the objectives are being achieved over a period of time, etc.

Brand Identity and Personality

Brand vision and objectives then need to be personified into the brand, so that it can be offered to the target audience (see Exhibit 5.2).

The process of building a brand identity and personality have been discussed in Chapter 2. In the strategic brand building process, we discussed that building the brand personality is the organization's task, but how the consumers perceive this personality can vary. Therefore, we need to research about the gap between the two. The following aspects can be researched:

- The extent to which the identity represents brand vision and values.
- The scope of the brand or the extent to which the brand can be stretched.
- The attributes and features of the brand.
- The organizational features (if they are being used to highlight the brand).
- The extent to which brand personality is in line with the brand vision.
- The extent to which the employees are in tune with the personality of the brand.
- The consumers' understanding of brand personality.
- The gap between the organization's design of and consumer's perception of the brand personality.
- The degree of influence of the brand symbols in strengthening the brand value, personality, etc.

Exhibit 5.2   Axe Effect on the Deodorant Market

Creating a market from scratch (in 1999) and ruling the roost is what Axe has done in the ₹500 crore (in 2009) deodorant market in India, which is growing at the rate of more than 40 per cent per annum. Axe had a market share of 25 per cent, far ahead of Henkel's Fa (market share of 8.5 per cent) and CavinKare's Spinz and Hi5 (7.4 per cent) in 2010. What made Axe click instantly and connect with the consumers was the positioning plank of 'babe magnet', i.e., 'wear Axe and women will begin to fall over you.' Research showed that Indian men were getting more conscious of their looks, including their body odour. Also, 'a young teenager is always looking to attract girls every day, the more, the merrier.' One of Axe's successful campaigns 'call me', showed 'beautiful women giving their mobile numbers to men who wore Axe. The campaign resulted in 3.5 million calls to the Axe number. This campaign was designed and finalized after a study of 750 girls across six cities in India regarding phone conversations. The study showed that getting a girl's phone number is the first step in the mating game and the girl would be willing to give her phone number to the guy she liked.' This successful plank helped Axe cut above the clutter and retain its number one position (Khicha 2010).

Brand Marketing Effort

Through brand marketing efforts, an organization delivers the experience of the brand to the customers. It includes the product that has been designed, the price of the same, the communication about this to consumers, and the channels through which it is made available to consumers. The performance of the employees towards the delivery of the brand experience is crucial and impacts the brand image. The aspects that can be researched here are:

- The degree to which the product features are in accordance with the brand value.
- Whether the price is as per the brand image.
- The degree to which brand positioning is in line with brand personality.
- The extent to which the various communication activities help in building the brand image.
- The extent to which the communication is in line with the brand identity.
- Whether the delivery of the brand is appropriate.
- The extent to which the choice of the channels are in line with the brand identity.
- The extent of the recruitment programme to reinforce the brand culture.
- The extent to which the brand behaviour of the employees is in line with the brand culture, etc.

Brand Image and Consumer Mindset

This aspect is different from the ones discussed so far, as this one is about the customer's orientation towards the brand, whereas the other factors are directly under the control of the organization. This factor measures what the customers think and feel about a brand, their brand purchase behaviour and trends, etc. (see Exhibit 5.3). The aspects that can be measured and studied here are:

- What the customers feel about the brand or the consumers' attitude towards the brand.
- The extent to which customer perception is in line with the brand identity.
- The extent to which brand personality matches the customers' perception of brand personality (Aaker's personality traits help in measuring this and are discussed in Chapter 2).
- The meaning of the brand for the consumers.
- Consumer purchase behaviour for the brand, etc.

Exhibit 5.3 Shoppers Stop Tracking Consumers

During testing times of the slowdown in 2008, when a majority of the organized players were pruning their brands, Shoppers Stop was busy rebranding itself as a 'premium-to-luxury retailer.' The strategy was simple—to issue loyalty cards (The First Citizen card) by charging shoppers a nominal fee of ₹200 to enroll in the programme. A number of organizations were using loyalty cards, but Shoppers Stop managed the data generated from these loyalty cards quite differently from the others. It used the loyalty cards to track its customers and the analysis of the loyalty cards was not limited to the shopping behaviour during festivals and for communities, but the information was also used to formulate brand strategies like merchandising, opening new stores, targeted communication, etc. As consumers came from places near major cities that Shoppers Stop wished to target, the purchases they made (as logged into the First Citizen card) were

Contd

Exhibit 5.3 *contd*

used to analyse the kind of products they bought, so that the store could be designed accordingly. For example, cardholders from Vashi showed a preference towards accessories like bags and shoes rather than for apparels. Therefore, when Shoppers Stop opened a store at Vashi in 2009, the beauty and accessories section was right at the entry and was much bigger compared to the beauty section in its other stores. 'Similarly women from Amritsar shopped more for ethnic wear and men for casuals (the absence of a corporate environment and more of a business one), which helped them stock accordingly. As there was more time at their disposal for even small outings, make-up was also a big draw. Shoppers Stop launched its full-fledged make-up brands including the top-end MAC in the Amritsar store. Large populations of non-resident Indians meant that they were already aware of premium brands.' A proper demand projection helped increase efficiencies and also kept the supply chain as lean as possible.

Apart from analysing information from the First Citizen Cards, Shoppers Stop also conducted sample-based market research and third-party surveys, such as wardrobe studies before opening a store in a new catchment area. 'Wardrobe studies help in ascertaining the aspirations as well as the actual mix in a town's wardrobes.' The other aspects that the retailer studied were, the kind of bank brands its customers belonged to, the number of credit cards they carried, the number of vehicles they possessed, telecom penetration in their cities or towns, etc., to fine tune the town's profile.

The existing customers were targeted with special offers on the basis of their shopping profiles. Consumers who had not used their cards for 12–18 months were wooed back with personalized offers. Loyal customers were targeted with advertisements through mailers and mobile phone messages. While marketing a jewellery brand (which had a tie-up with the store), Shoppers Stop sent out mailers to the 15,000 consumers who had shopped for jewellery at the store, but had not come back in the past 18 months. According to Vinay Bhatia, Vice-President (marketing and loyalty), Shoppers Stop, there was an increase of 40 per cent in jewellery purchase among this group over the ones who had not received any such communication (Kar 2011).

A brand can be evaluated on the basis of all these parameters and the feedback provided to the top management. As shown in Figure 5.1, the various stages of the brand chain are interconnected and influence each other. The top management needs to be perceptive about the gaps that exist between the various stages, so that it can take immediate corrective action for the holistic development of the brand. The brand chain is so called because the various stages together form the brand experience and each link is crucial for the development of a strong brand. Through qualitative techniques, relevant factors are delineated for the brand. These factors are then studied through quantitative techniques to understand their relevance on a mass scale. These are further discussed in the following sections.

 See how the Aditya Birla Group tracked its brand image.

RESEARCH TECHNIQUES

The techniques that can be applied to research a brand are broadly categorized into qualitative and quantitative research techniques. Boyd, et. al. 2005 have also termed these as exploratory and conclusive (as these are the objectives) rather than qualitative and quantitative (which tell you about the character of the data and the process of gathering data). Let us now study these techniques in relation to a researching a brand.

Exploratory Research Through Qualitative Techniques

As the name suggests, exploratory research helps explore the various relationships, associations, attitudes, feelings, etc., of the consumers towards a brand. The qualitative techniques used are helpful in identifying the various types of associations linked to a brand, the strength of the linkage, and the favourability and uniqueness of these associations. These techniques also help in identifying the sources of brand equity and so help in building strong brands. Some of the various qualitative techniques that can be used to measure brand equity factors such as awareness, attitude, etc., are as follows (Boyd, Westfall, and Stasch 2005, Keller 2004).

Secondary Data Search

An organization can make use of studies conducted by organizations or its own previous studies to gather data. This is an economical and quick way to research, as the organization has data about its own marketing activities and work done over the years. A number of government and private organizations, trade associations, etc., do a lot of research work, which can be used by companies. Some of these organizations are NCAER, MART, Nielsen, McKinsey, etc. A lot of secondary data is available and the spread of electronic media helps in expediting the research and making it convenient as well. Electronic data processing systems help in storing large volumes of data, which can be retrieved at the click of a button. The availability of a number of search engines on the Internet help in making secondary searches easier and at the click of a mouse. Through these searches, organizations can gather information about consumer behaviour, social trends, and industry trends, which help in developing brand strategies.

Survey of Knowledgeable People

Although studying secondary data is convenient and economical, it is limiting in its scope and other techniques need to be applied to research about specific brand attributes. While undertaking qualitative research, consumers who are knowledgeable about the brand can be researched in-depth to explore their feelings and behaviour towards the brand. This can be done by adopting any of the following techniques (Boyd et al. 2005, Keller 2004).

Depth interviews Consumers make decisions on the basis of conscious and sub-conscious reasons. Motives like jealousy, ego, superiority, etc., which are socially unacceptable are generally not reported by individuals in direct interviews. Therefore, in order to understand what motivated a consumer to purchase a particular brand, an organization is required to conduct depth interviews. These depth interviews are also called one-on-one, as individuals are interviewed in detail to explore their feelings and motivations about brands.

Method of conducting depth interviews Depth interviews are generally not based on questionnaires. They are semi-structured, where interviewers knows broadly what they need to explore about the brand, say the brand attributes, reasons for purchasing, brand image, etc. A good interviewer starts by putting the respondents at ease, so that the respondents can themselves explore (many times they are themselves not fully aware of what they feel, or why they feel so) and express their feelings about the brand and the various reasons that led them to purchase it. By probing as to why a consumer feels in a particular manner towards a brand, interesting aspects can be highlighted about the consumer's brand perception. Through depth interviews, organizations can elicit responses that would otherwise not be highlighted. The level of flexibility in such interviews is high and the interviewers can study the attitudes and motives in detail through the probing technique. The flip side is that due to this flexibility, different interviewers may get different results, making it difficult to compare.

Other drawbacks of this approach are that only trained people can conduct depth interviews, making them a costly affair. Also, the biases of the interviewers may be reflected in the results. Since consumers need to be interviewed in detail, it is time-consuming, therefore. soliciting the cooperation of the respondents might become difficult. Interpretation of depth interviews is also difficult, as they are subjective and can vary from one analyst to another.

Focus-group interviews   To overcome the drawbacks of one-to-one in-depth interviews, group interviews can be conducted. In this method, a group of six to twelve consumers is brought together and made to discuss the subject being explored. These consumers usually belong to the targeted market segment of the brand being studied. If an organization is targeting different segments, then consumers from different segments should not be put together in the same focus group. Different groups should be formed for different segments. The chosen respondents should also have prior knowledge of the product, the brand usage (can be current or recent users), and be involved in making the purchase decision. Also, some practitioners do not put men and women in the same focus group, as this leads to 'performing' when they are together. Strangers show less inhibition, and thus are more forthright about their opinions and feelings.

Method of conducting focus-group interviews   A focus group interview is conducted by bringing together a group of 6–12 consumers who satisfy the selection criteria. Just like depth interviews, here too the discussion is open and is not questionnaire based. The moderator can have an agenda of discussion, which broadly includes what parameters need to be explored. The topic is introduced to the group and the moderator only intervenes when the topic is exhausted to introduce a new topic that might not have been covered during the discussions or when the discussion goes off the track. The topic being researched is discussed in detail and the researcher can make notes of the discussions or tape/video-record the same for future reference. The rule of thumb is to have more than one focus group, and generally three to four focus groups are typical for a topic. Researchers can otherwise keep on running focus groups till no more new ideas are being recorded.

But focus group interviews too have their limitations. The success of a focus group is dependent on the skills of the moderator, as he or she is responsible for conducting the interviews, analysing the results, drawing conclusions, and making recommendations. A focus group composed of the same set of consumers, but a different moderator can have entirely different results and critics argue that the results are the creative *ides* of the researcher and should not be considered conclusive. The other drawback of this method is that aggressive people in the group can dominate the discussion and other individuals might not be able to express their views. People can also stray from the topic being discussed and so all the aspects being researched might not be covered during the allocated time (which is 'usually a maximum of two hours per group'). It is interesting to note that depth interviews, which were replaced by focus groups, are staging a comeback. However, focus groups are easy and cheaper to conduct, as information can be collected from several individuals at the same time. Most of the times this also results in the generation of new ideas.

Free associations This technique is used to profile brand associations formed by the consumers.

Method of conducting free associations The free associations technique involves asking the respondents what the brand means to them. Questions like 'what comes to your mind when you think of the brand'; 'what do you like best about the brand'; 'what do you dislike about the brand', etc., are asked. The question 'what comes to you mind when you think about the brand' helps find out the various brand associations that a consumer links with the brand. The associations that are stated first are the strongest and those stated later are weaker. The stronger associations have a greater impact on the consumer's decision-making process. By studying associations of competitor brands, the uniqueness of a particular brand can be delineated. The researcher needs to move from general questions about the product category to specific questions about the products and their brand image, while probing the respondents.

The benefits of this approach are that subconscious feeling of the consumers towards a brand can also be unearthed. The parameters that make up the brand image for the consumers and the reasons for brand equity can be identified. The drawback is that people conducting the probe need to be well-trained, so that they can get the consumers to relax and help them visualize the brand.

Projective techniques Sometimes, due to various reasons, consumers may not be able to express all their feelings towards a brand. To gain an understanding of these unexpressed feelings, organizations employ the projective technique. In this technique, respondents project their thoughts and feelings in a given situation and thereby reveal their inner feelings. By this, we can understand what the consumers' brand knowledge constitutes of and what the various sources of brand equity are. Some of the different ways of using this technique are as follows (Keller, 2004).

Completion and interpretation tasks The classic projective technique helps gain an understanding of the consumer's feelings by using incomplete stimuli. One such approach is the 'bubble exercise'. In the form of cartoon strips, people are shown buying or using a product. However, no dialogues are provided in the bubbles, and the respondents are asked to fill these in on the basis of their own thoughts and what they think is happening. This kind of an exercise helps gain an understanding of the 'user and usage imagery for a brand.'

Comparison tasks   In this method, consumers are asked to personify brands as people, animals, flowers, cars, vegetables, etc. Thus, respondents can be asked questions like, 'If Amul Butter were an animal, which one would it be? If it were a flower, which one would it be?' Each answer is then followed by a question about why the respondents made that particular comparison. This method helps gain an understanding of what image the consumers have about the brand.

The advantage of using this technique is that it helps to elicit information that the consumers are either not conscious of or might find difficult to express. The flip side is that such methods require time and effort on the part of the respondents, and so it makes it difficult to use frequently.

Analysis of Select Cases

Another type of exploratory research is the case study method, where select cases are studied. In this method, a marketing situation is studied in its actual context when the situation is 'obscure and multiple sources of evidence are used.' This is a variation of depth interviews, in which complex situations, where a number of individuals are interrelated, are studied. For example, a researcher can study how retailers can make their operations more consumer-friendly and compete with other stores. In this, the researcher needs to study the store in detail, and the manner in which the consumers behave in the store, along with the consumer's behaviour in competitor stores.

Method of conducting analysis of cases: For carrying out an analysis of the case, the researcher needs to study the situation and all the interrelated factors in detail. For example, to study the relationship of consumers with brands, the researcher needs to study in detail, the relationship the consumers have with brands and how they interact with the brands on a daily basis (Fournier 1998).

To conduct the analysis well, the researcher needs a good judgement to select the cases and have proper insight into analysing and interpreting them. The benefit is that inferences are drawn after studying real situations in entirety rather than from select aspects studied in general. The drawback is that there is a lack of objectivity and the researchers might only see the facts they want to see.

Qualitative research techniques help in exploring the consumer's perceptions, feelings, and images related to brands. They are flexible and because the sample size is small, they cannot be generalized on a larger scale. Thus, qualitative techniques help in generating research questions and guidelines, which need to be explored on a mass scale. This is where the second type of research, i.e., quantitative research comes in.

CONCLUSIVE RESEARCH THROUGH QUANTITATIVE TECHNIQUES

Qualitative techniques are exploratory in nature, i.e., they explore the feelings of the respondents. Due to the small sample size, in qualitative research, the findings cannot be generalized. Thus, to overcome this drawback, quantitative research techniques are employed and due to this aspect they are also referred to as conclusive research. The quantitative techniques help in measuring brand knowledge, 'depth and breadth of brand awareness, the strength, favourability and uniqueness of brand associations, brand judgments and feelings, and the extent and nature of brand relationships.' These techniques help in tracking the 'brand knowledge structures of consumers over time' (Keller 2004). They help in gaining an understanding of the 'cause-and-effect relationships' (Boyd et al. 2005). Some quantitative techniques are descriptive studies and experimentation (Keller 2004, Boyd et al. 2005).

Descriptive Studies

To gain a comprehensive and accurate description of a situation, this kind of study is used. The data generated from these studies are directly used for making branding decisions. Descriptive studies can be conducted using statistical methods as discussed below.

Use of Statistical Methods

This method is named after the techniques used to analyse the data that has been collected. The data collected is descriptive in nature. For example, how often is a brand or a product from the same category purchased, from where was it purchased, the brand image, consumers' beliefs about the brand, etc. The statistical method is different from the qualitative measures as it involves studying a number of cases, whereas in qualitative techniques, only a few cases are studied. Also, in qualitative techniques, in-depth studies are conducted, but here only a few factors are studied on a large scale to check whether the findings can be generalized for the target segment or not.

Method of conducting statistical method The factors to be studied are framed in the form of a questionnaire and data is collected from respondents on a large scale. The respondents should be drawn from that segment of consumers who form the target market of the brand being studied. For example, when studying online brand image, only people who have access to the Internet can form the target segment, and it is these people who should form the sample from where data is to be collected. The data so collected is tabulated and analysed with help of a number of techniques ranging from simple mean, percentages, to using specialized software for the analysis.

The data drawn from statistical techniques is analysed as a whole and not on an individual basis as in qualitative techniques. The benefit is that different researchers will get the same statistical result (such as averages, percentages, etc.), which generally does not happen in the case analysis method. Since the analysis is based on a larger sample-size than the case study method, the results so obtained can be generalized more accurately. The drawback of this method is that it can only suggest the cause-and-effect of relationships, but cannot prove them in the manner the experimental method does. The other problem is that the 'direction of the causal effect is not always clear. For example, where advertising and sales are found to vary together, it is not clear whether advertising causes sales or sales causes the expenditure of more advertising effort because of greater apparent potential sales results' (Boyd, et al. 2005).

Experimentation

As discussed, experimentation techniques help in establishing the cause-and-effect relationships more effectively than any of the other techniques. Experimentation is generally done by collecting data through an artificially controlled situation, so that the data measured is accurate. The 'artificiality' helps in controlling the factors that are being studied, which helps in obtaining conclusive evidence of cause-and-effect relationships.

Method of conducting experimentation   Experiments can be performed both in the field and in the laboratory. When conducting experiments in the field, say on the effect of variable pricing on sales, products can be placed in different stores and the prices varied in a controlled manner. The sales are recorded at each price level and the results drawn. To conduct the same experiment in the lab an artificial store can be created, where the respondents are asked to shop like they would in a real store. The prices at the store can be varied in the same manner as was done in the stores, and the selections of the respondents can be noted at different price points. Some of the ways for conducting experiments are as follows.

After-only-design method of experimentation   In this method, the dependant variable, for example, recall of a brand name by the consumers (who form the experimental group), is measured only after the application of the experimental variable. For instance, if an organization needs to see how many consumers recall their brand after a particular advertisement has been aired, it can conduct a study to measure this. However, if the brand recall of the consumers prior to the advertisement is not studied, this method will not give accurate results and the company cannot come to a conclusion about the impact of the advertisement by an 'after only design' method. However, for an organization that is launching a new brand, studying consumers before the launch will not be of much use and it is the 'after only' design that will help them gauge the brand recall by consumers.

Before-after design   In this method the dependant variable is measured at both times, that is before being exposed to the experimental variable and after being exposed to the experimental variable. The difference between the two gives a measure of 'the effect of the experimental variable.' For example, to study how advertising impacts brand recall, the brand recall for the respondents is tested before the advertisement is shown to them and then again after the advertisement is shown to them. The difference between the brand recall values gives the increase in brand recall due to the experimental variable (that is the advertisement).

The problem related to the use of the experimentation method in marketing is the time factor. Experiments measure only short-term effects and the cumulative long-term effects are generally ignored. The 'after' measurements should be done to cover long enough periods also, so that all the effects of the variables can be measured. This is generally not done, as management decisions cannot wait for the outcome of such lengthy experiments. The other drawbacks are that experimental research is costly and it is difficult to gain cooperation of the respondents (when done in the lab) or of the retailers (if the experiment is being done in the field). The other important factor is that when the experiments are done in the market, the competitors 'are apt to become aware of the test and are thus alerted to new developments. If the results of the test are measured in sales, the competitor may be able to learn as much from the test as the experimenter, and at considerably less expense.' To overcome this, the firm can come out with an 'emergency special promotion plan' (Boyd, et al. 2005), which can be used in the competitor's test market to confuse the competitors.

SOME QUANTITATIVE RESEARCH TECHNIQUES APPLIED TO BRANDING

To learn about brand awareness, experiments can be done to study the following.

Studying brand recognition This method requires respondents to identify the brand (or any of the brand elements) in a variety of circumstances. The most basic recognition test can be performed by giving consumers individual items and asking them if they have seen or heard of these items previously in the form of a 'yes' or 'no'. Brand name recognition can also be tested by giving consumers names of brands with some letters missing (see Exhibit 5.4 and test your own recognition of the brand names).

Studying brand recall Brand recognition only provides an approximation to a consumer's potential ability to recall. Brand recall can be demonstrated by the retrieval of the actual brand elements from a consumer's memory by providing some related cues. This can be done in the following ways.

Unaided recall In the unaided brand recall method, 'all brands' are provided as cues and the consumer will identify the strongest brands.

Aided recall In this method, cues such as product class, product category, etc., are provided to the consumers. Thus, consumers can be asked to name brands that come to their minds when they think of a bathing soap, or the brand that comes to mind when they think of butter, etc. This also helps us understand the breadth and depth of brand recall.

Brand Personality

In Chapter 2, we studied that brand personality is the human characteristics or traits associated with a brand. Aaker's brand personality framework was discussed in detail, as was the use of the same to measure brand personality.

Exhibit 5.4 Guess the Brand Name

Try and complete the brand names provided in the following list. See how you fare by comparing the answers with the answer key.

(1) _lle_ S_lly
(2) P_t_r E_gl__d
(3) A_ch_e_
(4) B_rb_e
(5) N_ro__c

(6) L__d_o
(7) P_r_e_
(8) _in_h_l
(9) _har_t G__
(10) _o_l_ck_

9) Bharat Gas 10) Horlicks
4) Barbie 5) Nerolac 6) Liaqdo 7) Parker 8) Cinthol
Answers 1) Allen Solly; 2) Peter England; 3) Archies.

Brand Image

To understand what the consumers think about the brand, marketers need to study the brand image dimension or the associations the consumers have formed with the brand. These associations can be in the form of beliefs or 'descriptive thoughts' about the brand. For example, a brand can be 'exciting', 'cool and hip', 'good graphic quality', etc. To study brand image, qualitative measures can be used to uncover the different types of associations consumers have with a brand. To study the strength of the brand image, we can ask consumers, 'What comes to your mind when you think of the brand?' To check the favourability of the brand image, consumers can be asked what they like and what they dislike about the brand. To check the uniqueness of the brand image, consumers can be asked what they feel is unique about the brand.

Brand Response

After studying brand image and brand awareness, marketers now need to understand what the consumers' intentions are towards a brand. If the consumers form a favourable brand attitude, it will reflect in their purchase intentions and in their willingness to purchase the brand. It has been studied that purchase intentions are 'most likely to be predictive of actual purchase' (Keller 2004).

Brand Relationships

The relationship that consumers form with the brand can be measured under the following heads.

Brand loyalty The willingness of the consumers to purchase a brand again and again is important for building strong brand equity. This aspect is, therefore, important and needs to be studied to strengthen a brand. Consumers can be at different levels of brand loyalty (see Chapter 1), therefore marketers will need to devise strategies for the different brand loyalists.

Brand substitutability 'Brands are bought not once but repeatedly, in many cases in predictably regular patterns, hence the truth of the saying that when we build brands we are making customers and not just sales. In marketing jargon, we are building a long-term franchise. In virtually every category examined empirically, it has been found that two-thirds of buyers normally buy (with varying degrees of irregularity) more than one brand. This introduces the extremely important concept of the repertoire of brands: the collection the homemaker buys in varying proportions, often (again) in predictably regular patterns.' (Jones 1999). Thus, we need to study the one brand in relation to these other brands. If consumers are purchasing the brand repeatedly, it results in high brand equity, but if they are willing to substitute the brand repeatedly depending on availability, etc., then it results in low brand equity (Keller 2004).

SUMMARY

Researching for a brand is an important aspect that helps in giving feedback to the organization about how the brand is being perceived by the customers and consumers. This feedback is an important input in further strategy formulations for the brand and brand strategies can be revised to keep the brand relevant for the consumers.

The brand chain provides an understanding of the broad activities involved in brand delivery. These activities help in tracing the process of brand creation and delivery and thus provide a broad framework of what to track. The brand chain is an important tool that helps decide what to track. It consists of the organizational vision and culture, brand objectives, brand identity and personality, brand marketing efforts, brand image and consumer mindset and brand evaluation.

There are various research techniques that can be applied to study and track the progress of the brand in the marketplace. Exploratory research through the various qualitative research techniques helps in exploring the various aspects of brand image, personality, equity, and the various relationships, associations, attitudes, feelings, etc. of the consumers towards a brand. Some of the qualitative research techniques that can be used are the survey of knowledgeable people and analysis of select cases.

Once the various parameters have been explored it needs to be followed by conclusive research so that the strength of the various parameters can be established. Quantitative research techniques are used for this purpose and the techniques are descriptive studies and experimentation.

Some techniques that can be used for studying brand awareness such as brand recall, brand image, brand personality etc. are discussed. Once the research findings have been gathered, they can then be generalized on a larger scale, the appropriate marketing and branding strategies can be worked out.

KEY TERMS

Brand chain The broad activities involved in the creation and delivery of a brand.

Brand tracking The collection of information about the brand from customers at regular intervals of time.

Conclusive research Helps draw conclusions, which can be applied to a large segment of consumers.

Depth interviews Exploring in-depth what the brand and product means to a consumers on an individual basis.

Exploratory research Helps explore the relationships that consumers share with a brand.

Focus-group interviews Exploring in-depth what the brand and product means to a group of consumers.

Projective technique A research technique, where the respondents have to project themselves into a situation to elicit their inner feelings.

EXERCISES

Concept Review Questions

1. Discuss the various stages in a brand chain.
2. Differentiate between exploratory and conclusive research. Discuss situations where these types of techniques can be applied. Which of these two techniques is better and why?
3. What is qualitative research? Discuss the various ways in which organizations can conduct qualitative research.
4. What is quantitative research? Discuss the various ways in which organizations can conduct quantitative research.

Critical Thinking Questions

1. Pick a brand and discuss how you can track the various stages in the brand chain.
2. Discuss the various methods you can use to measure the brand image for a particular brand. Give reasons to support your answer.

Internet Exercises

1. Visit the website http://www.nerolac.com/about/corporate-values and study the corporate vision,

values, and culture given here. Conduct an online research to see if the brand marketing activities are in line with the vision of the organization.
2. Visit the different blogs available on the Internet. Trace at least two brands on a minimum of two blogs. What conclusions can you draw about the brand image?

CD Exercise

Discuss various brand research exercises an organization can undertake to enhance their brand equity.

REFERENCES

Aaker, D. A. and Joachimsthaler, E. (2000), *Brand Leadership*, The Free Press, New York.

Alwi, S. F. and Da Silva, R. V. (2007), 'Online and offline corporate brand images: do they differ?' *Corporate Reputation Review*, Vol. 10, Issue no. 4, pp. 217–244.

Bergstrom, A., Blumenthal, D. and Crothers, S. (2002), 'Why internal branding matters: the case of Saab', *Corporate Reputation Review*, Vol. 5, Issue no. 2/3, pp. 133–142.

Boyd, Jr. H. W., Westfall, R. and Stasch, S. F. (2005), *Marketing Research: Text and Cases*, Seventh Edition, All India Traveller Bookseller, Delhi.

Dainik Bhaskar group, http://dainikbhaskargrou p.com/milestone.php, accessed on 19 April 2010.

de Chernatony, L. (2008), *From Brand Vision to Brand Evaluation*, Second Edition, Elsevier, New Delhi.

de Chernatony, L., 'A model for strategically building brands', *Journal of Brand Management*, Vol. 9, Issue no. 1, 2001, pp. 32–44.

Fournier, Susan, 'Consumers and Their Brands: Developing Relationship Theory in Consumer Research', *Journal of Consumer Research*, Vol 24, Issue 4, 1998, pp. 343–373.

Grace, D. and A. O'Cass, 'Brand associations: Looking through the eye of the beholder', *Qualitative Market Research*, Vol. 5, Issue no. 2, 2002, pp. 96–111.

Jevons, C., Gabbon, M. and de Chernatony, L. 'Customer and brand manager perspectives on brand relationships: A conceptual framework', *Journal of Product and Brand Management*, Vol. 14, Issue no. 4/5, 2005, pp. 300–309.

Jones, John Philip (1999), *How To Use Advertising To Build Strong Brands*, Sage Publications, New Delhi.

Kar, S., 'Consumers lead the way', *The Strategist, Business Standard*, 10 January 2011, p 1.

Keller, K. L. (2004), *Strategic Brand Management: Building, Measuring and Managing Brand Equity*, Prentice-Hall of India Private Limited, New Delhi.

Khicha, P., 'Can Axe retain its effect?' *The Strategist, Business Standard*, 22 November 2010, p 1.

Kotler, P. and Keller, K. L. (2005), *Marketing Management*, 12th Edition, Prentice-Hall of India, New Delhi.

Mahnert, K. F. and Torres, A. M. 'The brand inside: The factors of failure and success in internal branding', *Irish Marketing Review*, Vol. 19, Issue no. 1 & 2, 2007, pp. 54–63.

Mosley, R. W., 'Customer experience, organizational culture and the employer brand', *Journal of Brand Management*, Vol. 15, Issue no. 2, 2007, pp. 123–134.

Punjaisri, K. and Wilson, A. 'The role of internal branding in the delivery of employee brand promise', *Journal of Brand Management*, Vol. 15, Issue no. 1, 2007, pp. 57–70.

Steen, Eric Van den, 'On the origin of shared beliefs (and corporate culture)', *Rand Journal of Economics*, Vol. 41, Issue no. 4, 2010, pp. 617–648.

Superbrands (2009), *Superbrands: An insight into India's strongest consumer brands Volume III*, Superbrands India Private Limited, Gurgaon.

Vallaster, C. and de Chernatony, L. 'Internal brand building and structuration: The role of leadership', *European Journal of Marketing*, Vol. 40, Issue no. 7/8, 2006, pp. 761–784.

CASE STUDY

Branding and Its Effect on Purchasing Process Stages

Introduction

The biggest challenge for marketing professionals is their ability to create, maintain, and enhance brands. Branding is a major issue to be tackled in product strategy, as successful branding is one of the most potent tools for businesses to create and preserve the value of (Rio, Vazquez, and Iglesias 2001, Singhal 2004). Branding is an immensely challenging process, which requires intensive investment, building trust of consumers, delivering promises made to them. It takes many years, a lot of effort, and investment to create global brands. The concept of 'selling' is being replaced by 'purchasing' due to the rise in the number of brands, and so branding is important as it 'pre-sells' the product or service to the customer. Thus, branding is the most important activity for companies to become more profitable and more powerful. Branding is important in order to be competitive, and to be better able to deal with the fluctuating environment and market forces, marketers need to adopt branding strategies. Brand orientation is seen as a powerful tool for creating shareholder and long-term value (Simoes and Dibb 2001).

Postmodernists tend to believe that knowledge is 'time, culture, and context dependent.' They generally view consumption as a symbolic system as much as or more than an economic system (Hawkins et al. 2001). Consumer behaviour is studied to gain an understanding and knowledge of the factors that influence consumer behaviour to develop sound marketing strategies.

Consumers today are highly informed. Using new technologies like the Internet, email, and the mobile phone, consumers are able to acquire more detailed information about brands, products, and services in order to help them make smarter and more personalized choices on their own terms. They can validate a company's marketing and can more easily reject claims or statements based on their own knowledge (Ind and Riondino 2001).

The net result of the changing role of the consumer is that companies can no longer act independently. They need to understand how the consumers are behaving, how they are gathering information, what their major considerations are while purchasing a product, and what factors influence the purchase behaviour. Learning about how customers find and execute the optimum solution in a given market makes it easier for an organization to earn their long-term trust, purchases, and loyalty (Lawer and Knox 2006).

Branding, consumer behaviour, and the purchase process

In the postmodern consumer culture, it is believed that brands play an imperative role in the formation of consumer identity (Elliot and Wattanasuwan 1998 cited in Simoes and Dibb 2001). According to Davis (2000), 'to maximize the customer–brand relationship, a company must understand how customers think, act, perceive, and make purchase decisions.'

To be and remain successful, brand owners have to invest more time, effort, and money in trying to forecast changes in consumer behaviour and expectations (Singhal 2004). A review of the literature highlights some of the areas where brand research has been done to date. Studies conducted inform us about brands that stand out in people's lives (for example, Fournier 1998, Muniz and O'Guinn 2001), such that they are noticeably tied to and embraced by the informant and they represent the person in some way. Studies have also been conducted about the nature of brand images and explore the relationship of the image to concept of brand equity (Biel 1992). Brand, brand equity, brand image and hard and soft attributes of a brand have been studied in detail. In conclusion, the relation between brand image and behaviour has been drawn. However this data has been used to create a perceptual map of the image of the brands competing in the market. The aim has been to identify the brand attribute that would increase the brand's share of the market. Studies have also been conducted on the dimensions of brand personality (Aaker, Jennifer L 1997) with the focus on developing a reliable, valid, and generalizable scale to measure brand personality. Villarejo-Ramos and Sanchez-Franco (2005) have studied the impact of marketing communication and price promotion on brand equity. They have found that a positive relationship exists between spending and perceived quality, and that increased spending on advertising affects the perceived quality, as it increases the associated value of the brand, which helps in the purchase decision. Jevons et al 2005 have also done a conceptual study on the sources of understanding and managing brand meaning.

Researchers have tried to study the ritual dimension of consumer behaviour, which illuminates the psychological depth, conflict, and fantasy components of everyday consumer behaviour (Rook, Dennis W. 1985). This article introduces and elaborates the ritual construct as a vehicle for interpreting consumer behaviour and presents the results of studies that investigate the artificial and psychological contents of young adults' personal grooming rituals. Zeithaml (1988) studied consumer perceptions of price, quality, and value, and studied how consumers relate quality, price, and value in their deliberations about products and services. According to Zeithaml (1988), price, brand name, and the level of advertising are three extrinsic cues frequently associated with quality in research and which are general indicators of quality across all types of products. Brand name serves as a 'shorthand' for quality by providing consumers with a bundle of information about the product, which facilitates information processing and speeds decisions (Chernatony and Riley 1998).

Ataman and Ulengin (2003) conclude that investment in brand image and in the attributes of brand image provides a positive sales benefit. And this benefit can be quantified (within the expected limitations of all consumer research) providing additional ammunition in the argument that investing in brands is for consumer goods business the best way to deliver long-term profitability and real increases in business and shareholder value.

The buying decision process provides a framework for explaining the stages that consumers pass through in their decisions on purchasing (Blackwell, Miniard, and Engel 2006). This deals with the thought processes of the shoppers and how they decide what to buy. It consists of the following steps:

(a) Need recognition
(b) Information search
(c) Evaluation of alternatives
(d) Purchase decision
(e) Post-purchase evaluation

Need recognition This can arise when the shopper senses a deprived or unsatisfied need either as a 'cue' (due to the marketing effort of the firm or due to the social-cultural environment) or as a 'drive' (physical when the senses are stimulated). For example, a shopper sees his colleague using the latest palmtop and feels the need to purchase the same. Alternatively, the shopper can see the advertisement of the palmtop and feel the need for the same, or his current requirements necessitate the use of a palmtop. It is interesting to note that many researchers have associated product packaging as a brand communication vehicle and a big influencer on the nondurable product buying decisions (Lofgren 2005, Silayoi and Speece 2006).

Information search Once shoppers have identified a deprived need, they will try to search for information, and look for the different alternatives available to fulfill that need.

Evaluation of alternatives Olson (1978) pointed out that shoppers may use informational cues to develop beliefs about products, and that task response (i.e., choice or evaluation) may be a direct function of these mediating beliefs. Once the shoppers have collected information about different alternatives to satisfy their need, they have a list of the different brands they can purchase. The shoppers then evaluate these alternatives to identify the brand they are ultimately going to purchase. This evaluation can be based on a number of parameters, such as product attributes or features of the product, the pricing, brand name, after-sales services (if required), etc. Brand name serves as a 'shorthand' for quality by providing shoppers with a bundle of information about the product, which facilitates information processing and speeds decisions (Chernatony and Riley 1998). The shopper's decision-making process is also affected by a number of personal and psychological factors as discussed in detail in the section on factors influencing shopper behaviour.

Purchase decision Based on the decision-making process, shoppers will decide what course of action to take. They can defer the idea of purchasing if they feel that the offer is going to get better, or a better product is going to be launched in the near future, or club it with a festival, auspicious occasion, event (birthdays, anniversaries), etc. Marketing actions by the marketers, such as special discounts, bogof (buy one get one free offers, etc.), can also influence the purchase decision and motivate the customers to purchase a product immediately. If the customers are purchasing a particular product for the first time, especially if a shopping good (goods that are compared on the basis of price, quality, etc. at the time of purchase, such as clothing, cars, etc.), they can purchase the product in a smaller quantity than required, and this is called a trial purchase. But, if they have purchased the product previously and based on a favourable experience they have decided to purchase the product again, it is called a repeat purchase. Based on a number of favourable repeat purchases, shoppers can become long-term committed purchasers or loyal customers.

Post-purchase evaluation Once the customer has purchased the goods, it is followed by consumption of the same. During the consumption stage, the customer evaluates the goods against the perception and expectations formed during the pre-purchase stage. If the product performance matches the perception and expectations of the customers, it leads to satisfaction. If the experience exceeds customer expectations, the customers are over-joyed and this impacts the evaluation of the alternatives when the customer makes a similar purchase the next time. It also leads the customer to refer the products to family and friends. However, if the product performance falls below expectations, it creates dissatisfaction among shoppers and causes the customers to launch into an external search again to look for other products that can satisfy their needs and wants. Shoppers, in their post purchase evaluation, try to reduce their anxiety regarding their decision to purchase a particular product. This is called as cognitive dissonance. Shoppers can reduce their cognitive dissonance by

(i) seeking advertisements that support their choice and avoid those of the competitive brands.

(ii) confirming their own choice by influencing family and friends to purchase the same brand.

(iii) seeking reassurance from other satisfied owners.

It can be concluded that whatever the post-purchase evaluation (neutral, satisfied, or dissatisfied), it acts as an experience for the customers and impacts their input process. Feuss 2003 studied the effect of brand image on customers' post-purchase perceptions of the overall quality and found that brand image plays the role of an assimilator agent that 'pulls' post-purchase performance evaluations in the direction of the expectations embodied in the brand image.

A review of the literature on how branding affects the purchasing process gives us the following reasons for this:

Problem recognition—It is interesting to note that many researchers have associated product packaging as a brand communication vehicle and an increasing influencer on the nondurable product buying decisions at the store shelf level (Lofgren 2005, Underwood and Klein 2002, Underwood et al. 2001, Silayoi and Speece 2004).

Information search and evaluation of alternatives—Brand image affects the consumers' information search and evaluation of alternatives, and if the brand image is found to be congruent with the consumers' actual, ideal, social, ideal-social and situational-ideal-social image, then the brand is bound to be purchased (Ataman and Ulengin 2003). Souiden et al (2006) have studied in detail the effect of corporate branding on consumers' product evaluation and have found a positive correlation. Conrad 2003 studied the evolution of product evaluation, but here the focus was on buying situations, in which there is a time delay between the purchase and the delivery of the product and when consumers' evaluation of the product may change before the delivery occurs. Olson (1978) pointed out that consumers may use informational cues to develop beliefs about products, and that task response (i.e. choice or evaluation) may be a direct function of these mediating beliefs.

Purchase decision—Reast 2005 studied brand trust as a logical influence on evaluation and usage of brands. Reast talks about brand trust and how it can be used by organizations for brand extension strategies. According to him, investment in consumer-brand 'relationships' delivers a future pay-off in the ability to leverage the brand name in new categories. From this we can logically conclude that if brand trust can affect purchase decisions in extension categories, it will do so in the prevailing product line also.

Post-purchase behaviour—Feuss (2003) studied the effect of brand image on customers' post-purchase perceptions of overall quality and found that brand image plays the role of an assimilator agent that 'pulls' post-purchase performance evaluations in the direction of the expectations embodied in the brand image.

Thus, even though a number of studies have been undertaken in the area of purchase process stages, it is still not clear how branding impacts the various stages. To fill this gap in literature the following study was conducted (Dutta 2010).

About the study

The study mainly focuses on primary data collection. Primary data was collected using a structured, non-disguised questionnaire from women in Delhi and NCR as the universe, out of which convenience (non-probabilistic) samples were drawn. The secondary data was sourced mostly in the realm of macro-level indicators from published sources, both governmental and non-governmental reports and publications vis-à-vis this sector.

To study the impact of branding on the purchase process stages, the respondents were asked to rank their feelings on a five-point Likert scale (where one is not at all important and five is extremely important). The following questions were asked relating to each stage of the purchase process:

- Do you want to purchase the product by looking at the brand?
- When you want to buy a product and look around for information, is your decision influenced by the brand name?
- Does the brand name influence your evaluation of the different product choices?
- Do you base your purchase decision mainly on the basis of the brand name?
- In your post-purchase evaluation, does the brand name influence your evaluation?

The sample size was 326 and the respondents were from Delhi and NCR.

Results

The study revealed that for various purchase process stages, the effect of branding varies from not at all

important (0) to, of some importance (1), important (2), very important (3) and extremely important (4). If we see the average affect of the same for the different purchase process stages it is as given in Table 5.1 and Figure 5.2:

Table 5.1 Effect of branding on purchase process stages

Purchase process stage	Average
Problem recognition stage	2.78
Information search stage	2.781
Evaluation of alternatives	2.848
Purchase	2.413
Post-purchase evaluation	2.461

We see that branding impacts the purchase process stages and varies from being important to very important. The highest impact of branding is on the evaluation of alternatives, followed by the information search stage and then the problem recognition. The purchase stage is relatively least impacted by the brand name. Thus, if we keep the existent literature in mind and believe that branding plays a very important role at the time of purchase then the relative impact on the other purchase process stage is higher (Dutta 2010).

Conclusion

In conclusion we can say that there are various studies that have been undertaken on branding (as a strategy) and on brand equity. Instances of studies conducted on purchase decisions and post-purchase behaviour can also be found. Also, literature provides a rich source of studies conducted on family orientation towards purchasing behaviour. However, limited work has been conducted on the effect of branding on the purchase decisions of consumers like problem recognition, information search, and evaluation of alternatives.

A study of consumer behaviour at the purchase decision-making stage, highlights the trust levels of the consumers. These trust levels are not only associated with brand equity and brand loyalty but also with brand extension acceptance, as brands with higher trust will benefit in band extension strategies (Reast 2005). In terms of practical contribution, such a study enlightens marketers who are trying to market their goods and services in India.

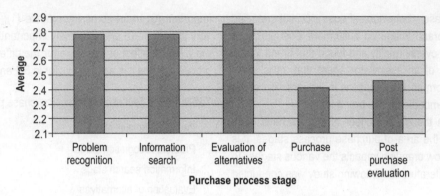

Figure 5.2   Impact of branding on purchase process stage

Discussion Questions

1. Trace the various steps involved in the research process conducted during the case study.

2. Discuss the various kinds of research methods used.

3. Discuss the findings in the light of their importance to brand building by marketers.

Case References

Aaker, Jennifer L., 'Dimensions of brand personality', *Journal of Marketing Research*, Vol 34, Issue 3, pp. 347–356, 1997.

Ataman, Berk, and Ulengin, Burc 'A note on the effect of brand image on sales' *Journal of Product and Brand Management*, Vol. 12, Issue no. 4, 2003, pp. 237–250.

Biel, Alexander L., 'How brand image drives brand equity', *Journal of Advertising Research*, Vol. 32, Issue 6, 1992, pp. 6–12.

Blackwell, R. D., Miniard, P.W. and Engel, J.F. 2006, *Consumer Behaviour*, 10th edition, Thomson South-Western, India.

Cherantony, Leslie de, and Riley, Francesca Dall'Olmo 'Defining a "brand": beyond the literature with experts' interpretations', *Journal of Marketing Management*, Vol. 14, Issue No. 7, 1998, pp. 417–443.

Davis, Scott M., 'The power of the brand', *Strategic Leadership*, Vol. 28, Issue no. 4, 2000, pp. 4–9.

Dutta, Kirti (2010), 'Effect of branding on purchase behaviour of urban Indian women', a PhD thesis submitted to M.G. Kashi Vidyapeeth, Varanasi.

Feuss 2003, 'The post purchase impact of brand image', a PhD thesis submitted to the faculty of Stevens Institute of Technology, Castle point on Hudson, Hoboken.

Fournier, Susan (1998), 'Consumers and Their Brands: Developing Relationship Theory in Consumer Research', *Journal of Consumer Research*, Vol 24, Issue 4, pp. 343–373.

Hawkins, D. I., Best, R. J. and Coney, K. A. (2001), *Consumer Behaviour*, 8th edition, McGraw-Hill Higher Education, New York.

Ind, N. and Riondino, M. C. 'Branding on the web: real revolution', *Brand Management*, Vol. 9, Issue no. 1, 2001.

Jevons, Colin, Mark Gabbott, and Mark Chernatony, 'Customer and brand manager perspectives on brand relationships: A conceptual framework', *The Journal of Product and Brand Management*, Vol. 14, Issue no. 4/5, 2005.

Lawer, C. and Knox, S. 'Customer advocacy and brand development', *Journal of Product and Brand Management*, Vol. 15, Issue no. 2, 2006.

Lofgren, Martin, 'Winning at the first and second moments of truth: an exploratory study', *Managing Service Quality*, Vol. 15, Issue no. 1, 2005, pp. 102–115.

Muniz, A.M. Jr. and O'Guinn, T.C. 'Brand Community', *Journal of Consumer Research*, Vol. 27, Issue 4, 2001, pp. 412–432.

Olson, Jerry C. (1978), 'Inferential Belief formation in the cue utilization process', *Advances in Consumer Research*, Vol. 5, Issue no.1, 1978, pp. 706–713, 8p.

Reast, Jon D., 'Brand trust and brand extension acceptance: The relationship', *Journal of Product and brand management*, Vol. 14, Issue no. 1, 2005, pp. 4–13.

Rio, A. Belen del, Rodolfo Vazquez, and Victor Iglesias, 'The role of the brand name in obtaining differential advantages', *Journal of Product and Brand Management*, Vol. 10, Issue no. 7, 2001, pp. 452–465.

Rook, Dennis W., 'The ritual dimension of consumer behaviour', *Journal of Consumer Research*, Vol 12, Issue 3, 1985, pp. 251–264.

Silayoi, P. and Speece, M. 'Packaging and purchase decisions: An exploratory study on the impact of involvement level and time pressure', *British Food Journal*, Vol. 106, Issue no. 8/9, 2006.

Simoes, Claudia, and Sally Dibb, 'Rethinking the brand concept: New brand orientation', *Corporate Communications: An International Journal*, Vol. 6, Issue no. 4, 2001, pp. 217–224.

Singhal, Arvind, 'Creating and preserving brand', *Strategic Brand Management*, Vol. 3, Issue no. 5, 2004, pp. 18–21.

Souiden, N., Kassim, N. M. and Hong, H. J. 'The effect of corporate branding dimensions on consumers' product evaluation: A cross-cultural analysis', *European Journal of Marketing*, Vol. 40, Issue no. 7/8, 2006, pp. 825–845.

Underwood, R. L. and Klein, N. M. 'Packaging as brand communication: Effects of product pictures on consumer responses to the package and brand', *Journal of Marketing Theory and Practice*, Vol. 10, Issue no. 4, 2002, pp. 58–69.

Underwood, R. L., Klein, N. M. and Burke, R. R. 'Packaging communication: Attentional effects of product imagery', *The Journal of Product and Brand Management*, Vol. 10, Issue no. 6/7, 2001, pp. 403–423.

Villarejo-Ramos and Sanchez Franco, 'The impact of marketing communication and price promotion on brand equity', *Journal of Brand Management*, Vol. 12, Issue no. 6, 2005, pp. 431–444.

Zeithaml, V. A., 'Consumer perceptions of price quality and value: A means-end model and synthesis of evidence', *Journal of Marketing*, Vol 52, Issue no. 3, 1988, pp. 2–22.

Measuring Brand Equity

6

LEARNING OBJECTIVES

After reading this chapter, you will be able to understand the following:

- Need for measuring brand equity
- Methods of measuring brand equity
- Financial measures
- Customer-based measures

ABOUT THE CHAPTER

In the chapter on brand equity (Chapter 2), we studied that it is the consumer perception regarding a brand that is responsible for creating the equity of a brand. Thus, brand equity resides in the minds of consumers and causes them to respond differently to an organization's marketing activities (Kotler and Keller 2005). This makes brand equity intangible. And as marketers, we need to know brand equity to better understand our brand since positive consumer perception resonates in the form of positive attitudes and intentions to purchase and negative perception can ring the death knell for a brand. This chapter gives an explanation about the financial perspective of brand equity or how much value is added to a product through the use of a brand name.

INTRODUCTION—NEED FOR MEASURING BRAND EQUITY

Brand equity is regarded as 'one of the key indicators of the state of health of a brand' (Pappu, Quester, and Cooksey 2006). The monitoring of this parameter elucidates the success of the brand in the marketplace and is believed to be a crucial step in the effective management of brands (Aaker 1992).

Measuring brand equity helps us in the following ways (Whitwell 2004):

- If we know the value of the brand, it is easier to accurately set royalty rates and transfer prices.

- The value of a brand can help in boosting the share price by generating positive public relations for the company.
- It helps the management effectively measure the return on investment (ROI).
- The brand valuation process helps throw light on a number of factors such as the performance of a brand relative to the competition; it also helps identify the strengths and weaknesses of the brand, and the various opportunities in the market, and the opinion of the customers. This objective opinion provides a useful insight into the performance of a brand.

MEASURING BRAND EQUITY

In the 1980s, companies started putting a value in their balance sheets for the brands they acquired. For example, Reckitt & Colman bought the Airwick brand and added a value for this brand on the balance sheet, Grand Metropolitan bought the Smirnoff brand and did the same. This recognition of the brand value of the acquired brands on the balance sheet resulted in a similar recognition of 'internally generated brands as valuable financial assets in a company'.

It was in 1988 that Rank Hovis McDougall (RHM), a leading UK flour miller, in defense against a hostile takeover bid by the Australian firm—Goodman Fielder Wattie—for the first time valued their portfolio of brands and included this value in the accounts books. Although this began as a defensive mechanism that helped fend off the takeover bid, it established the fact that it was possible 'to value brands that had been created by the company itself. In 1989, the London Stock Exchange endorsed this concept of brand valuation as used by RHM, by allowing the inclusion of intangible assets for shareholder approval during takeovers. This provided the impetus for major branded goods companies to recognize the value of brands as intangible assets in their balance sheets' (*Interbrand* 2010). There are a number of companies that measure brand equity. In India, *Brand Equity* (of *The Economic Times*) conducts surveys to identify the most trusted brands (see Exhibit 6.1).

Exhibit 6.1   Measuring the Most-Trusted Brands in India

A combination of factors can be used by organizations to measure the strength of a brand. For example, *Brand Equity* and The Nielsen Company use the following method to measure the Hundred Most Trusted Brands in India:

The most trusted brands are found from a survey of consumers across India and the survey primarily focuses on:
- The most familiar brands
- Brand provides quality
- Brand reassures consumers

Companies studied   A total of 300 brands were shortlisted for the study. Of the 300 brands, 83 were services brands and 217 consumer products; out of which thirty-five were new brands. The existing brands were selected on the basis of:
- Quality
- Price
- Consideration by customers at the time of purchase
- Popularity of the brand over the years
- Unique features

Contd

Exhibit 6.1 *contd*

- The confidence and pride that the brand evoked among users
- The unique feelings associated with the brand

New brands were included based on the following parameters:

- Sales
- Retail visibility
- Media visibility

Consumer profile As many as 8160 consumers across socio-economic classes, regions, ages, and incomes were surveyed. The top ten brands according to the survey conducted were as shown in Table 6.1.

Table 6.1 Top ten brands

Brand	Rank (2010)
Nokia mobile phones	1
Colgate	2
Lux	3
Dettol	4
Britannia	5
Lifebuoy	6
Clinic Plus	7
Pond's	8
Fair and Lovely	9
Pepsodent	10

Source: Brand Equity, 2010.

METHODS TO MEASURE BRAND EQUITY

Brand equity consists of two components—brand strength and brand value—and to understand how customers evaluate brand equity, we need to have an understanding of both these components (Lassar, Mittal, and Sharma 1995). We can measure brand equity in the following ways (Lassar et al. 1995; Sinha, Ashill, and Gazley 2008):

- Brand value or financial performance. Brand value is the financial gain accrued as a result of leveraging the brand strength. The financial performance is calculated to see how profitable the company is. This includes sector and regional analysis and the profitability of all its business units. Sector analysis includes the sector of which the brand is a part for example, the retail sector, FMCG sector, etc., and regional analysis includes the performance of the product category in a particular region. Both these parameters provide an understanding of the relative performance of the brand—that is the performance of the brand vis-à-vis the growth rate for the sectors and the regions.
- Brand strength or customers based measures. Brand strength is the brand association in the minds of the customers. This analysis helps in understanding what the customers think about the brand in relation to the competitor brands. As the study of the strength of the brand is done from the point of view of the consumers, it can also be termed as customer-based measure.

Brand Value

Conceptually, brand equity is 'the financial value endowed by the brand on the product' (Farquhar 1989), and this financial value generated can be measured by financial measures, which help investors in determining the value of a company or a brand. This is of particular relevance at the time of mergers and amalgamations. The limitations of using financial measures is that though they are beneficial for accounting purposes, they hardly provide guidance in the evaluation and implementation of marketing strategies responsible for building brand equity (Sinha et al. 2008). Haigh (2000) has suggested the following methods for calculating this.

Cost-based valuation The value of a brand is calculated on 'the basis of what it actually costs to create or what it might theoretically cost to recreate' the brand. Thus, 'historical advertising and promotion expenditures, campaign creation costs, trademark registration costs, etc.' (Tremblay 2008) are taken into account. This, however, does not correctly reflect the current value of the brand, as the cost of generating a brand does not truly reflect the income-generating potential of the brand.

Market-based valuation If information regarding 'market transactions involving comparable brands is available, it is possible to estimate one brand's value by comparing with another brand.' This method is rarely used, as such data is scarce and due to the fact that each brand is unique and it will be difficult to compare brands.

Royalty-relief method This method is based on the assumption that if the company did not actually own the brand, but had to license it from a third party, then what royalty would it have to pay for using the brand name. This is estimated by calculating the sales likely to occur in the future and 'then applying an appropriate rate to arrive at the income attributable to the brand royalties in future years. The notional brand loyalty is then discounted back to a net present value that is the brand value.' This method is widely used in India, as it is favoured by the fiscal and tax authorities and the courts, because the calculation is based on publicly available marketing and financial information (*Economic Times* 2007). The Brand Finance ratings discussed in Table 6.1 use this method of royalty relief to determine the value of the brand. First, 'the royalty rate that would be payable for its use were it owned by a third party' is determined. This royalty rate is then 'applied to future revenues to determine an earnings stream that is attributable to the brand. The brand earnings stream is then discounted back to a net present value' (Brand Directory 2011).

Economic-use method This method 'takes into account the economic value of the brand to the current owner in its current use.' This is the most widely used method and just like the valuation of shares, it is a 'cash-flow valuation'. This is measured by calculating the increase in gross profit due to selling a branded product versus selling an unbranded product.

Many research firms like Millward Brown Optimor, Brand Directory powered by The BrandFinance® Global 500, Interbrand, etc., study brands and come out with a brand ranking. The top twenty-five brands as ranked by Brand Directory are given in Table 6.2.

Brand Strength

Customer-based brand equity measures help in overcoming the limitations of the financial measures as they help managers evaluate marketing strategies. For example, promotional and positioning strategies can be evaluated by customer-based measures and this evaluation can help managers build sound long-term health of their brand (Sinha et al. 2008). The two models that have been widely used to measure brand equity are as follows:
• Brand Asset Valuator Model
• Aaker Model

Table 6.2 Brand Directory's brand rankings

Name	Country	Rank		Brand value (US$ millions)	
		2010	2009	2010	2009
Walmart	US	1	1	41,365	40,616
Google	US	2	5	36,191	29,261
Coca-Cola	US	3	2	34,844	32,728
IBM	US	4	3	33,706	31,530
Microsoft	US	5	4	33,604	30,882
GE	US	6	6	31,909	26,654
Vodafone	UK	7	8	28,995	24,647
HSBC	UK	8	7	28,472	25,364
HP	US	9	9	27,383	23,837
Toyota	Japan	10	10	27,319	21,995
AT&T	US	11	14	26,585	19,850
Bank of America	US	12	11	26,047	21,017
Santander	Spain	13	41	25,576	10,840
Verizon	US	14	15	23,029	18,854
Wells Fargo	US	15	23	21,916	14,508
Budweiser	US	16	19	21,279	16,692
Tesco	UK	17	20	20,654	16,408
McDonald's	US	18	12	20,192	20,003
Walt Disney	US	19	18	20,053	16,750
Apple	US	20	27	19,829	13,648
Nokia	Finland	21	13	19,558	19,889
The Home Depot	US	22	24	19,013	14,310
Samsung	Republic of Korea	23	28	18,925	13,541
China Mobile	Hong Kong	24	16	18,673	17,196
Orange	France	25	17	18,352	16,799

Source: http://www.brandirectory.com/league_tables/table/global_500, accessed on 20 January 2011.

 Go online to Millward Brown's Brand Directory at http://www.branddirectory.com, which gives global rankings of brands, along with their brand values and countries to which these brands belong.

Brand Asset Valuator Model

Young and Rubicam, an advertising agency, based on their research with more than 200,000 consumers in 40 countries, developed the Brand Asset Valuator (BAV) Model (Kotler and Keller 2005; Keller 2008). The key pillars for measuring brand equity as per this model are:

- Differentiation is the 'degree to which the brand is different from other' brands. It highlights the distinctive feelings that consumers develop for a brand and translates these feelings into the customer's choice, preference, and ultimately loyalty.

- Relevance refers to 'the breadth of the brand's appeal'. The more the brand appeals to the customer, the greater the household penetration.
- Energy is the ability of the brand to meet the future needs of the consumers and its ability to attract new customers. It measures the dynamic nature and momentum of the brand, and the changing financial performance of the brand.
- Esteem 'measures how well the brand is regarded and respected' by the consumers.
- Knowledge 'measures how familiar and intimate people are with the brand'.

Differentiation, relevance, and energy highlight the future value of the brand rather than just reflecting the past. Together, they represent the strength of the brand and form the 'Y' axis in Figure 6.1. Esteem and knowledge, on the other hand, are based on the past performance of the brand and form the stature of the brand represented on the 'X' axis in the figure. All the five pillars together form the 'power grid', which depicts the stages in the cycle of brand development.

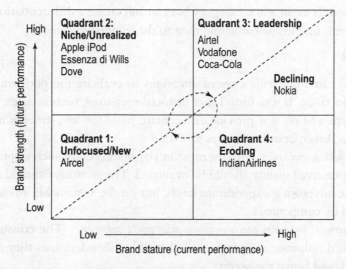

Source: Young and Rubicam's Brand Asset Valuator Model, cited in Kotler and Keller 2005 and Keller 2008, students' survey.

Figure 6.1 Brand Asset Valuator Model

The different quadrants, hence, formed by using brand stature and brand strength on the 'X' and 'Y' axis respectively are as follows:

Quadrant 1: New/unfocused In this quadrant, a brand has low levels of differentiation relevance, energy, esteem, and knowledge. All new brands start from this quadrant, where they are low on all levels.

Quadrant 2: Niche/unrealized potential Strong new brands that show a high level of differentiation fall in this quadrant. As the brand is highly differentiated, it targets a niche market. The other constructs of energy, relevance, esteem, and knowledge are however low and if the brand wants to become a brand leader it needs to build on these aspects as well.

Quadrant 3: Leadership These brands are high on all the five pillars. Just as it is not clear how long a product would occupy the various stages (introduction, growth, maturity, and decline) of a product life cycle, it is also not clear how long the brand would occupy in a particular quadrant before moving to another. If properly managed, brands can stay in the leadership quadrant for an indefinite period of time. A brand in this segment that loses on differentiation falls in declining leaderships.

Quadrant 4: Declining/eroding   Brands that have performed well in the past show a higher level of knowledge than esteem, differentiation, and relevance. Energy is lower still. Alternatively, when a brand can no longer maintain its differentiation and relevance from other brands, it falls into this quadrant.

The BAV model helps an organization understand how different its brand is from the competitors' and what its standing is in the marketplace. BAV also measures brands on the basis of forty-eight attributes, pertaining to brand image and brand personality, which helps to gain a clear understanding of the image of a brand that drives its strength and stature. This gives a measure of 'brand elasticity' or brand stretching. If a brand has an image consistent with other brands in the same category but can still create a differentiation for itself, then it is easier to stretch first to the niche and then to the leadership category.

Aaker Model

Aaker (1996) came out with a set of measures to evaluate the performance of brands in a company's portfolio. It was found that financial measures, such as sales, profit, margins, etc., are short term and do not provide an accurate basis for investments into building brands. According to Aaker, brand measures should:

Effectively evaluate brand equity   All the measures of brand equity, such as awareness, associations, loyalty, and perceived quality should be evaluated. The measures should not focus on tactical strategies like advertising expenditure levels, but on the sustainable advantage that cannot be easily copied by competitors.

Highlight constructs that prominently influence price levels, sales, etc.   The constructs that truly drive the market and influence the price levels should be considered, as they drive the future sales of the brand, and hence the profit.

Reflect the changes in brand equity over time   The measures should be sensitive to market changes and if brand equity falls/increases/remains constant (due to tactical strategies), then the measures should reflect this.

Be applicable across product categories and markets   Standard measures make it easier to evaluate brands across product categories and different sets do not have to be worked out each time. When the measures are constant across product categories, then they give a true reflection of the performance of the brands in the portfolio of the organization and make it easier to allocate resources across brands.

The ten set of measures as described by Aaker (1996) are grouped under five heads (see Figure 6.2) as follows:

1. **Loyalty measures**   Brand-loyal customers help create barriers to the entry of competing brands and are, therefore, important for an organization. They form the basis for premiums pricing and take time to respond to innovations, price cuts, etc., from the competitors. A strategy that does not connect well with the customers, impacts these loyal customers as

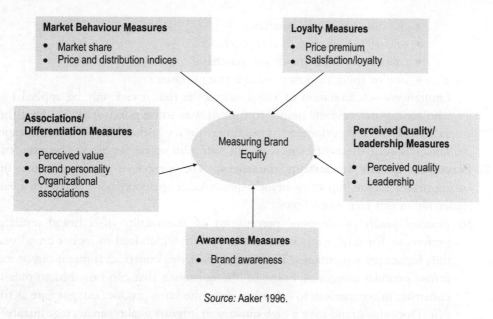

Source: Aaker 1996.

Figure 6.2 Measuring Brand Equity—Aaker's Brand Equity Ten

well and they respond strongly to such blunders. Brand loyalty can be indicated by the following factors:

(a) *Price premium*   Price premium measures the amount of money a customer is willing to pay extra for a brand as compared to a competing brand. If the price premium is positive, then a customer is willing to pay extra for the brand over the competing brand, but if it is negative, the company should reduce the price the same by percentage to induce customers to purchase the brand. The limitation of this is that other competing brands, which are not considered in the study, might be overlooked and that might eat into the market share of the brand. This construct can be measured by conjoint analysis that provides a series of choices to the customers, such as would they be willing to purchase a brand at a premium of ₹10,000 or at a discount of ₹5,000, etc., in comparison to another brand.

Limitations—This is possible only in sectors where there is a price difference. In sectors like banking, kerosene, urea, etc., where the prices are regulated, price premiums do not have any relevance and other measures come into play.

(b) *Customer satisfaction/loyalty*   This construct measures the satisfaction levels of customers after using the brand. This is especially useful in the services industries, such as hotels, banks, etc., and in the fast moving consumer goods (FMCG) category, where habitual purchase or customer loyalty results if the customers are satisfied with the brand. To measure this, consumers can be asked some of the following questions:

(i) Are you satisfied/dissatisfied/delighted with the brand?

(ii) Will you buy the brand the next time you need to purchase the same product?

(iii) Will you recommend the brand to others?

(iv) Is this brand

- the only brand you purchase?
- one of the two brands you purchase?
- one of the three brands you purchase?
- one of more than three brands you purchase?

Limitations—A limitation of this construct is that it can only be applied to people who have purchased the brand/consumed it at some point of time—be it the brand switchers, or loyal customers, or customers loyal to other brands. Thus, to capture the satisfaction of these different segments, different set of factors will be required.

2. **Perceived quality/leadership measures** The perceived quality of the brand is an important factor impacting brand equity. Aaker grouped both perceived quality and leadership in this factor as follows:

(a) *Perceived quality* Customers' perceptions of the quality of a brand result in their preference for it over other competing brands, which lead to higher brand usage and thus higher price premiums. The advantage of this construct is that it can be measured across product categories. Some of the questions that can be asked to measure this construct in comparison to other brands in the same product category are as follows:

(i) Does this brand have a high quality/an inferior quality/an average quality?

(ii) Is it the best/one of the best/the worst/one of the worst?

(iii) Does the brand have consistent quality/inconsistent quality?

Limitations—The limitations of this factor are:

(i) The meaning of perceived quality might vary among different sets of customers, such as those who are brand loyal, switchers, etc.

(ii) The perceived quality might not be a key driver and therefore may not impact customers. For example, while purchasing goods such as mobile phones, the factors impacting the purchase can be trendy design, features offered, customer care, etc., rather than only the perceived quality.

(iii) Other factors can also affect brand equity to which the perceived quality is not sensitive. For example, the entry of gel toothpastes (Close-Up), resulted in the loss of brand equity for the original white toothpastes (like Colgate), even though the perceived quality for white toothpastes was the same (Sagar et al. 2009).

These limitations led to the incorporation of the leadership variable 'to tap the dynamics of the market' as discussed below.

(b) *Leadership* The popularity of a brand and its leadership is an important construct of brand equity, as it reflects the number one syndrome, and if the brand is number one, it means that enough people are purchasing the brand and so it must be good. Also, if it is the leader in the product category, the brand will also be innovative technologically. Thus, leadership also measures the technological innovativeness of the brand. The questions that can be asked of customers to understand this are:

In comparison with other brands in the product category—

(i) Is this brand the leading brand/one of the leading brands/not one of the leading brands?

(ii) Is this brand growing in popularity?

(iii) Is this brand innovative and first with advances in products or services?

Limitations—Since leadership measures a number of variables, such as market size, popularity, and innovation, 'it is not a simple construct'. Also, literature does not show that it has been well-researched like the other constructs of loyalty, perceived quality, etc., and thus, the evidence in support of this construct is weak.

3. **Associations/differentiation measures**   These measures are meant to understand how the brand is associated in the minds of the customers and how it is different from competing brands in the same product category. The BAV model also treats differentiation as one of its key parameters. This is due to the fact that if a brand is not perceived as different from its competitors, then it would be difficult for organizations to charge a price premium, which will result in the slide of the brand to being just a commodity product. Thus, we can ask the customers if:

- The brand is different from competing brands?
- The brand is basically the same as competing brands?

This association/differentiation can further be explored by studying the brand under the following three perspectives:

(a) *The perceived value or how customers perceive the brand-as-a product*   The value proposition or the value provided by the brand is a function of the physical benefits provided by the brand due to the functions it performs. If the functional benefit provided by the brand is strong, consumers will prefer the brand over competitors. This functional benefit provides value to the brand and it is this value that is to be measured. This measure of the value can be applied across product classes and can be studied by asking the following questions:

  (i) Does the brand provide good value for money?
  (ii) Are there reasons to buy this brand over competitors?

Limitations—There is an overlap between brand value and perceived quality, and in certain contexts brand value can be considered as perceived quality divided by price.

(b) *Brand personality or how customers perceive the brand-as-a person*   This construct tells us what the customers would personify the brand as. This, thus, relies on the imagery that the users construct to understand brand association/differentiation. A dominant and interesting personality helps in attracting customers. For example, cosmetic firms should have an exciting personality; banks, hotels should have a friendly and reliable personality, trucks should have a rugged personality, etc. Customers can be questioned on the following lines to study brand personality:

  (i) Does this brand have a personality?
  (ii) Is this brand interesting?
  (iii) Do you have a clear image of the type of person who would use the brand?

Limitations   The key limitation is that not all brands have a personality. For brands that are positioned on the basis of their functional advantage and value, this construct might not be very relevant. Also, brand personality is stable and is not reflective of the changes in the market dynamics.

(c) *Organizational associations or how customers perceive the brand-as-an organization*   This is another aspect of brand association that highlights the organization—its people, values, and programs. This aspect is particularly important when consumers perceive brands to be similar to the organization with respect to their attributes or when the organization is clearly visible, such as in durable goods, for services firms, etc., or when a corporate brand is involved. This plays an important role in highlighting the fact that the brand is more than the products/services it sells. For example, Idea Cellular with its series of 'What an Idea Sirji' advertisements tried to highlight the organizational association. Their 'Save the Paper' ad campaign was also on the same lines. This, therefore, shows the concern that an organization has for its consumers and for society in general, as also the fact that they want to protect and sustain the environment on behalf of them. The various parameters that can be used for building organizational associations are:

(i) *Customer focus* Customers are important for the organization and the organization is concerned about its customers.

(ii) *Innovative products* Offering innovative products and being an innovative organization are two different things. The latter has a long-term effect, whereas the former can be effective only up to a point in time.

(iii) *High quality* Again, an organization can provide quality products, but this will be a short-term effect. If, however, the organization has an image of being committed to high quality at all times, then this has a more long-lasting impact on the customers.

(iv) *Orientation towards the community* This fact is important for customers who feel that the organization is committed towards society and that it does not exist only to fulfil its own motives.

(v) *Being a global player* An organization, which is a global player, highlights reliability factor to customers who in-turn feel that the products offered are world-class and the services provided are good.

To measure organizational associations, customers can be asked the following questions:

(i) Is this brand made by an organization they trust?

(ii) Do they admire the brand X's organization?

(iii) Do they believe that the organization associated with this brand has credibility?

Limitations—The limitation again is that this might not be relevant across all brands, and therefore can be misinterpreted.

4. **Awareness measures** The awareness measure has the following aspects:

(a) *Brand awareness* Brand awareness is an important component of brand equity, as it can affect customers' perception and attitude towards a brand. Awareness also drives brand choice and customer loyalty. The different levels of brand awareness are as follows:

(i) Brand recognition (Have you heard of brand 'xxx'?)

(ii) Brand recall (What brands can you recall in this product class?)

(iii) Top-of-mind (What is the first brand that comes to your mind when asked to recall brands in a product class?)

(iv) Brand dominance (When the brand named is the only brand recalled)

(v) Brand knowledge (When customers know what the brand stands for)

(vi) Brand opinion (When customers have an opinion about the brand)

New brands, such as Aircel, will be in the initial stages. Therefore, for Aircel it will make sense to measure brand recognition, but established brands, such as Airtel and Vodafone, which are in the advanced stages should measure top-of-mind recall or brand dominance or the opinion stage.

Limitations—Brand awareness levels differ in different industries. For example, for products in the software industry, brand recognition is important as a lot of customers are not tech-savvy and so do not update themselves about new launches. But for the automobile industry, comprising many established global players, a top-of-mind recall or brand dominance plays a more important role in influencing customers. Thus, the same measure cannot be used to compare brands in the software industry and those in automobile industry (Sagar et al. 2009).

5. **Market behaviour measures** This measure is different from the measures studied so far in the aspect that the measures studied hitherto require a survey, whereas this factor does not require a survey. Surveys can be time-consuming, expensive, and inconvenient, and can be difficult to implement and interpret. Brand loyalty is probably the only exception, as it can be studied from repeat purchase data. The various ways in which we can study market behaviour are as follows:

(a) *Market share* Market share, or share of the brand in the marketplace in comparison to its competitors, reflects the 'brand's standing with the customers'. Brands with high equity show a positive response from customers in the form of a high market share, and when competitors improve their brand equity their market share is bound to improve as well. Also, market share is easily available and accurate.

Limitations—The limitation of market share is that by providing promotional offers and discounts, market share can be increased and this will not be a true measure of brand equity. Also, market share needs to define the product class and the competitor set. So, for example, for gauging the market share of cold drinks, it has to be specified whether carbonated drinks, juices, along with lemonade, etc., will be considered.

(b) *Market price and distribution indices* To overcome the limitation of the effects of promotional strategies in market share, relative market price can be calculated as follows:

$$RMP = Avg\,SP_{brand} / Avg\,SP_{Total\,brands}$$

Where:

RMP = Relative Market Price

$Avg\,SP_{brand}$ = Average Price at which the brand is sold

$Avg\,SP_{Total\,brands}$ = Average Price at which all the brands in the product class are sold

It is the average price at which the brand is sold, divided by the average price at which all brands in the product class are sold. Market share is also affected by the distribution of the brand. Sales are sensitive to distribution and increase if the brand gains entry into a major market or enters a new geographic region. The opposite is also true and so a measure of the distribution coverage is also important while studying market share. This can be studied by measuring:

(i) the percentage of stores displaying and retailing the brand

(ii) the percentage of people who have access to the brand

Limitations—A common price platform will be difficult to create, as a brand can have different channels, variants, and a vast set of competitors. Also, there are various government taxes, duties, etc., which add to the problem. Distribution coverage also poses difficulties, as the brands have a number of sizes/varieties and distribution channels, which need to be sorted out.

A combination of consumer analysis and an analysis of the financial and business performance can also be undertaken. For example, 'Milward Brown, which is owned by advertising and communications giant WPP, generates its BrandZ Top 100 report by interviewing more than a million consumers worldwide and analysing each company's financial and business performance.' According to them, the twenty most valuable global brands are as given in Table 6.3.

Table 6.3 Top ten brands according to Millward Brown

| Brand | Rank | | Brand value | |
	2010	2009	2010 (US$ in millions)	2009 (US$ in millions)
Google	1	1	114,260	100,039
IBM	2	4	86,383	66,622
Apple	3	6	83,153	63,113
Microsoft	4	2	76,344	76,249
Coca-Cola	5	3	67,983	67,625
McDonald's	6	5	66,005	66,575
Marlboro	7	10	57,047	49,460
China Mobile	8	7	52,616	61,283
GE	9	8	45,054	59,793
Vodafone	10	9	44,404	53,727
ICBC	11	12	43,927	38,056
HP	12	17	39,717	26,745
Walmart	13	11	39,421	41,083
BlackBerry	14	16	30,708	27,478
Amazon	15	26	27,459	21,294
UPS	16	15	26,492	27,842
Tesco	17	21	25,741	22,938
Visa	18	36	24,883	16,353
Oracle	19	25	24,817	21,438
Verizon Wireless	20	34	24,675	17,713

Source: http://www.millwardbrown.com/Libraries/Optimor_BrandZ_Files/2010_BrandZ_Top100_Report.sflb.ashx.

Thus, it can be seen that there are various ways in which the value of brands can be calculated. An organization can use any or a combination of these ways. The result can be used to measure the performance of the brand and facilitate further decision-making by the organization.

SUMMARY

Measuring brand equity is important for an organization as it provides feedback about its branding activities. The measured equity is a report card of the organization and provides a backdrop for taking necessary action, so that the brand maintains its differentiation and lead in the market. The financial perspectives provide monetary value for brand equity and are important for mergers and amalgamations, whereas the customer perspectives provide a sound basis for the strategic and tactical marketing strategies of an organization.

The various ways by which both can be measured are discussed and the methods that may be used by the organization, keeping in mind the nature of the organization, are outlined. The ways in which brand value or the financial value can be measured are cost-based valuation, market-based valuation, the royalty-relief method and the economic use method. Brand strength or the customer-based measures that can be adopted by an organization are: The Brand Asset Valuator Model and the Aaker Model.

The Brand Asset Valuator Model developed by Young and Rubicam measures brands on the basis of differentiation, relevance, energy, esteem and knowledge. On the basis of the brand's performance along these parameters they are then categorized into four quadrants—unfocused/new, niche/unrealized potential, leadership declining and eroding. The Aaker Model consists of loyalty measures, perceived quality, awareness, differentiation measures and market-behaviour measures. These two measures can also be combined to measure the performance of an organization like in the example of Millward Brown discussed in the chapter.

KEY TERMS

Associations/differentiation measures These measures are used to understand how the brand is associated in the minds of the customers and how it is different from the competing brands in the same product category.

Brand dominance This is when the chosen brand is the only brand recalled in the product category.

Brand knowledge This is when the customers know what the chosen brand stands for.

Brand opinion This is when the customers have an opinion about the chosen brand.

Brand personality This is how the customers perceive the brand-as-a person. This construct tells us if the customers were to personify the brand what the brand would be to them.

Brand strength This is the brand association that exists in the minds of the customers. Analyzing brand strength helps us to understand what the customers think about the brand in relation to its competitors.

Brand value This is the financial gain accrued as a result of leveraging the brand strength. The financial performance is calculated to see how profitable the company is.

Conjoint analysis This is used to identify a combination of features which are most preferred by the consumers and which can be offered to the market

Cost-based valuation This is when the value of the brand is calculated on the basis of what it actually costs to create or what it might theoretically cost to recreate.

Customer satisfaction measure This construct measures the satisfaction level of the customers after using the brand.

Differentiation This is the 'degree to which the brand is different from other brands'.

Economic-use method This method 'takes into account the economic value of the brand to the current owner in its current use.'

Energy This is the ability of the brand to meet the future needs of the consumers and its ability to attract new customers.

Esteem This 'measures how well the brand is regarded and respected' by the consumers.

Knowledge This 'measures how familiar and intimate people are with the brand'.

Organizational associations This is how customers perceive brand-as-an organization. This is another aspect of brand association that highlights the organization—its people, values, and programs.

Perceived value This is how the customers perceive the brand-as-a product. The value proposition is a functional benefit provided by the brand.

Price premium measure The price premium measures the extra amount of money a customer is willing to pay for a brand compared to a competing brand.

Relevance This refers to 'the breadth of the brand's appeal' for the customers.

Royalty-relief method This method is based on the assumption that if the company did not actually own the brand, but had to license it from a third party, then what royalty it would have to pay for using the brand name.

Top-of-mind This is when the chosen brand is the first brand that comes to mind when asked to recall brands in a product class.

EXERCISES

Concept Review Questions

1. What do you understand by the term measuring brand equity? Discuss with the help of examples.
2. Delineate the various ways in which you can measure brand equity.
3. Out of the two ways—financial and customer perspectives—which do you think is more appropriate in calculating brand equity?
4. Discuss the Brand Asset Valuator Model with the help of the major brands in the category of fast moving consumer goods, such as soaps.

Critical Thinking Questions

1. Critically evaluate the statement, 'Brand equity measurement is important for the long-term success of a firm.'
2. Critically discuss Aaker's model for evaluating brand equity.

Internet Exercises

1. Visit the website http://www.interbrand.com/best_global_brands.aspx and study the ranking of brands. Discuss the methodology used by Interbrand to rank the brands.
2. Visit the website http://www.brandz.com/output/Branddynamicpyramid.aspx and study the model Brand Dynamic Pyramid developed by Brandz. Critically discuss the method used to evaluate the brands by them. How is this similar to or different from Interbrand's method?

CD Exercise

Pick a product category and list various brands in it. Place the brands in different quadrants of the Brand Asset Valuator model.

REFERENCES

Aaker, D. A., 'Managing the most important asset—brand equity', *Planning review*, Vol. 20, Issue no. 5, 1992, pp. 56–58.

Aaker, D. A., 'Measuring brand equity across products and markets', *California Management Review*, Vol. 38, Issue no. 3, 1996, pp. 102–120.

Brand Directory, http://www.brandirectory.com/methodology, accessed on 20 January 2011.

'Relief from royalty', *Economic Times* (2007), http://economictimes.indiatimes.com/news/news-by-company/corporate-trends/relief-from-royalty/articleshow/2245591.cms >, accessed on 2 February 2010.

Farquhar, P. H., 'Managing brand equity', *Marketing Research*, Vol. 1, Issue 3, 1989, pp. 24–33.

Haigh, D. (2000), 'Best practice in measuring the impact of marketing on brand equity and corporate profitability', *Journal of Targeting, Measurement and Analysis for Marketing*, Vol. 9, Issue no. 1, pp. 9–19.

Interbrand, http://www.brandchannel.com/papers_review.asp?sp_id=357, accessed on 19 May 2010.

Keller, K.L. (2008), *Strategic Brand Management*, Pearson Prentice Hall, New Delhi.

Kotler, Philip and K.L. Keller (2005), *Marketing Management*, Prentice Hall, New Delhi.

Lassar, W., B. Mittal, and A. Sharma, 'Measuring customer-based brand equity', *Journal of Consumer Marketing*, Vol. 12, Issue no. 4, 1995, p 11–19.

Pappu, R., P. Quester, and R.W. Cooksey, 'Consumer-based brand equity and country-of-origin relationships some empirical evidence', *European Journal of Marketing*, Vol. 40, Issue no. 5/6, 2006, pp. 696–717.

Sagar, M., Deepali Singh, D.P. Agrawal, and A. Gupta (2009), *Brand Management*, Ane Books Private Limited, New Delhi.

Sinha, A., N.J. Ashill, and A. Gazley, 'Measuring Customer-based brand equity using Hierarchical Bayes methodology', *Australian Marketing Journal*, Vol. 16, Issue no. 1, 2008, pp. 3–19.

Tremblay, C. (2008), 'A how-to guide to assessing brand value', http://www.brandchannel.com/brand_speak.asp?bs_id=193, accessed on 22 February 2010.

Whitwell, S. (2004), 'Brands on the balance sheet for IFRS', http://www.intangiblebusiness.com/Brand-services/Marketing-services/News/Brands-on-the-balance-sheet-for-IFRS~328.html, accessed on 25 May 2010.

Web resources

http://news.cnet.com/8301-1001_3-20003629-92.html, accessed on 20 January 2011.

http://www.brandirectory.com/league_tables/table/global_500, accessed on 20 January 2011.

http://www.millwardbrown.com/Libraries/Optimor_BrandZ_Files/2010_BrandZ_Top100_Report.sflb.ashx, accessed on 20 January 2011.

CASE STUDY

Measuring Brand Equity for Successful Celling*

Rihaan Khurana gazed out of his seventeenth floor office window for the zillionth time, deep in thought. His idle, bored mind reflected back to his life. Never having fared well in academics, Rihaan had always been crazy about gizmos—especially cell phones. In fact, that was probably his only passion. And ever since he had graduated from the 'Gizmo Guru' tag in college to managing his father's not-so-exciting mobile phone peripherals business, he thoroughly missed his good old days. Even though his company Mobi Tech Pvt. Ltd, was a well-known name in its field, his own personal interest was more towards the 'real' thing, as he called it, rather than just manufacturing earphones, Bluetooth devices, and the likes.

After a nine year long affair with them, at age 28, he now wanted to work officially with his first and only true love—cell phones. And why not? He could practically sense their pulse! The 'Gizmo Guru' was alive in him even today, and he had no intentions of letting it go! He wanted to establish a cell phone brand, which would be absolutely unique in its service offering. He decided to conduct a study of the mobile phone market in India, and so after a detailed research analysis, he came across some known, and some not-so-known findings:

Price premium

A survey on consumer awareness conducted by 'The Environmental Protection and Consumer Rights

---

*Tanya Seth is Assistant Manager–Marketing Support at Celfrost Innovations Pvt. Ltd.

Organization' (ECOCON), from 5 to 8 December 2005 acted as an effective tool to understand the mind of the consumer. Having covered 866 students in 23 colleges in and around Pune, of which, 457 were male and 409 female, it was brought to light that a whopping 88 per cent of the sample set preferred Nokia, with Samsung far behind at 3 per cent (ECOCON consumer awareness survey report cited in Nightingale. P.F, 2008). Undoubtedly, Nokia had an upper hand when it came to its pricing strategy. However, currently Nokia held 70 per cent of the market share (in November 2009) as compared to 78.8 per cent in 2005 (Govindkrishna 2006 cited in Nightingale P.F. 2008).

Conversely, although the first few years after launching its mobile handsets in 1999 were indifferent for Samsung, there had been a drastic increase in its market share from 7.8 per cent in November 2008 to 16.3 per cent exactly a year later (refer to Table 6.3).

Table 6.3   GSM market share in per cent

Brand	November 2008	November 2009
Nokia	71	70
Samsung	8	16
LG	4	6
Sony Ericsson	5	2
Others	12	6

Source: Industry cited in Bhandari, B. and Taneja, M., 19 January 2010.

Satisfaction/loyalty

Another recent survey done on youth preferences (refer to Appendix 1), of which 65 per cent of the respondents were between the ages of 22 and 28 (refer to Q10, Appendix 2), shows that 49 per cent of them currently use Nokia, as opposed to 10 per cent who own Samsung phones (refer to Q2, Appendix 2). When asked whether they are dissatisfied, satisfied, or delighted with their buy, as many as 56 per cent said they were satisfied, followed by 28 per cent of the people who were delighted (refer to Q4, Appendix 2). Another noteworthy point was that 74.7 per cent of the respondents said that they would recommend their current brands to others too (refer to Q5, Appendix 2).

The fact that a majority of the people, 42 per cent, change their cell phones every two to two-and-a-half years (refer to Q6, Appendix 2) and that almost two-thirds of the sample set would recommend their current brand to others (refer to Q5, Appendix 2), goes to say a lot about the kind of brand loyalty, the world leader in cellular phones, Nokia (Nightingale, P.F 2008), enjoys in India.

Perceived quality

When asked what factors were most crucial for them in a cell phone, not surprisingly, people said having the latest features; this factor was closely followed by trendy looks and good battery life (refer to Q7, Appendix 2). With the youth considering a 'good quality' phone as one having the latest features and trendy looks among other things, companies are now working towards providing the latest technologies in each of these spheres.

According to the Virgin Mobile Chief Marketing Officer, Prasad Narsimhan, 'The single largest phenomenon about the youth is that they network. The popularity of social networking sites is a symptom of this. They do this to create possibilities for themselves (Bhandari, Kar, and Iyer 2010). And, although some companies are still trying to understand how to incorporate the digital social media in their marketing plans, Samsung, late last year launched the Corby range of mobile phones targeted at the youth, which comes preloaded with popular social networking sites (*The Strategist, Business Standard*, 23 February 2010).

Astonishingly, even though an article dated 5 December 2009 in the Corporate Dossier, *The Economic Times*, labelled Samsung as one of 'The World's Most Inventive Companies', Nokia seems to have won the youth's heart, when it came to which brand they thought provided better quality phones. With a staggering 86 per cent people saying that Nokia provided superior phones than Samsung, the perceived quality of the latter definitely needs to be worked upon to match up to the standards of the Finnish organization.

Leadership

Even though, by now, it is clear that Nokia is the leader in India, in terms of market share as well as popularity, Nokia might have some things to worry about. According to Bhandari and Taneja 2010, 'The last one year has been a dream run for Samsung'. With their market share shooting from 7.8 per cent to 16.3 per cent in one year (as discussed above; refer to Table 6.3), Samsung's popularity seems to be growing at lightening pace.

As Ranjit Yadav, Samsung India Director (mobile and information technology) says, one of the reasons for this sudden growth could be that Samsung wants to be 'relevant to customers'. Samsung's strategy is to bundle more features than its rivals in the products it launches (Bhandari and Taneja 2010). According to Bhattacharjee 2010, the touchscreen market is already about 10 per cent of the market; and the industry reckons it could rise to over 20 in a year's time. At present, touch screens contribute to less than 10 per cent of Nokia's business in the country. Nokia claims that it launched the country's first touch screen phone—the 6108—in 2003, while Samsung and LG did so in 2008. Nokia has eight models in its portfolio at the moment, which is way short of Samsung's twenty and LG's twelve (Bhattacharjee 2010).

Samsung, which is the leader in the touch screen segment in the world, has decided to strengthen its portfolio even further; currently two-fifths of its models in the market are touch screen. In Yadav's words, 'At Samsung, we rely on our differentiated and innovative features to give superior value to customers' (Bhattacharjee 2010).

Perceived value

A majority of the respondents of the 'Preferences of the Youth' survey are willing to pay a maximum of ₹8,000 to 10,000 for a mobile phone (refer to Q8, Appendix 2). These budgetary constraints mean that the products and features must have long-term utility (*Brand Equity* 2010). The fact that 84 per cent are either satisfied or delighted with their phones (refer to Q4, Appendix 2), along with the finding that a majority of the people change their handsets every two years (refer to Q6, Appendix 2), indicates that the perceived value for the brands being discussed is quite high.

Although, going by the popularity of Nokia as a brand, it is safe to assume that the perceived value of Nokia is higher too.

Brand personality

As stated by Nightingale 2008, 'Since 1995, when Nokia entered India, this brand has been steadily growing and has gained wide acceptance in the market. Nokia is one of the most trusted brands in India and leads other cellular phone brands, in terms of market share, advertising, and customer services. The innovative technologies, user-friendly features, and affordable prices have contributed to Nokia's success.' Looking at this, it is evident that the Finnish brand is viewed more or less as a well-established company that has 'been-there-done-that'. On the contrary, Samsung might be far behind Nokia in terms of its market share, but it is definitely being accepted in the market. Bearing in mind that almost all of Samsung's line of cell phones is less than a year old (Bhandari and Taneja 2010), they seem to have done very well for themselves in the past year, having managed to convince 14 per cent of the respondents of the 'Preferences of the Youth' survey that they actually offer better quality phones than Nokia (refer to Q9, Appendix 2).

Yadav says, 'This business is all about change. The go-to-market time is extremely important'. To give the brand a high-tech image, Samsung, in March 2008, launched a mass-media campaign with Aamir Khan and the tagline, 'Next is what?' Samsung India's telecommunications expert, Mahesh Uppal claims that, 'Samsung's focus is on the youth. The company is conscious of the latest trends, new features, as well as attractiveness of the models' (Bhandari and Taneja 2010).

Organization associations

Organization associations that are often important bases of differentiation and choice include having a concern for customers and their needs, being successful, having quality, being a global player, and being trustworthy (Aaker 1996).

Taking into account the discussion till now and the 'Preference of the Youth' survey results (refer to Appendix 2), it is clear that Nokia is a global player that is highly trusted. Also, from what Uppal says, Samsung is quite focused on the needs of its target audiences (Bhandari and Taneja 2010). Focusing on 'a concern for customer needs', Samsung conducts continuous surveys on customer needs and products in the market. Good designs, impressive technology, and harmonious features are some of the predominating parameters that slot Samsung as one of the topmost contenders in the cellular phone market (Nightingale 2008).

Brand awareness

Brand awareness is an important and sometimes undervalued component of brand equity. Awareness can affect perceptions and attitudes. In some cases, it can be a driver of brand choice and even loyalty (Aaker 1996). When questioned about brand awareness, as much as 72 per cent of the sample set mentioned Nokia as the first brand that came to their mind when one said 'cell phones', followed by Apple, Blackberry, Sony Ericsson, and then Samsung at 10 per cent, 8 per cent, 5 per cent and 3 per cent respectively (refer to Q1, Appendix 2). Clearly, the top-of-the-mind recall of Nokia was the best.

What usually assists a company to achieve this kind of a brand recall is its advertising. According to *Brand Equity* (2 December 2009), Nokia stands at fourth position in the 'Top 20 List of Most Admired Marketers', leaving Samsung far behind at number twelve. Nokia's marketing spend is currently ₹200 crore. Add to that, a high decibel communication exercise, be it Priyanka Chopra as the brand endorser or Nokia's association with the high profile Kolkata Knight Riders, which ensures top-of-the-mind recall (*Brand Equity*, 2 December 2010). In another 'Analysis of Mobile Phones Advertising on TV in year 2006', 15 May 2007 (cited in Nightingale 2008), Nokia was the leader with 45 per cent slice of the ad pie, whereas Samsung stood at 9 per cent.

But, do celebrities actually help in creating brand recall for companies?

Although, *Brand Equity* (30 December 2009) mentions that the youth believe that 'sometimes celebrities do play a role in making a brand choice', another *Brand Equity* article dated 3 February 2010 states that according to the Celebrity Sensor Report released recently by MEC MediaLab, which covered over 1,000 respondents in India, only 35 per cent consumers felt that a celebrity helps them trust a product. Just 32 per cent believe that they can trust a celebrity when they are paid to endorse a brand; and

only 31 per cent say that celebrities make them want to recommend a brand. But for brand managers, the benefit of using celebrities comes from the fact that celebrities deliver quicker recall for brands in a clustered scenario.

Market share

As discussed above, in a fairly detailed manner, Nokia has a bigger market share than Samsung. As per the industry data of November 2009, the market standing of both companies in question is mentioned in Table 6.3.

According to *Brand Equity* (2 December 2009), even though Nokia today enjoys more than 60 per cent market share in mobile handsets, competitors like Samsung are close on its heels.

Market price and distribution coverage

Striving to keep their product offering relevant to consumers (Bhandari and Taneja 19 January 2010), Yadav says that 'an the entry level "essential" segment of below ₹3,000, the SamsungGuru comes with a Hindu calendar, tracker for misplaced handsets, Bluetooth (in some models), clamshell design, and a solar recharge facility (SolarGuru). In the multimedia segment, which is priced between ₹3,500 and ₹8,000, Samsung offers Metro with features like camera, pre-loaded social networking sites, and a card for storage. For small businessmen who travel to remote parts and rural consumers who are straddled with low connectivity, there is a dual-SIM handset. For young adventure-seekers, there is a 'Planet-proof Marine', which is a rugged phone that can be used even if it drops into water or is run over by a motorcycle. Then there is the world of touch-screen phones, which starts at ₹7,600 and goes up to ₹33,900. This is really Samsung's forte. The company claims it has 31 per cent share of the touch-screen market (Bhandari and Taneja 2010).

Apart from the consumer's mind, the battle has to be fought at the distribution level. And this is where, according to Yadav, Samsung has put in a lot of effort, 'The margins we offer to retailers are the best in the industry. We guarantee a 30 per cent return of investment on Samsung merchandize to retailers.' In India, there are some 1,20,000 dealers of mobile handsets. Samsung reaches about half of them and covers over 80 per cent handset sales in the country (Bhandari and Taneja 2010). Bhattacharjee 2010, states that 'large multi-brand stores have Samsung attendants to push the brand.'

When Vineet Taneja, Head of Marketing, Nokia India was asked if LG and other home-grown players with cheaper handsets, aggressive marketing strategies, and a big retail push were an area of worry for Nokia, he wasn't unduly perturbed. He felt that "there is no competitive advantage the local manufacturers have, and soon, one will kill the other" (Bhattacharjee , 2010).

Having conducted this detailed research on the current market scenario and market share holdings, Rihaan realized that it was not going to be easy to get a foothold into this industry. He would, as a first step, have to measure the brand equity of his own organization (Aaker 1996). But, he had always believed that where there's a will, there's a way, and even though, there were many challenges he would have to face, to get what he wanted— some that he could foresee right now, some not—he was willing to take his chances!

Discussion Questions

1. Already having a decent market share in the mobile accessories market in India, which target market should Rihaan Khurana focus on? Provide justification for your answer.

2. In the last few months, Mobi Tech Pvt. Ltd. has partnered with a leading radio channel to increase its brand awareness; giving out free coupons and gift vouchers to participants at the radio station was a conscious step the company took. Mobi Tech now has almost a 35 per cent of the pie.
   (a) How can the company manage its existing brand equity and try and use it positively to get a stronghold into the mobile phone market?
   (b) What other mediums or channels can Rihaan use as a mobile phone provider to position this brand well?

3. What are the basic challenges Rihaan needs to tackle to be able to step into the cell phone market?

Case References

Aaker, D., 'Managing brand equity across products and markets', *California Management Review*, Vol. no. 38, Issue no. 3, 1996, p 102.

Bhandari, B. and M. Taneja 'Bulking up', *The Strategist, Business Standard*, 19 January 2010, p.1.

Bhandari, B., S. Kar, and B. Iyer, 'The new age maharaja', *The Strategist, Business Standard*, 23 February 2010, p 1.

Bhattacharjee, A., 'Soft on touch', *The Strategist, Business Standard*, 19 April 2010, p 3.

Brand Equity, 'Cheeky singles', *Brand Equity, The Economic Times*, 30 December 2009, p 2.

Brand Equity, 'Neighbour's envy owner's pride', *Brand Equity, The Economic Times*, 2 December 2009, p 2.

Brand Equity, 'Top 20 list of most admired marketers', *Brand Equity, The Economic Times*, 2 December 2009, p 1.

Brand Equity, 'Woods for thought', *Brand Equity, The Economic Times*, 3 February 2010, p 2.

Brand Equity, 'Youth pulse Factors that influence Purchase choices among Urban Youth', *Brand Equity, The Economic Times*, 17 March 2010, p 3.

Corporate Dossier, 'The World's Most Inventive Companies', *Corporate Dossier, The Economic Times*, 5 February 2010, p 4.

Nightingale, P.F. 2008, Nokia the brand and its future in India, *Case Studies on Branding to Compete Leading Brands and their Strategies*, ICFAI Books, Andhra Pradesh, India.

APPENDIX 1

Cell Phones—Preferences of the Youth

1. Which is the first cell phone brand that comes to your mind?

2. Which mobile handset are you currently using?

3. When did you buy it?
   (a) Less than 4 months ago
   (b) 4 – 8 months ago
   (c) 8 – 12 months ago
   (d) More than a year ago

4. Are you dissatisfied/satisfied/delighted by it?
   (a) Dissatisfied   (b) Satisfied
   (c) Delighted

5. Would you recommend your current brand to others too?
   (a) Yes   (b) No

6. How often do you change your cell phone?
   (a) Every 6 – 8 months   (b) Every year
   (c) Every 2 – 2.5 years   (d) Every 2.5 – 5 years
   (e) After more than 5 years

7. What factors are crucial when you change your cell phone?
   (a) Battery life   (b) Trendy looks
   (c) Latest features (better camera, sound quality, etc.)
   (d) Exclusivity and uniqueness
   (e) Price

8. What is the maximum price you are willing to pay for a cell phone?
   (a) Less than ₹8,000   (b) ₹8,000 to 10,000
   (c) ₹15,000 to 18,000   (d) ₹20,000
   (e) Price doesn't matter, if I like it, I'll buy it anyway

9. Out of Nokia and Samsung, which brand according to you, provides better quality cell phones?
   (a) Nokia   (b) Samsung

10. What age group do you fall in?
   (a) 16 – 21 years   (b) 22 – 28 years
   (c) 29 – 35 years

Answers to the above questionnaire

1. Which is the first cell phone brand that comes to your mind?

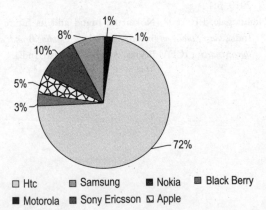

2. Which mobile handset are you currently using?

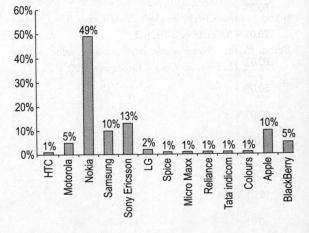

3. When did you buy it?

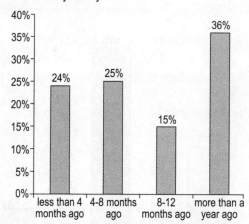

6. How frequently do you change your cell phone?

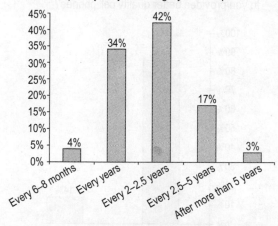

4. Are you dissatisfied/satisfied/delighted by it?

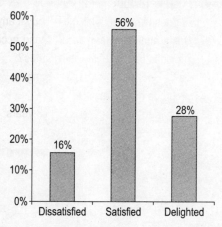

7. What factors are crucial when you change your cell phone?

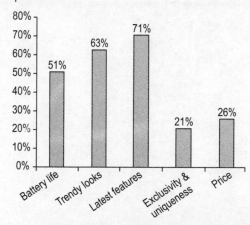

5. Would you recommend your current brand to others too?

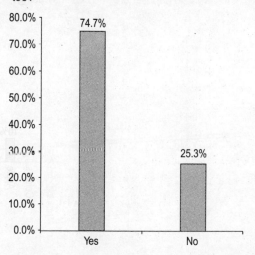

8. What is the maximum price you are willing to pay for a cell phone?

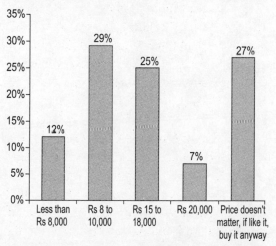

9. Out of Nokia and Samsung, which brand according to you provides better quality cell phones?

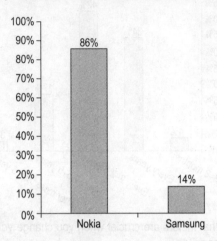

10. What age group do you fall in?1

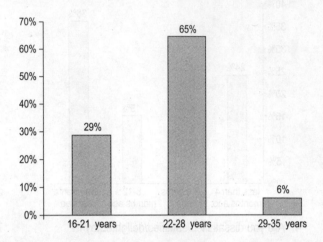

Part III
UNDERSTANDING CONSUMERS AND MARKETS

Part III

Understanding Consumers and Markets

Chapter 7   Consumer Behaviour and
Brand Buying Decisions

Chapter 8   Brand Architecture

Consumer Behaviour and Brand Buying Decisions

7

LEARNING OBJECTIVES

After reading this chapter, you will be able to understand the following:

- The concept of consumer behaviour with respect to branding
- Brand perception
- Changing demographic trends and lifestyles
- A model of consumer brand buying decision process
- Various factors affecting consumer behaviour
- Various factors affecting brand loyalty

ABOUT THE CHAPTER

This chapter provides an understanding of consumer behaviour in context of branding. Given that the core focus of marketing is to satisfy the needs and wants of customers, it is important for any organization to first understand the customers (Exhibit 7.1). Further, as the trend shifts from a buyer's market to a shopper's market, it is all the more necessary for marketers to understand the behaviour of customers so as to further influence them positively into buy their brands. The boom in information technology has further facilitated shoppers by giving them access to loads of information at the click of their fingers. Marketers, thus, need to remain on their toes in order to understand and be aware about how consumers think and behave. To facilitate this, the chapter enumerates and delineates an integrated approach to the main theories governing consumer behaviour, and outlines how the customer decides about a purchase, and as well as describes various factors affecting consumer behaviour vis-à-vis branding.

INTRODUCTION—WHAT IS CONSUMER BEHAVIOUR

In a postmodern consumer culture, it is believed that brands play a pivotal role in the formation of consumer identity (Elliot and Wattanasuwan 1998 cited in Simoes and Dibb 2001). According to Davis 2000 '... to maximize the customer-brand relationship, a company must

Exhibit 7.1   Understanding Consumers' Needs

Is it possible for brands that did not exist five years ago to have an estimated market size of ₹1500 crore with the potential to grow to ₹3000 crore by 2013 and grow at the rate of 20 per cent annually? The answer is yes, for the male grooming market in India. This highlights the fact that the consumers were there waiting for the right brands—their brand. Fair and Handsome, the first brand to enter the male face-care market, highlighted the need for a fairness cream specially manufactured for men. Overnight, they won over all the men, who were until at the time using women's fairness creams, and it became a ₹100-crore brand.

The requirements of Indian men in this area inspired companies like 'Unilever, Garnier, Nivea, Emami, Paras Pharma, Godrej, Sara Lee, etc., to launch skin care,

hair care, bath and shower brands, and deodorants only for men. P&G then announced plans to extend its Olay brand to men's products like pre-shaving thermal products akin to a hot towel at a barber shop' (Jacob 2010). The men's grooming brands have also therefore been contributing to their organizations' revenues. Nivea India attributes 15 per cent of its personal care products revenue to men's products. As much as 10 per cent of Emami's personal care revenue comes from the Fair and Handsome brand alone.

'The desire to purchase products to look good cuts across classes today. A man earning just ₹50 a day saves money for hair colouring', Manish Goenka, Director, Emami (Jacob 2010).

understand how customers think, act, perceive, and make purchase decisions.' This highlights the need for brand managers to understand the consumer's brand purchase behaviour (see Exhibit 7.2).

Consumer behaviour, being an interdisciplinary science, has witnessed a number of research attempts to understand it in the past two decades. New data, relationships theories, and models have been worked out. The term consumer behaviour is defined as 'the behaviour

Exhibit 7.2   Ghari Gains

The ₹12,000 crore detergent market saw the brand Ghari gaining at the expense of brand Nirma in the year 2010. Currently, Unilever has a market share of 36–37 per cent of the overall detergent market (both bars and powders) followed by Ghari at 10 per cent, P&G at 10 per cent, and Nirma at 8 per cent. Both Nirma and Ghari cater to the economy segment of the market, while HUL and P&G cater to the mid-market segment. However, in the year 2010, due to an inflation in the food prices, most consumers opted to buy the lower-priced detergent variants. As they could not cut down on food, consumers tightened their purse strings when it came to buying other products. The money they

managed to save in this manner, they spent on food. One of the products that the consumer down-traded on was the detergent used for washing clothes. Ghari, by consolidating its distribution system in the north, was there when the customers wanted it. North India has a 35 per cent share of the detergent market compared to 30 per cent in the west, 25 per cent in the south and 10 per cent in the east. Thus, by being present where the consumers are and by cashing in on their sentiments, Ghari gained over Nirma, which was leading at 13 per cent three years ago when Ghari had a market share of just 10 per cent (Pinto 2010).

Exhibit 7.3   TVS Gets Street Smart to Become a Significant Third

The two-wheeler motorcycle industry is dominated by two formidable players—Bajaj and Hero Honda. The segment crossed the 10 million unit level in March 2010; it has Hero Honda as the market leader at 4.6 million units followed by Bajaj Auto at 2.5 million units. TVS trails at 1.5 million units. A look at the consumers delineates the Ram and Krishna consumer segments that are well-catered to by the industry players. 'Ram is the good guy who buys a bike for functional reasons, while Krishna is the naughty guy who wants some fun with his bike. Between the two they command the lion's share of the bike market in India' (Rajiv Bajaj, MD,

Bajaj Auto, cited in Gupta 2010). To capture a foothold in this competitive market, TVS is focusing on niche segments. It has thus launched TVS Jive (with an auto clutch and an urban focus) as against the commuter bikes and sporty motorcycles. The TVS Wego scooter (with a unisex metal body) is again different from the Hero Honda's vehicle for women. TVS's strategy of being focused and targeting niche segments seems to be paying off. It clocked a growth of over 20 per cent in the first three months of 2010. This was comparable to Hero Honda's 23.6 per cent and Bajaj's 30 per cent growth in 2009–2010 (Gupta 2010).

that consumers display in searching for, purchasing, using, evaluating, and disposing of products and services that they expect will satisfy their needs' (Schiffman and Kanuk 2004). Consumer behaviour focuses on how individuals arrive at decisions about spending their available resources (time, money, and effort) on consumption related items. It includes what they buy, why they buy it, when they buy it, where they buy it, how often they buy it, how often they use it, how they evaluate it after the purchase, the impact of such evaluations on future purchases, and how they dispose of it. The focus of marketers should not be objective reality, but instead consumer perceptions. These perceptions may be altered either by changing objective reality or by reinterpreting objective reality for consumers (Jacoby and Olson 1985). This is possible through developing an understanding of consumer behaviour. The net result of the changing role of the consumer is that companies can no longer act independently. They need to understand how consumers are behaving, how they are gathering information, their major considerations while purchasing the brand, and the factors influencing this. Learning about how the customer finds and executes the optimum solution in a given market makes it easier for an organization to earn their long-term trust, purchases, and loyalty (Lawer and Knox 2006). The postmodern study of consumer behaviour is not meant to predict and manipulate consumer behaviour, but to better understand it. It is believed that knowledge of the factors that influence consumer behaviour can, with practice, be used to develop sound marketing strategies (see Exhibit 7.3). These marketing strategies need to be integrated with the brand development activity for holistic development of the firm in the long term.

CONSUMER BEHAVIOUR AND THE ROLE OF BRANDING

The last decade has seen the marketplace flood with brands both national and international. The customer has a number of options to choose from and the consumer's attitude towards a brand is very influential in the purchase decision-making process (Grant and Stephen 2006).

Some brands are purchased 'not once but repeatedly, in many cases in predictably regular patterns; hence the truth of the saying that when we build brands we are gaining customers and not just sales. In marketing jargon, we are building a long-term franchise.' It has been studied that 'two-thirds of buyers normally buy, with varying degrees of irregularity, more than one brand. This introduces the extremely important concept of the repertoire of brands: the collection the homemaker buys in varying proportions, often in predictably regular patterns' (Jones 1999). This consistent habit of repeat purchase in most of the markets highlights the need to build strong brands. The brand name serves as a 'shorthand' for quality by providing consumers with a bundle of information about the product. 'Brands are at the very heart of marketing. When a company creates a strong brand it attracts customer preference and builds a defensive wall against competition' (Doyle 1993). A brand promises consumers quality and value and communicates a distinct advantage to them. Companies recognize the value of having strong brands in their portfolio as they help them build a loyal customer base (Grant and Stephen 2006).

The Concept of Perception

The biggest challenge for marketing professionals is their ability to create, maintain, and enhance brands (see Exhibit 7.4). Branding is a major issue to be tackled in product strategy, as successful branding is one of the most potent tools for businesses to create and preserve value (Rio, Vazquez, and Iglesias 2001; Singhal 2004).

Branding is an immensely challenging process, which requires intensive investment, building an element of trust with consumers and delivering promises made to the consumer. It takes many years of effort and investment to create global brands. Branding is a complex process, but its goal is simple. It leads to the creation and development of a specific identity for a company, product, commodity, group, or person (Levine 2003). 'Marketing is branding' or branding is the

---

Exhibit 7.4   Brands and Customers

The brand name is the bridge that connects consumers with the firm's product. Consumers, on the basis of their experience during various touch points with the brand, assign meaning to the brand. But when the meaning transforms from being significant to irrelevant, the brand name becomes powerless. Take the example of the brand, Bajaj. The 'Hamara Bajaj' campaign had catapulted the brand to an iconic status. It symbolized a 'family's wealth and social prestige' and carried along a generation of middle class families. However, this heritage brand name was recently dropped from the models of motorcycles and rear engine auto-rickshaws, which Bajaj Auto currently manufactures.

Brand Maggi, from the house of Nestlé, on the other hand has been able to retain its connection with the customers. The brand, along with its extensions, continues to enjoy customer affection and it has graduated from the '2-minute noodles' to the 'taste bhi, health bhi' platform.

Brand HMT, once the 'timekeepers to the nation', became obsolete due to its 'inability to identify the metamorphosis of the target audience and attract new customers' (Koshy 2010). Brands need to keep track of the changing consumer trends, and a vigilant customer feedback can help insulate them.

glue that holds the marketing functions together (Ries and Ries 1999). The concept of 'selling' is being replaced by 'purchasing' due to the rise of brands, and so branding is important as it 'pre-sells' the product or service to the customer. Thus, branding is the most important activity that helps companies become more profitable and more powerful. Branding is important as it provides the competitive advantage, and branding strategies help the organization deal with the changes taking place in the external environment. Brand orientation is seen as a powerful tool for creating shareholder and long-term value (Simoes and Dibb 2001).

The brand helps the manufacturer or service provider by creating a unique positioning for them, legally protecting the features, associating a distinct quality expectation, providing a source of competitive advantage, and ensuring distinct returns. 'Brand perceptions affect consumers' buying decisions.' Strong brands help the marketing managers to meet the challenges of today's highly volatile markets (Simoes and Dibb 2001) by positively influencing the purchase behaviour of consumers.

Rio et al. 2001 studied the role of the brand name in obtaining differential advantages and stated that brands have a functional and utilitarian component and a symbolic as well as expressive component (see Figure 7.1). The functional dimension describes brand evaluation in a rational and practical manner. Consumers evaluate the performance capabilities of the product, along with perceptions about usage effectiveness, value for money, availability, and reliability of the brand. Therefore, this dimension represents the more intrinsic advantages of the product and usually corresponds to product related attributes. At a more emotional level, the symbolic evaluation of the brand is considered. Here, consumers use personal or subjective criteria, such as taste, pride, desire to reinforce their membership to a particular social group, and for expressing something about themselves in their consumption decisions. These benefits are the more extrinsic advantages and usually correspond attributes related to the brand name.

Thus, by investing in a brand, organizations can attain differential advantages for their products. The idea is not only to promote the functional benefits and differentiation, but also the brand related symbolic attributes. The overall brand perception affects consumer-buying decisions (Simoes and Dibb 2001).

Consumer research has traditionally viewed the question of brand preference in terms of brand attributes, product benefits, and the actual decision-making process (Keller 2003). Phenomenological studies (Fournier 1998; Kozinets 1999; Muniz and O'Guinn 2001), however, offer a different perspective. These studies demonstrate that the consumer is an active partner with the marketer in brand-meaning formation. As marketers, we can influence the customer, but ultimately consumers form their own perceptions about the brand and what the brand means or stands for, for them. For example, consumers may develop different types of relationships with brands based on their experiences (Fournier 1998) or form brand communities and subcultures with other consumers around important brands (Kozinets 1999; Muniz and O'Guinn 2001).

These studies also suggest that consumers appropriate brand meanings in ways that make the brand meaningful to them (Coupland 2005). Coupland's research studied how the habits and patterns of home life impact the meaningfulness or meaninglessness of brands. Thus, as brand managers we need to study the context in which the brand is being consumed by the

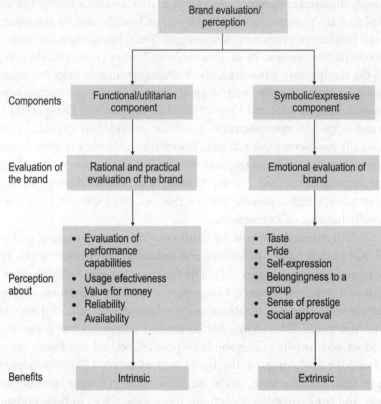

Figure 7.1 Brand evaluation and perception by customers

consumers to better understand the degree of relevance of the brand for them. Companies can develop the trust and commitment of consumers by building a greater understanding of customer attitudes, values, relationships, and their perceptions of value, thus necessitating the understanding of consumer attitude and consumer decision-making. All this leads to the formation of an image of the brand by the consumers. If this image is different from the image of the brand portrayed by the organization, it leads to a 'brand gap.'

Brand image is defined as 'the customer's perception of brand identity.' Brand identity portrayed by the organization can be same or different from the brand image formed by the customers on the basis of their experience. (This has already been discussed in detail in the second chapter that deals with creating a brand.) If the brand image is the same as the brand identity then there is no brand gap. For this to happen, companies need to have a clear understanding of the attitudes and purchase processes of the consumers.

THE CONSUMER ATTITUDE—THE INDIAN CONSUMER

India is the twelfth largest consumer market in the world, roughly equivalent to that of Brazil (in terms of area), but has a population six times larger. It is said that by 2015, the Indian consumer market will match Italy's, and by 2025 it will only be preceded by the US, Japan, China, and UK. India, currently (2009–2010), has around six million households that spend more than $28 billion per year and are considered 'rich' (Pinckney 2009). Both consumption and consumerism in India are on the rise as the population and purchasing power increases.

Changing Demographic Trends and Lifestyles

Most retailers start with a demographic segmentation to better understand the profile of their consumers. 'India is experiencing certain socio-demographic changes, which are furthering the growth in organized retail' (Cygnus 2006) (see Exhibit 7.5). It, thus, becomes imperative to understand the changing demographic trends of the Indian consumers. These trends can be studied under the following heads:

1. The young Indian consumer
2. Rising household income
3. Spending habits and brand behaviour
4. Rise of the Indian woman as a consumer
5. Changing consumer expectations
6. Changing lifestyles
7. Regional differences

Exhibit 7.5   The Indian Social Expression

The Indian social expression industry (gifting) has seen the steady rise of an organized player—Archies. Archies has slowly been changing the predictable Indian mindset. The evolving customer base with 'an increased exposure to developed markets, rising per capita and disposable income, a more liberal view of western cultural practices, and the sheer joy of being alive that Indians are wont to display has added a whole new dimension to social occasions.' Archies has risen to each occasion by designing a range of merchandise to help customers express their sentiments. There are cards for all occasions—from birthdays and anniversaries to 'Thinking of You', 'Miss You', 'Get Well Soon', etc. Customers find it easy to express their emotions through the Archies cards which come with the lines to express their feelings (see Image 7.1). The sentiments that the cards help to express, 'appeal to all age-groups and domographics'. It has really become a 'special way to say you care'.

The company is a unique example of supply creating demand. The credit of celebrating special occasions like Mother's Day, Father's Day, etc., goes to the Archies' ability to focus on them and develop marketing strategies around them. It is credited with bringing the concept of Friendship Day to India. Children are getting pocket money to spend and Archies is targeting this disposable income. The pester power of children helps them get what they want to gift on Friendship Day. Other occasions, such as Valentine's Day, also see the shop flooded with merchandise ranging from teddy bears and soft toys to chocolates and other gift items. The footfalls also increase during this period and a number of teenagers can be seen coming to the Archies stores.

Archies invented and instituted the fourth Sunday in September as Daughter's Day and backed it with an effective communications campaign. This has led to more people expressing their affection towards the girl child in an otherwise narrow and orthodox Indian society. The increasing number of working women has lead to the paucity of time that parents have with their children. Parents look forward to such occasions so that they can make their children feel special.

Contd

Exhibit 7.5 *contd*

Courtesy: Superbrands.

Image 7.1 Archies cards; also see Plate 6

Gifting as an expression is not confined to individuals but is relevant to corporate India too. Corporates look for innovative gifts that match their brand identity. Archies, in 2007, launched the 'Giftworks' brand, through which it provided a wide range of products to corporate houses. These are custom-made and include items like wine boxes, executive table clocks, exquisite chess sets, etc. Thus, Archies, by the dint of its understanding of the consumers and its ability to influence consumer behaviour has survived and grown to become a ₹138-crore brand (2008–2009) (based on *Superbrands,* 2009, pp. 18–19).

The Young Indian Consumer

Consumers in India are characterized by the fact that they are very 'young'. Among the highly populated countries, India has the lowest median age of 24 with 45 per cent of its population below the age of 25 years and 81 per cent below 45 years of age (Cygnus 2006). This young population is the major driver of consumption as they have both the ability and the willingness to spend and are more brand conscious.

Rising Household Income

The disposable income in households across rural and urban India is increasing. On an all-India basis, the growth in average household disposable incomes was at the rate of 3.6 per cent until 2005, the same is forecasted to grow at a rate of 5.3 per cent till the year 2025 (McKinsey

2007). The increase in income gives the Indian consumers the purchasing power to invest in brands.

Spending Habits and Brand Behaviour

It has been observed that there is a category shift in consumption patterns of the Indian consumers. Historically, the focus was more towards savings, but with increased media exposure, influx of consumer brands, and urbanization, consumers' aspiration levels are increasing. This has caused a shift towards spending, which has been growing at an average of 11.5 per cent a year for more than a decade. Consumers who were traditionally unwilling to spend on leisure and entertainment, have started spending money on movies, vacations, and eating out. Consumers, in general, are spending on a trendier lifestyle with an inclination towards trying out new things. The Indian lifestyle is shifting from austerity to complete self-indulgence and there is an aspiration for a global lifestyle (PwC 2006). From the time of the economic liberalization in 1991, the number of foreign players in the domestic market has increased. The Indian consumers, who have always preferred foreign goods, now have a range of brands to choose from, thus shifting the focus from the sellers' market to the buyers' market (Cygnus 2006; KSA Technopak-Consumer Outlook 2004). It has been studied that 79 per cent of the consumers in India said that they were willing to trade up for a brand (that is customers are encouraged to buy the more expensive brand) and that the brand name would make them spend more (McGregor 2009) (see Exhibit 7.6).

Rise of the Indian Woman as a Consumer

Rapid urbanization and industrialization in India has brought about a social change—the gradual breakdown of the joint family system and the equality of job opportunities for the urban, middle class, educated Indian woman (Ghosh and Roy 1997). This has led to a definite improvement in the status of Indian women, which is reflected in the growing number of women in public services occupying positions of political power and authority (Upreti 1988 cited in Ghosh and Roy 1997). Since 80 per cent of all the shopping is done by women (Cygnus 2006), they form an important segment for marketers' branding activities. Exhibit 7.7 discusses how two-wheeler manufacturers are targeting women purchasers.

Exhibit 7.6 Mercedes to Sell Pre-owned Cars

Mercedes-Benz, a top player in the Indian luxury car market, has realized that India has car enthusiasts with the propensity to spend money on ₹1 crore-plus cars. It had launched its AMG range starting from ₹1 crore in India in 2008, and seeing the response introduced its S-600 Guard at ₹6 crore. It has realized that there are consumers who are willing to upgrade to a price point of ₹15–18 lakh. They 'want to buy a Mercedes Benz family, but don't want to enter the price point of a C-class (starting at ₹26 lakh)'. To tap these customers and to facilitate the 30,000 existing Mercedes owners who might want to trade in their vehicles, Mercedes plans to sell used cars in India. The Proven Exclusivity Program or the pre-owned car business will have financing options also to facilitate the customers (Chauhan 2010).

Exhibit 7.7 Two-wheeler Manufacturers Targeting Women Purchasers

More than 6 per cent of all two-wheeler buyers in the country are women and analysts say that the current purchase level of scooters by them (about 450,000 units annually) is largely a conservative one (Baggonkar 2008). The gearless scooter segment has been seeing a rapid demand from college girls and housewives, with more than 50 per cent of the Scooty buyers being women. This has resulted in the segment becoming the second largest segment in the two-wheeler category after bikes. This has lead two-wheeler manufacturers to come out with strategies to tap this profitable segment. Manufacturers, such as Hero Honda, Bajaj Auto, TVS Motors, etc., are coming out with gearless scooters backed with special sales promotion schemes to woo the fairer sex. Bajaj Auto launched its Kristal gearless scooter meant for college girls (Kaushik 2006) and TVS Motor Company launched its first electric scooter, Scooty Teenz Electric for women in Gujarat in 2008 (domaint.com, 2010). Mahindra & Mahindra, 'which took over the two-wheeler business of Kinetic Motor in 2008, has already launched three 125 cc scooters—two power scooters, Mahindra Rodeo and Duro—and the Mahindra Flyte'. The Flyte is targeted towards women commuters (*The Hindu* 2010).

Hero Honda had 'adopted an entirely women-oriented positioning for its first launch in the segment—the Hero Honda Pleasure, a 100 cc gearless scooter' in 2006. '... there is a huge untapped segment of women customers, which offers immense growth potential. With this launch, we are now ready to extend our products and services to this vast customer profile,' said Pawan Munjal, Managing Director, Hero Honda. The company has taken its strategy a step further by opening twenty-two exclusive women's outlets called 'Just4her', across the country. These outlets 'offer special facilities to women customers and have female service supervisors and sales executives' (Kaushik 2006). These outlets, apart from contributing to the brand building exercise, are targeted exclusively at the women buyers to ensure that they feel comfortable while visiting the showroom both during and after the purchase process. With this they have also launched the 'Lady Rider Club with special benefits like milestone rewards, personal accident insurance, invitation to special events, etc.' The Pleasure scooter's advertisements featuring Priyanka Chopra were targeted at women with the punch line, 'Why should boys have all the fun?'

In addition, 'companies like Yamaha and Honda are even going to colleges for organizing events like choosing youth icons and giving test rides, while initiating competitions with prizes. Companies are showcasing products in malls, shopping arcades, and other recreational areas that attract large footfalls of women buyers.

TVS Motors has come out with the concept of 'women on wheels' to promote scooters in 150 tier I and tier II cities. This concept is aimed at improving product familiarity among potential buyers. The company also plans to help women buyers obtain a learner's and permanent license at the end of the six-day course. 'In addition, there will be a special financing package lined up for the customer, which will have convenient EMI schemes and easy down payment load. Even the paperwork required for owing the vehicle will be done by TVS Motors' (Baggonkar 2008).

Source: Kaushik, Neha 2006, 'Ungeared for growth', Business Line, The Hindu, http://www.thehindubusinessline.com/catalyst/2006/02/09/stories/2006020900030100.htm, accessed on 22 April 2010; http://www.domain-b.com/companies/companies_t/TVS_Motor/20080215_electric_scooter.html accessed on 22 April 2008; Baggonkar, S 2008, 'Two-wheeler makers target women to up sales', (online) available from http://www.business-standard.com/india/news/two-wheeler-makers-target-women-tosales/321682/ accessed on 22 April 2008; Hero Honda 2010, available from http://www.herohonda.com/media_archives.htm accessed on 22 April 2010; The Hindu 2010, 'M&M eyes double-digit growth in two-wheelers', dated 18 April 2010, available from http://beta.thehindu.com/business/companies/article402533.ece accessed on 23 April 2010; domaint.com, 2010.

Changing Consumer Expectations

Indian consumers place a lot of emphasis on value orientation and prefer opting for brands that provide them value for money. This characteristic makes them stand out as one of the most discerning consumers in the world. Even though consumer expectations have only just begun to evolve, it is observed that consumers still pay a lot of importance to this characteristic even though their prime focus is on the quality of the product. It is observed that consumers now seek a wider variety of products and brands and look for products that reflect the latest in style and fashion (Cygnus 2006). This allows marketers to invest in brand building and brand extensions, so that they provide a number of options to choose from. In 1998, the customer expectations were as follows (Cygnus 2006):

1. Value for money
2. Quality of products
3. The politeness of salesman
4. Exchange and return policies
5. Salesman non-interference
6. A wide variety of products and brands

In 2004 the evolved consumer expectations of the Indian consumer were as follows (Cygnus 2006):

1. Quality of products
2. Value for money
3. A wide variety of products and brands
4. Products reflecting the latest styles and fashions
5. The politeness of salesman
6. Exchange and return policies

Thus, we can see that consumer expectations are changing and they are looking for a wide variety of products and brands, which in turn is providing opportunities for companies to introduce more brands and products.

Changing Lifestyles

It has been observed that the influx of consumer brands and the increasing exposure of consumers to these brands and the world in general through the use of information technology has driven the consumer aspiration levels higher. Consumers are increasingly spending on eating out, personal care items, movies and theatre, books and music, as well as clothing (Cygnus 2006). This shows that consumers' lifestyles are changing and they tend to go out more and spend more on personal care items and clothing.

Regional Differences

'Words like 'heterogeneous' and 'plural' do not even begin to convey the extent of India's diversity and the varied dimensions or aspects of that diversity. And it is not just the twenty-three languages, the geographic and climatic diversity, the different religions living together, and the many shades of rich and poor people that exist or coexist, in this vast, continental country. India has twenty-eight states, and there are wide income and social development disparities among them' (Bijapurkar 2007). According to a study by KSA Technopak 2005, it was seen that consumers in the western part of India were the highest spenders across regions on emerging lifestyle categories like furniture, computers or laptops, mobile phones, etc., and hence provided a lot of opportunities for various brands. On the other hand, it was observed that consumers in the eastern part of India were more conservative when it came to spending. Their spending was the lowest on products like personal care, clothing and footwear, movies, and lifestyle products. Brand managers in these areas need, therefore, to focus on providing value for money to tap into this segment of price-conscious consumers.

 See the Max New York Life (MNYL) Insurance presentation to see how an understanding of the changing demographic trends helped it connect to its customers.

BRANDS AND CONSUMER DECISION-MAKING

Companies can build trust and commitment by gaining a greater understanding of customer attitudes, values, relationships, and their perceptions of value. To be and to remain successful, brand owners have to invest more time, effort, and money in trying to forecast changes in consumer behaviour and expectations (Singhal 2004). Consumer decision-making has been studied extensively and many models have been proposed regarding how consumers make purchase decisions. It has been found that consumers go through a sequential decision-making process before and after making a purchase and various researchers have proposed various models for this. These different models can be integrated under the Input-Process-Output model. The model is highlighted as under (see Figure 7.2) with special reference to branding.

Input

Inputs are all the external factors that influence a consumer's purchase decision. These can either be the marketing efforts of firms or socio-cultural influences.

Marketing efforts of firms Firms use various marketing communication tools in an attempt to inform, persuade, and remind consumers of their existence and thus influence their purchase decision. Brand name, along with product, pricing, and distribution of the products has also been found to influence the consumer's purchasing decision. And in the case of services, people, physical evidence, and processes also influence the customers. Marketers can influence customers by highlighting a problem that has always existed and then providing a solution to it. For example, Paras Pharmaceuticals Limited realized through qualitative research that itching can be normal for which no medication is sought, or persistent, due to infection and poor hygiene, for which special remedies were sought. Paras then educated consumers about 'intertrigo' or itching caused due to sweat in the folds of the skin and offered a solution— ItchGuard. The response to this brand was overwhelming, and in no time it became the star performer at Paras. 'It had addressed an issue, which was so common, so personal to everyone, yet so unspoken. And by doing this, it projected, in a very strong manner, the philosophy of Paras—of providing solutions where none existed, to make lives healthier'. Thus, the problem recognition for customers came as a response to the marketing efforts of the organization which was trying to communicate about an existing problem and the benefit that their product would bring to to potential customers.

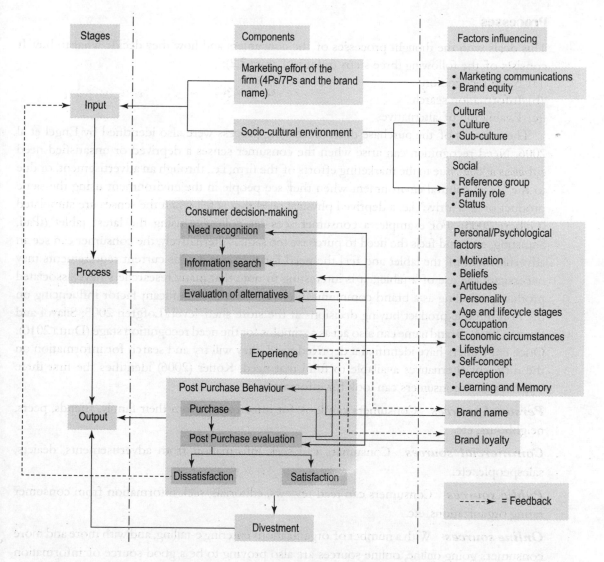

Stages | Components | Factors influencing

Input

Marketing effort of the firm (4Ps/7Ps and the brand name)

Socio-cultural environment

- Marketing communications
- Brand equity

Cultural
- Culture
- Sub-culture

Social
- Reference group
- Family role
- Status

Consumer decision-making

Process

Need recognition

Information search

Evaluation of alternatives

Personal/Psychological factors
- Motivation
- Beliefs
- Attitudes
- Personality
- Age and lifecycle stages
- Occupation
- Economic circumstances
- Lifestyle
- Self-concept
- Perception
- Learning and Memory

Experience

Post Purchase Behaviour

Purchase

Output

Post Purchase evaluation

Brand name

Brand loyalty

Dissatisfaction | Satisfaction

- - - - - ➤ = Feedback

Divestment

Source: Based on Schiffman and Kanuk 2004, *Consumer Behaviour*, Delhi, 8th edition, Pearson Education, pg 565; Blackwell Miniard and Engel 2006, *Consumer Behaviour*, 10th edition, Thompson South-Western, Haryana, India, pp. 85; Dutta, Kirti 2010, 'Effect of Branding on Purchase Behaviour of Urban Indian Women', a Ph D thesis submitted to M.G. Kashi Vidyapeeth, Varanasi.

Figure 7.2 Model of consumer decision-making

Socio-cultural environment Socio-cultural factors can also act as cues and influence customer's attitude towards a brand. It consists of the cultural and social environment. The cultural environment is further made up of the sub-categories culture and sub-culture, and the social environment includes references to groups, family roles, and to status. These form the 'invisible hand', which guides the activities of individuals and thus impacts the what, why, and how of an individual purchases (Schiffman and Kanuk 2004). These have been discussed in detail in the section on factors influencing consumer behaviour.

Processes

This deals with the thought processes of the consumers and how they decide what to buy. It consists of the following three steps (refer to Figure 7.2):
 (a) Need recognition
 (b) Information search
 (c) Evaluation of alternatives

These stages of the purchase decision-making process were also identified by Engel et al 2006. Need recognition can arise when the consumer senses a deprived or unsatisfied need either as a 'cue', due to the marketing efforts of the firm, i.e., through an advertisement, or due to the social-cultural environment when they see people in the environment using the same product or as a 'drive', i.e. a deprived physical need that is felt when the senses are stimulated (Gilbert 2003). For example, a consumer sees his colleague using the latest tablet (iPad, Samsung, etc.) and feels the need to purchase the same. Alternatively, the consumer can see an advertisement of the tablet and feel the need for the same, or his current requirements may necessitate the use of a tablet. It is interesting to note that many researchers have associated product packaging as a brand communication vehicle and a significant factor influencing on the non-durable product buying decisions at the store shelf level (Lofgren 2005; Silayoi and Speece 2004). Brand name can also act as a stimulus for the need recognition stage (Dutta 2010). Once consumers have identified a deprived need, they will try and search for information on the different alternatives available to fulfil that need. Kotler (2006) identifies the first three ways in which consumers can look for information:

Personal sources   Consumers can look for information from their family, friends, peers, neighbours, etc.

Commercial sources   Consumers can seek information from advertisements, dealers, salespeople, etc.

Public sources   Consumers can read reviews, editorials, seek information from consumer rating organizations, etc.

Online sources   With a number of organizations entering e-tailing, and with more and more consumers going online, online sources are also proving to be a good source of information for consumers interested in comparing different brands before purchasing one.

Past experience   This situation arises when the customer has already satisfied a similar need in the past and on the basis of the previous experience, positive or negative, may want to satisfy the need from a same or a different source. Past experience is an important and dominant aspect while making a purchase decision (Dutta 2010).

Consumers may use informational cues to develop beliefs about brands and task responses, i.e., choice or evaluation, may be a direct function of these mediating beliefs (Olson 1978). Brand image affects consumers' information search and evaluation of alternatives. If the brand image is found to be congruent with the consumer's actual, ideal, social, ideal-social, and situational-ideal-social image, then the brand is bound to be purchased (Ataman and Ulengin 2003). Once the consumers have collected information about different alternatives to satisfy their need, they have a list of the different brands they can purchase. The consumers then evaluate these alternatives to identify the brand they are ultimately going to purchase. This evaluation can be based on a number of parameters, such as product attributes or features of the product, pricing, brand name, after sales services, etc. Brand name serves as a 'shorthand' for quality by providing consumers with a bundle of information about the product, which facilitates information processing, speeds decisions (Chernatony and Riley 1998), and impacts the information search and evaluation of alternatives stage (Dutta 2010). The consumer decision-making process is also affected by a number of personal and psychological factors as discussed in detail in the section on factors influencing consumer behaviour.

 See MNYL ads to know how they are providing information cues to parents.

Family members also influence the purchase decision, and Howard and Sheth proposed the model for family buying behaviour. Their model highlighted the fact that purchase is influenced by the other members of the family and the predisposition of the father, mother, or other members of the family impacts the family buying behaviour (Gilbert 2003). For further discussion on this aspect, see the section on the role of family in factors influencing consumer behaviour.

The time-span involved at the processes stage varies according to the type of goods being purchased, i.e., convenience, shopping, or speciality product with the time involved increasing from convenience (like fast moving consumer goods—toothpaste, detergents etc.) to speciality goods (like luxury clothes, TV, etc.). The experience that individuals gain from this process has a bearing on them when they purchase the product again or recommend it to family and friends. This is also affected by the post-purchase evaluation by the consumer and if the post-purchase evaluation is satisfactory, it will positively reinforce consumers the next time they make a similar purchase decision. Also, this step is influenced by the kind of product being purchased.

Output

Output is related to the action the consumer is going to take based on the input and the process. It consists of the purchase decision and the post-purchase evaluation.

Purchase decision Based on the process, consumers will decide what course of action to take. They can defer the idea of purchasing if they feel that the offer is going to get better or a better brand is going to be launched in the near future, or club it with a festive or auspicious occasion, etc. Marketing actions by the marketers, such as special discounts, buy-one-get-one-free or bogof offers, etc., can also influence the purchase decision and motivate customers to purchase goods immediately. If the customers are purchasing something for the first time, especially if it is a shopping commodity (like furniture, clothing, etc.), they may purchase in smaller quantities; this purchase is called a trial purchase. But, if they have purchased the brand before and based on a favourable experience they have decided to purchase it again, it is called a repeat purchase. Based on a number of favourable repeat purchases, consumers can become long-term committed purchasers or loyal customers. Thus, when a retail outlet opens for the first time, customers will go and purchase from it to see the quality of the products, services offered, the ambience, etc. And if the customers are satisfied after this trial purchase, then they go back for repeat purchases. It is important to note that consumers need not necessarily go through these steps, i.e., a customer can make a purchase without going through a trial purchase, if they feel that the brand quality is good and the retailer is located conveniently. Brand trust is a logical influence on the evaluation and usage of brands. If consumers trust the brand they are more likely to adopt and purchase brand extensions from the firm (Reast 2005). Thus, investment in consumer brand 'relationships' delivers a future pay-off in the ability to leverage the brand name in new categories. From this, we can logically conclude that brand name and trust can affect purchase decisions in the same category and in the extension categories as well.

Post-purchase evaluation   The purchase of a brand is followed by its consumption. During the consumption stage, the customer evaluates the brands against the perception and expectations formed during the pre-purchase stage. Feuss (2003) studied the effect of brand image on customers' post-purchase perceptions of overall quality. He found that brand image plays the role of an assimilator agent, which 'pulls' post-purchase performance evaluation in the direction of the expectations embodied in the brand image. If the product performance matches the perception and expectations of the customers, it leads to neutral feelings. If the experience exceeds customer expectations, the customers are satisfied and this satisfaction impacts the evaluation of the alternatives when customers make a similar purchase the next time. It also leads customers to refer the brand(s) to family and friends. However, if the brand performance falls below expectations, it creates dissatisfaction among consumers and acts as an input and causes customers to launch into an external search again to look for other brands that can satisfy their needs and wants. Also, if the price of the brand purchased is high and the resulting purchase causes dissatisfaction to the customers, the organization should immediately undertake recovery strategies. (For further information, see the chapter on recovery strategies in *Services Marketing Operations and Management* by Jauhari and Dutta.)

Consumers in their post-purchase evaluation try to reduce their anxiety regarding their decision to purchase a particular product. This is called as cognitive dissonance. Consumers can reduce their cognitive dissonance by:
 (a) seeking advertisements that support their choice and avoid those of competitive brands
 (b) confirming their own choice by influencing family and friends to purchase the same brand
 (c) seeking reassurance from other satisfied owners

It can be concluded that the brand name does impact the post-purchase evaluation of customers (Dutta 2010). The post-purchase evaluation (neutral, satisfied, or dissatisfied) acts as an experience for customers and impacts the input process of customers during their next purchase. This experience also impacts brand image, and positive evaluations help build brand equity, whereas negative evaluations lead to deductions from brand equity. If the evaluations are positive, they will lead to favourable perceptions of the brand and ultimately to brand loyalty (for a detailed discussion on brand loyalty see Chapter 3). A consumer who is brand loyal will look for that brand and purchase it exclusively on every transaction (Cataluna,

Garcia, and Phau 2006). For brand loyal customers, the purchase process does not exist and they look to purchase that brand only irrespective of the marketing strategies of competitors. The experience with the brand is the major motivating factor for brand loyal behaviour and marketers need to influence these experiences by attributing the brand with desirable and quality features so that it consistently delivers as per the customers' expectations.

Divestment

The final stage in the consumer purchase process is divestment or how customers ultimately dispose the brand. Consumers can do this by recycling, or selling the brand. With consumers becoming more conscious about environmental issues, the divestment stage should be given due consideration by the marketers. They can provide options for recycling and/or remarketing the brand. The Internet is a medium affecting this step, as a number of sites are available where customers can log on and offer their brands for auction or sale; the most popular site being e-bay.

VARIOUS FACTORS AFFECTING CONSUMER BEHAVIOUR

The purchase decision-making process is influenced by a number of factors. In the Indian context the factors influencing the purchase behaviour are as follows.

Socio-cultural environment   The socio-cultural factors are less tangible but imperative for marketers, as they affect the customer's evaluation and adoption or rejection of the brand. To build iconic brands, marketers need to gain 'cultural knowledge', which includes culture, sub-culture, social changes, class, and gender, rather than the 'knowledge about individual consumers' (Holt 2004). A cultural environment is made up of the following.

Culture

In the context of consumer behaviour, culture is defined as, 'the sum total of learned beliefs, values, and customs which serve to regulate the consumer behaviour of members of a particular society' (Schiffman and Kanuk 2004), where beliefs and values guide consumer behaviour and are the ways in which customers/consumers behave and it is what is considered usual and acceptable.

Managerial implications   It is important for marketers to understand the culture and coordinate their marketing accordingly, since culture is imbibed from a very early age and takes long periods of time to be changed. For example, when Kellogg's launched their breakfast cereal in India, they had to face the fact that it would be very difficult to change the eating habits of consumers. In India, people have *paranthas* and other local foods for breakfast. Health conscious consumers were on the rise, but then they wanted to eat the cornflakes in warm milk and not cold (as in western countries). Thus, Kellogg's had to make changes in its product offering accordingly. Also, to cater to their taste buds, Kellogg's launched Crispix Banana, Crispix Chocos, Froot Loops, Cocoa Frosties, etc., in the year 2000 (Mukund 2002).

Sub-culture

In the cultural profile of a society we can identify members who tend to possess certain beliefs, values, and customs, which set them apart from other members of the same society and this group is referred to as the sub-culture.

Managerial implications Sub-cultural analysis helps marketers identify profitable segments of sub-cultures within the cultural segment and target them with their marketing policies (Schiffman and Kanuk 2004). For example, in India there are different sub-cultures existing as per the geographical distribution. We can see different cultures across north, south, east, and west India and people differ in their food consumption, dressing habits, etc. So in north India wheat forms a part of the staple diet, but south Indians prefer rice.

Social Class

Consumers, whether individuals or families, in a society, can be segmented on the basis of wealth, status, lifestyle, education, economic status, reference group, and family role; such a segmented group is called a social class (Schiffman and Kanuk 2004; Blackwell et al. 2006).

Managerial implications Practitioners should realize that consumers in a particular social class are bound to show similar consumerism habits, as the purchasing power of consumers within a social class is similar. The social environment is made up of the reference group, family role, and status. A reference group comprises the group of people who have an impact on an individual's consumption behaviour. Consumer behaviour is also influenced by family roles. As discussed in the section on the changing demographic trends, the role of women in the family is changing, as they are no longer confined to only being home-makers.

Motivation

Motivation drives individuals to follow a specific course of action. Unfulfilled needs drive individuals to behave in a manner that they hope will fulfil their aroused need, and thereby reduce the tension caused by the unfulfilled need. Motivational theories help marketers understand the thinking process of consumers, as the thinking process along with the previous learning influences the specific course of action consumers take to fulfil their need. According to Maslow's hierarchy of needs, individuals satisfy their needs as follows:

Physiological needs This includes the most basic level of needs like food, clothing, water, shelter, etc. These needs are the first level of needs individuals satisfy.

Safety needs These needs are satisfied after physiological needs and examples include savings accounts, insurance policies, etc.

Social needs Need for belonging, love, and affection are the main highlights of this need. Advertisers of fast moving consumer goods generally highlight this need in their advertisements to motivate consumers to purchase their products.

Esteem needs This need includes prestige, position, and self-respect. Advertisements of premium goods, clothing, and accessories are generally targeted towards this need.

Self-actualization needs This includes the need for self-fulfilment. This varies from individual to individual. As individuals, people might feel that need to satisfy their creative instinct and want to paint, write; a spiritual person might want to learn more from the holy texts, etc.

Courtesy: Superbrands.

Image 7.2 Bank of Baroda ad—Be online not in line; also see Plate 6

Courtesy: Superbrands.

Image 7.3 Bank of Baroda ad—Bill payment on line; also see Plate 6

Managerial implications Marketers can position their products based on this understanding of the consumer's motivation to purchase products. Motivation can also help marketers identify the segment that will be most interested in their product, thereby serving as a segmentation tool (Schiffman and Kanuk 2004). Thus, Bank of Baroda tries to motivate customers by highlighting their different needs related to Internet and mobile banking like bill payments, money transfers, not standing in a line, etc. (see Images 7.2 and 7.3).

Beliefs

These reflect the understanding and opinion of consumers about something, a product, brand, retail outlet, etc. Marketers can position themselves as the most trusted organization, but if the consumer tends to differ, the advertisements will not be effective.

Managerial implications Marketers need to align themselves with the beliefs of the customers. Customers should feel that the brand that is being offered is the best in the category for them. For example, Everest spices draws its unique selling proposition from the belief that most Indians have—that their mother is the best cook, and are always nostalgic about their mothers' cooking. Taking this cue Everest positioned its brand as, 'Taste mein best, Mummy aur Everest', (Best in taste, Mummy and Everest), which means to say that Everest helps create food just like mother (see Image 7.4).

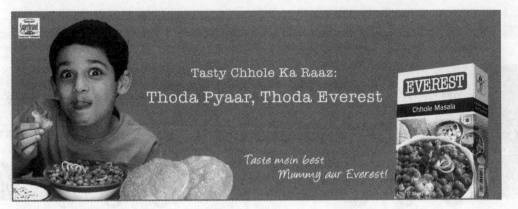

Courtesy: Superbrands.

Image 7.4   Mom's cooking and Everest spices; also see Plate 7

Attitude

Attitude is the way a consumer behaves towards something, such as a product or a brand. It is a viewpoint that can either be favourable or unfavourable, is learned and consistent. Consumers' attitudes will determine whether they will respond favourably or not towards a particular advertisement, strategy, and hence towards purchasing the product. Marketers can overcome attitudinal issues by being innovative.

Managerial implications   As attitude is learned, managers need to focus on how they can help consumers learn about their brand in a fun-loving manner. This helps in developing a positive attitude towards the brand. For example, when Knorr launched its soupy noodles, it was positioned as a quick hunger filling snack. Given that kids do not find soup exciting, the noodles were added to make it attractive. Also, to overcome children's initial hesitation to try something new, Kajol was roped in to make the experience fun. The 'Thoda Khao, Thoda Piyo' television commercial helped on two fronts—it helped the children understand how to consume the brand and at the same time made it fun (Chamikutty 2010).

 See how MNYL is leveraging on the attitude of parents towards their children.

Personality

Personality is the inner quality, character, persona, and mannerisms that determine an individual's response to their environment. The personality determines the manner in which a customer is going to respond to particular brands, product features, pricing, and promotion. Hence, it can be taken as an important segmentation variable (Schiffman and Kanuk 2004).

Managerial implications   Brand managers try to build a perception of their brand that is in line with the consumer's perception of their own existing personality or the personality they want to portray to their friends. Consumers, whose favourite celebrity is endorsing a brand, would like to consume the brand to show that they have a personality closely resembling their chosen celebrity. Thus, we have a number of brands that are being endorsed by celebrities, such as Amitabh Bachchan, Shah Rukh Khan, Priyanka Chopra, etc.

Age and Life-Cycle Stages

The age and the family life cycle stage is another important variable influencing the purchase decision-making of an individual. Consumers show different preferences for products according to the stages in their life cycles and their age. Thus, while a teenager may be interested in the latest electronic gadgets, music, and fashion trends, a middle-aged man with a family may be interested in household items, products for his children, etc. Also, the life cycle stage has a special significance in the Indian context, as it has been observed that all family members influence the purchase decision.

Managerial implications Consumers are interested in brands that fulfil their requirements as per their age and the life cycle stage they are in. Managers, therefore, need to build brand communications around the specific product category need that their brand satisfies and both the point of parity and point of differentiation need that to be highlighted. A study by Nielsen highlights the fact that 20 per cent men in Delhi, Mumbai, and Bangalore from the SEC (Socio-Economic Classification) A and B households use anti-ageing products. Since currently all the anti-ageing products are marketed for women, the men are forced to use these same products. This leaves scope for anti-ageing products targeted at men who are more than 35 years old. This is in line with the fairness creams market for men not so long ago (see Exhibit 7.1). 'Nivea India is in the process of rolling out a premium anti-ageing men's product' (Bhushan 2010).

 See how MNYL is focusing on life cycle stage of parents with young children.

Occupation and Economic Circumstances

Occupation influences purchase decisions, as a high-level occupation means a higher income, which gives consumers a higher paying capacity; these customers, therefore, tend to shop in high-end retail outlets and malls such as the Emporio Mall in Delhi, which house the most expensive brands. Consumers in the middle income bracket would be more interested in value for money and can be found shopping in outlets such as Big Bazaar, Subhiksha, etc.

Managerial implications Organizations can design their brands around the type of occupation and economic circumstances of their customers. For example, Tata, through its Taj Hotels, Resorts, and Palaces, focuses on the luxury and premium segment of customers. For the value segment, it has a chain of budget hotels under the brand name of 'Ginger'.

Lifestyle

Lifestyle includes the activities and behaviour of people. Different consumers choose different products based on their lifestyle. Thus, people who are health conscious will opt to go to gyms and will be more interested in health and fitness products; they will look for organic and healthy food.

Managerial implications Brand managers can build a brand preference by highlighting how the use of their brand can help consumers keep pace with their chosen lifestyle. Thus, for consumers who have an active lifestyle, Bank of Baroda launched its International Debit Card (see Image 7.5).

Self-concept and Perception

How individuals perceive themselves also determines how they are going to decide about what, how, and where they purchase. Thus, people who feel that they are social would like to visit malls, restaurants, etc., with family and friends, unlike a loner who would like to order over the phone or the web. Perception is related to how an individual distinguishes sensory inputs into a logical image.

Managerial implications The manner in which an individual perceives the marketing inputs decides the image of the company in relation to its competitors and is an important variable for deciding whether the individual is going to purchase the product or not. For example, Idea Cellular is promoting the e-bill facility to curb the

Courtesy: Superbrands.

Image 7.5 Bank of Baroda International Debit Card; also see Plate 7

use of paper. People who are conscious about preserving natural resources might opt for this brand. For youngsters with a self-concept of being independent, Bank of Baroda launched its education loan for higher studies (see Image 7.6).

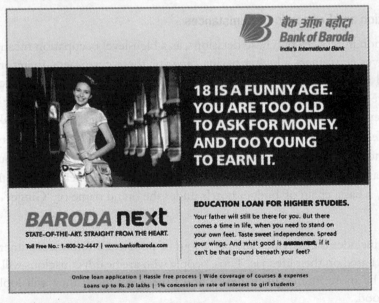

Courtesy: Superbrands.

Image 7.6 Bank of Baroda Education Loan; also see Plate 7

Learning and Memory

Learning is the manner in which individuals acquire knowledge about different products and if the learning is positive and the experience with the product good, then their memory retains the experience and affects the future manner in which the individual is going to respond towards purchasing the product. For example, ITC (Indian Tobacco Company) launched Fiama Di Wills soaps and shampoos. Consumers who have had a favourable experience with ITC brands will want to try out their new products also.

Managerial implications Brand managers, by increasing the frequency of communications with the customers, can help in committing the brand to the memory of the consumers. They need to focus on each 'moment of truth' or each interaction of the consumer with the brand. All the interactions add to the learning the consumers have about the brand. All positive learning and reinforcements lead to a strong and favourable memory about the brand.

Role of the Family

The importance of the family in the decision-making process cannot be ignored in the Indian context. A study by KSA Technopak 2005 shows that it is the family that decides on household purchases like home textiles, home appliances, electronics, movies, eating out, cars, and two-wheelers. Children are also found to influence these purchases. As is expected, men have a higher say than women in big purchases like cars, appliances, electronics, etc., and women have a bigger say in purchases such as food and grocery, home textiles, etc. The role of children in household purchases is more evident when they are 16 years or above, especially in the purchase of expensive or big ticket products such as a new car, TV, mobile phone, etc. Children in the age group of 8–15, termed as tweens, impact purchase decisions of movies and eating out the most. Children start demanding brands since the time they start going to school and the tween brand loyalty lasts through to adulthood. The family buying patterns are found to influence brand loyalty of kids in adulthood and they feel that they should also purchase the same brand that was purchased by their parents (Cincotta 2006).

Managerial implications The preferences built in childhood stay with consumers throughout their lives. These preferences are bound to influence brand loyal behaviour. Managers, therefore, need to focus on their consumers from an early age. Their advertisements can focus on the entire family and show the mother, father, child, and grandparents consuming the brand. A number of brands follow this policy, for example, Dhara refined oil has the tagline, 'My Daddy Strongest' and uses the family to showcase the brand.

 See how MNYL is highlighting the role of the family (parents in this case).

BRAND LOYALTY AND BRAND COMMITMENT

To build brand loyalty, marketers need to build brand awareness, so that the brand is imprinted in the minds of the consumers. The more the consumers see the brand, hear about it, or think about it, the higher the probability of the brand being registered in their memories. The next step is to build a brand image as per the brand identity. If the consumers' brand image satisfies their expectations of the brand, they feel more comfortable while purchasing the brand. This increased familiarity with the brand and the favourable signals sent by the brand at the time of consumption enhances the comfort the consumers have with the brand, as they believe that the brand will meet their expectations. This ultimately leads to the formation of brand credibility, which adds to brand equity. Brand loyalty is defined as consumers' commitment towards a particular brand, so much so that they are constantly looking out for marketing activities associated with the brand and are motivated to obtain the brand exclusively on every purchase (Cataluna et al. 2006).

In Figure 7.2, the ultimate output of brand consumption is to create brand loyalty. Companies benefit from brand loyalty as it:

(a) lowers vulnerability to competitors' marketing strategies (Keller 2004)
(b) increases marketing communication effectiveness and reduces marketing costs (Keller 2004; Rundle-Thiele and Bennet 2001)
(c) allows companies to charge higher margins (Keller 2004)
(d) increases the probability of success in brand extension and licensing opportunities (Keller 2004)
(e) means that customers are less price-sensitive (Krishnamurthy and Raj 1991), therefore they do not readily shift over with a change in prices by competitor brands
(f) can induce loyal customers to buy more of the brand than they normally would when it is promoted, while non-loyal customers are likely to purchase the promoted brand only in small quantities (Cataluna et al. 2006)
(g) has more influence on purchase decisions than price promotions (Cataluna et al. 2006).

Research shows that a 1 per cent increase in customer loyalty equals to a 10 per cent cost reduction, and a 5 per cent increase in customer loyalty increases the profitability of the company by 40–95 per cent (Kim, Morris, and Swait 2008). Also, the cost of attracting a new customer is five times more than the cost of retaining an existing customer (Reichheld and Sasser 1990). The five levels of brand loyalty have been discussed in Chapter 1. Let us now look at the factors affecting brand loyalty (see Figure 7.3):

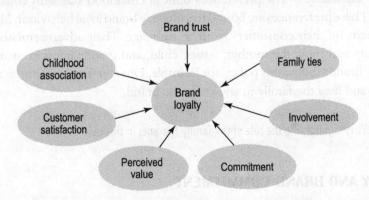

Source: Derived from Cincotta 2006; Punniyamoorthy and Raj 2007.

Figure 7.3   Factors affecting brand loyalty

Family ties   Family ties influence brand loyalty and kids choose the brands that their parents always chose (Cincotta 2006).

Childhood association   Brand alliances formed in childhood influence brand loyalty, therefore marketers should form a brand communication strategy targeted at the young population (Cincotta 2006).

Brand trust   Brand trust is the trust that consumers have in a brand to reliably fulfil their expectations (Andaleeb 1992). High trust leads to a positive and favourable attitude.

Customer satisfaction   An increase in customer satisfaction with the brand experience increases brand loyalty (Bloemer and Kasper 1995). Customer satisfaction, apart from impacting repurchase intention, also impacts word of mouth and word of mouse and so cannot be ignored (Westbrook and Oliver 1991).

Involvement   Involvement with the product impacts brand loyalty. Involvement includes commitment from consumers in the form of thoughts, feelings, and behavioural response. It is the motivation, interest of the customer towards the brand that leads to brand loyalty (Park 1996).

Perceived value   The customer's assessment of the utility of the brand is based on the benefits received and the monetary and non-monetary cost for acquiring the same (Dodds, Monroe, and Garewal 1991). The following dimensions describe perceived value (cited in Punniyamoorthy and Raj 2007).

Functional value   The brand utility that is derived from the quality of the product and the level of performance that leads to functional value. Thus, the functional value of a mobile phone can be that the battery lasts long, the product is user-friendly, etc.

Emotional value   The emotional value or feelings derived from the consumption of the brand affect brand loyalty. So, an emotional bonding or the warm feeling on using a Nokia mobile phone might influence the consumer to purchase the same brand the next time.

Price-worthiness   A reduction of the perceived cost adds to the value of the brand. Thus, when a trusted brand like Nokia reduces the price of its E-series, it might influence consumers to readily purchase the brand, as now the brand is more worthy to purchase at the reduced price.

Social value   The utility obtained from the brand's ability to increase the social self-concept is known as social value. Thus, using a Nokia mobile phone would elevate one's status among peers and anyone who sees the consumer using the brand.

Brand commitment   Consumers' commitment links them to the marketing organization, and it is 'the act of maintaining a relationship with a commercial partner' (Gordon 2003). If a customer is committed towards a brand, it can be safely presumed that the customer is brand loyal, will frequently purchase the brand, and has a favourable attitude towards the brand. Commitment can be built by building brand communities online or by forming clubs. For example, Exhibit 7.7 tells us that Hero Honda formed the Lady Rider Club to build consumer commitment towards the brand.

Thus, to build long-term customer loyalty and derive advantages of the same, marketers need to build their marketing strategies focused around the above parameters.

SUMMARY

Consumers are the focal point of all the marketing activities. Marketers need to know how the consumers behave, so as to target them with such strategy, which is bound to have the maximum influence. The perception of the consumers towards the brand is important as consumers evaluate the brand both in term of the functional (utilitarian) and the symbolic (expressive) aspects. The changing demographic trends and lifestyles of consumers is important as is the rising household income, consciousness towards brands, spending habits and behaviours, etc., all of which influence consumption and purchase behaviour.

Consumer behaviour is very complex and is influenced by a number of factors. An understanding of these factors act in-depth as a guiding force for the marketers and helps them in better influencing the consumers' behaviour. Since the Indian consumer market forms a lucrative portion of the global consumer force, marketers need to understand that this is a segment from which they can target profitably, provided they develop an understanding of the behaviour of the consumers.

The way in which a brand impacts this consumer purchase behaviour is of paramount importance in branding strategy success and has been studied through the input, process and output purchase stages of consumer buying.

The chapter concludes with a discussion on brand loyalty and the factors that influence brand loyalty in consumers for example brand trust, family ties, involvement, commitment, childhood associations, etc. Marketers need to be aware of these factors so that they can successfully retain customers and convert them into loyal customers for increasing the profitability of the firm.

KEY TERMS

Attitude   It is the way a consumer behaves towards a product, brand, etc.

Beliefs   These are the understandings and opinions of consumers about a product, brand, retail outlet, etc.

Commercial sources   This includes advertisements, dealers, salespeople, etc.

Consumer behaviour   It is the behaviour that consumers display in searching for, purchasing, using, evaluating, and disposing of products and services that they expect will satisfy their needs.

Cultural environment   The cultural environment is made up of culture and sub-culture, as well as social class, which in turn includes reference groups, family roles, and status.

Culture   This is the sum total of learned beliefs, values, and customs, which serve to regulate consumer behaviour of the members of a particular society.

Input   These are all the external factors that influence a consumer's purchase decision, including the marketing efforts of the firms or the socio-cultural influences.

Objective reality   Objective reality is whatever remains true whether you believe it or not.

Online sources   This includes all the sources available on the Internet.

Output   This is related to the action the consumer is going to take based on the input and the process stages.

Personal sources   This includes family, friends, peers, neighbours, etc. as a source of information.

Personality   It is the inner quality, character, persona, and mannerisms that determine an individual's response to their environment.

Phenomenological studies   Phenomenological studies relate to the study of a phenomenon, i.e., it studies the meaning of appearances rather than reality.

Process   This deals with the thought processes of the consumers and how they decide what to buy.

Public sources   This includes reviews, editorials, seeking information from consumer rating organizations, etc.

Social class Consumers (individuals and/or families) in a society can be segmented on the basis of wealth, status, lifestyle, education, economic status, reference group, and family roles.

Sub-culture This includes members who tend to possess beliefs, values, and customs that set them apart from other members of the same society.

Word of mouse When consumers communicate over the Internet through e-mails, chat rooms, social networking sites, etc., about their experiences with the brand, it is called word-of-mouse. This is not company initiated and the company cannot influence this directly except by providing a good experience with the brand.

EXERCISES

Concept Review Questions

1. What is consumer purchase behaviour? Why do we need to study it with reference to branding?
2. How does branding impact the behaviour of consumers?
3. Delineate any three factors influencing the process stage of the purchase decision-making process. Which according to you is the most important factor for branding strategy and why?
4. Discuss any three factors that influence the consumer purchase decision-making process.
5. What is brand loyalty? What are the factors impacting consumers' brand loyalty?

Critical Thinking Questions

1. Critically evaluate the statement, 'Branding impacts all purchase process stages.'
2. Comment on the statement, 'Brand loyalty only impacts the profitability of the firm and there are no benefits for the consumers.'
3. Does 'brand gap' exist? With the help of an example, discuss the existence or absence of a 'brand gap'.

Internet Exercises

1. Visit the Internet site of a retailer selling in the UK market and another in the Indian market. What similarities or differences can you draw in the context of consumer behaviour?
2. Visit the Internet site of a bank operating in any foreign country and the site of the same bank in the Indian market. How is the branding strategy same or different keeping in mind the varying consumer behaviour in the two countries?
3. You are the manufacturer of garments and wish to export your product to a developed country. Visit the government site of that country. What information can you draw regarding the consumer behaviour in these countries and how will this help you in your brand formulation strategy?

CD Exercise

View Max New York Life Pension Plan ad and discuss how they have made retirement 'aspirational'.

REFERENCES

Andaleeb, S.S. (1992), 'The trust concept—Research issues for channels of distribution', *Research in Marketing*, Vol. 11, pp. 1–34.

Ataman, Berk, and Burc Ulengin (2003), 'A note on the effect of brand image on sales', *Journal of Product and Brand Management*, Vol. 12, no. 4, pp. 237–250.

Baggonkar, S. (2008), 'Two-wheeler makers target women to up sales', http://www.business-standard.com/india/news/ two-wheeler-makers-target-women-tosales/321682/, accessed on 22 April 2010.

Bhushan, R., 'Angry young men....always—men in Delhi, Mumbai, Bangalore using anti-ageing products marketed for women', *The Economic Times*, New Delhi, 9 August 2010, p. 4.

Bijapurkar, Rama (2007), 'We are like that only', Penguin Portfolio, New Delhi.

Blackwell, R.D., P.W. Miniard, and J.F. Engel (2006), *Consumer Behaviour*, 10th Edition, Thompson South-Western, India, Chapter 3.

Blomer, J.M.M. and H.D.P. Kasper (1995), 'The complex relationship between consumer satisfaction and brand loyalty', *Journal of Economic Psychology*, Vol. 16, Issue no. 2, pp. 311–329.

Cataluna, F.J.R.; A.N. Garcia, and I. Phau (2006), 'The influence of price and brand loyalty on store brands versus national brands', *International Review of Retail and Distribution and Consumer Research*, Vol. 16, Issue 4, pp. 433–452.

Chamikutty, P., 'Storm in a bowl', *Brand Equity, The Economic Times*, 23 June 2010, p. 2.

Chauhan, C., 'Now, Mercedes to sell used cars in India', *Economic Times*, New Delhi, 29 June 2010, p. 4.

Cherantony, Leslie de, and Francesca Dall'Olmo Riley (1998), 'Defining a 'Brand'—Beyond the literature with experts' interpretations', *Journal of Marketing Management*, Vol. 14, pp. 417–443.

Cincotta, K. (2006), 'Family ties define brand loyalty', *B & T Weekly*, 10 November issue, pp. 18.

Coupland, Jennifer Chang (2005), 'Invisible brands—An ethnography of households and the brands in their kitchen pantries', *Journal of Consumer Research*; Gainesville; Vol. 32, Issue 1, pp. 106–118.

Cygnus Business consulting and research (2006), *Industry insight—Indian retail industry*, Cygnus Business Consulting and Research, Hyderabad, pp. 11.

Davies, Andrea, and Richard Elliott (2006), 'The evolution of the empowered consumer', *European Journal of Marketing*, Vol. 40, Issue 9/10, pp. 1106–1121.

Dodds, W.B., KB Monroe, and D. Grewal (1991), 'Effects of price brand and store information on buyers' product evaluations', *Journal of Marketing Research*, Vol. 28, Issue 3, pp. 307–319.

Doyle, P. (1993), 'Building successful brands—the strategic options', *Journal of Consumer Marketing*, Vol. 7, Issue no. 2, pp. 5–20.

Dutta, Kirti (2010), 'Effect of Branding on purchase behaviour of urban Indian women', a Ph D thesis submitted to M.G. Kashi Vidyapeeth, Varanasi.

Elliott, John (2007), 'India's retail revolution', http://money.cnn.com/magazines/fortune/fortune_archive/2007/07/09/100122335/index.htm, accessed on 4 April 2010.

Feuss (2003), 'The post-purchase impact of brand image', a PhD thesis submitted to the Faculty of the Stevens Institute of Technology, Castle Point on Hudson, Hoboken.

Fournier, Susan (1998), 'Consumers and their brands—developing relationship theory in consumer research' *Journal of Consumer Research*, Vol. 24, Issue no. 4, pp. 343–373.

Ghosh, R.N. and K.C. Roy (1997), 'The changing status of women in India—Impact of urbanization and development', *International Journal of Social Economics*, Vol. 24, Issue 7/8/9, pp. 902–917.

Gordon, F. (2003), 'When does commitment lead to loyalty', *Journal of Service Research*, Vol. 5, Issue 4, pp. 333–344.

Grant, I.J. and G.R. Stephen (2006), 'Communicating culture—an examination of the buying behaviour of 'tweenage' girls and the key societal communicating factors influencing the buying process of fashion clothing', *Journal of Targeting, Measurement and Analysis for Marketing*, Vol. 14, Issue 2, pp. 101–114.

Gupta, N.S., 'Focus on clever niches to drive TVS' two-wheeler biz', *Economic Times*, New Delhi, 16 April 2010, p. 4.

Holt, D. (2004), *How Brands become Icons—The principle of cultural branding*, Harvard Business School Press, Cambridge, MA.

http://www.mckinsey.com/mgi/reports/pdfs/india_consumer_market/MGI_india_consumer_full_report.pdf, accessed on 29 March 2010.

Jacob, S. (2010), 'In all fairness, men going for facelift—HUL, Garnier, Nivea, Emami vie for pie of men's grooming market', *Economic Times*, New Delhi, 12 November 2010, p. 4.

Jacoby, J.R. and Jerry C. Olson (1985), *Perceived quality*, Lexington Books, Lexington, MA, cited in Zeithaml, 1988.

Jones, John Philip (1999), *How to use advertising to build strong brands*, Sage Publications, New Delhi.

Kaushik, Neha (2006), 'Ungeared for growth', *Business Line, The Hindu*, http://www.thehindubusinessline.com/catalyst/2006/02/09/stories /2006020900030100.htm, accessed on 22 April 2010.

Keller, K.L. (2004), *Strategic Brand Management—Building, Measuring and Managing Brand Equity*, Prentice-Hall of India Private Limited, New Delhi.

Kim, J., J.D. Morris, and J. Swait (2008), 'Antecedents of true brand loyalty', *Journal of Advertising*, Vol. 37, Issue 2, pp. 99–117.

Koshy, A. (2010), 'When brand turns burden', *Economic Times*, New Delhi, dated 16 April 2010, p. 4.

Kozinets, Robert V. (1999), 'E-tribalized marketing? The strategic implications of virtual communities of consumption', *European Management Journal*, Vol. 17, Issue 3, pp. 252–265.

Krishnamurthi, L. and S.P. Raj (1991), 'An empirical analysis of the relationship between brand loyalty and consumer price elasticity', *Marketing Science*, Vol. 10, Issue 2, pp. 172–183.

KSA Technopak (2005), *Consumer Outlook 2005—Changing Paradigms*, KSA Technopak, Gurgaon.

Lawer, C. and S. Knox (2006), 'Customer advocacy and brand development', *Journal of Product and Brand Management*, Vol. 15, Issue 2, pp. 121–129.

Levine, M. (2003), *A Branded World*, John Wiley, New Jersey.

Lofgren, Martin (2005), 'Winning at the first and second moments of truth—an exploratory study', *Managing Service Quality*, Vol. 15, Issue 1, pp. 102–115.

McGregor, J. (2009), 'Consumer spending in a recession', http://www.businessweek.com/careers/managemen-tiq/archives/2009/04/consumer_spendi.html, accessed on 16 April 2010.

McKinsey (2007), 'The Bird of Gold—The rise of India's Consumer Market'.

Modi, Ajay (2007), 'Retail', http://www.business-standard.com/general/storypage_test.php?&autono, accessed on 15 April 2010.

Mukund, A. (2002), 'Kellogg's Indian Experience', *Marketing Management*, Vol. 1, Dutta, S. and Mukund, A. (eds.), ICFAI Press, Hyderabad, pp. 48–55.

Muniz, A.M. Jr. and T.C. O'Guinn (2001), 'Brand Community', *Journal of Consumer Research*, Vol. 27, Issue 4, pp. 412–432.

Olson, Jerry C. (1978), 'Inferential Belief-formation in the cue utilization process', *Advances in Consumer Research*, Vol. 5, Issue 1, pp. 706–13.

Park, S.H. (1996), 'Relationships between involvement and attitudinal loyalty constructs in adult fitness programs', *Journal of Leisure Research*, Vol. 28, Issue 4, pp. 233–250.

Pinckney, W.S., 'Reaching out to users far and wide', *The Economic Times*, New Delhi, 29 December 2009, p. 4.

Pinto, V.S., 'Detergent war—Ghari gains at Nirma's expense', *Business Standard*, New Delhi, 13 September 2010, p. 4.

Poston, Toby (2006), 'Countdown to India's retail revolution', http://news.bbc.co.uk/1/hi/business/4662642.stm, accessed on 15 April 2010.

Punniyamoorthy, M. and M.P.M. Raj (2007), 'An empirical model for brand loyalty measurement', *Journal of Targeting, Measurement and Analysis for Marketing*, Vol. 15, Issue 4, pp. 222–233.

Rai, N. and Pallavi Bisaria (2007), 'Small retailers fight a losing battle against the giants', http://www.business-standard.com/common/storypage_c.php, accessed on 5 October 2009.

Reast, Jon D. (2005), 'Brand trust and brand extension acceptance—the relationship', *Journal of Product and Brand Management*, Vol. 14, Issue 1, pp. 4–13.

Reichheld, F. and W.E. Jr. Sasser (1990), 'Zero defections—quality comes to services', *Harvard Business Review*, Vol. 68, Issue no. 5, pp. 105–111.

Ries, Al and Laura Ries (1999), 'World-class brands', *Executive Excellence*, Vol. 16, Issue 3, p. 11.

Rio, A.B. del; Rodolfo Vazquez and Victor Iglesias (2001), 'The role of the brand name in obtaining differential advantage', *Journal of Product and Brand Management*, Vol. 10, Issue 7, pp. 452–465.

Rundle-Thiele, S. and R. Bennet (2001), 'A brand for all seasons? A discussion of brand loyalty approaches and their applicability for different markets', *Journal of Product and Brand Management*, Vol. 10, Issue 1, pp. 25–37.

Schiffman, L.G. and L.L. Kanuk (2004), *Consumer Behaviour*, 8th edition, Pearson Education, New Delhi, pp. 8-9.

Silayoi, P. and M. Speece (2006), 'Packaging and purchase decisions—An exploratory study on the impact of involvement level and time pressure', *British Food Journal*, Vol. 106, Issue 8/9, pp. 607–627.

Simoes, Claudia, and Sally Dibb (2001), 'Rethinking the brand concept—new brand orientation', *Corporate communications—An International Journal*, Vol. 6, Issue 4, pp. 217–224.

Singhal, Arvind (2004), 'Creating and preserving brand', *Strategic Brand Management*, Vol. 3, Issue 5, pp. 18–21.

Superbrands (2009), Superbrands—An insight into India's strongest consumer brands, Volume III, Superbrands India Private Limited, Gurgaon.

Talwar, S.L. (2007), 'Malls are here, India is shopping', *Retailer*, June-July issue, pp. 108–127.

The Hindu, 'M&M eyes double-digit growth in two-wheelers', http://beta.thehindu.com/business/companies/article402533.ece, accessed on 23 April 2010.

Westbrook, R.A. and R.P. Oliver (1991), 'The dimensionality of consumption emotion patterns and consumer satisfaction', *Journal of Consumer Research*, Vol. 18, Issue 1, pp. 84–91.

Zeithaml, V.A. (1988), 'Consumer perceptions of price quality and value—A means-end model and synthesis of evidence', *Journal of Marketing*, Vol. 52, Issue 3, pp. 2–22.

Web resources

http://www.domain-b.com/companies/companies_t/TVS_Motor/20080215_electric_scooter.html, accessed on 22 April 2010.

http://www.paraspharma.com/content.php?SecID=2&CatID=12&SubCatID=13, accessed on 19 April 2010.

http://www.herohonda.com/media_archives.htm, accessed on 22 April 2010.

CASE STUDY 1

Consumer Behaviour towards Cold Drinks Brands

The McKinsey 2007 report forecasts that the aggregate consumption of cold drinks in India will grow to 34 trillion by 2015 and to 70 trillion by 2025. This soaring consumption will vault India into the premier league among the world's consumer markets. The consumer market in India which stood in the twelfth position in 2007 will be almost as large as Italy's market by 2015 and by 2025, India's market will be the fifth largest in the world. This vast pool of consumers is bound to attract business leaders, as they scan for opportunities over the coming decade. To cash in on this lucrative position and to be successful, knowledge of consumer behaviour is going to play an extremely critical role.

To back this prediction, the Indian fast moving consumer goods (FMCG) sector has shown growth even during the period of economic slowdown following the sub-prime crisis. (refer to Table 7.1 for breakup of FMCG industry) This sector is estimated at ₹120,000 crore or US$25 billion and is growing at a compound annual growth rate (CAGR) of 12 per cent and is expected to reach ₹206,000 crore or US$43 billion by 2013, and ₹355,000 crore or US$74 billion by 2018.

Table 7.1 FMCG industry breakup

Category	Share (%)
Food and beverages	53
Personal care	20
Tobacco	15
Household care	10
Lighting	2

Source: FICCI Technopak 2009, FMCG Sector: The Road Ahead, FICCI Technopak.

It is observed that unlike other consumption categories that are dominated by urban growth, personal non-durables will see a strong growth in both the rural and urban areas. The total urban market will grow tenfold, to almost 1000 billion Indian rupees by 2025. The rural consumption will also grow significantly, adding 700 billion rupees of spending over the next twenty years. It is felt that with rising incomes and increasing exposure, rural consumers will shift from traditional solutions to higher-value packaged goods, giving a boost to the rural market growth (*Business World* 2008).

Soft drinks

The soft drinks market size in India stands at ₹8500 crore. As the mercury soars, the cold drinks market also heats up. All the major players come out with a number of strategies, be it advertising, promotion, channel management, or launching new variants. PepsiCo has come out with its new 'Youngistaan ka WOW!', Coca-Cola has launched Minute Maid Nimbu Fresh and Burn, a premium energy drink, and has a number of variants like Minute Maid mixed fruit, Minute Maid apple, etc. (Singh, Zachariah, and Mukherjee 2010). With so many established brands in the market, an unaided brand recall across the family life cycle stages helps in identifying the brand that is most remembered by consumers.

The study

Over the years, the Indian woman has evolved from being a homemaker into a working woman, stepping outside the home. The literacy rate among women is also increasing. Women are having a greater say in decision-making at home as well. This segment of Indian women is an increasingly important segment for markets to cater to. The purchase behaviour of the urban woman in India can be categorized according to the family life cycle stages. A study was conducted to see if the purchase behaviour of women varied according to the family life cycle stages across the six life cycle stages like: teenagers or college students, life cycle (LC) stage 1; young women, unmarried, working, or non-working, LC stage 2; young married women, without children, LC stage 3; married women with young children, up to 13 years of age, LC stage 4; married women with grown-up children, above 13 years of age, LC stage 5; married women, empty nest, LC stage 6. Urban women from Delhi and the National Capital Region were asked to list the top three cold drink brands that came to their mind. The weighted average was then calculated for each brand and summed for all the respondents in each life cycle stage. The results are highlighted in Tables 7.2 and 7.3 and Figure 7.4.

Table 7.2   Brand preferences—Cold drinks

Brands	LC1	LC2	LC3	LC4	LC5	LC6	Aggregate
7 Up	0.98	1.98	2.15	1.81	1.32	1.49	9.73
Mirinda	1.81	2.3	0.16	1.65	1.81	1.31	9.04
Fanta	2.31	4.27	3.31	1.64	8.11	2.15	21.79
Limca	4.61	6.42	5.27	5.91	4.59	5.27	32.07
Dew	2.48	4.14	1.3	2.8	3.28	0.81	14.81
Sprite	2.79	6.08	3.44	4.29	8.06	1.63	26.29
Thums Up	1.96	4.47	3.12	4.1	3.95	4.46	22.06
Pepsi	14.77	11.77	14.59	14.24	9.95	14.24	79.56
Maaza	1.49	2.14	2.29	2.48	2.13	0.99	11.52
Coca-Cola	13.72	8.57	13.07	14.08	12.26	12.25	73.95

Table 7.3   Anova—Single factor—Cold drinks

Groups	Count	Sum	Average	Variance
7 Up	6	9.73	1.621667	0.192617
Mirinda	6	9.04	1.506667	0.537227
Fanta	6	21.79	3.631667	5.695057
Limca	6	32.07	5.345	0.51927
Dew	6	14.81	2.468333	1.535697
Sprite	6	26.29	4.381667	5.482937
Thums Up	6	22.06	3.676667	0.950747
Pepsi	6	79.56	13.26	3.8292
Maaza	6	11.52	1.92	0.31856
Coca-Cola	6	73.95	12.325	3.93819

Source of variation	SS	df	MS	F	P-value	F-crit
Between groups	993.1111	9	110.3457	47.97742	1.58516E-21	2.073349
Within groups	114.9975	50	2.29995			
Total	1108.109	59				

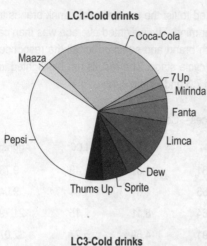

LC1-Cold drinks

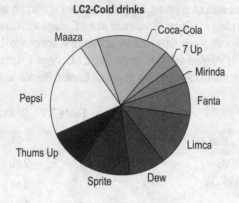

LC2-Cold drinks

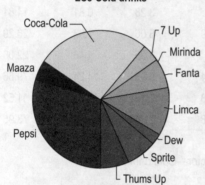

LC3-Cold drinks

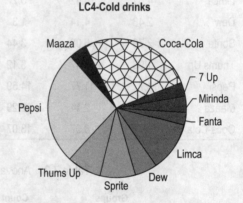

LC4-Cold drinks

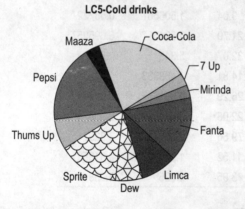

LC5-Cold drinks

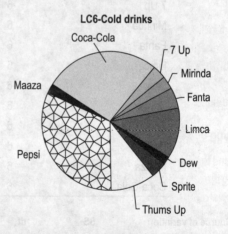

LC6-Cold drinks

Figure 7.4 Brand preferences across life cycles—Cold drinks

Conclusion

With so many brands vying for consumer attention, an understanding of the consumer behaviour towards a soft drinks brand is interesting and enlightening. The results have been depicted and some interesting observations can be made across the life cycle stages.

Discussion Questions

1. How is India becoming an attractive destination for international brand marketers?
2. Do you agree with the observation that consumer preference shifts across the life cycle stages in the same product category? Why or why not?
3. What inferences can you draw from the results depicted in the case study?
4. What strategies can you recommend to the cold drink marketers in the light of the above discussion?

Case References

Business World 2008, *The Marketing Whitebook*, *Business World*, New Delhi, pp. 229.

McKinsey 2007, 'The Bird of Gold—The rise of India's Consumer Market', http://www.mckinsey.com/mgi/reports/pdfs/india_consumer_market/MGI_india_con-sumer_full_report.pdf, accessed on 29 March 2010.

Singh, Namrata, Reeba Zachariah, and Rupali Mukherjee, 'Summer Sale—Cos step up the heat', *Times of India*, New Delhi, 29 March 2010, p. 21.

CASE STUDY 2

Housing Finance and Brand LIC

Introduction

Housing is a basic necessity and an aspiration for many of the one billion plus people of India. 'A burgeoning middle class with a high percentage of working age population, rapid urbanization and migration to cities and the breakup of joint families and the subsequent emergence of nuclear families are strong growth drivers for the housing finance market. Tax breaks on interest and principal repayment on housing loans' give a further impetus to this sector. The demand-supply gap is an estimated 24 million dwelling units.

Changing consumer trends

The home loan market has been an important barometer in gauging the upward mobility of the middle-class customers. The upward mobility has added to the purchasing power. The last decade has witnessed a demographic change in the borrowers also. Yesteryears borrowers were in the late-40s and now the borrowers are in their mid-30s.

Indian home loan market

The housing finance companies (HFCs) constitute the Indian home loan market. They are 'overseen by the National Housing Bank and commercial banks regulated by the Reserve Bank of India.' The huge demand-supply gap has attracted a number of players. The industry has clocked a spectacular compounded annual growth rate of 30 per cent in the period between 2003–04 and 2007–08. The housing loan market is one of the most competitive in the country. There are a large number of pan-India-and local players.

LIC Housing Finance Limited

LIC Housing Finance Limited (LICHFL) had been able to maintain a strong foothold in the market for over twenty years. It is a giant in the home loan segment and has seen a 100 per cent increase in approvals of loans for the first five months of the fiscal year 2009–2010. The average size of the loan has also grown from ₹12 lakh to ₹13 lakh. The annual disbursement for the financial year 2009–10 is estimated at ₹130,000 crore or US$27.10 billion, as against the previous year's ₹117,000 crore or US$24.40 billion. LICHFL offers a range of housing loan schemes. These include loans to individuals for purchasing new houses, repairs, and renovations. To professionals, they provide loans for self-owned office premises. Employees

Courtesy: Superbrands.

Image 7.7 LIC Housing Finance ad; also see Plate 8

of reputed corporate houses can get special schemes. For senior citizens a reverse mortgage is also possible. Apart from individual consumers, reputed builders and developers can also avail loans for residential projects and 'against securitization of rental receivables.'

Communicating with the customers

To reach the customers, LICHFL employed a multimedia campaign. TV, radio, print, online, mobile (see Image 7.7), and outdoor media were used besides organizing events. LICHFL sponsored 'Blockbuster Budhwar' programme

has been running on 'FM Radio Mirchi for the past three years.' It also has tie-ups with premier property exhibitions.

Brand value

'Transparency, trust, and credibility—these qualities are synonymous with the LICHFL brand. The organization believes in putting the interests of its customers above all—a belief that is accepted and shared by more than a million satisfied customers.' The same has been claimed in its ad also (see Image 7.8).

Ghar aapne banaya.
Hum ne sirf saath diya.

You made up your mind, to have your own address.
Our wide range of products only complemented it.

Property sections, estate agents and builders,
you looked through every little detail.
Our indepth legal and technical appraisal just added assurance.

Small sacrifices to big decisions, you made them all.
Our simple and fast processes just supported them.

You put everything you had on the line.
*Our zero hidden cost with no fine print is the
least you could expect.*

Aapko salaam

LIC HOUSING FINANCE LTD.

Courtesy: Superbrands.

Image 7.8   LIC ad 'zero hidden cost'; also see Plate 8

Conclusion

LICHFL is a formidable and well-entrenched player in the home loan market. It has understood the customers and its advertisements target young achievers who are the current home loan borrowers. It has also tried to attract them through innovative schemes from 'hire-purchase and re-financing to mortgage and loans against property.'

Discussion Questions

1. Discuss the home loan market scenario in India.
2. Describe the consumer behaviour of the home loan customers.
3. Apply the consumer purchase process model and discuss the stages the customers can probably go through while 'purchasing' a home loan.

Case References

Superbrands 2009, Superbrands—An insight into India's strongest consumer brands Volume III, Superbrands India Private Limited, Gurgaon, pp. 126–127.

Brand Positioning

8

LEARNING OBJECTIVES

After reading this chapter, you will be able to understand the following:

- The concept of brand positioning
- Brand values
- Brand positioning statement
- Crafting the positioning strategy
- Guiding principles for positioning
- Repositioning

ABOUT THE CHAPTER

Increased global competition and stagnant market conditions have added to the woes of organizations and driven home the need to build strong brands (Low and Lamb 2000). To be strong, brands must be perceived to have a distinct and favourable identity by the customers. A favourable perception of the brand by the target market is found to be strongly associated with brand choices and market shares and in turn with profitability (Achenbaum 1972; Buzzell and Gale 1987 cited in Ghosh and Chakraborty 2004). Marketers, thus, need to understand how to build a favourable perception of the brand among the consumers who constitute the target market and constantly strive to make the brand relevant for them over a period of time.

INTRODUCTION

Branding is all about building a strong brand that is remembered for all the good reasons both by the customers and consumers. However, customer perception is a variable that organizations can only hope to influence. Organizations can communicate all the good things about a brand, but how consumers will perceive the brand will depend upon a number of variables including the customers' own experience with the brand. The unique place the brand occupies in the minds of the customers is called positioning. A brand cannot be successful if it is not well positioned in the minds of the consumers. Positioning a product is therefore integral to the success of a brand. Brand perceptions impact business-customer relationships in the long term (Fournier 1998) and are therefore of strategic importance (Morris 1999). The positioning model that is based on consumer perception is an invaluable tool for portraying visually the competitive marketplace and also for its diagnostic capability (Desarbo et al. 2002). For successful brand positioning, companies need to primarily influence the perception of the consumers, and an organization can use various brand elements to achieve this objective (see Exhibit 8.1).

Exhibit 8.1   Positioning Starbucks

The Starbucks story began in 1971 with a single store in Seattle as 'a roaster and retailer of whole bean and ground coffee, tea and spices.' The brand was named after the 'first mate in Herman Melville's 'Moby Dick'. It evoked the romance of the high seas and the seafaring tradition of the early coffee traders. The logo was also inspired by the sea—featuring a twin-tailed siren from Greek mythology' and Starbucks Coffee was inscribed around the siren (see Images 8.1 and 8.2). Over the years the logo underwent some changes and the Siren was given 'small and meaningful updates'. However, Starbucks Coffee was always a part of the logo.

As Starbucks celebrates its 40th anniversary, the brand has evolved further. It wants to utilize the potential of its presence in over 16,000 neighbourhoods across 50 countries to the fullest. Starbucks will continue to retail coffee, but at the same time it wants to widen its portfolio to include other products as well. Keeping this in mind it has retained the siren in the logo, but has removed Starbucks Coffee from it (see Images 8.3 to 8.5).

This new brand identity will give Starbucks 'freedom and flexibility to explore innovations and new channels of distribution that will keep us in step with current customers and build strong connections with new customers.'

Source: http://www.starbucks.com/blog/looking-forward-to-starbucks-next-chapter.

Image 8.1   Starbucks logo in 1971

Image 8.2   Logo in 1987

Contd

Exhibit 8.1 *contd*

1992-Present

Source: http://www.starbucks.com/blog/
looking-forward-to-starbucks-next-chapter

Image 8.3 The logo from 1992 till the end of
December 2010

1992   2011

Source: http://www.starbucks.com/blog/looking-forward-to-
starbucks-next-chapter

Image 8.4 The new logo launched in 2011

1971

We start by selling coffee beans in
Seattle's Pike Place Market.

1987

We add handcrafted espresso
beverages to the menu.

1992

We become a publicly
traded company.

2011

We mark 40 years and begin
the next chapter in our history.

Source: http://assets.starbucks.com/assets/5a106e41fe954581999566a4293ced89.jpg.

Image 8.5 The logos over the years

CONCEPT OF BRAND POSITIONING

The success or failure of a product depends upon the customers. How the customers perceive the product and what they feel about the product is therefore crucial to the success of the organization. Brand positioning implies that a brand is positioned in the minds of the customers and it is not internal to an organization. Organizations can, through their various marketing communications, try and build as well as guide customers towards a particular positioning. It is, therefore, important to understand the concept of positioning. For example, Godrej launched its Ezee brand for 'special clothes and delicate garments like woollens, silks, baby clothes, wool blends, premium cottons, lingerie, etc. The biggest worries of consumers washing clothes with powder and bar detergents were shrinkage and colour fading. Ezee addresses both these worries through its unique pH neutral formulation.' The tagline, 'Garam kapde rahein naye jaise' (keeps woollen clothes new) and communicating to consumers about 'Chaali di Chaati' (saying that woollens shrink from a chest size of 40 to 36 after using the normal detergent, but with Ezee the size remains 40) also drove home the positioning for warm clothes (see Images 8.6 and 8.7) (Godrej 2011; *Superbrands,* 2009).

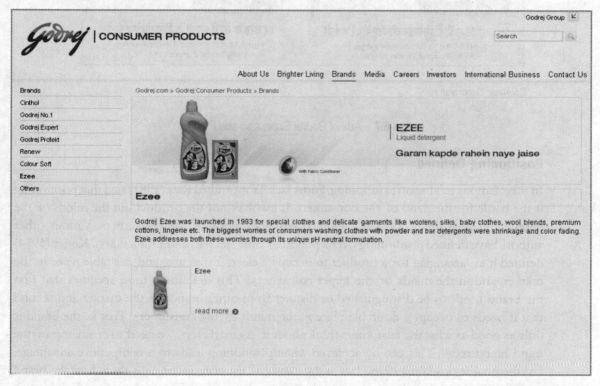

Source: http://www.godrej.com/godrej/GodrejConsumerProducts/our-brands.aspx?id=5&menuid=195&catid=330&subcatid=0&subsubcatid=0&productid=0.

Image 8.6 Positioning Ezee

Courtesy: Superbrands.

Image 8.7   Ads of Godrej Ezee; also see Plate 9

Positioning Defined

In their famous treatise on positioning, gurus Jack Trout and Al Ries (1981) said that positioning is the battle for the mind of the consumers. It involves not the product but the minds of the people and how the product is ingrained into the minds of the consumers. Various other authors have defined positioning over a period of time (Jauhari and Dutta 2009). Kotler (1984) defined it as 'arranging for a product to occupy a clear, distinctive, and desirable place in the market, and in the minds of the target consumers.' This definition, thus, specifies that first the brand needs to be distinguished or distinct from other brands in the market and second that it needs to occupy a desirable place in the minds of the consumers. That is, the brand is only as good as what the customers think about it. As marketers, we need to create top of the mind brand recall. This can be achieved when positioning leads to a competitive advantage, i.e., the unique position a brand has in the minds of the consumers, tells them how the brand is different from the other competing brands in the market. For example, see Exhibit 8.2. It takes a look at malt-based health drinks and the major players' positioning plank. The resulting market share has also been given.

Brand positioning, thus, gives an edge to the brand in a global village cluttered with a number of regional, national, and international brands in different product categories. Services

Plate 1

Tupperware's high level of association with style (Chapter 1, p. 4)

The best in business.
Served by the best in the business.

Kingfisher ad (Chapter 1, p. 18)

Castrol ad (Chapter 2, p. 42)

Plate 2

Juhi Chawla endorsing
Catch (Chapter 2, p. 49)

Ranbir Kapoor endorsing
Panasonic
(Chapter 2, p. 49)

Plate 3

Lux and Katrina Kaif
(Chapter 2, p. 60)

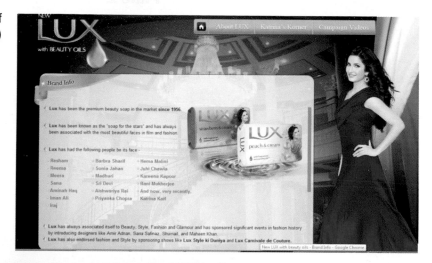

Lux promotion
(Chapter 2, p. 61)

Apollo Hospitals
(Chapter 3, p. 65)

Plate 4

Taj Mahal Palace, opposite
the Gateway of India
(Chapter 3, p. 78)

The Kingfisher experience
(Chapter 3, p. 85)

Kingfisher 'Fly five star' (Chapter 3, p. 83)

Plate 5

The Aditya Birla Group
Transcending business

A US$ 30 billion corporation, the Aditya Birla Group is in the League of Fortune 500. It is anchored by an extraordinary force of 131,000 employees, belonging to 42 nationalities. The Group operates in 28 countries. Over 60 per cent of its revenues flow from its overseas operations.

Beyond Business -
The Aditya Birla Group is:

- Working in 3,000 villages. Reaching out to 7 million people annually through the Aditya Birla Centre for Community Initiatives and Rural Development, spearheaded by Mrs. Rajashree Birla.

- Focusing on: Health Care, Education. Sustainable Livelihood, Women Empowerment Projects, Infrastructure and espousing social causes.

Highlights 2010

- Over a million patients treated at 3,000 Medical Camps and its 18 hospitals. More than 800 children learnt to smile again as they underwent cleft lip surgery. We helped immunise 6 million children against polio.

- At our 42 Schools across India we provide quality education to 45,000 children. Of these 18,000 students receive free education. Merit Scholarships are given to an additional 8,000 children from the interiors.

- Our Vocational Training Centres and the Aditya Birla Rural Technology Park accord training in sustainable livelihood projects to 27,000 people.

- Our 4,000 Self-Help Groups have led to the empowerment of 38,000 women.

- Working closely with Habitat for Humanity, we have so far built more than 350 houses as part of our community outreach programme, besides supporting the building of an additional 1,550 houses.

- We are also engaged in creating model villages in rural India. We have chosen 300 villages for this transformation - whereby in a five year time frame the villages would be self-reliant in every aspect, moving out of the "below the poverty line" status. So far more than 80 villages in India's hinterland have already reached the level of model villages.

- To embed CSR as a way of life in organizations, we have set up the FICCI - Aditya Birla CSR Centre for Excellence, in Delhi.

- In line with our commitment to sustainable development, we have partnered the Columbia University in establishing the Columbia Global Centre's Earth Institute in Mumbai.

  Transcending the conventional barriers of business because we believe it is our duty.

ADITYA BIRLA GROUP

www.adityabirla.com

Aditya Birla Group ad (Chapter 4, p. 115)

Plate 6

Archies cards (Chapter 7, p. 184)

Bank of Baroda ad—Be online not in line
(Chapter 7, p. 195)

Bank of Baroda ad—Bill payment on line
(Chapter 7, p. 195)

Plate 7

Mom's cooking and Everest spices ad (Chapter 7, p. 196)

Bank of Baroda International Debit Card ad
(Chapter 7, p. 198)

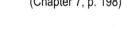

Bank of Baroda Education Loan ad
(Chapter 7, p. 198)

Plate 8

LIC Housing Finance ad
(Chapter 7, p. 210)

LIC ad 'zero hidden cost'
(Chapter 7, p. 211)

Exhibit 8.2 Positioning for Malt-based Health Drinks

Malted food drinks (MFD) account for ₹2,400 crore of the ₹3,000 crore health drinks segment in India. The white malted food drinks dominate the malted food drinks category and account for 70 per cent of the malted food drinks category. Southern and eastern markets, which are milk-scarce, drive the category growth, where it acts as a milk substitute. The brown drinks account for 30 per cent of the market. The MFD market has been growing at a modest 6–8 per cent, as the products are priced high (₹138/500gm). For this reason, MFD lack mass appeal. Another reason for their slow growth is the competition from the new products launched on the health platform. Table 8.1 takes a look at the major players and their positioning strategies.

Table 8.1 Positioning strategies of major players

Company	Brand	Positioned as	Ad campaign	Market share
GSK Consumer Healthcare India	Horlicks (1930s)	Pleasurable nourishment to increase performance and growth	'Taller, Stronger, Sharper'	GSK has a 70 per cent share in the MFD category. Horlicks has 55 per cent share and other brands' Boost, Maltova, Viva have a 15 per cent share
Cadbury India	Bournvita (1948)	To take on physical and mental challenges	Daily dose of energy for the mind and body ('din bhar ki tan aur man ki shakti)	15 per cent
Heinz India	Complan (1969)	'Complete planned food' for children and adults	'I'm a Complan boy, I'm a Complan girl' shifted to 'twice as fast' height gain since 2004	13 per cent
Amul	Nutramul (1980s)	Highest protein content	'Every Cup Builds You Up'	2 per cent
Dabur, India	Dabur Chyawan Junior (2009)	Ayurvedic malt food drink with 35 ayurvedic herbs having properties like antioxidant, energy-giving and immunity building	More growth days	

Source: Adapted from Jacob 2009 and Consumer Monopolies Report 2009.

organizations can overcome the intangibility characteristic of services by positioning the product specifically in the mind of the customers. Specific positioning of services firms will lead to an understanding by the customers as to what the brand stands for and what to expect from the brand. This is also because once organizations decide on their positioning strategies, they need to develop other marketing mixes in line with this strategy (Gupta 2005).

We can thus summarize that

1. Positioning is how the brand is unique and relevant for consumers.
2. It is how the brand is different from other brands in the product category.

3. It gives a raison d'être to customers to buy the product.
4. For service organizations, positioning also helps overcome the concept of intangibility.
5. Further, how the firm positions products also acts as a guiding hand in the development of the marketing mixes.

 Look at the various Zoozoo ads and see how various services like background music, beauty alerts, etc. have been positioned.

Brand Values

A brand has to compete at various levels in a given market. The task is to develop a distinctive image that leads to a competitive advantage for the brand (see Exhibit 8.3). The characteristics of the brand that are highlighted (by the organization while positioning) lead the consumer to develop various attributes specific to a particular brand. Over a period of time, as the brands evolve and expand across categories, the core brand values help define the five to ten most important elements of the brand and what the brand stands for. The core brand values for a brand can be mapped by asking customers for 'their top-of-mind brand associations'. These are then grouped into categories, and each category description then acts as a core brand value (Keller 2004). For example, Reliance Mutual Fund 'endeavours to be a trusted wealth creator' and it has been able to do so by becoming India's number one mutual fund (Superbrands, 2009) (see Image 8.8).

Courtesy: Superbrands.

Image 8.8   Reliance ad; also see Plate 9

Exhibit 8.3   Brand Values of Ashok Leyland

Ashok Leyland's brand promise, 'Engineering your tomorrows' delivers at two levels—the engineering/technology level and the aspirational level. At 'the technology level it promotes the values of safety, comfort, economy, and ecology. On the aspirational level, it communicates a warm and caring relationship with the "your" as singular, i.e., it is meaningful to each stakeholder in a unique way. The Leyland in the company name cues the international aspect of the brand, while Ashok underlines the custom-built relevance of the company to the Indian context. To the customer, it is a strong, sturdy reliable and caring brand. To the initiated, it is appropriate technology that makes economic sense. For all its stakeholders, however, it means a lasting relationship built on trust.' (*Superbands* 2009)

Positioning Statement

The company's positioning can be effectively described to the customers with the help of a positioning statement. A positioning statement is 'the message that communicates the brand image to consumers… it conveys to consumers how one firm's offerings are differentiated from a competitors' and signals how the firm wishes to be seen or perceived. A strong and consistent positioning statement is necessary to stand out against competitors and should help sharpen and strengthen the brand identity' (Runyan 2006). The positioning statement elucidates what a company is, what it does, and how it is different from competitors. It should be brief and more importantly defensible. If it can be copied easily and does not help in differentiating the organization from the other players in the category, then it would not give the desired positioning. The statement should be 'a short, compelling declarative sentence that states just one benefit, and addresses your target market's No. 1 problem. It must be unique, believable and important, or your target market will ignore you and your product' (Abinati, n.d.).

The template of the choice of the positioning statement was authored by Geoffrey Moore (cited in *The Beaupre Buzz* 2003), and is as follows:

For (target customers)
Who (have the following problem)
Our product is a (describe the product or solution)
That provides (cite the breakthrough capability)
Unlike (reference competition)
Our product/solution (describe the key point of competitive differentiation).

For example, consider the brand positioning statement of Nirula's, which is given in Exhibit 8.4.

Thus, we can see that Nirula's has started with 'our product is' followed by 'for'; 'that provides'; 'our product/solution' for their positioning statement.

A consistent positioning statement, which enables an organization to convey a clear image to consumers, helps in building a strong brand identity and in distinguishing the brand from competitors (Runyan 2006). Organizations can also develop single-lined positioning statements. For example, Dominoes says, 'Khushiyon ki home delivery', which means delivering happiness to your house, and Thums Up—'Taste the thunder'.

Exhibit 8.4 Positioning Brand Nirula's

The positioning statement of Nirula's is: 'Brand positioning'.

Nirula's is a warm, contemporary, accessible, eating place for families including children and young adults, serving the widest variety of Indian and International food, beverages and desserts, at affordable prices.'

The tagline for Nirula's is, 'It's desilicous' (Nirulas 2010).

See how Idea is using its positioning statement 'an idea can change your life' to position itself. See how Idea is using its positioning statement 'an idea can change your life' to position itself.

CRAFTING THE POSITIONING STRATEGY

Strategy is defined as 'the direction and scope of an organization over the long term, which achieves advantage in a changing environment through its configuration of resources and competencies with the aim of fulfilling stakeholder expectations' (Johnson, Scholes, and Whittington 2008). Positioning strategy is thus the strategy to position the services in a dynamic environment with an aim to fulfil organizational goals. To create successful brands, organizations need to choose their positioning strategy carefully. The aim of the brand is to create a positive position in the minds of consumers. The consumers should have a clear understanding as to what the brand stands for, and the brand should have the maximum recall in a particular product category. On an average, the human mind is exposed to hundreds of messages in a day, be it on TV, in newspapers, magazines, or even online. The concepts of selective attention, selective perception, and selective retention are well-documented. The idea is not to create something unique that consumers reject, but to match the emotions and feelings, knowledge, and experience of the customers so that it creates a favourable perception and makes a lasting impression on them (Ries and Trout 1981). Marketers, therefore, need to understand the consumers, their feelings, and emotions, so that they can connect favourably with them. An overview of how the positioning strategy can be chosen is given in Figure 8.1.

Segmentation

Since the core focus of the concept of marketing is the need and want of the consumer, organizations need to develop an understanding of their market first. Secondly, positioning as a concept always comes after segmentation and targeting. Thus, first organizations need to segment the market. Broadly, organizations can choose either the consumer-based variable, on the basis of geographic location, demography or psychographic factors, or the buying situation, such as a special occasion when consumers buy the product on the basis of benefits they are seeking, their loyalty, etc. Please see Chapter 5 Segmentation, Targeting and Positioning for a Services Firm in *Services Marketing Operations and Management* by Jauhari and Dutta, 2009 when the consumers buy the brand.

See the use of segmentation by Vodafone in its various Zoozoo ads.

Targeting

After segmenting the market, an evaluation of the various segments is done, and the segment structural attractiveness is studied. Factors such as the nature and number of competitors, substitute products, the bargaining power of buyers and suppliers as well as the threat of new entrants, company objectives and available resources for the market segment to be serviced are identified.

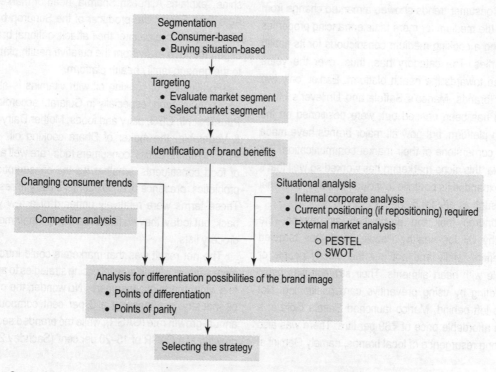

Source: Adapted from Kumar 2001; Keller 2003; Gupta 2005; Jauhari and Dutta 2009.

Figure 8.1 Crafting the positioning strategy

Identification of Brand Benefits

Marketers need to identify the benefits that the targeted consumers are looking for in a particular product category. They need to understand the factors important to the consumers. For example, if the consumers are looking for a convenience good (like washing powder, soap, etc.), price may be important to them, whereas in a shopping good, the features may be more important than the price and the consumer might be willing to spend more for better features. Thus, the various brand benefits that can be provided to the consumers in a particular category can be identified. The various brand benefits that can be highlighted for refined cooking oil are discussed in Exhibit 8.5.

See how Vodafone is highlighting its brand benefits in the Zoozoo ads.

Exhibit 8.5   The 'Health' Platform

The Indian consumers have made a gradual transition from using saturated cooking mediums such as Vanaspati to using non-saturated refined oils. They have also made a transition from loose oil to packaged oils. Consumer trends showed a marked change from using the medium for mere taste enhancing properties to using a cooking medium conspicuous for its health properties. The category has, thus, over the years worked towards the health platform. Earlier, only two major brands, Marico's Saffola and Unilever's Flora, which has been phased out, were positioned on the health platform, but now all major brands have made it the cornerstone of their market communication. For Saffola, this niche marketing has worked so well that it has expanded its portfolio to include salt and functional food such as *atta* for diabetics.

Sundrop took the proposition as generic—'the Healthy Oil for Healthy People', and thus targeted the entire family and not just the elderly people or people with heart ailments. Their strategy was mass marketing by using preventive care positioning. Not to be left behind, Marico launched Saffola Gold at a more affordable price of ₹89 per litre. There was also a strong resurgence of local brands, namely Gemini at

₹52 per litre, Gold Winner at ₹50 per litre, Dhara at ₹48 per litre, and Crystal Soya at ₹42 per litre.

'This was the time when the premium segment began to fade and the economy segment began to shine,' explains Asheesh Sharma, head of marketing, Agro Tech Foods, the producer of the Sundrop brand of refined oils. 'To counter their attack, national brands began to move away from the curative health platform to the generic family health platform.'

'Fortification of cooking oil with vitamins is also a very popular tend, especially in Gujarat,' according to Paul Thachil, CEO, dairy and foods, Mother Dairy Fruit & Vegetable, the maker of Dhara cooking oil. 'With evolving eating habits, consumers today are well aware of food constituents, whether it's the consumption of probiotics, presence of antioxidants, dietary fibres, etc. These terms were relatively unheard of a few years back, but today, they do find a mention on their monthly grocery lists.'

The net result was that marketers could introduce more variants with differential pricing strategies to appeal to a wider range of consumers. 'No wonder, the overall oil industry is witnessing a 6 per cent compounded annual growth rate (CAGR), while the branded sector is growing at a CAGR of 15–20 per cent' (Sachdev 2009).

Consumer Behaviour and Changing Consumer Trends

These variables are also studied so that brand positioning is realistic and close to what the consumers want. Many brands have achieved success by positioning themselves vis-à-vis the changing trends. A case in point is the refined cooking oils, which are focusing on the consumer trend of health consciousness. For example, Sunflower cooking oil focuses on 'Healthy Oil for Healthy People'. Keeping in mind the consumer trends, the brand benefits that can lead to successful positioning are identified.

Competitor Analysis

An organization needs to do a competitor analysis to identify the positioning bases of the competitors. This helps the organization make an informed decision. The objective is to create a unique positioning in the minds of consumers and be different from other players in the category. Exhibit 8.5 shows how various players in the cooking oil category used the same health platform, but were able to differentiate themselves in the minds of the consumers.

Situational Analysis

The identification of various brand benefits, consumer trends, and competitor analysis needs to be matched with the organization's situational analysis, which comprises the following.

Internal Corporate Analysis

The corporate needs to do a reality check as to which of the various brand benefits it can provide efficiently and effectively. An analysis of operations, marketing, finance, and human resources is done to highlight the strengths and weaknesses of the organization.

Current Positioning

This is valid if the organization plans to reposition its brand organizations, over time, feels that their positioning is no longer valid and that they need to change to make themselves more relevant, current, and exciting for the consumers. Take the case of the Bank of Baroda—one of the most prominent banks in the Indian banking industry. The logo of the bank was designed in 1908 by Maharaja Sayajirao Gaikwad III. It was blue in colour and consisted of an ear of corn, symbolizing agriculture, a cogwheel, symbolizing industry, and an upraised hand blessing the populace stating, '*Akshayyam te Bhavishyati*', i.e., Thou shall forever be prosperous. Over the years, consumer behaviour changed, liberalization led to a number of players, both private and foreign, entering the market and the bank's market share declined by almost 20 per cent. To attract new customers and to cut above the clutter, the bank decided to reposition itself. Thus, it designed the new logo of the morning sun, symbolic of change from night to day, with five rays, symbolizing the global presence of the bank. The logo was in vermilion colour to symbolize loyalty and was positioned at an angle to represent the dynamic nature of the bank (see Image 8.9).

Image 8.9   Logo of Bank of Baroda

Rahul Dravid was chosen as the brand ambassador to denote trustworthiness, as Dravid is trusted for his performance in the cricket matches he plays. The bank initiated many new schemes and emphasized ATMs, Internet banking, and credit cards to match foreign bank facilities. Eight to eight banking, i.e., from 8 a.m. to 8 p.m., was introduced in 500 branches and nine 24-hour human banking branches were also introduced, where people were available twenty-four hours. This rebranding exercise led to the bank being named one of the five strong public sector banks shortlisted for leading consolidation in the Indian banking industry (Rathore 2006; Sagar et al. 2009, Superbrands, 2009).

External Market Analysis

As organizations do not work in isolation, an analysis of the external market situation is important. To study the external market, the organization needs to study the various politico-legal, economic, social, technological, and environmental factors, PESTE in short, and the changing trends related to these in the external environment. A careful study of the PESTEL factors leads to the identification of opportunities and threats in the external market, which the organization can cash in on in the long run. An understanding of these factors and positioning according to these helps the organization stay relevant for the target audience over a longer period of time. Based on both internal analysis and external market analysis, the organization can then plot the strengths, weaknesses, opportunities, and threats, SWOT, to identify the areas they can work on in the future to tap market opportunities. Generally, organizations focus and position themselves on the basis of their strengths, keeping in mind the opportunities in the external market environment. For example, keeping in mind the economic environment of rural settings, Unilever came out with the 'Shakti' programme. As part of project 'Shakti', Unilever dovetailed its corporate social responsibility of empowering women at the bottom of the pyramid, which stands for the semi-urban and rural population, into a revenue earning model, wherein women acted as distributors of Unilever. This resulted in creating rural entrepreneurs, and while the women were able to earn their livelihood, Unilever benefited from the sales of its products (Unilever 2010).

Analysis of Differentiation Possibilities

When customers choose a brand of a particular product category, they choose brands towards which
 (a) those they have the most favourable attitude; and
 (b) those which provide them product-related benefits (James 2005).

   This signifies that the customers must develop a favourable attitude towards a brand vis-à-vis other brands in the same product category, i.e., they must feel that the brand is better than other brands. This is called the point of differentiation (POD). A second point signifies that the brand must provide product-related benefits, i.e., the brand must be able to perform the functions of that particular product category to the hilt. This is called the point of parity (POP). According to Kotler and Keller (2005), POP is of two types:
 (a) Category POP—These associations tell customers that the brand belongs to a definite product or service category. These associations tell the customers that the product performs the necessary functions of a product category. Thus, a mobile phone's primary function is to provide communication apart from the add-on features such as a camera, an MP3 player, SMS, music download, etc.
 (b) Competitive POP—These are the 'associations designed to negate the competitors' POD'. Thus, a brand that provides all the benefits that the competing brands provide and is also able to differentiate itself or has unique selling propositions, would be a brand that is in a stronger position in the eyes of the customers.

   POP tells a customer that the brand fits into a particular product category or whether it is at par with its competitors. POD, on the other hand, establishes unique associations for the brand and informs the customers how the brand is different or more favourable than the other brands. It is important to note that the POD highlighted should be distinctive and believable and should be the one that is relevant to the customers. The various PODs that can be selected are highlighted in the section on the guiding principles for positioning.

Selecting the Strategy

Out of the various POPs and PODs, the organization can then decide on specific ones to represent the brand. These POPs and PODs should be specific to an organization and should add value to the brand by building brand equity. For example, in the refrigerator category, Kelvinator used 'the coolest one' as its positioning statement. The new players could also have focused on this aspect, but they realized that the new generation of Indians were extremely health conscious and so Samsung used the 'Bio-Fresh' technology to position its refrigerator saying that it keeps food fresh longer, thus keeping it healthier (Mahim et al. 2009).

GUIDING PRINCIPLES FOR POSITIONING

To create favourable positioning and top-of-the-mind brand recall, brands should be dubbed as the best in their product category. It is always easier to recall the best brand in a product category, for example, Xerox, IBM, Coke, etc. But it is equally important that the number one brand does not explicitly say it is the best, as customers may perceive it negatively and feel that the brand is desperate (Sagar, Singh, Agarwal and Gupta 2009). The brand should do a regular environmental analysis and change in order to meet the changing needs of the people or to overcome competitors' launches (see Exhibit 8.6).

Successful brands can also try entering different segments with new brands, also called multi-branding. For example, ITC retails premium clothing under the brand, Wills Lifestyle

Exhibit 8.6   Men's Fairness Cream Market in India

Winds of change have been blowing in the men's personal grooming category. Men are now more interested in personal grooming, and there is more pressure to look good now than in the previous generation. The net result is that Indian men are now investing more money and time to enhance their looks.

"In the last few years we have seen Indians indulging in grooming, health, and wellness. The Indian market is now mature enough to accept specialized products meant for specific purposes rather than a mass general product. Now, it's for marketers to promote products, which cater to these niche requirements and the sooner someone identifies and understands the need, more lies the chances of success," said Sarang Panchal, Executive Director, Customized Research Services, The Nielsen Company, South Asia' (AC Nielsen 2007).

A study by Gillette reveals that Indian men spend 20 minutes on an average in front of the mirror, compared to the 18 minutes spent by women. Surveys show that men are using 30 per cent of the fairness creams sold in India (Bhushan 2007). To tap this segment, Emami launched 'Fair and Handsome' in 2005. Fair and Handsome was a category creator and its launch was supported by heavy promotion. The theme of the company's advertisements revolved around bringing out the fact that a large number of men used women's

Contd

Exhibit 8.8 *contd*

fairness creams. Shah Rukh Khan was roped in as the brand ambassador and the potential for men's fairness cream was put at ₹600 crore. Hindustan Lever Limited, now Hindustan Unilever Limited, which was already catering to the fairness cream market for women, however came out with Fair and Lovely Menz Active fairness cream in 2006.

and its economic range of clothing under the brand John Players (Sagar, et. al. 2009). Such brand extensions (for more discussion on this see the chapter on brand extension) provide a flanking strategy, i.e., providing a range of brands so that consumers have a number of options to choose from and do not look for competitors brands, and help the firm target the price conscious customers as well. Late entrants should shy away from a me-too strategy and should try to differentiate themselves from other players in the category. The different strategies that organizations can use to differentiate themselves (Kotler and Keller 2005; Masterson and Pickton, Hiremath 2009) are as follows.

Product

The product provides the maximum number of variables for differentiation of the brand. This differentiation can be the bases of tangible attributes and intangible attributes (Ramaswamy and Namakumari 2009). Some of the various possibilities are discussed as below.

Differentiation on the Basis of Tangible Attributes

Organizations can choose to concentrate on physical variables to position themselves. Here are the various factors that can be considered for product differentiation.

Product form   Product form such as the shape, size, or physical structure can be used to differentiate a product. For example, Doy soap targeted towards children was introduced in the shape of animals and characters such as King Leo, Fundoo Teddy, etc. (see Image 8.10).

Product ingredients   Organizations can position their offerings on the basis of the ingredients in the product. For example, Dabur has a range of brands in the toothpaste product category (see Image 8.11), differentiated on the basis of the ingredients used. Babool toothpaste is positioned to contain the benefits of the Babul tree (Arabic tree or Acacia Arabiaca), Meswak toothpaste is made with the extract of the toothbrush tree (also called Miswaak or Salvadore Presica), etc.

Product attributes   The unique attribute of the product can be highlighted to position the brand. For example, Dove uses the moisturizing attribute of the soap to position itself. DermiCool focuses on the cooling effect of the talc. Appy Fizz highlights the carbonated apple juice concept to position itself.

 See how Idea is communicating this in its ads.

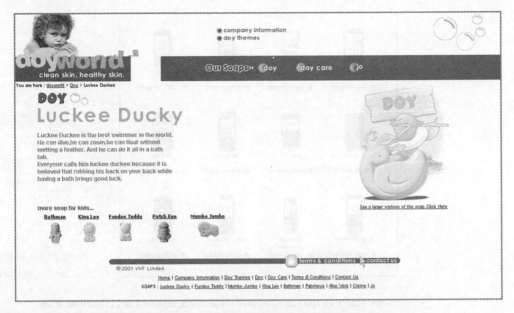

Source: http://www.doyworld.com/sitefiles/doy_luckeeducky.htm, accessed on 28 December 2009.

Image 8.10   Different shapes of soap by Doy

Source: http://www.dabur.com/Products-Health%20Care-Oral%20Care, accessed on 21 December 2009.

Image 8.11   Dabur's range of toothpastes

Product functional features   This means providing differentiation on the basis of the various functions that the product can perform. Most of the mobile companies have introduced

Source: http://www.nokia.co.in/find-products/products, accessed on 21 December 2009.

Image 8.12 Nokia products

products on the basis of a number of features such as camera, music player, Internet browser, etc. (see Image 8.12).

Product characteristics and customer benefits Product characteristics and the benefits it offers consumers can be used to create differentiation as well. For example, Bajaj Auto launched bikes in 220 cc, 125 cc, 135 cc and now 100 cc bikes with digital twin spark ignition technology (DTSi). Dabur has launched the Uveda skincare range including 2-in-1 moisturizer (with SPF 8), which helps build moisture from within and also protects the skin from damages due to the sun. Reliance Mutual Fund uses the benefits of growth potential and tax savings to the customers (*Superbrands*, 2009) (see Image 8.13).

 See how Idea is communicating this in its ads.
Also see use of product characteristics in the Zoozoo ads.

Product use The manner of use of the product can also be employed to position the product. Mamy Poko Pants diapers have used this effectively to differentiate their brand. Their diapers for babies can be worn like a pant, the waistband and leg gathers are soft and stretchable preventing red marks, and they are also easy to take off by tearing both the sides of the 'pants'.

 See how Idea is communicating this in its ads.

Product class To get an instant connect for the point of parity, organizations can also use the product class to classify themselves and then give their point of differentiation. For

Courtesy: Superbrands.

Image 8.13   Reliance Mutual Fund ad

example, Nestlé India sells skimmed dahi or yoghurt, dahi and fruit yoghurt in the country. In 2007, it launched 'NesVita' for healthy digestion (Image 8.14). Amul also launched Amul ProLife Probiotic Dahi (Image 8.15). They said the probiotic (POD) dahi (product class) contains good bacteria that help in digestion.

 Take a look at the Idea 3G ad to see the positioning of services like live TV, video calling, etc.

Source: http://www.nestle.in/images/nesvita_yoghurt_flash.jpg, accessed on 24 December 2009.

Image 8.14   Probiotic yogurt from Nestlé Nesvita

Image 8.15   Amul ProLife Probiotic Dahi ad by Amul

Differentiation on the Basis of Intangible Attributes

Intangible attributes like prestige, status, sentiments, and beliefs can be used to create brand differentiations. Raymond has used the emotional theme of, 'The Complete Man' over the years to position its brand successfully. Raymond Ltd group president and whole time director P.K. Bhandari said, 'Raymond has always played on the emotional chord in its communication. We have always aimed at creating something unique and different, yet relevant to the Raymond brand.' Reid and Taylor differentiate its men's range of suiting through its distinctive tagline, 'Bond with the best' *(Superbrands,* 2009) (see Image 8.16).

Price-Quality

This is a positioning approach based on providing quality products at low prices. For example, Big Bazaar says, 'Is se sasta aur accha kahin nahi!' (see Image 8.17), i.e., nowhere will you find stuff cheaper and better than this.

Symbols

Symbols are also used to position a brand in the market, for example, the golden arches of McDonald's and the multicoloured apple logo of Apple. Symbols can be very effective if used to reflect a desired quality in the brand. For example, there is Airtel's new symbol to position itself (see Case Study 2) and Pillsbury's Poppin' Fresh, Pillsbury Doughboy, which reinforces the unique relationship between the housewife and the Doughboy. The Doughboy is one of the top ten advertising icons in the world. He is 'over eight inches tall, wears a baker's costume and has the colour and texture of fresh dough. He also comes with expressive blue eyes and a mild swagger when he walks and is used to position the *chakki* fresh *atta* or dough fresh from the mill' *(Superbrands,* 2009) (see Image 8.18).

Image 8.16   Reid and Taylor ad

Source: http://bigbazaar.futurebazaar.com/indexBigBazaar.jsp;jsessionid=B45D623D5E0C1107EBA1BB71FCCDEE03?_requestid= 75657, accessed on 26 December 2009.

Image 8.17   Big Bazaar—Accha and Sasta

Competition

Organizations can also position their products against well-entrenched competitors in the market. This can be effective, since the image of the competitors in the marketplace can be used as a reference point. Coke and Pepsi are usually seen indulging in this type of positioning especially to counter each other's campaigns (see Exhibit 8.7).

Exhibit 8.7   Comparative Advertising for Successful Positioning

Companies have long used the plank of comparative advertising to position themselves and overcome the POD of the competitors. Earlier, tricky lines that were ambiguous enough were used to keep consumers guessing. When Coca-Cola bagged the official sponsorship of the World Cup in 1996, Pepsi came out with the campaign, 'Nothing official about it'. 'Coke responded with the 'Baaki Sab Bakwass' (all others are nonsense) campaign which mocked PepsiCo's 7-Up ads (Brahma 2009). Again, when Pepsi launched its Youngistaan campaign with the 'Saawariya' kid, Ranbir Kapoor, Deepika Padukone, and Shah Rukh Khan, it targeted the youngsters of the nation. Coke came out with the 'Jashn Mana Le' campaign starring Hrithik Roshan. Sprite, a subsidiary of Coke, came out with direct spoof of 'Yeh hai Hindustan Meri Jaan' (Management Paradise,

Contd

Exhibit 8.7 *contd*

2009). However, when Horlicks blatantly showed the Complan brand in a TV commercial and compared how Horlicks was a smarter choice, Complan raised an issue and took Horlicks to court. Complan launched a campaign, wherein it was claimed that children who drink Complan regularly grow twice as fast as the other kids since it contains '100% milk proteins and 23 vital nutrients'. According to Manish Bhatt, VP and ECD, Contract Advertising, 'Comparative advertising, when tastefully executed, can be an example of successful advertising' (cited in Anand 2008).

Personnel

People can also be used to differentiate the brand in the marketplace. The people can be both employees of the organizations and customers. These are discussed as below.

Employees

Organizations, especially the service organizations for whom employees form an integral part of the product or service, can also use their employees to differentiate themselves. For example, Singapore airlines has long used the flight attendants to differentiate themselves. The flight stewardesses are commonly referred to as Singapore girls and encapsulate Asian values of providing warm, caring, and gentle hospitality. The 'Singapore Girl' is a brand icon in itself (see Image 8.19) and in 1994 the famous Madame Tussauds Museum in London displayed it as the first commercial figure ever (Roll 2004).

Courtesy: Superbrands.

Image 8.18 Pillsbury Doughboy

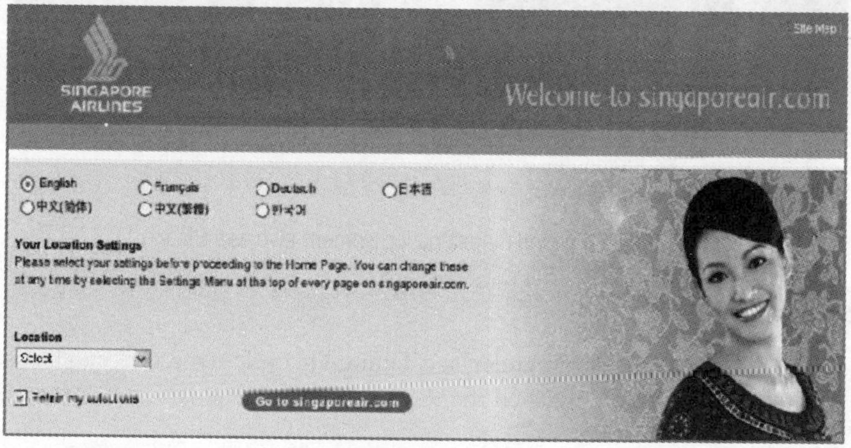

Source: http://www.singaporeair.com/saa/index.jsp.

Image 8.19 The Singapore Girl

Product user

The product user can also be used to differentiate the brand. For example, Complan was first launched by Glaxo, UK during World War II as a ration for soldiers. However, post war the brand was positioned as 'supplementary nutrition for adults in convalescence'. It was recommended by doctors and was positioned as 'a sick man's source of nutrition'. This positioning gave limited success and Glaxo had to review the positioning, because though the health drink market was growing, Complan sales were not. Finding the 'growing child' segment to be a big market, Complan repositioned itself for this market by becoming 'a complete planned food for children'. However, now Complan has positioned itself as the 'only health drink that is complete and suits varied occasions and users. Only Complan, with 23 nutrients, is complete for the body and is targeted towards the child, who is a problem eater', the young executive who is too busy to eat, the grandpa who is too ill to eat, and the young housewife who needs the extra nourishment for all the strain she undergoes (Ramaswamy and Namakumari 2009). Vodafone has come out with a fresh 'Power to You' brand positioning and Yahoo has launched an ad campaign with the tagline, 'It's You' (Ramsay 2009). Femina has always positioned itself as the complete and wholesome magazine for women (*Superbrands*, 2009) (see Image 8.20).

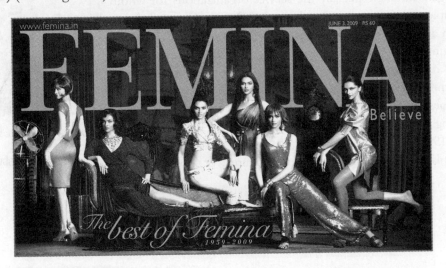

Courtesy: Superbrands.

Image 8.20   Femina magazine for women; also see Plate 10

Demographics

Demographic variables, such as gender, age, family, life cycle stage, etc., can be used to position brands. For example, Titan launched the Raga collection of wristwatches for women.

Channel

The strategy used to distribute the product can also be used to position the services. In India, Eureka Forbes was the pioneer in direct marketing for selling its vacuum cleaner and water purifier equipment and used the same to differentiate itself (*Superbrands*, 2009) (see Image 8.21).

Image

Organizations can formulate a distinct positioning by creating powerful images that strike a responsive chord with the target audience. This is generally appropriate for service organizations, where the basic product is the same and hence companies can create differentiation on the basis of their image (Kotler, Bowen, and Markens 2006). For example, most of the tourist destinations on the coast try to create differentiation by portraying the image of the beach, sand, clear water, etc., to entice the customers. SOTC, the outbound division of Kuoni Travel India private limited, uses the image of fun and its tagline, 'Expect More', which adds to the anticipation of good times (*Superbrands*, 2009). The ad promises beaches, scuba diving, shopping, etc., in the Philippines (see Image 8.22).

Courtesy: Superbrands.

Courtesy: Superbrands.

Image 8.21   Euroclean selling directly to customers; also see Plate 11

Image 8.22   Holidays by SOTC; also see Plate 11

Customer Care and Service

Customer care and service can be used for brand differentiation. Domino's Pizza has used this plank by promising the delivery of the ordered pizza within thirty minutes, failing which the pizza would be given free. This is of course subject to certain terms and conditions.

Corporate Identity

Brands that are well-entrenched in the market can also use their corporate identity as a positioning basis. Godrej has served the Indian market since 1897 and is currently one of India's most trusted brands. Despite having companies in varied sectors like real estate, FMCG, industrial engineering, appliances, furniture, security, and agri-care, it still uses the corporate name of Godrej to position itself. Reliance and Tata follow the corporate umbrella branding strategy for their products and ITC also uses its corporate brand name to endorse products like Fiama di Wills, Kitchens of India (*Superbrands*, 2009), etc. (see Image 8.23).

 See the Aditya Birla logo at the end of the Idea ad.

Courtesy: Superbrands.

Image 8.23   Kitchens of India by ITC; also see Plate 11

Positioning by Brand Endorsement

A well-known brand in the market can be used to give backing to a sub-brand. For example, when Lakme launched the cosmetic collection—Bridal Sutra—it used the brand name of Lakme to endorse it (Hiremath 2009). This concept of endorsement helps organizations leverage the new launch in the market by building on the trust and quality of the endorser.

Positioning Related to Specific Category of Customers

A company can target a niche market or a specific category of customers so as to gain their attention and earn higher profits. Vicco Vajradanti launched Vicco Vajradanti SF, i.e., sugar free—a toothpaste for diabetics who preferred a toothpaste without sugar.

Usage Occasion and Time

The usage occasion or the use of the same product for different purposes and situations can be used to position the product. For example, when we think of dry skin, Vaseline comes to mind immediately and when we think of chapped lips and winter care, Boroplus comes to mind.

Using Corporate Social Responsibility

The recent years have witnessed a renewed interest in corporate social responsibility (CSR) by the corporate world. Consumer research shows that CSR does play a role in 'consumers' brand and product evaluations over and above economic and rational considerations' (Klein and Dawar 2004; Anselmsson and Johansson 2007). Thus, CSR can also be used in marketing communication to influence consumers and favourably position the brand. Aircel is the fifth GSM service provider in India, the other four being Bharti, Vodafone, Idea, and BSNL, and is targeting a subscriber base of a hundred million by 2012. To build a strong brand differentiation, it has come out with the 'Save the Tiger' initiative and hopes to influence the young audience in India (Singh 2010). Idea Mobile Service Provider has also been using this in the form of the 'What an Idea Sirji' series. When their 'walk when you talk' ad ran into troubled waters (Advertising Standards Council of India (ASCI) had slammed the company for encouraging potentially unsafe activities), they came out with the commercial on saving trees and reducing paper use (Govindassamy 2010). Another successful example is Tata Tea's 'Jaago Re', i.e., Wake Up campaign, where Tata came out with campaigns to encourage young adults to vote and take a stand against social evils like paying bribes (Superbrands, 2009). This helped the brand achieve instant leadership (Paul 2010) (see Image 8.24).

Courtesy: Superbrands.

Image 8.24 Wakeup campaign of Tata Tea; also see Plate 12

REPOSITIONING

When a brand tries to alter the position it occupies in the mind of customers, it is termed as repositioning. There can be a number of reasons for an organization to want to change the position its brand occupies in the minds of consumers. Some of them are (Sagar et al. 2009; Ramaswamy and Namakumari 2009) as follows.

Lacking in achieving the desired position   An organization's current positioning strategy might not have achieved the desired results, thereby compelling the organization to rethink and change its positioning. For example, when Alto was launched by Maruti, it was positioned as 'the hottest car in town'. However this positioning failed to click with the target market and Alto was repositioned as a vehicle for 'young India' with the 'Let's Go' campaign.

To penetrate the market   Increased market penetration can be achieved by repositioning to increase the usage occasion or to widen the target market. An example is Milkmaid, which was launched in the 1960s for use in tea and coffee as a convenient form of milk. The 1980s saw Milkmaid sales plateau and the company repositioned Milkmaid as an ingredient for sweets and other preparations apart from use in tea and coffee. Recipes were printed on the packaging and well-planned advertising campaigns were launched.

To match consumer preferences   Consumer preferences change with time. When Margo, which has been in existence since 1920, was launched as a medicinal soap with the natural qualities of *neem,* it was well-received. However, over a period of time, Margo lost its appeal due to the onslaught of new beauty soaps and consumers' preference for the same. The recent years have seen herbal soaps and personal care products regaining their favour with the masses. Henkel Spic, which bought the brand from Calcutta Chemicals, the original owners, consequently gave the brand a facelift and it was repositioned as a regular-use soap, and the herbal fragrance was moderated to shed the medicinal image. To appeal to the 20–25 years segment of consumers, the core ingredient *neem* was retained but it was also ensured that the soap generated more lather (Shashidhar 2003).

Crafting the brand as current   Brands become obsolete and need to be upgraded to make them contemporary and relevant. The section on situation analysis discusses how Bank of Baroda had to change its positioning to overcome the outdated and boring bank image to an exciting brand with new schemes and modern-day facilities. Another example is Hamam, which was initially launched by Tomco in 1931 as a men's soap and was later repositioned as a family soap. In 1994, the product was repositioned as a 'herbal skincare soap' that could be trusted for skincare.

Change in market or market conditions   Change in the existing market conditions or entry into a new market calls for repositioning as well. For example, McDonald's tried to reposition itself as an economic brand by launching the happy price menu and the, 'Baap ke Zamaane ke Daam', or prices that were charged during the times of your father, campaign.

To overcome competition   A rethink in the positioning can be forced by increasing competition in the segment. For example, Philips has been a dominant player in the Indian electronics market for many years. The arrival of Korean players, such as Samsung and LG, however, heated up the market for Philips. To overcome the competition, Philips launched the 'Sense and Simplicity' campaign. They studied that many 'modern-day gadgets saddle consumers with more features than they can handle and functions they will never need'. Thus, Philips incorporated the 'Simplicity Litmus Test', whereby each product was designed around specific user needs, was easy to experience, i.e., was not complex and the features could be understood easily, and at the same time was technologically advanced and innovative.

If an organization manages its brand positioning well by re-positioning and staying current then the product life cycle can be extended and the company can generate profitability through continued consumer interest and preference. It has been studied that repositioning leads to a turnaround and positively impacts the performance of the company (Boyne 2004).

Repositioning Strategies

The generic repositioning strategies discuss the following ways by which organizations can attempt to reposition themselves:
  (a) Image repositioning
  (b) Product repositioning
  (c) Intangible repositioning
  (d) Tangible repositioning

Image repositioning   When the same product of an organization is launched again in the same market it is termed as repositioning. The idea is to change the image of the organization, so that it is perceived favourably by the target audience. When Maruti launched Omni, it was positioned as a Multi-Utility-Vehicle (MUV). The car had to face tough competition from Matador and Tempo and could not acquire a dominant position in the van market. Maruti then repositioned the van as 'the most spacious family car at the lowest price', which proved to be more advantageous. Another example is Dettol, which was positioned as an antiseptic liquid for cuts and bruises. It was then positioned for multiple uses like after-shave purposes, washing babies' clothes, cleaning, etc. This repositioning helped it increase its use and hence its sales.

Product repositioning   Targeting the same market with a different product is called as product repositioning. This is done to make the product more relevant and attractive to the current target market. Most of the organizations come out with product modifications and newer variants to attract customers. For example, automobile companies launching their latest models. Hyundai, for instance, launched Santro in India in 1998 and in 2003 the Santro Xing as the new improved version of the earlier car with better performance, international design, etc.

Intangible repositioning   When the same product is launched for a different target market, it is called as intangible repositioning. For example, Cadbury's Dairy Milk was earlier targeted at children. Saturation of the market made them shift the target to the youth as well with the 'Asli Swaad Zindagi Ka' or the 'Real Taste of Life' campaign. During festive seasons like Diwali, Rakhi, and Bhaidooj, it was positioned as a substitute for sweets and as the ideal gift for a brother or a sister. Currently, adults are also being targeted with the campaign 'Meetha Hai Khana Aaj Pehli Taarikh Hai', which means eat something sweet, as today is the first date of the month.

Tangible repositioning   When a new product is launched for a different target market, it is termed as tangible repositioning. For example, Lifebuoy launched Lifebuoy Plus—the old Lifebuoy with a different perfume, liquid Lifebuoy and Lifebuoy Gold—a white coloured soap with a different fragrance and even priced higher to tap the market (Ramaswamy and Namakumari 2009; Sagar et al. 2009; University of Nottingham 2009).

To be successful and relevant to consumers, brands need to occupy a favourable position in the minds of the consumers. If the positioning does not have the desired effect, organizations can attempt to reposition their brands. The end result is to ensure that the brand occupies a favourable position in the particular category it operates in. However, the environment is dynamic and brands also need to adapt themselves with the changing social, political, economic, and technological factors. This calls for repositioning exercises over a period of time. The strategy adopted for repositioning can be chosen according to the type of repositioning the organization wishes to undertake.

SUMMARY

A brand is worth what the consumers think about it, not more, not less. To build strong brands, it is therefore important for customers to develop positive perceptions about the same. This can be done by highlighting the core brand values the organization wishes to associate with the brand and build consumer perception around the same. This is known as positioning.

A positioning statement can be developed so as to inform the customers how the brand is relevant for the consumers and the unique characteristic it possesses vis-à-vis its competitors.

The positioning strategy gives a step-by-step easy to follow process by which organizations can successfully position the brand. It starts with segmentation, targeting, and the identification of brand benefits. An understanding of the changing consumer trends, situational analysis and competitor analysis identification of the different points of parity and differentiation for the differentiation possibilities have been discussed. This helps in the identification of the various ways by which the brand can be positioned to gain a distinct image from the other players in the market for example on the basis of product, price quality, intangible attributes, etc.

For brand longevity, it is imperative that it stays relevant over a period of time. Organizations can rejuvenate their brands, so that the consumers' existing positioning is changed to a new more favourable association with the brand. This can be affected by brand repositioning strategies such as image repositioning, product repositioning, tangible repositioning and intangible repositioning.

KEY TERMS

Brand value   Brand value helps define the five to ten most important elements of the brand and what the brand stands for.

Image repositioning   When companies have not changed the product but still want to change the manner in which the customers perceive them, they go for image repositioning to alter the manner in which they are perceived as an organization.

Intangible repositioning   When companies want the same product to be consumed by a different target market they go for intangible repositioning, since the physical aspects are the same.

Positioning statement This elucidates what a company is, what it does, and how it is different from its competitors, and is used to convey the brand image to the consumers.

Positioning strategy It is the strategy to position the services in a dynamic environment with an aim to fulfil organizational goals.

Positioning Arranging for a product to occupy a clear, distinctive, and desirable place in the market, and in the minds of the target consumers.

Product repositioning When companies come out with a new product in the same target market, and they want the consumers to perceive this as a new product which is more relevant and attractive they go for product repositioning.

Repositioning This is the exercise that companies adopt to change the position that they currently occupy in the minds of consumers to something new and different.

Tangible repositioning When a new product is launched for a different target market, they focus on the physical aspects of the product, this is called tangible repositioning.

EXERCISES

Concept Review Questions

1. What is positioning? Discuss with the help of examples.
2. How can organizations decide on the positioning strategy?
3. Out of the various options available to position brands, which do you think are the four most important ones and why?
4. Discuss the relevance of repositioning brands.
5. With the help of examples discuss the ways in which an organization can reposition a product in the market.

Critical Thinking Questions

1. Pick a product category that is dominated by 2–4 players. Critically discuss the brand positioning strategies for these players.
2. Choose a brand that you feel is not appropriately positioned. Delineate the reasons for the same.

What strategy can you suggest to gain favourable positioning for this brand?
3. Identify a brand that has been in the marketplace for more than two decades. Critically examine its brand history. Identify the areas of strengths and weaknesses and how you might have built the brand differently.

Internet Exercises

1. Visit the website of an organized retail organization. Can you identify the target market and the positioning strategy? How would you like to reposition the player?
2. Pick up any two hospitality firms serving the same target market. Compare and contrast their online branding strategy.

CD Exercise

View Max New York Life ads and discuss how the company has repositioned itself from 'Your Partner for Life' to 'Karo Zyada ka Irada'.

REFERENCES

Nielsen, A.C. (2007), 'Indian males no more shy away from personal grooming—Nielsen', http://in.nielsen.com/news/20070402.shtml, accessed on 16 February 2010.

Abinanti, L. (n.d.), 'Messages that matter—Positioning starts with a message strategy', http://www.messagesthatmatter.com/columns/positioning_strategy.shtml, accessed on 21 December 2009.

Anand, T (2008), 'Comparative advertising Too hot to handle', http://www.exchange4media.com/e4m/news/fullstory.asp?section_id=1&news_id=33411&tag=28367&pict=, accessed on 31 December 2009.

Anselmsson, J. and U. Johansson (2007), 'Corporate social responsibility and the positioning of grocery brands—

An exploratory study of retailer and manufacturer brands at point of purchase', *International Journal of Retail and Distribution Management*, Vol. 35, Issue 10, pp. 835–856.

Beaupre Buzz Newsletter (2003), 'Make a statement', http://newsletter.beaupre.com/e_article000209887.cfm>, accessed on 25 December 2009.

Bhushan, Ratna (2007), 'Gender neutral—Shah Rukh to pitch for Emami fairness', *The Economic Times*, New Delhi, 18 June 2007.

Boyne, G.A. (2004), 'A "3Rs" strategy for public service turnaround—Retrenchment, repositioning and reorganization', *Public Money and Management*, Volume 24, Issue no. 2, pp. 97–103.

Brahma, M. (2009), 'Name of the game', *Business World*, New Delhi, Vol. 6, Issue 12.

Business (2000), 'Cadbury extending the product life cycle through repositioning', http://www.business2000.ie/pdf/pdf_9/cadbury_9th_ed.pdf, accessed on 22 December 2009.

Consumer Monopolies Report (2009) Motilal Oswal, http://www.motilaloswal.com/researchreport/Downloadfile.aspx?mode=112&filename=63396037912268 1532.pdf, accessed on 22 December 2009.

Desarbo, W.S., J. Kim, S.C. Choi, and M. Spaulding (2002), 'A gravity-based multidimensional scaling model for deriving spatial structures underlying consumer preferences/choice', *Journal of Consumer Research*, Vol. 29, Issue 1, pp. 1–16.

Fournier S. (1998), 'Consumer and their brands—Developing relationship theory in consumer research', *Journal of Consumer Research*, Vol. 24, Issue 4, pp. 343–373.

Ghosh, A.K. and G. Chakraborty (2004), 'Using positioning models to measure and manage brand uncertainty', *Journal of Product and Brand Management*, Vol. 13, Issue 5, pp. 294–302.

Govindassamy, Manoj (2010), 'Advertising standards slams Reliance comm. and Idea mobile for misleading TV commercials 'Don't walk when you talk', http://www.moneymint.in/advertisement/advertising-standards-slams-reliance-comm-and-idea-mobile-for-misleading-tv-commercials-dont-walk-when-you-talk, accessed on 11 February 2010.

Gupta, S.L. (2005), *Brand Management Text and Cases* (an Indian perspective), Himalaya Publishing House, New Delhi, Chapter 8, pp. 178–189.

Hiremath, C. (2009), 'Branding perspectives', *Marketing Mastermind*, Issue November 2009, pp. 18–21.

Jacob, Sarah, 'Sipping health for strong future', *The Economic Times*, New Delhi, 25 December 2009, p. 4.

James, D. (2005), 'Guilty through association—brand association transfer to brand alliances' *Journal of Consumer Marketing*, Vol. 22, Issue 1, pp. 14–24.

Jauhari, V. and Kirti Dutta (2009), *Services Marketing—Operations and Management*, Oxford University Press, New Delhi, Chapter 5, pp. 143–178.

Johnson, G.K. Scholes and R. Whittington (2008) *Exploring Corporate Strategy*, 8th edition, Prentice Hall, London.

Keller, K.L. (2003), *Strategic Brand Management—Building Measuring and Managing Band Equity*, 2nd edition, Prentice Hall of India Private Limited, New Delhi, Chapter 3, pp. 118–173.

Klein, J. and N. Dawar (2004), 'Corporate social responsibility and consumers' attributions and brand evaluations in product-harm crisis', *International Journal of Research in Marketing*, Vol. 21, Issue no. 3, pp. 203–217.

Kotler, Philip and K.L. Keller (2005), *Marketing Management*, Prentice Hall, New Delhi.

Kotler, Philip, John T. Bowens, and James C. Makens (2006), *Marketing for Hospitality and Tourism*, Fourth Edition, Pearson Education Inc., New Jersey, Chapter 9.

Kumar, S.R. (2001), *Managing Indian brands—Marketing Concepts and Strategies*, Vikas Publishing House, New Delhi, pp. 138.

Low, G.S. and C.W. Lamb (2000), 'The measurement and dimensionality of brand association', *Journal of Product and Brand Management*, Vol. 9, Issue 6, pp. 350–368.

Maldar, N.J. and R.S. Rathore (2006), 'The rising Baroda sun—Reaching the global customers', *Effective Executive*, July, ICFAI University Press.

Masterson, R. and D. Pickton (2004), *Marketing—An Introduction*, McGraw Hill Education, London.

Morris, K. (1999), 'The brand's the thing', *Business Week*, New York, 26 July, Issue no. 3639, p. 4.

Paul, Josy, 'Create more acts, not ads', *The Economic Times*, New Delhi, 16 February 2010, p. 4.

Ramaswamy, V.S. and S. Namakumari (2009), *Marketing Management*, MacMillan, New Delhi.

Ramsay, F. (2009), 'After Vodafone and Yahoo, Asda too takes a YOU turn' *The Economic Times*, New Delhi, 13 October 2009, p. 4.

Ries, A. and J. Trout (1981), *Positioning, The battle for Your Mind*, Warner Books—McGraw-Hill Inc., New York.

Roll, Martin (2004), 'Singapore Airlines flying tiger' http://www.brandchannel.com/features_profile.asp?pr_id=209, accessed on 13 February 2010.

Runyan, R.C. (2006), 'Tourist dependent small towns—Understanding competitive advantage', *Journal of Vacation Marketing*, Vol. 12, Issue 4, pp. 329–343.

Sachdev (2009), 'Banking on health', http://www.financialexpress.com/printer/news/500370/, accessed on 19 December 2009.

Sachdev, Radhika (2009), 'Banking on health', http://www.financialexpress.com/printer/news/500370/accessed on 19 December 2009.

Sagar, M, D. Singh, D.P. Agarwal, and A. Gupta (2009), *Brand Management*, Chapter 7, Ane Books Pvt. Ltd, New Delhi.

Shashidhar, Ajita (2003), 'Margo soap re-launched to target youngsters', http://www.thehindubusinessline.com/2003/06/17/stories/2003061700470600.htm, accessed on 27 December 2009.

Singh, Shalini (2010), 'Aircel eyes pan-India GSM, 100m subscribers', http://articles.timesofindia.indiatimes.com/2010-02-04/india-business/28122136_1_aircel-plans-pan-india-subscriber-base, accessed on 14 February 2010.

Web resources

http://assets.starbucks.com/assets/5a106e41fe954581999566a4293ced89.jpg, accessed on 6 January 2011.

http://bigbazaar.futurebazaar.com/indexBigBazaar.jsp;jsessionid=B45D623D5E0C1107EBA1BB71FCCDEE03?_requestid=75657, accessed on 26 December 2009.

http://economictimes.indiatimes.com/News/News-By-Industry/Auto/Two-wheelers/Bajaj-Auto-to-sue-TVS-on-IPR-infringement, accessed on 10 December 2009.

http://www.airtel.in/wps/wcm/connect/392ba98044b487778923e9bd155 abeed/Airtel_Logo.jpg?MOD=AJPERES&CACHEID=392ba98044b487778923e9bd155abeed, accessed on 15 January 2011.

http://www.amul.com/cooking-probioticdahi.html, accessed on 24 December 2009.

http://www.doyworld.com/sitefiles/doy_luckeeducky.htm, accessed on 28 December 2009.

http://www.henkel-india.com/cps/rde/xchg/henkel_inh/hs.xsl/body-881.htm?iname=Margo&countryCode=in&BU=cosmetics&brand=000000QWHO, accessed on 15 February 2010.

http://www.hyundai.co.in/MileStones.asp?pagename=comp, accessed on 19 February 2010.

http://www.indiantelevision.com/mam/headlines/y2k6/apr/aprmam63.htm, accessed on 10 December 2009.

http://www.mamypokoclub.com/Menu_Console/Content_Management/frmContentRender.aspx?PageID=52>, accessed on 2 December 2009.

http://www.managementparadise.com/forums/archive/index.php/t-57613.html, accessed on 28 December 2009.

http://www.nestle.in/images/nesvita_yoghurt_flash.jpg, accessed on 24 December 2009.

http://www.new.godrej.com/godrej/godrej/aboutgodrej-group.aspx?id=1&menuid=1163, accessed on 2 January 2010.

http://www.nirulas.com/brand-quality.html, accessed on 19 February 2010.

http://www.nokia.co.in/find-products/products, accessed on 21 December 2009.

http://www.singaporeair.com/saa/index.jsp, accessed on 6 March 2011.

http://www.starbucks.com/blog/looking-forward-to-starbucks-next-chapter, accessed on 6 January 2011.

http://www.unilever.com/sustainability/casestudies/economic-development/creating-rural-entrepreneurs.aspx, accessed on 15 February 2010.

www.nottingham.ac.uk/ttri/docs/positioning.doc, accessed on 30 December 2009.

CASE STUDY 1

Positioning Gone Wrong

Häagen-Dazs probably did not realize that a sign that was meant to tempt the Capital's crème de la crème to its premium "international-quality" ice-creams would instead land it in hot water.

– Dasgupta 2009

Introduction

Häagen-Dazs ice cream, the super-premium frozen dessert segment, opened up its first store in India in December 2009. Within a few days, it managed to hurt the sentiments of a number of people, and everybody began blogging, tweeting, and discussing about it, and not for the right reasons. This case study traces the history of Häagen-Dazs and the sequence of events immediately after it opened up its first outlet at Select City Walk in Saket, Delhi.

History of Häagen-Dazs

Häagen-Dazs was the brainchild of Reuben Mattus and was launched in the year 1960 in New York. Mattus was a young entrepreneur with a passion for quality and a vision for creating the finest ice cream. He worked in his mother's ice cream business selling fruit ice and ice cream pops from a horse drawn wagon in the bustling streets of the Bronx, New York. To produce the finest ice cream available, he insisted on using only the finest, purest ingredients. The family business prospered throughout the 1930s, 40s, and 50s. By 1960, Mattus, supported by his wife Rose, decided to form a new company dedicated to his ice cream vision. He called his new brand Häagen-Dazs, to convey an aura of the old-world traditions and craftsmanship to which he remained dedicated. Häagen-Dazs initially started out with only three flavours—vanilla, chocolate, and coffee.

The Häagen-Dazs brand quickly developed a loyal following. Its early success was created by word of mouth. Without the benefit of advertising, the story of an incredibly rich and creamy confection spread rapidly. At first, it was only available at gourmet shops in New York City, but soon the distribution expanded throughout the east coast of the US and by 1973 Häagen-Dazs products were enjoyed by discerning customers throughout the United States. Then in 1976, Mattus's daughter Doris opened the first Häagen-Dazs shop in Brooklyn, New York. It was an immediate success, and its popularity led to a rapid expansion of Häagen-Dazs shops across the country.

In 1983 Mattus sold Häagen-Dazs to The Pillsbury Company, and since then it has become a global phenomenon, available in 50 countries. The careful attention to quality was maintained and ice cream lovers the world over recognize the unique Häagen-Dazs logo as synonymous with the ultimate super-premium ice cream. Häagen-Dazs' constant endeavour to innovate and bring new frozen dessert experiences to its customers enabled it to be the first to introduce the world to ice cream bars for a grown up palate. It introduced Häagen-Dazs® ice cream bar line in 1986 and other super premium innovations followed, with Frozen Yogurt in 1991 and Sorbet in 1993.

'Häagen-Dazs loves Honey Bees' campaign

In 2009, the brand came out with a campaign 'Häagen-Dazs loves Honey Bees' to save the vanishing honeybees in North America. The brand won the Cannes PR Lion award at the Cannes International advertising festival for this campaign. The campaign also 'received recognition with the Gold CLIO title for its strategic communications/public relations at the global CLIO Awards in Las Vegas, besides several other awards and a huge response from consumers' (Bhushan 2009). A screenshot of the same campaign is given on page 36 (Image 8.25).

The Indian foray

They debuted in China in 1996 and have since successfully operated eighty stores across twenty cities with huge accompanying fanfare, especially among young professionals. Häagen-Dazs, armed with the success it had in China planned to enter India. They felt that today's India was similar to the Chinese market in 1996 and were confident of opening thirty or forty outlets in India. This despite the fact that Nestle, which has a long standing in India, did not venture to introduce its own super-premium global ice-cream brand Mövenpick on account of the limited size of the category. Häagen-Dazs ice cream was already available in limited select stores, such as Sugar & Spice in Delhi and Nature's Basket in Mumbai apart from a few 5-star hotels. But then, General Mills India Pvt. Ltd signed a franchisee deal with RTC restaurants and gave them the exclusive rights to Häagen-Dazs. RTC then opened the first flagship outlet of Häagen-Dazs at the Select City Walk Mall on 10 December 2009 (Bhushan 2009).

Arindam Haldar, Director, Häagen-Dazs & Business Processes, said, 'Our first flagship outlet in India will provide consumers with the opportunity to enjoy Häagen-Dazs in a cosmopolitan yet relaxed setting, the perfect reflection of Häagen-Dazs' 'commitment to innovation, natural goodness, and sophistication. The area of this outlet is 1400 square feet and we are delighted to serve a wide range of tempting ice-creams from Häagen-Dazs—

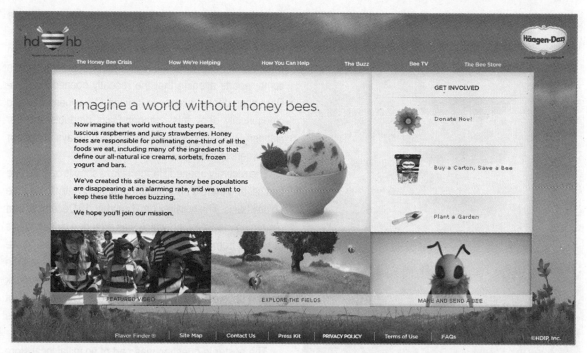

Source: www.helpthehoneybees.com, accessed on 3 January 2010.

Image 8.25   Häagen-Dazs loves Honey Bees campaign

Belgian Chocolate, Choc-choc-chip, Coffee, Vanilla, Chocolate, Mango Sorbet, Raspberry Sorbet, Strawberries Cheese Cake, Summer Berries and Cream, Mango and Passion Fruit, Vanilla Caramel Brownie, Cookies and Cream, Strawberry, etc., along with different cookies and brownies' (cited in Kumar 2009).

The campaign and after

'A day before the US brand opened its first outlet in a south Delhi mall, it put up signboards around the area for a "preview for international travellers" with the telling rider, "Entry restricted only to holders of international passports"', (Dasgupta 2009).

On 15 December, one of the consumers who visited the outlet to taste the ice cream could not entre the store. He called up his friend, Rajesh Kalra, to vent his feeling and clicked a few photographs on his mobile phone and sent it to him. According to Kalra, 'I couldn't believe what I saw. Was I in India, sixty-two years after gaining independence, and years after South Africa officially

ended apartheid? The banners outside the outlet said, "Exclusive Preview for International Travellers". And under that, in an even finer print, the real bombshell—"Access restricted only to holders of international passports."' Kalra posted the photo on his blog and within minutes it had gone around the globe, 'Sorry, Indians not allowed' 'stirring up a number of protests that left the company red-faced' (Dasgupta 2009). The photo of the controversial sign was also pasted on the blog (see Image 8.26).

Times of India updated the above blog with a post on 17 December 2009 as under:

'Dear readers,
A director of Häagen-Dazs, Arindam Haldar, called me Wednesday evening and wanted to discuss this post and the reaction it has generated from Indians all over the world. He tried to explain that their banner, which has resulted in such heat, was merely a teaser and that the company can never say no to an Indian. He admitted that the company may have erred in its choice of words and he was sorry.

Source: http://blogs.timesofindia.indiatimes.com/randomaccess/ entry/sorry-indians-not-allowed,1 accessed on 2 January 2010.

Image 8.26 Photo of the controversial Häagen-Dazs banner

When I said I merely did the job of a journalist and that the apology should actually be addressed to Indians all over the world, and even non-Indians, who have expressed disgust at your company's insensitivity, he said he'd send out an apology to the media. While he sounded apologetic on the phone and said he was genuinely sorry, I present below the 'apology' the managing director of the company that manages the brand in India sent out. You can decide for yourself if this really constitutes an apology.

Media statement from Mr Anindo Mukherji, Managing Director, General Mills India Pvt. Ltd, 'There have been some reports alleging that the recently opened Häagen-Dazs shop denied access to Indians. We vehemently and categorically deny this. Häagen-Dazs products and our Häagen-Dazs shop in India are and will always be for our consumers in India.

The recently opened Häagen-Dazs shop is open to one and all, and there's no question of barring entry to anyone on any basis. The preview on Thursday, 10 December had a morning media event, which was attended by journalists of repute from the Indian media. The same evening we had a launch party for our friends and families, less than 5 per cent of who were foreigners. Also, during the mock training days at the shop leading up to 10 December, a lot of interest was generated and hundreds of walk-ins were given samples of our ice cream.

The poster in question was part of an initial local store communication at a few locations within the same mall announcing the opening of the new Häagen-Dazs shop in the mall. The message was intended to suggest that you can enjoy, for instance, a taste of the French Riviera without travelling to France by enjoying Häagen-Dazs. Unfortunately, the reference to the international passport holder on the poster may have led to a significant miscommunication. This was completely unintended and we apologize for creating the misimpression that may have hurt our sentiments as Indians' (*Times of India* 2009).

Conclusion

The year 2009 saw Häagen-Dazs receive accolades for its campaign 'Häagen-Dazs loves Honey Bees' and also criticism for its 'exclusive preview for international travellers' campaign. The positioning was meant to attract the crème de la crème to the super premium ice cream joint. Unfortunately, the choice of words was wrong. If we believe Brendan Behan, an Irish poet and author who is known for his quotable quotes, and consider that 'There is no such thing as bad publicity except your own obituary', then it means that all this led to a lot of publicity for Häagen-Dazs.

Discussion Questions

1. Do you think the choice of words finally worked to garner publicity for the company?
2. Do you agree with the saying that there is no such thing as bad publicity? Does it apply to Häagen-Dazs?
3. What strategy would you suggest that Häagen-Dazs follows to position itself appropriately and recover lost ground in the minds of customers?

Case References

Behan, Brenda 2010, 'Brenda Behan quotes', http://www.brainyquote.com/quotes/quotes/b/brendanbeh103369.html, accessed on 4 January 2010.

Bhushan, R., 'Häagen-Dazs' first café coming up in Delhi', *The Economic Times*, New Delhi, 27 November 2009, p. 6.

Dasgupta, R.R. 2009, 'No Indians allowed here—Häagen-Dazs—Wrong choice of words', http://economictimes.indiatimes.com/news/news-by-industry/services/hotels-/-restaurants, accessed on 4 January 2010.

Kumar, D. 2009, 'Häagen-Dazs enters India with Select City Walk Store' http://www.indiaretailing.com/news.aspx?topic=1&Id=4377, accessed on 2 January 2010.

Web resources

http://blogs.timesofindia.indiatimes.com/randomaccess/entry/sorry-indians-not-allowed1, accessed on 2 January 2010.

http://www.Häagen-Dazs.com/company/history.aspx, accessed on 1 January 2010.

www.helpthehoneybees.com, accessed on 3 January 2010.

CASE STUDY 2

Airtel—Reinventing the Brand*

Bharti Enterprises, the Indian behemoth with business as varied as telecom, retail, and insurance amongst others, began its journey from a small loss-making telecom company in the 1990s. The company from the very onset has challenged industry wisdom and with a deep understanding of the Indian psyche has harnessed consumer trends with great panache. Never to be seen as a complacent player, it has repeatedly introduced innovations that have redefined industry dynamics. It not only entered new areas of telecom, broadband, 3G, value added services (VAS) in the domestic market, but also spread its wings to seek greener pastures abroad.

Background

Bharti debuted in the Indian telecom arena through its subsidiary Airtel in November 1995. With this entry, Airtel became the first company to launch mobile voice services when the market comprised one million phones, all fixed lines. It was a time when a mobile handset cost as high as ₹45,000 with call charges to the tune of ₹16/minute. Logically, the target audience comprised of the elite up-market executives and entrepreneurs. Airtel was, thus, positioned as an aspirational brand competing more for badge value with less focus on the mobile service. The lifestyle brand's logo was black, uppercase in bold letters with the baseline stating, 'The Power to Keep in Touch'. This tag line was chosen to make the user feel in control and powerful. The decision that the brand should connote leadership in all spheres, such as network, innovations, and service offerings was taken at the very onset. Moreover, this was a time when customers had limited knowledge but high curiosity for cellular services. Hence, Airtel had to educate the market. It released full and half-page print advertisements addressing apprehensions related

*Dr Swati Singh, Faculty Marketing, Bhavan's Usha and Lakshmi Mittal Institute of Management, New Delhi.

to roaming, coverage areas, and making international calls. The success of the campaign provided Airtel with a marginal increase in subscriber base taking it up to 0.38 million (year 1999) in Delhi, its key market (Kumar 2010).

The company provided the Indian cellular market with a number of category firsts, such as opening its first showroom 'Airtel Connect' in Delhi, where customers could buy handsets, get new connections, subscribe to VAS, or pay their mobile bills all under the same roof. In its endeavour to innovate faster than its competition, Bharti added more VAS, such as smart mail, fax, call hold, call waiting, etc. The success of the campaign provided the Airtel brand, along with its pre-paid card service brand 'Magic', which was launched in 1999, top-of-the-mind recall amongst users, and a leadership position in markets of operation. Industry experts attributed this to Bharti's phenomenal brand building and positioning activities. The initiatives undertaken in the late 1990s won Airtel numerous accolades. It was named 'Best Cellular Service' in the country and won the 'Techies' award for four consecutive years from 1997 to 2000 (Saxena 2005).

'Touch Tomorrow'

The new telecom policy of 1999 replaced the license fee by a revenue sharing scheme and extended the license period from ten to twenty years. This allowed telecom players to slash prices and focus on the price sensitive SEC B. Airtel was forced yet again to relook at its strategies. A host of brand-tracking studies conducted to tap into the consumer mindset in early 2000 indicated that the 'leadership' campaign, in spite of its success, had made the brand appear cold, distant, but efficient. The campaign had succeeded in attracting the crème de la crème of society, but failed to connect with the value conscious customer. Another revelation that the study unearthed was that family and friends were key influencers in the choice of cellular phone services. In order to create stronger bonds with existing customers and use the channel of word of mouth, it launched the 'touch tomorrow' campaign in August 2000 with an advertising budget of US$11.5 million (Kumar 2010). The commercials featuring cellular users surrounded by caring family members not only made the brand appear more humane, warm, and approachable, but also highlighted the benefits that Airtel as a brand

could provide. The entire repositioning exercise was accompanied by a rebranding initiative, wherein the Airtel brand was given a new logo endowed with red, black, and white colours with 'Airtel' enwrapped in an ellipse. The tag line 'touch tomorrow' was cleverly placed below the lower case typography (see Image 8.27).

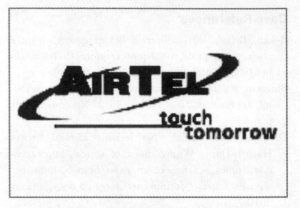

Source: http://www.icmrindia.org/images/airtel%20touch%20 tomorrow.JPG, accessed on 21 February 2011.

Image 8.27 Airtel 'touch tomorrow' logo

While the early advertising by Airtel positioned mobile phones as a business-cum-lifestyle tool, the new advertising strategy was two-pronged. The more rational communication highlighted new offerings like the 'Magic' prepaid card and the emotional element showed a younger target group in an attempt to garner the loyalty of the youth.

With this campaign, the company also shifted focus from SEC A to SEC B audiences. The repositioning was extended to the length and breadth of the company's network. The company also increased its touch point network, i.e., shop in shops located at a number of departmental stores and malls. It revamped the Airtel connect centres giving them a contemporary look by putting into place a host of e-kiosks, fasades, signages, and merchandising items. The colour scheme was redone in red, white, and black, in line with the new logo, likewise a dress code was incorporated to create a soothing, soft, yet classy feel. The dress code for men was black trousers and white shirt bearing the Airtel logo topped with a red tie, while the women wore red tops, black trousers, and ivory chiffon scarves. The repositioning strategies stood the company in good stead, making it the leader in most circles of operation in early 2002.

'Live Every Moment'

In early 2002, Bharti again took the world by storm by embarking on yet another repositioning exercise. The decision to exit the 'touch tomorrow' and launch the 'Live Every Moment' campaign surprised many. The logo underwent a change to appear more symbolic of innovation, energy, and friendliness (see Image 8.28).

Source: http://2.bp.blogspot.com/_VE87FAggTF8/TOtY0PZmdrl/
AAAAAAAAAmQ/omWRFoVcYTs/s1600/airtel-logo.png.

Image 8.28   Airtel's logo that continued up to 2010

Airtel managed to rope in music maestro A.R. Rahman to create the signature tune for the campaign. The tune went on to become the most downloaded ring tone in India. These brand-building activities were unleashed to establish Bharti as a global telecom player and at the same time give Airtel a younger international appeal.

With increased competition in the telecom market attributes, such as superior connectivity and clarity became generic offerings forcing Airtel to look for a new differentiator. It chose to bet on intangible benefits. Hence, the two basic emotions of expressing and communicating became central to the campaign 'express yourself'. The campaign that was launched in 2003 roped in celebrities like Sourav Ganguly, Sachin Tendulkar, Shah Rukh Khan, Kareena Kapoor, and Karishma Kapoor. With this campaign, Airtel continued its focus on tier 2 and 3 towns as well as villages. The 'Express Yourself' campaign was replaced by the *'Baat Karne Se Hi Baat Bantee Hai'* campaign in 2010, which highlighted various service features like STD, roaming, SMS, night calling, and mobile Internet that were more relevant to the youth, the logo, however, remained the same (see Image 8.29).

Source: http://4.bp.blogspot.com/_VE87FAggTF8/TOtYzbI8jnI/
AAAAAAAAAmM/EqboOsV1MnM/s1600/airtel.jpg.

Image 8.29   Airtel logo under Express Yourself campaign

The next level

In June 2010, Bharti Airtel acquired the African operations of the Kuwait based telecom service provider Zain. With this acquisition, Airtel's presence across the globe went up to eighteen countries, of which fifteen are African nations and the others being Sri Lanka, Seychelles, and Bangladesh. This led the company to launch another rebranding exercise. The rationale behind the rebranding was twofold. As a global player, it needed to undertake a mammoth rebranding exercise to provide the brand a uniform presence across the countries of operation. At the same time, the digitalization wave that has swept the Indian market place heralded Airtel's entry into 3G, social media, and e-commerce requiring an altogether new positioning. The launch of the new identity also marked the 200 million customers' milestone for Airtel in November 2010 (Krishnamurthy 2010). The campaign was rolled out in all the relevant markets starting November 2010. The evolution of the telecom industry, coupled with the brand's expansion, required movement of the brand 'Airtel' to the next level.

The new identity

Work on the campaign began towards the middle of 2010 when Bharti invited a pitch from the world's top brand specialists. The company shortlisted Brand Union, which had previously worked with it in 2005, to design its new logo. Brand Union was provided the makeover brief with the built-in caution to retain the red colour. The decision to retain the red colour came after consumer research suggested that the colour was the core to Airtel's identity and held positive connotations in the African subcontinent too. Telecom players in Africa had particularly focused on blue, purple, and green colours, therefore, red would serve as a clear-cut differentiator. The company came up with over a hundred potential logos which comprised permutations and combinations representing air, bubbles, etc. (Bhandari and Khicha 2010). Two were finally shortlisted and presented before Sunil Mittal, the CMD of the Bharti Group. The one he finally selected evolved from the Zain logo—a swirl emanating from the solar system (see Image 8.30).

Source: http://www.airtel.in/wps/wcm/connect/392ba98044b487778 923e9bd155 abeed/Airtel_Logo.jpg?MOD=AJPERES&CACHEID= 392ba98044b487778923e9bd155abeed.

Image 8.30 The new logo of Airtel

Since the countries in which the brand is present comprise a primarily young population, the new image had to be modern, youthful, and bright. The new logo is therefore modern, vibrant, and friendly, signalling its accessibility to all stakeholders. The lower case lends the brand more humility. The red colour that has been retained, reiterates the heritage, energy, and passion that the brand is famous for. Digging deeper to unearth the anatomy of the new logo, we see that the small letters represent the informality of the email or the net generation, the swoosh lends the logo a touch of class, speed, and modernity, while the red colour lends the brand a dash of aggression, appeal, and vibrancy. J. Walter Thompson, the telecom company's creative partner, was given the responsibility for creating the new positioning for India 'Dil jo chahe pass laye', i.e., get closer to what you love. The new signature tune is again by Rahman. In order to zero in on the name of the symbol, Bharti relied on customer co-creation, wherein it launched a competition to name the symbol. About half a dozen entries would be shortlisted by an internal team after which the entries would be subjected to an online vote. Within a few days of the campaign launch, the company received over 7200

entries (Bhandari and Khicha 2010). The company is of the opinion that the new identity will help the brand extend beyond telecom and hence will not create any hindrances in case Airtel wants to extend into newer and more varied services. To ensure complete success of the rebranding exercise, Bharti had to make sure that the change was implemented across all signages of the company. This included all touch points, such as glow signs, drop boxes, visiting cards, letterheads, etc. The change of signages across all mediums was achieved within a fortnight of the rebranding exercise.

Conclusion

Rebranding and repositioning exercises are activities that require considerable forethought and planning, and are clearly not mere whims and fancies of the top management. Airtel is one of the few brands that has from the onset understood the pulse of its target market and proactively changed itself to remain contemporary and relevant to its stakeholders. Any change however insignificant or mammoth is always accompanied by some resistance. Fortunately for Airtel, its previous repositioning and rebranding activities have till now managed to strengthen the brand. The naysayers will however opine that the company should have spent the whopping ₹300 crore (Rastogi Assem 2010) on improving customer service and decongesting its network rather than on a makeover. Others are critical of the choice of colour being 'too similar to Vodafone', and the symbol, which according to most, doesn't really mean anything unlike the Vodafone logo, which represents a quote or speech blurb. The company, however, is confident that it has embarked on the right path. The makeover is already being supported by changes in processes, systems, as well as in investments in information technology to take customer service and employee engagement to new heights. How far Airtel will be able to deliver on the new found promise, only time will tell.

Discussion Questions

1. What triggered the changes in positioning strategies of Airtel since the time of its inception?

2. Airtel spent a phenomenal amount of money in the year 2010 to create its new global identity. Do you think the money was well spent, why or why not?

Case References

Bhandari, Bhupesh, and Preeti Khicha, 'Reinventing brand Airtel' http://www.business-standard.com/india/news/reinventing-brand-airtel/417198/, accessed on 18 December 2010.

Krishnamurthy Jagadeesh, 'Airtel reveals new global identity', http://www.campaignindia.in/Article/239173,airtel-reveals-new-global-identity.aspx, accessed on 12 December 2010.

Kumar Praveen, 'Airtel – Positioning (And Repositioning)—From 'Touch Tomorrow' to 'Live Every Moment'' http://corporatesolutionsug.com/marketing/airtel-positioning accessed on 10 December 2010.

Rastogi Aseem, 'Airtel's New Logo & Signature tune—Better or Worse?' http://trak.in/tags/business/2010/11/18/airtel-new-logo-tune-rebranding/, accessed on 8 February 2010.

Saxena Rajan (2005), *Marketing Management*, 3/e, Tata McGraw Hill, New Delhi.

Web resources

http://timesofindia.indiatimes.com/business/india-business/Bharti-completes-acquisition-of-Zains-Africa-biz-for-107bn/articleshow/6023848.cms, African Analyst, accessed on 12 December 2010.

http://www.airtel.in/wps/wcm/connect/392ba98044b487778923e9bd155 abeed/Airtel_Logo.jpg?MOD=AJPERES&CACHEID=392ba98044b487778923e9bd155abeed, accessed on 15 January 2011.

http://www.superbrandsindia.com/images/brand_pdf/consumer_1st_edition _2004/airtel/index.htm, accessed on 19 January 2011.

http://www.authorstream.com/Presentation/jakan-543652-airtel/, accessed on 19 January 2011.

www.dot.gov.in/osp/Brochure/Brochure.htm, accessed on 16 January 2011.

Part IV
MANAGING BRANDS

Part IV

MANAGING BRANDS

Branding and the Marketing Programme

9

LEARNING OBJECTIVES

After reading this chapter, you will be able to understand the following:

- Product strategy
- Pricing strategy
- Distribution strategy

ABOUT THE CHAPTER

A brand that has been successfully built over a period of time draws its equity not only from the brand elements and positioning, but also from the marketing strategies and the subsequent activities that revolve around it (see Exhibit 9.1). These marketing strategies are related to the 4Ps—product, price, place, and promotion—and the first three will be discussed in this chapter and the fourth in the next chapter. The impact of these marketing strategies on the brand equity of an organization will be the main focus of this chapter.

Exhibit 9.1   Paras Targets Niches to Create Successful Brands

Paras Pharmaceuticals, makers of a strong set of over-the-counter brands, such as Moov, Dermicool, D'Cold, Krack, Ring Guard, and Setwet, reported revenues of ₹401.4 crore in the financial year 2010 (Kurian 2010). Moov and D'Cold are both examples of niche categories that Paras successfully targeted, as these categories already have strong established brand players, such as Iodex by GlaxoSmithKline and Vicks by Proctor and Gamble. The brand power of Paras Pharmaceuticals can be gauged by the fact that when in December 2010 it was put on the block, it was purchased at a blow-away premium of eight times the sale at ₹3260 crore by none other than the British consumer goods giant Reckitt Benckiser.

Paras Pharmaceuticals in its twenty-five years of its existence was able to build strong brands by identifying 'need gaps and creating niche segments that larger players had not tapped or categories where the leader had not been too vibrant.' These were then followed by clever marketing strategies that helped Paras challenge the existing leaders (Kar 2010).

BRANDING AND THE MARKETING PROGRAMME—AN INTRODUCTION

The focus of marketing is the customers, the people who make or break a brand. Marketers are doomed when their organization's product attributes do not better the product features of other brands. It is important to note that the purchase decision is influenced by a 'bundle of satisfaction' offered by the marketers, which includes the convenience of purchase or the place aspect, the style of advertising, or the promotion aspect (Kuehn and Day 1962), and the price of the product along with the manufacturer's reputation. Thus, what is important is how the customers perceive the whole bundle of satisfaction. Therefore as marketers, while making decisions regarding the product, pricing, promotion, and place, we need to keep in mind how these are going to impact the brand as a whole. Let us now study these factors and their impact on the brand equity of a firm in the marketplace.

PRODUCT STRATEGY

Introduction

The product that forms the core of all marketing efforts along with its features are the factors that majorly impact the purchase decision of consumers (Kuehn and Day 1962). The product features form the core of brand equity, and the product decisions should be such that they enhance brand image and brand resonance (Keller 2008) (see Exhibit 9.2). The gaps in the product offering need to be plugged to provide a wholesome experience to the customers (see Exhibit 9.3).

What Is a Product?

A product is defined as 'a tangible object, or an intangible service, or an idea, which a marketer has to offer to satisfy the needs and wants of the customers' (Jauhari and Dutta 2009). The product should be built around the needs of the customers and should be able to satisfy them. For example, for parents who are worried about the effect that constant TV viewing will have on their children's vision, Sony launched the LX3D television model. This is a super-smart TV, which uses face recognition technology to identify children from adults and judge how far these children are from the TV. The moment the child is too close to the screen it goes fuzzy and remains so until the child moves back to a safe distance. It also senses the fact that the viewer has left the room and switches itself off to save energy (ANI 2010).

Exhibit 9.2   Moov's Product

Moov was launched by Paras Pharmaceuticals in 1986 as an over-the-counter pain reliever. This category already had well-entrenched brands, such as Iodex from GlaxoSmithKline and Zandu, which is now with Emami (Kar 2010). In order to differentiate Moov from the others, Paras positioned it as a specialist joint-pain reliever and later as a back-pain reliever targeted at the woman of the house. The product took the competitors head on—it came in an attractive packaging, with a nice fragrance, and was easy to apply. The non-greasy nature of the cream did not leave a stain and all these strategies helped in endearing Moov to the customers.

Exhibit 9.3 Product Offerings at Marks & Spencer

For the first time in 125 years, Marks & Spencer seeks to fill the gaps in its product offerings and provide a complete weekly shop to the consumers. Sectors that are not represented by the retailer's own brands or where the retailer has a low market share, such as confectionary, alcohol, personal care, pet food, and laundry, will be filled with other reputed brands, such as Cadbury Wispa, Kellogg's Cheerios, Coca-Cola, Pantene, etc. The presence of these 'essential, must-have brands' at M&S will help in saving the consumers' time by making everything available to them under one roof. The filling of the gaps in product offerings will also remove a barrier to launching an online food delivery service, as the limited size of the product offering and logistical challenges involved are the main concerns in going online (Quilter 2009).

The 'product' refers to the physical product, such as the Apple iPod or Sony television, or the services product, such as banking services, or a mix of both, such as a coffee at Café Coffee Day. Products can broadly be thought about at three levels.

Core product This aspect looks at the question— 'What does the consumer buy?' and 'What is the company offering?' Thus, we first define the 'core problem-solving benefits or services that consumers seek' and then design the product around that.

Actual product At the next level, marketers develop the features of the product, the quality, the design, brand name, and the packaging (see Exhibit 9.4).

Augmented product The augmented product is built around the core and the actual product. This involves providing additional benefits and services to customers, such as delivery and credit facility, after-sales service, product support, and warranty. For example, one of the reasons for the sale of assembled computers being higher than that of branded computers is that computers require a lot of after-sales service in the form of software support, as there may be problems of computers not functioning due to software dysfunction. Vodafone

Courtesy: Superbrands.

Image 9.1 Vodafone ad; also see Plate 12

is another example of a brand that has been developing value products at affordable prices to empower its customers to 'go mobile and make the most of the opportunities that come their way or even create new ones.' Customers can use features like SMS, MMS, caller tunes, ring tones, wallpapers, voice SMS, alerts, etc. Consumers can also find partners on shaadi.com through their mobile (see Image 9.1) (*Superbrands*, 2009).

Exhibit 9.4   Kohinoor Basmati Rice—The Transition from a Product to a Brand

Every year, 650 million metric tonnes of rice are produced globally. The bulk of this is produced in China, Indonesia, Bangladesh, and India. The Basmati variety of rice comprises less than one per cent of the global production. Basmati is generally preferred by consumers over the other varieties, as it elongates a 100 per cent on cooking without increasing in girth and has a rich desirable aroma (Graham 2002). The cost differential between Basmati and the other varieties is therefore high.

In 1976, three brothers from Amritsar started a venture with a capital of ₹80. They paid all this money to an artist for designing a logo and then with the help of a metal sheet transferred the logo onto a 35 kg bag of Basmati rice. Thus, a commodity was converted into a brand—the Kohinoor brand of Basmati Rice (see Image 9.2).

Kohinoor offers the best Basmati rice 'from select farms, ages it in special containers under strictly controlled conditions for between 1–2 years,' which when cooked provides a sweetish, nut-like flavour, and a heady aroma. (See Image 9.3.) Kohinoor is recognized as the first company to brand a commoditized product and also as the first brand to recognize the power of celebrity endorsements. The early commercials of Sharmila Tagore and the Nawab of Pataudi have a high recall value even today. Kohinoor is now a ₹635-crore or $132.30-million empire and has offices globally along with two world-class plants in India and two rice mills in Dubai and the UK (*Superbrands,* 2009).

Courtesy: Superbrands.

Image 9.2   Kohinoor brand of Basmati rice

Contd

Exhibit 9.4 *contd*

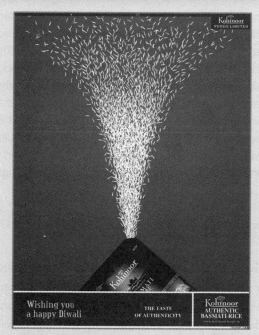

Courtesy: Superbrands.　　　　　*Courtesy: Superbrands.*

Image 9.3　Kohinoor ads wishing Happy Diwali and Happy Onam; also see Plate 12

Consumers purchase a 'complex bundle of benefits' to satisfy their needs and wants. As marketers, we need to identify the value drivers for the customers and build our core, actual, and augmented product around these to satisfy and delight the customers (Kotler, Armstrong, Agnihotri, and Haque 2010). Thus, we need to build a brand with the best of features at all levels to enhance brand equity (see Exhibit 9.4).

Product Strategy and Branding

Product decisions are made at three levels—'individual product decisions, product line decisions, and product mix decisions' (Kotler et al. 2010). The product line and product mix decisions are discussed in the chapter on brand strategy, and the individual product decisions, which include product features, perceived quality, etc., are discussed here as follows.

Product features　The features of a product should help the brand reach out to its target market (see Exhibit 9.5). For example, when Nokia's market share slipped from 56.2 per cent in 2008 to 54.1 per cent in 2009 due to 'strong competition from domestic brands like Micromax, Lemon, Karbonn, BlackBerry, and iPhone in the smart-phone segment, it launched a mobile phone with a qwerty keypad, email service, and access to social networking sites at ₹5300' (*The Economic Times,* 2010a).

Exhibit 9.5 Fruity Variants for Chyawanprash

Everyone knows that Chyawanprash is good for health, but not many take to its spicy and sour taste. Dabur rules the chyawanprash market, which is estimated at ₹400 crore with a 65 per cent market share (Singh 2010). Their regular consumers are in the age-group of below 13 years and above 30 years as these groups 'need to develop immunity to fight diseases.' In order to target the 13–30 year olds, Dabur launched fruity variants of its chyawanprash—mango and orange flavours—in November 2010. Emami's Sona Chandi Chyawanprash, with a market share of 7–8 per cent, was the first to come out with flavoured variants by launching Chocoprash, Chyawanprash that tasted like chocolate and could be used as roti and bread spread (Singh 2010), in March 2010 (Mukherjee 2010). However, it had to be taken off the shelves as people could not mix chocolate, which is 'not seen as healthy and which many believe is the cause of tooth decay', with chyawanprash (Singh 2010). Emami is now watching the response of the market to Dabur's fruity variants and plans to come out with its own variants in the year 2011 if consumer response is good (Singh 2010).

Perceived quality An organization can have high technical standards and quality control systems in place, but it is the extent to which the product satisfies the wants of the customers that is important. In other words, the perceived quality of the product impacts the customers and they need to be assured that the product is superior and the workmanship excellent (Kuehn and Day 1962). Product quality is a major factor impacting perceived quality (Yu and Fang 2009). Branding helps in influencing the perceived quality of the product as has been discussed in the chapter on brand equity. Bad product quality also impacts perceived quality and results in lowering brand equity (see Exhibit 9.6). It has also been studied that the brand name impacts the consumers the most and allows companies to charge a price premium 'regardless of whether they have a quality advantage or not' (Apelbaum, Gerstner, and Naik 2003).

Packaging Packaging communicates and advertises, it attracts customers, and at the same time communicates information about the brand and the product to them (Pantin-Sohier

Exhibit 9.6 Toyota's Recall of Cars

Toyota, the world's largest car manufacturer, suffered a major blow in the year 2010, when it recalled 6 million cars in North America, 75,000 vehicles from China, and 2 million units in Europe approximately. The reason was that the floor mat trapped accelerator pedals caused sudden, unintended acceleration. Though this is not the first major recall in the US auto industry (in 2008–09, Ford recalled 14.3 million cars with faulty switches; in 2004 GM recalled 4 million pickups worldwide as the tailgates could break without warning; in 1996 Ford recalled more than 8 million cars to replace the ignition switches), it also saw a sales and production halt in North America. Eight models of Toyota Motors including the Camry, which is a best-seller, were affected and this has damaged Toyota's 'once unshakeable record for safety and reliability.'

Source: Adapted from Reuters 2010.

2009). Within an organization, packaging has different perspectives for different departments. The brand or product manager wants it to effectively protect the quality of the product until it reaches the final customers. The sales manager wants it to be attractive so that it fulfils its sobriquet of the 'silent salesman'. The purchase department looks at the pricing aspect, while designing the packaging. Packaging has to fulfil a number of functions, such as attracting the customer's attention, giving a description of the product, and affecting the sales, since 70 per cent of the purchase decisions are made in the stores (Kotler et al. 2010). Packaging influences brand equity, both directly as a brand element and indirectly by impacting the brand image. The importance of packaging has been discussed in the chapter on brand equity.

Product support services The support services provided by the organization also help in building the brand and contribute to its brand equity. Ashok Leyland, an iconic brand in India, has buses carrying around 60 million people every day, which is many times more than the people carried by the Indian Railways. More than 50,000 of these vehicles are used by the Indian Army alone. One of the reasons for Ashok Leyland achieving a superbrand status (*Superbrands*, 2009) is the product support services it provides (see Exhibit 9.7).

Customer experience The experience of customers with the product is an important factor impacting brand equity and brand recall. Creating memorable experience leads to enhanced brand recall and also builds brand demand. These experiences can be created at the time of the purchase of the products and services, or the first moment of truth, and also after the purchase of the product, especially a tangible product. Customer experiences built during the first moment of truth result in high brand equity for repeat buyers, and the product quality impacts brand image for first time buyers (Yu and Fang 2009). 'Aftermarketing' is the trend in marketing that focuses on the marketing activities that occur after the consumers have purchased the product. This is done to enhance the consumption experience of the customers, also called as the 'second moment of truth'. The instruction manual or the user manual is an example of aftermarketing as are the customer service departments (Keller 2008).

Conclusion The product is at the heart of all marketing activities and also of brand equity. Marketers should choose product features and benefits that the consumers desire and should sell the product and provide after-sales services in a manner that forms 'strong, favourable,

Exhibit 9.7 Support Services at Ashok Leyland

Ashok Leyland has over six lakh vehicles plying on Indian and foreign roads. To provide customer support services, the company has 170 dealership outlets, thirty sales offices, and a nationwide chain of franchisee service centres. Apart from this, its genuine spare parts are available through more than 1000 outlets.

Ashok Leyland has also undertaken a host of initiatives aimed at providing support services to customers and channel partners. ALWAYS is the company's national helpline, which provides emergency services and speedy assistance around-the-clock. To promote good customer services and reward excellent practices, it created the 'MITR' project—'a nationwide loyalty programme for 2400 parts retailers and 8200 mechanics' (*Superbrands,* 2009).

and unique brand associations' which in turn leads to brand equity in the form of greater brand resonance.

 See Yamaha Motor ads and the three different roles of John Abraham to flaunt the different colours of the FZ bikes. Also how it has helped the company increase its market share.

PRICING STRATEGY

Introduction

Of the four Ps of marketing, pricing is the most important factor for an organization, since the other Ps result in expenses for the organization, and price is the only revenue-generating element in the marketing mix. Consumers form their quality judgements about a new product either on the basis of the brand name, if the product is a brand extension, or on the basis of the price (Taylor 2009). Building strong brands results in a 'brand halo' effect, wherein 'perceptions of a brand's overall attributes affect pricing beyond the effect of the specific qualities of a particular product within the brand' (Betts and Taran 2002). This means that by building strong brands, companies can charge a price premium for their products. Prices once set and announced to the consumers are very difficult to increase or decrease. Price discounts result in a negative effect on the consumer reference prices (Hardesty and Bearden 2003), product quality reference (Dark and Chung 2005), and on brand image and brand equity (Yoo, Donthu, and Lee cited in Palazon and Delgado 2009). An increase in the prices is equally difficult (see Exhibit 9.8), especially during times of recession. In this section, we will explore the pricing strategy of an organization in context with branding.

What Is Pricing?

In simple terms, price is the amount of money charged for a product or service. Historically, price has been a major factor affecting buyer choice. In recent decades, non-price factors have

---

Exhibit 9.8   Whither Price Rise?

Rising inflation and commodity cost has put pressure on the fast moving consumer goods (FMCG) firms, as their profit margins have been hit. If that was not enough, the increase in excise duty from 8 per cent to 10 per cent and the minimum alternative tax from 15 per cent to 18 per cent, the rising packaging prices, diesel, and petrol costs have all had a cascading effect on the prices. The price of packaging material has risen by 25 per cent, and so far, the companies have absorbed the price hike. They, however, feel that any further hike in prices will have to be passed on to the consumers. But, companies are wary of increasing prices and want to keep their ₹2, ₹5, and ₹10 price points intact. Godrej Consumer Products, Cavinkare, Dabur, all feel that they will have to hike the prices of their brands to some extent but cannot increase them significantly due to competitive pressure and feel that they will drive up their profit margins through volumes. The entry levels of ₹2 shampoo sachets, ₹5 biscuit packs, and ₹10 chips will remain, but the quantity or the grammage will be reduced. Manufacturers are reluctant to touch these price points as these entry-level price points have high volume growth and add to their profit margins (Bhushan 2010; Vyas 2010a).

gained increasing importance, but price still remains one of the most important factors. A number of factors influence the price, and the cost incurred in manufacturing the product forms the building-block that determines the final price of the product. This cost incurred is a fact but what the company charges for the product is a policy (Kotler et al. 2010). Pricing decisions are based on a number of factors. After settling on a price and keeping in mind the environmental factors, the competition, and the consumers, organizations can offer discounts and various promotional schemes on these prices. Brands that are available globally need to be sensitive to pricing issues; otherwise, it will lead to a grey marketing situation, allowing grey marketers to source brands from markets where prices are low and sell them in markets where prices are high. It has been studied that brands sold in grey markets have lower brand equity than authorized goods (Chen 2007).

Organizations incur certain costs in manufacturing a brand and making it available to customers for purchase. On the other hand, customers, in order to consume a brand, go through a series of activities to acquire the brand—the effort to go and procure the brand, pay the price or cost of the brand, consume it, and then dispose the brand if it is of the durable kind or the remnants if it is the non-durable kind. The customers, on consuming a brand, form their own perceptions of the value of the brand, and the price paid for it should thus be in line with this perception of the value. If the price paid is higher, it will result in a loss of sales, as consumers will not purchase or repurchase the brand. On the other hand, if the price is lower, it will result in loss of revenue for the organization. This suggests that for marketers, the price range starts with the cost incurred in manufacturing the product and ends with the customer perception of value (Keller 2008; Kotler et al. 2010). The benefit of building strong brands is that this upper ceiling of price can be increased by enhancing customer value. Organizations can also offer attractive price points, so as to influence customers to try out and consume their brand (see Exhibit 9.9).

The two main strategies of value-based pricing (Kotler et al. 2010) are as follows.

Good value pricing This entails offering the right combination of price, quality, and service. Customers today are very discerning and perceptive and form their own price and quality perceptions. Indian customers are value conscious and are motivated by 'what they get for what they pay.' To appease these customers, marketers can launch products at lower

---

Exhibit 9.9   The New Price Point

Shampoo has long been available in the market in sachets. Inflationary pressure pushed organizations to come out with low price points and experiment in other areas of packaged foods as well. It now seems that the ₹5 price point is here to stay. It is not surprising as the ₹5 pricing has the benefits of convenience of coinage and 'single-serve usage.' Apart from fighting inflation, it also 'drives trials, engages consumers, and demolishes basic entry-level barriers.'

For PepsiCo India, the ₹5 price point contributes to '45 per cent of the overall food sales. Two-thirds of sales in the ₹11,300 crore biscuits market takes place at sub-₹10 price points.' Telecom services providers, such as Idea Cellular, Tata DoCoMo, Airtel, and Vodafone are all offering ₹5 recharge options. '₹5' is, thus, the 'magic word for marketers across products' (Bhushan and Pande 2010).

price points. For example, McDonald's 'value menus' provide products at lower prices. Maruti Suzuki is revamping its portfolio and the new variants are cheaper than the outgoing ones. For example, the Zen Estilo is ₹50,000 cheaper than the outgoing model, the new multipurpose Eeco is ₹1 lakh cheaper than the Versa, etc., providing greater value for money (Chauhan 2010). However, good value does not always mean a low price. Luxury products, though expensive, can also spell good value to their target customers. Till recently, in India, products were sold at their maximum retail price (MRP) and this concept is fairly new. Good value pricing at the retail level can be either of the following.

Everyday low pricing (EDLP)   This strategy entails charging a low price on a daily basis with no price discounts. First movers like Subhiksha, pioneered the concept in India for the organized retail sector (Ramalingam 2008). MakeMyTrip is another example of an organization that focuses on lowest priced travel tickets and even provides the lowest airfare guarantee.

High-low pricing   This strategy allows the marketers to charge a higher price on an everyday basis, but offer price promotions on select items at various intervals of time. Heritage foods, promoted by Chandrababu Naidu, practises this concept at its 'Fresh@' stores in Bangalore, Chennai, and Hyderabad. It offers deals and discounts on select items. It also offers a 'bill-buster scheme, where customers are rewarded for making purchases above a certain value' (Ramalingam 2008).

Value-added pricing   To differentiate and to protect themselves from price wars, organizations can add value to their product offering. This helps in enhancing customer perception of the value and at the same time allows the organization to charge a premium. For example, the ₹1500 crore retail packaged water market is highly fragmented, and the smaller players account for three-fourths of the market. Bisleri who pioneered the packaged water industry retails at ₹10 for 500 ml, ₹13 for 1 litre, is also a dominant player in the bulk segment following a 'direct-to-home and direct-to-institution delivery model.' Apart from the small players, it also faces competition from big players like Coca-Cola's Kinley and Pepsi Co's Aquafina. As the margins in the retail packaged water market are already wafer-thin, Bisleri has gone premium with the launch of 'Vedica'—a natural mineral water sourced from the Himalayas. Natural mineral water accounts for 2–3 per cent of the total packaged water category. Vedica, priced at ₹20 for 500 ml and ₹30 for 1 litre, is available at 'select outlets including malls, fine dining restaurants, hotels, and grocery stores in big cities' (Bhushan 2009; Franchise Mart 2010).

Pricing Strategy and Branding

The pricing strategy impacts the brand image and perceived quality of an organization. Consumers generally associate a higher price with higher quality. Brand equity helps in creating acceptability of a higher price for a branded good vis-à-vis a commodity. On the other hand, psychological pricing, say for instance the use of the 99 price endings, favourably impacts both the brand image and the perceived quality (Fortin, Cleland, and Jenkins 2008). The organizational brand strategy for pricing can also impact the pricing strategy to be followed while launching a new product or service. For example, when India's Tata and Japan's NTT Docomo entered the GSM space in July 2009, they triggered a churn in the market by 'offering tariffs at one paisa per second.' Tata Docomo's subsequent entry into the 3G spectrum will be in line with its earlier pricing strategy. Docomo is averse to giving it a 'premium' label like the other operators and plans to 'incentivize' the 3G usage, so that consumers pay less if usage increases. As a special Diwali gift, in 2010, it offered its subscribers in nine circles, the opportunity to experience the 3G services for free for seven days (Naidu 2010).

The pricing strategy over the portfolio of brands can be divided into product line and product mix pricing as follows.

Product line pricing To offer a range of brands at different price points, organizations can launch different brands in its product line, which has been discussed in the chapter on brand strategy. For example, Suzuki, the Japanese two-wheeler major, offers super bikes at different price points of ₹12.75 lakh for the GSX-R1000 model, ₹8.5 lakh for the Bansit 1250S model, and the ₹12.5 lakh for the Hyabusa and Intruder models in India (PTI 2010). Different brands should provide various options according to the different value perceptions of customers by offering different features at different prices. Brands with a number of variants, sizes, or flavours can add more brands to their basket of offerings at different price points which results in the addition of one or more brands to the consideration set of the consumers. (Mehta, Rajiv, and Srinivasan 2003). This helps in targeting different customers, and brands can be purchased by a larger segment of customers (see Exhibit 9.10).

Another strategy that organizations can follow is optional product pricing. This is when organizations sell optional products that customers can purchase along with the main product. These are generally the accessories that go with the main product. Car companies follow this strategy by advertising the stripped down variant of the car and then offering additional variants with more features at higher prices (Kotler et al. 2010). For example, Ford India launched 'Figo' in India with a price range starting from ₹3.49 lakh and going up to ₹4.42 lakh for the petrol variant and ₹4.47 to ₹5.29 lakh for the diesel variant (*The Economic Times*, 2010c).

Product mix pricing The product mix decisions can further be divided on the basis of the different brands being manufactured by the organization. Unrelated brands can be

---

Exhibit 9.10 Segmenting Foodies

KFC, Dominos, Pizza Hut, and McDonald's have all looked at their pricing strategies to endear themselves to the Indian masses. The year 2009 saw Pizza Hut introduce 'two price points of ₹99 targeted at college students and ₹199 targeted at young working professionals. A global restaurant chain to join this 'food wagon' is Thank God It's Friday (TGIF). TGIF is offering the afternoon two-course meal for a flat ₹199 on weekdays, which is in tune with their 'global strategy of introducing revamped and more localized menus with attractive prices'. This will also help them get more customers and help battle 'lower footfalls during lunch hours'. 'Rohan Jetley, Vice-President, Marketing and Development, Bistro Hospitality, which runs the TGIF chain in India feels that this strategy has helped them segment the customers. TGIF doesn't fear any dissonance amongst its premium clients with such a mass marketing pricing move. "Evenings and dinners are for the premium consumers, while lunch time is suitable for the cost-conscious consumer", says Mr Jetley.' (Ambwani 2010).

priced individually. Related products in the brand portfolio can be priced keeping in mind the following strategies.

Captive product pricing To sell products that can be used with the main product, companies use captive product pricing. For example, Hewlett-Packard sells its printers and also the ink-cartridges that need to be used with them. Gillette is another example; it sells low-priced razors, but the replacement cartridges are priced high. This can be a deterrent when consumers will not purchase the product fearing the high recurring cost involved.

Product bundle pricing When several brands are bundled together and sold at a lower price, this is called product bundle pricing. Product and service bundles are strategically used by companies to enhance profits through stimulated demand (Sheng, Parker, and Nakamoto 2007). Service firms like restaurants offer this by bundling complimentary food items together, for example, McDonald's packages its burgers, french fries, and a soft drink at a 'combo' price (Kotler et al. 2010).

Conclusion

Pricing is the only marketing mix that brings revenue for an organization. Prices once set are difficult to increase and organizations need to be very careful, as pricing also impacts the brand image of the organization. Companies can use pricing strategically to bundle their brands and drive sales across categories for the organization. The image of the brand can be reinforced through the pricing and should be used strategically to build and cash in on brand equity.

DISTRIBUTION STRATEGY

Introduction

Distribution enables the brand to be present where a customer can purchase it. This includes making the brand available from its place of manufacture to the place where the final consumer can purchase or consume the brand (in case of a services product). Organizations can sell their brands directly to the final consumer or take the help of intermediaries like wholesalers, distributors, etc., to reach the final consumer. Organizations can manufacture the best of products, promote it well, and price it accurately, but all this will be wasted if it is not available where and when the customer needs to purchase it. To make the product available and to tap the consumers, KFC, for example, is opening a number of outlets in various convenient locations (see Exhibit 9.11).

What Is Distribution?

A brand that is not available in a store when the consumer wants to purchase it results in the following situations (Corsten and Gruen 2003):

1. Store switching—consumers can purchase the brand in another store.
2. Postpone purchase—consumers can postpone their purchase till the time it is available in the same store.
3. Lost sale—consumers will not purchase the brand at all, resulting in loss of sale.
4. Same brand substitution—consumers can substitute the brand with a different size of the same brand or a different type of the same brand, for example, purchasing a 600 ml pack instead of the 1-litre pack or vice-versa; purchasing Thums Up instead of Coca-Cola.

Exhibit 9.11   The KFC Brand in India

Euromonitor, one of the world's leading independent providers of business intelligence on industries, countries, and consumers, estimates the eating-out market in India to be worth $64 billion and that it is growing at about 10 per cent a year annually. This is constituted by the branded chains, unbranded food outlets, mom and pop stores, street food stalls, bakeries, etc. Branded chains hardly control 2 per cent of the market share. This has motivated KFC to expand at a rapid pace and come out with one KFC within a 3 km radius of every major locality.

The company has a brand image of a hard-core non-vegetarian brand. India is a country densely populated by vegetarian consumers, about 35 per cent. This 35 per cent is found in the north and west of India with Rajasthan and Gujarat having 95 per cent plus vegetarian population. Delhi and Punjab have about 50 per cent vegetarian population, and in the south just 2–3 per cent people are vegetarian. The company plans to tweak its menu in the coming 3–4 years to serve good vegetarian food to the non-sensitive vegetarians. At the same time, to reach out to these people it plans to increase the number of outlets from 74 in 2010 to 500 by 2015 (Varma 2010).

5. Brand switching—consumers can substitute the brand with another brand of another organization, for example, buying Pepsi instead of Coca-Cola.

Of all of the above, it is the lost sale and the brand switching, which are detrimental to a brand. The importance of distribution in brand decisions can be gauged by the fact that the iconic brand from United Kingdom—Hamleys—major reason for a tie-up with Reliance Retail in India was due to their expertise in the supply chain management. According to Mr Gudjon, CEO Hamleys, 'Creating a sustainable supply chain for toys or any other retail chain is a major challenge for any organized player here, that is the reason we have a partner like Reliance Retail here, who are known for their expertise in this end of retail management' (Vyas 2010b). The various strategies that companies can employ for distribution are as follows.

Intensive distribution   When an organization makes its services available through as many outlets as possible, it is called intensive distribution. A brand that falls in the FMCG category, especially that of convenience products, should follow the intensive distribution strategy, since 'availability of products is the new battleground in the FMCG industry' (Corsten and Gruen 2003).

Selective distribution   When an organization chooses some outlets to distribute its brand, it is called selective distribution. Brands that are less frequently purchased and require a comparison regarding their features, quality, price, etc. use this type of distribution.

Exclusive distribution   When an organization chooses only limited number of outlets to distribute its brand, it is called exclusive distribution. Organizations generally indulge in this strategy to create an aura of exclusivity and class around their brands. For example, Christian Dior, one of the largest fashion houses in the world opened its first store in Mumbai at the Taj Mahal Palace and Towers (Raghavendra 2010).

Organizations can also link together their various businesses to make a foray into other categories. For example, Tata Chemicals launched a range of pulses branded as i-Shakti Dal. See Exhibit 9.12 for further details.

Exhibit 9.12 Branded Pulses

Tata Chemicals has identified 'pulses as the staple facing a chronic shortage, not yet addressed by the government.' The prices of pulses have risen in the last few years due to poor supply. The company estimates the annual demand for pulses will rise to 34 million tonnes by 2030. The packaged staples have seen flour, rice, salt, etc., but not pulses. Tata Chemicals hopes to overcome this by announcing the launch of branded pulses—i-Shakti Dal, which will be used as their umbrella food brand (see Image 9.4).

Tata Chemicals already has '690 rural outlets called Kisan Sansar in north and east India. Rallis, its subsidiary, with a range of agro-chemical products, has a customer relationship programme called Kisan Kutumb in the south and west. Together, they touch base with over 5 million farmers across the country.' They have also launched a 'public private partnership with the government of Tamil Nadu for urad dal and of Punjab for moong dal called "Grow more pulses"'. They also plan to educate farmers to grow more pulses, introduce them to the best practices, better seeds, and inform them about irrigation. The pilot project in Tamil Nadu has 4000–5000 farmers cultivating 5000–7000 acres of urad dal. Uttar Pradesh, Maharashtra, and Karnataka will be supplying toor dal. The pulses will be priced between ₹85–100 per kilo. The distribution will be taken care of through the Tata Salt-i-Shakti distribution chain, which includes 1.5 million outlets. Starting with Tamil Nadu and Maharashtra, i-Shakti will reach the rest of India by June 2011 (Kar 2011).

December 21, 2010

- *Introduces four variants of dals i.e.,* moong, chana, toor and urad
- *To leverage Rallis India's close farmer relationships and Tata Chemicals' existing wide distribution network of traditional* kirana *stores and large format food malls to market the dals*

Mumbai: If there is a single food dish that reaches the core of every Indian's heart, it is a warm cup of a simple, home-cooked *dal* (pulses). *Dals* are not only a rich source of protein, but also the mainstay of every Indian's diet. India is probably the only nation that depends heavily on pulses as its staple food. Extending the i-Shakti brand from salt to other food essentials, Tata Chemicals (TCL), today, unveiled as India's first national brand of pulses — i-Shakti Dals — and has launched four popular varieties of pulses i.e., *chana, toor, urad* and *moong* (including whole green *moong* and green *chilka*) in the Indian market.

The pulses range has been reasonably priced between MRP Rs95 to Rs100 for a one-kg pack and will be available in SKUs of one kg, 500g and 250g. Apart from the traditional *kirana* stores and modern format food retail chains, TCL will utilise its Tata Kisan Sansar outlets as well as its existent strong salt-distribution network to distribute the i-Shakti Dals range across the country.

The i-Shakti Dals range of pulses will be rolled out in a phased manner and will be initially available in Tamil Nadu, Maharashtra, Gujarat and then available in the rest of the country.

Speaking on the pulses foray, R Gopalakrishnan, chairman, Rallis India (Rallis), and vice chairman, TCL, said, "*Dal* has been an integral part of almost every Indian meal, we are happy to introduce an initiative that is holistic in nature and takes due care in every process — from seed to food, therefore the term 'from farm to fork'. Through this we aim to work towards creating a healthier future for our country."

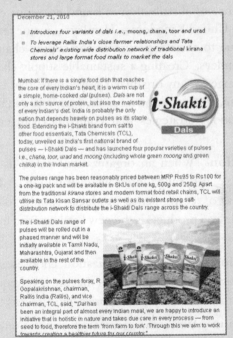

Source: http://www.tatachemicals.com/media/releases/201012dec/20101221.htm, accessed on 22 January 2011.

Image 9.4 Branded pulses from Tata Chemicals

Distribution Strategy and Branding

The distribution of the product has to be in line with its brand image. Thus, for example, a diamond jewellery brand like Orra is set to open a number of anchor stores more than double the size of its retail outlets. The cost of each store of an average size of 3000 square feet will take ₹15–20 crore to set up. Each such store, a total of five stores being planned in the coming three years, will focus on premium customers and the first such store will come up in New Delhi's posh South Extension market (*The Economic Times,* 2010b). Gucci, with an image of producing exclusive designer goods, has one store located in Delhi and Mumbai each; it plans to open stores in other metros including Bangalore (PTI 2009). Why does it not plan to open other stores in Delhi and Mumbai? The answer is simple, it wants to maintain the 'exclusive' image of its brand and thus wants to go for an exclusive distribution and not selective or intensive distribution, which will dilute its brand image. Companies have also adopted the strategy of acquisitions to help them in the distribution of their brands. For example, Coca-Cola in 1993 paid ₹180 crore to Parle to acquire the iconic brand Thums Up, so that it could gain 'access to more than 5 lakh retailers through Parle bottlers' (Sabharwal 2010).

Another example of brand building through distribution is the TTK group, makers of the Prestige brand of cookware that was founded in 1928 and was initially the distributor of pressure cookers imported from the UK. In 1959, TTK set up a production facility for pressure cookers in Bangalore, and has since then introduced a host of cookware, mixer-grinders, gas stoves, etc., which were distributed through multi-brand dealer networks (see Image 9.5).

Prestige cashed in on the reality boom by foraying into the modular kitchen segment. This helped it transform from a pressure cooker company to a total kitchen solutions provider and set up its own exclusive Prestige Smart Kitchen outlets (see Image 9.6).

It further sensed a measurable shift of the Indian rural market towards branded kitchen products (*Superbrands,* 2009). To reach this vast audience, Prestige formed an alliance with HPCL (Hindustan Petroleum Corporation Ltd) 'for the distribution of Prestige's products through the LPG outlets in the country' (*Superbrands,* 2009).

Bank of Baroda also uses its presence in different states throughout India to distribute its services through its network of more than 1950 branches (*Superbrands,* 2009) (see Image 9.7).

Courtesy: Superbrands.

Image 9.5 Prestige ad for its pressure cooker

Courtesy: Superbrands.

Image 9.6 Prestige Smart Kitchen

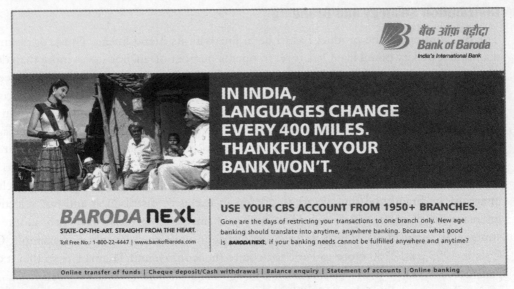

Courtesy: Superbrands.

Image 9.7 Bank of Baroda's 1950 and more branches

India has a mix of unorganized and organized retail in the form of mom-and-pop or kirana stores and malls respectively (Misra 2008). The global meltdown and the resultant slowdown in the market have forced organizations to take a re-look at their brand portfolio—especially in the $20 billion organized retail sector (Mukherjee 2010). Thus, Aditya Birla Retail has closed thirty-nine stores of its 'More Supermarkets' (Sruthijith 2010); the Future group has decided to 'rejig its operations to just six large formats—Pantaloons, Big Bazaar, Food Bazaar, Central, Home Town, and eZone. The smaller formats like Depot, Lee Cooper, Fashion@Big Bazaar, Blue Sky, etc., have been merged and will be pursued as shop-in-shop concept rather than stand-alone stores' (Mukherjee 2009). Retailers, through the shop-in-shop concept, reduce their costs by 25 per cent and can exploit synergies with other retailers from non-competing categories to provide a wider choice to consumers in the same store (Mukherjee 2010).

Conclusion

Effective distribution is necessary to make the brand available where the consumers can conveniently purchase them. Where the brand is retailed and how it is sold also communicates with the customers and has a bearing on the brand image. Organizations, thus, need to strategize carefully the distribution aspect of their brands, so that it enhances brand image, and ultimately brand equity.

SUMMARY

An integrated marketing concept provides an understanding that all the Ps communicate with the customers. Thus, directly or indirectly they impact brand image, and hence brand equity. In this chapter, we studied how we can enhance brand equity through product policies and initiatives. Product decisions regarding product features, perceived quality, packaging, product support services and customer experience all have a bearing on the customers' experience of the brand and therefore influence the brand image. This can be further reinforced by selling the product at a price that is in line with the brand image. Lifestyle brands cannot just adopt price discounts to enhance sales without impacting their brand image. Therefore, for the long-term growth of the brand, organizations need to be very careful. For a portfolio of brands, the pricing strategies that can be adopted are product line pricing and product mix pricing. Product mix pricing further includes strategies like captive product pricing and product bundle pricing.

How and where the brand is being sold also speaks volumes for the brand. FMCGs need to be available readily, so that consumers can purchase them easily. If the product is not available it leads to store-switching, postponed purchase, lost sales, brand switching and same brand substitution. However, a Nike shoe can afford to be present at select outlets in a city and consumers will come looking for it. Thus, a company can choose between intensive distribution, selective distribution and exclusive distribution depending on the kind of product it is marketing. The brand, thus, needs to look at all the aspects of the product, pricing, and distribution for strong brand equity.

KEY TERMS

Brand spiralling Using the traditional media to promote and attract consumers to an online website is called brand spiralling.

Captive product pricing To sell products that can be used with the main product, companies use captive product pricing.

Convenience products These are products that are purchased frequently by the consumers with minimum comparison and buying effort. Minimum or no planning is required before the purchase of these products.

E-business It is the use of the digital media or the electronic media to reach out and connect with the consumers.

Everyday low pricing (EDLP) EDLP stands for an organization charging a low price on a daily basis with no further price discounts.

Exclusive distribution When an organization chooses only a limited number of outlets to distribute its brand, it is called exclusive distribution.

Good-value pricing Good value pricing is offering brands at the right price and providing quality and service accordingly, so that customers get good value for their purchases.

High-low pricing This strategy allows marketers to charge a higher price on an everyday basis, but offer price promotions on select items at various intervals of time.

Intensive distribution When an organization makes its services available through as many outlets as possible, it is called intensive distribution.

Price Price is the amount of money charged for a product or service.

Product bundle pricing When several brands are bundled together and sold at a lower price, it is called product bundle pricing.

Product A product is a tangible object, an intangible service, or an idea, which a marketer offers to satisfy the needs and wants of customers.

Selective distribution When an organization chooses only some outlets to distribute its brand, it is called selective distribution.

Social networking sites A number of independent online communities, such as Facebook, Orkut, etc., which have come up and that provide options for customers to congregate and exchange information online.

Value-added pricing To differentiate and to protect themselves from price wars, organizations can add value to their product offering and then pricing them accordingly.

EXERCISES

Concept Review Questions

1. Discuss the concept of a product. While deciding upon the product strategy, what factors should be kept in mind?
2. Elucidate the type of pricing strategies an organization can adopt. Discuss with reference to branding.
3. Discuss how the distribution strategy of an organization impacts its brand image.
4. Enumerate the various e-business strategies an organization can adopt to build a brand. Discuss any two strategies an organization should adopt and discuss why you think these two are important.

Critical Thinking Questions

1. How can we differentiate between a product and a brand? Can we transform a product into a brand?
2. In an age where consumers seek convenience, do you think an exclusive distribution strategy is no longer valid?

3. With Internet penetration at 7 per cent in India, do organizations need to have an online strategy?

Internet Exercises

1. Visit the website of Asian Paints at http://www.asianpaints.com. Identify the Ask Aparna icon. Click on this and experience the same. What is the strategic relevance of this? Why according to you has Asian Paints used this feature on their website?
2. Visit the website of Kingfisher at http://www.flykingfisher.com. On the top right hand corner, click on the 'Kingfisher World' icon. Describe the same? What is the benefit of incorporating this on the website?

CD Exercise

View the Idea ad and discuss how it helps in positioning the brand's products.

REFERENCES

Ambwani, M.V., 'Have lunch @ ₹199. Thank God it's a weekday', *The Economic Times*, New Delhi, 13 November 2009, p. 4.

ANI, 'Smart TV blurs if kids get too close', *Times of India*, New Delhi, 12 June 2010, p. 17.

Apelbaum, E., E. Gerstner, and P.A. Naik, 'The effects of expert quality evaluations versus brand name on price premiums', *Journal of Product and Brand Management*, Vol. 12, Issue no. 3, 2003, pp. 154–165.

Betts, S. and Z. Taran, 'The "brand halo" effect—brand reliability influence on used car prices', *Proceedings of the Academy of Marketing Studies*, Vol. 7, Issue no. 1, 2002, pp. 19–24.

Bhushan, R. and B. Pande, 'Packing a paanch', *The Economic Times*, New Delhi, 24 December 2010, p. 4.

Bhushan, R., 'A basket of woes', *The Economic Times*, New Delhi, 1 March 2010, p. 4.

Bhushan, R., 'Thirst for premium drive', *The Economic Times*, New Delhi, 29 December 2009, p. 4.

Chauhan, C.P., 'Maruti tweaking models to take on rivals', *The Economic Times*, New Delhi, 11 January 2010, p. 5.

Chen, H.L., 'Gray marketing and its impacts on brand equity', *Journal of Product and Brand Management*, Vol. 16, Issue no. 4, 2007, pp. 247–256.

Corsten, D. and T.W. Gruen, 'Desperately seeking shelf availability—an examination of the extent, the causes and the efforts to address retail out-of-stocks,' *International Journal of Retail and Distribution Management*, Vol. 31, Issue no. 12, 2003, pp. 605–617.

Darke, P.R. and C.M.Y. Chung, 'Effects of pricing and promotion on consumer perceptions—It depends on how you frame it', *Journal of Retailing*, Vol. 81; Issue no. 1, 2005, pp. 35–47.

Fortin, David R., Sarah Cleland, and Anna Jenkins (2008), 'Effects of advertised pricing on brand image for an on-line retailer', *Proceedings of the 2008 American Academy of Advertising Annual Conference*, S. Rodgers ed. San Mateo, CA US, March, 263–75.

Graham, R. (2002), 'A proposal for IRRI to establish a grain quality and nutrition research center,' IRRI Discussion Paper Series No. 44, International Rice Research Institute, Los Baños (Philippines), p. 15.

Hardesty, D.M. and W.O. Bearden (2003), 'Consumer evaluations of different promotion types and price presentations—The moderating role of promotional benefit level', *Journal of Retailing*, Vol. 79, Issue no. 1, pp. 17–25.

Jauhari, V. and K. Dutta (2009), *Services Marketing Management and Operations*, Oxford University Press, New Delhi, Chapter 2.

Kar, S., 'Chemistry of pulses', *The Strategist, Business Standard*, New Delhi, 3 January 2011, p. 2.

Kar, S., 'Why Paras is a hot buy', *Business Standard*, New Delhi, 11 October 2010, p. 14.

Keller, K.L. (2008), *Strategic Brand Management—Building, Measuring and Managing Brand Equity*, 3rd Edition, Prentice-Hall of India Private Limited, New Delhi.

Kotler, P., G. Armstrong, P.Y. Agnihotri, and E. ul Haque (2010), *Principles of Marketing—A South Asian Perspective*, 13th Edition, Prentice Hall, Delhi.

Kuehn, A.A. and R.L. Day (1962), 'Strategy of product quality', *Harvard Business Review*, Vol. 40, Issue 6, pp. 100–110.

Kurian, B. (2010), 'UK giant buys maker of Moov for ₹3,260 crore' http://timesofindia.indiatimes.com/business/india-business/UK-giant-buys-maker-of-Moov-for-Rs-3260-crore/articleshow/7096196.cms, accessed on 21 January 2011.

Mehta, N., S. Rajiv, and K. Srinivasan, 'Price uncertainty and consumer search—A structural model of consideration set formation', *Marketing Science*, Vol. 22, Issue no. 1, 2003, pp. 58–84.

Misra, D.P., 'FMCG distribution channels in India—Challenges and opportunities for manufacturers and retailers', *The Journal of Global Business Issues*, Vol. 2, Issue 2, 2008, pp. 175–182.

Mukherjee, P. (2010), 'Emami wants bigger bite of food business', http://www.emamiltd.in/press/Business%20Standard%2011%2003%202010.pdf, accessed on 21 January 2011.

Mukherjee, W., 'Recession shapes Biyani's biz plan', *The Economic Times*, New Delhi, 27 November 2009, p. 6.

Mukherjee, W., 'Sharing space to expand specialty chains', *The Economic Times*, New Delhi, 9 April 2010, p. 6.

Naidu, K., 'Tata Docomo to play pricing game in 3G too', *Business Standard*, New Delhi, 4 November 2010, p. 10.

Palazon, M. and E. Delgado, 'The moderating role of price consciousness on the effectiveness of price discounts and premium promotions', *Journal of Product and Brand Management*, Vol. 18, Issue no. 4, 2009, pp. 306–312.

Pantin-Sohier, G., 'The influence of the product package on functional and symbolic associations of brand image', *Recherche et Applications en Marketing*, Vol. 24, Issue no. 2, 2009, pp. 53–71.

PTI, 'Gucci set for single-brand India foray', *The Economic Times*, New Delhi, 4 December 2009, p. 4.

PTI, 'Suzuki launches ₹12.75 lakh bike', *The Economic Times*, New Delhi, 15 June 2010, p. 5.

Quilter, J., 'Now, Marks & Spencer lets in other brands—First in 125 years—British retailer seeks to plug gaps in product offering', *The Economic Times*, New Delhi, 5 November 2009, p. 4.

Raghavendra, N., 'Dior to open first Mumbai store at Taj', *The Economic Times*, New Delhi, 28 January 2010, p. 4.

Ramalinga, A. (2008), 'Everyone loves a good discount', http://www.financialexpress.com/news/everyone-loves-a-good-discount/286531/0, accessed on 10 June 2010.

Reuters, 'Toyota extends recall of cars to Europe', *The Times of India*, New Delhi, 29 January 2010.

Sheng, S., A.M. Parker, and K. Nakamoto, 'The effects of price discount and product complementarity on consumer evaluations of bundle components', *Journal of Marketing, Theory and Practice*, Vol. 15, Issue no. 1, 2007, pp. 53–64.

Singh, P., 'New flavours of the season—Chyawanprash makers have lined up fruity variants for a wider reach', *Business Standard*, New Delhi, 9 December 2010, p. 8.

Sruthijith, K.K., 'Less is more for Aditya Birla Retail', *The Economic Times*, New Delhi, 1 April 2010, p. 4.

Superbrands (2009), *Superbrands—An insight into India's strongest consumer brands*, Vol. III, Superbrands India Private Limited, Gurgaon.

Taylor, V., 'Brand name and price cue effects within a brand extension context', *Academy of Marketing Studies Journal*, Vol. 13, Issue no. 2, 2009, pp. 59–75.

The Economic Times (2010a), 'Nokia plays to masses to outsmart rivals', *The Economic Times*, New Delhi, 27 April 2010, p. 4.

The Economic Times (2010b), 'Diamond in style', *The Economic Times*, New Delhi, 12 April 2010, p. 4.

The Economic Times (2010c), 'Figo drives into India with a tag of ₹3.49 L', *The Economic Times*, New Delhi, 10 March 2010, p. 4.

Varma, U., 'As a brand, we are targeting non-sensitive vegetarians', *The Economic Times*, New Delhi, 12 April 2010, p. 4.

Vyas, M. (2010a), 'FMCG firms facing package ordeal—price of packaging materials up by 25% during last three months', *The Economic Times*, New Delhi, 6 April 2010, p. 4.

Vyas, M. (2010b), 'Barbie may go for sarees and bindis', *The Economic Times*, New Delhi, 22 January 2010, p. 4.

Yoo, B., N. Donthu, and S. Lee, 'An examination of selected marketing mix elements and brand equity', *Journal of the Academy of Marketing Science*, Vol. 28, Issue no. 2, 2000, pp. 195–211.

Yu, H. and W. Fang, 'Relative impacts from product quality, service quality, and experience quality on customer perceived value and intention to shop for the coffee shop market', *Total Quality Management*, Vol. 20, Issue no. 11, 2009, pp. 1273–1285.

Web resources

http://www.thehindubusinessline.com/2006/10/20/stories/2006102001001200.htm, accessed on 19 January 2011.

http://www.tatachemicals.com/media/releases/201012dec/20101221.htm, accessed on 22 January 2011.

http://www.franchisemart.in/retail_news-62.html, accessed on 6 February 2011.

CASE STUDY

Micromax—The Indian War Horse*

Introduction

The turf war in the Indian handset market has reached a pinnacle with the advent of a slew of Indian brands eating away at the feet of the behemoths. One such homegrown gladiator is Micromax. Understanding the pulse of the customer, riding popular trends, making good use of government policy changes, and outsourcing judiciously, the company has redefined the market place. The Indian mobile landscape has been dominated by foreign players, such as Nokia, Samsung, LG, Motorola, etc. Micromax is amongst the first homegrown thoroughbreds to challenge this foreign supremacy. It is presently eyeing the dicey second position previously occupied by the likes of Sony Ericsson, Motorola, and currently Samsung. Founded by Rajesh Aggarwal, the formidable challenger commenced its journey in 1991 as a modest distributor of computer peripherals for companies such as LG, Sony Inc., Dell Corp. (Dharamkumar 2010). Sumit Arora, Rahul Sharma, and Vikas Jain came on board in the year 1998. In the subsequent year, the company expanded operations to include the marketing of telecommunications equipment (i.e., making PCO phones for Bharti). The entry into the mobile handset market came only in 2007. An important development in the macro environment that went in the company's favour was the decision by the Department of Telecommunication to ban handsets lacking valid international mobile equipment identity (IMEI). This stemmed the influx of cheap Chinese phones. At the same time, Nokia which had previously dominated the mobile handset category also acceded some space due to the non-availability of appealing models. Since, Micromax initially lacked customer base and did not want to challenge the might of the existing players, it chose the road less travelled by concentrating on the rural market first. Lets us examine how the Indian David challenged the supremacy of the colossal Goliaths.

Designing the product and building the brand

The company from the very beginning relied heavily on consumer insights to develop and market its phones. According to company folklore, in the year 2007, while on a trip to Behrampur (West Bengal), Rahul Sharma chanced upon an Airtel PCO powered by a truck battery. The owner of the PCO would haul the battery 12 km on his bicycle to an adjacent village for overnight charging and return with it the subsequent morning (Philip 2010). When

*Dr Swati Singh, Faculty Marketing, Bharatiya Vidya Bhavan's Usha and Lakshmi Mittal Institute of Management, New Delhi.

Micromax diversified into mobile handsets, the inspiration for its first product was drawn from this very episode. The product that culminated from this insight was the X1i with a battery capable of lasting thirty days and providing seventeen hours of talk time on a single charge. Priced at ₹2249, it was a runaway success in the rural belt. Buoyed by the success of the phone, the company aggressively set about designing its handset brigade. All its product launches have been designed meticulously to cater to a specific consumer requirement. Micromax X235 doubled as a master remote for TVs or air conditioners; priced at ₹3000, its unique feature was previously unheard of in the Indian market. Understanding the consumer's need to carry two mobiles, two SIMs, it launched dual SIM phones priced between ₹1,999–12,999, the Q7—a dual SIM phone came with a QWERTY keypad priced economically between ₹4500–₹5000. To cater to rapidly growing social networking trends amongst the youth, it launched the Q5—a Facebook phone (Ghosh 2010). Endorsed by the glamorous Twinkle Khanna, the Swarovski-encrusted Bling, priced at ₹5500, was a fashion statement that was lapped up by young girls and women alike. Selling 35,000 pieces per month, it is the most successful product from the Micromax stable. It co-branded with MTV for the Micromax MTV X360, which has built-in Yamaha amplifiers. Spotting the growing trend of gaming across the urban youth, Micromax launched yet another formidable gadget, the G4 Gamolution. The primary focus as the name suggests is gaming and the star power is provided by its brand ambassador, action hero Akshay Kumar. The company promoted the set during IPL 3 matches. Just like the previous models, the G4 is fully loaded with features that include a 4 GB expandable memory, 2-megapixel camera, and a web camera.

Pricing across the portfolio

The lethal combination of aggressive pricing coupled with deadly features across the board has given Micromax's competitors sleepless nights. Strategically, therefore, the communication from Micromax is bereft of price emphasis, focusing primarily on the features. Micromax had confined itself to small towns and rural belts in the initial 12–18 months of its launch in 2007. It served this market by providing a host of handsets priced between ₹1,800 and ₹2,400. By pricing models at 30 per cent lower than established players and loading its handsets with previously unimagined features, Micromax till now has been able to achieve margins of 10 per cent. It understood very early in the race that the multinational players had slightly misunderstood the market. The rural and semi-urban markets did not want less for less but aspired to get more for less. This gap was plugged by Micromax by loading its phones with features, and at the same time pricing them equivalent to a 'basic phone' from the MNC stable. Floored by coloured screens, camera, torches, back up, etc., the semi-literate and illiterate market took to Micromax with great enthusiasm. The company realized that it could not resist the urban charm for long and, hence, drafted its expansion plan. For its urban expedition, the company launched high-end sets that could run on Google's Android and Microsoft's Windows Mobile operating systems and yet not burn the customer's pocket. To announce its urban entry, it advertised with a vengeance, sponsored Khatron ke Khiladi–3, Asia Cup 2010, and acquired the title sponsorship rights for the 11th IIFA Awards held in Sri Lanka during June 2010. To increase visibility, the company signed on Akshay Kumar as its brand ambassador and sponsored the Bryan Adams tour to India in February 2011.

Distribution and servicing

The company was well aware that success in the Indian market requires a strong brand as well as an efficient distribution system. Hence, it went about creating a distribution network comprising 34 super distributors, 450 distributors, and approximately 55,000 retailers (Dharmakumar 2010). A difficult task for mobile companies had been the payment collection from dealers. Micromax was able to overcome this hurdle by offering dealers additional margins for making payments in advance. Paying upfront for the handsets, prevented the trade from overstocking, and at the same time, pressurized the dealers to push the Micromax products more aggressively. Moreover, Micomax has kept the trade in good spirit by giving margins as high as 5 per cent against the 2 per cent generally given by established players (Dharmakumar 2010). Another element of success in the mobile market is the post-sales service. Micromax has ramped up its service centres to 450. However, it still has a long way to go to take on established players with over 600 plus centres (Philip 2010).

Research and production

Micromax's product strategy was carefully devised so that it did not fall into the 'me too' trap, but ensured that despite being priced low each of its offerings had a unique proposition. Therefore, the responsibility of designing the phones as well as the software was assigned to an in-house research team. The company sources chips from the likes of MediaTek Inc., Qualcomm Inc., and Infineon Technologies AG. It outsources manufacturing to companies in Taiwan, South Korea, and China. Unlike the larger players, smaller companies like Micromax first zero-in on the features desired for a model and then invite bids from Chinese companies. The company capable of manufacturing the desired model at the desired cost is given the contract. This competitive bidding reduces the cost of the mobile, and on the other hand allows the company to bring forth new models more frequently. However, following a phenomenal surge in demand, the dynamics that previously existed have undergone a change, requiring greater stability and certainty across the supply chain. Therefore, Micromax invested ₹100 crore in setting up a manufacturing facility in Baddi, Himachal Pradesh. It expects to produce 5,00,000 handsets a month from this plant by 2011. The success of Micromax encouraged TA Associates, a US-based private equity firm to buy around 20 per cent stake in the company for approximately ₹210 crore in December 2009 (Joseph 2010).

Global aspirations

Having created products that appealed to the value-conscious customer, it was but logical for Micromax to look for similar customers in other countries. It made a foray into Nepal, Bangladesh, and Sri Lanka in July 2010. Its entry into the Middle Eastern countries like Oman, UAE, Kuwait, and Qatar was achieved through a wholly owned subsidiary, Micromax Informatics FZE in October 2010.

The road ahead

There is a popular saying, 'Well begun is half done'. Micromax, till now has played its cards well. It has sent jitters amongst the established players. However, the road ahead is full of uncertainty and will require greater focus in building brand affinity, through not only quality products, but also upgraded software. Supply chains will have to be streamlined and success will depend on volumes. Besides, there is also the lingering requirement of scaling up service centres and bracing for attacks from bigger players fighting to regain lost turf. The future, thus, depends on the agility and nimble-footedness that Micromax displays in understanding and riding future developments and trends.

Discussion Questions

1. What product strategies has Micromax followed to establish itself as a brand in the handset industry?
2. Discuss the pricing strategies followed by Micromax. Is this in line with its branding strategy?
3. Discuss the various distribution strategies followed by Micromax. Is it in line with the brand image created by the product and pricing strategies?
4. What do you think about the various strategies followed by the Micromax brand? What can be the reason for choosing the specific foreign markets for entry? Discuss the implications of the same for the brand Micromax?

Case References

Dharamkumar, Robin (2010)'Micromax Mobile Advantage' http://business.in.com/article/work-in-progress/micromax-mobile-advantage/10472/1, accessed on 19 August 2010.

Ghosh, Arnab (2010)'Micromax Q6 Qwerty Phone Launched' http://gadgetophilia.com/micromax-q6-qwerty-phone-launched/, accessed on 21 August 2010.

Joseph, Lison (2010)'Micromax challenges Samsung, LG in mobile phone stakes' http://www.livemint.com/2010/02/08221833/Micromax-challenges-Samsung-L.html, accessed on 21 August 2010.

Philip, Thomas Jogi (2010), 'Upwardly mobile—Nothing micro about Micromax', http://economictimes.indiatimes.com/articleshow/6165036.cms, accessed on 20 August 2010.

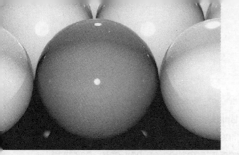

E-branding—Building the Brand Online

10

LEARNING OBJECTIVES

After reading this chapter, you will be able to understand the following:

- The concept of e-business
- E-business strategies
- Building a brand online

ABOUT THE CHAPTER

The recent years have seen the rise of a new media—the Internet. More and more companies are now going online to tap a wider audience at a minimal cost (see Exhibit 10.1). The online strategy of an organization is, therefore, equally important in building brand equity and cannot be ignored in the times to come. The convenience and the 24/7 accessibility of the Internet make it an attractive media for both buyers and sellers. Considering the fact that consumers in rural India are as gadget-savvy as urban Indians and that half the mobile phones sold in rural India are Internet-enabled (Aulakh 2011), the scope of online branding pan-India is huge.

Exhibit 10.1   A Whole New World

Young consumers today are increasingly becoming 'immune to clichéd prime-time television advertising and prefer to spend intimate time with their PCs (personal computers). A study of 475 active online consumers revealed the following:

- 91 per cent rely on the web for current news and information

- 60 per cent personalize homepages by adding features like RSS or content feed
- 70 per cent read blogs regularly
- 67 per cent regularly watch videos online

People are increasingly empowered by their social media and the second-by-second frenzied analysis of the relationship status on Facebook profiles is a stark truth.'

Contd

Exhibit 10.1 *contd*

The social media both excites them and empowers them to stay connected with their friends 24/7. This makes the Internet the 'hottest real estate'. Since great brands need to 'continuously engage and connect with their consumers, be a part of their conversation, listen to them as much as they speak to them', the Internet is the place to be. Many brands are providing the option of 'Follow us on Twitter' or 'Join us on Facebook' (marked 'a' on the Image 10.1 ahead). One of the brands to log on to this media early on in India was Sunsilk, a shampoo from Unilever, with its 'Gang of Girls (GoG)', an exclusive online girls' community.

They provide information on hair care, hairstyle, latest trends, and fashion reports with information on style news, make-up trends, and beauty treatments. The makeover machine (marked 'c' on Image 10.2) allows a mix and match method to create a new look before physically experimenting with it. The show and share icon (see Image 10.2) allows forums for discussions and debates, sharing of 'fab moments',

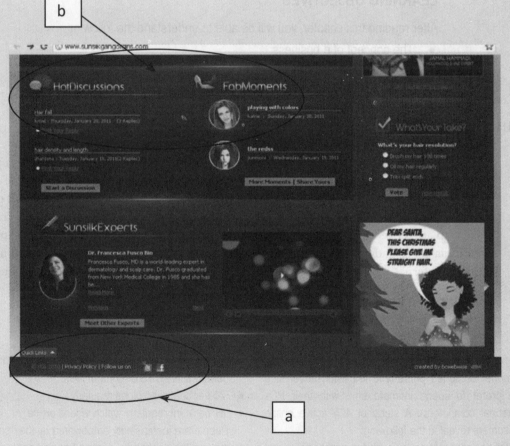

Source: http://www.sunsilkgangofgirls.com/

Image 10.1 Icons on Sunsilk Gang of Girls

Contd

Exhibit 10.1 *contd*

talent parades, etc. Thus, it provides a platform for both self-expression and a space for interaction with hot discussions and fab moments (marked 'b' on the Image 10.1 and is that moment when you donned your best hairstyle, the most glamorous outfit—your most memorable look). All this makes this online community a part of the consumers' life and allows the brand to be a friend that consumers willingly interact and communicate with (Sachdev 2010; Sunsilk Gang of Girls 2010).

Image 10.2 Sunsilk Gang of Girls

INTRODUCTION

The World Wide Web has opened a set of new opportunities for organizations. From the traditional brick and mortar firms, we now have click and mortar firms (see Figure 10.1), i.e., firms are these days present online besides the physical store that you can actually go visit, for example, HP Laptops, Amul, etc. There are also organizations that have a presence only in the virtual world, i.e., they are present only online and do not have physical stores, for example, amazon.com.

The online media enables firms to reach a wider cross-section of people and attain a global audience. Organizations have the opportunity to be present online, do business, service customers, and communicate with the target audience effectively and efficiently. With the global Internet penetration still at 26.6 per cent and the penetration in India at 7 per cent (Internet World Stats 2010), the media is still in its infancy and the opportunity it offers is humongous. The availability of content in a number of local languages further promotes the adoption of the Internet by consumers. The Internet Corporation for Assigned Names and Numbers (ICANN), the global body that sets the standards for the Internet, decided to make addresses available in non-Latin scripts as well from 27 October 2009 onwards. This enabled non-English speaking Indians to type 'dot bharat' (.bharat) in the Devanagari script, while accessing popular websites, thus offering huge possibilities to small and medium enterprises (Shivapriya 2009) (see Exhibit 10.2). Apart from the Internet, there are mobile phones, dedicated kiosks, etc. that enable the use of digital commerce to help in building the brand.

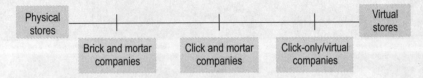

Figure 10.1   Progression from physical to virtual stores

Exhibit 10.2   Future's E-bazaar

Kishore Biyani's Future Group has been one of the first modern retailers to adopt digital commerce in a big way. Its online retail arm—'Future E-commerce'—already has an e-commerce portal, FutureBazaar.com, and is now planning to launch new initiatives like 'sms short codes, teleshopping, proximity marketing through mobile phones, and virtual shopping through manned kiosks.' It will be competing with portals like indiatimes.com, eBay.com, rediff.com, and websites like Landmark, Shoppers Stop, etc. The size of online marketing at ₹500 crore a year, and teleshopping at ₹900 crore, along with the fact that urban consumers spend 8–10 hours a day on any one of the screens, whether computer, mobile, television, or dedicated kiosks, is what has inspired this decision.

The brands purchased through e-bazaar will be 5–20 per cent cheaper compared to the in-store prices. This is because of the fact that brands will be sent directly from the warehouse to the consumer without taking up shelf space. The online store—Futurebazaar.com—will be updated with more stock-keeping units and more information about brands on the website, including videos. The company is in talks to acquire an IT company with 150 personnel to maintain and develop the content and website for Futurebazaar.com. For the teleshopping initiative, bulk airtime on TV channels will be purchased. Dedicated manned kiosks will be erected, where consumers can browse 'through products and gather information, watch videos, even place an order and pay cash. The SMS short codes will also be promoted extensively and will also carry out proximity marketing using Bluetooth and cell tower based technologies.' Three to four products will be heavily promoted across all the digital platforms every week.

Source: Sruthijith 2010.

WHAT IS E-BUSINESS STRATEGY?

E-business is the use of the digital media or the electronic media to reach out and connect with consumers. It includes buying and selling goods and services, servicing customers, collaborating with business partners, and conducting electronic transactions within an organization (Turban and King 2009). An e-business strategy complements the traditional means of marketing rather than cannibalizing it. It adds value and an integration of the traditional and Internet methods 'creates potential advantages for established companies' (Porter 2001). Organizations can conduct business electronically, for example through mobile phones or the Internet, and leverage the experience and know-how to maximize value for the customers. For example, according to Mr Levent Demirel, Deputy General Director of Promotion, Ministry of Culture and Tourism, Turkey, the 'power of digital' is being leveraged for marketing Turkey as a tourist destination. They 'visit people online, on Facebook, and invite them to visit Turkey.'

With 471 million mobile phone subscribers in India (Ray 2009) already, a number of Indians are experiencing the Internet first on their mobile devices (Bartz 2009). This has helped in the growth of both Internet marketing and mobile commerce, and it cannot be ignored as a tool to reach the relevant market. The following activities can be done to reach the customers online (Kotler et al. 2010).

Create a website Organizations can create their own websites online and use that to reach customers with information about their products, promotions, the nearest outlets, after-sales service, etc. As discussed, a number of organizations are now turning from 'brick and mortar' to 'click and mortar', for example, Asianpaints.com (see Image 10.3) to virtual organizations, only having a virtual presence, such as amazon.com, ebay.com, etc.

Source: http://www.asianpaints.com/, accessed on 3 July 2010.

Image 10.3 Website of Asian Paints

Image 10.4   Online Ads on the website of the Indian Railways

Place ads online   Organizations can place their advertisements online. For example, on the Indian Railways website—irctc.com (see Image 10.4)—you can see the advertisement of Aircel, My Bill Seva, etc. (see the section on marketing and the Internet for a further discussion on online advertising).

Using e-mail   Organizations can use their database to send e-mails to customers to inform them about promotional offers from time to time. However, with the explosion in spam mails, customers are prone to deleting mails even before reading them. Thus, to overcome this, organizations are adopting the practice of 'permission based e-mail marketing', wherein they ask customers if they want to receive newsletters, etc. For example, Future Bazaar at the time of registering customers seeks their permission to send newsletters and other information (see Images 10.5 and 10.6).

Setting up or participating in online social networks   A number of independent online communities like Facebook, Orkut, etc., have come up, which provide options for customers to congregate, and exchange information online. Companies can either participate in the existing communities or set up their own communities. For example, Nokia (India) has a Facebook account, where 449,224 people like it (as on 21 March 2011) (see Image 10.7).

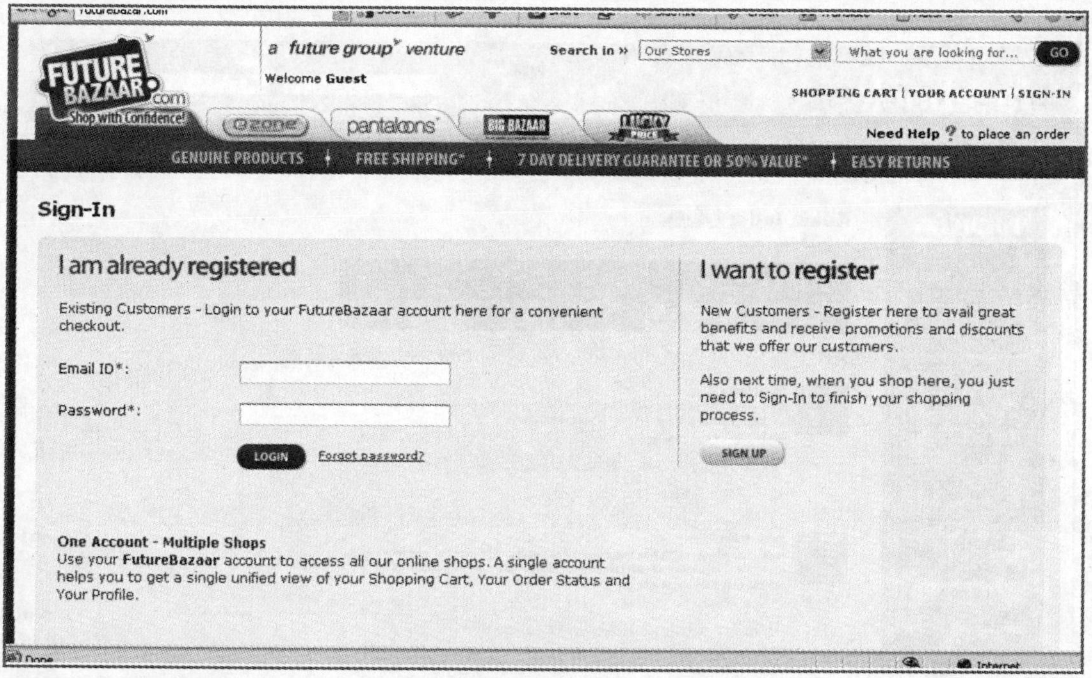

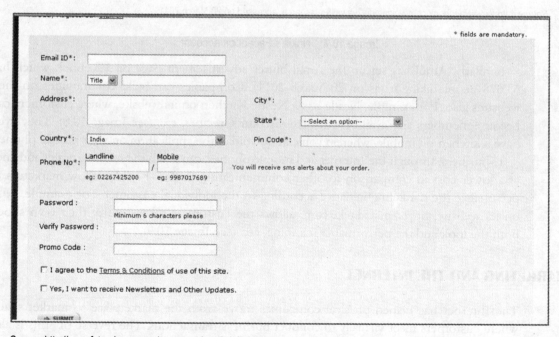

Image 10.5   Website of Future Bazaar

Source: http://www.futurebazar.com/, accessed on 3 July 2010.

Image 10.6   Details required while registering on the Future Bazaar website

Image 10.7 Nokia's Facebook account

Similarly, Amul has set up the Amul butter advertisement page on Facebook which has 63,678 people liking it (as on 20 March 2011). Companies can build communities on their websites also. For example, Nestlé has a Nestlé Kitchen on its website, where customers can become members and avail benefits like discounts, recipes, etc. (see Image 10.8). They even have a kitchen on mobile, wherein you can download the application on your mobile phone.

E-business, through the Internet and mobile phones, can reach the relevant target audience at a lower cost in comparison to other communication tools. They also allow marketers to personalize the marketing initiative according to the individual customer. For example, Nike on its website, http://nikeid.nike.com, allows the customers to customize their own shoes, both the look and the performance, clothing, etc. (see Image 10.9).

MARKETING AND THE INTERNET

The Internet has helped physical companies move from the marketplace to market space, where customers meet virtually to conduct business transactions. The reverse of this is also true, wherein companies after establishing themselves successfully in the market space, have come to the marketplace (see Exhibit 10.4). The Internet provides a number of benefits over the traditional stores and helps companies stay connected with consumers at the click of a

Source: http://www.nestle.in/nestle_kitchen/home.aspx, accessed on 4 July 2010.

Image 10.8 Nestlé Kitchen

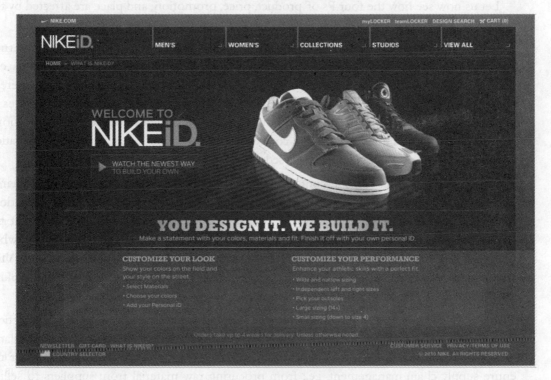

Source: http://nikeid.nike.com/nikeid/index.jsp#feature,whatisnikeid, accessed on 3 July 2010.

Image 10.9 NIKEiD site

Exhibit 10.3   What You Did Not Know about MakeMyTrip.com

- It is the first online travel company in India to offer its services through the internet, telephone, retail, and mobile.
- It introduced the concept of hotel pictures and guest reviews to sell hotel rooms.
- Each month over 3 million unique visitors visit its website.

- Each day it sells approximately 12,000 air tickets, 1000 hotel room nights, and 200 holiday packages.
- It offers the revolutionary 'search-book-pay' SMS service for flight ticketing.

Source: Superbrands 2009.

---

mouse. Consumers can easily access information from their homes, offices, and even on the move through their laptops and mobile phones that help them to stay connected online. The Internet provides a wealth of information about brands, their prices, what the brand-owning organizations have to say about themselves, and also what consumers say on different blog sites, i.e., the online word of mouth or 'word of mouse'. The Internet has helped organizations to progress from just providing information about their products to selling their brands and to helping build customer relationships online (see Exhibits 10.3 and 10.4).

Let us now see how the four Ps of product, price, promotion, and place are affected by the Internet.

Product   Some products can be completely digitalized for easy distribution on the Internet, for example, music, books, software, etc. For other types of products, organizations can get direct feedback from consumers about their expectations and experiences, and thereby tailor their products according to the tastes and preferences of the consumers. Changes in brand experience can be incorporated with the help of consumers' feedback and suggestions. Consumers can also be involved in the co-creation of a product by accessing customization options like the NIKEiD example discussed above.

Pricing   The Internet helps in connecting directly with the consumers. The intermediaries are removed and, therefore, the margin can then be an extra profit for the organizations or can be passed on as discounts to the consumers. For example, it is estimated that the costs of the banking service through the Internet is just a fraction of the cost involved when using conventional methods. Rough estimates assume teller cost at ₹1 per transaction, ATM transaction cost 45 paise, phone banking 35 paise, debit cards 20 paise, and Internet banking at 10 paise per transaction (RBI 2001).

Place   The Internet, as a distribution media, has been discussed in the preceding section. Websites of organizations are online places, where they interact and provide brand-related information and experience to consumers. Companies can also use these websites for the entire supply chain management, i.e., from procuring raw material from suppliers to selling finished products to customers. For procuring raw materials online, also called e-procurement, companies can put their requirements online and place request for quotations. Suppliers can

Exhibit 10.4   Online Travel Booking Revolution

Deep Kalra started MakeMyTrip.com in the year 2000 to service non-resident Indians (NRIs), who were looking out for economical travel tickets to visit their home country—India. By 2005, it became the 'foremost travel website in the US-India space' (see Image 10.10). Around 2005, the LCC (low-cost carriers) revolution hit the Indian market, which provided a plethora of choices for consumers. For consumers, the competitive fares brought to the fore the need to conveniently compare these prices and book tickets online. MakeMyTrip.com provided all this and more with its 'lowest airfare guarantee'.

The competitive advantage that MakeMyTrip.com had was the first mover advantage. This fact along with their constant innovation and upgradation of technology helped them stay ahead of competition. For example, they have come out with a MakeMyTrip application for the BlackBerry smartphone, offering the ease of availing all the services of MakeMyTrip.com on the go too.

Product   MakeMyTrip.com diversified and evolved from a travel portal to a 'one-stop-travel-shop' with a range of online and offline travel products and services. Its portfolio of products includes international and domestic air tickets, holiday packages, and hotels, domestic bus and rail tickets, private car and taxi rentals, MICE (meetings, incentives, conference, and exhibitions), and B2B and affiliate services. (Also see Image 10.11.)

Pricing   Its powerful search engine allows comparison and booking of both low-cost as well as full service airlines.

Source: http://www.makemytrip.com

Image 10.10   MakeMyTrip website

Contd

Exhibit 10.4 *contd*

Courtesy: Superbrands.

Marriages are made in heaven. To make your honeymoon though, simply call on 0285‑3098747 or visit makemytrip.com. Walk in to our Travel Shop, Vadodara "SAARTH" Complex, Opp Nutan Bharta Club, Above Reliance Fresh, Nutan Bharat Society, Alkapuri

Courtesy: Superbrands.

Image 10.11   MakeMyTrip.com ads

Contd

Exhibit 10.4 *contd*

Place Besides being present online, MakeMyTrip.com realized that people still prefer the traditional touch-and-feel method of booking tickets. To satisfy this need, it opened offices in twenty cities across India.

Promotion MakeMyTrip.com entered the Indian market with its lowest airfare guarantee, which made people sit up and take note of this new entrant. The money back guarantee helped it to build recognition and brought instant success to the brand. The famous slogan 'Hamne Toda Vaada Toh Pay Only Aadha' (if we break our promise, you pay only half) revolutionized the international travel market. The strategic use of print, radio, television, and online marketing helped bring recognition and brand recall.

Consumer insights After understanding and satisfying the Indian consumers' habit of bargaining by offering the lowest airfares, it was time to move on. On opening physical stores, MakeMyTrip.com realized that not all consumers wanted air tickets. To satisfy this need, it diversified into bus and rail ticket bookings.

MakeMyTrip is the 'undisputed online leader, with its share of the travel market extending to more than 50 per cent of all online sales, a fact evinced by the trust placed in it by millions of happy customers' (company website and Consumer Superbrands 2009).

send in their bids and the company can then decide from where to procure the materials. For spot purchases, that is immediate buys or for purchasing utilities like office stationery, etc., there are a number of sites that provide price comparisons, for example www.naaptol.com. 'Launched in January 2008, Naaptol is India's comparison-based social shopping portal—the one-stop destination for all shoppers, merchants, and market enthusiasts.' Image 10.12 shows various product ranges such as mobile phones, cameras, computers, etc., which are available on the Naaptol website. Image 10.13 shows that once a particular product category is chosen, the products appear with the option to compare prices, etc.

Bizrate.com is another online search portal (Image 10.14), which allows the convenience of searching for products, 'comparing' at reputed stores, and 'conquering' or getting the best deals and prices (see Image 10.15 and Exhibit 10.4: Online Travel Booking Revolution). Customers' ratings for stores are also provided (see Image 10.16), which helps prospective customers decide before making the final purchase.

Companies can also use their websites for tracking and tracing orders placed. For example, www.dhl.com provides the customers a unique tracking number, which helps them trace their packages/shipments sent via DHL (Image 10.17).

Through intranet and by using various software packages available, organizations can provide order processing and procurement information for the concerned employees, which helps in saving time and in reducing the duplication of tasks.

Promotion The Internet is used to promote and communicate about the brand to consumers. Online ads are of the following types (IAMAI 2010).

Text ads These are ads that are in the form of text and are generally visible on search engines, like Google and Yahoo. They are hyperlinked to the advertiser's website and when clicked on by a potential customer, they direct customers to these websites. For example, in Image 10.18, the first two links—HP and PC World—are paid text ads.

Image 10.12   Products available at Naaptol.com

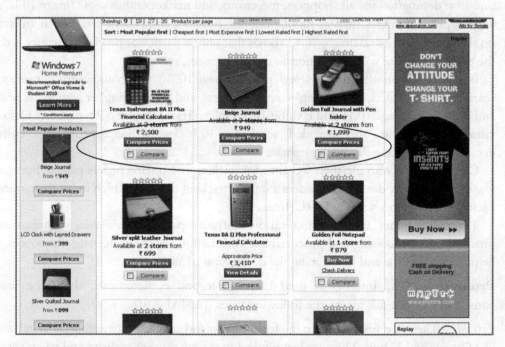

Image 10.13   Price comparison at Naaptol.com

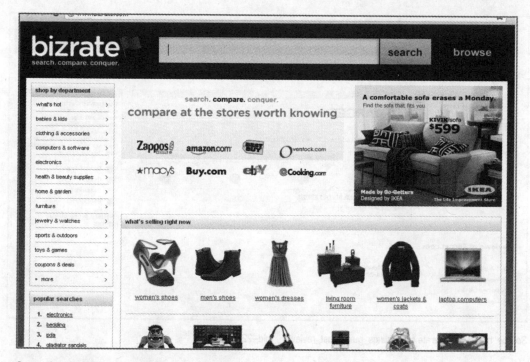

Source: http://www.bizrate.com

Image 10.14 Bizrate—Search, Compare, Conquer

Source: http://www.bizrate.com/womens-shoes/dr.-scholl's-fast-flats,-fits-sizes-5-6--pid2349350362/

Image 10.15 Bizrate—Comparing Dr Scholl's Fast Flats

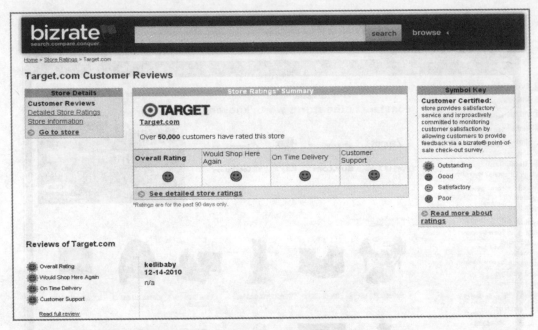

Source: http://www.bizrate.com/ratings_guide/cust_reviews__mid--22731.html

Image 10.16   Bizrate—Customer review for Target.com

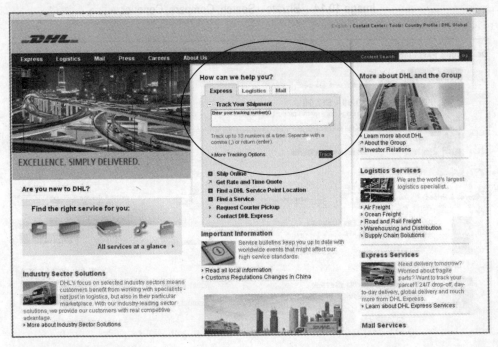

Source: http://www.dhl.co.in/en.html

Image 10.17   DHL—Tracking shipment online

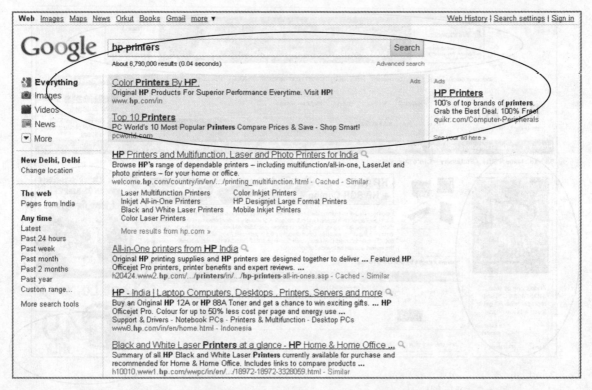

Source: http://www.google.co.in/#hl=en&biw=1024&bih=677&q=hp+printers&aq=f&aqi=g10&aql=&oq=&fp=989aa0e6667459e.

Image 10.18   Text ad on Google

Display ads   These are ads that contain text, logo, photographs, etc., and are placed at various points on a web page. Banner ads are a form of display ads (see Image 10.19).

Organizations can place their text ad or display ad classifieds, like naukri.com or monster. com. They can pay these sites a fee for listing their organization or can follow any of the following models (IAMAI 2010).

CPI/CPM   Cost per impression (CPI)/cost per mille (CPM) is the most fundamental model that is used for display ads. This is an extension of the traditional media broadcast model, where the advertiser pays per impression or image of the ad shown. The limitation of this model is that it is not performance-based. Thus, if the ad is placed on Google, *The Economic Times* website, etc., the organization will have to pay Google or *ET* for say a thousand impressions of the ad that are shown on these websites.

CPC   Cost per click (CPC) is mostly used by the new advertisers. Contrary to CPI, here the payment is made only when a prospective customer clicks on the ad and views the ad or the hyperlinked site. For example, out of the thousand impressions of the ad that were shown on a website, say only one hundred people clicked on the ad to see it further. The advertiser will then pay Google or any other website only for these hundred clicks rather than the one thousand ad impressions shown.

Source: http://www.naaptol.com/buy/gifts/stationary/office_stationary.html.

Image 10.19   Banner ad of Dell and other brands on Naaptol.com website

CPL   Cost per lead (CPL) takes the cost per click a step further. It derives from the fact that all prospective customers who view the ad do not purchase the product and could only be information seekers. 'Auto and IT industries have moved from CPC to CPL now' (IAMAI 2010). Thus, say out of the hundred people who clicked on the ad, only twenty-five had an intention to purchase the brand, then payment will be made to Google for these twenty-five leads only that were generated out of the ad (rather than the thousand impressions as in CPI or hundred clicks as in CPC).

CPA   Cost per acquisition (CPA) is purely based on performance, and here the advertisers pay only if they have acquired a customer from the ad that was shown on the website. 'Veteran online advertisers like travel agencies, banks, insurance companies, etc., are using this model the most' (IAMAI 2010). Thus, say out of the twenty-five leads that were generated, if only five people actually purchased the brand, then the advertiser will only pay for these five rather than thousand impressions as in CPI or hundred clicks as in CPC or twenty-five leads as in CPL.

The total Indian online advertising market was estimated at ₹785 crore for 2009–2010 and is expected to reach ₹993 crore in 2010–2011 (see Table 10.1). A further breakup of the text and display ad market is given in Table 10.2.

Table 10.1   Total online advertising market

Online ads	Year 2009–10 (crore)	Year 2010–11* (crore)	Growth (%)
Text ad	368	459	26
Display ad	417	534	28

* Expected figures.

Source: IAMAI 2010.

Table 10.2   Text and display ad spend by industry

Advertisers	Text ads (2009–10) (in crores)	Display ads (2009–2010) (in crores)	Total spend on ads (in crores)
BFSI	89	52	141
Travel	74	59	133
Online publishers	58	37	95
IT	33	33	66
Telecom	23	51	74
Auto	17	39	56
Education	16	25	41
FMCG	13	26	39
Consumer durables	10	34	44

Source: IAMAI 2010.

BFSI (banking, financial services, and insurance) includes banks, non-banking financial companies, insurance companies, asset management companies, credit rating agencies, etc. Further discussion on how the e-business strategy can be used for building a brand is discussed in the next section.

E-BUSINESS STRATEGY AND BRANDING

The Internet has the potential to facilitate new business concepts and also provide improved competitiveness by increasing efficiencies in the purchase and delivery of products. However, just rushing in to adopt new technologies without strategizing for the overall brand-building and delivery of value to the customers can be a 'recipe for disaster' (Lovelock 2001). The Internet as a medium gives rise to new branding opportunities for third parties that 'neither produce a product nor deliver a primary service' (Evans and Wurster 1997). For example, www.mouthshut.com provides opinions, advice, and information written by users on a range of products, from automobiles to restaurants to mobiles to movies. While searching for a product or service, potential customers have access to a plethora of reviews. Also, by writing reviews, members create a buzz about brands and products, which in turn influence consumer decisions.

This also brings to light an important fact that the consumers' power is increasing. They have access to loads of information at the click of a mouse and they can even spread word of mouth or rather word of mouse at minimal cost to a wider audience. Online search tools make the search for information and comparison of brands much easier (Sinha 2000). The Internet technology has opened a level playing field for a wider participative audience. The increased efficiencies, enhanced competition with low barriers to entry, transparent and excessive flow of information, and increased customer power, highlight the need to build strong brands. A strong online brand helps shift the balance of power from the competitive marketplace and 'fickle' or less loyal customers towards the brand (Ibeh, Luo, and Dinnie 2005).

Strong and successful brands reinforce and enhance the effectiveness of the online brand strategy and lead to success on the Internet (Ibeh et al. 2005).

 See Zoozoo online downloads of e-cards and wallpapers.

The various techniques that organizations can adopt to enhance their brand equity through e-business are as follows.

Integration of the online and offline brand experience   The online and offline brand experience should be integrated. This can be possible when the online brand experience is built around the brand promise. The 'look and feel of the brand's site should be consistent with the brand values' (de Chernatony and Christodoulides 2004).

User-friendly site   'The brand's site should speak the language of the customers rather than that of the IT department' (de Chernatony and Christodoulides 2004), i.e., the site should be consumer-friendly and the information should be easily available rather than making the consumers hunt around.

Interactive chats   Live chats can also be set up to support customers' experience of the brand.

Lively online communities   Organizations can set up 'lively online communities' to create a 'worldwide buzz' for their brands (Ibeh et al. 2005). The online communities should help build interaction between the customers and with the brand too (discussed earlier in the chapter).

Domain names   To enhance worldwide brand recognition, companies can use standardized domain names and further internationalize them like www.google.co.in (for India), www.google.cn (for China), www.google.co.uk (for United Kingdom), www.sony.com.au (for Australia), www.sony.com.pa (for Panama), www.sony.com.sg (for Singapore), www.sony.co.in (for India), etc. This enables the companies to provide standardized product and marketing information to customers in their local languages, and through the symbols and colours that are prevalent and preferred there.

Brand spiralling   Companies can use traditional media to promote and attract consumers to an online website. From television, radio, newspapers, magazines, and billboards to simple shopping bags, consumers are encouraged to visit the firm's website. The firm should 'provide a compelling reason for the consumers to visit the brand online' (de Chernatony and Christodoulides 2004). 'One goal of each advertising campaign should be to encourage traffic to the site and enhance brand recognition. The interactive nature of the Internet makes it possible for a firm to learn more about each customer. This information can then be used to target more specific messages' (Clow and Baack 2009).

Mobile marketing   Companies can use this media to target niche customers and also build communities (refer to the above point and related discussion earlier in the chapter). They can send ads on mobiles and reach a number of relevant customers at the cost of a few paisas per customer.

Location-based mobile   Bluetooth technology allows marketers to communicate with customers and target them with specific information when they are in the vicinity of their store. So, if a consumer is visiting a mall, he/she can get information on the latest deals available in the store. A McDonald's outlet can entice them with their menu and offers of the day, Café Coffee Day can give them special offers on select coffees, etc. This enables marketers to target relevant customers who are in the vicinity and, hence, most likely to drop in and execute a purchase. An application called Shopkick was launched in August 2010 (for iPhone users and another one for Android phones), which 'tracks and offers promotions to shoppers as they move from outside the store to counters, cash registers, and even inside the dressing room.' Major mall operators like Macy's, Best Buy, and American Eagle Outfitters in New York City, San Francisco, etc., were the early adopters of this application (Clifford 2010).

M-commerce   The introduction of m-commerce has led to mobile adaptations of social networking sites like Facebook and Orkut, where advance bookings can be made for movie tickets, regular commuters between Delhi and Gurgaon can get their toll tags recharged through their mobile phones, etc. With the global mobile-payment transactions projected at $1.13 trillion for 2014, Google is working on a mobile payment service that will allow users to purchase milk, bread, etc., by 'tapping or waving mobile phones against a register at the checkout'. It is based on a near-field communication (NFC) technology that 'beams and receives information wirelessly from 4 inches away' (Kharif 2011).

Customers are co-creators   The customers should be seen as co-creators of the brand experience (de Chernatony and Christodoulides 2004). The Internet tools can be used to build a complete brand experience and for this, the brand managers need to listen to the voice of their consumers and customers. One-to-one relationships should be encouraged, and brand managers should learn from the consumers and then incorporate the learning to build a relevant brand experience for them.

SUMMARY

E-business helps organizations achieve the shift towards the customers by providing information where and when the customers want it. The 24/7 nature of the online media helps companies stay connected with their customers and provides information at the click of a mouse across geographical boundaries. Companies can explore a number of options to move from physical stores to virtual stores like brick and mortar, click and mortar and click only companies or virtual stores. Using online media is also an effective strategy and the recent global recession saw companies adopt this media to reach specific audiences for their brands. Companies can create websites, place their ads online, email, participate on social networks to reach their consumers and customers. The cost efficiency of the media is an added bonus. The Internet has also revolutionized the manner in which the product, pricing and delivery of the brand occurs to the customers. Products can be digitalized or changes can be incorporated by gaining feedback from the consumers. Online promotion can be in the form of text ads and display ads. A number of business models can be used like cost per impression, cost per click, cost per lead and cost per acquisition. There are a number of strategies that can be adopted to enhance the brand equity online like integration of online and offline media, developing user-friendly sites, interactive chats, lively online communities, etc. The opportunities provided by this media are immense and with Internet penetration still in its infancy, it is a sunrise media.

KEY TERMS

Brand spiralling   Using the traditional media to promote and attract consumers to an online website is called as brand spiralling.

Cannibalization   The decrease in demand for an existing product due to the introduction of a new product by the same manufacturer.

Cost per acquisition (CPA)   This online advertising model is purely based on performance and here the advertisers pay only if they have acquired a customer from the ad that was shown on the website.

Cost per click (CPC)   An online advertising model in which the advertiser makes the payment for the ad shown only when a prospective customer clicks on the ad and views the ad or the hyperlinked site.

Cost per impression/mille (CPI/CPM)   An advertising model that allows advertisers to pay for the number of impressions of the ad shown online.

Cost per lead (CPL)   Another type of online advertising, wherein the advertiser makes payment for the ad shown only when a lead is generated out of the ad.

Display ads   Online ads that contain text, logo, photographs, etc.

E-business   It is the use of the digital media or the electronic media to reach out and connect with consumers.

Proximity marketing   It is the dissemination of marketing information, by using wireless technology, to customers in real time when they are present at a particular location.

Social networking sites   A number of independent online communities such as Facebook, Orkut, etc., have come up providing options for customers to congregate, and exchange information online and these are called as social networking sites.

Text ads   Online ads that are in the form of text matter only.

EXERCISES

Concept Review Questions

1. Enumerate the various e-business strategies an organization can adopt to build a brand. Discuss any two strategies an organization should adopt and discuss why you think these two are important.
2. Discuss the marketing concept with respect to online marketing.
3. How has the Internet impacted the traditional method of doing business?

4. Discuss the various business models available for online advertising. Which out of these would you recommend to an organization and why?

Critical Thinking Questions

1. With Internet penetration at 7 per cent in India, do organizations need to have an online strategy?
2. Critically discuss the various methods available for organizations to advertise their brands online.

3. Critically discuss the e-business strategy with respect to branding for an organization.

Internet Exercises

1. Visit the website, http://www.beinggirl.co.in/main/home. php. Compare this with http://www.sunsilkgangofgirls. com/. What similarities and differences can you draw regarding the brand promotion activities?

2. Visit the website, http://pepsicoindia.co.in/. How has the organization used the online media to build and reinforce its brand?

CD Exercise

Go online to the official Vodafone Facebook and Twitter pages and see how the brand is using this media to build its brand image. What other online marketing tools are being applied by Vodafone to build its brand online?

REFERENCES

Aulakh, G., 'Rural India gadget-savvy too—Gfk Nielsen', *The Economic Times*, New Delhi, 27 January 2011, p. 5.

Bartz, C.A., 'Power at click of mouse—The best of both worlds', *The Economic Times,* New Delhi, 12 November 2009, p. 6.

Clifford, S., 'Aisle by aisle, an app pushes bargains', *The Economic Times*, New Delhi, 18 August 2010, p. 4.

Clow, K.E. and D. Baack (2009), *Integrated Advertising, Promotion and Marketing Communications*, Third Edition, Pearson Education Inc., New Delhi, Chapter 13, pp. 428–457.

De Chernatony, L. and G. Christodoulides, 'Taking the brand promise online—Challenges and opportunities', *Interactive Marketing,* Vol. 5, Issue 3, 2004, pp. 238–250.

Demirel, L. (2011), 'Destination Marketing—Turkey as a tourism and investment destination'. At AIMA World Marketing Congress 'Expect miracles every day!' on 4–5 February 2011 at Hotel Lalit, New Delhi.

Evans, P.B. and T.S. Wursterm (1997), 'Strategy and the new economics of information', *Harvard Business Review,* Vol. 75, Issue 5, 1997, pp. 71–82.

Ibeh, K.I.N., Y. Luo, and K. Dinnie, 'E-branding strategies of Internet companies—Some preliminary insights from the UK', *Journal of Brand Management,* Vol. 12, Issue 5, 2005, pp. 355–373.

Internet and Mobile Association of India (IAMAI) (2010), 'Online advertising in India', IAMAI, http://www.iamai. in/Upload/Research/OnlineAdvertising_46.pdf, accessed on 5 February 2011.

Internet World Stats 2010, http://www.Internetworldstats. com/stats.htm, accessed on 27 June 2010.

Kharif, O., 'In the works—A Google mobile payment service? You'll be able to walk into a store and do commerce, says Eric Schimdt, And it'll eventually replace credit cards', *The Economic Times,* New Delhi, 6 January 2011, p. 4.

Kotler, P., G. Armstrong, P.Y. Agnihotri, and E. ul Haque (2010), *Principles of Marketing—A South Asian Perspective,* 13th Edition, Prentice Hall, Delhi.

Lovelock, C., 'The dot-com meltdown—What does it mean for teaching and research in services?', *Managing Service Quality,* Vol. 11, Issue 5, 2001, pp. 302–306.

Porter, M.E., 'Strategy and the Internet', *Harvard Business Review,* March 2001, Volume 79, Issue 3, pp. 62–78.

Ray, S. (2009)'Mobile Internet in India', Internet and Mobile Association of India, http://www.iamai.in/Upload/ Research/MobileInternetinIndia_39.pdf, accessed on 27 June 2010.

RBI (2001), 'Report on Internet banking', http://www.rbi.org. in/scripts/PublicationReportDetails.aspx?ID=243>, accessed on 8 January 2011.

Sachdev, H., 'Brave new world of web marketing', *The Economic Times,* New Delhi, 6 June 2010, p. 4.

Shivapriya, N., 'Net turns truly Indian as Bharat goes online from 2010', *The Economic Times,* New Delhi, 12 November 2009, p. 6.

Sinha, I., 'Cost transparency—The nets real threat to prices and brands' *Harvard Business Review,* Volume 78, Issue 2, 2000, pp. 43–51.

Sruthijith, K.K., 'Future gets ready for big e-bazaar', *The Economic Times,* New Delhi, 6 May 2010, p. 4.

Turban, E. and D. King (2009), *Introduction to e-Commerce,* 2nd Edition, Prentice Hall, US.

Web resources

http://www.facebook.com/NokiaIndia?v=wall&ref= search, accessed on 4 July 2010.

http://nikeid.nike.com/nikeid/index.jsp#feature,whatisnikeid, accessed on 3 July 2010.

http://www.naaptol.com/buy/gifts/stationary/office_stationary.html, accessed on 3 February 2011.

http://www.bizrate.com/womens-shoes/dr.-scholl's-fast-flats,-fits-sizes-5-6--pid2349350362/, accessed on 3 February 2011.

http://www.bizrate.com/ratings_guide/cust_reviews__mid--22731.html, accessed on 3 February 2011.

http://digitalenterprise.org/models/models.html, accessed on 3 February 2011.

http://www.google.co.in/#hl=en&biw=1024&bih=677&q=hp+printers&aq=f&aqi=g10&aql=&oq=&fp=989aa0e6667459e, accessed on 3 February 2011.

http://www.asianpaints.com/, accessed on 3 July 2010.

http://www.irctc.co.in/, accessed on 3 July 2010.

http://www.futurebazar.com/, accessed on 3 July 2010.

http://www.naaptol.com, accessed on 3 February 2011.

http://www.bizrate.com, accessed on 3 February 2011.

http://www.dhl.co.in/en.html, accessed on 3 February 2011.

http://www.makemytrip.com/, accessed on 5 February 2011.

http://www.sunsilkgangofgirls.com/, accessed on 6 February 2011.

http://www.nestle.in/nestle_kitchen/home.aspx, accessed on 4 July 2010.

http://www.mouthshut.com/help/aboutus.php, accessed on 28 June 2010.

CASE STUDY

Marketing IPL Online

This changes the world of sports broadcasting. The Internet has changed the lives of everyone and this will do the same for sport.

– Lalit Modi, IPL Commissioner,
Daily Telegraph, 20 January 2010.

Introduction

In June 2007, Lalit Modi, the then Vice-President of the Board of Control for Cricket in India (BCCI), brainstormed with Andrew Wildblood, Vice-President of International Management Group (IMG), to give rise to what is arguably one of the most successful/controversial/talked about cricketing events—the IPL T20. IMG is a global sports, media, and fashion management organization with footsteps in thirty countries. The idea was to start a domestic cricketing event consisting of professional cricket players from all over the world. Thus, IPL or the Indian Premier League was born as a sub-committee unit of the BCCI. The format consists of a cricket match played between franchise squads and is limited to twenty overs per team. The teams are owned by franchises. Each team consists of players acquired through an auction arranged by BCCI/DLF IPL. The franchises can spend a maximum amount of $5 million to acquire the players. Post auction, they can purchase additional players; Indian players not included in the auction can be signed any time and foreign players can be approached via IPL.

The auction

On 20 February 2008, an open auction was conducted 'by an independent professional auctioneer, Mr Richard Madley, in the presence of all the franchises. Seventy-eight national and international players were put up for bidding. There was an annual 'base player fee' (i.e., the fee at which the bidding for the player starts), 'adjusted on a pro-rata basis depending on the player's availability for the IPL season in the first year.

While bidding, franchises had to be cautious not to cross the $5 million limit that was set. Once made, a bid could not be withdrawn. The bidders included a number of India's powerful and rich industrialists and movie stars. DLF, a leading Indian real estate firm, won the IPL exclusive sponsorship right and became the main sponsor for five years (Schwartz 2009). The other sponsors are Sony Entertainment Television as official broadcaster, Kingfisher Airlines, official umpire partner and official airline, Pepsi, official pouring supplier, etc.

Season 1—2008

The opening ceremony for the 2008 season, held on 18 April, contributed to the building up of fervour, and the public was enthralled by the matches. The presence of Bollywood personalities like Shah Rukh Khan, owner of the Kolkata franchise, Preity Zinta, co-owner of the Kings XI Punjab, etc. added to the excitement. Over a forty-six day period, fifty-eight of the fifty-nine matches scheduled were played, one was washed out due to rain. The saw each 'team playing with all the other teams both at home and away in a round robin system. In the final match, Rajasthan Royals defeated Chennai Super Kings in a last ball thriller.'

Season 2—2009

In the year 2009, for the second season, each franchisee had a sum of $2 million to spend on player fees. This included new players acquired in the 2009 auction or 'through signing uncapped new players or re-signing any 2008 temporary replacements'. The matches for the second season were held in South Africa due to the 'clash with the general election dates in India and related security concerns' (Doctor 2009). 'The format of the tournament remained the same as the inaugural one. Deccan Chargers, who finished last in the first season, came out eventual winners of the tournament.'

Season 3—2010

During the third season, matches were again held in India and 'an auction for sixty-six players was held in January with only eleven players being sold...' This season saw the Chennai Super Kings defeat Mumbai Indians by twenty-two runs.

Season 4—2011

The Season 4 auction was a first in some aspects—first, Sourav Ganguly and Chris Gayle were not even bidden for by any franchise, and second 'two new teams—Sahara Pune Warriors and Kochi Tuskers Kerala took part in the auction for the first time after successfully winning bids to be part of the fourth season. The increase in franchises from eight to ten also lead to an increase in the number of matches from sixty to ninety-four under the 'round-robin' format being used. 'A hectic international calendar and

fears about injury to players' required a relook at the format, and so it was decided that the tournament be played in a group format, where the teams would be divided into two groups of five each through a draw of lots. In all, seventy-four matches were now proposed. The amount allowed for purchase of players was increased to $9 million and each franchise was allowed to have a squad of thirty players (Basu 2010).

DLF IPL brand elements

Some of the brand elements being used by IPL are the DLF-IPL logo, the logos of each of the ten IPL franchises, the words—Indian Premier League, IPL, DLF Indian Premier League, DLF-IPL etc., the names of the IPL franchises, and www.iplt20.com (see Images 10.20 and 10.21).

Source: http://www.iplt20.com/

Image 10.20 DLF IPL logo

Source: http://www.iplt20.com/.

Image 10.21 Logos of some of the franchises

Online marketing

The DLF-IPL website address www.iplt20.com is easy to remember and provides a world of information to IPL fans. The news icon provides news, but the latest news posted is of 29 April 2010 (see Image 10.22).

Source: http://www.iplt20.com/.

Image 10.22 IPL home page

Source: http://www.iplt20.com/.

Image 10.23 IPL teams information

The information about the teams is still limited to the original eight (see Image 10.23).

The fan zone is however current with the posts being updated every second (see Image 10.24).

The results icon leads to the page where all the results for matches throughout the different seasons of IPL are highlighted, along with detailed match reports and the scoreboard. The videos and photos section is updated with exciting videos and photos of the three seasons. A number of cricketing statistics are provided for the different years and for the different franchises. IPL also advocates two causes through its icon 'partners' on its website's

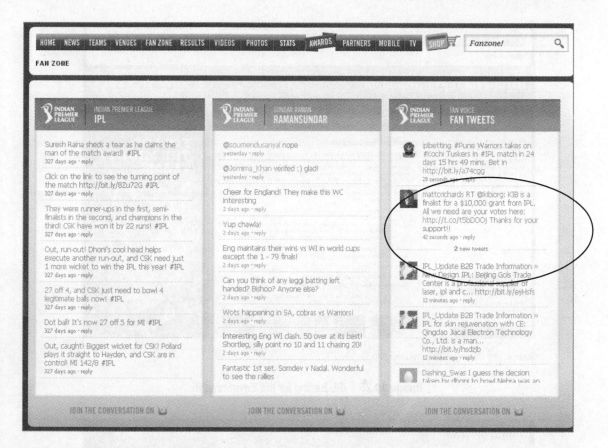

Source: http://www.iplt20.com/fanzone.php.

Image 10.24   IPL Fan Zone

homepage. The first is the cause of UNEP (United Nations Environment Programme) and encourages its fans to do the same (see Image 10.25).

The other is the NGO Room to Read (see Image 10.26), which works 'to transform the lives of millions of children by addressing literacy and gender equality in education'. Through its website, IPL appeals for donations to promote the cause.

The last icon on the home page is for 'Shop' and it takes you to the online store, where you can purchase merchandise, jerseys, T-shirts, etc. (see Image 10.27).

Discounts are provided in the 'deals of the day' (see right hand side of Image 8), where a 36 per cent discount is being offered on a roti maker. A click provides further information about the product and an incentive in the form of free shipping within India. There is an option of paying cash on delivery and you can track the order as well (Image 10.27).

In 2010, IPL made a landmark agreement with Google, whereby IPL's 2010 season was broadcast live on a dedicated YouTube channel across the world (except in the US), along with re-broadcast options. 'The agreement gives Google exclusive online rights for IPL content' for a period of two years and the revenue earned from advertising and sponsorship will be shared between the two. 'The most significant aspect of the deal is the amount of control it gives the viewers, who will be able to customize their viewing experience by choosing between different camera angles. Additionally, they will be able to freeze, fast-forward, and rewind the feed, as

Source: http://www.iplt20.com/unep.php.

Image 10.25 IPL Batting for the Environment

Source: http://www.iplt20.com/room2read.php.

Image 10.26 IPL and Room to Read

Source: http://www.infibeam.com/IPL/.

Image 10.27   IPL online shopping

well as watch replays any time during the day, a choice that is unavailable to television viewers who are bound by broadcast schedules. This became the first such deal in the cricket world. This also made the event truly global, as it gave access to 500 million pairs of eyes every single moment of the day' through Google (see Image 10.28). It also provided the sole medium for fans to watch matches, especially in countries like the UK, where there was no live telecast arrangement.

IPL also advertises this fact on its home page (see Image 10.22) by asking fans to capture the front row seats on www.youtube.com/ipl. On YouTube, one can watch previous matches or the highlights (see Image 10.29) with 56,634,144 channel views. It had 94,569 subscribers as on 20 March 2011. The subscribers get regular notifications of new videos on this channel.

Mobile marketing

The IPL homepage provides options for mobile browsing through the browser m.iplt20.com (see Image 10.28), where one can watch live videos, catch the latest updates, and scores. The contest link here provides the option of playing cricket games through one's Facebook account.

There are exciting contests. For instance, for April 2011 IPL Season 4, whoever scores the highest runs by 3 April, gets a chance to win the XBOX 360 and there are other exciting prizes like Bioshock PS3, DVDs, etc., for twenty-four other top scorers (see Image 10.30).

This is not all. The site promises other events throughout the year with a number of exciting prizes to be won.

For retailing tickets, a number of options are available online, such as www.ticketgenie.in (see Image 10.31), which are the ticketing partners for teams Knight Riders, Deccan Chargers, and Royal Challengers. Tickets for matches played by the Mumbai Indians and Delhi Daredevils can be purchased from www.kyazoonga.com

Ticketgenie provides detailed information about the venue and the entire pricing range for customers to choose from (see Image 10.32).

Tickets for Kings XI matches can be purchased from www.bookmyshow.com (see Image 10.33).

On 24 April 2008, IPL entered into a long-term contract with Ticketpro for selling tickets online at www.ticketpro.in.

Other sites like iplticket.net (Image 10.34) also offer online tickets where tickets for all the teams can be purchased.

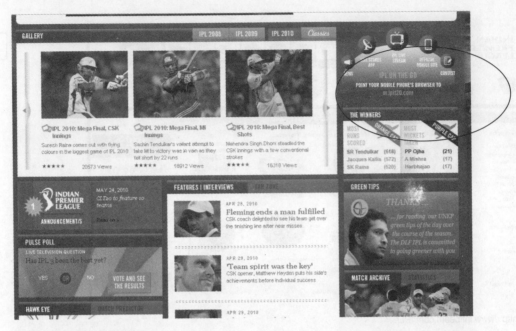

Source: http://www.iplt20.com/.

Image 10.28   IPL on the go

Source: http://www.youtube.com/ipl.

Image 10.29   IPL on YouTube

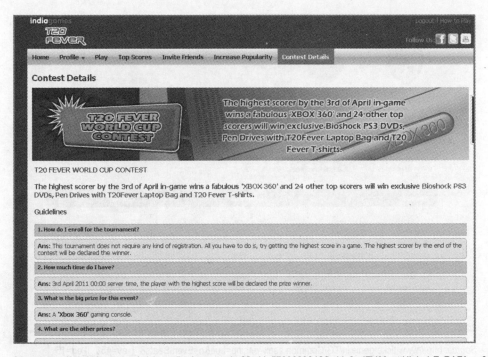

Source: http://ipl.t20fever.com/cricketonline/contest.php?fbuid=570062964&fbsid=2.wlZY03vcttUL4p4rEyRAFA__.3600.13005
61200-570062964.

Image 10.30   IPL online games

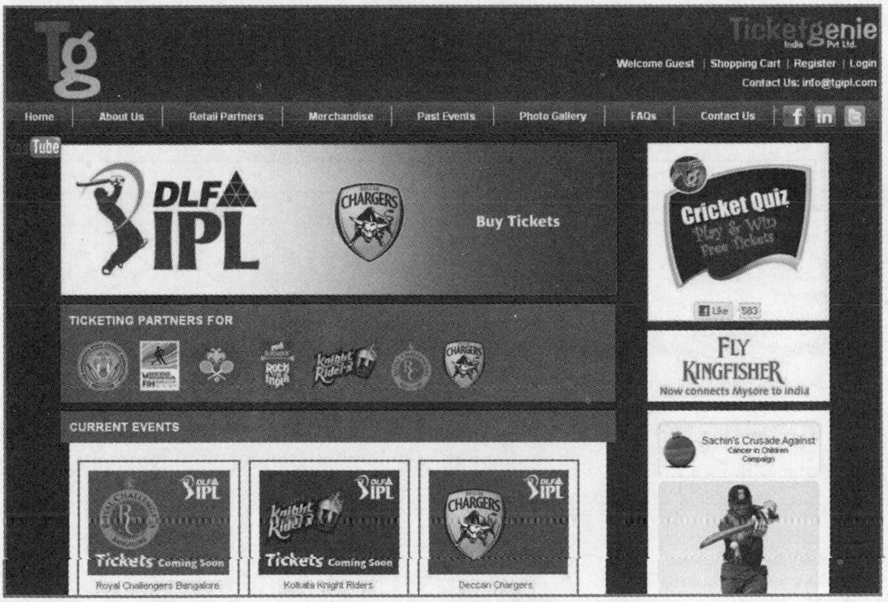

Source: http://www.ticketgenie.in/TG/Common.aspx?p=Home&engine=false.

Image 10.31   Purchase IPL tickets on Ticketgenie

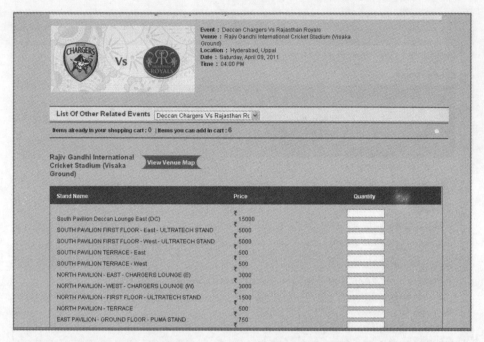

Source: http://www.ticketgenie.in/TG/Common.aspx?engine=true&p=EventSeats&_i_ev=45&_i_eg=15.

Image 10.32   Online pricing at Ticketgenie

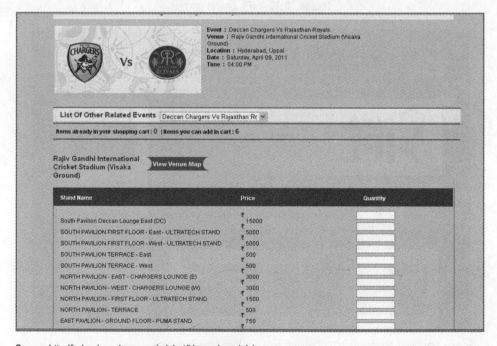

Source: http://in.bookmyshow.com/cricket/kings-xi-punjab/.

Image 10.33   Booking tickets on Bookmyshow.com

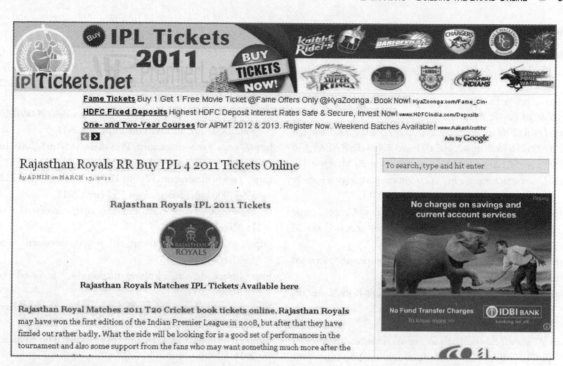

Source: http://www.ipltickets.net/rajasthan-royals-rr-buy-ipl-4-2011-tickets-online/

Image 10.34   IPL ticket on iplticket.net

Conclusion

The word 'cricket' has always raised a frenzy in India and Indians can never have enough of their favourite game. It is, therefore, not surprising that DLF-IPL is a grand success. In the year 2009, it secured the fourth position in Forbes' list of 'World's hottest sporting properties' (Schwartz 2009). In the year 2010, its brand value became $4.13 billion, which was more than double that of the previous year, when it was valued at $2.01 billion. IPL has also made effective use of the Internet to capture the global audience. The stage is now set for the fifth season with a spectacular line-up of matches.

Discussion Questions

1. Discuss the concept and journey of IPL as a brand.
2. Delineate the various online strategies used to promote the brand IPL. What further suggestions can you make to increase the brand value?
3. Delineate the various e-commerce strategies used to distribute the brand IPL. What further suggestions can you make to increase the effectiveness of online delivery?

Case References

Basu, I. (2010), 'IPL to have 74 matches for next three seasons', http://timesofindia.indiatimes.com/iplarticleshow/6498994.cms, accessed on 19 March 2011.

Doctor, V. (2009), 'South African elections and IPL 2' http://economictimes.indiatimes.com/news/news-by-industry/et-cetera/south-african-elections-and-ipl-2/articleshow/4311273.cms, accessed on 19 March 2011.

Schwartz, P.J. (2009), 'The world's hottest sports league' http://www.forbes.com/2009/08/27/cricket-india-ipl-business-sports-ipl.html, accessed on 19 March 2011.

Web resources

http://www.hindustantimes.com/Ground-rules-for-the-IPL-Auction/Article1-277109.aspx, accessed on 15 March 2011.

http://www.facebook.com/group.php?gid=1091-63002458616, accessed on 19 March 2011.

http://ipl.t20fever.com/cricketonline/contest.php?fbuid=570062964&fbsid=2.wlZY03vcttUL4p4rEyRAFA__.3600.1300561200-570062964, accessed on 20 March 2011.

http://www.ticketgenie.in/TG/Common.aspx?p=Home&engine=false, accessed on 20 March 2011.

http://www.ticketgenie.in/TG/Common.aspx?engine=true&p=EventSeats&_i_ev=45&_i_eg=15, accessed on 20 March 2011.

http://in.bookmyshow.com/cricket/kings-xi-punjab/, accessed on 20 March 2011.

http://www.infibeam.com/Kitchenware/i-Roti-Maker/P-H-KW-Others-NS-1054.html?id=Black, accessed on 20 March 2011.

http://www.telegraph.co.uk/sport/cricket/twenty20/ipl/7033597/IPL-to-broadcast-live-on-YouTube.html, accessed on 20 March 2011.

http://www.espncricinfo.com/ipl2010/content/story/445173.html, accessed on 20 March 2011.

http://timesofindia.indiatimes.com/sports/cricket/news/IPL-brand-value-doubles-to-413-billion-Study/iplarticleshow/5713042.cms, accessed on 20 March 2011.

http://www.hindu.com/2008/02/20/stories/2008022056622000.htm, accessed on 15 March 2011.

http://www.kyazoonga.com/PressRelease/Apr8-2008-Indianbytes.pdf, accessed on 20 March 2011.

http://www.hindu.com/2008/12/18/stories/2008121859971900.htm, accessed on 15 March 2011.

http://www.imgworld.com/about-us.aspx, accessed on 15 March 2011.

http://www.iplt20.com/about_IPL.php, accessed on 15 March 2011.

http://iplschedule.in/ipl-player-auction/14, accessed on 19 March 2011.

http://www.infibcam.com/IPL/, accessed on 20 March 2011.

http://www.iplt20.com/fanzone.php, accessed on 20 March 2011.

http://www.ipltickets.net/rajasthan-royals-rr-buy-ipl-4-2011-tickets-online/, accessed on 20 March 2011.

Branding and Marketing Communications

11

LEARNING OBJECTIVES

After reading this chapter, you will be able to understand the following:

- The importance of marketing communication in brand-building
- The influence of marketing communication on consumers
- Various communications tools used by an organization
- Advertising
- Sales promotion
- Publicity and public relations
- Internet marketing
- Integrating the brand communications

ABOUT THE CHAPTER

This chapter discusses marketing communication in the context of branding. Marketers need to communicate with their target market about their product offering. The third chapter on consumer behaviour and brand buying decisions highlighted the fact that consumers' attitude towards the brand influences the purchase decision process. Marketers aim to influence this attitude by communicating with the current and potential customers during the different stages of the purchase process (see Exhibit 11.1). This chapter looks at this communication by the marketers from the perspective of building a brand and maintaining and enhancing brand equity.

Exhibit 11.1   Transition from Hutch to Vodafone

On 21 September 2007, '40 million subscribers of the much-loved iconic brand', Hutch, shifted seamlessly to a brand few had heard about—Vodafone. The success of the transition can be gauged by the fact that one week after the launch on 28 September 2007, it 'had achieved an awareness level of 80 per cent.' How was a completely new entity able to achieve this difficult task and evoke the same emotions in the customers as the iconic brand, Hutch? The answer is very simple. It took the most 'endearing brand icon of Hutch—the

Contd

Exhibit 11.1 *contd*

pug—and gave it a new 'home' called Vodafone.' This was supported by a twenty-four hour roadblock on Star TV's thirteen channels. This was followed by the 'Happy to help' initiative, which highlighted the breadth of its service network. (See Image 11.1.)

Vodafone also launched various other service-oriented initiatives, which were designed to simplify lives and helped in differentiating it from the other players (*Superbrands*, 2009).

Courtesy: Superbrands.

Image 11.1   Vodafone ad; also see Plate 13

NEED FOR MARKETING COMMUNICATION IN BRANDING

Given the cultural diversity in India, brand managers need to educate customers about their brands using terms that the consumers would understand, so as to build the bond that enhances the organizations' credibility and fosters brand-related attitudes and purchase intentions. There is a significant relationship between firm-sponsored education activities, and positive customer brand attitudes, and purchase intentions. Organizations, through their marketing communication activities, can impact the way consumers consume brands by influencing their beliefs and attitudes. Thus, an organization's marketing communications can be used to educate consumers about their brands' attributes and develop positive associations, so that consumers feel that the brand is the best consumption choice for them given their values and lifestyles (Martinez 2003). Olson (1978) pointed out that consumers may use informational cues to develop beliefs about products (see Exhibit 11.1), and that their final choice for purchase may be directly influenced by these beliefs.

MARKETING COMMUNICATION AND PROMOTION AND THE INFLUENCE ON CONSUMERS

Promotion is defined as 'the managerial process of communication an organization has with its target audience to generate attitudinal and behavioural responses and facilitate exchanges for mutual benefit' (Jauhari and Dutta 2010). A consumer can develop, modify, or reinforce attitudes toward a brand depending on the exposure to the brand (see Exhibit 11.2). The Internet environment, sales activities, brand-driven advertising, or promotional activities all provide means of brand interaction and significantly influence the attitude of the customers towards the brand. This highlights the increasing usefulness of communications and brand interactions as marketing vehicles used by companies to boost the effectiveness of their brand value efforts. Marketing communication is undertaken so as to reinforce brand loyalty and enhance brand consumption, thus communication has brand-building implications as well (Jones 1999).

Exhibit 11.2   What You Did Not Know about Vodafone

- When 'the pug' was first shown in the Hutch ad in 2003, it instantly connected with the Indian consumers and Pug pup prices shot up to ₹80,000, $1670.
- The Zoozoos are actually real people wearing body suits and are not animated as is widely believed.
- Zoozoo theme birthday parties, cakes, and cookies have become a rage.

- 'The Zoozoo campaign is the first-ever Indian entry to reach Advertising Age's top viral film list. In 2009, Ad Age in New York listed it as the world's top viral campaign, two weeks in a row. The Zoozoos entered the chart at number one position—the first time any campaign had achieved this on its debut (*Superbrands,* 2009).

In the consumer purchase process, the customer purchases a product or service from the awareness set, i.e., the brands the customer is aware of out of the total number of brands, the total set, available in the marketplace. If the service meets the initial buying requirements of the customer, it forms the consideration set and as the customer gathers more information, the strong contenders form the choice set, from which the customer makes the final choice (Kotler and Keller 2006). It can, thus, be said that if the customer is not aware about the service, it would not fall within the awareness set and so would consequently not form the final choice for the purchase of services. Hence, it is of utmost importance to communicate to the customer the details about the product being offered by the organization and influence the customer so that the product is the final choice for purchase. Once the communication has been initiated, it is important for the organization to continue the communication with current and potential customers in different ways to cover pre-purchase, purchase and consumption, and post-purchase stages. This communication can be in the form of advertising, sales promotion, personal selling, direct marketing and public relations. All these are discussed in detail in the section on communication options. Over a period of time, the perception of the customers towards these various communications leads to the building of a brand image in their minds. Thus, what is being communicated and how it is being communicated is important and crucial to the brand-building exercise. Marketing communication can help us in the following (Jauhari and Dutta 2010).

Building brand awareness   On entering a market, organizations need to communicate the qualities and inherent features of their brands to the target audience. Organizations can build their brand awareness by communicating the brand values to the stakeholders. For example, Aquaguard's brand value resides in product development and the customer services that they offer (*Superbrands,* 2009). They communicate this in their ad (see Image 11.2). They communicate

Courtesy: Superbrands.

Image 11.2   Aquaguard advertisement

about the water purification technology to the consumers in order to build trust and preference for their brand. Brand awareness is built to enhance brand recall and recognition.

Enhancing brand knowledge   Brand knowledge builds on brand awareness and provides further information to reinforce the fact that as a brand they are the best in the class. In Image 11.3, Aquaguard can be seen to be building the consumers' brand knowledge by informing them about the state-of-the-art technology, which has been used to design the product. It also informs about after-sales service centres and water-testing labs (*Superbrands*, 2009).

Courtesy: Superbrands.

Image 11.3   Another Aquaguard advertisement

Favourable brand attitude Brands need to build a favourable brand attitude so that customers like the brand and prefer the brand to the other brands in the same category. In Image 11.3, Aquaguard is seen educating people about how only Aquaguard Total has the unique e-boiling+ technology, which eliminates all the disease-causing bacteria and virus, certification from the Indian Medical Association, 1500 after-sales service centres, and its labs. By highlighting the fact that over sixty lakh mothers trust the brand and that a money back guarantee is offered, they are further trying to influence the consumers' attitude towards their brand.

Remember that the communication process starts with the objective of the communication. Here, the Aquaguard ads show that due to the different objectives, the advertisement copy differs, requiring different ads.

COMMUNICATION OPTIONS

Marketing communication, in simple terms is a dialogue of the organization with the various audiences of the brand. The idea is to position the brand in the minds of the consumers, so that consumers respond to this communication by purchasing the brand or by responding favourably to organization related activities (Fill 2002). An organization can communicate with its various audiences in the following ways (Kotler and Keller 2006; Jauhari and Dutta 2010):

1. Advertising
2. Personal selling
3. Sales promotion
4. Events and campaign marketing
5. Direct marketing
6. Publicity
7. Word of mouth
8. Internet marketing

Advertising

Advertising is 'any paid form of non-personal presentation and promotion of ideas, goods or services by an identified sponsor' (Kotler and Keller 2006). It is advertising that transforms a product that provides functional benefits and no more into a brand that offers the consumer psychological rewards in addition to the functional ones (Obermiller et al. 2005). According to Zeithaml (1988), price, brand name, and the level of advertising are three extrinsic cues frequently associated with quality in research and which are general indicators of quality across all types of products. Research suggests that advertising received prior to an experience can exert the most influence (La Tour and La Tour 2005) on the consumer.

Advertising is the most visible form of brand communication and can reach the customers through any of the media available, such as television, radio, Internet, out-of-home hoardings, banners, posters, etc., and through the print media, via newspapers, magazines, leaflets, etc. The year 2009 witnessed an economic slowdown in more ways than one. It was a tough year for the advertising industry as well. According to the Pitch-Madison Media Advertising Outlook 2010, the year 2009 saw the advertising industry drop to ₹18,670 crore, a 10 per cent drop as compared to 2008 when the industry size was ₹20,717 crore (Exchange-4-Media 2010). The Internet as a medium for marketing communications and advertising is discussed in detail further in the chapter.

For a brand, advertising can serve the following purposes (Sagar, Singh, Agrawal, and Gupta 2009).

Brand information   Companies can advertise in order to inform the customers about the brand. For example, the Dominoes' promise of 'delivery in thirty minutes, otherwise free pizza' (also see Exhibit 11.3, the Vodafone Zoozoos). The government also indulges in a lot of advertising for social benefits, such as the pulse polio advertisements, advertisements against female infanticide, etc.

 See making of the Zoozoos video.

Exhibit 11.3   Vodafone Zoozoos

In 2009, Vodafone had three ongoing campaigns—the pug campaign was used to convey customer service, Bollywood actor, Irfan Khan was used to convey 'the brand's value for money products', and the Zoozoos to communicate the various product and service offerings (Shah 2009). The first Zoozoo commercial, shown at the time of the Indian Premier League's second season matches (Shah, 2009), became an instant hit. 'Each of the twenty nine Zoozoo commercials revolved around a Vodafone product or service.' They dominated all the ads for Vodafone (some ads can be seen in Image 11.4)—from the TV to magazines and newspapers to the Internet. There was a Facebook page dedicated to the Zoozoos, while the Zoozoo YouTube channel became the most subscribed to channel. Zoozoo became the fourth most searched word on Google' (*Superbrands* 2009).

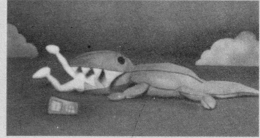

Courtesy: Superbrands.

Image 11.4   Zoozoo ads; also see Plate 13

Brand positioning To position the brand in the minds of the consumers, companies can take the help of advertising. For example, Cinthol has long used the freshness plank to position itself. Club Mahindra positions itself as providing fun for the family during their vacations. A brand can position itself on a number of variables and this has been discussed in detail in the chapter on brand positioning.

Brand recall Advertisements, with the help of humour, jingles, and catchy slogans try to catch the attention of the consumers. The 'U and I in this beautiful world...' jingle immediately connected with the customers and helped in building a high brand recall for Hutch, now Vodafone. Similarly, the Zoozoos of Vodafone were very successful in creating top-of-the-mind brand recall for Vodafone.

Brand personality and identity With the help of advertising, marketers can easily convey what the brand stands for, i.e., its personality and identity to a large number of people. Consumers get to know what the identity of the brand is. For instance, Nike tells consumers that it is a daring brand; Maruti comes across as a brand that cares for its customers; Idea is associated with bright ideas for society, such as the education of children in rural areas, saving paper, protecting the trees, etc. Even in this online advertisement, Idea is talking about growing a virtual tree and saving paper (see Image 11.5).

Source: http://www.123greetings.com/events/holi/thank_you/thank2.html, accessed on 25 February 2010.

Image 11.5 An Idea ad posted on an online greetings website

Brand repositioning To change a perceived unwanted brand image or to provide a fresh new image to a brand, organizations can undertake repositioning strategies. When the Bank of Baroda went in for a change of image, it advertised heavily to promote and inform consumers about the same. Similarly, due to the perception of customers that private banks have more ATMs, the State Bank of India ran the advertisement, wherein a person comes to the office without his trousers, since he has lost a bet with his friend who had said that SBI had the maximum number of ATMs. Airtel's repositioning has been discussed in the chapter on positioning.

Advertising Media and Influence on Branding

The attitude of the consumers towards advertising impacts the consumer brand attitude, which in turn influences the purchase decision of the customers. With the spread of communication technology, consumers have greater control over their ad exposure, and their feelings about advertisements depend on the medium in which the advertisement appears (Shavitt et al. 2004). There are several media options available for the marketer and each media is promising, and hence which media to choose can be confusing for the marketer. Since consumers have more control over their ad exposure, they make their exposure choices based on their opinions of advertising in the medium. It is argued, therefore, that a good understanding of consumer attitude and perceptions toward advertising in specific media is essential. Since advertising influences both the brand attitude and purchase intention, special attention needs to be given to this aspect of marketing communication. It is, therefore, important to understand how consumers' perceive advertising, and what their reactions are to the different media options available for the marketers to formulate effective strategies.

The various media through which organizations can reach consumers are TV, the radio, magazines, newspapers, out-of-home (OOH) media, and the Internet. A brief overview of the market scenario and growth rate of each media is discussed below.

Television The TV is estimated to have grown at 6.8 per cent since 2008 and reached ₹257 billion in 2009. This growth can be attributed to increased TV penetration. There has also been a rise in the number of digital homes, which has led to increased subscription revenues for broadcasters and distributors. The advertising revenues thus increased by 7 per cent (FICCI; KPMG Frames 2010). TV as a mass media is effective and brand managers can use both audio and visuals to create a highly persuasive dramatic effect. TV has high believability, broad acceptability, and has a better reach than even newspapers. It helps in communicating about the brand to the illiterate rural masses. However, due to the proliferation of television channels, it is getting to be more and more challenging to reach the target audience. Organizations are indulging in a 'roadblock' to capture the attention of the target audience. *My Name Is Khan* was the first film to use a roadblock across all Star Networks to showcase a trailer of the film for three minutes. This was followed by Kites with a roadblock across 40 channels on 29 March 2010 at 9:30 p.m. to launch its music (Raghavendra 2010). General Motors used a mix to reach the different segments for its different brands. For example, Chevrolet Cruz was launched on the 'Big Boss—Season 3' show on the Colors channel (Bhushan 2010). Regional advertising is also growing and is partly driven by new sectors like real estate, hospitality, education, etc., which being local brands prefer to advertise through local channels (FICCI; KPMG Frames 2010). The top five advertisers on TV are as follows (Table 11.1).

Print media The Indian print media industry, which includes both newspapers and magazines at the national and regional level, stood at ₹175 billion in 2009 and grew by 2 per cent compared to the year 2008. The growth in circulation offset the deteriorating advertising revenues, as corporates spent less on advertising during the economic slowdown. The regional market for print media however showed a positive growth. The print media is emerging as a promising platform for advertising with improved literacy levels and emerging sectors like

Table 11.1 Top five advertisers on TV

Name of the advertiser	Rank in 2000	Rank in 2010
Hindustan Unilever	1	1
Reckitt Benckiser (India)	10	2
Coca-Cola India	2	3
Cadburys India	25	3
SmithKline Beecham	12	5

Source: The Economic Times 2009; Exchange-4-Media, 2011

Exhibit 11.4   The 'Talking' Print Ad

India has seen a flurry of activity in the auto market with all the major global brands trying to gain a share of the Indian pie. The Volkswagen group came to India in 2001 with its Skoda brand, which was followed by the Audi, and the Volkswagen brand in 2007 (Volkswagen 2011). In spite of being present in the Indian market for a few years now, it has low brand awareness (IST; ET 2010). What Volkswagen required was clutter-breaking ideas to connect with the mass audience in general, and with the target audience in particular. It decided to use the print ad to reach this audience. It used roadblocks in the *Times of India* and the innovative 'hole in the paper campaign for the Polo car launch.' (IST; ET

2010). In September 2010, Volkswagen advertised its Vento brand with a 'talking' print ad in *The Hindu* and *The Times of India*. A small black electronic device was added to the full-page ad of Volkswagen with 'a picture of a Vento and an engineer crying next to it' and the moment the paper opened the ad would play the following:

'Best in class German engineering is here. The new Volkswagen Vento built with great care and highly innovative features. Perhaps that's why it breaks the heart of our engineers to watch it drive away,' (IST IANS, 2010). The ad was innovative and helped in creating a lot of buzz along with free publicity as well.

---

telecom, organized retail, and education (see Exhibit 11.4). Some of the other factors for the emergence of the print media are optimization of the cover price, growth in sales volume due to improved penetration, and the increasing importance of regional print.

Through newspapers, immediate information, such as sales, discounts, etc., can be passed on to consumers. The choice of a newspaper or a magazine helps in reinforcing the brand image and therefore care should be taken in selecting these by the brand managers. The top five brands using the print media for their marketing communications are as in Table 11.2, and Table 11.3 shows the top five advertisers.

Radio   The radio industry was worth ₹7.8 billion by the end of 2009, 0.3 per cent less than in 2008 (FICCI; KPMG Frames 2010). Due to its wide coverage and cost effectiveness, radio is becoming an attractive media to reach the Indian masses. Advertising on the radio is cheaper and has a captive audience during the traffic rush hours. Channels such as Radio Mirchi with over 41.2 million listeners are drawing the support of the youth and helping in the revival of radio as a media (IBEF 2010).

Table 11.2 Top five brands in print media in 2000 and 2009

Top five brands in year 2000	Top five brands in year 2009
Bajaj two-wheelers	IIPM
Aiwa	Department of Income Tax
Sansui	Maruti cars
Akai	State Bank of India
UTI	Ministry of Consumer Affairs

Source: The Economic Times 2009.

Table 11.3 Top five advertisers in the year 2009

Rank	Advertiser
1	Tata Teleservices
2	Hindustan Unilever
3	Lufthansa
4	Pantaloons Retail India
5	Petroleum Conservation and Research Association

Source: The Economic Times 2009.

Cinema advertising The filmed entertainment sector, i.e., film and television, worth ₹89 billion in 2009, showed a negative growth primarily due to the 'multiplex producer stalemate, shelving of expansion plans of multiplex players, impact of IPL, and the dismal performance of the films at the box office. However, product placement in films is still common and some of the recent examples are L'Oreal and Volkswagen's yellow Beetle in the film *Aisha*. Barista Lavazza Espresso Bars also adopt this technique and have appeared in films and commercials (*Superbrands* 2009).

Out-of-home (OOH) media The OOH media was worth ₹13.7 billion in 2009. The economic slowdown impacted this media and it witnessed a negative growth of 15 per cent over 2008. New technologies have added a lot of excitement to this media, which has evolved from being mere sketches on walls. The year 2009 saw an increased investment in tier two and three cities. This media is latent in the top six metros, as they account for only 30 per cent of the consumption and 60 per cent of the spend. The impact of OOH media on the human brain is subtle but strong, 'Every poster, panel, banner, flyer, message behind a truck, etc., subtly imparts information to our brains and sways our brand perception on a daily basis. The message gets stored subliminally and plays its role when required.' The OOH is more than just billboards and kiosks now; there is a lot of technology, art and skill involved in the media. Brand campaigns are being launched primarily through OOH media (Joshi 2009). The effective use of the out-of-home media to build brand Aircel has been discussed in the chapter on brand equity.

Online advertising   Online advertising is considered be the fastest growing advertising medium now (FICCI; KPMG Frames 2010) (see Table 11.4). It is expected to grow from ₹6 billion in 2009 to ₹15 billion by 2014 (PricewaterhouseCoopers Entertainment and Media Outlook Report 2010). Some of the ways of advertising online are 'banner ads, digital videos, sponsored links, etc. Classified advertising dominates the online ad industry with a 48 per cent market share and search-based advertising has a 24 per cent share (Singh 2009).

Table 11.4   Advertising media size and growth rate

Media	Size (2009) (in billion ₹)	Projected size (2014) (in billion ₹)	Growth rate (%) (2010–2014)
TV	257	521	15
Print	175	269	9
Radio	7.8	16.4	16
Filmed entertainment	89	137	9
Out-of-home	13.7	24.1	12
Online advertising	6	15	20.1

Source: FICCI, KPMG Frames 2010; PricewaterhouseCoopers Entertainment and Media Outlook Report 2010.

The other important factor impacting brands while advertising is the use of celebrities. To reinforce the brand image, the image of the celebrity endorsing the brand has to be in line with the characteristics of the brand the organization needs to communicate to the customers. The top five celebrities for the year 2009 is shown in Table 11.5.

Table 11.5   Top celebrities in 2009

Rank	Celebrity
1	Priyanka Chopra
2	M.S. Dhoni
3	Kareena Kapoor
4	Saif Ali Khan
5	Deepika Padukone

Source: Bhushan 2009.

The consumers' exposure to a particular media will decide whether they view the brand advertisement or not. An understanding of the consumer's media consumption habits helps in deciding which media to choose. Brand managers can also use a combination of the various media options to reach their target audience. In such an eventuality, a diverse set of consumers and customers can be reached. The overlap, i.e., when the same consumer is exposed to all or a couple of the media used, will help reinforce brand awareness and brand recall (see Exhibit 11.5).

Exhibit 11.5   Advertising Nirma

The brand that churned the FMCG detergent segment and changed the entire perspective of the detergent market is Nirma. Launched in 1969 by Gujarati entrepreneur Dr Karsanbhai Patel from the backyard of his house in Ahmedabad, it was the David that challenged the Goliath— Unilever's established brand, Surf, which was also the market leader at that time. Nirma's advertising strategy focused on the value-for-money angle. It used a catchy jingle 'Doodh si safedi Nirma se aye, Rangeen Kapde bhi khil khil jaye' (Nirma's whiteness is as white as milk, even the most resplendent clothes blossom with it)' and was first aired on the radio in 1975. The same jingle was used to advertise the brand on television and was first broadcasted in 1982. It is one of the longest running jingles and has seen very few changes since the time it was first aired (*Superbrands* 2009). Now with a lot of companies advertising online, Nirma hasn't stayed behind either (see Image 11.6).

There is a page dedicated to Nirma on Facebook (see Image 11.7) with 57 people liking it, as on 13 February 2011, and Nirma ads can also be viewed on YouTube (see Image 11.8).

Thus, through the use of a mix of media, Nirma has effectively reached its target audience and is one of the largest selling detergent brands in the world (*Superbrands,* 2009).

Source: http://www.nirma.co.in/.

Image 11.6   Nirma's online presence

Contd

Exhibit 11.5 *contd*

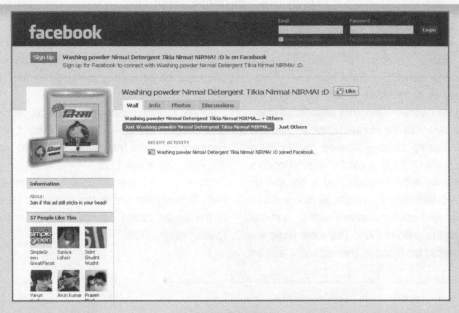

Source: http://www.facebook.com/pages/Washing-powder-Nirma-Detergent-Tikia-Nirma-NIRMA-D/123164721028320?v=wall.

Image 11.7   Nirma on Facebook

Source: http://www.youtube.com/watch?v=i-sx_NduQZs.

Image 11.8   The Nirma advertisement on YouTube

Personal Selling

Personal selling, unlike advertising, is the interpersonal interaction between the representatives of an organization and its customers. It is defined as a 'face-to-face interaction with one or more prospective purchaser for the purpose of making presentations, answering questions, and procuring orders' (Kotler and Keller 2006). Personal selling is helpful in building a brand, as the manner in which the brand is communicated and sold to the ultimate customer is directly controlled by the brand owners. This helps them create a brand experience at the time of sales, which can be the start of building brand relationships. A salesperson can be trained by the organization to deliver the brand experience to the customer rather than be pushy and deceitful. Companies like Life Insurance Corporation, Eureka Forbes, etc. have adopted personal selling for their products and services. The various ways by which organizations can do personal selling are as follows.

Going where the customer is   Organizations can approach customers to sell products to them within the convenience of their homes, for example Eureka Forbes, Tupperware, etc. (see Exhibit 11.6: Selling at Eureka Forbes). This is also possible in a business-to-business selling scenario, where the salesperson can contact the end-user directly.

At a retail outlet where the customer goes   Organizations can do personal selling by hiring sales executives at company-owned outlets, where customers may come for buying a product.

In both cases, the ultimate aim is to impress upon the customer the fact that the brand has features that will satisfy the needs and, wants of the customers in the best possible way, and inform them about the various uses of the brand.

Exhibit 11.6   Selling at Eureka Forbes

Eureka Forbes Limited (EFL) was set up in the year 1982 and is now a ₹12 billion 'multi-product and multi-channel' company dealing in domestic and industrial vacuum cleaners, air purifiers, water purification systems, and home security solutions. It is Asia's 'largest direct sales organization with 7000 direct personnel that touch 1.5 million homes. They have one of the largest networks catering to more than 131 cities and 398 towns across the country. This is not all; they are also represented by a 10,000 dealer sales network and over a 58-distributor strong industrial sales network.'

A vacuum cleaner in 1982 'was a product category that had "market resistance" written all over it. Especially with the proverbial Kanta Bai doing all the cleaning and that too without any capital expense.' EFL decided to overcome this resistance by reaching out to the customers in their house when they had ample time to listen and see the demonstration of a product (see Image 11.9). Each salesperson was called a Eurochamp and was responsible for interacting, demonstrating, convincing, installing the product, and providing servicing to customers. He was the single point contact between the customer and

Contd

Exhibit 11.6 *contd*

Courtesy: Superbrands.

Image 11.9 Euroclean ad

EFL and was responsible for building the brand that has now reached 1.5 million homes. The Eurochamps were professionals who were well-educated, well-groomed, and who built on customer relationship rather than focused on the transactions involved. They assessed the needs of the customers and offered them solutions that enhanced their life and came to be recognized as 'friendly men' and came to be known as 'friends for life'.

Source: http://www.eurekaforbes.com/aboutus/aboutus-profile.aspx, accessed on 10 July 2010 and Superbrands 2009.

Sales Promotions

Both advertising and personal selling are aided by sales promotions. Sales promotions are 'a variety of short-term incentives to encourage trial or purchase of a product or service' (Kotler and Keller 2006). It, therefore, influences and motivates the customer to make the purchase 'now'. As a brand manager, the choice of tool for sales promotion is critical, because it should be in line with the long-term brand strategy and should strengthen the same. The various sales promotion tools (Kotler, Armstrong, Agnihotri, and Haque 2010) that can be adopted and their implications on branding are discussed below.

Coupons A coupon can be mailed to the customers, inserted in newspapers or attached to a menu pamphlet. A coupon generally offers a discount on the customer's next purchase.

Coupons can be used at the introductory stages to attract the customers to the brand launched or can be used at the maturity stage to boost sagging sales. Organizations can also indulge in the same at other times. For example, Dominoes provides coupons that can be redeemed at the time of the next purchase. A brand that is newly launched in the market can attract trials with the help of this. Brand managers can use innovative ways to dispense their coupons, for example through SMSes on the mobiles, sending emails online, etc. This also helps to cut above the clutter of the number of coupons being offered.

Samples Giving samples of a brand as a trial can be done to introduce a new brand or create a buzz about the existing brand. These samples can be delivered to customers' doors, attached to a fast moving product, attached to a magazine, or handed out in a store. Samples can help in building awareness about the brand and once customers are satisfied with the brand they will indulge in repeat purchase.

Price packs These are savings offered on the regular packs of the product. If customers purchase the brand that has been packaged together, they will be able to buy it at a lower price. For example, Lux, sometimes, comes in packs of three at a discounted price, or two related products can be bundled together, a toothpaste and toothbrush, for instance.

Cash refund These are different from coupons in the sense that here price reduction occurs after the purchase when some proof of purchase is sent. A successful and popular cash refund strategy of MakeMyTrip.com that revolutionized the international travel market was, 'Hamne Toda Vaada Toh Pay Only Aadha', i,e., if we break our promise to you, pay only half the rate. This innovative campaign, which offered a refund of half the money to the traveller who wasn't completely satisfied with his international holiday, was a huge success' (Consumer Superbrands 2010 p. 135).

Premiums These 'are goods offered either free or at a low cost as an incentive to buy a product'. McDonald's offers a variety of premiums in its Happy Meals; Bournvita also provides premiums to attract children. At Big Bazaar, you can purchase two shirts at a special discount. HCL once offered a free Nokia phone worth ₹6289 free with the purchase of an ME laptop. Shoppers Stop offered a complimentary Gili diamond pendant for making purchases worth ₹30,000 between the October to December period (Basu and Mukherjee 2009).

Advertising specialties or promotional products These are useful articles like pens, mugs, calendars, T-shirts, caps, etc., which are imprinted with the 'brand name/organization name, logo, or message that are given as gifts to consumers'. These articles are used by the consumers and subtly keep reminding them of the brand name. This is a strategy adopted by pharmaceutical companies, which offer doctors promotional products that can be kept on their tables. Sitting on the table, these products will remind doctors of the medicine's brand name.

Point-of-purchase promotions These include displays and demonstrations at retail outlets or any other place where the customer makes a purchase. Barista Lavazza offers live music performances, tarot card exhibits, handwriting analysis sessions, etc., to provide excitement for guests at their outlets.

Contests, sweepstakes, and games   Sales can also be promoted by organizing contests, around activities such as making a jingle, providing suggestions, etc., and the best entry is then selected by a panel of judges. For example, Lays organized a contest in which people were asked to send in new names of flavours to Lays. The flavours that were chosen were to get a percentage of the sales or a fixed amount up front. Sweepstakes are when consumers submit their names for a draw. A game, on the other hand, is when some consumers get something—a bingo, numbers, missing letters every time they buy, which may or may not help them win a prize. They help to create brand attention and consumer involvement. For example, Castrol uses contests and sweepstakes to attract customers. In 2011, it used the ICC World Cup to promote itself (see Image 11.10) by offering the winner a chance to watch a match in style (see Image 11.11).

Source: http://www.castrol.com/castrol/castrolhomepage.do?categoryId=3230.

Image 11.10   Castrol's ICC World Cup promotion

Events and Campaign Marketing

Brands have long been associated with sponsoring events like the various cricket matches, football tournaments, etc. Companies can also organize their own events such as the Standard Chartered Mumbai Marathon organized on 17 January 2010, or the Swasthya Chetna, Healthy Awakening campaign of Lifebuoy, which educates rural communities about the importance of washing hands with soap. 'In India, over six lakh children under the age of five, die annually from diarrhoea,' which can be prevented by washing hands. These areas are otherwise difficult to reach through the usual marketing campaigns on TV or through the press, etc.

The Kitply brand of plywood, through their association with cricket, for example built a high visibility for themselves. By association with icons like Sachin Tendulkar and giving among cheques at the end of matches, a remarkable franchise for the brand was created. They also organized a tri-nation ODI series, which was telecast by Neo Sports in 2008 and received 42.6 million tune-ins, which was 20 per cent higher than the IPL final (*Superbrands*, 2009). Organization of such events or campaigns increases brand recall, and association with a big event inculcates trust in the customers and convinces them that the brand is a big brand.

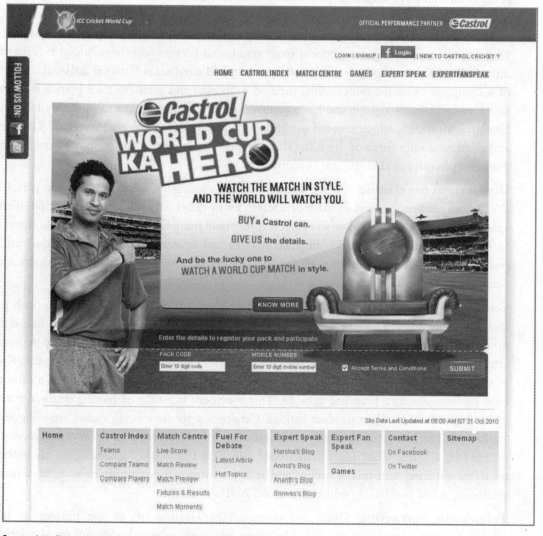

Source: http://www.castrolcricket.com/world-cup-ka-hero/.

Image 11.11   Castrol promotion details

Direct Marketing

Direct marketing can be defined as the 'use of mail, telephone, fax, e-mail, or the Internet to communicate directly with, or solicit response from, or dialogue with specific customers and prospects' (Kotler and Keller 2006). Electronic shopping, telemarketing, television shopping, etc., are various ways in which organizations can do direct marketing. Dell Inc. has always relied on and championed the direct sales method for selling its personal computers. However, in India it is also selling products to the consumers through retail stores and also through Perot Systems which it acquired in 2009 for $3.9 billion, and which is now spearheading its entry into the selling services *(The Economic Times,* 2010a). Amazon and eBay are examples of companies that have been able to create a brand name for themselves by adopting the direct marketing route.

The direct selling industry in India stands at ₹3330 crore and is growing at a rate of 17 per cent. It is facing competition from traditional players who have added e-tailing and direct selling to increase their reach to semi-urban and rural areas (Sharma 2010). An example of a company using the direct selling method to market and establish their brands is Amway, which entered India in 1998 and has a turnover of ₹1128 crore and a sales force of 5.5 lakh. Similarly, Modicare, which entered the Indian market in 1996, has a turnover of ₹100 crore and employs a sales force of 1.5 lakh (Sharma and Ghosh 2009). The various forms of direct marketing (Kotler et al. 2010) are as follows.

Direct mail marketing   When through 'letters, catalogues, ads, brochures, samples, CDs, DVDs', organizations send an offer or a reminder or other items to prospective customers at a particular address, physical or virtual, it is direct mail marketing. This allows brand managers to send information to a highly targeted market and an easy measurement of the result is possible. Email and SMS options allow for quick delivery of direct mail and are discussed in detail in the section on Internet marketing.

Catalogue marketing   This allows brand managers to mail their catalogues, both print and digital, to select customers. By going online, brand managers can upload a number of options for customers to choose from. However, in India people like to purchase items only after physical inspection and therefore catalogue marketing is not highly successful (Kotler et al. 2010). 'Catalogues are enjoying a Renaissance' and along with being used as a sales tool have become essential branding vehicles. This is evident from the increasing editorial content in catalogues and not just product listings. Catalogues are now being called 'magalogues' or 'catazines'. The increased branding content leads to consumers spending more and more time on the magalogues, which leads to increased sales (see Exhibit 11.7). Catalogues are powerful tools for pushing consumers online and it is reassuring for consumers to hold a printed catalogue, while purchasing online (Bashford 2010).

Telephone marketing   With the increased penetration of mobile phones in India, telephone marketing is on the rise. Marketers use both inbound and outbound telephone marketing to receive orders and sell to customers directly. Teleshopping in India is estimated at ₹900 crore a year (Sruthijith 2010).

Exhibit 11.7   Branding through Catalogues

The electronics brand giant, Bang and Olufsen's catalogues are printed bi-annually in twenty-one languages and 'target up to one million existing and potential customers and dealers.' To be used both as a marketing vehicle and a branding tool for customers and dealers, it is designed as a 'half catalogue (B&O Collection) and half editorial (B&O Magazine).' Research proves that this strategy is working and readers 'spend an average of thirty-seven minutes examining the catalogue, and comparing readers with non-readers, 29 per cent more readers of strongly agree that B&O stands for 'timeless design' and 12.5 per cent more believe it stands for craftsmanship.'

Marks and Spencer's Home gets its 320-page catalogue printed twice a year along with mini-books, smaller versions of the catalogue and leaflets. As all the retail outlets cannot display the entire range, the catalogues account for the 'lion's share of the business'. These catalogues act as an inspiration for customers, and they can view the entire range of furniture at leisure (Bashford 2010).

Mobile phone marketing   Increasing use of mobile phones makes this an attractive media for marketers. Some of the mobile phone promotions include ring-tone giveaways, retailer announcements of discounts, special sales, etc. Location-based marketing via Bluetooth is also possible when customers get messages from marketers on the basis of their proximity to retail outlets.

Publicity and Public Relations

Publicity is 'a variety of programmes designed to promote or protect a company's image or its individual products' (Kotler and Keller 2006). Organizations can maintain public relations through company magazines, annual reports, donations, etc.

News releases are a popular means of disseminating information about the brand. However, if the release is not in favour of the brand, it can harm the brand image. For example, brand Coca-Cola's bottling plant, Hindustan Coca-Cola Beverages, at Plachimada, in Kerala, which was shut down in the year 2004, was recently in the news. The Kerala government panel had been studying the charges of depletion of ground water and dumping of solid waste that had both harmed farming activities in the area and loss of health. Coca-Cola now has been asked to pay ₹216 crore for the damages and even though Coke has denied the charges *(The Economic Times,* 2010b), such publicity is bad for the company, and the company will need act to see that its brand equity is not affected. The news of the bidding battle between Kraft Foods and other rivals for Cadbury in the year 2009 had resulted in the share prices reaching a new high (Jones 2009). These examples highlight the need to manage the publicity of the organization so that brand equity is enhanced and not lost.

Other ways by which publicity can be created is through newsletters, magazines, and annual reports, and this also helps in disseminating the relevant information about the brand, which helps the organization build higher brand equity. 'Public service activities' carried out by organizations also helps in creating goodwill for the brand. 'Corporate identity material like business cards, logos, stationery, buildings, websites, company cars and trucks', etc., all help in creating brand identity in the minds of customers (Jauhari and Dutta 2010; Kotler et al. 2010).

Publicity is an important brand-building tool and should not be overlooked at the time of deciding the communications strategy. According to Dr Pragnya Ram, Group Executive President—Corporate Communications, Aditya Birla Group, '80 per cent of the consumers' perception is formed by what they are reading in the media and media is taken at face value'. Thus, the need to maintain good public relations is vital for the success of a brand.

Word of Mouth

This includes the customer-to-prospective customer interaction, which is not directly under the control of the organization. 'In developed countries, it is advertising that affects the purchase choice the most, but in developing countries like India and Indonesia it is word of mouth that affects the purchase decision the most. Indians are a closely knit society and are easily influenced by their peers, relatives, etc.' (Jauhari and Dutta 2010). Brands can create a positive word of mouth for themselves by consistently delivering during the moments of truth for the customers. Also, during the initial days of a start-up when organizations cannot invest money in advertising, word-of-mouth publicity is the best way to spread the word about the brand and create brand awareness and ultimately footfalls. For example, 'when Dutch national Lalita de Goederen opened Bagel's Café in Gurgaon in June 2009 she depended on word-of-mouth publicity. Bagel's saw 500 billings a month in July and August. September 2009 onwards, Lalita started updating the fan page regularly. Billings doubled within a month and in November 2009 she opened a ten-seater cafeteria in a commercial building' (Sivakumar 2010). A brand, therefore, has to create the right marketing mix and communicate this effectively to customers, so that customer expectations from the brand do not surpass their perception about the brand performance. The Internet now makes it possible to spread the word of mouth quicker and to a wider audience through message boards, virtual communities, blogs, etc.

Internet Marketing

The Internet and its related platforms are considered as the new age media. The Internet scores over traditional media, that is print, television, radio, etc., by providing current information with the minimum lead time to the relevant target audience and the impact is far more measurable. Customers also benefit by receiving relevant advertising.

Online product demonstrations and product usage facilitate the selling process. E-advertising is global in nature and assists consumers in choosing their brands at their own convenience and pace (see Exhibit 11.8). It provides a high quality and an interactive multimedia option to reach the customers (Ramprasad 2009). The flip side is that it can transform the corporate reputation in an instant when consumers use the web to vent their disapproval and expose wrongdoings. The British Petroleum (BP) oil leak was highly talked about and commented upon, resulting in its reputation being severely damage in 2010. The online media cannot be ignored and needs to be monitored so that organizations can protect their reputations (Jones 2010). The various methods by which an organization can communicate and advertise in the new age media are as follows (Ramaswamy and Namakumari 2009).

Viral marketing Viral marketing is an effective tool of brand communication, where an information or communication is passed through the Internet from one mouth to many and

Exhibit 11.8   The Net Savvy India Post

India Post, with 1,55,333 post offices across the country, now has another post office—the virtual post office launched at the end of the year 2010. This virtual post office made it possible to sell stamps, transfer money, and provide various other postal services at the click of a mouse. This enabled 'the Internet savvy educated urban consumers' to use the services of India Post, which turned 246 years old in 2010, more easily. The services include railway ticketing, foreign remittance, collection of mobile bills, etc. India Post is now planning to expand these services to also include pre-paid cards, which will support cashless transactions at retail outlets (Sanyal and Ghosh 2010).

from there to many more till the information spreads like a virus. 'The Dove Evolution viral ad is effective because it sends a unique, positive message about the true definition of beauty. And this video really did spread like a virus. Not only did it get nearly 2 million hits within a month's time, but it also received attention from top TV shows like Ellen, The View, and Entertainment Tonight.'

Social networking sites   Social networking sites such as Facebook, Orkut, etc., are gaining popularity and helping people connect across geographical boundaries and time. They also provide a wealth of personal information about the customers online, and can be used effectively by marketers to finetune their offerings. YouTube allows marketers to upload videos and ads about their products and is increasingly becoming popular among onliners. It is effective in India as customers here depend more on word of mouth and prefer talking to family and friends before making a purchase decision. However, the drawback here is that the marketers do not have control over what is being said and both types of information can be sent out—good and bad. Marketers need to monitor various websites like Mouthshut.com and keep tabs on what is being said about the brand (Sagar et al. 2009). Any negative comments should be redressed immediately. Thus, a lot of content creation and content-sharing is possible here. These sites are also becoming the largest source of on- or offline friend networks (Irani 2010). Brand managers can leverage networking sites in the fashion that Cadbury promoted the 'virtual gifting phenomenon' on Facebook during Diwali when gifting is common. Through their gifting application, users could 'send virtual Cadbury chocolates to friends, family, and colleagues and this was visible on the person's entire social network.' (Menon 2010)

3-D digital shops   These are high quality environments in three dimensions, which are slated to become the next big phenomenon on the Internet. Here, there are ample opportunities for marketers to explore and communicate with their target audience. For example, Second Life, http://education.secondlife.com/about/, is an open-ended virtual game, where residents can create their own buildings, vehicles, etc. This will help marketers understand consumer behaviour and place their brands in the game and in virtual stores, where consumers can purchase the product online.

Blogs   Blog is the short name for web logs. These are web pages, where individuals can post their opinions about various issues and communicate them to the whole world. Consumers, whether they purchase online or offline, do go online to check the reviews of the brands they intend to purchase, especially cars, tickets, hotel rooms, etc., as well as electronic products. According to a global study on online purchasing by Nielsen (Nielsen Wire 2010), 'one of the great benefits of shopping online is the ability to read others' reviews of a product, be they experts or simply fellow-shoppers.' Brands that fail to deliver according to their brand promise need to specially pay attention, as 41 per cent of the customers said that they were most likely to write a review about their negative experiences. Evalueserve and Empower Research are companies that are providing the services for scrutinizing blogs for their clients. 'Various blog search programmes are also available, such as Nielsen Buzzmetrics, which uses crawlers to sieve through consumer "buzz" on blogs and arrive at marketing insights' (Ramaswamy and Namakumari 2009).

Web TV   This technology provides the facility of downloading TV programmes and watching them at leisure and not necessarily at the scheduled time. Web TV will also impact television advertising and needs to be looked at as a potential medium in the future when more and more people begin adopting this medium.

Mobile phones   With the increased adoption of mobile phones by the Indian consumers, it is fast becoming an attractive media to specifically select and target the relevant audience. There are 671.69 million mobile subscribers in India (June 2010 data from Dash 2010) who can be relevantly targeted by various brands. IBM is testing a product called Presence. This enables the detection of shoppers, who have signed up for Presence, as soon as they enter a retail store and it then offers real time discount coupons through the mobile. Also, the spending habits of the shoppers, their browsing time in the different departments, etc., can be collected and analysed to provide a better shopping experience for them (Rosenbloom 2010). Thus, a promotion for lady's-finger can be sent on the mobile phone once customers enter the fresh vegetables aisle, or they can get advice for purchasing matching accessories once they buy a new dress, etc.

SMS   Instead of calling on the mobile phones, companies can also send SMSes. The benefit of sending an SMS is that it can be stored and reconsidered later. With commercial SMS now costing less than a paisa, all companies from insurance, to vastu, geyser manufacturers to builders have adopted this media taking the score of SMSes across the country above the 100 million a day mark (Dash 2010).

Podcasts   These are pre-recorded programmes that can be made available on a website for download, which people can watch later on their computers or mobile phones. Podcast takes its name from Apple's iPod line of products, but is not limited to the same (*Entrepreneur*, 2010).

Company websites   The websites of organizations also communicate with the target audience. The benefit is that consumers can visit these websites at their leisure and convenience, since they are available 24/7. Also, information on the Internet can be processed in real time and the latest communications, promotional campaigns, product updates, etc. can be provided to the customers with a minimum time lag (also see the section on branding and marketing strategies in Chapter 6).

Online advertising   Companies can post links to their websites or even advertisements on the websites of other organizations. These ads can be in the form of banner ads or pop-up ads.

In-store TV   This is a form of point-of-purchase display, where customers inside a store can watch the ads for the brands in the store on the screen. For example, Big Bazaar and Shoppers' Stop use in-store TV to 'narrowcast' or broadcast information to a narrow focused audience in the store at that point of time.

In-programme brand placement   Brands are now placed in TV programmes or serials or in films, where they can catch the eye of the viewers and thus achieve a higher brand recall. Embedding products in the storyline helps to cut the clutter and leads to a higher awareness on part of the audience. For instance, in the show, 'Big Boss 3' (2008) on the Colors channel, the Airtel music was played to wake the participants up in the morning. Financial services like ICICI Prudential Life Insurance launched their Jeete Raho campaign through the film *Cheeni Kum*. Reliance Capital tied up with *Three Idiots* to promote its All Izz Well insurance plans and Bajaj Allianz tied up with the movie *Paa* for its children's plans. 'Bajaj Allianz claims that the tie-up has doubled its promotion frequency.' The flip side is that the tie-up can result in brand overkill and may have negative implications if the film does not do well at the box office (Sharma and Dhall 2009).

One of the strategies, using which marketers can connect with customers online, is by 'crowdsourcing for advertisements'. In crowdsourcing (Howe 2006), organizations take the work from one employee and entrust it to a large group of people (crowd) that leads to a community-based design (Howe 2006; Kaufman 2008). This allows consumers to have a say in the brand, be it in the product design, promotions, designing, innovations, etc. Marketers are benefited as it allows them to get feedback from consumers in time for them to incorporate into their brand-building strategy. Unilever is an example of an organization using the idea of crowdsourcing its ads (Tiltman 2010).

INTEGRATING BRAND COMMUNICATIONS

Marketers can communicate with their target audience via a number of media and various communications tools. In actual life, the choices that consumers have are not simple, especially given the fact that there are a multitude of brands to choose from. Also, a consumer is influenced by a number of parameters prior to the purchase of the same (Joshi 2009). Thus, marketers need to be present and touch the lives of the customers at more than one point with information about the brand that they are offering, by educating the customers about the brand, the various brand attributes, brand prices, etc. The information that goes out via all the tools and media used should be consistent and deliver the same message (see Exhibit 11.9). This helps in building a strong consistent brand image and reinforces the brand attributes in the minds of the customers.

Exhibit 11.9   Managing Brand Communications at Tata Sky

The brand Tata Sky is a satellite service provider in the direct to home (DTH) category (see Image 11.12).

It has positioned itself under the DTH category and uses search engine optimization, as can be seen from Image 11.13, to ensure that it comes out at the top in the organic search for 'DTH'.

Tata has also launched its Tata Sky Plus and Tata Sky Active services. The former is positioned as a

Courtesy: Superbrands.

Image 11.12   Tata Sky advertisement

Contd

Exhibit 11.9 *contd*

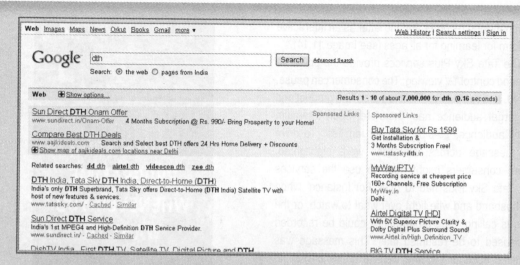

Source: http://www.google.co.in accessed on 17 August 2010.

Image 11.13   Tata Sky in DTH Google Search

Courtesy: Superbrands.

Image 11.14   Tata Sky ad of Actve Wizkids; also see Plate 14

Contd

Exhibit 11.9 *contd*

personal video recorder and the latter as an interactive platform for learning for all ages (see Image 11.14).

The Tata Sky Plus services provide the power to plan and control TV viewing. The consumer can pause, record, and rewind live TV. It is a premium product and the target audience has, therefore, been 'premium metro audience, 25-plus, affluent families'. To drive the message across, situations were highlighted, where consumers might need to use the services that Tata Sky Plus had to offer. For instance, when the husband and wife fight over what to watch, or the boss is calling, etc., programmes could be recorded or paused to be resumed later. This message was modified according to the website on which the ad was run. Thus, for a cricketing websites, the ad was as given in Image 11.15.

This was followed by the ad message 'pause, record, rewind, live TV' for an entertainment website (see Image 11.16).

Source: http://www.media2win.com/case_studies_tata_sky_plus.html, accessed on 17 August 2010.

Source: http://www.media2win.com/case_studies_tata_sky_plus.html, accessed on 17 August 2010.

Image 11.15 Tata Sky online ad for cricket lovers

Image 11.16 Tata Sky online ad on entertainment websites

Contd

Exhibit 11.9 *contd*

For the financial website, the message was as given in Image 11.17.

This highlights the fact that even though the ad copy was personalized according to the website, the basic message of 'pause, record, and rewind live TV' was consistent throughout.

The Tata Sky Active series provides a platform for interactive TV. The organic search for 'interactive TV' shows the Tata Sky link on the first page. Thus, it has positioned itself in this category also (see Image 11.18).

For Tata Sky Active, there were a series of ads on TV, print, outdoor media, and the Internet. These ads highlighted how learning was made fun and easy. Their brand ambassador, Aamir Khan, drives across the brand message. Image 11.19 shows that they have highlighted the same brand communication on their website also.

Thus, we can see that Tata Sky has provided uniform brand communication across all the platforms, and finds a place in the Superbrands category.

Source: Based on *Superbrands* 2009; Media2win 2010.

WANT A SECOND LOOK AT STOCKS ON THE MOVE?

LET US REWIND IT FOR YOU.

REWIND A PROGRAMME WHENEVER YOU WANT TO

PAUSE
RECORD
REWIND
LIVE TV

Click here for demo

TATA Sky +

Source: http://www.media2win.com/case_studies_tata_sky_plus.html, accessed on 17 August 2010.

Image 11.17 Tata Sky ad on financial websites

Contd

Exhibit 11.9 *contd*

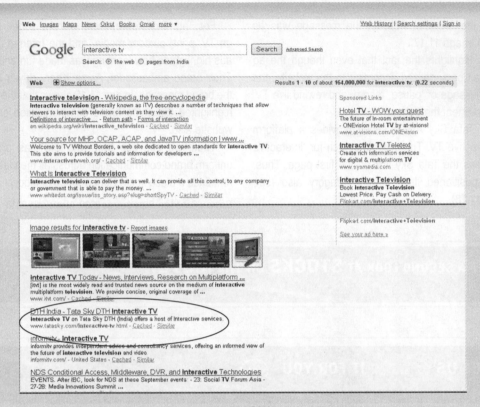

Source: http://www.google.co.in, accessed on 17 August 2010.

Image 11.18   Tata Sky on Google search for Interactive TV

Source: http://www.tatasky.com, accessed on 18 August 2010.

Image 11.19   Tata Sky official website

SUMMARY

Communicating with the target audience is imperative in building a brand. Consumers need to be aware and knowledgeable about the offering—the brand—that has been designed for them. The awareness and the image that the consumers have about the brand can make the brand successful and easily acceptable and adoptable by the customers. This chapter talks about the various ways in which an organization can communicate with the target audience be it through advertising, personal selling, sales promotion, events and campaign marketing, direct marketing, publicity, word-of-mouth, or Internet marketing. The advertising section delineates the various perspectives that advertising can help develop for consumers like brand information, positioning, brand recall, etc. It covers the various media options available to the marketers and the impact they have from the branding perspective. Personal selling also looks at the various ways in which

marketers can use this as a tool to build their brand. The sales promotion section looks at the various sales promotion tools and their impact on branding. Event and campaign marketing can also be used for communicating and building a perspective of the brand and this has been discussed in that section. This is followed by direct marketing: its various ways and the impact of the same on branding. The publicity and public relations section and word-of-mouth section focus on the use of these as a tool to build a brand. The new age media—the Internet is also discussed in detail. The various options available like viral marketing, social networking sites, 3-D digital shops, etc. have been highlighted. The integrated marketing concept then talks about the selection and choice of media and the various communication options, keeping in mind the brand image that organizations need to portray.

KEY TERMS

Advertising Communication that is paid for by an identified sponsor with the object of promoting ideas, goods, or services.

Brand attitude It is the attitude that consumers develop towards a brand on the basis of their association, direct and indirect, with the brand.

Brand awareness It is the ability of the consumer to recognize or recall the brand as a member of a particular product class category.

Brand knowledge It is the understanding that the consumers have about a brand and constitutes brand awareness and brand image.

Brand positioning It is arranging for a product to occupy a clear, distinctive, and desirable place in the market, and in the minds of the target consumers.

Brand response This is the customers' response to the marketing activities and the brand meaning they have derived.

Direct marketing Selling by means of dealing directly with the consumers rather than through retailers. Traditional

methods include mail order, direct mail selling, cold-calling, telephone selling, and door-to-door calling. More recently, telemarketing, direct radio selling, magazines, TV and online computer shopping have been developed.

Marketing communication It is a dialogue between the organization and the various audiences of its brand.

Personal selling Person-to-person interaction between a buyer and a seller in which the seller's purpose is to persuade the buyer of the merits of the product, to convince the buyer of their need for it, and to develop with the buyer an ongoing customer relationship.

Promotion The managerial process of communication an organization has with its target audience to generate attitudinal and behavioural responses and facilitate exchanges for mutual benefit.

Public relations Influencing the public so that they regard an individual firm, charity, etc., in a favourable light compared to their competitors, since a good corporate image is an important asset for an organization.

Sales promotion An activity designed to boost the sales of products or services. It may include an advertising campaign, a free-sample campaign, offering of free gifts, etc.

Word of mouth The customer-to-prospective customer interaction, which is not directly under the control of the organization.

EXERCISES

Concept Review Questions

1. What is promotion and how does it impact branding?
2. Critically discuss the statement, 'It is advertising that transforms a product, which provides functional benefits and no more, into a brand that offers the consumer psychological rewards in addition to the functional ones.'
3. How can sales promotions help in building a brand?
4. Enumerate the various ways in which the Internet can be used to communicate about the brand. Highlight any two that you think are the most important, and explain why?

Critical Thinking Questions

1. 'Marketers can communicate with their target audience via a number of media and various communications tools'. Critically discuss this statement in the light of branding.
2. An FMCG company is deciding to launch a shampoo. What promotional tools would you recommend to build their brand and why?

3. Evaluate the use of publicity and public relations in building a brand.

Internet Exercises

1. Visit the Indian Railways online reservation website http://www.irctc.co.in/ and list the various ads that you can see. Do these ads deliver the brand message? What perception of the brand can you form from these ads?
2. Visit the website http://www.makemytrip.com. Can you find the brand communications of MakeMyTrip on other websites like http://economictimes.indiatimes.com? Do you think MakeMyTrip is following an integrated brand communications approach?

CD Exercises

1. Discuss the kind of communication option being exercised in the 'Up Close and Personal' video of the Aditya Birla Group.
2. Discuss the ad of Fortune and how it helps in building the brand.

REFERENCES

Bashford, S., 'Still in Vogue', *Brand Equity, The Economic Times,* New Delhi, 24 February 2010, p. 4.

Basu, S.D. and W. Mukherjee, 'Buy, Buy 2009: Cos, retailers add value to year-end offers', *The Economic Times,* New Delhi, 29 December 2009, p. 4.

Bhushan, R, 'Priyanka is first queen of endorsements', *The Economic Times,* New Delhi, 17 December, 2009, p. 4

Bhushan, R., 'Madison bags ₹100-cr GM media account for 3 years', *The Economic Times,* New Delhi, 25 March 2010, p. 4.

Dash, D.K., 'Junk SMS mess: Over 100m a day', *Times of India,* New Delhi, 2 August 2010, p. 1.

Dutta, Kirti (2009), 'Consumer information sources and effectiveness of advertising media: An analysis of India, Turkey and New Zealand' presented at the *4th International Conference on Services Management held at Barceló Hotel, Oxford* organized by the Oxford Brookes University, Pennsylvania State University, US and IIMT on 8–9 May 2009.

Dutta, Kirti (2010), 'Effect of Branding on purchase behaviour of Urban Indian Women' a PhD thesis submitted to M.G. Kashi Vidyapeeth, Varanasi.

Exchage-4-media (2010), 'Pitch-Madison Media Ad Outlook 2010: Indian ad pie at ₹21,145 cr; 13 pc growth projected in 2010', http://www.exchange4media.

com/e4m/news/fullstory.asp?section_id=1&news_id=37257&tag=2528&search=y, accessed on 11 July 2010.

FICCI KPMG media report - 2010 http://www.kpmg.com/IN/en/Press%20Release/Media%20n%20Entertainment%20Industry%20projected%20to%20grow%20at%2013percent%20over%20next%20five%20years%20to%20INR%201091%20bn%20FICCI-KPMG%20report.pdf, accessed on 25 July 2010.

Fill, C. (2002), *Marketing Communications Context, Strategies and Applications,* 3rd edition, Prentice Hall.

Howe, J. (2006), 'The rise of crowdsourcing', http://www.wired.com/wired/archive/14.06/crowds.html, accessed on 15 August 2010.

IST ET Bureau (2010), 'Media room Volkswagen "talking" ad', http://economictimes.indiatimes.com/features/brand-equity/Media-Room-Volkswagens-talking-ad/articleshow/6646039.cms, accessed on 10 February 2011.

IST, IANS (2010), 'Volkswagen pushes new Vento with "talking" print advertisement' http://economictimes.indiatimes.com/news/news-by-industry/services/advertising/Volkswagen-pushes-new-Vento-with-talking-print-advertisement/articleshow/6600104.cms, accessed on 10 February 2011.

Jauhari, V. and K. Dutta (2010), *Services Marketing Management and Operations,* Chapter 14, Oxford University Press, New Delhi.

Jones, D., 'Be there or be square', *Brand Equity, The Economic Times,* New Delhi, 11 August 2010, pp. 1.

Jones, D., 'Cadbury shares lap up attention, hit new high', *The Economic Times,* New Delhi, 24 November 2009, p. 17.

Jones, John Philip (1999), *How to Use Advertising to Build Strong Brands,* Sage Publications, New Delhi.

Joshi, Prasoon, 'It's fun but tough out of home', *The Economic Times,* New Delhi, 15 December 2009, p. 4.

Kaufman, W. (2008), 'Crowdsourcing turns business on its head', http://www.npr.org/templates/story/story.php?storyId=93495217, accessed on 15 August 2010.

Kotler, P., G. Armstrong, P.Y. Agnihotri, and E. ul Haque 2010, *Principles of Marketing: A South Asian Perspective 13th Edition,* Prentice Hall, Delhi.

Kotler, Philip and Kevin Lane Keller (2006), *Marketing Management 12e,* Prentice Hall of India Private Limited, New Delhi, p. 193.

LaTour, Kathryn A.B. and M.S. LaTour, 'Transforming consumer experience when timing matters', *Journal of Advertising,* Vol. 34, Issue 3, 2005, p. 19–30.

Martinez, Trevino (2003), 'Firm to consumer educational practices: Enhancing firm credibility to foster brand related attitudes and purchase intentions' a PhD degree submitted to University of Memphis.

Menon, R., 'The games brands play', *The Economic Times,* New Delhi, 10 August 2010, p. 4.

Nielsen, Wire (2010), 'Global online shopping report', http://blog.nielsen.com/nielsenwire/consumer/global-online-shopp.ing-report/, accessed on 25 July 2010.

Obermiller, Carl, Eric Spangenberg, and D.L. MacLachlan, 'Ad skepticism the consequences of disbelief', *Journal of Advertising,* Vol. 34, Issue 3, 2005, p. 7–17.

Olson, Jerry C. (1978), 'Inferential Belief formation in the cue utilization process', *Advances in Consumer Research,* Vol. 5, Issue 1, p. 706–13.

PricewaterhouseCoopers Entertainment and Media Outlook Report 2010, http://www.pluggd.in/internet-advertising-media-forecast-for-india-297/, accessed on 30 July 2010.

Raghavendra, N., 'Kits music to hit air with 1-min roadlock', *The Economic Times,* New Delhi, 25 March 2010, p. 4.

Ramaswamy, V.S. and S. Namakumari (2009), *Marketing Management,* MacMillan, New Delhi.

Ramprasad, V. (2009), 'Modern trends in advertising', *Advertising Express,* November issue, pp. 19–22.

Rosenbloom, S., 'Buy, buy time: Cellphones let shoppers point, click and purchase', *The Economic Times,* New Delhi, 1 March 2010, p. 4.

Sagar, M., D. Singh, D.P. Agarwal, and A. Gupta (2009), *Brand Management,* Ane Books Pvt. Ltd, New Delhi, Chapter 6.

Sanyal, S. and A. Ghosh, 'India post turns net savvy, plans virtual PO', *The Economic Times,* New Delhi, 16 April 2010, p. 6.

Shah, G. (2009), 'Zoozoo rakhis anyone?' http://www.livemint.com/2009/07/24235030/Zoozoo-rakhis-anyone.html, accessed on 10 February 2011.

Sharma, A. and D. Ghosh, 'Makeover time for direct sellers', *The Economic Times,* New Delhi, 17 November 2009, p. 4.

Sharma, A. and Dhall, A., 'All Izz Well, Insurance companies reel off products with filmy touch', *The Economic Times,* New Delhi, 18 December 2009, p. 4.

Sharma, A., 'Global biggies plan direct-selling foray', *The Economic Times,* New Delhi, 6 July 2010, p 4.

Singh, H., 'Online display ads to grow 32%: Study', *The Economic Times,* New Delhi, 15 December 2009, p. 4.

Sivakumar, N., 'Facebook spices up startups' food business', *The Economic Times,* New Delhi, 16 March 2010, p. 4.

Sruthijith, K.K., 'Future gets ready for big e-bazaar', *The Economic Times,* New Delhi, 6 May 2010, p. 4.

Superbrands (2009), *Superbrands: An insight into India's strongest consumer brands Volume III*, Superbrands India Private Limited, Gurgaon.

The Economic Times 2010a, 'Kerala panel asks Coca-Cola to pay ₹216-crore damages', *The Economic Times*, New Delhi, 23 March 2010, p. 6.

The Economic Times 2010b, 'India key market for us: Dell, Company keen on participation in UID project, eyes smartphone market', *The Economic Times*, New Delhi, 24 March 2010, p. 5.

The Economic Times, 'Service Return', *The Economic Times*, New Delhi, 21 December 2009, p. 4.

Tiltman, D., 'Unilever experimenting with crowdsourcing for ads', *The Economic Times*, New Delhi, 28 April 2010, p. 6.

Zeithaml, V.A., 'Consumer perceptions of price quality and value: A means-end model and synthesis of evidence', *Journal of Marketing*, Vol. 52, Issue 3, 1988, pp. 2–22.

Web Resources

http://digitallabz.com/blogs/11-examples-of-viral-marketing-campaigns.html, accessed on 16 August 2010.

http://education.secondlife.com/about/, accessed on 23 July 2010.

http://mumbaimarathon.indiatimes.com/ index1.html, accessed on 14 July 2010.

http://www.castrol.com/castrol/castrolhomepage.do?categoryId=3230, accessed on 13 February 2011.

http://www.castrolcricket.com/world-cup-ka-hero/, accessed on 13 February 2011.

http://www.entrepreneur.com/encyclopedia/term/159122.html, accessed on 20 July 2010.

http://www.eurekaforbes.com/aboutus/aboutus-profile.aspx, accessed on 10 July 2010.

http://www.exchange4media.com/e4m/news/fullstory.asp?section_id=1&news_id=40527&tag=33021, accessed on 1 June 2011.

http://www.facebook.com/pages/Washing-powder-Nirma-Detergent-Tikia-Nirma-NIRMA-D/123164721028320?v=wall, accessed on 13 February 2011.

http://www.google.co.in, accessed on 17 August 2010.

http://www.ibef.org/artdispview.aspx?in=49&art_id=25980&cat_id=124&page=3, accessed on 27 July 2010.

http://www.lifebuoy.com/swasthya_chetna.html, accessed on 15 July 2010.

http://www.media2win.com/case_studies_tata_sky_plus.html, accessed on 17 August 2010.

http://www.nirma.co.in/, accessed on 13 February 2011.

http://www.tatasky.com, accessed on 18 August 2010.

http://www.volkswagen.co.in/en/volkswagen_world/volkswagen_india.html, accessed on 10 February 2011.

http://www.youtube.com/watch?v=i-sx_NduQZs, accessed on 13 February 2011.

CASE STUDY

Advertising Medias

Introduction

The sixty-four years since independence have witnessed many revolutions: the green in 1960s, the white in the 1970s, the family entertainment in the 1980s, and 'the mobility revolution of the millennium' (Sivakumar 2010). The family entertainment revolution was heralded in the 1980s by the launch of the national television, but the television industry in India came into being in 1957, when each day, for a limited period, black and white programmes were aired in New Delhi. The Asian Games in India in 1982 saw a revolution in the form of colour television. The liberalization of the economy in 1990s drove in a number of international channels with several local offerings. This proliferation of media was not limited to the channels alone.

There are approximately 300 dailies and a number of magazines to choose from. The out-of-home advertising is also an attractive means to catch the attention of customers on the go. With 637 million mobile phone subscribers who are using the same for a number of applications and connectivity on voice as well as for accessing the net, the proliferation of media is huge. Also, to reach a diverse consumer market, geographically, culturally, and linguistically, in a country like India, keeping in mind the budget of an organization can be a task.

Understanding of the consumer attitude towards the media

A study of the consumer attitudes towards the various media was conducted with about 350 respondents participating in the study. The consumers were asked to rank the influence of the media on their purchase decision-making. The results are shown in Table 11.6.

Table 11.6 Overall ranking of media influences

Options	Rank
Past experience	1
Publicity	2
TV commercials	3
Shows/Exhibits	5
Magazines/Newspaper ads	4
Brochures	7
Billboards (out-of-home)	8
Point of purchase displays	6
Internet ads	9
Radio	10

Source: Dutta 2010.

Past experience with the brand is the number one influence on a customer at the time of purchase. This is followed by the brand image of the firm based on publicity rather than of company-influenced communications. TV commercials come at number three followed by magazines and newspaper ads, and shows and exhibits.

A further correlation analysis showed perfect correlation between TV and the Internet. This shows that when customers view information on the TV, they go online to determine the validity or to gain further information about the company/product before purchasing. As far as the other media are concerned, the information is unique and impacts the buying process differently and further highlights the importance of understanding each media.

The consumers were also asked to rank their opinions towards the various media based on the following: how informative, how helpful as a buying guide, how irritating, how believable, how exaggerated, how boring, how misleading, and what kind of a negative influence on the kids they were. The overall ranking for the various media is shown in Table 11.7.

Advertisements in newspapers and magazines were found to be most informative and the ads in these media in the reverse order were considered helpful as a buying guide. For consumers, newspaper and magazine ads were most believable, exaggerated, and boring. They were also found to be least misleading and were ranked as having the least negative impact on children. Ads in the movies were the most irritating, but least boring. They did not score well as a believable, informative, and helpful buying guide

Table 11.7 Overall attitude towards media

Media	Informative	Helpful in buying	Believable	Irritating	Exaggerated	Boring	Misleading	Negative impact on children
Newspapers	1	2	1	6	1	2	7	7
Magazines	2	1	2	7	2	1	6	6
Films	5	6	6	1	5	7	3	3
Radio	6	5	5	2	6	5	1	5
TV	4	4	4	3	4	4	4	1
Internet	3	3	3	5	3	3	5	2
OOH	7	7	7	4	7	6	2	4

Source: Dutta 2010.

either. Radio also scored low as informative and helpful buying guides and on the believability factor. These ads were also found to be irritating and misleading. TV was found to have the maximum negative impact on children and was placed fourth as a source of information and a help in being a guide for buying. The television ads were also thought to be exaggerated but believable, boring, and misleading. The Internet, though found to have a negative impact on children, scored well as an informative and helpful buying guide that was believable as well. Out-of-home was found to be the least informative, the least helpful as a buying guide, and the least believable.

Conclusion

'The heavy reliance on past experience reiterates the importance of moments of truth and getting it right the first time. Organizations should, thus, focus on the experience of the customers and try to be more innovative so as to create a memorable impact on the customers. Organizations should study their positioning in the minds of the customers, as these individuals also constitute the reference-set for family and friends as well as for other customers. The Internet banner ads and Internet pop-up ads were found to be the least important in comparison

to magazines and newspapers as important sources of information. One can infer that the traditional sources of information continue to be important sources for customers. In spite of the popularity of the Internet, these traditional sources cannot be overlooked. The use of the Internet for promoting products should not be ignored even though it is considered as the least important medium, because it is rated very high on being informative and helpful in making purchase decisions. Another factor is the increasing penetration and use of the Internet in India (Johar and Bhatia 2008), which shows that it will become an important media in the near future. TV and Internet have been ranked as having the maximum negative impact on children and this aspect should also be taken into consideration while formulating the media strategies' (Dutta 2009).

Discussion Questions

1. Which media affects the consumers the most? Keeping this in mind, what promotional strategy would you formulate for a company that wants to sell ceiling fans in India?
2. Keeping in mind the consumer's attitude towards the media, what media mix would you recommend to the same organization?

Case References

Dutta, Kirti 2009, 'Consumer information sources and effectiveness of advertising media—An analysis of India, Turkey and New Zealand' presented at the 4th International Conference on Services Management held at Barceló Hotel, Oxford organized by Oxford Brookes University, Pennsylvania State University, US and IIMT on 8–9 May 2009.

Dutta, Kirti 2010, 'Effect of branding on purchase behaviour of Urban Indian Women' a PhD thesis submitted to M.G. Kashi Vidyapeeth, Varanasi.

Johar, J. and P. Bhatia, 'Widening Net—India Inc logs on to search portals for wider audience', The Economic Times, New Delhi, 12 September 2008.

Sivakumar, D., '15 years of revolution called mobility', The Economic Times, New Delhi, 26 July 2010, p. 13.

Part V
BUILDING RESILIENT BRANDS

Brand Strategies 12

LEARNING OBJECTIVES

After reading this chapter, you will be able to understand the following:

- The concept of brand strategies
- Naming a brand extension
- Brand extension strategies—line and category extension
- Brand stretching
- Advantages and disadvantages of brand extensions
- Launching new brand extensions

ABOUT THE CHAPTER

Brands are built over time through carefully thought-out strategies. They are the assets of a firm and can be used to leverage the entry of the firm in the same or different product categories. Consumers base their purchase decisions on a limited number of product attributes; therefore, launching a new product in a product category with established competitors can be difficult (Aaker 1990). Firms need to carefully plan their product launch, and one of the best and proven ways to gain success is to use their established brands to gain entry, i.e., brand extension. Having a well-thought-out brand strategy can be a key contributor to the success of an organization in the marketplace.

Consumers encode the functional and emotional values of the brand in their minds, which helps them identify the point of difference among competing brands (Martinez and Chernatony 2004). Consumers' attitude towards the extension and the perceived quality of the brand influence the general brand image. This highlights the importance of managing brand extensions carefully so as to achieve the desired results.

NEED FOR DESIGNING BRANDING STRATEGIES

Human effort, time, and money are required in abundance to build a brand from scratch. Once the brand is established and doing well, companies realize that to stay competitive and to tap other opportunities in the market, they need to come out with more products to attract consumers. The new product can be branded under the existing brand or the organization can give an entirely new brand name to the same. These decisions are strategic and have implications for the organization as a whole. Thus, over a period of time, a company can have a number of brands in its basket of offering for consumers in the same or different product categories. This is called brand portfolio and includes all the brands and brand lines that a company has to offer in the market (see Exhibit 12.1).

Exhibit 12.1   Extending Brands

The lifestyle trends of consumers are changing. With increasing overseas travels, more Indians are getting exposed to 'new flavours and textures. Brand extensions are catering to this need. For example, Britannia's new Britannia Treat Choco Decker is nothing, but its 'Treat jam biscuit with a layer of chocolate'. These are available in both biscuit racks and confectionery counters. Thus, by innovating, packaging changes, and 'cross-category placements', the same product can be extended to different categories. This extension expands the target audience and also helps in tapping new consumption opportunities (Jacob 2011). Britannia also has the 'NutriChoice' high fibre biscuits, which it has extended to introduce the NutriChoice diabetic friendly range of cookies. These are available in two variants—oats and ragi (see Image 12.1).

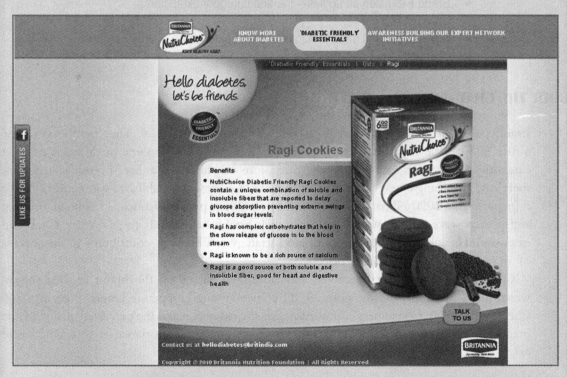

Image 12.1   Britannia NutriChoice Diabetic Friendly Essentials

An organization's product width includes all the different product lines it is offering in the market. The organization can come out with a number of related products, which form one product line; or a number of unrelated products, which form different product lines, i.e., a product mix. An organization's product width denotes the number of product lines it has. In the product line, it can have a single brand or a number of brands. All the brand lines that an organization has to offer are called brand mix or brand assortment (Keller 2004).

Thus, for example, Britannia Industries, which started as Britannia Biscuits in 1892 and was rechristened in 1979, has now diversified into cakes, dairy products, etc., all of which form the product width for Britannia. The biscuits, cakes, dairy products, etc. constitute different product lines for Britannia. If we talk of one product line such as cakes, then with in that it has different brands like Britannia bar cakes, Britannia cup cakes, Britannia chunk cakes, and Britannia veg cakes. All these form the product line length for the product line of cakes. Now, if we talk of Britannia bar cakes, it comes in different flavours, such as fruit, butter sponge, chocolate, pineapple, vanilla, etc. All these constitute the product line depth for Britannia bar cakes. This concept of product mix width, length, and depth has been further clarified with the help of Figures 12.1 and 12.2.

If we consider the example of Britannia biscuits, it has eleven brands of biscuits. Each brand is further composed of a number of sub-brands. Figure 12.2 shows the sub-brands of Tiger biscuits. Similarly, Good Day has thirteen sub-brands like Good Day Butter, Good Day Coconut Cookies, Good Day Honey and Raisin Cookies, etc. Thus, the brand portfolio of biscuits has a number of brands.

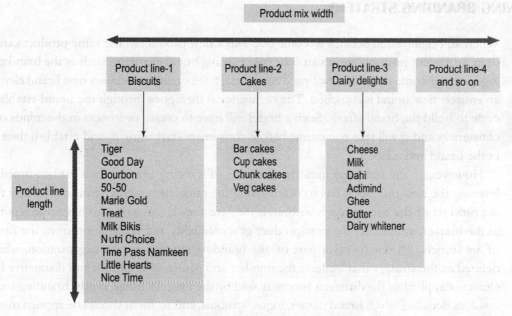

Source: Based on http://www.britannia.co.in, accessed on 25 March 2010; Keller 2004.

Note: The list shown in the figures is illustrative, not exhaustive.

Figure 12.1 Product mix and product lines for Britannia

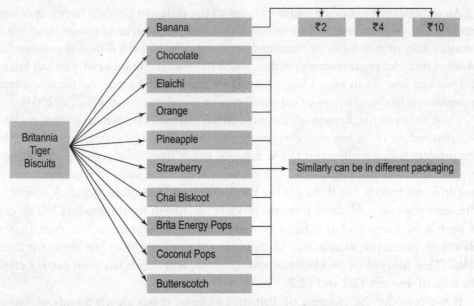

Source: Based on http://www.britannia.co.in, accessed on 25 March 2010; Keller 2004.

Note: The list shown in the figure is illustrative, not exhaustive.

Figure 12.2   Product line depth—Britannia Tiger Biscuits

DEFINING BRANDING STRATEGY

When an organization decides to come out with a new product in the same product category or in a different product line, it can either use existing brand elements, such as the brand name, logo, etc., or come out with new brand elements. If the organization uses new brand elements, an entirely new brand is launched. The organization then goes through the brand establishing cycle to build the brand afresh. Such a brand will have to create awareness in the minds of the consumers and it will take some time before consumers start using it, and establish their trust in the brand and adopt it.

However, if the company uses the elements of existing brands, then it can immediately leverage the new product it has to offer. Using the same elements reminds consumers that it is a product of the company whose brands they are already using or who has some reputation in the market, and hence, the new product gets credibility and recognition from the first day of its launch. All this forms a part of the branding strategy for an organization, which is defined as the strategy that 'reflects the number and nature of common and distinctive brand elements applied to the different products sold by the firm. In other words, branding strategy involves deciding which brand names, logos, symbols, and so forth should be applied to which products and the nature of new and existing brand elements to be applied to new products' (Keller 2004).

Thus, while devising a branding strategy, organizations need to answer the following questions:
1. How many brands can an organization effectively and efficiently offer to the market?

2. Whether to come out with new brand launches or not?

3. Where to place these brand launches as line extension or category extension (see the section on branding strategies and opportunities for growth for further details)?

4. Which brand elements to use—existing, new, or a combination of the two?

As discussed, organizations can use the equity of an existing brand to leverage the new product, which is called brand extension. Brand extension is defined as 'when a firm uses an established brand name to introduce a new product' (Keller 2004). The new brand so launched is called a sub-brand and the existing brand is called the parent brand. If the parent brand name has already been used in various product lines, it is also called a family brand (Kotler and Keller 2006). When HUL launched their shampoos, they named them after their famous brand of beauty bathing soap—Lux. The Lux soap was the parent brand and Lux shampoo was the sub-brand.

STRATEGIES FOR CHOOSING A BRAND NAME

A company is represented by a name—the corporate name. This name is important as it identifies the organization and builds a frame of reference for the consumers. Many companies use this corporate name to represent the individual brands they launch in the market. For example, Tata uses its corporate name to brand all the products it sells in the market. It brands both commodity products such as salt and the more sophisticated products such as cars, consultancy services, etc. with the same corporate name—Tata.

There are also instances where companies do not use their corporate brand name to represent the products launched. For example, Yum! Brands, which owns KFC, Pizza Hut, Taco Bell, and Long John Silver's restaurant brands, does not use its corporate brand name to represent any of its brands. It uses individual names to represent these brands and each brand is an individual brand with its own brand elements. This discussion shows that when a company decides to launch its product in the market it can choose any brand name. The general strategies discussed by Keller (2004) and Kotler and Keller (2006) for naming brands are as under:

1. Corporate brand name combined with individual name
2. Individual names
3. Blanket family names
4. Separate family names for all products

Corporate Brand Name Combined with individual Name

A corporate can use its established name to launch various brands in the market. As discussed, large corporate houses in India are using this strategy to brand their products. For example, the Aditya Birla group have used the name Birla in combination with white cement, Carbon, Sunlife Insurance, etc. In such cases, they have branded individual products with a combination of corporate and individual brand names. Similarly, Reliance also uses a combination of its corporate name, Reliance, with individual names, such as retail (Reliance Retail), gas (Reliance Gas), and aviation fuel (Reliance Aviation). Britannia is another example of brand name and individual name constituting the final product-brand name, for instance, Britannia Cheese, Britannia Daily Fresh Dahi, Britannia cakes, etc.

Individual Names

An organization can come out with a number of products in a product category and give different names to each. For example, HUL offers a number of detergent powders, such as Surf, Rin, and Wheel. It also provides a basket of bathing soaps, such as Lux, Lifebuoy, Breeze, Hamam, Liril, etc., each targeted towards different market segments and with its own unique positioning. In individual branding, the brand name is not accompanied by any other family or corporate brand name.

Blanket Family Names

When the same name is used to represent the brand in different categories, it is called a blanket family name. This can be the company name also. For example, General Motors uses the name Chevrolet for its range of sedans, SUVs, coupes, vans, hatchbacks, etc. It similarly offers a range of cars in the brand names of Cadillac, Buick, etc.

Separate Family Names

As a strategy, an organization can also come out with separate family names. For example, Tata's retail segment has four retail chains, all targeting different product categories. The Croma retail arm has a range of Croma brands like Croma refrigerators, Croma notebooks, Croma air conditioners, etc., apart from other manufacturers' brands. The Westside chain of retail stores offer a range of garments, accessories, and home products; Landmark retail stores offer books, music, etc, and Star Bazaar, the fourth retail arm offers a range of fresh goods, apparel, luggage, consumer durables, household products, etc. Tata's hospitality section is again composed of broadly two brands—Ginger, the budget hotels, and Taj, the luxury, leisure, and business hotels. Similarly, HUL has the brand Lakmé for cosmetics, Brooke Bond for tea, Kissan for sauces and jams, etc.

After deciding on the type of naming strategy that is to be adopted for naming the brands, organizations can then add variants to the same by coming out with modifier brands. Modifier brands are the items or models that are added to the brands. For example, Tata Indica Vista, Tata Indica V2 Xeta, and Tata Indica V2 are all variants of the Indica car, based on the different features and add-ons provided by the organization. Lux has introduced modifiers in the individual brand variants. For example, Lux bathing soap is available in Lux Strawberry and Cream, Lux Festive Glow with Honey, Lux Peach and Cream and Lux Creamy White. Lux is the individual brand in each of these products and the strawberry and cream, peach and cream, etc. are the modifiers.

 See the use of modifiers by Fortune in the various ads.

The idea of having the corporate name combined with the individual name or family name is that the organization can add sub-brands to these brands and offer more options or choices for the consumers to choose from. With individual names again, organizations can keep adding more brands to their portfolio.

BRANDING STRATEGIES AND OPPORTUNITIES FOR GROWTH

To create a buzz and excitement and to be relevant at all times, brands need to constantly innovate and come out with new variants of products. Taking brand and product to be the two important factors around which organizations can strategize, we see that the following scenarios can arise for the organization (Tauber 1981):

(a) Launch a new brand in an existing product category—flanker brand
(b) Launch a new brand in a new product category—new product
(c) Launch an existing brand in an existing product category—line extension
(d) Launch an existing brand name in a new product category—category extension/franchise extension/brand extension

Flanker brands   These are brands launched in existing product categories. These brands provide a range of brands with various features in the same product category, giving a wide range of choices to consumers so that they do not have to look elsewhere. For instance, Unilever provides a number of bathing soaps, such as Lux, Pears, Liril, Rexona, Dove, Hamam, etc., which act as flanker brands to each other. ITC has introduced Fortune hotels in the mid-priced category as a flanker brand to its Maurya, Maratha, Windsor hotels, all of which belong to the five-star category, pan India.

New product   A firm can grow by tapping the potential in a different product category. Launching a new brand in a new product category—called new product—requires a lot of time, effort, and money. For example, Dabur in the home care category has Dazzl, a disinfectant floor cleaner, Odomos mosquito repellent, Odonil room freshner, Sanifresh toilet cleaner, etc.

The cost of introducing a new name runs into millions of rupees, but even such spending does not guarantee success. The use of an established brand name can increase the probability of success and substantially reduce investment in the introduction of a new brand (see Figure 12.3). Brand names are 'the most real and marketable assets of many firms' (Aaker 1990). Thus, the other growth option is to use this brand name to launch other brands—either in the same or different product category (Tauber 1981; Aaker 1990). Companies can use the existing brand name and leverage the brand equity of the same while launching a new product in the market. Research indicates that brands launched as extensions 'capture a greater market share and realize greater advertising efficiency than individual brands' (Smith and Park 1992).

The terms stretching and extension are often used interchangeably. However, some have delineated extension as the addition of product variants or new products under the established brand name in the same 'product field' or product category as the established brand. On the

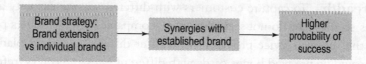

Source: Based on Tauber 1981; Aaker 1990; Smith and Park 1992; Pitta and Katsanis 1995.

Figure 12.3   Effect of brand extension

other hand, stretching refers to a brand in a new 'product field' or product category (Sarkar and Singh 2005). Brand stretching is discussed in detail later in the chapter. Extension can be of the two types: line extension and brand/category extension.

Line Extension

When a new product is added to an existing brand in the same product category, it is called line extension. The new product could be a new flavour, colour, package size, etc., which targets a different set of customers. An example is Nestlé's Maggi 2-Minute Noodles. It is available in different flavours like masala, chicken, tomato, and curry. For the health conscious consumers, the company launched Maggi Vegetable Atta Noodles. This variant was launched based on ingredients: 'more vegetable in its garnish and packed with the power of fibre'. To target consumers on the go who face paucity of time, the company has came out with the Maggi Cuppa Mania variant. Consumers just need to add hot water to the cup; there is even a fork inside, making it ready to eat.

 See the ads of Adani Wilmar that show line extension strategy for Fortune.

Why Line Extension?

Line extensions are undertaken for the following reasons (Quelch and Kenny 1984).

Diversity of customers Consumer groups are getting diversified based on their consumption needs and wants. To cater to these different segments of customers, organizations need to come out with more variants by following the line extension strategy.

 See diversity provided by Adani Wilmar's Fortune Kachi Ghani and Fortune Soya Oil.

Customers' need for variety Consumerism is now underlined by a variety seeking behaviour of consumers who want to experiment and try out different products. As an organization, retaining these customers is very important. To provide the variety that consumers need, organizations go for line extensions. Thus, we see the fast moving consumer goods (FMCG) sector offering variety in their brands with different ingredients/flavours, form, size, etc.

 See the Fortune Soya and Fortune Sunlite Oil ads to satisfy need for variety.

Pricing breadth To capture customers with different paying capacity and provide them with options so that they do not seek elsewhere, companies offer products priced variably. An example is the mobile service providers who offer different pre-paid plans. Thus, we have Vodafone providing pre-paid bonus cards with different rates and offers (refer to Image 12.2).

Capacity utilization Many times companies come out with different variants for optimum utilization of their plant capacities. To recover the fixed cost invested in the plant and to

Image 12.2   Offers of Vodafone

also achieve efficient cost of operations, companies come out with new brand extensions by effecting minor changes in the plant (Verma 2009).

Increasing profitability   By launching line extensions, organizations increase their overall sales performance. Also, the cost involved in launching a line extension is much less than launching and establishing a new brand. It costs approximately five to six times more to launch a new brand than a line extension (Verma 2009). Thus, line extensions lead to increased profitability, as they increase the sales, are relatively inexpensive, and lead to optimum capacity utilization also.

Competitive reasons   Companies with extensive product lines capture a higher shelf space in retail markets. This leaves little space for competitors and they find it difficult to make their presence felt. HUL, Nestlé, and P&G all follow this strategy of providing a number of brand extensions so as to capture a higher percentage of the shelf space.

Trade demands   Emergence of new forms of retail outlets, especially organized retail outlets in India has put pressure on the FMCG companies. It has been studied that Indians increasingly prefer the modern organized retail formats for shopping. This has brought retailers to the forefront and has resulted in a shift in the bargaining power from FMCG companies to retailers. This has resulted in FMCG companies offering special brands/packaging for these retailers (see Exhibit 12.2).

Counter competition   Keeping an eye on the competition and the products they are offering is imperative for sustainability in the marketplace. Thus, if the competition launches a new variant or product, companies need to offset the same with their own offering. For example, Pepsi Company launched Nimbooz (lemon-based drink) and Parle Agro launched its lemon drink LMN in the year 2009. Coca-Cola also came out with its lemon offering in the form of Nimbu Fresh under the Minute Maid brand in January 2010 (*The Economic Times*, 2010)

Exhibit 12.2   Special Brands for Big Bazaar by HUL, P&G

India's overall retail sector market is forecasted to rise to $833 billion by 2013 and to $1.3 trillion by 2018, at a compound annual growth rate (CAGR) of 10 per cent. Also, organized retail, which is pegged at around $8.14 billion, is expected to grow at a CAGR of 40 per cent to touch $107 billion by 2013. It has been predicted that organized retail, which in February 2010 stood at 5 per cent of the retail market in India, will witness the maximum number of large format malls and branded retail outlets in the coming two years (India Brand Equity Foundation 2010). Catering to this organized retail calls for a different strategy as is evident from the following.

Players like Big Bazaar are requesting FMCG companies to make 'customized' products in specific pack sizes and variants that are not necessarily going to be available at the mom-and-pop stores and that too at attractive prices. So, chances are that 'the next time you decide to buy a Clinic All Clear shampoo you might just get a cheaper and more exciting variant at the nearest Big Bazaar outlet than at your local grocery store.'

According to Mr Sadashiv Nayak, President, Big Bazaar, 'Considering we are getting a different set of customers in our stores there is a need to create specific products with different stock keeping units (SKUs) and variants and we have made proposals to our vendors. In this way, both the retailer and the vendor can make better margins. We are confident that vendors can create different products and brands that can blossom in modern trade and take them to a different level. After all, we have big properties and such brands can meet their objectives and at the same time also meet the specific demands of our customers.'

Hindustan Unilever Ltd (HUL) and Procter & Gamble (P&G) have expressed their willingness to 'collaborate to win' with retailers to make it a 'win-win situation for both'. According to Mr Manish Tiwary, Vice-President, Customer Management, HUL, 'We are looking at bringing out customized shampoos at a lower cost soon and are checking out this proposition with the shoppers.' In the case of P&G too, there are chances of it launching new pack sizes to cater to the modern trade. In fact, P&G has been 'relying on modern trade to build categories such as feminine hygiene for its Whisper brand and creating separate SKUs to further penetrate the category'.

Source: Adapted from India Brand Equity Foundation 2010, http://www.ibef.org/artdispview.aspx?in=63&art_id=25318&cat_id=376&page=2, accessed on 5 April 2010; *BusinessLine* 2010, http://www.thehindubusinessline.com/2010/02/05/stories/2010020551750700.htm, accessed on 28 March 2010.

Image benefits   Organizations can also come out with line extensions to recharge the image of a brand. We will study more of this in the chapter on brand revitalization.

Types of line extensions

Line extension can be realized in a number of ways. They can be classified as horizontal and vertical extensions (Pitta and Katsanis 1995) (see Figure 12.4).

Horizontal line extension   When an established brand name is used to enter a new segment of the market in the same product class, it is called horizontal line extension. For example, Coca-Cola used the established brand name of Coke to launch Diet Coke, which catered to a different segment of cola drinkers—the diet conscious segment, which was not being catered to by the parent brand.

Vertical line extension   When an established brand name is used to 'introduce a related brand in the same product category but with a different price and quality balance', it is called vertical line extension. The automobile sector generally goes for vertical line extensions, wherein they provide a range of models at different prices so as to attract diverse market segments.

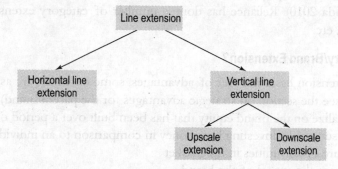

Source: Based on Pitta and Katsanis 1995.

Figure 12.4   Types of line extensions

Vertical extensions are again of two types.

Upscale extension   An existing brand name is used to launch a product with higher price and better quality than the original brand. Prestige products are more acceptable in upscale extensions. The limited editions of high-priced Montblanc pens fall in this category. For instance, its writer's edition was based on famous authors such as Ernest Hemingway, Charles Dickens, Oscar Wilde, and Voltaire.

Downscale extension   An existing brand name is used to launch a product at a lower price and with lower quality. This offers the chance of sampling to new market segments and hence results in some enhancement of the market share. For example, Levi's launched Levi Strauss Signature for the value conscious consumer. Functional products generally allow downscale extensions.

Line extension gave rise to products in categories that were already dominated by the parent brand. This led to cannibalization and resulted in small share gains only, which produced very little profit. Firms then started searching for new markets rather than a further segmentation of the existing market, and this resulted in the launch of new products for these markets. However, the cost of introducing an altogether new brand was high and underlined the monetary benefits of extending an existing brand to a new product category (Tauber 1988). This gave rise to category extension, which is discussed below.

Category Extension

When an existing brand name is used to launch a new product in a different product category, it is called category extension. Tauber (1988) popularized the notion of category extension by developing a disciplined approach to producing new products by 'leveraging an established brand name into categories new to that brand and called it brand franchise extension'. Category extension is also referred to as brand extension by some authors (Sarkar and Singh 2005; Verma 2009).

For example, Mirc Electronics, the manufacturers of Onida brand, started with Onida televisions. Now, they have a number of products under this brand like Onida washing machine, Onida DVD player, Onida microwave oven, Onida LCD TV, and even Onida mobile phones (Onida 2010). Reliance has done a number of category extensions into petroleum, textile, retail, etc.

Why Category/Brand Extension?

Category extension has a number of advantages, some of which are as follows (for detailed discussions see the section on strategic advantages for the parent brand). It allows
1. To capitalize on the brand equity that has been built over a period of time
2. To gain success by investing less money in comparison to an individual brand
3. To capture opportunities in the market
4. To enhance the appeal of the brand
5. To manage the fewer brands better in the portfolio
6. To increase advertising efficiencies

Types of Category Extension

From the example of category extension discussed above (Onida), we can highlight the fact that extension can be in related and unrelated categories. Whether related or not, they are all horizontal extensions. Some authors (Moorthi 1999; Sagar et al. 2009) have also highlighted image-related brand extensions. Thus, category extension can be of the following types.

Category-related extension The organization launches a brand related to the same category as the parent brand. Amul has long been associated with butter and its use as a spread for bread. Keeping in line with this and the fact that Indian consumers are getting more health conscious, Amul introduced Amul Lite—a low fat, low calorie, and low cholesterol bread spread.

Image-related brand extension The company leverages its image to launch new products. For example, Britannia has the image of a biscuit company and it has used this image to launch breads and cakes.

Unrelated extension   The company launches a brand in a product category that is entirely new, like Reliance's venture into retail from petroleum, textile, etc.

For brand extensions to be successful, they should evoke associations with the parent brand, which is both favourable and unique. Tauber (1988) gave the term 'competitive leverage' to the set of benefits conveyed by the brand name to the product that is being extended in the new category. The following types of leverages were identified by Tauber for category extension of brands that can be considered by organizations.

Extension of the product in a different form   To leverage a product in a different category, the form of the product can be changed. When a product is launched in a different form, for example, when an organization selling dairy whiteners starts selling condensed milk, and it constitutes an entirely different product category, it is called a category extension and not line extension, as it is catering to a different category. This is because dairy whiteners are used for purposes entirely different from those of condensed milk.

Companion/complementary product   Launching complementary products for the parent brand is also category extension. A complementary or companion product is a product that is used with other products. For example, Hewlett-Packard manufactures computers, notebooks, various types of printers, and even accessories required for the printer, such as ink cartridges, network cards, etc., in the form of companion or complimentary products. Research shows that when complimentary products are promoted together, they are evaluated more favourably even if the extensions differ considerably from the parent brand (Shine, Park, and Wyer Jr. 2007). Tauber (1988) identified some companion products as 'close-in' products, for example, Colgate toothbrush and Colgate toothpaste, and some that lead to forward or backward integration, for example, Duracell batteries and Duracell flashlights.

Same customer base   An organization has a customer base to which it can 'sell something else'. It can launch a range of products to meet the needs of this group of consumers. For example, Lakmé caters to the beauty needs of women by offering a range of cosmetics from lip colour to eye shadows, foundations, nail colour, etc. They have also launched salon services, wherein they provide beauty salon services, such as make-up, hair, draping sarees/dupattas in different styles, etc., under the brand name Lakmé Salon.

Company expertise   Companies can use their expertise to launch brand extensions in different product categories. This type of extension is generally successful, as customers believe that the company has experience, knowledge, or expertise in this area. For example, Japanese companies generally use this strategy. Thus, Honda, known for its excellent small engines, has leveraged its expertise to make Honda cars, Honda gensets, Honda scooters, Honda lawnmowers, etc. Sony also uses this concept to come out with a range of extensions, such as TV, stereo, handy cam, play station, etc., from the original tapes and transistors in 1950s.

Distinct features or benefits of the brand   A brand can achieve distinction in the form of novel attributes, features, or benefits provided, which form unique associations with the brand. An organization can cash in on this unique distinction to provide products in other categories. For example, Himani Navratna Hair Oil brand from the house of Emami has

Navratna Cool Talc is a brand extension of Navratna oil, which today enjoys the leadership position as ayurvedic Cool Oil.

Navratna Cool Talc provides a refreshing break from the usual talcs...read more

duniya ka sabse chotta AC

Source: http://www.emamigroup.com, accessed on 5 April 2010.

Image 12.3 Distinct feature of Navratna Cool Talc

achieved a unique differentiation in the form of providing a cooling effect. It is positioned as the world's smallest air conditioner to denote its cooling effect. Emami has used this differentiation to come out with Himani Navratna Cool Talc again with the same positioning plank to denote the cooling effect of the powder for consumers suffering from the scintillating heat of the sub-continent summers (see Image 12.3).

Brand image or prestige   Status brands offer prestige, and hence create an image of the product. This image can be used by organizations to extend themselves in unrelated categories. Lifestyle or designer brands associated with prestige generally end up with this type of extension. For example, Montblanc offers writing instruments, jewellery for women and men, watches, etc.

Distinctive taste/ingredient   To launch a brand in a different category, an organization can take the taste/an ingredient of the existing product and use it to launch other extensions based on the same taste/ingredient. For example, Häagen-Dazs ice cream launched its Häagen-Dazs' cream liqueur.

Brand Stretching

As has been discussed earlier, the terms stretching and extension are often used interchangeably. However, some have delineated extension as the addition of product variants or new products under the established brand name in the same product field as the established brand. On the other hand, stretching refers to a brand in a new product field (Randall 2003; Sarkar and Singh 2005). For example, if Coca-Cola launches Coca-Cola strawberry flavour, it will be called as brand extension. If Coca-Cola uses the same brand name to launch say a garment line or computers, cars, etc., which is not related to the cold drink sector, then it will be called brand stretching.

It has been studied that the more the number of products associated with a brand, the higher the customer confidence. Customers even tend to evaluate extensions more favourably (Dacin and Smith 1994). Companies like Tata and Reliance show that a brand can be stretched to different unrelated categories. Research also shows that successful brand extensions in diverse categories may reduce the effects of fit on the succeeding extensions (Dain and Smith 1994) (for further discussion on effects of fit, see the section on potential pitfalls of brand extension). Effect of fit is the consumer's perception of a brand and applies to the extended (new) product, and the new product should fit this perception. There are various factors that support and also operate against brand stretching (Randall 2003).

Factors that Support Brand Strength

Awareness and reputation of the parent brand   High consumer awareness and a good brand reputation translate into an advantage for the brand. Thus, a brand that has a number of extensions and holds a good reputation in the market results in higher customer confidence in the brand.

Applicability of the brand essence   The core value of the parent brand should be retained in the brand stretch for it to be successful.

Expertise and know-how   Transferability of the expertise and the know-how in the new brand as well.

Consumers' perception of the difficulty to manufacture the new brand   The higher the difficulty, the more positive the perception.

Offering complementary products   The new brand offers a complementary product that goes with the original brand.

Filling a market gap   The existence of a real market gap that is filled by the new brand.

Factors that Operate against Brand Strength

Inappropriate association between the parent brand and the new brand   If the association between the parent brand and the new brand is not appropriate, it will not support the stretch, as it will be difficult for the consumers to relate the latter with the former.

Wrong associations between parent and new brand also lead to a disadvantage   If an association does not fit well with the new brand being launched, then it fails to support the stretched brand.

Consumers' perception of the organization   A claim that is not perceived to be true for the organization will not be believed by the customers. If the organization still makes such a claim, the consumers are not bound to believe it, thus leading to a disadvantage for the firm.

Types of Products that Can Be Extended

Brand extension can be successfully applied to the following two types of products (Pitta and Katsanis 1995).

Products with function-oriented image If the focus of a product is on the performance, then such a product is called a function-oriented product. For example, Gillette razors, Nokia mobile phones, where the focus is on the functional aspects, such as talk time, battery backup, features like alarm, torch, radio facility, etc.

Products with prestige-oriented image Products that are visualized on the basis of 'consumers' expression of their self-image' are called prestige-oriented products. For example, Bang and Olufsen, which has a premium prestige-oriented image, manufactures high-end speakers, mobile phones, flat TV, etc.

BRAND EXTENSION DECISION—AN ANALYSIS

A brand is an organizational asset built painstakingly over a period of time. This calls for careful evaluation of the brand extension strategy, and managers should take a call as to when to protect the brand name and when to exploit it. This requires a careful understanding of the various advantages and pitfalls associated with using an established brand name to launch a new product in the market. It has been studied that brand extensions offer a number of benefits are not provided by the traditional new product development. Some of the benefits that make brand extensions important strategic tools for the organization are as follows (Tauber 1981; Aaker 1990; Sagar, Singh, Agarwal, and Gupta 2009; Volckner and Sattler 2006; Keller 2004).

Strategic Advantages for the Parent Brand

Brand extensions provide some strategic advantages for the parent brand as follows.

They enhance appeal for the parent brand The introduction of a brand extension enhances the appeal of the parent brand among prior non-users and prior non-loyal users of the parent brand. This results in the purchase of the parent brand and translates into an increase in market share (Swaminathan, Fox, and Reddy 2001).

They reinforce key associations Brand extensions help the core brand by reinforcing key associations and enhancing brand name recognition. The associations of the brand extension not only garner favourable positioning for them, but also strengthen the associations of the parent brand and its positioning (Park, Jaworski, and MacInnis 1986). For example, Pril, after its successful entry into the dish wash category, launched Pril Multi-Degreaser, a surface cleaner (see Image 12.4). This reinforces the Pril tagline of 'tough on grease, soft on hands' (Consumer Superbrands, 2009).

They strengthen parent brand 'memory structures' and 'facilitate retrieval processes' It has been studied that extensions result in strengthening the consumer's memory structure, which facilitates the speed with which brands are recalled in various buying situations in the parent brand category. The retrieval of the brand is easier and results in quicker brand recall (Morrin 1999). Thus, if a consumer is using Pril dish wash soap, then the Pril multi-degreaser surface cleaner is bound to come to mind in case the consumer has the need for such a product.

They maximize comparative advantage   Brand extensions can be used as a strategy to enhance the life cycle of a product. As a product class matures and more and more competitors are added, companies launch new entrants in the form of brand extensions. These brand extensions have an advantage over the new competitor brand names and are found to be more successful than the latter. These extensions also help to be in tune with the changing consumer demands and competitor activities and thus stay relevant for the consumers. For example, Life Insurance Corporation was only in the insurance segment, but now seeing the demand for housing loans, it is also providing LIC Housing loans.

Courtesy: Superbrands.

Image 12.4   Pril advertisements; also see Plate 14

Courtesy: Superbrands.

Image 12.5   Cinthol Advertisement for soap, talc, and deodorant; also see Plate 15

They lead to fewer brands that need to be managed   Brand extensions of a parent brand lead to fewer brands in the company portfolio, and thus, effort can be concentrated on these few brands rather than on a number of brands.

They increase advertising efficiencies   Advertising efficiencies are increased and expenditure reduced, as the company advertises for fewer brands and all the varieties and sub-varieties are included. Also, the exposure to advertising of brand extension facilitates the recall for the parent brand (Morrin 1999). For instance, in the advertisement for Cinthol (see Image 12.5), we see the Cinthol soap, talc, and deodorant (Consumer Superbrand, 2009) all being advertised, thus distributing the advertisement spend.

They defend a brand   Brand extensions help defend the parent brand in the market. Line extensions result in offering brands at different price points/variants, etc., and thus provide a bundle of products to choose from. Category extensions can save the company by moving into relevant product categories and further add to the brand equity of the parent brand.

They enhance the life cycle of the brand   A product has a life cycle and the brand if associated with only one product will follow this life cycle and eventually decline. To keep the brand growing, an organization can launch extensions of the brand, which give a new lease of life to the parent brand.

They help target a particular segment of customers   Companies realize that by extending a brand and by introducing some slight changes in the product, they can attract a different segment of customers. This is evident in the market of fairness creams, which is now targeting men. Another example is the launch of Pril Bar's mango-vinegar variant, as it was found that 'the mango peel is used as a scrub in the state of Uttar Pradesh' (Consumer Superbrands, 2009).

Strategic Advantages for the Sub-Brand

Like the parent brand, the sub-brand also gets an added advantage because of brand extensions. These are as follows.

Positioning a brand   Using an established brand and forming strong associations with the same to launch a new product helps communicate complex messages and position the brand effectively in the minds of the consumers.

Introducing from a position of strength   A new product launched under an existing brand name immediately leverages the product with customer awareness and impressions associated with the existing brand. There may also be reduced risk of failure of the new product due to its association with an established brand name. Thus, when the Birla group launched Birla White cement, it was with the intention of transferring the brand equity of Birla to the new product. The subsequent extensions of Birla White Wallcare Putty, Birla White Textura, which provides a textured wall finish, Birla White Kool and Seal for wall protection, etc., were introduced from a position of strength due to the established brand name of Birla White.

Minimizing introduction expense   In comparison to a new brand, the investment outlay required for an extended brand is less. Its association with the existing brand transfers an image to the new brand and the company does not have to start from scratch in building customer awareness and winning the trust of consumers, thus reducing the introduction expense.

Minimizing marketing expenses   The marketing expenses of distribution, packaging, labelling, etc. are reduced. Thus, in the Cinthol advertisement (Image 12.5), the packaging of the soap, deodorant, and talc are all similar and the various extensions of the same also have a similar packaging, except for a difference in the colour combinations.

Quality association   Customers are intelligent and study proves that they base their purchase decisions on their own experience with the brand (Dutta 2009). Thus, a brand that has high quality association in the minds of consumers can successfully transfer this image to the new product launched. For example, Boroline Antiseptic Cream has long been associated with quality and this was transferred to the Eleen Hair Oil launched by the company GD Pharmaceuticals Private Limited (Consumer Superbrand, 2009) (see Image 12.6).

Encouraging trial purchase   The association with a reputed brand denotes that the company has been around and is established. It thus reduces the risk associated with trying out the products and builds confidence that the products are unlikely to be flawed and would be supported by the company.

Source: http://www.boroline.com/eleen.php, accessed on 24 May 2010.

Image 12.6   Boroline's Eleen hair oil

Satisfying variety-seeking behaviour   By providing a number of variants, companies provide a range of products to choose from. This satisfies the variety-seeking behaviour of consumers and they do not have to look towards other brands for options. For example, Catch brand of the DS Group, has a range of table spices like black salt, table salt, pepper, etc. (Consumer Superbrand, 2009). Seeing the need for fresh ground garnishes on the table, the company came out with the fresh ground range of pepper, garlic salt, rock salt, etc. (see Image 12.7).

Increasing advertising efficiencies   An important corollary to brand extension is that a brand extension increases the sales of the parent brand. The advertising of the extended brand has a synergistic effect on the original product and the umbrella effect creates advertising efficiencies. As can be seen from Image 12.7, all the variants are advertised in the advertisement of Catch, thus increasing the awareness for Catch brand as a whole.

Clarifying what the brand means to consumers   Extensions also help organizations gain an understanding of how consumers think about a brand and relate to it. This understanding helps them in extending the brand in the same general direction for a higher probability of success and also results in new brand meanings. For example, Kellogg's originally launched cereals as a healthy alternative for the breakfast category. Then they extended into Nutri-Grain Bars, Special K Challenge, etc., and associated the brand with a new meaning of 'healthy snacking'.

Courtesy: Superbrands.

Image 12.7 Catch advertisements

Increasing market coverage   The sub-brands, when launched with specific new features, result in attracting segments of consumers who were hitherto not their customers. This results in increasing the market coverage of the brand. Thus, when Crocin (a tablet for pain relief) launched its Crocin Cold n' Flu, it was promoted as a medicine that provided relief from fever, pain, and cold, thus increasing the usage to a wider segment of consumers.

Permitting subsequent extensions   A sub-brand that is successful as an extension results in reinforcing the favourable brand associations in the minds of consumers. The enhanced brand equity can then be cashed in by bringing out subsequent extensions and the cycle is repeated. The various examples of brand extensions discussed are all witness to this.

Potential Pitfalls of Brand Extension

Like the two sides of a coin, brand extension also has its flip side. According to Tauber (1981) and Aaker (1990), some of the drawbacks of using an existing brand to launch new brands are as below.

Failure of brand name to add value   The association with a successful, established brand in itself does not guarantee success, unless it is backed by a product that has both competitive parity and a point of differentiation. The differentiation can flow from superior production, and/or distribution, and/or merchandizing, and/or advertising capability, and/or superior technological product. For instance, Coke came out with Vanilla Coke in 2004, but the new variant could not capture the target audience and a successful brand name like Coke failed to add value to the extended product.

Negative association   Consumers perceive the parent brand to be associated with certain characteristics. When the new product does not fall in this perception level, it is said to be negatively associated with the brand. Such an association then does not add value to the extended product and undermines the credibility of the new product line. For example, Lux, from HUL, extended itself to Lux Shampoo and failed, as the parent brand was strongly positioned as a 'beauty soap', which was in dissonance with the property that was being transferred, i.e., hair care.

Problem of fit   Consumers have a perception of a brand and if the extended product fits this perception, then the consumers are likely to adopt the new product. The converse is also true, and if the extended product is far removed from how the consumers perceive the parent brand then they are not likely to accept the extended brand. For example, Dettol is perceived as a germ killer and this image was used to extend the brand to soaps and liquid hand wash, which was well received by the consumers. In case Dettol had used its brand name to extend into confectionery or manufacturing cars, it would have been difficult for consumers to fit these into the perception of the brand.

According to Aaker and Keller (1990), fit construct is made up of three dimensions:
- Extent to which extension complements the brand's primary product.
- Extent to which extension is a substitute for the brand's primary product.
- Consumers perception of the ability of the organization to transfer the skills acquired in making existing products to manufacture the extended product.

For a brand to fall in the consumer's 'category of fit', it should complement the primary product, but at the same time offer some extra benefits not offered by the primary product and the brand equity of the primary product should be transferred to the new product.

Cannibalization of parent brand's sales   Line extensions mean adding variants of the brand for the same customer base. This results in competition among the same brand's extensions and eventually leads to loss in sales for the variants of the brand. Thus, for example, if a consumer purchases only Cinthol Deo Musk spray and does not look at any of the other five variants offered by Cinthol in the same category, it leads to loss in the sale of the other brands.

Perception of poor quality   A brand that has the perception of being the best in quality alone should be extended. If the perception is to the contrary for some consumers, then the extension is bound to limit the market for the new product.

Creation of undesirable associations   An extended brand, over a period of time, develops its own association with the consumers. These associations if favourable, strengthen the parent brand and if unfavourable lead to the creation of undesirable associations that can weaken the parent brand and cause damage. However, if the parent brand associations are stronger than the extended brand, then the negative transfer of failure of the extended brand is less likely to affect the parent brand. For example, when Reliance launched Reliance mobile phones promising consumers the cheapest communication service and later consumers realized that a there were a lot of hidden charges involved, it led to consumers developing negative associations with the mobile phone. However, the association with the parent brand was so strong that the negative transfer did not much hamper the image of the parent brand and the other extensions were quite successful.

Weakening of existing associations   The extension of a brand within a product class or related product class strengthens the association with that product class. However, extension into unrelated categories blurs the boundary of the brand and can result in weakening of the existing associations. The Tata brand name has been used to brand products extending from salt to software, and thus it is difficult to associate the brand Tata with a particular product category.

Dilution of the parent brand image resulting in confusion   Rampant extension can lead to the dilution of the parent brand image and to confusion in the minds of the consumers as to what the brand stands for. Also, ill-fitting brand extensions lead to dilution of the parent brand positioning (Ries and Trout 1981).

Reduced identification with any one category   Another aspect of brand extension is that though they might be successful, as they are into a number of product categories, related and unrelated both, extensions might result in lack of identification with any one category. Companies such as Tata and Reliance, which adopt corporate branding, have to confront this issue.

Effect of a brand crisis   If a brand crisis occurs, such as the incidence of Cadbury's chocolates being infested with worms, then all the products bearing the name of the brand will be negatively affected by the crisis.

Foregoing the opportunity to create a new brand   Brand extensions result in using the same brand to launch different products. The alternative of launching and establishing a new brand is foregone, which could otherwise have been extended to cover related products. Thus, Everest has launched its various brands, such as Everest Henna Powder, Everest Kesari Milk Masala, etc., with the same brand name (see Image 12.8). It could have launched its herbal beauty care with a different brand name and could have used the same brand name to extend in the beauty-care product category.

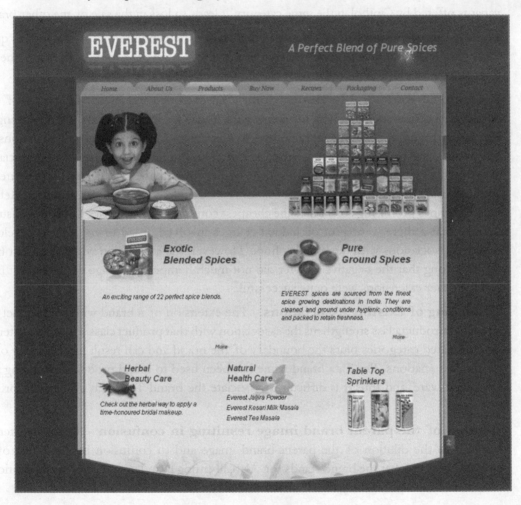

Source: www.everestspices.com/product, accessed on 24 May 2010.

Image 12.8   Brand extension by Everest

Encounter retailer resistance   A brand with a number of extensions means a higher stockholding cost for the retailers and a higher occupation on the shelf space. Also, many times not all the brand variants might be fast moving, thus, increasing the holding cost. For example, Big Bazaar decided not to stock Kellogg's breakfast cereals till higher margins were not given, as the 'cost of holding Kellogg's stocks was high, because its large-sized packages take up significant shelf space in stores. Also, only a few of the breakfast cereal makers' several variants do well' (Vijayraghavan and Bhushan 2009).

These potential pitfalls highlight the fact that extension of brand image, though a beneficial strategy for the organization, needs to be applied judiciously and in a disciplined systematic manner.

CRITICAL FACTORS FOR BRAND EXTENSION SUCCESS

The study of brand category extension underlines the fact that for successful brand extensions, companies should consider the following determinants of success for brand extension (also see Figure 12.5).

Parent Brand Characteristics

Perceived quality of the parent brand   The perceived quality of the parent brand is a crucial factor in the evaluation of brand extensions. It is, therefore, important that customers have a high perception of the quality of the parent brand. Thus, investing in and building a favourable reputation of the parent brand builds a positive customer disposition towards the parent brand and its brand extension (Lahiri and Gupta 2005).

Conviction   Confidence in the parent brand results from high parent brand knowledge, formation of strong brand associations on the basis of personal interaction and marketing activities of the firm, and good memories associated with the brand (Volckner and Sattler 2006).

Experience   The consumer's experience with the parent brand builds customer perception of the brand. This in turn builds conviction towards the parent brand and influences the

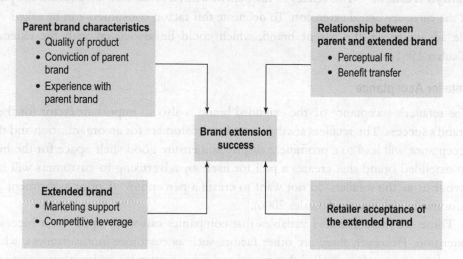

Source: Derived from Tauber 1981; Smith and Park 1992; Lahiri and Gupta 2005; Volckner and Sattler 2006.

Figure 12.5   Factors affecting the success of brand extensions

consumer to form favourable outlook towards the parent brand and in turn the extended brand (Volckner and Sattler 2006).

All these factors result in a favourable predisposition towards the brand. Both conviction and experience are built over a period of time due to the interaction between the parent brand and the consumer. Therefore, while selecting a brand to extend from the company's portfolio, managers should give due importance to both these characteristics by choosing a brand that performs favourably in terms of both factors.

Extended Brand

Marketing support   The marketing support provided to the extended brand in the form of advertising and similar other means increases the awareness of the extended brand and elevates consumer's perception of the same (Volckner and Sattler 2006).

Competitive leverage   The new product provides benefits that the existing competitive products do not provide. To identify this, consumers are asked to list the competitor brands and highlight how the brand is different—both point-of-differentiation and point-of-parity—from the competitor brands (Tauber 1981).

Relationship Between Parent Brand and Extended Brand

Perceptual fit   Perceptual fit is when the consumer perceives that the new product is consistent with the parent brand. This can be decided by asking the question, 'how likely are the consumers to accept alternative products from the same brand?' For example, if Colgate extends itself to Colgate Dental Clinics, then how likely are the consumers to adopt them (Tauber 1981)?

Benefit transfer   This relates to the benefit wished to be transferred from the parent brand in the category brand extension. To delineate this factor, consumers can be asked to highlight the advantage of the parent brand, which could be associated with the extended brand (Tauber 1981).

Retailer Acceptance

The retailer's acceptance of the extended brand is also an important factor for the extended brand's success. The retailers are the immediate customers for an organization and their higher acceptance will lead to a prominent display and ensure good shelf space for the brand. Also, an extended brand that creates a pull for itself by advertising to customers will be a strong favourite, as the retailers do not want to create a perception of poor assortment among the customers (Volckner and Sattler 2006).

These are the controlled variables that companies can work upon for a successful brand extension. However, there are other factors such as customer innovativeness, which impact brand extensions. It is studied that more innovative customers evaluate extensions favourably. Such type of customers should be targeted by organizations for efficient brand extensions (Lahiri and Gupta 2005).

LAUNCHING A BRAND EXTENSION

According to Tauber (1981), Aaker (1990), and Aaker (1991), a category extension can be identified as a six-stage process (see Figure 12.6) as discussed below.

Stage 1 Company identifies the brand to be extended from its portfolio of brands; of course, if there is only one brand then only this brand can be chosen. Organizations can choose from their range of brands and highlight one or more brands depending on the financial strength and ability of the organization. For example, Amul has always used its name to extend itself into other product categories. ITC has the Fortune brand in the mid-priced hotel category and the Maurya brand in the five-star hotel category. And when it wants to extend itself further in the hotels category, it can decide whether to extend the Fortune brand or the Maurya brand.

Stage 2 The next stage is to identify key associations of the brand. The associations can run to over a hundred and should be reduced to the most promising set of 5–15 strong associations for the brand. For brand extensions, associations that can provide a competitive leverage by providing a link with other categories are most helpful. For example, for Amul the key association would be 'quality milk product'.

Stage 3 In this stage, on the basis of each key association, alternative definitions of the business are highlighted, along with idea generation for possible related categories. So, for Amul, the key definitions would be butter, milk, curd, ice cream, etc.

Stage 4 Identification of products related to each category. Thus, for the definition of cheese the key related categories can be processed cheese, cottage cheese, cheese spreads,

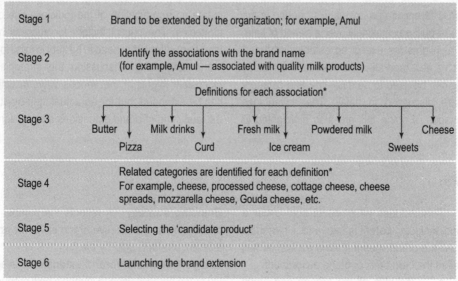

Note: The list is indicative, not exhaustive.
Source: Based on Tauber 1979; Aaker 1990; Aaker 1991, and www.amul.com.

Figure 12.6 Stages in launching a brand extension

mozzarella cheese, Gouda cheese, etc. For the definition of milk drinks, Amul has extended into flavoured milk, buttermilk, lassi, energy drink Nutramul, etc.

Stage 5 Selecting the 'candidate products' out of the different products identified, the next stage is to select a limited number and test them to see if they fit the extension and provide some point of advantage. For a successful launch, the 'perceptual fit, competitive leverage, and benefit transfer' should be there. Thus, for Himalaya Herbals, in the definition of baby-care range, where they are offering wipes and diaper rash creams, the perceived similar benefit can be to launch a diaper that moisturizes the skin and does not cause diaper-induced rashes on the delicate skin of babies. The perceived similar benefit for powder in the category of baby care can be 'for delicate skin'.

Stage 6 The final stage is to launch the extended brand. While launching the brand extension, companies can reduce the risk of brand extension by not linking the brand name too closely with the new product. The brand name's function here is to endorse the new product and yet distance itself from the new product. This is particularly beneficial when companies go for vertical brand extension, i.e., company extends to a low-quality product and it, therefore, becomes imperative for it to ensure that 'the original price/quality positioning is unaffected by the extension'. Thus, at the time of launch of Fiama Di Wills, the focus was more on the brand name Fiama Di Wills than on ITC, the parent company.

SUMMARY

Brands help in differentiating a company's offering in the market. They are built painstakingly over a period of time. This chapter highlights the use of an established brand name to launch a new product in the market. The various strategies that can be used to do this—line and category extensions—are discussed in detail. The advantages and disadvantages of doing this are also highlighted to create an appreciation of the judicious use of extension strategies. The critical factors for success highlight the important criteria that need to be kept in mind for successful brand extensions. Discussing the strategies of brand extensions highlight the various ways in which a brand can be extended, but for an actual step-by-step strategy, the launching of brand extensions are highlighted.

KEY TERMS

Brand lines This includes all products sold under a particular brand, including parent brands and sub-brands.

Brand mix All the brand lines that an organization has to offer are called the brand mix or brand assortment.

Brand portfolio It includes all the brands and brand lines that a company has to offer the market.

Brand stretching This refers to launching a brand in a new product field as the parent brand.

Branding strategy It reflects the number and nature of common and distinctive brand elements applied to the different products sold by the firm.

Category extension/brand extension When an existing brand name is used to launch a new product in a different product category, it is called category extension.

Flankers These are brands that are launched to fight competitors' brands, so that the main brand of the organization retains the desired positioning in the minds of the consumers.

Line extension   When a new product is added to an existing brand in the same product category, it is called line extension.

Product line   The organization can come out with a number of related products that form one product line or a number of unrelated products that form different product lines.

Product mix   The unrelated product lines that a brand has in its portfolio are called a product mix.

Product width   It includes all the different product lines a company is offering to the market.

EXERCISES

Concept Review Questions

1. What is a brand portfolio? Discuss with the help of industry examples.
2. Differentiate between product mix and brand mix.
3. While launching a new product, what strategies can be adopted by organizations? Discuss with help of examples.
4. Differentiate between the following:
   (a) Line extension and category extension
   (b) Brand extension and brand stretching
5. Discuss any two-line extension strategies and give reasons why you think these are important.
6. Discuss any two-category extension strategies and explain why you think these are the most important.

Critical Thinking Questions

1. Critically evaluate the statement, 'Brand extensions are important growth strategies for a firm.'
2. Organizations like Tata and Virgin show that brands can be stretched successfully. Do you think that organizations should follow this strategy?

3. Pick an organization that has a number of brand extensions. Discuss whether these extensions have been successful or not and the reasons for the same.

Internet Exercises

1. Visit the website of Hindustan Unilever Limited at http://www.hul.co.in/brands/. Evaluate how the company has been using a mix of brand extensions and new brand launches in its portfolio of brands for the food/personal care/home care category.
2. Visit the website of Godrej Ezee, www.ezeefabcare.com. Identify the various products and critically discuss the use/absence of brand extensions as a strategy.

CD Exercises

1. See the Amul ad and discuss various categories into which Amul has extended itself. What kind of extension strategy is it following?
2. Discuss the brand naming strategy adopted by Max New York Life for its various products.

REFERENCES

Aaker, David and K.L. Keller, 'Consumer evaluations of brand extensions', *Journal of Marketing*, Vol. 54, Issue 1, 1990, pp. 27 41.

Aaker, David (1991), *Managing Brand Equity Capitalizing on the Value of a Brand Name*, The Free Press, New York, Chapter 9, pp. 206–237.

Aaker, David, 'Brand extensions the good, the bad, and the ugly', *Sloan Management Review*, Vol. 31, Issue 4, 1990, pp. 47–56

Dacin, P.A. and D.C. Smith, 'The effect of brand portfolio characteristics on consumer evaluations of brand extensions', *Journal of Marketing Research*, Vol. 31, Issue 2, 1994, pp. 229–242.

Dutta, Kirti (2009), 'Consumer information sources and Effectiveness of Advertising Media an analysis of India, Turkey and New Zealand' presented at the 4th International Conference on Services Management held at Barceló Hotel, Oxford organized by Oxford Brookes

University, Pennsylvania State University, US and IIMT on 8–9 May 2009.

India Brand Equity Foundation 2010 http://www.ibef.org/artdispview.aspx?in=63&art_id=25318&cat_id=376&page=2, accessed on 5 April 2010.

Jacob, S. (2011), 'Is it a biscuit or jam? Or both?' *The Economic Times*, New Delhi, 2 February 2011, p. 4.

Keller, K.L. (2004), *Strategic Brand Management Building, Measuring and Managing Brand Equity*, Prentice-Hall of India Private Limited, New Delhi.

Kotler, P. and K.L. Keller (2006), *Marketing Management*, 12th Edition, Prentice-Hall of India, New Delhi, pp. 280–283.

Lahiri, I. and A. Gupta, 'Brand extensions in consumer non-durables, durables and services a comparative study', *South Asian Journal of Management*, Vol. 12, Issue 4, 2005, pp. 25–37.

Martinez, E. and L. De Chernatony (2004), 'The effect of brand extension strategies upon brand image', *Journal of Consumer Marketing*, Vol. 21, Issue 1, pp. 39–50.

Moorthi, Y.L.R. (1999), *Brand Management the Indian context*, Vikas Publishing House, New Delhi, Chapter 3, pp. 79–108.

Morrin, M., 'The impact of brand extensions on parent brand memory structures and retrieval processes', *Journal of Marketing Research*, Vol. 36, Issue 4, 1999, pp. 517–525.

Park, C., W.B.J. Jaworski, and D.J. MacInnis, 'Strategic Brand concept-image management', *Journal of Marketing*, Vol. 50, Issue 4, 1986, pp. 135–145.

Pitta, D.A. and L.P. Katsanis, 'Understanding brand equity for successful brand extension', *The Journal of Consumer Marketing*, Vol. 12, Issue 4, 1995, pp. 51–64.

Quelch, J.A. and D. Kenny (1984), 'External Profits not Product Lines', *Harvard Business Review*, Volume 62, Issue 5.

Ramaswamy, V.S. and S. Namakumari (2009), *Marketing Management*, MacMillan, New Delhi.

Randall, G. (2003), *Branding a practical guide to planning your strategy*, Kogan page limited, London, Chap. 5.

Ries, A. and J. Trout (1981), *Positioning The battle for your mind*, McGraw-Hill, New York.

Sagar, M., D. Singh, D.P. Agrawal, and A. Gupta (2009), *Brand Management*, Ane Books Pvt. Ltd, New Delhi.

Sarkar, A.N. and J. Singh, 'New paradigm in evolving brand management strategy'. *Journal of Management Research*, Vol. 5, Issue 2, 2005, pp. 80–90.

Shine, B.C., J. Park, and R.S. Wyer Jr, 'Brand synergy effects in multiple brand extensions', *Journal of Marketing Research*, Vol. 44, Issue no. 4, 2007, pp. 663–670.

Smith, D.C. and C.W. Park, 'The effects of brand extensions on market share and advertising efficiency', *Journal of Marketing Research*, Vol. 29, Issue 3, 1992, pp. 296–313.

Superbrands (2009), Superbrands An insight into India's strongest consumer brands Volume III, Superbrands India Private Limited, Gurgaon.

Swaminathan, V., R.J. Fox, and S.K. Reddy, 'The impact of brand extension introduction on choice', *Journal of Marketing*, Vol. 65, Issue 4, 2001, pp. 1–15.

Tauber, E.M., 'Brand Franchise Extension new product benefits from existing brand names', *Business Horizon*, Volume 24, Issue no 2, 1981, pp. 36–41.

Tauber, E.M., 'Brand leverage strategy for growth in a cost-controlled world', *Journal of Advertising Research*, Volume 28, Issue 4, 1988, pp. 26–30.

The Economic Times (2010), http://economictimes.indiatimes.com/news/news-by-industry/cons-products/food/Tangy-flavour-to-Cola-wars-Coke-launches-Nimbu-Fresh/articleshow/5477452.cms, accessed on 3 April 2010.

Verma, H. (2009), *Brand Management Text and Cases*, 2nd Edition, Excel Books, New Delhi.

Vijayraghavan, K. and R. Bhushan, 'Scorn Flake Biyani not to have Kellogg's for breakfast', *The Economic Times*, New Delhi, 12 November 2009, p. 4.

Volckner, F. and H. Sattler, 'Drivers of brand extension success', *Journal of Marketing*, Vol. 70, Issue 2, 2006, pp. 18–34.

Web resources

http://www.amul.com, accessed on 4 April 2010.

http://www.boroline.com/eleen.php, accessed on 24 May 2010.

http://www.britannia.co.in, accessed on 25 March 2010.

http://www.britannia.co.in/Hello_Diabetes/Ragi.html, accessed on 14 February 2011.

http://www.emamigroup.com/index.php?brand_id=55, accessed on 5 April 2010.

http://www.everestspices.com/product, accessed on 24 May 2010.

http://www.himalayaherbals.com, accessed on 18 May 2010.

http://www.nestle.in/PreparedDishes_CookingAids, accessed on 25 March 2010.

http://www.onida.com/products.aspx?prodcat=6, accessed on 27 March 2010.

http://www.thehindubusinessline.com/2010/02/05/stories/2010020551750700.htm, accessed on 28 March 2010.

http://www.vodafone.in/existingusers/prepaid/offers/bonuscards/pages/bonuscard_offers_del.aspx?cid=del, accessed on 1 April 2010.

CASE STUDY

Brand Extensions at ITC

Introduction

Indian Tobacco Company (ITC) belongs to the select group of Indian business conglomerates that focus on diversification into new businesses as a growth propellant for their brand business (Pandey 2009). It is one of 'India's foremost private sector companies with a market capitalisation of over $22 billion and a turnover of over $5 billion as on 31 March 2009.

ITC is rated among the World's Best Big Companies, Asia's Fab 50, and the World's Most Reputable Companies by *Forbes* magazine; among India's Most Respected Companies by *BusinessWorld;* and among India's Most Valuable Companies by *Business Today*. ITC ranks among India's 10 Most Valuable (Company) Brands, in a study conducted by Brand Finance and published by *The Economic Times*. ITC also ranks among Asia's fifty best-performing companies compiled by *Business Week*.

ITC has a diversified presence in cigarettes, hotels, paperboards and specialty papers, packaging, agri-business, packaged foods and confectionery, information technology, branded apparel, personal care, stationery, safety matches, and other FMCG products. While ITC is an outstanding market leader in its traditional businesses of cigarettes, hotels, paperboards, packaging, and agri-exports, it is rapidly gaining market share even in its nascent businesses of packaged foods and confectionery, branded apparel, personal care, and stationery.

The strategy for a new product launch—The brand portfolio

The organization, since its humble beginnings in 1910 as Imperial Tobacco Company of India, Virginia House, with the group headquarters in Kolkata, has been the proud witness to many successful new business scripts in the company's long and varied journey. It mainly focused on the cigarette business and integrated backwards into printing and packaging mainly to support its cigarette business. Today, it is a sophisticated packaging house.

In 1975, the company launched its hotel business with the acquisition of a hotel in Chennai, which was rechristened ITC-Welcomgroup- Hotel Chola. It now has more than hundred properties under its hotel business. Due to the strong winds of change in the external environment—political, social, regulatory, etc.—the company had to diversify from its tobacco business not only to save itself financially, but also to protect the company's image. This marked the start of an exercise to create a new brand image and the philosophy of investments in new business categories such as apparel, personal care, etc. It drew on the expertise developed so far in distribution, for instance, to create synergies and help develop the new businesses.

The year 2000 saw the launch of Wills Lifestyle, a premium branded apparel business. ITC did not stop here but moved on to the FMCG sector through ITC Foods in 2001 and from there to personal care in 2005. It launched brands like Essenza Di Wills, Fiama Di Wills, Vivel Di Wills, Vivel, and Superia. ITC has a presence in paperboards, greetings, gifts, stationary, and agri business with its much acclaimed e-Choupal initiative.

Branding strategy

The branding strategy of ITC is well thought out and employs a strategic approach. It does not rely on acquiring weaker brands to grow inorganically into new segments, but has created its own range of personal care and apparel brands.

ITC has entered different sectors with a combination of individual brand names and brand extensions. The branding in the various categories sees a mix of family brand name and individual brand name strategy. Some of these examples are discussed below.

Apparel business

The branded apparel business saw them start with Wills Sport. Wills was their cigarette brand and according to the Tobacco Bill if a brand name is associated with a tobacco product, it cannot be extended to a different line of business. ITC, thus, discontinued with its Wills cigarettes brand and carried it to its retail foray of Wills Lifestyle chain (*The Economic Times* 2007). This was then expanded to include Wills classic formal wear in 2002 and Wills clublife eveningwear in 2003. They company also forayed into youth fashion segment with the brand John Players in 2002.

Education and stationery products

Here the three dominant brands are Expressions greeting cards, Paperkraft, and Classmate. Paperkraft started in 2002 as a premium range of notebooks and has been extended into the office consumable segment with the launch of text liners, permanent ink markers, and white board markers in 2009. The Classmate brand of notebooks, launched in 2003, was to cater to the masses of students and has extended to schoolbags, children's books, slam books, geometry boxes, pens, etc.

Food business

The year 2001 marked the entry of ITC into the food business with its brand Kitchens of India. This brand catered to the ready-to-eat gourmet dishes sector. The following year witnessed ITC's entry into the confectionary segment with Minto and Candyman brands, and Aashirvaad Atta, wheat flour, marked its entry in the staples segment. With the Sunfeast brand, the company entered the biscuits segment, and with Bingo!, it entered the snacks category. All these six brands collectively have more than two hundred products under them.

Personal care

ITC's personal care portfolio includes Essenza Di Wills, Fiama Di Wills, Vivel Di Wills, Vivel, and Superia brands. Essenza Di Wills includes a range of fragrances and bath and body-care products for both men and women. 'So far the effort has been to keep the focus on the main brands through brand extensions, rather than confusing consumers with many sub-brands with different names' (Pandey 2009).

'But the same does not apply to its luxury Essenza Di Wills range, which has sub-brands like Inizio, Aqua, and Mikkel to cater to exclusive and individualistic desires of its rich target audience. The Inizio sub-brand caters to men with Inizio Homme and to women with Inizio Femme. If Essenza is about luxury, Fiama is about premiumness. This second product line, launched in September 2007, caters to the premium segment with the mid and upper middle-class as its prime target group, and it is pitched against HUL's Dove and Vaseline, Nivea, L'Oreal and Garnier shampoos and conditioners' (Pandey 2009). The Fiama range includes shampoos, conditioners, shower gels, and soaps. The Vivel Di Wills soaps caters to the upper middle-class consumers, and the Vivel brand offers soaps and shampoos and caters to consumers in the mid and upper middle-class segments. To cater to the popular mass segment, especially in the hinterlands, where HUL's Lifebuoy, Hamam, Breeze, Godrej No. 1, etc. compete, ITC launched the Superia range of soaps and shampoos. The Superia soap range is available in four variants; the shampoos come in two variants, besides an antidandruff variant.

Discussion Questions

1. Discuss the product mix and brand mix of ITC.
2. Is the brand extension strategy being followed at ITC? Give examples where it is/where it is not following this strategy.
3. What suggestions would you like to give ITC to effectively manage their branding strategy and why?

Case References

Pandey, O., 'Marketing @ ITC', *Pitch*, Vol. 6, Issue 7, 2009, pp. 30–45.

The Economic Times 2007 'Smokers can opt for Rock, Jazz or Blues', http://economictimes.indiatimes.com/articleshow/2101580.cms, accessed on 14 April 2010.

Web resource

http://www.itcportal.com/sets/itc_frameset.htm, accessed on 15 April 2010.

Managing Brand Architecture

13

LEARNING OBJECTIVES

After reading this chapter, you will be able to understand the following:

- Brand architecture and the relationship between brands
- Product market brand context
- Choosing the right position
- Rationalizing brand portfolio

ABOUT THE CHAPTER

The previous chapter discussed how established brands can leverage new product offerings. Brand extensions lead to a portfolio of brands, which has its own life cycle, and needs to be pruned regularly to maintain a beautiful bouquet of brands. This chapter highlights the various roles brands play in the market and the rationalization strategies for the same.

BRAND ARCHITECTURE AND RELATIONSHIP BETWEEN BRANDS

In a brand portfolio, each brand should be unique and should result in maximizing the equity of all the other brands in the portfolio and/or should not harm the equity of the other brands (Exhibit 13.1). Each brand has to be unique and should cater to different segments in the market. Therefore, while devising a brand portfolio, marketers need to be careful and come out with brands that maximize the coverage of the market and minimize the overlap between brands, so that the threat of cannibalization is minimized. An organization can launch new brands either to satisfy a particular need of the target market or to offset competition. This results in brands playing a specific role in the portfolio of brands of an organization. Kotler and Keller (2006) have highlighted four specific roles of brands: flankers, cash cows, low-end entry, and high-end prestige (See Figure 13.1).

Flankers are the brands that are launched to fight competitors' brands, so that the main brand of the organization retains the desired positioning in the minds of the consumers. Hindustan Unilever Limited (HUL) is an organization that uses the strategy of flanker brands. For

Exhibit 13.1   Consolidating Brands at Jet Airways

Jet Airways is currently offering three brands: Jet Airways, a full-service airline, and Jet Lite and Jet Konnect, both low-cost airlines. Jet Lite was created by acquiring Air Sahara in 2007 to fulfil its need for a low-cost carrier. However, soon after Jet took over Air Sahara, the deal ran into some legal hassles. During this period of slowdown, some Jet flights were operating at 'abysmally low seat utilization' and Jet wanted to transfer some aircrafts to its low-fare operation. Due to legal hassles, these plans did not immediately see the light of day, and Jet came out with another low-cost carrier, Jet Konnect.

Jet Lite had a distinct position in the minds of customers as a low-cost carrier from Jet Airways. The brand elements were different from that of Jet Airways, as the logo was slightly modified and the crew had different uniforms and the interiors were also different. The communication strategy of 'different, yet same' helped in driving home the 'quality levels and trust of Jet Airways, but in a no-frill environment'. Jet Konnect, on the other hand, uses the same imagery and brand elements of Jet Airways everywhere, including crew uniforms. This similarity has many times resulted in creating confusion, with customers buying Jet Konnect tickets when they actually wanted to fly Jet Airways. Such confusion has more often than not resulted in unhappiness, as the customers were expecting the service of Jet Airways.

Thus, Jet Airways is spending on two brands that offer 'more or less the same value to the customer. So the decision to consolidate the brand makes total sense' (Bajaj 2010).

example, in the 1970s and 1980s, when Surf faced stiff competition from Nirma Chemicals' low-priced washing powder Nirma, it launched the brand Wheel to cater to the masses at a lower price. In 1993, when Proctor and Gamble (P&G) launched its brand Ariel, in India, in the premium plank as a superior product with superior technology, Surf launched Surf Ultra, positioning it directly against Ariel (Ramaswamy and Namakumari 2009).

Cash cows are brands that have dwindling sales, but still have sufficient customers to maintain a profit for the organization. As a strategy, organizations need to offer cash cow products in the market as consumers prefer the brand and may not trade up or down, i.e., purchase another brand of higher or lower value, for the other brands in the portfolio. Thus, to retain these groups of consumers, organizations need to maintain these cash cows in their brand portfolio. For example, Singer still sells the very basic models of its sewing machines, in spite of the newer electronic models and embroidery and sewing machines, which are technologically far more advanced with additional features. Though, Colgate has come out with Colgate Gel, it still sells the Colgate White toothpaste. This is because consumers who use Colgate White will not purchase the gel variant and will switch to some other toothpaste if Colgate White is withdrawn from the market.

The *low-end entry* and the *high-end prestige brands* are the low-priced and high-priced brands in the portfolio. The low-end entry-level brands are to entice consumers, for example, the ₹20 burgers from McDonald's. These brands are strategically used to attract customers and once customer footfalls are achieved, then they can be traded up to the other variants. The high-end prestige brands, on the other hand, add 'prestige and credibility to the entire portfolio'. The Gitanjali Group offers a range of brands in the jewellery sector, right from Nakshatra and D'Damas, both diamond jewellery set in gold, to the Rivaaz brand, which has gemstones resembling diamonds set in silver and steel, and the Lucera brand, which has silver jewellery starting from ₹700 (Gitanjali group 2010). All these and other brands in the brand portfolio of Gitanjali Group were launched so that the group can provide a range of brands to different market segments and thus maintain or enhance their market share.

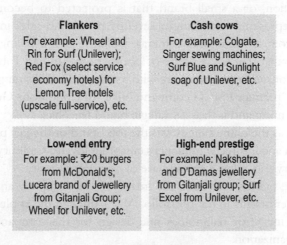

Flankers	Cash cows
For example: Wheel and Rin for Surf (Unilever); Red Fox (select service economy hotels) for Lemon Tree hotels (upscale full-service), etc.	For example: Colgate, Singer sewing machines; Surf Blue and Sunlight soap of Unilever, etc.
Low-end entry	**High-end prestige**
For example: ₹20 burgers from McDonald's; Lucera brand of Jewellery from Gitanjali Group; Wheel for Unilever, etc.	For example: Nakshatra and D'Damas jewellery from Gitanjali group; Surf Excel from Unilever, etc.

Source: Adapted from Kotler and Keller 2006.

Figure 13.1 Brand roles in the brand portfolio

The initial step of brand portfolio organizing is done with the help of brand architecture. According to Aaker and Joachimsthaler (2000), 'Brand architecture specifies the roles played by the brand, the relationship among brands, and different product-market brand contexts'. This definition talks about the following two aspects, which are discussed in detail later in the chapter:

(a) Roles played by the brands
(b) Product-market context roles

According to Aaker and Joachimsthaler 2000, an understanding of brand architecture is important to

- Build powerful brands
- Lead to optimal allocation of brand-building resources
- Provide clarity of offering, so that the brand identity is clearly perceived by the consumers, providing an opportunity to extend the brand
- Provide synergy in creating association building
- Provide a platform for future growth

Roles Played by the Brands

In an organization that has a portfolio of brands, the management of each brand requires a lot of brand-building resources. If there are a number of brands, then the organization might not have adequate resources to support all the brands. Treating brands as silos or verticals leads to wrong allocation of resources. Also, the synergies across brands can neither be created nor exploited. Kotler and Keller (2006) identified the four roles played by brands—flankers, cash cows, low-end entry, high-end prestige—discussed in the previous section. Aaker and Joachimsthaler (2000b) identified the portfolio roles played by the brands: strategic brands, linchpin brands, silver bullets, and cash cow brands.

Strategic brand can be a 'currently dominant brand also called megabrand, which can maintain or grow its position, or a small brand that is projected to become a major one'. Thus, a strategic brand represents a meaningful level of profit and sales in the future. For example, Kodak moved from its traditional cameras, which it is still selling in India, towards digital cameras, as it felt that that is the future of photography. Indian Tobacco Company (ITC) has moved towards consumer personal care with its Fiama Di Wills range, which is in line with its aspiration to be a premier FMCG company. Nike All Conditions Gear helps position Nike in the outdoor-adventure and is thus a strategic brand for Nike.

Linchpin brand, as the name suggests, is the top brand or the key player. It provides a source of differentiation and indirectly influences customer loyalty. Cadbury's Dairy Milk is a linchpin brand for Cadbury's, as it has a strong base of customer loyalty.

Silver bullets are brands that build the image of the company and positively influence the image of the other brands in the portfolio. iMac launched by Apple in the late 1990s resulted in generating an image of technology and design for the company and was thus the silver bullet for the organization.

Cash cow brand is a brand that has a loyal group of customers and does not require the level of investment required by others. Their sales may be stagnant, but the loyal customers do not leave the brand and hence the margin generated is strategically invested in other brands that are the bases of future growth for the organization. For example, Nivea as a brand has extended into a number of skin care products, but Nivea Crème continues to do well and is a cash cow for the company.

The first three types of brands require investment and need to be managed actively, so that they fulfil their strategic mission. Companies thus need to have some cash cow brands in their portfolio, which can fund the strategic, linchpin, and silver bullet brands.

Product-Market Context Roles

It is the manner in which 'a set of brands combine to describe an offering in a particular product-market context' (Aaker and Joachimsthaler 2000b). Aaker and Joachimsthaler further identified the following four types of product-market context roles: endorser and sub-brand roles, benefit brands, co-brands, and driver roles.

Endorser and sub-brand roles   The umbrella parent brand is the point of reference for consumers. At the time of brand extension, organizations can use this umbrella brand, along with the name of a sub-brand to define the new offering. For example, Chevrolet Spark, where Chevrolet plays the role of the endorser and Spark is the sub-brand.

Benefit brands   As the name suggests, benefit brand is a 'branded feature, component, ingredient, or service that augments the branded offering'. It provides a branded feature that is an integral part of the brand and delivers some benefit to the consumer, for example, Revlon ColorStay Lipcolor.

Co-brands When two established brands, either of different organizations or different businesses in the same organization, come together to create an offering, in which each brand plays the driver role, that is each brand plays a prominent role in influencing the customers through their brand image, they are called co-brands. The belief is that the presence of both the brand names will strengthen the purchase intention and help reach a new target audience (Kotler and Keller 2005). For example, 'the first Platinum airline co-branded credit card in India, the Jet Airways Citibank Platinum Credit Card' (Jet Airways 2010).

Driver roles A brand with a driver role 'drives the purchase decision and defines the use experience' or influences the purchase and the experience of the customers with the brand. A driver brand has a loyal following of consumers who would not be as comfortable with the product if the brand were missing. For example, Cadbury Dairy Milk has a major driver role in the portfolio of Cadbury.

BRAND RELATIONSHIP SPECTRUM

A powerful brand architecture tool is the brand relationship spectrum (Aaker and Joachimsthaler 2000a), which depicts the relationship between the various brands of an organization on a spectrum (see Figure 13.2). Thus, we can have the following kinds of brands and relationships.

House of brands This is one of the extremes, where an organization has a number of brands and all these are stand-alone brands that are independent of each other. Proctor and Gamble (P&G) follows this strategy and sells more than fifty brands in India. These brands are 'not connected' to each other. 'Shadow endorser' brand is a variant in the house of brands, where 'the endorser brand is not visibly connected to the endorsed brand, but many consumers know about the link'. For example, Mountain Dew, which is the endorsed brand, and Pepsi, which is the shadow endorser brand.

Endorsed brands Many organizations use their established brands to endorse new brands, as discussed in the earlier point. The degree of relationship varies as follows.

Token endorsement This is a variant of the endorser strategy, where the master brand is involved in a number of product markets and is less prominent than the endorsed brand. For example, Marico, a leading Indian company in consumer products and services in the global beauty and wellness space, has a number of well-known brands such as Saffola, Parachute, etc.

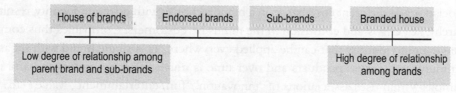

Source: Adapted from Aaker and Joachimsthaler 2000a and 2000b.

Figure 13.2 The brand relationship spectrum

'Hair and Care' hair oil is also well known and is endorsed by Marico, a fact that is relatively lesser known among consumers.

Linked name   Here, the endorser brand name is linked to another name with common elements. For example, Nestea, where *Nes* stands for Nestlé by Nestlé; Chicken McNuggets, where *Mc* links to McDonald's, etc.

Strong endorsement   Here, the endorser brand strongly endorses the sub-brand. For example, Unilever launched a drink in the fruit juice category in March 2011 and used its well-known brand Kissan to launch this new drink. The three variants—apple juice and soya, mango juice and soya, and orange juice and soya—are strongly endorsed by the Kissan brand name.

 See the use of Fortune brand name to strongly endorse their refined oil, Kachi Ghani Oil, etc.

Sub-brands   These are brands that are connected to the parent brand and supplement or modify the parent brand's association. The parent brand provides the 'primary frame of reference' and the sub-brand provides the attribute association. For example, Sony Walkman, where Sony provides the parent brand's association of technological innovation and Walkman provides the attribute of listening to music on the go. Sub-brands are further graded into the following.

Sub-brand as co-driver   This is the 'co-driver' situation, where the endorser brand and the sub-brand both play a major role. For example, Nestlé Kit Kat, where both Nestlé and Kit Kat have strong brand equity.

Master brand as drive   Here, the parent or master brand primarily drives the success of the sub-brand. For example, HP Deskjet, where the primary driver for the sub-brand, the Deskjet printer, is the parent brand name HP or Hewlett-Packard.

Branded house   In a branded house, the 'parent brand moves from being the primary driver to play a dominant driver role across a multiple offering.' It has the following variants.

Branded house with different identity   A branded house that uses the same brand name but maintains different brand identities and positions, as different associations are needed in different contexts. Thus, though the Tata brand name is used for Tata Salt, it stands for different associations than when the brand name is used in connection with the Tata Consultancy Services.

Branded house with same identity   Many times, companies feel that having different associations in different contexts as in a branded house with different identity, results in brand anarchy, i.e., chaos and confusion in the minds of customers. Companies thus come out with a single brand identity that can be applied everywhere, as 'a single brand with set associations communicated across products and over time is much easier to understand and recall.' For example, Virgin uses associations of 'innovation', 'fun/entertainment', 'value', etc., which can be applied to a range of products across product categories, be it Virgin Atlantic Airlines, Virgin mobiles, etc.

A further understanding of managing brands can be gained by studying the *brand portfolio structure* of the organization, i.e., the number of groups of brands the organization has, the brand hierarchy, and the extent to which a brand can be stretched. A *brand hierarchy* is a graphical representation (see Figure 13.3) of the branding strategy of an organization. It displays the brand elements across the firm's products by portraying the number and nature of distinctive and common brand elements and thus reveals the ordering of the brand elements (Keller 2004).

The brand hierarchy can have corporate brand level, i.e., the corporate or company brand, for example, Tata, Reliance, General Motors, etc.; family brand level, i.e., a brand used in more than one product category, for example, Chevrolet, Optra, etc.; individual brand level, i.e., brand restricted to one product category, for example, Park Avenue, Real juices, etc.; and the modifier, i.e., a special item, for example, Spark 1.0, 1.0 PS, 1.0 LS, etc. Once the

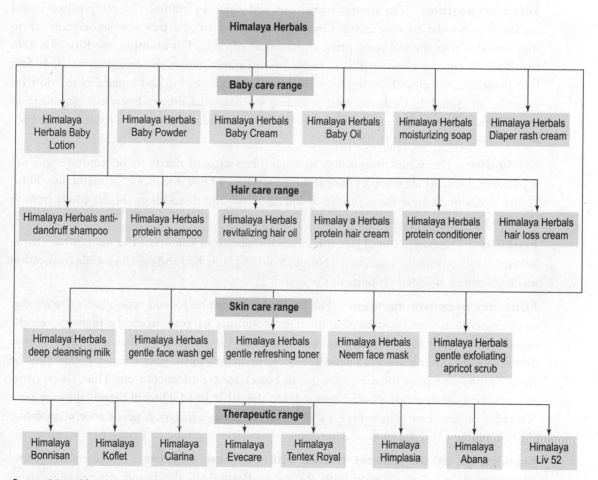

Source: Adapted from Himalaya Herbals, 2010. Available at http://www.himalayaherbals.com, accessed on 18 May 2010 (please note that the brands depicted in the figure are not exhaustive but illustrative).

Figure 13.3 Himalaya brand hierarchy

portfolio hierarchy is identified, portfolio graphics, such as logo, symbols, packaging, etc., are delineated.

CHOOSING THE RIGHT POSITION

In light of the above discussion, it is clear that a brand can play any role in the market according to the corporate strategy. The brand relationship spectrum offers a number of categories to choose from. It is for the organization to decide whether it wants to gravitate towards a branded house or a house of brands. For an organization to choose branded house as a strategy, the following factors need to be studied (Aaker and Joachimsthaler 2000b).

Contribution made by the master brand to the new offering This needs to be in terms of any, some, or all of the following.

Value proposition The master brand can add value by transferring its positive brand associations to the new offering. Organizations need to see that the association being transferred is relevant and appropriate for the new offering. For example, the Birla Sun Life Insurance Company Limited (BSLI) retails life insurance under the brand name Birla Sun Life Insurance, which reflects the trust of the Aditya Birla group and highlights the domain expertise of Sun Life Financial Inc., a leading international financial services organization from Canada, thus providing a value proposition of 'formidable protection for the customers' future' (Birla Sun Life 2011).

Credibility The value proposition that has been created needs to be credible and the organization should see whether the parent brand can add this dimension of credibility. Thus, Dettol Antiseptic Liquid has an image of killing germs and this adds credibility to the brand's extension into the soap category.

Visibility The parent brand can enhance the visibility of the new offering if it has strong linkages with consumers. Thus, when Minute Maid was launched and the Coca-Cola connection was highlighted, it added visibility to the brand.

Efficiency in communication The parent brand can help build economies of scale due to the synergy in brand communication. The economies of scale would be higher when the brand plays a driver role and comparatively lesser when the brand acts as an endorser, because in that case the other brands still need to be communicated to the customers. For example, the Amul brand name plays the driver role for its butter, ice cream, cheese, etc. Thus, when Amul is advertising, all its products are benefited. On the other hand, Himani brand endorses both Navratan oil and Boroplus powder, and therefore the organization needs to communicate about both the products to the customers.

Association of the master brand with the new offering Is the master brand strengthened by its association with the new offering? If the brand extension helps in strengthening the master brand, then the organization should gravitate towards the branded house. On the other hand, an organization can gravitate towards a house of brands under the following two situations.

There is a compelling need for a separate brand   A new brand can be created when there is a compelling need for the same. This can be in case of any of the following:

(a) When there is a need to highlight a key association that is not being supported by the existing brand. For example, Pantene for strong hair and Head & Shoulders for dandruff by P&G.

(b) When the company is offering something new or different. ITC has a portfolio of brands for different offerings. For example, its FMCG foods business unit has brands such as Bingo snack foods; Minto-o and Candyman brands in the confectionary sector; Aashirwad, which includes staples such as atta, spices, ready meals, etc.

(c) To avoid association with the current brand, especially when the brands cater to different segments of the market. For example, ITC's Lifestyle retails premium apparels under the Wills brand for working professionals. It offers Wills Classic, work wear, Wills Sport, relaxed wear, etc., and for the male youth, it offers fashion wardrobe under the brand John Players.

(d) To retain customers in case of acquisitions, such as Kraft retaining the brand name of Cadbury even after acquiring the company.

(e) To avoid a channel conflict, organizations can come out with different brands that are targeted for different channels, such as the special brands by Unilever and P&G for Big Bazaar, as discussed in the chapter on brand strategy.

The business can support a new brand   Developing a brand requires investment of time and money. The brand architecture for an organization that owns multiple brands is complicated and needs expertise, in terms of its human resources, to be managed. All this adds to the investment required in building a new brand, and the organization needs to do a cost-benefit analysis to make the final decision.

The organization needs to decide which position to take after careful consideration (see Exhibit 13.2).

Exhibit 13.2   Extending Brand Kissan

The Kissan brand name turned sixty-two years old in 2011 and leads the market in ketchups, jams, and squashes category. This brand is a part of Unilever, a 'Rs 18,000-crore giant with more than thirty-five consumer brands mostly in food, personal care, and home care segments. Unilever, which has fruit-based beverages only in a few markets including Brazil,' plans to foray into this segment in the Indian market to cash in on 'the health-conscious mindset of the Indian consumer'. The fruit-based beverage market is estimated at ₹1500 crore (2011) and has dominant players like Dabur, Parle Agro, PepsiCo, and Coca-Cola. To leverage the new entrée, Unilever will launch it under the established brand name of Kissan and it will be available in tetra packs. This announcement has evoked different responses. According to 'Mr Anand Halve, co-founder of brand consultancy firm Chlorophyll, "Kissan is a brand associated with kids and no adult consumer would like to be seen with such a brand out of home. The tetra pack category is mainly driven out-of-home and Unilever would face problems in positioning it as an adult brand"' (Malviya 2011).

RATIONALIZING THE BRAND PORTFOLIO

Over a period of time, due to more product launches, an organization can build a portfolio of brands. The performance of these brands needs to be monitored over time, so that organizations can effectively rationalize their brand portfolio. In the rationalization of brands, companies decide on the brands to be retained after the necessary pruning of its portfolio of brands.

Rationalization can be done using any of the following ways (Sarkar and Singh 2005):

- liquidation
- merging
- selling
- milking
- elimination
- consolidation

Liquidation is when the firm terminates business and uses its assets to discharge its liabilities. If the brand is important and the firm wishes to retain it, then it can also be *merged* with another brand. *Selling* the brand is another option and Cadbury's sale to Kraft is an example. Deriving maximum sales and *milking* the brand is another option for the firm. However, if the firm feels that selling and merging are not possible, it can *eliminate* the brand (see Exhibit 13.3). Also, if the brand is doing well, it can further *consolidate* the brand, i.e., build it further. The brands of the company are evaluated and placed on one of the lists identified above. The non-performing brands are placed in any of the first five categories and the well-performing brands are placed in the last category for consolidation. The enhancement of core brands is a well-thought-out strategy and it is these brands that the company should focus on as growth drivers for the organization. Thus, we can summarize the brand architecture strategies as follows.

1. The portfolio strategy, where the relationship between the various brands and the role to be played by each brand are identified, i.e., whether they should be endorsers/sub-brands, co-brands, driver roles, strategic brands, linchpin, silver bullets, or cash cows.

Exhibit 13.3   Phasing Out Getz

Getz was launched by Hyundai Motors in 2004 at a price point of ₹4.5 lakh. The brand was targeted at customers who 'wanted to upgrade from the entry-level hatchbacks, such as Maruti 800 and Alto, and its own popular Santro'. The sales of Getz in 2004 peaked to 3000 units a month. Getz was packed with quality and performance, but its sales dropped. The wilting sales were due to the launch of Maruti Swift in May 2005, which was priced at ₹4 lakh and had a retro design. The dismal performance in sales by Getz combined with the robust demand for its i10 and i20 brands helped Hyundai decide to end the production of Getz and focus on i10 and i20, which had a 'waiting period of up to two months due to capacity constraints'. This helped further the success of its high-selling i20, which witnessed a demand for more than 5000 units a month as against the targeted 2000 units. Hyundai is not new to the practice of weeding out products that are not performing well. It has earlier done the same with the Elantra sedan and the Terracan SUV since its entry in India in 1998 (Chauhan 2010).

2. Brand strategy, where the brand hierarchy levels are identified.
3. Extension strategy, where the introduction of further brands as line or category extensions is identified.

SUMMARY

This chapter helps brand managers understand how to manage a portfolio of brands. The various roles played by the brands provide an understanding of how and where different brands fit in the scheme of things. This helps in deciding on the extension/pruning strategy for established brands and in keeping the portfolio of brands relevant and current for the target market. With the help of brand architecture, organizations can focus on their power brands, i.e., high performing brands, and rework on the strategy for the brands that have ceased to perform in the market.

KEY TERMS

Brand hierarchy This is a graphical representation of the branding strategy of an organization.

Brand portfolio structure The number of groups of brands the organization has, the brand hierarchy, and the extent to which a brand can be stretched.

Brand rationalization When companies decide on the brand to be retained after the necessary pruning of its portfolio of brands.

Cost-benefit analysis Analyzing cost effectiveness of the different available alternatives in order to see if the benefits outweigh the costs.

Linchpin brand This is the top brand or the key player for the organization.

Silver bullets These are brands that build the image of the company and positively influence the image of the other brands in the portfolio.

Strategic brands These are brands that are either currently dominant and can retain their position or have the potential to become major players in times to come.

EXERCISES

Concept Review Questions

1. Discuss the various roles that can be played by a brand in the market.
2. Delineate the various roles that the brand can perform in light of the product market.
3. What is the brand relationship spectrum?
4. Delineate the various strategies available for rationalizing the brand portfolio.

Critical Thinking Questions

1. Do you agree with the statement, 'The decision to consolidate the brand makes total sense.' Why or why not?
2. Critically discuss the relevance of brand architecture for an organization.
3. Critically discuss what strategy should be adopted by an established FMCG brand catering to the detergent

market while trying to establish itself in the grooming category.

4. According to you, which strategy is better: to have a branded house or a house of brands? Why?

Internet Exercises

1. Visit the Montblanc website at www.montblanc.com/ and work out the brand architecture. Comment on the brand architecture strategy being adopted.

2. Visit the Dabur website at http://www.dabur.com and draw out the brand hierarchy for the organization. What strengths and weaknesses can you identify for the organization? Discuss the suggestions that you can recommend to them.

CD Exercise

Study the Idea ad and discuss the brand architecture for the same.

REFERENCES

Aaker, David A. and Erich Joachimsthaler 2000a, 'The Brand relationship spectrum—The key to the brand architecture challenge', *California Management Review*, Vol. 42, Issue 4, 2000, pp. 8–23.

Aaker, David A. and Erich Joachimsthaler 2000b, *Brand Leadership*, The Free Press, New York.

Bajaj, Shashank, 'Jet Lite vs Jet Airways Konnect', *Business Standard,* New Delhi, 29 November 2010, p. 14.

Chauhan, C.P., 'Getz ready for phaseout—Hyundai to end production of hatchback on poor sales, focus on high-selling i20', *The Economic Times*, New Delhi, 25 June 2010, p. 4.

Keller, K. L. 2004, *Strategic Brand Management—Building, Measuring and Managing Brand Equity*, Prentice-Hall of India Private Limited, New Delhi.

Kotler, P. and K. L. Keller 2006, *Marketing Management*, 12th Edition, Prentice-Hall of India, New Delhi, pp. 280–283.

Malviya, S., 'HUL to take a sip of fruit drink with Kissan', *The Economic Times,* New Delhi, 7 February 2011, p. 4.

Sarkar, A. N. and J. Singh, 'New paradigm in evolving brand management strategy', *Journal of Management Research*, Vol. 5, Issue 2, 2005, pp. 80–90.

Web resources

http://insurance.birlasunlife.com/AboutUs/Company-Profile/tabid/167/Default.aspx, accessed on 28 March 2011.

http://www.himalayaherbals.com, accessed on 18 May 2010.

CASE STUDY

Brand Architecture of Emami Group

Introduction

In 1974, the Emami Group was founded in Kolkata by childhood friends—R.S. Agarwal and R.S. Goenka. They 'left their high profile jobs with the Birla Group to set up Kemco Chemicals', which manufactured Ayurvedic medicines and cosmetics. The business environment was fragile, as the market was dominated by multinationals and there was labour unrest and political problems in West Bengal and companies located there were contemplating shifting out of the state. Not to be bogged down by all this, the two friends, with a meagre amount of ₹20,000, combined the wisdom of Ayurveda with modern manufacturing techniques and the brand Emami was formed.

'Emami Talcum, Emami Vanishing Cream, and Emami Cold Cream were great favourites with the quality conscious consumers in the mid-seventies. The company soon became adept in selling beautiful dreams to Indian women interested in finding their own identity. The signature tune of Emami played over radio and TV became a household favourite.'

'In 1995, Kemco Chemicals, the partnership firm was converted into a public limited company under the name and style of Emami Ltd In 1998, Emami Ltd was merged with Himani Ltd and Himani Ltd's name was changed to Emami Ltd In 2000, with a view to concentrate on its core FMCG business, Emami's investment undertaking was demerged and Pan Emami Cosmed Ltd issued its fully paid up shares to shareholders of Emami in the ratio of 1:1. In 2003, a new factory unit was set up at Amingaon, Guwahati. A public issue of fifty lakh equity shares of ₹2 each at a price of ₹70 followed in 2005. The issue was oversubscribed within few seconds of its opening with an overall over subscription of thirty-six times of the issue size.'

Brand strategy

In 1978, they acquired Himani Ltd, a 100-year-old company that had turned sick. Himani was also into cosmetics and

had good brand equity in the eastern part of India with a well-laid-out factory in Kolkata. The financial risk was high and it was a mammoth task to turn around a sick unit into profitable venture, but it proved to be a turning point for Emami.

In 1984, they launched the Boroplus antiseptic cream 'with the twin positioning of antiseptic cream and protective cream ideal for harsh weather conditions and minor skin problems such as chapped, cracked, and dry skin', under the Himani umbrella. This was followed by brand extension in the form of Boroplus prickly heat powder. The Boroplus family consists of antiseptic cream, icy cool talc, icy sandal talc, long acting body lotion, and triple action light moisturizing body lotion (see Image 13.1). The Boroplus brands are currently endorsed by celebrities such as Amitabh Bachchan and Kareena Kapoor.

In the nineties, the flagship brand of Navratna Cool Oil came into being again under the Himani umbrella. 'The company extended the brand to launch Navratna Extra Thanda Oil and Navratna Lite Oil. While the former competed with other strong cooling oils in the market, the

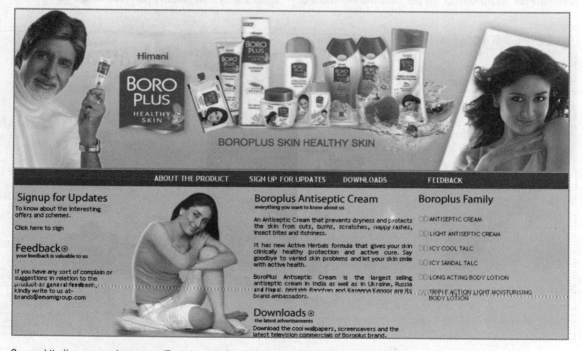

Source: http://www.emamigroup.com/Boroplus-Anti-Septic-Cream, accessed on 15 February 2011.

Image 13.1   Himani Boroplus

latter was targeted at consumers who are more comfortable with lighter aroma, are appearance conscious, and want less sticky oil. Emami has adopted a number of steps to drive growth, such as the launch of the ₹10 SKU (Stock keeping unit) and its focus on retailing through men's parlours. The company inducted market-specific brand ambassadors such as Surya, Chiranjeevi, Mahesh Babu, and Upendra in South India and Amitabh Bachchan in the rest of India (see Image 13.2).'

In 1998–99, Sona Chandi Chyawanprash was launched and in May 2002, the company launched Sona Chandi AmritPrash, a chyawanprash that was also an ayurvedic health tonic, conceived by Himani Ayurveda Science Foundation (see Image 13.3). The acquisition of Zandu Chyawanprash and Zandu Kesari Jivan has strengthened Emami's presence in the chyawanprash segment. Shah Rukh Khan and Rituparna Sengupta endorse the brand.

The Emami brand endorses the Mentho Plus balm, which was introduced in 1990 as a 'specialist pain reliever for common ailments, such as headache, back ache, cold, tiredness, sprain, and muscular pain'. In 2009–2010, Mentho Plus accounted for 18 per cent market share of the ₹380-crore pain balm market. 'Following the Zandu acquisition in 2008, Mentho Plus and Zandu Balm possess a combined 61 per cent share in the pain-balm category with a minimal geographical overlap. While Mentho Plus is strong in South India, 80 per cent of revenues, Zandu enjoys a pan-India presence.' Mentho Plus uses the Ravana mascot to advertise itself (see Image 13.4) and 'Zandu is the only balm brand in India to be endorsed by a celebrity. The brand entered into a strategic tie-up with the Mumbai Indians team in 2009–10. Its advertisements featured Sachin Tendulkar, Zaheer Khan, and Harbhajan Singh, showcasing the national presence of the brand and its effectiveness against headaches, body aches, and cold. The company roped in Virendar Sehwag, Dinesh Karthik, and Amit Mishra as brand ambassadors.

In the year 2005, Emami created marketing history by launching a fairness cream for men—Fair and Handsome. It was a category creator that helped create a category of a ₹14-billion fairness cream market for men. The brand crossed ₹100 crore in revenues in 2009–10 and grew at 32 per cent CAGR during 2007–10. This brand is being endorsed by Shah Rukh Khan (see Image 13.5).

Source: http://www.emamigroup.com/Navratna-Oil, accessed on 15 February 2011.

Image 13.2 Himani Navratan Oil

Source: http://www.emamigroup.com/Sonachandi-Amritprash, accessed on 15 February 2011.

Image 13.3 Himani Sona Chandi Amritprash

Source: http://www.emamigroup.com/Mentho-Plus, accessed on 15 February 2011.

Image 13.4 Emami Mentho Plus balm

Source: http://www.emamigroup.com/Fair-&-Handsome, accessed on 15 February 2011.

Image 13.5 Emami Fair and Handsome

The company introduced a Health Care Division in 2006 and launched a number of ayurvedic over-the-counter (OTC) medicines. 'Emami Limited, with an investment of ₹700 crore, acquired major stake in Zandu Pharmaceuticals Works Ltd in 2008 to capitalize on the huge business synergy between Zandu and Emami. Post its acquisition, a century-old household name in India, with some of its prominent brands like Zandu Balm, Zandu Chyawanprash, Zandu Kesri Jeevan, Zandu Pancharishta, Sudarshan, and Nityam Churna also came under Emami's basket of brands' (Emami 2008). In 2009–10, 'new products—Boroplus Winter Lotion and Emami Malai Kesar Soap and new product variants such as Navratna Oil—were launched.'

Conclusion

The Emami Group has shown strong and commendable performance over the years consistently. According to its 2009–10 performance report, it had a 27 per cent CAGR in the top line and 42 per cent CAGR in the bottom line of the Emami Group in the five years leading to 2009–10. It has over ₹5000 crore ($1 billion) of capitalization and has crossed ₹1000 crore in revenues in 2009–10. 'Navratna Oil, Boroplus Antiseptic Cream, Fair and Handsome Fairness Cream for Men, and Zandu Balm continued to enjoy the number one status in their respective categories.' More than ₹200 crore revenues were derived from Navratan and Boroplus brands. In total, it has over 300 products, which retail in 4,25,000 outlets in sixty-five countries.

Discussion Questions

1. Tabulate the brand architecture for Emami Limited.
2. Discuss the various strategies used by the company to launch its different brands. Evaluate the pros and cons of the strategies used.
3. Discuss the brand elements used for the various brands. What can you suggest to the organization to further increase their brand equity?
4. Visit the website of the Emami Group and highlight the use of brand elements for the brands not discussed in the case study.

Case References

http://www.emamigroup.com/Boroplus-Anti-Septic-Cream, accessed on 15 February 2011.

http://www.emamigroup.com/Boroplus-Prickly-Heat-Powder, accessed on 15 February 2011.

http://www.emamigroup.com/Fair-&-Handsome, accessed on 15 February 2011.

http://www.emamigroup.com/Mentho-Plus, accessed on 15 February 2011.

http://www.emamigroup.com/Navratna-Oil, accessed on 15 February 2011.

http://www.emamigroup.com/Sonachandi-Amritprash, accessed on 15 February 2011.

http://www.emamiltd.in/investor-relations.asp?detail=financial-information, accessed on 15 February 2011.

Brands Over Time

14

LEARNING OBJECTIVES

After reading this chapter, you will be able to understand the following:

- The importance of managing brands over a period of time
- Brand growth challenges—brand reinforcement
- Sustaining a brand long term—brand revitalization
- Brand turnaround

ABOUT THE CHAPTER

This chapter helps in providing an understanding of how brands can be managed over a period of time. The previous chapter helped brand managers understand the relationship between brands in the portfolio. This chapter helps understand the managing of brands, so that their equity can be reaped for a longer period. Brands need to attract new customers to be successful and this chapter explores how brands can remain young for consumers even as they grow old.

INTRODUCTION

A brand, once launched, needs to be carefully managed and nurtured during the initial stages of its launch and also over a period of time. If an organization is like a garden, then brands are like plants. Just as plants need constant watering, weeding, and pruning, brands need to be constantly monitored for changes in the external and internal environment. Any weaknesses or threats need to be attended to, and every strength and opportunity needs to be exploited to the hilt. As time passes, the need for managing brands increases, as consumers' tastes and preferences change and the brand has to satisfy these changing needs and wants to sustain itself in the market. Strong brands, such as Lux, Amul, Cadbury's, etc., have stood the test of time and have been able to generate revenues for their organizations year after year. On the other hand, there are brands that were launched and backed with a lot of investment, such as

Exhibit 14.1   Need for Revitalization

Vicco Turmeric and Vajradanti were both 'once marquee (leading) ayurvedic skincare and oral care brands. Founded in 1952 by late K.V. Pendharkar, the Vicco group had carved its niche as a maker of distinct ayurvedic products. Vicco Vajradanti powder and paste, Vicco Turmeric skin cream and sunscreen cream, and Vicco Narayani cream were its best-known products.'

Today, Vicco may not command a high valuation as it 'failed to keep pace with consumer trends, though it continues to hold brand recall and strong brand equity.' According to Harish Bijoor, Chief Executive Officer at Harish Bijoor Consults Inc., 'It could not capture new consumers and remained static—that was Vicco's big problem' (Bhushan and Vyas 2010).

Bajaj Scooters, Vicco, etc., and still remained static and could not beat the competition and generate volumes year after year (see Exhibit 14.1).

MANAGING BRANDS OVER TIME

One of the most important issues facing brand managers is how to revitalize a brand and keep it relevant and current. Honest and rigorous dedication is required to build strong brands. Exhibit 14.1 shows that the brand needs to attract new customers year after year, so that volumes and revenues can be generated. At the same time, the brand experience, which includes brand promise, brand delivery, communication, etc., also needs to be consistent, so that it does not alienate the existing customers. For example, Cadbury has been able to reposition itself and has successfully attracted new customers and at the same time been able to retain the existing customers (see Exhibit 14.2).

Exhibit 14.2   Cadbury's Brand Communications—Then and Now

The year was 1994, the brand was Cadbury Daily Milk—a chocolate which was till then 'restricted to and targeted at children'. The game changer was the TV commercial 'the real taste of life'. This advertisement was based on the 'larger universal insight that at the end of the day we are all kids at heart'. Cadbury focused on this and appealed to the child within each of us, by launching an ad that showcased the product being consumed by people of all ages. 'It gave the adult population license to enjoy chocolates. The ad was also called "Shimona" after the girl who ran out on the cricket field.'

In 2010, the ad for the same brand was the 'Shubh Aarambh' one. This is based on the Indian cultural insight of eating something sweet before embarking on a new journey or at the start of a new beginning. Though based on a strong cultural truth, it has a contemporary youthful twist that allows people to easily connect with it. Both campaigns, though perceptibly different, share the same brand values of joy and shared happiness. The 'real taste of life' was a timeless ad with 'great insight, great creative, great music, and great performances.' 'The Shubh Aarambh campaign came after a long brand journey and evolution' (Avasthi 2010). Why does Cadbury need to reconnect with the youth and make itself contemporary?

BRAND CHALLENGES

As discussed in Chapter 1, brand managers need to constantly ensure the success of their brands. Otherwise, once successful brands can ride into oblivion. The success ratio for a new brand launch is only 5 per cent. According to the Black Eye Ratio, if ten brands are launched in a year, only two survive and do well in twenty-four months and this comes down to one brand in seventy months (Pinto 2010). This shows that for an organization to have a strong brand in its portfolio, it requires effort not only prior to the launch, but post-launch as well. The brand has to consistently deliver in an environment that is dynamic—be it consumers, competitors, or political and legal environment. There can be a number of challenges that have to be managed on the path to success for a strong brand. Some of them include the following.

Quality aspect The quality of a brand's product is very important and is the prime satisfier of the need and want of the consumer. The consumer has constant interactions with the product at the time of consumption, which can vary from many times for consumer durables to a few or one time for non-durable products. All these moments of truth build customer perception about the quality of the product, and consistent performance by the product results in high brand equity. It has been studied that over a period of time, brands that provide good financial performance are the brands that have 'relative perceived product quality'. That is the highest quality of the product at a given price point (Berry 1988). The organizations, therefore, not only have to design a quality product but also need to deliver consistent quality over a period of time. Implementation of total quality management (TQM) can help organizations deliver quality products.

Changing consumer trends The world is getting hypercompetitive and consumer trends are evolving. A brand that is stagnant and does not adapt to the changing times is bound to die a natural death. Brand managers, thus, need to track the changes in the social environment, such as consumer purchase behaviour, changing consumption patterns, evolution of the taste and preferences of the people, etc. Brand managers need to grow and sustain their brand long term, so that the coming generation adopts the brand with the same alacrity as the previous generation did. This is a challenge for marketers and all the great brands have stood the test of time and are still relevant to customers today. For example, Maggi, from Nestlé, is a brand that has come a long way since the time of its launch in 1982 as the '2-minute noodles' to the 'taste bhi health bhi' platform through a number of brand extensions. The brand has been a category creator and has inspired other established players to launch brands in this category, such as Knorr Soupy Noodles, Horlicks Foodles, etc. (See case study in Chapter 1—Cooking up Maggi Noodles.)

Introducing technologically advanced products Brands need to evolve to keep pace with advances in technology. Adoption of technology helps the brand create a buzz and stay young and relevant for consumers over time. For example, the brand value of HMT watches, which was a 'timekeeper to the nation', has declined due to its 'technological obsolescence' (Koshy 2010).

Growing number of private labels, or the retailers own labels The organized players have established themselves as brands that the consumers recognize and trust. This, combined with the fact that the Indian customer trusts and seeks advice from retailers at the time of purchase, has increased the bargaining power of the retailers. Retailers stand to gain by launching their own private labels as they get a gross margin of 60–70 per cent on the private labels compared to the 30 per cent from manufacturer brands (Mehta 2011). This, in turn, has encouraged retailers to launch private labels, which are giving competition to manufacturers' brands. It has been studied that 70 per cent of product categories sold at supermarkets are store brands (Sayman and Raju 2004). According to The Nielsen Shopper Trend Study (2011), in India, private labels account for 6 per cent of modern trade or organized retail sales. The awareness among shoppers for private labels increased to 78 per cent in 2010 as against 64 per cent in 2009 (Mehta 2011). Retailers advertise established brands to attract footfalls to their stores and then 'sell store brands to price sensitive customers'. This allows retailers to negotiate better deals with manufacturers for stocking and selling their wares (Cataluna, Garcia, and Phau 2006).

Brands becoming generic   There are instances of dominant brands in a product category that were so widely used that they became generic for that product category (Kapferer 2008). For example, the Surf brand name is used for all blue-coloured washing powders, Xerox brand name is generally used to mean photocopying, etc. Organizations need to be very careful when their brand becomes a market leader. They constantly need to protect, nurture, and communicate the differences of their brands from the other competing brands to avoid falling into this trap.

Lack of effective and consistent communication   A brand has to communicate with its target audience to attract new customers, as inability to attract new customers hastens the decline of the brand. A brand that advertises itself and creates top-of-the-mind brand recall denotes that it is a key player in the market. Consumers will develop high brand awareness, and thus, the chances of the brand being purchased are higher. A brand that ceases to advertise will be lost in the maze of products being offered. It will be a task to sustain such a brand for the long term.

Keeping the brand young   One of the challenges for brand managers is to keep the brand young over a period of time (see Exhibit 14.3). Consumers need to feel that the brand belongs to them and is not a 'brand of yore'. They should feel excited about using the brand and consider it as their own rather than as their fathers' or grandfathers' brand.

 See how Amul manages to keep its brand young.

Exhibit 14.3   Old Spice—Vying for a Comeback

Old Spice is a popular American brand of male grooming products. The brand was acquired by P&G in 1990 from the Shulton Company. The first Old Spice was launched as a fragrance for women in 1937, while Old Spice for men was introduced in 1938 (P&G 2011). Schultz developed the Old Spice brand, along a colonial nautical theme and used a colonial sailing ship as the trademark. Its strong masculine positioning through

Contd

Exhibit 14.3 *contd*

the tag line 'mark of a man' conjures up old memories. After P&G took over, the old ship was replaced by a sail boat/yacht in 1992. Following the acquisition of Gillette in 2005, P&G garnered substantial market share in the male grooming category, thereby reducing its reliance on Old Spice and it appeared that the brand had been put on the back burner, so much so that it slowly began to fade from consumer memory.

As the male grooming category grew substantially over the years, younger brands, such as Axe from Unilever, began to eat into Old Spice's market share. Old Spice became a brand associated with older men and even in some cases 'brand of yore', failing to appeal to the younger audience. So, in an attempt to capture the imagination of the youth and bring them back into its fold, P&G decided to utilize the power of social networking.

During the super bowl (the National Football League's Championship game in the US) of 2010, P&G unleashed a viral marketing campaign for Old Spice, which redefined the rules of social network marketing. The campaign introduced the brand's character 'the Old Spice man' played by sports star-turned-actor Isaiah Mustafa. The ad promised women that he was 'the man your man could smell like'. The campaign was an instant success with over thirteen million hits on YouTube. Following the release of the video, the level of interaction with the target audience was enhanced further with P&G releasing a host of quick hit videos of Mustafa responding to fan messages on FaceBook, Yahoo, and Twitter. The videos of Mustafa responding to individual queries of fans became a further rage with people flocking to YouTube to play and replay them.

The videos were not only entertaining, but also made the company appear new and trendy. The interactive nature of the videos enabled consumers and non-consumers to participate. Although a regular ad takes months to plan and execute, the Old Spice campaign, which sought inputs from consumers, produced over 150 different video responses in a matter of two days with the help of Mustafa, social media experts, videographers, and marketers alike (Gaudin 2010).

The advertising agency hired by P&G for this purpose was Wieden+Kennedy, which had to its credit iconic campaigns such as 'Just do it' for Nike. The task at hand for them was to transform the staid old but classic brand into an iconic brand. Wieden+Kennedy spent about a year working on the relaunch of the brand. The company realized that the brand had to be made 'relevant' for the younger generation, which is more inclined towards male grooming products. Thus, a number of racy print ads were created targeting the 18 to 34 year olds.

The campaign had Mustafa reply to questions posted by celebrities, such as Demi Moore, Christina Applegate, Olympic speed skater Apolo Ohno, talk show host Ellen DeGeneres, etc. The team deliberately zeroed in on these celebrities who were not only credible but had a substantial fan following on the Internet. The buzz that was created resulted in an increase of Old Spice's Twitter followers by 2700 per cent since the launch (Weiden+Kennedy 2010). The campaign successfully put the brand on the youth's radar and helped push sales for the brand.

BRAND GROWTH CHALLENGES—REINFORCING BRANDS

Brands that are successful in a product category invite competition. This leads to the entry of other players and competition heats up. The brand, therefore, needs to reiterate, remind, and reinforce itself to the customers, so that they are constantly reminded about the brand benefits, the needs it satisfies, and how it is superior to other brands in the same category. This reinforcement can be successfully done by following the strategy for effective reinforcement.

To retain its position, the brand needs to adopt strategic marketing activities, which flow from the brand vision (see Figure 14.1). These strategies are fulfilled through marketing tactics that lead to customer perception and these perceptions constitute brand knowledge for customers, which impacts their attitude towards the brand. Thus, all tactics should be formulated from the brand strategy with a perspective of building strong brand equity. These strategies and tactics result in creating knowledge about the brand and consumers. Consumers' attitude towards the brand is formed on the basis of the brand knowledge and their own moments of truth with the brand. Over a period of time, keeping in mind the response of customers, competitors, and in order to tap new markets, brand managers may come out with new marketing strategies. These new strategies can impact the brand awareness, and thereby the brand image the consumers have. The intention is that the brand should be able to retain the desirable brand image or reposition itself as a desirable brand in the minds of consumers. Such a brand will be 'relevant' and 'current' for the consumers and they will want to purchase it and be associated with it.

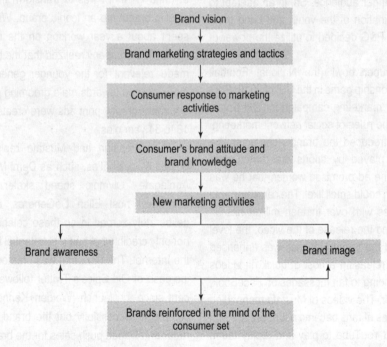

Source: Adapted from Keller 2008.

Figure 14.1 Reinforcing brands

While reinforcing brands, both brand awareness and brand image are important. Customers need to be aware of the products being represented, the needs they satisfy, and the benefits of using the product. The brand image transfers the superiority of the brand due to the presence of the brand name. Organizations can achieve a high brand awareness and image by strategic brand actions such as follows.

Brand awareness   The objective of brand awareness and what needs to be communicated should be clear as ineffective advertising leads to decreased brand awareness and effective advertising leads to increased brand awareness. For example, Aquaguard initially wanted to position the Eurochamps, i.e., the salespeople selling Aquaguard, to the target audience, so that the concept of direct selling is acceptable to them. Once this was established, they shifted gear and focused on communicating the importance of drinking water 'in improving the quality of life' (*Superbrands*, 2009).

Consistent brand image communications   This is a crucial point in building strong brands. The existing customers need to be comfortable about a brand, and thus they need to be told that the brand is their same old favourite brand. At the same time, the brand needs to be sensitive, dynamic, adaptive to the evolving consumer needs, and this needs to be communicated to the prospective customers. This requires tightrope walking by balancing the new with the old. As brand managers, it is, therefore, important to understand what to retain (old) and what to add (new). For example, Cadbury's chocolate has always focused on the happy moments of life—in the 'Shimona' ad, the 'Pappu paas ho gaya' (Paapu has passed in his exams) ad, the 'kutch meetha hai khaana, aaj pehli taarikh hai' (eat something sweet, as it is the first day of the month) ads, and the 'Shubh aarambh' (auspicious start) ads.

Protecting 'value creators' for the brand   The factors that lead to strong brand equity should be identified and retained (Keller 2008) for reinforcing the brand. For example, the jingle of Nirma, the moppet of Amul, etc. (see Image 14.1 and Exhibit 14.4) are value creators for their respective brands.

 See how Amul is using its topical ads to protect itself.

Courtesy: Amul.

Image 14.1   Amul Topical ads; also see Plate 15

Exhibit 14.4   Amul's 'Unrivalled' Moppet

The Amul moppet has endeared herself to millions of people through the years. The story began in 1966 'when Sylvester daCunha, the then managing director of the advertising agency, ASP, clinched the account for Amul Butter. The butter, which had been launched in 1945, had a staid, boring image.' On the other hand, the rival Polson's butter girl was a 'sexy village belle, clothed in a tantalizing *choli* all but covering her upper regions.' According to daCunha, 'Eustace Fernandez, the art director, and I decided that we needed a girl who would warm her way into a housewife's heart. And who better than a little girl? And so it came about that the famous Amul Moppet was born.' The girl was first put on hoardings and lamp kiosks in 1966 and the response generated was phenomenal.

'For the first one year, the ads made statements of some kind or the other, but they had not yet acquired the topical tone. In 1967, daCunha decided that giving the ads a solid concept would give them extra mileage, more *dum*, so to say. In 1969, when the city first saw the beginning of the Hare Rama Hare Krishna movement, daCunha and the creative team working on the Amul account came up with a clincher—"Hurry Amul, Hurry Hurry". That was the first of the many topical ads that were in the offing' (Amul 2011). Over the years, Amul has played the role of a social observer and has consistently come out with topical ads that have been documented from 1976 till date on Amul's website (see Image 14.1). The moppet is a highly visible source of brand equity for Amul and is one of the oldest running outdoor ads that appeals to all age groups of consumers. It consistently reinforces the brand image, and the topical ads that are based on current happenings revitalize the brand and keep it young.

Exhibit 14.4 highlights the fact that a brand not only needs to be reinforced from time to time but should also be energized and rejuvenated, so that the people who are growing up and subsequently graduate to represent the target market feel that the brand is meant for them. For example, a brand with a target market of people from 25–35 years should in time cater to the other people who grow up to be 25 years old. Let us now see how brands can be revitalized and rejuvenated.

SUSTAINING A BRAND LONG TERM—BRAND REVITALIZATION

There are various examples of brands that were once prominent and performing well but could not maintain the same performance over a period of time and faded from consumers' memories. Forhan's, a non-foaming fluoride toothpaste brand, was a successful brand of the 1960s. It was positioned as the 'toothpaste created by a dentist', but failed to continue appealing to consumers when confronted with the aggressive marketing of companies such as Colgate-Palmolive and Unilever (Vijayraghavan and Philip 2009). Examples of other once-strong brand players include Halo shampoo by Colgate-Palmolive and Keo Karpin hair oil, which had to give up their position as national brands to become regional players. Let us now see how brands can be managed successfully over a period of time (see Figure 14.2).

To revitalize itself, a brand has to start from the branding strategy that it is following. This would include segmentation-targeting-positioning (STP), the four/seven Ps, the brand elements, etc., which the brand is following and which leads to brand knowledge. To revitalize

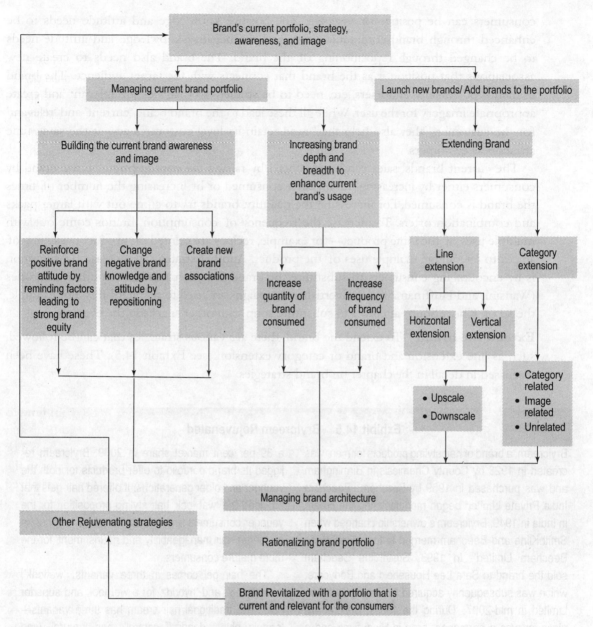

Source: Adapted from Munthree, Bick, and Abratt 2006; Keller 2008.

Figure 14.2 Revitalizing the brand portfolio

the brand, the organization can strategize at two levels: manage the current brand portfolio or extend the brand.

Manage the current brand portfolio To manage current brands, the brand knowledge of consumers for each of the brands needs to be studied. This brand knowledge of the consumers can be positive or negative. The positive knowledge and attitude needs to be enhanced through brand communications, and the negative knowledge and attitude needs to be changed through repositioning of the brand. The brand also needs to create new associations that position it as the brand that connects with the target audience. The brand elements, personality, endorsers, etc. need to be studied, so that they are relevant and create appropriate imagery for the user. While all these lead to the brand being 'current' and 'relevant' for the customers, they also help the brand retain its loyal customers and at the same time attract new customers.

The current brands' sales can be enhanced by raising the consumption of the brand by consumers either by increasing the quantity consumed or by increasing the number of times the brand is consumed. For increasing the quantity, brands try to come out with larger packs and combination offers. To increase the frequency of consumption, brands come out with multiple uses of the same product—for example, recipes are printed on product packaging of spices to encourage multiple uses of the product. Another strategy to increase consumption is by encouraging consumers to substitute the brand for other products in other categories (Wansink and Huffman 2001). Advertising campaigns are used to highlight this. For example, the ad of Knorr Soups attempts to substitute soup with other snacks in the evening.

Extend the brand   To extend the brand, there are various strategies that can be followed, such as line extension and brand or category extension (see Exhibit 14.5). These have been discussed in detail in the chapter on brand strategies.

Exhibit 14.5   Brylcreem Rejuvenated

Brylcreem, a brand of hair styling products for men, was created in 1928 by County Chemicals in Birmingham and was purchased in 1939 by Beecham. 'Beecham India Private Limited began manufacturing the cream in India in 1949. Brylcreem's ownership changed when SmithKline and Beecham merged to form SmithKline Beecham Limited'. In 1993, SmithKline Beecham sold the brand to Sara Lee Household and Bodycare, which was subsequently acquired by Godrej Sara Lee Limited in mid-2007. 'During the 1960s, Brylcreem's glass jar was a permanent prop in Hindi films and a must-have for the well-groomed, fashion-conscious man of the day. The new parent reworked the entire positioning strategy and re-launched it as a young, cool, and upwardly mobile brand' that was accessible to all. This helped re-energize Brylcreem and it dominated the hair styling and grooming segment with a 39 per cent market share in 2009. Brylcreem re-jigged its brand portfolio to offer products for both the younger and older generations. It offered hair gels that provided the 'wet look' hair styling proposition for the younger consumers and traditional red tub hair cream for 'better hair manageability and nourishment' for the more mature consumers.

The hair gel comes in three variants, 'wetlook', 'ultrastrong', and 'hybridz' for a wet look and superior hold. The traditional hair cream has three variants—'protein plus', 'dandruff control', and 'natural' (see Images 14.2 and 14.3).

Thus, the company has a range of products that target distinct usage and hair types. While focusing on the common aspiration of men to 'look good' but not wanting to alienate the mass markets, Brylcreem hired Indian cricket captain—M.S. Dhoni—as its brand

Contd

Exhibit 14.5 *contd*

Courtesy: Superbrands.

Image 14.2 Brylcreem ads for wet look and ultra strong gel; also see Plate 15

Courtesy: Superbrands.

Image 14.3 Brylcreem protein plus and naturals

Contd

Exhibit 14.5 *contd*

Image 14.4
Brylcreem 'Style
is for everyone' ad

Courtesy: Superbrands.

ambassador. The ad showed Dhoni returning to his hometown anxious as he has a new hairstyle. However, all his apprehensions vanish when he finds that everyone from the 'owner of the corner tea-shop, the local goon, the postman, the gym owner, and even his mamaji have undergone a style metamorphosis.' The tagline, 'Style is for everyone' drives home this change (see Image 14.4).

Some lesser-known facts of Brylcreem include:

- 'Fred Flintstone's famous 'Yabba Dabba Doo' is derived from the Brylcreem motto 'a little dab'll do ya!'
- One of the early brand ambassadors for Brylcreem in India was the legendary singer Kishore Kumar.
- Footballer David Beckham promoted Brylcreem until he shaved off his hair.
- At a show in 1967, the original lead singer and guitarist of Pink Floyd reportedly crushed a tube of Brylcreem over his head, while the band's co-founder Syd Barrett was its regular user' (*Superbrands*, 2009).

Brand extensions, over a period of time, result in a number of brands that have to be managed by an organization. Brand architecture helps in managing these brands strategically by listing the various brand elements being used by the organization and providing clarity for the use of these brand elements (more discussions on brand architecture in the chapter on managing brand architecture). This rationalization (see the section on relationalizing the brand portfolio in Chapter 13) helps in maintaining brands that have positive brand equity and are in sync with the consumers. Thus, the organization has a portfolio of brands, which are according to the current demands and need trends of the market. However, this is a cyclical process and brand managers need to consistently check that the brand is according to the current needs of the customers and can follow some rejuvenation strategies if it is not.

 See the various topical ads of Amul and how they help in revitalizing the brand.

BRAND TURNAROUND—OTHER REJUVENATING STRATEGIES

The marketplace has seen the death of many brands, which lost relevance for consumers and faded away. For good brands, brand managers need to 'salvage and leverage the equity that has been built over the lifetime of the brand. Brands die because of neglect and consumer indifference' (Wansink and Huffman 2001). Thus, it is important for the brand managers to revitalize their brands, so that they create excitement, buzz, and constant consumer attention. There are various strategies that brand managers can follow to keep their brand from ageing and for revitalizing them. Some of them include the following.

Product innovations   Brand managers can follow the strategy of innovation to create a buzz about their brand. By coming out with new innovations, they can leverage the brand according to the technology used or the product design. This refreshes the brand as current and up-to-date (see Exhibit 14.6).

Exhibit 14.6   Innovating to Stay Ahead—Bata

Bata was launched in 1894 by 'Tomas Bata, in Zlin, a small town in erstwhile Czechoslovakia, now the Czech Republic', and the Bata Shoe Company set up store in India in 1932. Over the years, the aim of Bata to provide 'shoes-of-choice to its customers' has helped it grow from strength to strength and has established it as a superbrand (see Image 14.5).

Bata is a brand that draws trust and nostalgia from old timers and through 'constant innovations in designs and product development using cutting-edge technology research, it continues to enjoy the trust and support of consumers.' Bata has revamped its stores using the 'Bata global format' and stocked it with 'stylish new range of superior quality products' (see

Courtesy: Superbrands.

Image 14.5   Bata spring summer collection ad

Contd

Exhibit 14.6 *contd*

Image 14.6). The new format makes the store visually alluring with separate sections for children, women, and men.

The exciting product range with innovative designs is backed with its message 'Be surprised—New range, Great prices' (*Superbrand*, 2009) (see Image 14.7).

Courtesy: Superbrands.

Image 14.6   Bata Store; also see Plate 16

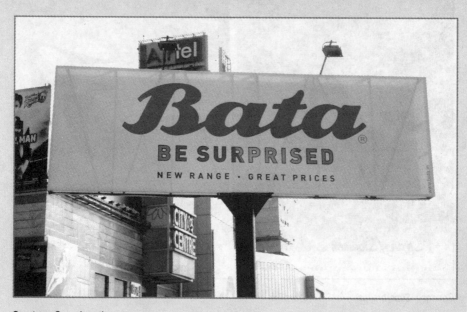

Courtesy: Superbrands.

Image 14.7   Bata Be Surprised

Exhibit 14.7　Back with a Bang

Some of the successful brands that faded into oblivion with the entry of international players are getting 'inspired for a comeback by the success of several Indian mobile phone brands, such as Micromax, G'Five, and Spice Mobile'.

Weston This was a domestic brand that was synonymous with black-and-white television sets in the 1980s. With the entry of the international players, it became an original equipment manufacturer (OEM) and was heard no more. In 2010, it decided to relaunch its brands with a range of products, such as TVs, DVD players, washing machines, irons, grinders etc. For distributing its brands, it has a dealer network pan-India and is looking at a presence in the Croma stores.

Sonodyne A successful brand of the 1980s, it was India's first big brand of audio and music systems. It gave giants like Philips and Panasonic a tough fight but could not stand the heat when Japanese and Korean players entered the market. Its entrepreneur, Ashoke Mukherjee, is coming back with new-age products, such as home theatres, dockers, LCD/plasma TVs,

etc. to target the ₹25,000-crore durable market, which is growing at approximately 10 per cent per annum. It has 'tied up with Croma and eZone to set up shop-in-shop brand outlets'.

Kelvinator Kelvinator was a successful brand that became synonymous with refrigerators. Videocon is planning to relaunch it in Gujarat, Tamil Nadu, and the east, where the brand had enjoyed high loyalty. The Videocon group acquired the operations of Electrolux in India, along with the brand rights for Kelvinator and Allwyn in 2005 (ET 2005).

Akai Akai, a Japanese brand based in Singapore, was another brand that was highly successful in the 1980s and early 1990s. It gave tough competition to Onida and Videocon, but eventually lost ground. Akai is also looking at a comeback with value-for-money propositions. It plans to venture from TV production into producing microwave ovens, mobile phones, washing machines, and home theatres.

Source: Mukherjee, Basu, and Jacob 2010.

Re-launching the brand　Re-launching the brand in a new avatar or variant also helps rejuvenate the brand. A number of brands that were once successful, but later lost their charm are coming 'back with a bang' (for examples, see Exhibit 14.7).

Repositioning the brand　A brand that is out of sync with consumers needs to be upgraded and the same needs to be then communicated to the consumers, as Bank of Baroda did through its ad (discussed in the chapter on brand positioning). A brand can also evolve over a period of time and offer services that were not in its purview earlier. This again calls for repositioning; for example, the repositioning of Airtel (see case study on Airtel in the positioning chapter).

New uses of the brand　By identifying new uses of the brand, the organization can enhance their sales. For example, Dabur Honey was positioned on the basis of purity at the time of its launch in the 1990s. However, as the consumption of honey in India is limited to medicinal or religious purposes, the challenge for Dabur was to identify ways to enhance sales. The strategy was to identify needs and drive the consumption of honey. Dabur then launched a number of ads showing honey being consumed with *paranthas*, as bread spreads, etc. Subsequently, honey was elevated to the health platform and promoted by the brand ambassador Amitabh Bachchan. Image 14.8 shows Dhoni, another brand ambassador, touting the use of the product as a sugar substitute. This helped the brand come out of the kitchen closet on to the dining table and increased its sales. The food usage aspect has also helped overcome the seasonal bias of sales (Mitra 2010). Honey was previously consumed typically during winters to provide energy and warmth.

Distribution changes   A brand can be revitalized by making it available through a number of distribution channels. This promotes the brand and creates value as compared to an unknown brand. For example, Amul, besides being present in the market through its distributor retailer network, is now present at railway stations also through its parlours, at malls through its scooping parlours, and online as well (see Images 14.9 and 14.10).

Multiple placements on shelves in shop floor   It has been observed that sales can be increased by placing the brand on different shelves, where they compliment the products that have been placed on these shelves. 'Multiple placements provide multiple opportunities for the consumers to be confronted with the brand and to purchase' it (Wansink and Huffman 2001). For example, once the brand Dabur Honey had established itself as the 'fitness from the healthy alternative' it was carefully positioned on the shelves of fruits or cornflakes on the organized retail shop floors as a food complement. The other strategy adopted was to place a concave mirror, which depicts the image of the object in a leaner form at the entrance 'with reminders of Dabur Honey leading to the primary shelf' (Mitra 2010). Other examples of multiple placements include Kelloggs and Britannia Treat Choco

Source: http://www.dabur.com/Products-Health%20Care-Honey%20Home

Image 14.8   Dabur Honey promoted as substitute for sugar

Image 14.9   Railway parlour at Palanpur, Gujarat

Image 14.10   Amul scooping parlour at Shukan Mall, Ahmedabad

Decker. Kelloggs has leapt from the breakfast bowl to the snack box and is now also available in ₹10 packs alongside chips at supermarkets 'to tap into the evening snack opportunity for children'. Britannia Treat Choco Decker is available at the biscuit rack and the confectionery counter as well. Unibic's upcoming chyawanprash cookie (Jacob 2011) will be targeting both the ₹400-crore chyawanprash market (Malaviya 2011) and the ₹11,000-crore cookie market (Banerjee 2010).

Effective communication   Brands need to communicate with and remind the consumers about themselves for top-of-the-mind brand recall. Brands use a number of strategies to cut above the clutter and communicate effectively. Celebrity endorsements, humour, jingles, etc. are some of the ways. For example, Alpenliebe used a jingle, Disney cartoon characters, a crocodile, and actor Kajol for top-of-the-mind recall. Organizations using event sponsorship for effective communication have to be wary of 'ambush marketing' by competitors (Crow and Hoek 2003). Ambush marketing is when a non-sponsor of an event advertises in a manner in which they pass off as the official sponsors (Sandler and Shani 1989) and thus attempt to gain the benefits available to the official sponsors (Bean 1995; Meeghaghan 1996). It is defined as 'the practice whereby another company, often a competitor, intrudes upon public attention surrounding the event, thereby deflecting attention toward themselves and away from the sponsor' (Meehaghan 1994). Cricket matches have always evoked mass responses in India and companies can be seen indulging in ambush marketing (see Exhibit 14.8).

The use of topical ads by Amul helps in effective communication at regular intervals of time.

Conclusion

There are a number of strategies for revitalizing brands. The question is which strategy to choose. Brands that have a high share in the market tend to enjoy positive brand perception and high customer loyalty. The strategy for such brands should be those that strengthen

Exhibit 14.8   Cricket and Cola

The Cricket World Cup 2011 was not just limited to in-field team battles. It again ignited a scuffle between the two soft drink giants—Coca-Cola and Pepsi. At a time when every campaign churns out loads of money for their brands (Manohar 2011) and with just thin lines setting them apart in the combat for the numero uno position, Coca-Cola and Pepsi have looked at striking the best chord during the ICC Cricket World Cup 2011.

The cola giants had a face-off, which was not just limited to endorsements. It pitted Sachin Tendulkar and M.S. Dhoni against ICC and created an off-field battle between the cricketers and the ICC. Some of the official sponsors for the World Cup were Pepsi, Nokia,

Philips, Maruti, Hero Honda, Vodafone, etc. According to ICC guidelines, no player can endorse a sponsor's rival brand during the World Cup. Despite this, both Dhoni and Sachin endorsed rival sponsor brands. Sachin endorsed Coca-Cola, Pepsi's rival, even though Pepsi was being endorsed by the Indian Team during the world cup, and Dhoni endorsed Sony and TVS. These endorsements could have led to Sachin and Dhoni being banned from playing the World Cup (Rao 2011). However, after the two cricketers met with the ICC board officials, the guidelines were relaxed to non-appearance in rival brand ads from seven days before the start of the matches (Kannan 2011).

Contd

Exhibit 14.8 *contd*

Choke-a-Cola

Coca-Cola, not being the official sponsor for World Cup 2011, tried very hard to get on to the list of non-official advertisers, so that it could do regular ads without taking into account anything related to the World Cup and still be visible during the biggest phenomenon for advertisers (Pinto and Mukherjee 2011).

A Blast from the Past

The rivalry between Coke and Pepsi during cricket's biggest tournament is not new. For the 1996 World Cup, Coca-Cola had paid a huge amount of money to become the official sponsor. But once the tournament began, Pepsi stole the thunder through a massive advertising blitz with an ambushing tag line, 'Nothing official about it'. This did not go down well with ICC and its sponsors, Coca-Cola. After this incident, ICC made its sponsor rules more stringent with the aim of protecting the sponsors from such ambushes (*Hindustan Times*, 2011).

the perceptions and at the same time enhance usage levels. A brand that has a low share in the market suffers from low awareness and lack of widespread positive perception among consumers (Wansink and Huffman 2001). Such a brand should encourage consumers to choose them by building brand awareness and offering price promotions to encourage trial and usage. The brands that lie in-between should follow increased distribution, alternate shelf placements, and so on.

SUMMARY

Brands are painstakingly established over a period of time. Brand managers, therefore, need to nurture them, so that the benefits can be reaped for a longer time. On the path to longevity, a brand faces many challenges, which have to be dealt with proactively. Brand managers need to look at the portfolio of brands in their basket for effective strategizing, so that maximum profitability can be reaped.

Brands that are not performing need to be researched for the reasons and invested in or hived off accordingly. Brand managers need to be innovative and constantly revitalize their brands. This helps in creating a buzz and keeps consumers excited about the brand. The trick for the brand is to get older but not age and fade away.

KEY TERMS

Ambush marketing Gaining public attention during an event and diverting attention from the official sponsors of the event.
Brand reinforcement Reminding consumers about the brand benefits, the needs it satisfies, and how it is superior to other products in the same category.

Brand revitalizations Rejuvenating and renewing the brands for consumers.
Relative perceived product quality This refers to the customer perception of the product quality in comparison to the other products available at a given price point.

EXERCISES

Concept Review Questions

1. What is brand reinforcement? Discuss how an organization can effectively reinforce its brands.
2. What is brand revitalization? How can a brand revitalize itself? Discuss any three strategies.
3. Differentiate brand reinforcement from brand revitalization.

Critical Thinking Questions

1. Critically discuss the need for brands to revitalize themselves.
2. If a brand is reinforcing itself, does it still need to revitalize? Discuss.
3. What revitalization strategies would you recommend to a brand that is a market leader in its category, such as sports shoes, aerated drinks, packaged foods, etc.?

Internet Exercises

1. Visit the following website: http://www.nestle.in/ PreparedDishes_CookingAids.aspx?OB=3&id=31. Delineate the strategies adopted to reinforce and revitalize the brand.
2. Visit the website: http://www.britannia.co.in/ brandstories_cookies.htm and discuss how the new positioning statement of 'Zindagi mein life' impacts the brand perception. Does it reinforce or revitalize the brand? How?

CD Exercise

Design a topical ad for Amul on contemporary issues while maintaining uniformity with the topical ads shown in the CD.

REFERENCES

Avasthi, A., 'Then and Now', *Brand Equity, The Economic Times,* New Delhi, 27 October 2010, pp. 4.

Banerjee, R., 'Not just a cookie clutter', *Brand Equity, The Economic Times,* New Delhi, 22 December 2010, p. 3.

Bean, L. (1995), 'Ambush marketing—Sports sponsorship confusion and the Lanham Act', *Advertising* Age, Vol. 75, pp. 1099–1134.

Bhushan, R. and M. Vyas, 'Vicco Turmeric, Vajradanti on the block', *The Economic Times,* New Delhi, 19 November 2010, p. 4.

Cataluna, F.J.R.; A.N. Garcia and I. Phau, 'The Influence of price and brand loyalty on store brands versus national brands', *International Review of Retail, Distribution and Consumer Research,* Vol. 16, Issue 4, 2006, pp. 433–452.

Crow, D. and J. Hoek (2003), 'Ambush marketing—a critical review and some practical advice', *Marketing bulletin,* Vol. 14, Issue 1, pp. 1–14.

Gaudin, Sharon (2010)'Old Spice smells like social media success', http://www.computerworld.com/s/ article/9179253/Old_Spice_smells_like_social_media_ success, accessed on 30 January 2011.

Hindustan Times (2011), 'Those Jarring Notes', http://www. hindustantimes.com/Those-Jarring-notes/Article1- 654267.aspx, accessed on 13 February 2011.

Jacob, S. (2011), 'Is it a biscuit or jam? Or both?' *The Economic Times,* New Delhi, 2 February 2011, p. 4.

Kannan, S. (2011), 'ICC goes easy on players endorsing rival brands', http://www.thehindubusinessline.com/ industry-and-economy/marketing/article1153513.ece, accessed on 31 March 2011.

Kapferer, J.N. (2008), *The New Strategic Brand Management,* 4th Edition, Kogan Page, New Delhi.

Keller, K.L. (2008), *Strategic Brand Management—Building, Measuring and Managing Brand Equity,* 3rd Edition, Prentice-Hall of India Private Limited, New Delhi.

Koshy, A., 'When brand turns burden', *The Economic Times,* New Delhi, 16 April 2010, p. 4.

Malaviya, S., 'SRK, Dhoni, Ravi Kishan do wonders for chyawanprash', *The Economic Times,* New Delhi, 26 January 2011, p. 4.

Manohar (2011), 'Off Field Battle—Tendulkar and Dhoni Endorse Rival Brands' http://www.indiamag.in/ off-field-battle-tendulkar-and-dhoni-to-endorse-rival-brands.html, accessed on 13 February 2011.

Meenaghan, T. (1994), 'Point of view—Ambush marketing - Immoral or imaginative practice?' *Journal of Advertising Research,* Vol. 34, Issue 3, pp. 77–88.

Meenaghan, T. (1996), 'Ambush marketing—A threat to corporate sponsorship', *Sloan Management Review*, Vol. 38, Issue 1, pp. 103–113.

Mehta, S.G., 'Private unlimited labels', *The Economic Times*, New Delhi, 21 January 2011, p. 4

Mitra, M., 'Just what the doctor ordered', *Brand Equity, The Economic Times*, New Delhi, 10 November 2010, p. 3.

Mukherjee, W.; S.D. Basu and S. Jacob, 'Dead Brands walking—Old favourites such as Akai, Panorama, Weston, Kelvinator, Oscar, and Maharaja Whiteline are staging a comeback', *The Economic Times*, New Delhi, 26 November 2010, p. 4.

Munthee, S., G. Bick, and R. Abratt, 'A framework for brand revitalization through an upscale line extension', *Journal of Product and Brand Management*, Vol. 15, Issue 3, 2006, pp. 157–167.

Pinto, V. and S. Mukherjee (2011), 'There'd better be something official about it' http://www.business-standard.com/india/news/there/d-better-be-something-official-about-it/424522/, accessed on 23 February 2011.

Pinto, V.S., 'India sees three brand launches a day, but only 5 per cent survive', *Business Standard*, New Delhi, 17 July 2010, p. 1.

Rao, Sujan 2011, 'Sachin Tendulkar, MS Dhoni to miss ICC World Cup, 2011?' http://www.cricindian.com/news/sachin-tendulkar-msdhoni-miss-icc-cricket-world-cup-2011, accessed on 13 February 2011.

Sandler, D. and D. Shani (1989), 'Olympic Sponsorship vs "ambush" marketing—Who gets the gold?' *Journal of Advertising Research*, Vol. 29, Issue 4, pp. 9–14.

Sayman, S. and J. Raju, 'Investigating the cross-category effects of store brands', *Review of Industrial Organization*, Vol. 24, Issue 2, 2004, pp. 129–141.

Superbrands (2009), Superbrands—An insight into India's strongest consumer brands Volume III, Superbrands India Private Limited, Gurgaon.

The Economic Times (2005), 'Kelvinator promises coolest December', http://articles.economictimes.indiatimes.com/2005-08-23/news/27472292_1_kelvinator-video-con-group-sansui, accessed on 30 March 2011.

Vijayraghavan, K. and L. Philip (2009), 'Forhans set to lose its anchor again' http://economictimes.indiatimes.com/news/news-by-industry/cons-products/fmcg/forhans-set-to-lose-its-anchor-again/articleshow/4422112.cms, accessed on 20 February 2011.

Wansink, B. and C. Huffman, 'Revitalizing mature packaged goods', *Journal of Product and Brand Management*, Vol. 10, Issue 4, 2001, pp. 228–242.

Web resources

http://www.amul.com/hits.html, accessed on 20 February 2011.

http://www.amul.com/story.html, accessed on 20 February 2011.

http://www.dabur.com/Products-Health%20Care-Honey%20Home, accessed on 23 February 2011.

http://www.nielsen.com/content/dam/corporate/us/en/reports-downloads/Retail%20and%20Shopper%20Trends%202010.pdf, accessed on 23 February 2011.

http://www.uk.pg.com/products/products/oldSpice.html, accessed on 14 February 2011.

http://www.wk.com/campaign/digital_response#, accessed on 14 February 2011.

https://picasaweb.google.com/amulretail/RaiwayParlours#5436203279870050354, accessed on 20 February 2011.

https://picasaweb.google.com/amulretail/ScoopingParlours#5457612202665372530, accessed on 20 February 2011.

CASE STUDY 1

LIC—Staying Ahead in the Game*

Introduction

The Life Insurance Corporation (LIC) of India was established in 1956 by the Indian government as a separate entity dealing with life insurance. The corporation was created by a nationalization process, under which 245 Indian and foreign insurance companies were merged.

*Dr Swati Singh, Faculty Marketing, Bhartiya Vidya Bhavan's Usha and Lakshmi Mittal Institute of Management, New Delhi.

The brand was given a logo of two hands protecting a lamp (see Image 14.11). The acid test for the life insurer came in 1999 with the de-regularization of the Indian insurance sector. The opening up of the sector was undertaken to improve the penetration of insurance products, provide better services, and at the same time, reduce government intervention.

With the advent of foreign players, the market share of LIC shrank by 22 per cent, while the annual premiums declined from 564 per cent to 109 per cent between 2000–01 and 2002–03. However, the entry of foreign players served as a silver lining for LIC, since it resulted in considerable growth in the life insurance industry and life insurance penetration rose to 4 per cent in 2008–09 from 2.15 per cent in 2000–01 (Manickavasagam and Pandikuma 2010). Ever since the entry of private players in the insurance industry, experts have been writing off LIC, but the company has displayed considerable resilience and foresight, which has helped it grow from strength to strength.

Gearing up

The LIC management was quick to realize that to tide over the challenges, which had emerged, some key changes

भारतीय जीवन बीमा निगम
LIFE INSURANCE CORPORATION OF INDIA

Image 14.11 Logo of LIC

had to be undertaken. Hence, the company began to focus on three core areas for improvement (Narain 2000):

- upgrading the marketing skills of its mammoth workforce
- energizing the entire organization and awakening it from years of slumber
- initiating steps to enhance speed, quality, and adoption of technology

The steps taken by the company in this regard over the years include the following.

Harnessing people power   Government organizations have been seen to buckle under the huge employee costs that accrue to them. However, LIC was able to utilize the same people power to fuel its growth. Rather than handing out voluntary retirement schemes (VRS) to reduce its salaried employee base, it initiated a host of HR initiatives to improve employee productivity. Its post recruitment orientation training (PROT) is believed to transform average sellers into top performers. Under this programme, 4 lakh agents were provided intensive training in 2010. Another initiative that was started in 2009 was 'senior business associates' (development officers), who were hired at very low costs and reimbursed as part of office expenses. In 2009, 550 such officers were able to generate premiums worth ₹2600 crore. Encouraged by their performance, the senior business associates were increased to 1000 in 2010 (Nair and Kurup 2010). Another practice that has served to motivate employees at LIC is the discouragement of lateral hiring, as it believes in acquiring and nurturing talent and spending tremendous sums of resources over 8–10 years in shaping recruits into officers. Every year, it relocates 10 per cent of its workforce through transfers and promotions to develop better functional and regional understanding. In 2009 alone, it moved 10,500 employees across 2853 offices all over India. To ensure successful adoption of the new roles, managers at select career levels are provided a week-long induction programme to ensure that the movement is seamless. While most organizations adhere to the culture of the boss training the juniors, the reverse is true in the case of the learning culture at LIC. Here junior officers coach the senior executives. Most transferees and promotees at LIC learn the intricacies of their new roles from their juniors. This practice of bottom-up coaching is reflective of the 'unconditional' trust that exists in the interpersonal relationships in the organization (Machado 2009).

Claim settlements   Claim settlement has been a major source of consumer apprehension. Moreover, government organizations, due to their cumbersome procedures and apathetic attitudes, often drove customers towards private players. However, LIC successfully improved performance on this parameter and became the most credible life insurer based on actual claim performance.

This is no small feat for a company that receives over 45,000 claims on an average working day (ET-Brand Equity 2008). During the year 2008–09, it settled claims worth ₹1.49 crore, settling 97 per cent claims on or before the due date and settling 93 per cent non-early death claims (i.e., claims that fall after three years from the commencement of the policy) within twenty days of intimation. With its continued dedication, LIC managed to achieve the best claim settlement ratio in the industry— 96.54 per cent for the year 2009–10.

Taking up technology LIC began to leverage information technology in servicing its business from the onset. The company introduced computers in 1964 by replacing unit record machines that had been introduced in the 1950s. During the 1990s, standardization of hardware and software was initiated. To increase responsiveness towards customers, in 1995, LIC began offering online service to policyholders and agents. This facilitated the availability of policy status report, acceptance of premium and revival, and loan quotation on demand. LIC also set up interactive voice response system (IVRS) in fifty-nine centres across the country and 150 interactive touch screen-based multimedia kiosks in strategic locations in metros and larger cities to disseminate information. These kiosks also accepted premium payments. In 2008, it introduced Entrepreneur Data Management System (EDMS) across all its branches in a phased manner. This enabled LIC to maintain paperless records of its customers.

Channels of distribution Till the year 2000, LIC relied only on agency channels of distribution, but with the entry of private players, it started to consider alternative forms of distribution. The channels it adopted include bancassurance or selling insurance through banks, brokers, and corporate agents. Over the years, LIC has collaborated with thirty-nine banks for the bancassurance mode, including nine nationalized banks. Other than this, it also utilizes the services of over 510 corporate agents and 125 insurance brokers. In 2010, it tied up with Net Ambit, a company engaged in the distribution of financial services, to further enhance its alternative distribution system. Through this arrangement, LIC's products are now available across 140 offices of Net Ambit. Other than this, the direct channel was launched in August 2009 to cater to tech-savvy customers. This helped the company in lead generation; the customer's interest is captured by the server, which passes on the information to the direct sales executive for approaching the customer.

Rural focus Through its high level of accessibility and availability, LIC has been able to increase proximity with the target group, irrespective of their location and status. While the private players restricted themselves to the more affluent classes, it was LIC's duty to extend its services to cover the poorest and remotest customer. For its rural drive, it not only hired agents from rural areas, but also opened up satellite offices to cater to the rural masses.

The Jeevan Mangal (see Image 14.12) and New Jana Raksha polices were rural specific products and hence were complete hits there. In 2009–10, as much as 26 per cent of LIC's business came from the rural areas. The company sold 15 lakh micro policies to people below the poverty line during the same period (Kurup 2010). Its rural strategy also worked wonders due to a number of pertinent innovative schemes like Bima Gram—a programme wherein a portion of the premium collected

Courtesy: Superbrands.

Image 14.12   LIC Jeevan Mangal; also see Plate 16

from select villages was put back into the system for the village's development, and Bima School—which aimed to spread insurance awareness among school children. LIC also launched products targeting agricultural and landless labourers as well as marginal land owners. These policies offer up to ₹30,000 in life cover and ₹75,000 accident cover. Moreover, the premiums have been structured keeping in mind the uncertainty of income of these groups. For the Aam Aadmi Yojna, the premium is as low as ₹25 for a ₹5000 cover. To ensure reach to such groups, LIC tied up with self-help groups and nongovernmental organizations (NGOs) (Banerjee and Ramanathan 2007).

Wide portfolio As the needs of consumers' underwent changes, LIC upgraded its portfolio to launch schemes for every pocket and every need. Currently, it offers over fifty different plans that range from the conventional plans such as endowment assurance (Jeevan Anand), term assurance (Jeevan Mangal), and money back plans to contemporary unit linked plans (LIC Market Plus 1) (see Images 14.12 to 14.13). Other than this, it also has plans for women, children, pensioners, etc. (*Superbrands*, 2009).

Promotion Just like any other industry, in the insurance sector too promotion is critical for a firm's survival. Initially, most insurance companies relied on the print media for advertising since insurance is a high involvement product. However, slowly their advertising spends across other mediums, particularly television, began to rise. LIC also upped its advertising spends over the years and has consistently ranked amongst the top ten advertisers in print and television mediums. In an attempt to lure the youth towards its brand, LIC also sponsored spots on Kaun Banenga Crorepati and Zee Cine Awards in 2005. Its advertising spend in the same year was to the tune of ₹116-crore. Prior to 2007, the company was dealing with forty-five advertising agencies, thirteen at the national level and thirty-two at the zonal level. In 2007, it decided to empanel just four agencies, thus, breaking away from a twelve-year-old practice (Exchange for Media 2004). In 2010, it chose four agencies—RK Swamy BBDO, Mudra, J Walter Thompson, and DraftFCB Ulka—for creative and media duties. The media budget for the same year was a massive ₹250-crore spread across print, digital, television, radio, and below the line (communication targeted to

Courtesy: Superbrands.

Image 14.13 LIC Jeevan Anand; also see Plate 16

Courtesy: Superbrands.

Image 14.14 LIC Market Plus 1

individuals like through emails, etc.). The seriousness that LIC has displayed towards its communication strategy has also added to its image as a marketer to reckon with.

Focus on customer service   LIC identified quite early that one of the key ways to bringing in new customers and retaining existing ones was to improve the level of services delivered. Operating in a market where insurance is primarily a push product, with customers having low levels of financial literacy, the company has worked extremely hard to tap into the minds and hearts of its target audience. In 2004, LIC hired the services of Wipro and IBM for its customer relation management project at a cost of ₹50 crore. Under the project, both companies worked together to compile data of over fifteen crore policyholders of the company. A thorough analysis of this data enabled the company to study consumer behaviour and chalk out its marketing strategy (Pandey 2004). It also introduced a host of customer friendly initiatives such as facilitated settlement of survival benefits without calling for policy documents, concessions to customers for reviving their lapsed policies, and alternate channels for payment of premium through ATMs, ECS (electronic clearance system), the Internet, and even SMS. It is through such customer-centric measures that despite the entry of a slew of private players, LIC has still been able to hold on to its dominant position.

Road ahead

Many believed that the multinational giants with their deep pockets and smart marketing think tanks would eat into the market share of LIC. However, much to their chagrin, LIC over the years has managed to retain consumer trust and has built on its image. This trust was demonstrated by the company topping *Brand Equity's* most-trusted brands survey for five consecutive years from 2004 to 2008. It was able to leverage its brand aura to extend to businesses like housing finance, asset management, etc.

In January 2011, LIC crossed the landmark 2.5 crore policies and received ₹34,137.12 crore in first premium income, i.e., first premium received in a particular financial year, in the financial year 2010–11. The endowment plan launched in September 2010 garnered 1017,560 policies with a first premium income of ₹4804.12 crore, in just over four months. Thus, with such superior performance and highest brand recall in the industry, brand LIC has clearly proven that far from extinguishing, the lamp is going to burn stronger and brighter lighting up more and more lives.

Discussion Questions

1. What have been the key success factors that have helped LIC tide over competition?
2. How did LIC mange to gain a foothold in rural India?
3. What role has LIC's promotion strategy played in brand building?

Case References

Banerjee, Gargi, and Gayatri Ramanathan, 'LIC to build on rural presence for higher growth', http://www.livemint.com/2007/10/10234054/LIC-to-build-on-rural-presence.html#, accessed on 28 January 2011.

http://www.bimabazaar.com/index.php?option=com_content&view=article&id−111·modern-market-driven-strategies-of-lic-an-overview&catid=45:life-insurance&Itemid=70, accessed on 21 January 2011.

Kurup N.K., 'LIC investments guided by various regulations', http://www.thehindubusinessline.in/2010/12/13/stories/2010121350241000.htm, accessed on 16 January 2011.

Machado, Noel, 'Leadership Next Research Study—LIC' http://www.shrmindia.org/leadership-next-research-study-lic, accessed on 24 February 2011.

Manickavasagam, and P. Pandikuma, 'Modern Market Driven Strategies of LIC—An Overview',

Nair, Remya, and NK Kurup, 'LIC bets on customer service to stay ahead' http://www.thehindubusinessline.in/2010/06/03/stories/2010060353050800.htm, accessed on 25 February 2011.

Narain D.S. 'Competition in insurance sector -Will LIC still be market leader?' http://www.thehindubusinessline.in/2000/11/27/stories/042741ju.htm, accessed on 23 February 2011.

Pandey, Piyush, 'LIC ropes in Wipro, IBM for CRM project' http://www.business-standard.com/india/news/lic-ropes-in-wipro-ibm-for-crm-project/150982/, accessed on 24 January 2011.

Superbrands (2009), Superbrands—An Insight into India's Strongest Consumer Brand, Volume III, Superbrands Pvt. Ltd, Gurgaon.

Web resources

http://economictimes.indiatimes.com/articleshow/3118904.cms?prtpage=1, accessed on 25 January 2011.

http://www.exchange4media.com/e4m/news/fullstory.asp?section_id=1&news_id=12248&tag=6983&pict=, accessed on 24 January 2011.

http://economictimes.indiatimes.com/personal-finance/insurance/insurance-news/lic-crosses-25-crore-policies-target/articleshow/7398387.cms, accessed on 23 January 2011.

http://economictimes.indiatimes.com/articleshow/3118904.cms?prtpage=1, accessed on 28 January 2011.

http://www.financialexpress.com/news/lic-to-hike-advertising-spend-to-target-youth/131089/0, accessed on 23 February 2011.

http://www.afaqs.com/news/story.html?sid=26073, accessed on 23 February 2011.

http://www.seasonalmagazine.com/2009/11/how-lic-remains-life-insurance-leader.html, accessed on 27 January 2011.

http://www.seasonalmagazine.com/2009/11/how-lic-remains-life-insurance-leader.html, accessed on 22 February 2011.

http://www.thehindubusinessline.in/2010/08/18/stories/2010081851940600.htm, accessed on 28 January 2011.

http://www.licindia.in/it_lic.htm, accessed on 25 February 2011.

http://www.business-standard.com/india/news/edms-in-lic%5Cs-berhampur-division-by-2010/351451/, accessed on 23 January 2011.

CASE STUDY 2

Pond's—A New Lease of Life*

Background

The Indian skincare industry has been displaying considerable growth at over 10 per cent since the last few years (Shree Shilpa 2011) and is expected to register a CAGR of nearly 19 per cent during 2010–13 (RNCOS Report 2010). The changing lifestyles and increasing disposable incomes has made both women and men more conscious of their appearance. Pegged at ₹3500 crore (in 2010), the skincare segment has two primary growth drivers anti aging and skin whitening creams apart from moisturisers, face washes, etc. Estimated at ₹80–100 crore, the anti aging category is growing at 40 per cent compared to the ₹600-crore whitening segment, whose growth rate is pegged at 15–20 per cent (Chatterjee 2010). The anti-aging segment has attracted a host of players, both domestic and international, which include Elder Pharma, Hindustan Unilever Limited (HUL), Proctor and Gamble (P&G), Garnier, and L'Oreal to name just a few.

HUL is Unilever's Indian subsidiary and market leader in most categories of FMCG products in which it operates. The major challenge for HUL in the anti-aging category came from Olay, P&G's anti-aging brand. Launched in 2007, Olay has been an aggressive player in this segment from the very onset and leads the category with 36 per cent market share in 2010 (Sagar 2010). Since HUL lacked a brand that could cater to this segment, it decided to extend the Pond's brand to address to both the anti aging as well as whitening segments. Pond's Age Miracle was thus launched in 2006 with a promise to bring back candlelight dinners, long drives, and the lost romance into the lives of women aged 35 and above.

*Dr Swati Singh, Faculty Marketing, Bhartiya Vidya Bhavan's Usha and Lakshmi Mittal Institute of Management, New Delhi.

Extending the brand

Pond's was invented by a New York based pharmacist Theron T Pond. It has been present in the Indian market since 1947 and Unilever bought Pond's in 1987. Until a few years ago, Pond's was a brand restricted to cold cream and talcum powder. The brand displayed minor changes in the form of extension into moisturizer through Pond's Body Lotion, which did not meet with a lot of success. Always known as the hardworking women's brand, the anti aging category posed formidable challenge for Pond's, since the category was premium in nature and, therefore, required an image change. Despite owning a number of successful brands in the skincare segment, such as Vaseline, Lakme, Fair & Lovely, HUL still had to identify a brand that could help it plug the gaps in the anti aging segment. Ponds, thus, became a natural choice, since it had connotations of a heritage brand that stood for international quality. Pond's success became slightly easier as the international brands present had limited equity in India, especially in the masstige (mass + prestige) segment. The Pond's brand was also extended to include skin-lightening products.

The anti-aging products in India had initially catered to the 35+ women who had the disposable income to purchase anti aging products that were priced at a premium, but later even 20+ women and men began using these products as awareness of preventive care grew. To cater to the mass premium market, pricing of the Pond's Age Miracle range was restricted to less than ₹1000, thus avoiding head-on competition with counterparts. It was positioned as a solution to tell tale signs of aging brought about by rising pollution levels, hectic work schedules, and growing stress. Rising disposable incomes, growing consciousness towards personal grooming, and the presence of organized retail also fuelled the rapid growth acceptance of the brand. Banking on its heritage and international equity, the brand was able to register with the target group. As the market for complete skincare in India was evolving, HUL extended the Pond's Age Miracle range to include products, such as cleanser, toner, serum, cream, under-eye cream, and Pond's double white and botanical hydration range. Buoyed by the success of its age miracle range, HUL launched a slew of products under the Pond's range to include Flawless white, White Beauty, and Perfect result. The growth of organized retail

also ensured that the products could be sold in a manner akin to international brands, with skin analyzers/ experts available at counters to address and guide consumers. Though initially the range was imported from Thailand, HUL began manufacturing 'Pond's Age Miracle' in India in 2008. With local manufacturing, the prices of Pond's age miracle were further reduced, making the new price points at ₹299, ₹199, and ₹99, thereby making the products more accessible to consumers (PTI 2010). Having gained considerable foothold in the lower end of the anti aging market, Ponds now required an equally strong presence in the premium end of the category. Hence, in 2010, HUL launched Pond's Gold Radiance range, priced between ₹500–₹1000. This became the most expensive brand in HUL's skin care range. The new range came infused with real gold micro particles and included youth serum, glow day cream, youth reviving eye cream, etc. Launched after years of research by the Pond's Institute, the range is said to revitalize across four key dimensions—texture, colour, evenness of tone, and hydration. The move was also undertaken in light of numerous global players, such as L'Oreal, P&G, Beiersdorf-owned Nivea increasing their presence in mass premium and premium segments.

Campaigning for a miracle

The transition of Pond's from a mass brand to a premium one was achieved by a series of well-planned and executed campaigns. The launch pad for Pond's age miracle range in 2007 was a campaign that featured users giving their feedback on the product. This was followed by a 'romance revival' campaign that featured a husband turned chef vying to bring romance back into his married life. These campaigns were followed by the launch of miracle boutiques, where women could consult beauty experts as well as post their queries and feedback on the website. To induce trial of the anti aging products, it launched the '7 day challenge with money back guarantee' campaign from 1 September to 20 October 2007. The seven-day challenge was a truly unique campaign since nothing like it had been previously tried. It played a major role in developing a favourable attitude towards the range (Media news line 2007).

In December 2008, HUL took a major step towards enticing the affluent class by launching a concept show titled Pond's Age Miracle Salaam–e-Ishq on Star One. The show showcased real life couples reliving the romance of their relationships. With this move, HUL attempted to move beyond product placement to co-creation of entertainment, ensuring that the brand's proposition remained central to the show's theme. To appeal to the price conscious customer, HUL offered trial packs of Pond's Age Miracle cream at ₹295 for 50 ml; it followed rival Olay's strategy by giving away new jars of cream in exchange for old ones. HUL also followed up the campaign by an endorsement programme featuring the likes of Mehr Jesia Rampal, former Miss India and supermodel, and Rina Dhaka, fashion designer, all discussing how the product had changed their lives. As the brand was extended to include skin-lightening products, a number of titillating campaigns were unleashed. HUL brought back the previously successful seven-day challenge, however, this time for the Flawless White range. The campaign guaranteed women positive effects on the skin post a seven-day usage of the cream. Promoted from the 1 March to 30 April 2008, the campaign was supported by a massive multimedia presence (Business Wire 2008). Under the campaign, women were invited to try the cream for seven days, if they were unsatisfied by the product they could call a toll free number mentioned in the TV commercial, following which Pond's helpline would get in touch with them, collect the product, and reimburse their money if the claim was valid. The company also used Malaika Arora Khan to endorse its products, and Pond's Gold Radiance was the title sponsor for Zee Cine Awards 2011.

The road ahead

As consumer needs and lifestyles undergo a change, brands need to resonate the change to stay contemporary and meaningful for its consumers. HUL made the Pond's magic work by seizing an emerging opportunity. The extension of the Pond's brand to other categories helped HUL plug a gaping hole in its portfolio and simultaneously provided the aging Pond's brand with a new lease of life. How Pond's is able to cope with skincare experts, such as L'Oreal, Nivea, Garnier, and P&G, in the long run as they garner stronger footholds remains to be seen.

Discussion Questions

1. Why did HUL extend Pond's into the skincare segment and not launch a new brand instead?
2. Why has the anti aging segment grown lucrative in India?
3. Which competitors did HUL fear the most and why?
4. What were the promotion campaigns that helped Pond's Age Miracle establish itself as a key contender in the anti aging category?

Case References

Chatterjee, Purvita, 'Skin-care brands add anti-aging allure' http://www.thehindubusinessline.in/2010/12/03/stories/2010120350800500.htm,accessed on 14 January 2011.

http://articles.economictimes.indiatimes.com/2010-11-01/news/27574405_1_anti-ageing-olay-hul-chairman-harish-manwani, accessed on 21 March 2011.

RNCOS – Report, 'Skin Care Market Set to Shine in India', http://www.pubarticles.com/article-skin-care-market-set-to-shine-in-india-rncos-1297685083.html. accessed on 16 February 2011.

Sagar, Malviya, 'HUL's Pond's to counter P&G's Olay'.

Shree Shipla, 'Forever young—India's anti-ageing cream market coming of age', http://www.tehelka.com/ story_main47.asp?filename=Ws231110CONSUMER_GOODS.asp, accessed on 23 March 2011.

Web resources

http://www.financialexpress.com/news/Pond's-flawless-white-range-launches-its-7-day-challenge-campaign/283959/1, accessed on 15 March 2011.

http://www.indiareport.com/news-details/print_news.php?id=941518, accessed on 28 March 2011.

http://www.medianewsline.com/news/120/ARTICLE/1443/2007-09-20.html, accessed on 11 March 2011.

Brands in a Borderless World

15

LEARNING OBJECTIVES

After reading this chapter, you will be able to understand the following:

- How to manage brands across geographical boundaries
- Challenges and issues in going international
- Branding strategies that can be adopted while going international
- Critical factors for success
- Ethical brand positioning

ABOUT THE CHAPTER

So far, we have been discussing the various strategies that organizations can adopt to build a sustainable brand worth high equity. An organization can leverage such a brand and come out with strategies that will help penetrate the market and gain high market share. Once the opportunities in the market have been utilized, the question is, 'what next?' What does the organization now do to enhance its sales and profitability? The organization now needs to look beyond its current market for greener pastures. It needs to look at opportunities available in other countries/markets and try to exploit those as well (see Exhibit 15.1). In this final chapter, we will see how an organization can manage global brands.

Exhibit 15.1 GlaxoSmithKline's Second Innings in the Oral Care Market

GlaxoSmithKline Consumer Healthcare (GSKCH) has a number of well-known brands in its portfolio, such as Horlicks, Eno, Crocin, Iodex, etc. (GSK 2011). In 2003, it had launched the Aquafresh toothpaste in the Indian market but had to withdraw it in the same year due to its unsuccessful stint in the marketplace. GSKCH, with an annual global sale of $750 million (₹3403 crore), has started its second innings in the Indian oral care market with its biggest and fastest growing global toothpaste brand—Sensodyne. The overall toothpaste market in India is approximately ₹2700 crore. Sensodyne is a toothpaste for sensitive teeth and has

Contd

Exhibit 15.1 *contd*

been test marketed for a year in four states—Tamil Nadu, Kerala, Karnataka, and Andhra Pradesh. It plans to target 5 per cent share of the urban oral care market in India, which is worth approximately ₹1850 crore. GSKCH launched a toothpaste for sensitive teeth, as its research shows that 17 per cent of the consumers suffer from sensitive teeth. This category of sensitive toothpaste is estimated at ₹180 crore and is growing at double the growth rate of regular toothpaste, i.e.,

18 per cent as compared to the 9 per cent for regular toothpaste. Some of the players offering toothpaste for sensitive teeth are Colgate Sensitive from Colgate, Thermoseal from ICPA Health Product, and Glister from Amway. The Sensodyne brand will be available in two variants in India—fresh gel and fresh mint, priced at ₹45 and ₹42, respectively. It will be sold through 16 lakh outlets and ₹20 crore has been allocated to promote the brand (Kar 2011).

MANAGING BRANDS ACROSS BOUNDARIES

Brands are 'ubiquitous' and consumers are consuming the best brands available to them. Brands such as Coca-Cola and Nike have global cognitive salience and their ability to arouse passion across different countries is undeniable (Cayla and Arnould 2008). If we look at the car segment alone, there are a number of global brands present in India, such as Toyota, Hyundai, General Motors, etc.; and also luxury carmakers, such as Rolls-Royce, Bentley, Porsche, Bugatti, etc., with Bugatti Veyron 16.4 Grand Sport being the most expensive car with a price tag of ₹16 crore (Economic Times Bureau 2011). The availability of a number of competitor brands necessitates a brand to be present in a particular market. For example, Mercedes Benz reintroduced its super premium sedan Maybach in India in February 2011. The maximum price tag is ₹5.10 crore (ex-showroom Delhi) and the starting price is ₹4.85 crore (Economic Times Bureau 2011) (also see Exhibit 15.2).

Global brands are looked upon with envy and have a uniform positioning, personality, look, feel, and advertising strategy across different countries. However, they are not exactly

Exhibit 15.2   India to See Fifty New Cars in 2011

The year 2010 saw the launch of more than a dozen new cars, which was just the beginning of the exciting offerings Indians were set to receive. With the rise in the disposable income and backed by a booming economy, India is becoming the destination for global auto majors. Cash-rich people in smaller towns and cities exhibit a new desire to flaunt their wealth. A group of 150 local businessmen decided to purchase en masse a Mercedes Benz each in the October of 2010, signalling the rising yen for luxury products.

January 2011 started with the launch of Maruti's Kizashi priced at ₹16–18 lakh. Its SX4 sedan is being fitted with a diesel engine, in keeping with the customers' preference for diesel products. The other cars lined up for their Indian innings are Toyota Etios Liva (₹3.8–5.5 lakh), Honda Brio (₹4.5–6 lakh), Nissan Sunny (₹7–9.5 lakh), Volkswagen Tiguan (₹28 lakh), Porshe Panamera (₹1.5 crore), Mercedes Maybach (₹6 crore), etc. (Chauhan 2011).

identical. Slight changes may be there in the product offering, communication, promotions, etc. There are a number of reasons for a brand to go global (Evans and Burman 2007; Kotler and Keller 2006), which include:

1. Slow growth in the domestic market
2. Increased competition at home and saturation of the domestic market
3. Opportunities for higher profitability in the global market
4. Tax incentives and government policies that promote international marketing
5. Identification of similar market segments and consumer needs in different country markets
6. Diversified risk by being present in multiple countries

These factors provide a rationale for going global.

Advantages of Global Brands

There are a number of advantages a firm can reap by selling a brand in multiple country markets. These advantages include:

Economies of scale   Going global helps the firm reap advantage of economies of scale. A standardized brand with a global brand name can help reap economies of scale not only in production, but also in research and development, logistics, communications, and packaging costs. These savings are translated to reduced prices and help in enhancing the financial performance of the brand (Schuiling and Kapferer 2004). For example, Timex entered India through a joint venture with Titan in 1992, and a few years down the line, in 1996–97, decided to part ways. At that time, Timex was running at a loss and it was predicted that it would not last long in the market. However, Timex proved the critics wrong. According to Mr V.D. Wadhwa, Timex India's Managing Director, 'Net sales for the quarter ended June 2010 grew 45 per cent, while profits grew 107 per cent over the corresponding period. The company declared a profit of ₹5 crore in the last quarter as compared to the corresponding quarter last year. This is the fourth year in a row when we are on the profit track. We are going on a high-growth trajectory and planning to double our revenue in the coming year.' He attributes this to a number of strategies (discussed later in the chapter) and also due to the company 'taking advantage of the entire supply chain expertise that exists in different parts of the world. We are trying to integrate much more with the Timex organization worldwide and leverage the strength at a global level.' The connection with the global design centre in Milan enables Timex to develop world-class watches. According to Mr Kapil Kapoor, Timex Group's COO (Chief Operating Officer), 'What is unique about Timex? It is the only global brand with a strong supply chain and manufacturing facility in India. That gives us a unique advantage, where we can leverage our global technology, through the global design centre in Milan, to be able to bring to the consumer watches at the best possible price.'

Increased brand life cycle   A brand that is at a mature or declining product life cycle stage in the home country can identify an opportunity in a host country with the market potential for it to enter at the introduction stage. This helps sustain the brand long term by finding new markets and opportunities and provides the brand with a fresh lease of life. For example, brands that retail in developed countries need to consistently develop new models due to technological advancements and research and development activities. However, the developing and underdeveloped countries face a time lag before the demand for such technologically advanced products arise; for example, the demand for 3G phones in India is at the introductory stage right now.

Availability 'Global mobility of customers' (Keller 2004) makes it imperative for brands to be present in different countries, so that they are available when the customer wants them. For example, brands such as Coke, Pepsi, McDonald's, etc.

Perception of brand superiority A brand that is present in diverse markets is perceived to be successful, of high quality, signals prestige, and social status (Keller 2004), and is therefore preferred over local brands (Benedict, Steenkamp, Batra, and Alden 2003). Quality is an important construct that drives the preference of consumers towards a brand (Schuiling and Kapferer 2004) and a global brand image is helpful in positioning intangible services, such as banking, financial services, etc. (Wright 2002).

High prestige and status Global brands are associated with high prestige and status. This aspect motivates customers who want to be seen consuming brands that are globally admired.

Decrease in marketing cost Adoption of uniform marketing strategies across the country markets helps in increasing efficiency and provides a cost advantage. Similar marketing strategies across countries are easier to manage rather than managing a number of country-specific strategies. For example, Microsoft for its XP campaign was able to save $30 million in man hours and production costs over the previous similar campaigns by standardizing the core concept ('yes you can') and sending this core concept to different local agencies in different country markets for adaptation. Thus, in the UK the focus was on working women who can look after their home and still attend an online official meeting; in the US, the features highlighted were photography and file sharing; in China the focus was 'you can do as you wish' and features highlighted were music, messaging, office use, etc. (Cateora and Graham 2004).

Uniform brand image The other benefit of adoption of uniform marketing strategy is that it results in a uniform brand image as well, which leads to enhanced brand equity.

Barrier to entry A global brand, which has a strong presence across country markets and operates on economies of scale with high prestige, status, etc., is a strong brand that creates barriers to entry (Schuiling and Kapferer 2004). For example, Bang and Olufsen's collection of audio systems, TV, telephones, etc. are retailed in more than a hundred countries (Bang and Olufsen 2011) and the products are exclusive and lend high prestige, thus creating barriers to the entry of other new players. Unilever and Nestlé both have strong established brands in the FMCG category, which are being retailed globally, and thus they create strong barriers to the entry of other new players.

Opportunity to tap similar segments in different geographical markets Similar segments of customers are present globally. For example, there are working women who are always hard pressed for time and welcome brands that help in saving their energy and time; all young mothers are concerned about their baby's health and hygiene; teenagers who want to be in sync with the latest fashion trends, etc., and these segments of consumers can be found in different country markets.

Enhanced strategic flexibility Global operations provide firms with multiple sourcing opportunities. This reduces dependence on a particular supplier and better cost-effective suppliers can be tapped. Orders can be redirected to locations that are operational at under capacity utilization and the overall efficiency can be increased. A global logistics system helps in reducing the time to market brands (Craig and Douglas 2000). For example, Zara (an international fashion company belonging to Inditex, an international fashion retailer) has shortened its delivery time by linking its retail outlets with a centralized system, which tracks the design, size, and colour of the outfit sold and stocks outlets with latest trends, in line with the preferences of consumers and at the same time removes products that are not selling well. It has managed to reduce the order fulfilment cycle (time duration between receiving an order at the distribution centre and delivery of the goods to the store) to an 'average 24 hours for European stores and a maximum of 48 hours for American or Asian stores' (Fibre to Fashion 2011).

All the points above are valid when an organization offers a standardized brand in all the country markets.

See how creating a global brand has helped McDonald's leverage on the advantages available for a global brand.

Disadvantages of Global Brands

However, many times it is not possible to provide a standard brand everywhere. There can be a number of reasons for this. Let us now discuss the disadvantages of a global marketing programme.

Needs and wants Selling a uniform brand across different country markets does not recognize the fact that there can be different needs and wants of the consumers in each of these different markets. The lifestyle and consumption habits vary in different country markets and are strongly influenced by the cultural habits of the consumers. Thus, for example, cows are sacred for the Hindus in India and it is against their religion to consume beef. Thus, McDonald's, famous for its hamburgers (with beef patty) the world over, does not retail it in India.

See how Mc Donald's overcame the disadvantage of different needs and wants. The Indian ad showcases McAloo Tikki, Soft Serve, Chicken McGrill, and Pizza McPuff and it does not retail its world famous hamburgers in India.

Different usage patterns The manner of consumption of brands can vary in different country markets. This provides opportunities for national players who can retail their brands. For example, hair oil is largely used in South Asia, and therefore does not figure in the portfolio of organizations that provide brands that can be sold globally. For example, Unilever, which retails a number of FMCG brands, does not have hair oil in its portfolio of brands. Emami has used this to its advantage and its brand Navratan Hair Oil is worth over ₹100·crore (Kar 2010).

Difference in consumer response Consumer response to the marketing mix may be different in different countries according to their cultural conditioning. This is especially true for advertising, and cultural differences might make it difficult to use a global campaign. Thus, in India, Axe Dark Temptation deodorant ads that explicitly depict women pursuing the model wearing the deodorant was found 'objectionable, indecent, and vulgar' by the Ministry of Information and Broadcasting, which led to the advertisement eventually being pulled off air (PTI, 2008). However, it did not face this problem in Western countries, where a more explicit ad was aired.

Preference for local brands Research shows 'that consumers tend to evaluate local products more highly than foreign products and this behaviour varies across countries' (Schuiling and Kapferer 2004). Thus, countries with high preference for local brands would not prefer a global brand, highlighting a need to launch local brands. For example, P&G was retailing its laundry detergent in Europe under the local brand name Fairy. In the year 2000, it decided to change the same detergent to a global brand named Dawn. It had not anticipated the preference of the consumers towards the local brand and the resistance towards the Dawn brand. The result was that by the end of 2001, the market share of Dawn had fallen drastically in Germany, even though the product formulation was the same. 'P&G's experience with Dawn shows that companies which respond to local preferences may have an advantage over those that address a standardized market, because significant numbers of consumers do resist global brands, preferring local ones that seem more familiar' (Frost 2005).

Uniform brand image not necessarily relevant A uniform brand image that is adopted in global branding might not be relevant in some country markets. For instance, Honda in the US stands for quality and reliability. In Japan, where quality is a norm for most of cars, Honda stands for youth, speed, and energy (Aaker and Joachimsthaler 1999).

CHALLENGES IN GOING INTERNATIONAL

Going global is a challenging process. Various countries across the globe are at various stages of development. The needs and wants of people across the countries might be the same, but the brand consumption can vary depending upon economic, social, and cultural factors. An organization needs to study these factors to gain an understanding of them vis-à-vis its brand and accordingly try to tailor the brand (see Exhibit 15.3). Some of the factors that need to be looked into are as follows.

Politico-economic factors The politico-economic factor is a primary area of concern, as brand managers need to know whether the country is operating at a sound level and if it would be 'safe' for them and their employees to conduct business in that country. Factors such as the political set-up of the country, stability of the government, monetary policies of the government, gross domestic product (GDP), inflation, etc. should be considered and then brand managers can decide which country to enter and what brands to offer.

Socio-economic classifications The socio-economic classification is another important factor that should be considered by brand managers. The number of people belonging to the

Exhibit 15.3 Cracking the African Market

Africa is seen as a continent that has unstable governments, weak governance, poor infrastructure, corrupt regimes, and many other such weaknesses. Yet, a number of Indian companies—be it conglomerates, such as the Tata Group, Godrej Group, Essar, Vedanta, Apollo Tyres, Dabur, or smaller companies, such as Nihilent Technologies based in Pune—are busy with their African ventures. This is because Africa offers a mixed bag—there are opportunities galore in Kenya, South Africa, and Ghana, and places once considered dangerous, such as Sierra Leone, are making honest efforts to change. Indian companies are pursuing a 'mix of buy and build strategies to grow'. The experience of some of the Indian players in the African market is provided below.

Apollo Tyres For Apollo Tyres, the African market was strikingly similar to the Indian market. An acquisition opportunity available at an attractive price was too good to resist. It acquired Dunlop SA for ₹290 crore in 2006. In the case of Apollo, 80 per cent of its sales in India was to the replacement market and 20 per cent to the original equipment partners, whereas 95 per cent of Dunlop's sales was to the replacement market and 5 per cent to the original equipment makers. According to Neeraj Kanwar, Vice Chairman and MD, Apollo Tyres, 'With the purchase, we got global purchasing power and our raw material purchasing cost nosedived by 17–18 per cent.'

Godrej Group Godrej's initial foray into Africa in 1996–97 was not very fruitful. It had formed a joint venture with Sara Lee to launch its Good Knight brand, but withdrew in the early 2000s when it realized that 'Sara Lee was restricting its growth ambitions. It was only accidentally that in 2006 they woke to the potential of South Africa when they acquired 'the African hair colour business of Rapidol.' It has set up its 'One Africa' strategy, wherein four hubs that spread across Africa will cover 'south, west, east, and central Africa'. A separate R&D team has been entrusted with the task of designing products at different price points to satisfy the needs of the African consumers.

Dabur Dabur entered Africa in 2007 (Reuters 2007) with toothpaste and has realized that the key to success is localization. Nigeria being a predominantly gel market, it launched Dabur Herbal Green Gel and targeted the youth with its 'Change to Green' campaign. The use of rap music, which is popular among the target youth segment, helped it become the fastest growing brand in the segment (Mitra, Carroll, and Mahanta 2010).

different strata is important as brand managers need to know whether the target audience, who can afford to pay for their brand as well, is there in sufficient numbers.

Social factors Social factors and the manner in which the society is developing affect the consumption patterns. These are important as they help decide whether the brand will be relevant for the target audience or not.

Legal aspects The laws prevalent in the country are of importance while deciding to go global. Laws regarding product descriptions, labelling, advertising, etc. should be studied before entering the country. The law machinery is also important, especially in times of dispute, which can arise when an organization is going global.

Technological factors Studying the level of technology in a country is important to understand the technology that is being used by the consumers. Organizations should offer

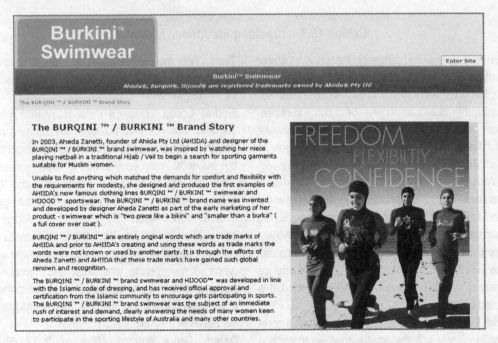

Source: http://www.burkini.com

Image 15.1   Burkini Swimwear

brands that are in line with the level of technology being used so that there is easy adoption by the consumers and they are not put off by the over simplistic nature or scared by the complexities.

Cultural factors   The culture of a country influences the consumption patterns of the people there. This can also vary within the country, which is especially true for a huge country like India with a rich cultural diversity. Brands need to adapt or come out with completely new products, keeping the culture in mind. For example, keeping in mind the Islamic code of dressing for Muslim women, the Burkini brand was designed for women who wish to participate in water sports. 'The sun, sand, and surfing constitute an Australian way of live, but for many orthodox Muslim women in the country, a visit to the beach meant trudging though the sand in heavy full-length robes.' This was till Sydney-based designer Aheda Zanetti designed the Burkini (see Image 15.1) made of 'manufactured waterproof polyester', and it 'covers the whole body except for the feet, hands, and face'. The idea was so appealing that it caught not only Australia in its rage, but also Dubai, Egypt, Syria, etc. (Chaturvedi 2007).

ISSUES IN GOING INTERNATIONAL—LOCAL OR GLOBAL?

An issue that needs attention when going global is the decision whether to have local brands or to go ahead with a global brand. A local brand is a brand that is available in one country or a limited geographic area (Wolfe 1991). A global brand, on the other hand, is a brand that uses a uniform marketing strategy and marketing mix in all the markets it serves (Levitt 1983). An organization, while marketing brands across boundaries, can either develop different brands for different markets, which leads to a number of local brands in its portfolio that have to be managed, or it can treat the world as one market and offer one brand globally. This leads to the development of few global brands in the brand portfolio, which becomes easier for the organization to manage. The advantages and disadvantages of a global brand have been discussed in the beginning of the chapter.

 See the McDonald's presentation and ads to understand how they strike a balance between local and global.

Advantages of Local Brands

According to Schuiling and Kapferer (2004), the advantages of developing local brands are as follows.

Satisfying local needs   A local brand is designed such that it caters specifically to the needs and wants of the people in a particular geographic area.

Socio-economic factors   The purchasing power of the target audience across different countries can be different, and to capture a wider market, brands at different price points might need to be introduced.

Flexibe pricing   A local brand can be better managed from the pricing aspect, as it does not have any implications on the brand in other country markets. This also helps in tackling price comparisons across country markets and serious issues such as parallel importing can be avoided. Organizations can retail the same brand in different country markets. However, the cheaper prices of the brand in one country can provide lucrative options to retailers, who instead of using the company authorized delivery channels, can import the brands on their own to gain higher profit.

Hedging risks   A portfolio of local brands reduces risks for the organization, as now the risk is divided between all the local brands rather than a few global brands. Also, the failure of a brand in a particular market does not impact the brand image of other local brands in different country markets.

Gaining entry into a new market   In order to gain quick entry into new markets, companies can also acquire a brand from the local market and use it as a platform to sell its brands. For example, when Coca-Cola re-entered India in 1993, it acquired a strong national player, Thums Up, and used its distribution channel to sell its Coca-Cola brand.

Thus, pursuing a local brand strategy does make sense and it can be recommended that an organization maintains a balanced mix of strong local and global brands in its portfolio for increased profitability and reduced risk. To avoid a number of local brands, firms are also following the regional strategy, where brands are developed for a particular market region. The idea is not to have only standardization, i.e., global brands, or only localization, i.e., offering local brands, but to follow both standardization and customization as a strategy, i.e., the 'glocal' approach or the 'think global, act local' approach.

BRANDING STRATEGIES

When firms decide to sell their brands across geographic boundaries and enter new markets, critical and strategic entry decisions have to be made regarding the brand name, brand positioning, and product.

Brand name The brand name is of utmost importance in a global marketplace, where 'local names can add to or destroy the established brand equity' (Aaker 1991). There are ample examples of brands that made gaffes while naming products in foreign markets, such as the classic 'Nova' blunder. Nova in Spanish means 'no go'. And then there was the Coca-Cola name written in Chinese; the Chinese characters representing Coca-Cola meant 'bite the wax tadpole' and were changed to mean 'tastes good and makes you happy' (Zhang and Schimitt 2001). This again calls for careful analysis to see whether to use a global brand name or to give it a local name.

Brand positioning The other important decision is regarding the positioning of the brand. Here again organizations can follow a standardized strategy with a similar image across country markets or they can adapt their positioning strategies. Brands such as Coca-Cola and McDonald's follow a uniform positioning strategy, but Honda's example at the beginning of the chapter supports the need for adaptation.

Product Decisions regarding the product—design, colour, features, warranties, guarantees, etc.—are to be considered while launching a brand in another country. Here again, an organization can adopt either standardization or localization strategies. Products that require technical variations due to differences in different countries in terms of voltage current, tastes, preferences, climatic variations, etc. need to be adapted. For example, in China, due to variations in climate, especially heat and humidity, L'Oreal had to design 'four types of skin balance from north to south and east to west' (Kapferer 2009). If we look at the branding strategy from a local to a global brand, then different strategies can be worked out as shown in Figure 15.1.

A local brand is a brand, whose the product, positioning, and brand name are modified to suit local needs. A global brand, on the other hand, has all the three aspects standardized with

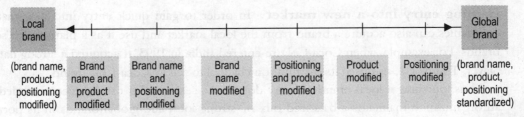

Source: Based on Schuiling and Kapferer 2004; Kapferer 2005; Kapferer 2009.

Figure 15.1 Localization to standardization

a few adaptations in detail. As we move from a global brand towards a local brand, we can have a combination of the strategies as follows.

Positioning modification   In this strategy, the brand name and the product are the same, but the positioning is modified to suit local needs. For example, Levi's has the same brand name and product globally, but modifies the positioning in different countries.

Product modification   Here, the brand name and positioning are the same, but the product is adapted to suit the local requirements. For example, Starbucks, which is famous for its coffee, also retails tea in Japan to cater to the tea-loving consumers there. Henkel's detergent brand (Persil) is sold in Germany, France, and the Netherlands with separate product formulations that address local preferences in each country (Frost 2005).

Positioning and product modification   The brand name is same, but the product has been modified, which might now warrant a different positioning of the same. For example, Henkel's detergent brand (Persil) is sold in Germany, France, and the Netherlands and the product formulations are different to address the local preferences. 'Henkel markets the whiteness of Persil in Germany and France, but in the Netherlands, a green version of the brand was positioned as an environmentally-friendly product' (Frost 2005).

Brand name modification   The same brand name cannot be used everywhere due to issues in translation (as discussed) or due to legal reasons and so it needs to be modified. The product and positioning can be the same. For example, Unilever's brand of margarine retails under the name of Becel in Canada, Promise in US, and Flora in Europe and they are positioned as a healthy heart spread (McMains 2009).

Brand name and positioning modified   If the brand name is modified as discussed above, the positioning might also be required to be changed according the cultural perspectives and perceptions of the consumers in the host country. For example, Tata Indica cars are being retailed in Europe under the brand name of Rover (through an agreement with the MG Rover group of the UK) (PTI 2002).

Brand name and product modified   In some countries, it is possible to continue with a particular positioning strategy, but brand managers still need to identify usage patterns, local requirements of the people, and modify the product along with the brand name accordingly. For example, P&G retails different detergent brands, such as Cheer, Era, Tide, Gain, etc., and in different formats, such as powder, liquid, and bar detergent, according to the washing needs in the different markets.

However, these are not the only considerations while deciding to enter different country markets.

Process of Brand Strategy

Going global consists of a sequence of activities and these can be described with the help of Figure 15.2.

Organizational drivers   The first step is the organizational driver. Organizational drivers are the internal factors in an organization that influence or drive the employees to work towards a specific goal. An organization needs to be committed to sell brands across geographical boundaries. Along with the commitment, there should be resources, monetary and non-monetary, which includes personnel resources also, and the required skill sets to go global.

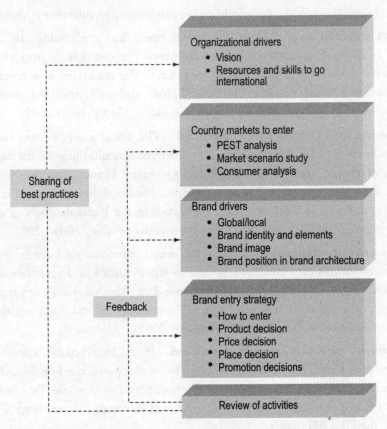

Source: Adapted from Samiee 1994; Aaker and Joachimsthaler 1999; Douglas and Craig 2001; Cateora and Graham 2004; Kotler and Keller 2006.

Figure 15.2 Brand strategy process for a borderless world

Country markets to enter The next stage is to decide which country markets to enter. While studying country attractiveness, the PEST, i.e. political, economic, social, and technological factors (discussed earlier in the chapter), should be studied, along with the consumer analysis—their socio-economic classification and cultural factors. All these help in understanding the need requirements of the consumers, so that the brand offering can be customized accordingly. One important aspect not to be overlooked is the market scenario study or the competitor analysis. The number of competitors present and their offerings will further help in deciding the branding strategies in the particular country market.

Brand drivers After the country market to enter has been decided, the next step is to study the brand drivers. This includes the following.

Global or a local brand As discussed in detail at the start of the section, there are a number of strategies to choose from, and the organization, keeping in mind the country factors, can decide on the strategy to follow.

Brand identity and elements The brand elements that will help in building brand awareness and image have to be designed globally. Here again, the organization can have a uniform logo and brand identity, but aspects, such as celebrity endorsers, packaging, brand name, and slogans, need to be considered for adaptation according to the local requirements. All brand identity and brand element theories need to be applied for the country market and decisions need to be made.

Brand image The brand image that the brand intends to portray is important and a uniform global brand image helps avoid confusion in the minds of the consumers.

Brand position in brand architecture The global/local brand so designed in the different country markets should be according to the brand architecture and should fit in with the same. This positioning will further help the organization in strategizing the brand.

Brand entry strategy The next important step is to decide on the brand entry strategies. This includes how the brand is going to enter the foreign market—through licensing, joint ventures, etc. For example, Starbucks has formed a strategic alliance with Tata Coffee to set up stores in the Tata group's retail outlets (BS Reporter 2011). The four Ps for that particular market also have to be considered.

Product The product to be offered for a particular market needs to be identified and the level of standardization and customization required needs to be evaluated. For example, McDonald's has adapted its product offering according to the different country markets. Thus, in France it retails wine along with the food, in Germany it retails beer also, and in India it retails the McAloo Tikki Burger.

Price Pricing is an important aspect that should be considered while going global. The price of the brand vis-à-vis the competitors in the same market segment communicates with the consumers in terms of prestige, quality, and performance of the brand (Kapferer 2009). The global mobility of the consumers and the availability of information on the Internet make it important to reduce the brand's price variance across country markets. Also, to encourage customers to purchase from company authorized retail outlets and discourage parallel markets, the pricing strategy should be carefully considered in the different country markets. If the price variance is high, then local brand names should be encouraged, so that the brand does not fall in the trap of grey markets.

Place How and where the brand can retail is important. In India, 100 per cent foreign direct investment (FDI) in single brand retail is not allowed and so companies need to think through their brand distribution strategy (see Exhibit 15.4). For example, the German luxury brand Montblanc is a maker of high-end writing instruments and has extended its brand to luxury leather goods, watches, jewellery, cufflinks, etc. It was established in the year 1908 and has been retailing in over seventy countries. Montblanc retains its exclusive image by taking special care of where it is retailing its brand, which is primarily done through exclusive boutiques.

Exhibit 15.4   Ellesse Italia to March into the Indian Market

Ellesse was founded in 1959 by Leonardo Servadio in Perugia, Italy, and draws the name from his initials (L & S, i.e., elle-esse). It started off as a skiwear brand, but then diversified into sportswear. It is now 'part of the UK-based brand management firm, Pentland Group, which also owns other iconic sportswear brands, such as Speedo and Lacoste.' It is a brand that has been endorsed by legendary players like Boris Becker and Muhammad Ali. It is currently retailing in forty-five countries across the globe. In India, it is entering into a five-year licensing deal with S Kumars Nationwide. India is a hot destination for international luxury brands, post the stagnation in consumer demand in most western markets. There are several international sports lifestyle wear brands already wooing the young Indian consumers, such as Reebok Classics, Adidas Originals, Puma, US Polo, etc. Ellesse will be introduced at a premium positioning against Adidas Originals and will be setting up at least five stores to start with. S Kumars has brands such as Belmonte, Reid and Taylor, etc. It became a global player in '2009 by acquiring US-based formal wear company Hartmarx Corporation with Emerisque Brands UK in a deal valued at ₹571 crore. This was followed with a joint venture with the luxury group Louis Vuitton Moet Hennessey (LMVH), giving it the worldwide license to market Donna Karan New York's (DKNY) menswear.' S Kumars Nationwide is looking at the profitable segment of young Indians with a 'desire to dress casually and contemporarily even at the workplace.' Keeping this in mind, it also plans to launch the casual premium brand Kruger, designed by renowned Italian designer Renalto Grande (Fibre2fashion, 2010), for both men and women (Jacob 2011).

Montblanc found it hard to enter the luxury retail space in India and according to Karl-Heinz Handke, President, Western Hemisphere, Montblanc, 'When you go to New York, you go to Madison Avenue, in Paris you go to Avenue Montaigne; in India there is no street you can go to. It is very difficult to find good space or good retail shop.' In India, they operate through sixteen boutiques, mostly located in metros. They are present in hotels, luxury malls such as Emporio in Delhi and UBS in Bangalore and a couple of very well-known jewellers (Rai 2010). Their distribution is very selective and this helps them maintain their exclusive brand image.

Promotion   The manner in which a brand is promoted in different places, the advertising message and the manner of portrayal of the same, and the choice of a celebrity for endorsing the brand are all very important and can impact the brand image (see Exhibit 15.5). It has been studied (Pae, Samiee, and Tai 2002) that consumers prefer locally produced commercials to foreign-sourced ones, therefore, even if global brands are being offered, the advertising should be localized for higher brand familiarity effectiveness.

Review of activities   The review of the strategies over time is very important and it helps the organization to decide about the future course of action. For example, when Timex Group, headquartered in Middlebury, Connecticut (US), entered India in 1992, it formed a joint venture with Titan. Titan was handling the distribution for Timex through 5000 retail outlets, 2500 showrooms, 220 direct dealers, 100 multi-brand outlets, and 20 exclusive showrooms. However, after a few years, Timex broke away from the joint venture and moved from integrated manufacturing to the assembly model. Its product offerings were at the lower price point, less than ₹1000, which was reworked and higher ranges were also included; their price points are now between ₹500 and ₹5000. The watch retail environment was veering towards branded stores. Timex opted for a multi-brand outlet, rather than mono brand stores to provide an exciting shopping experience for customers. These stores are called Time Factory and have grown to seventy in number. Apart from these stores, other store formats being employed to retail the brand are a smaller format version of the Time Factory and kiosks in malls (*The Strategist*, 2010). This can help provide feedback at two levels—at the country market level and at the brand decision level. If the brand is not performing well, the organization can withdraw the brand from the country market or it can rework the brand strategy. The best practices of the brand in different country markets can be shared at the organizational level for the enhancement of knowledge and skills of the employees.

 See ads of McDonald's and how it is a global brand.

Exhibit 15.5   Celebrity Endorsement—Gone Wrong...Or Didn't It?

The use of celebrities to represent brands is a common marketing practice. Accenture, a global giant in the field of consulting, used Tiger Woods as their corporate face since most people were not aware of what Accenture was all about. Their tagline 'Go on. Be a tiger' extolled the corporate virtue of performance and risk taking. This was until Tiger Woods was caught in the bizarre car accident that lead to embarrassing revelations about a series of affairs he had had with other women. Woods was 'no longer the best representative' for Accenture (Arango 2009). Nike decided against dropping Woods and had to face the consequence of its reputation falling from thirty, on the date of the crash, i.e., 27 November 2009, to twenty-one on 11 December 2009, among women over 18 years. Gillette also observed similar trends—its buzz score fell from 21.8 on 27 November 2009 to 15.1 on 4 December 2009, among men more than 18 years old. 'Since the company's announcement that it would limit marketing featuring Woods notably the Fusion MVP razor ads, also featuring Roger Federer and Derek Jeter, scores have rebounded to 20.4.'

Gatorade was smarter and was able to increase the buzz score among men over 18 by announcing on 8 December that 'Tiger Focus sports drink was being phased out'; the buzz score on 8 December was 21.3 and on 11 December it was 25.1.

'However, high-end watchmaker Tag Heuer not only sees a continued role for Tiger in its marketing efforts, but it is also boosting its association with Woods, because of the scandal. But the brand's strategy assumes some interesting cultural stereotypes' (Sauer 2010).

According to Jean-Christophe Babin, President and CEO of TAG Heuer, 'The partnership with Tiger Woods will continue, but we will downscale the use of his image in certain markets for a period of time... We recognize Tiger Woods as a great sportsman, but we have to take account of the sensitivity of some consumers in relation to recent events' (O'Leary 2009). Thus, they dropped Woods in America but realizing that for consumers in China, the success of a man is measured by the number of women he has, TAG Heuer increased the association with Woods. 'In an interview with *The Sydney Morning Herald*, Babin said, 'In China, conversely you have TAG Heuer with Tiger Woods everywhere because (with) the Chinese it rather increases their esteem' (AsiaOne 2010). The strategy seems to be working and sales are strong (Sauer 2010).

CRITICAL FACTORS FOR SUCCESS

The competition globally is heating up with more and more brands viewing the world as their market. Brands can be successful in a particular geographic region, but might struggle in another (see Exhibit 15.6).

Some of the critical factors that need to be kept in mind for global success are as below.

Standardizing and customization   For a global branding success, it has been postulated that at first the core essence of the brand should be standardized across the country markets and then the adaptation and the execution should be carried out as per the country market requirements (de Chernatony, Leslie, Halliburton, Bernath 1995). Once the core brand essence has been standardized, the execution of a global brand image will be relevant and the core values of the brands can be leveraged. Brand managers can easily internalize the brand values and then implement them in different market scenarios.

Support global brand-building process   For global branding success, it is important to have a brand planning process in place and a person in charge of the same to ensure that the brand planning is executed on the global scale. The brand planning process should focus on the strengths of the brand and create sustainable brand advantages. The global brand strategies should be translated into country-specific strategies, so that the brand identity that

Exhibit 15.6   Bottling Pepsi in Morocco

RJ Corp, owned by Ravi Jaipuria, is a ₹3000-crore company with international presence across industries. It has the Indian franchisee rights for Yum! Restaurants International, KFC, Pizza Hut fast food chains, and Costa Coffee. In recent years, it has increased its global presence, especially in Africa, where it is already bottling Pepsi in Mozambique and Zambia. It also operates dairy business in Kenya and Uganda, where it sells packaged milk, milk powder, butter, processed cheese, and yoghurt (Bhushan 2011).

RJ Corp is one of PepsiCo's biggest bottler in South Asia and has acquired its entire franchisee bottling operations in Morocco for about $100 million in February 2011. PepsiCo is a distant second to Coca-Cola in the African market and wants to scale up its presence in Morocco, which has an estimated market size of soft drinks at $1 billion (Bhushan 2011). Table 15.1 shows that 70 per cent of PepsiCo Inc. revenues come from the Americas, whereas for Coke, a majority of its revenue comes from the overseas

markets. The Asian, Middle East, and African markets are clearly dominated by Coca-Cola (Vannucci 2010).

Table 15.1   Revenue from different country markets for Coca-Cola and Pepsi

Region	PepsiCo Inc. Revenue for 2009 (%)	Coca-Cola Co. Revenue for 2009 (%)
Americas	72	39
Europe	16	17
Asia, Middle East, Africa	13	23
Others	0	21

Source: Vannucci 2010.

RJ Corp will have access to the entire North African market and will play a key role in challenging Coca-Cola in Africa, as it will take care of both the manufacturing and distribution of Pepsi.

is reinforced in the different markets is consistent (Aaker and Joachimsthaler 1999). The top management should be committed and provide financial backing to build the brand globally.

Build coherent international brand architecture Brands play a critical role in establishing visibility and position of the firm in international markets. A firm can develop global brands or endorse local country brands with the corporate brand or logo, thus establishing a common image and identity across country markets. While going global, an organization can acquire other brands, form alliances with other organizations to retail their brands, etc. Typically, the firm's international branding strategy is formed through an evolutionary process that results from decisions to enter new country markets or expand product offerings within an existing country. Often, firms make these decisions piecemeal on a country-by-country, product division, or product line basis, without considering the overall balance or coherence of branding in international markets from a strategic perspective. With the spread of information technology and availability of information at the click of the mouse, markets are becoming integrated and consumers are aware of happenings the world over (Douglas and Craig 2001). A coherent and integrated international structure is therefore important, which helps in enhancing the brand equity and leverages the brands in other markets as well.

Assign managerial responsibility 'The firm must decide how to manage brands that span different geographic markets and product lines. It must determine who should have custody of international brands and who is responsible for coordinating their positioning in different national or regional markets, as well as making decisions about the use of a given brand name on other products or services' (Douglas and Craig 2001). The brand management responsibility can be assigned to any one of the following (Aaker and Joachimsthaler 1999).

Management team This includes the top managers who are responsible for formulating the branding strategies and view the brands as key assets for their organization. P&G has a 'global category team', which consists of managers responsible for R&D, manufacturing, and marketing in their region. This team is chaired by the executive vice president who also has a second line job, for example, heading health and beauty aids, along with chairing the hair care global category team. The team meets at regular intervals in a year and is responsible for the implementation of the branding strategy. The idea is to build local brand strength to create strong global brands.

Brand champion A senior executive, possibly the CEO, can serve as the primary brand advocate and nurturer, especially, when the top executive has a passion and talent for brand strategy. For example, Nestlé has a brand champion for each of its corporate strategic brands and just like the leaders in P&G, the brand champion in Nestlé also has a second assignment. The brand champion is responsible for all the brand-related activities such as extension, stretching, etc.

Global brand manager In high-tech and service industries, the top management might lack the branding experience; here, the brand responsibility is passed on to the manager just below the top line managers. In some organizations, they may have authority, but when authority is not provided, the global brand manager needs to create a planning process and convince the top management for support. For example, MasterCard's global brand manager convinced the organization to form a mini-board of six board members and to nominate one of them to be its chair. That person became the brand's voice during board meetings. Companies should be sensitive to the issue of brand management and should provide an environment conducive for the brand manager to work and take decisions. They should train, mentor, and reward employees who can fill this role.

Global brand team   A global brand manager has a lot of responsibility and it can be an uphill task to manage the brand alone. A team, on the other hand, makes it easier for the global brand manager to convince individual country brand managers about the importance of global brand management. The global team can be formed by choosing representatives from different geographic areas at different stages of brand development and different functional areas, such as market research, advertising, promotion, etc. The disadvantage is that as no one person heads the team, the responsibility for strategy implementation cannot be assigned to any one person.

Share best practices   Communication is an important aspect of any strategy. For a global branding strategy, it is essential that the brand communicates with its target audience and with the other internal members involved in the brand-building process as well. Brand managers in different countries should be privy to the information about what worked well or did not work well in other country markets. This is hard work, as in day-to-day practice, the managers have to implement their strategies, and meet deadlines and targets as well. So, it requires a lot of effort in documenting, understanding, and explaining what worked well and what did not, and then there is also the issue of criticism. Companies, therefore, need to build an encouraging environment where the best practices in a country market are highlighted and shared across the organization and different country markets. For example, Frito-Lay holds a 'market university' in Dallas three times a year, wherein marketing directors and general managers meet and discuss their brand concepts for a week. The best practices can be documented and a knowledge bank made available for reference (Aaker and Joachimsthaler 1999).

Create cross-country synergies   In supporting global brand building strategies, a top down approach is advocated, wherein the global brand strategy is delineated and from that flow the country-specific strategies. However, the bottom-up approach is also possible, where the country brand strategies are formulated, from which the global brand strategy is built. In such a case, the cross-country synergies should be created so that the brand strategies in different countries complement each other rather than speak different vocabularies. If a common strategy is not possible, the country strategies can be grouped by similarities. For example, countries in the same level of market maturity, say developed, emerging, etc., or same level of competition, where the brand is a challenger, leader, etc., can be grouped together and the brand strategies in these similar countries should be in line with each other (Aaker and Joachimsthaler 1999). These strategies can be documented for cross-reference when further strategizing in different markets (see Exhibit 15.7).

ETHICAL BRAND POSITIONING

It is imperative for organizations to be ethical to build credibility and long-term brand equity. The brand Satyam was the fourth largest software company in India until 2009, when the

Exhibit 15.7   Kellogg's Brand Learning

Kellogg's has set up Brand Learning, a London-based international specialist consultancy in marketing capability development, an initiative aimed at embedding common working processes across Kellogg's territories. Initially, Brand Learning will develop and lead 'master classes' for Kellogg's portfolio directors and 100 senior managers who are each responsible for a group of brands. Kellogg's subsequently plans to extend it to the entire marketing team. According to Mark Baynes, Chief Marketing Officer at Kellogg's, 'We (are aiming) to create a team inspired, equipped, and enabled to drive stronger returns in this increasingly complex consumer landscape.' According to Harriet de Swiet, the Brand Learning group account director, 'The speed of marketing has changed so much that if you are going to work with global brands, you need people who are all on the same agenda.'

Ford has also developed a similar plan called One Ford to encourage a consistent approach to marketing across regional markets (Charles 2011). Organizations need to develop cross-country synergies for a consistent global marketing strategy and higher brand equity that translates into sales.

exposure of internal fudging of accounts, which 'overstated their books by ₹5000 to ₹6000 crore leading the stock price to inflate and helping the top management make money' (CNN IBN 2009), was made public. The brand took a severe beating and in 2009, Tech Mahindra acquired 31 per cent stake in it and the brand was rechristened Mahindra Satyam. It takes consistent application of resources, in terms of money, time, and effort to build a brand and it can be ruined by the reckless activities of individuals. Following an ethical path is a matter of choice, but working ethically and in the larger interest of the brand will help reap the benefits of the brand for ages.

Thus, a brand that has been painstakingly built over time can be brought to nothing due to the reckless behaviour and ulterior motives of some people in the organization. Managing a brand should intertwine ethical practices into the organizational internal brand-building activities and the organizational culture should motivate employees towards the same. While revitalizing and rejuvenating the brands, special attention should be paid so that brand life along with brand equity is enhanced.

SUMMARY

This chapter focuses on the need for organizations to explore opportunities beyond their geographical boundaries for further growth and profitability of the brand. There are numerous advantages for going global, such as economies of scale, increasing the brand life cycle, availability of brand for globally mobile customers, higher prestige and status, etc. However, just like the two sides of a coin, there are disadvantages as well, such as variation in the needs and wants of consumers, differences in the consumption patterns and consumer responses in different country markets, preference for local brands, and perhaps the irrelevance of a uniform brand image. The firm should look at the politico-economic, socio-economic, social, legal, technological, and cultural factors before deciding its markets. The path to global reach is also not easy and there are challenges that firms can face, such as deciding whether to develop a local or a global brand. The branding strategies to be followed for the brand name, product, and positioning has to be decided by the firms. The steps that help in a systematic global development of the brand have been delineated, starting from organizational drivers, country markets to enter, brand drivers, brand entry strategies, followed by review of activities, feedback, and sharing of best practices. Some critical factors that should be kept in mind for the brands' global footprint such as standardization and customization, support for global brand-building process, building coherent international brand architecture, assigning managerial responsibility, sharing best practices, and creating cross-country synergies have been highlighted. The chapter ends with the need to be ethical in brand practices as this will help reap the benefits of the brand for a longer period of time.

KEY TERMS

Economies of scale   When an increase in the number of goods being produced increases the efficiency of production.

Global brand   A brand that uses a uniform marketing strategy and marketing mix in all the markets it serves.

Local brand   A brand that is available in one country or a limited geographic area.

Localization   Adapting a brand's marketing programme according to the country in which it is to be sold.

Standardization   A brand that follows the same marketing programme across countries.

EXERCISES

Concept Review Questions

1. Why does a brand need to go global? List any five reasons for going global.
2. Discuss the pros and cons of going global.
3. Discuss any two important factors that need to be studied before choosing a country to market the brand. According to you, why are these factors the most important?
4. Delineate the various strategies that organizations can follow while selling the brand in a borderless world.
5. Discuss the organizational drivers and brand drivers in the brand strategy process.

Critical Thinking Questions

1. Critically discuss which one of these factors—socio-economic factor or the cultural factor—is more important while deciding on the marketing strategy of the brand.
2. What strategy would you recommend for managing a brand in the borderless world—local or global? Why?

3. Critically discuss any three key factors for successfully selling a brand globally. According to you, why are these most important?

Internet Exercises

1. Visit the website of Dabur at http://www.dabur.com/ Overseas-International%20Range. Identify the various brands being retailed in the overseas market. What similarities and differences can you draw in the brand elements?
2. Visit the Harley-Davidson websites http://www.harley-davidson.in/harley-davidson-india-our-motorcycles. html (for India) and http://www.harley-davidson.com/ en_US/Content/Pages/home.html (for the US). Try to delineate the brand strategy followed by Harley-Davidson for selling its brand in India.

CD Exercise

Look at the Aditya Birla ad and discuss how the company has managed to 'take India to the World'.

REFERENCES

Aaker, D.A. and E Joachimsthaler, 'The lure of global branding', *Harvard Business Review*, vol. 77, issue 6, 1999, pp. 137–144.

Aaker, D.A 1991, *Managing Brand Equity*, The Free Press, New York.

Arango, T, 'Lost in the Woods—risks of advertising with one-man brand', *The Economic Times*, New Delhi, 15 December 2009, pp. 4.

AsiaOne 2010, 'Tiger still big in China', http://www.asiaone.com/News/Latest%2BNews/Sports/Story/A1Story20100303-202101.html, accessed on 27 February 2011.

B.S. Reporter, 'Tata coffee brings Starbucks to India,' *Business Standard*, 14 January 2011, pp. 1.

Benedict, J., E.M. Steenkamp, R. Batra, and D.L. Alden, 'How perceived brand globalness creates brand value', *Journal of International Business Studies*, vol. 34, issue 1, 2003, pp. 53–65.

Bhushan, R., 'Jaipuria to bottle Pepsi in Morocco', *The Economic Times*, New Delhi 4 February 2011, pp. 1.

Cateora, P.R. and J.L. Graham 2004, *International Marketing*, 12th edition, McGraw-Hill, New York.

Cayla, J. and E. Arnould, 'A cultural approach to branding in the global marketplace', *Journal of International Marketing*, vol. 16, issue 4, 2008, pp. 86–112.

Charles, G., 'Brand new breakfast', *Brand Equity, The Economic Times*, New Delhi, 26 January 2011, pp. 4.

Chaturvedi, A. 2007, 'Bikini turns burkini down under', http://origin-www.ibnlive.com/news/bikini-turns-burkini-down-under/31295-2.html, accessed on 27 February 2011.

Chauhan, C.P., '50 new cars in '11', *The Economic Times*, New Delhi, 5 January 2011, pp. 4.

Craig, C.S. and S.P. Douglas, 'Configural advantage in global markets', *Journal of International Marketing*, vol. 8, issue 1, 2000, pp. 6–27.

De Chernatony, L., C. Halliburton, and R. Bernath, 'International branding—demand- or supply-driven opportunity?' *International Marketing Review*, vol. 12, issue 2, 1995, pp. 9–21.

Douglas, S.P. and C.S. Craig, 'Integrating branding strategy across markets—building international brand architecture', *Journal of International Marketing*, vol. 9, issue 2, 2001, pp. 97–114.

Economic Times Bureau 2011, 'Bach with a bang', *The Economic Times*, New Delhi, 2 February 2011, pp. 4.

Evans, J.R. and B. Berman 2007, *Marketing Management*, Cengage Learning, New Delhi.

Frost, R. 2005, 'Should global brands trash local favourites', http://www.brandchannel.com/features_effect.asp?pf_id=253, accessed on 2 April 2011.

http://www.brandchannel.com/home/category/celebrity-brandmatch.aspx

Jacob, S., 'S Kumars set to launch sportswear brand Ellesse Italia', *The Economic Times*, New Delhi, 26 January 2011, pp. 4.

Kapferer, J.N. 2009, *The New Strategic Brand Management—Creating and sustaining brand equity long term*, Kogan Page, New Delhi.

Kapferer, J.N., 'The post global brand', *Journal of Brand Management*, vol. 12, issue 5, 2005, pp. 319–324.

Kar, S., 'Boro plus more', *The Strategist, Business Standard*, New Delhi 29 November 2010, pp. 4.

Kar, S., 'Second time lucky?' *The Strategist, Business Standard*, New Delhi, 14 February 2011, pp. 2.

Keller, K.L., 2004, *Strategic Brand Management—Building, Measuring and Managing Brand Equity*, Prentice-Hall of India Private Limited, New Delhi.

Kotler, P. and K.L. Keller 2006, *Marketing Management*, 12th Edition, Prentice-Hall of India, New Delhi.

Levitt, Theodore, 'The globalization of markets', *Harvard Business Review*, vol. 61, issue 3, 1983, pp. 92–103.

McMains, A. 2009, 'Unilever shifts Flora/Becel line to DDB', http://www.adweek.com/aw/content_display/news/account-activity/e3i1239cf1a1e13f6239b4fe217-be896b43 accessed on 1 April 2011.

Mitra, M., A.M. Carroll, and V. Mahanta, 'How India Inc is cracking the African market', *Corporate Dossier, The Economic Times*, New Delhi, 20 August 2010, pp. 1.

O'Leary, N. 2009, 'TAG Heuer stands by Tiger Woods—Company said it would continue endorsement deal', http://www.adweek.com/aw/content_display/news/client/e3i992f0a307665b901fac5762aa067a882, accessed on 27 February 2011.

Pai, J.H., S. Samiee, and S. Tai, 'Global advertising strategy—the moderating role of brand familiarity and execution style', *International Marketing Review*, vol. 19, issue 2/3, 2002, pp. 176–189.

PTI 2002, 'Tata Rover in pact to sell Indica in Europe', http://articles.economictimes.indiatimes.com/2002-12-21/news/27343287_1_indica-kevin-howe-tata-engineering, accessed on 2 April 2011.

PTI 2008, 'Axe's chocolate deo ad raises stink with Govt.' http://ibnlive.in.com/news/axes-chocolate-deo-ad-raises-stink-with-govt/71879-3.html, accessed on 1 April 2011.

Rai, A.R., 'It's hard to find luxury retail space in India', *The Strategist, Business Standard*, New Delhi, 22 November 2010, pp. 3.

Samiee, S. 1994, 'Customer evaluation of products in a global market', *Journal of International Business Studies*, vol. 25, issue 3, 1994, pp. 579–604.

Sauer, A. 2010, 'Tag Heuer stays with Tiger Woods in China', http://www.brandchannel.com/home/category/celebrity-brandmatch.aspx, accessed on 27 February 2011.

Schuiling, I. and J.N. Kapferer, 'Real Differences between local and international brands—Strategic implications for international marketers', *Journal of International Marketing*, vol. 12, issue 4, 2004, pp. 97–112.

The Strategist, 'The Indian market is Timex's top priority', *The Strategist, Business Standard*, New Delhi, 9 August 2010, pp. 2.

Vannucci, C. 2010, '2010 will be challenging for PepsiCo', http://news.medill.northwestern.edu/chicago/news.aspx?id=157896, accessed on 28 February 2011.

Wolfe, Alan 1991, 'The single European market—national or euro –brands?' *International Journal of Advertising*, vol. 10, issue 1, pp. 49–59.

Wright, A., 'Technology as an enabler of the global branding of retail financial services', *Journal of International Marketing*, vol. 10, issue 2, 2002, pp. 83–98.

Zhang, S. and B.H. Schimitt, 'Creating local brands in multilingual international markets', *Journal of Marketing Research*, vol. 38, issue 3, 2001, pp. 313–326.

Web resources

http://www.adweek.com/aw/content_display/news/client/e3i35216ec6c243332181ee7bf39ebc99cd, accessed on 27 February 2011.

http://ibnlive.in.com/news/the-inside-story-of-how-satyam-scam-unfolded/83158-7.html, accessed on 25 February 2011.

http://fashiongear.fibre2fashion.com/brand-story/zara/logistics.asp, accessed on 27 February 2011.

http://www.fibre2fashion.com/news/textile-news/news-details.aspx?news_id=86864, accessed on 28 February 2011.

http://www.icmrindia.org/casestudies/catalogue/Business%20strategy1/Business%20Strategy%20Timex%20in%20India.htm, accessed on 1 April 2011.

http://in.reuters.com/article/2007/11/20/idINIndia-30600220071120, accessed on 28 February 2011.

http://www.gsk-ch.in/crocin.aspx, accessed on 23 February 2011.

http://www.burkini.com/, accessed on 27 February 2011.

http://www.bang-olufsen.com/about-us, accessed on 31 March 2011.

CASE STUDY

Keepers of the flame—Taking 'Aditya Birla' to the World*

Introduction

Kumar Mangalam Birla was barely 28 when he took over the Aditya Birla group of companies on the untimely demise of his legendary father, Adita Vikram Birla. The passing away of his father, more than sixteen years ago, in the year 1995, had left a huge void in Kumar Mangalam's heart and a clutch of companies each operating in its own stratosphere.

As a youngster, the son would often goad the father to weave his far-flung empire under one cohesive brand. Aditya Birla was an iconic figure in the Indian industry and

*Dr Pragnya Ram is the Group Executive President, Corporate Communications & CSR of the Aditya Birla Group

what better brand than the much acclaimed and renowned Aditya Birla. But the father would not concede, as he thought it was totally inappropriate and presumptuous. So, the matter was canned until the 53rd birth anniversary of Aditya Birla. On 14 November 1996, Kumar Mangalam Birla paid homage to his father by unveiling the new group logo under the Aditya Birla Group banner. He leveraged upon the uniqueness of his father and the bank of goodwill that came with the legacy.

The corporate logo—The rising sun

The 'rising sun' was chosen as the corporate logo. It was depicted in vibrant, earthy colours and was visually very arresting. The sun rises over two circles: an inner circle, symbolizing the internal universe of the Aditya Birla Group, and an outer circle, symbolizing the external universe. Textured within it is a dynamic meeting of rays converging and diverging between the two. A corporate anthem followed as a sequel to the corporate logo. Captioned as 'Homage to the sun—Aditya vandana', this captivating Sanskrit hymn extols the greatness of the sun and its never-ending journey towards excellence. To make it culturally acceptable, renditions were done.

'Aditya' is the Sun God in the holy scriptures of not only the Hindus, but for people all over. The history of human civilization in Egypt, Babylon, Persia, Peru, Southeast Asia, and so on sees the sun as a source of inspiration, the source of all power. It evokes gratitude, reverence, and at times awe. The sun as an illuminating source and as godhead transcends religions and cultures.

The brilliant radiance and energizing effulgence of the sun—the corporate mark of the group—became a unifying force. In Birla's words, 'the intent at one level was simply to have a group identity that would serve as a corporate logo. We chose the rising sun. That the impact of a symbol can be so enormous is something that took us by surprise. At a time when the organization was going through emotional turmoil, the symbol of the rising sun brought the different parts of the group together, helped us as an organization to re-energize ourselves, cross the bridge, and to get started on the path to change. The learning was quite striking. The need to relate, to belong—to a club, to an association—basically to some sort of fraternity is inherent in all of us. The corporate identity served that need, also as a

proxy for a charismatic leader who was missed greatly. At another level, it made an emotional connect that weaved the group into an integrated whole.'

Brand ownership

In creating the Aditya Birla Group corporate identity, Birla had signalled a new beginning and an expectation that the image should live up to the name Aditya Birla. The Aditya Birla identity used globally is the insignia of the group, the visible recognition of the brand, and a great visual trigger. The corporate identity serves as an umbrella for the group. It signals the common values and beliefs that guide the behaviour in all entrepreneurial activities. It provides a sense of unity, pride, and belonging to all of the employees in whatever function or business area they work. And therefore, everyone tries to live up to the brand in every respect, regardless of the geography in which they work.

A tough slog

In the transformational process and in building the brand identity, the group had to go through a tough slog. Between the times of the father and the son, there was a sea-change in the environment. From an insular protected regime, India, as a nation, was taking its first, albeit hesitant, steps towards liberalization, deregulation, and globalization. For our group, globalization was nothing new, having operated in the open economies of Southeast Asia much earlier. Aditya Birla had a pioneering spirit and had dared to venture into the free economies of Southeast Asia, way back in 1970, when globalization was unheard of in the corporate lexicon.

In the then vibrant and free market Southeast Asian countries, he ventured to set up world-class production bases. He had foreseen the winds of change and staked the future of his business on a competitive, free market-driven economy order. He put Indian business on the globe, twenty-two years before economic liberalization was formally introduced by the then Prime Minister, Narasimha Rao, and the then Union Finance Minister, Dr Manmohan Singh. He set up nineteen companies outside India, in Thailand, Malaysia, Indonesia, the Philippines, and Egypt. Indo Thai Synthetics Company for synthetic yarn manufacture; Thai Rayon Public Company for Viscose Staple Fibre; Thai Acrylic Fibre Company Limited for acrylic fibre; Thai Carbon Black Public Company for carbon black, integral to tyre manufacturing. Besides these, manufacturing companies in the chemical sector set up by him included Thai Polyphosphates and Chemicals Company for sodium phosphates and a joint venture company Thai Peroxide Company Limited with FMC Corporation, US. In Indonesia, he built a significant presence in the textile sector through three major companies—PT Indo Bharat Rayon, PT Elegant Textile Industry, and PT Sunrise Bumi Textiles. In the Philippines, he set up the first Indian Pilipino joint venture with the Indo Phil Group of Companies. In Malaysia, Pan Century Edible Oils and Pan Century Olio Chemical—which were essentially in the palm oil refining sector and production of fatty acids and glycerine—were the companies set up by Aditya Birla.

Envisioning the future

In India, the situation changed dramatically from being production driven in the 'license raj' and quota system, wherein whatever you manufactured would be sold to the customers in a market-driven economy. This was a paradigm shift that entailed a razor-sharp eye on the bottom-line. This was earlier a no-brainer, as the market was controlled. In sum, it meant a change every which way. The change journey began in 1997.

Building an exemplarily meritocratic organization, and unrelentingly working to make the group a great place to work in became a priority. The concept of performance itself underwent a radical change, from hard numbers to include service, quality excellence, employer brand, and talent development. Together, with the board of directors, Birla ushered in a culture of performance management, celebration, and eulogizing success.

At the same time, Birla constructed, deconstructed, and reconstructed businesses. He, supported by the Aditya Birla Management Corporation Limited (ABMCL) Board, evolved a range of non-conformist strategic options, moving into new businesses, along with acquisitions, mergers, restructuring, and ensuring that in every sector that the group operates in, it is perched at the top or among the top three. To do so, he put each of the businesses under the microscope, his rationale being to provide a sharper focus, target resources better, sharpen the competitive edge, and enhance shareholder value. Throughout the group, value creation became the mantra. Simply put, he articulated the group vision—'to be a premium global conglomerate with a clear focus on each business'.

The leadership across several levels in the organization is sharp, smart, quick thinking, has tremendous passion, acts with speed, and is flexible enough to adapt to the ever-changing environment, and ambitious enough to dream audaciously. The goal is to become a $65 billion group by 2015 from $30 billion in March 2011.

Taking Aditya Birla to the world

Over the years, manufacturing plants have been acquired in Canada, China, Indonesia, palm plantations in Laos, mines in Australia, and new plants have been set up in Egypt, Thailand, and China. Alongside, capacities in all of the group's manufacturing units have been expanded exponentially.

In India as well, Birla made major acquisitions, the most notable being the cement division of Larsen & Toubro, Indal from Alcan, and Madura Garments from Coats Viyella. Under his stewardship, the Aditya Birla Group enjoys a position of leadership in all the major sectors in which it operates.

Hindalco, the group's flagship company, through a number of acquisitions coupled with Brownfield and Greenfield expansions, has grown to become a metals behemoth. It is ranked among the world's top five aluminium majors, and Hindalco Novelis is the largest aluminium rolling company globally. Hindalco has thirty-three plants crisscrossing thirteen countries. The acquisition of Novelis in 2007 has taken Hindalco to an altogether new level and it is truly global corporation. It has manufacturing plants in North America—US and Canada, Europe—France, Germany, Italy, Luxembourg, Switzerland, and the United Kingdom. Asia—Malaysia and South Korea, South America—Brazil, and India.

Likewise, in cement, with a spate of acquisitions and consolidating Grasim's cement business with that of

Ultratech, the group in 2008–2009, became the eighth largest cement producer globally and India's numero uno. In the year 2010, the group acquired ETA Star Cement Company in Dubai, together with its operations in the UAE, Bahrain, and Bangladesh. This move too was in line with Birla's long-term strategy of expanding their global presence and taking 'Aditya Birla to the world'.

In the viscose staple fibre (VSF), used in the textile value chain, its position as the largest producer of VSF in the world remains unassailable. The VSF and pulp, the raw material for the fibre, operations are spread in India, Thailand, Indonesia, China, Canada, Laos, and Sweden and VSF business enjoys a 22 per cent share of the global market.

In the acrylic fibre business, the group's companies, Alexandria Fibre Company in Egypt and Thai Acrylic Fibre Company in Thailand, have catapulted the group to become the fifth largest producer of acrylic fibre in the world, with a capacity in excess of 150,000 metric tons annually.

In carbon black, Alexandria Fibre Company in Egypt, Thai Carbon Black in Thailand, Liaoning Birla Carbon in China, and three carbon black plants in western and northern India make it the world's fourth largest producer of carbon black in 2011. In June 2011, it gained the EU regulatory clearance for the acquisition of Columbian Chemicals. This further bolstered its position as the world number one carbon black producer. Carbon black is the most critical ingredient in making tyres for automobiles, besides its use in other sectors.

In India,

- Madura Fashion & Lifestyle is a top fashion (branded apparel) and lifestyle player
- Indian Rayon is the second largest player in viscose filament yarn
- Aditya Birla Chemicals is the second largest in the chlor-alkali sector
- Idea is among the top three telephone companies
- Aditya Birla Financial Services is a leading player in life insurance and asset management
- Aditya Birla More is among the top three supermarket chains in the retail business
- Aditya Birla Minacs is among the top ten BPO companies

Our strategy—Alignment of the communications/brand vision

Envisioning also is an evolutionary process. When the journey began, the first challenge was to build the brand from scratch. Fourteen years down the line, the story is very different. So now as a service-driven, bottom-line oriented, value-adding function, the vision is: 'To make the Aditya Birla Group brand well recognized in the countries in which we operate, by 2015, while continuing to enhance the brand in India, among its multiple internal and external stakeholders'.

Igniting brand passion internally and enhancing brand image externally is necessary for ensuring brand loyalty. To make this happen, a meticulously thought out and carefully crafted strategy has been put in place. The Aditya Birla brand values epitomize the group values—integrity, commitment, passion, seamlessness, and speed. These values form the glue that binds a multi-cultural, diverse set of people across the globe.

That said, as we become more and more global, acquiring new companies, we go to great lengths to examine—what does the name/brand of the acquired company bring to the table. An in-depth research process follows. A perception study of the acquired company brand in the geographies that it operates is done by an external agency among its multiple stakeholders. The findings determine the brand architecture. In case there is no need to reinvent the wheel or fix what is not broken, then it is left as it is.

By a simple act of branding, and taking the acquired company under the Aditya Birla umbrella, we have been able to communicate the change with a great degree of sensitivity, and alongside leverage our brand equity. For instance, Novelis' image has been successfully integrated into the Aditya Birla group image. Our companies, globally, are not regarded as distant appendages of the parent company. As a matter of fact, we work towards global convergence.

We respect the unique culture and diversity that exists in our companies in all the twenty-seven countries where we are present. All of them have one truly major force in common and that is 'the Aditya Birla character' defined by our values.

Open two-way communication

Our strategy rests on proactive, honest, open two-way communication with all of our stakeholders. Our brand delivery continues to reach out through multiple vehicles/ channels. This is germane to the brand building and communication strategy across the world. Globally, while the broad contours are well defined, each company has the leeway to adapt these principles to their local environment. The brand identity and brand usage is non-negotiable. A detailed brand identity manual serves to ensure that the Aditya Birla brand logo is used identically. The group's insignia, which is the rising sun, is clearly recognized globally and is seen in a positive light. A selective view of our strategy includes:

- Leveraging the image of the chairman, the overwhelming respect and admiration that he enjoys as a visionary and values' driven leader, and on these wings raising our brand.
- Rock solid internal communications comprising leadership communications, a vibrant intranet, on-line communication, world-class publications, supporting market communication, and more.
- Enhancing the corporate image identity and reputation management through a multiple of measures and ongoing image measurement.
- Proactively working with the media to ensure honest and balanced reportage on the group.
- The www.adityabirla.com site receives more than 15 lakh page views every month. Having German, French, Spanish, and Arabic websites help build our global brand.
- Investor relations support by using the annual report to beam the group's value creation processes and the highest standards of corporate governance.
- Servicing business sectors, introducing for the first time in the industry, the concept of business communication managers. Members of our team service distinctive businesses and provide them with expertise in communication with all their stakeholders.
- Alongside, one is on the strategy table, providing strategic advice and guiding communications in various companies during restructuring, mergers, acquisitions, and divestments. Here, the chairman specially addresses employees and other stakeholders in the value chain, such as distributors, franchises, and key customers in an unfettered environment, providing total transparency on the moves made.
- Advertising campaigns, TV, press, digital, and sponsorships are part of the process. It is critical is to ensure that the tools that are being used are in sync with the brand image and brand vision.

For the first time in 2011, the group have recoursed to beaming our messages on the best in class, high coverage digital media; for example reuters.com, bloomberg.com, ft.com, and fortune.com. Globally, we have a series of activities that take our brand to an altogether different level. For example, our company Novelis' can recycling programme; globally, Novelis recycles nearly 36 billion aluminium beverage cans, rendering it the world's largest can recycler. The energy saved from one recycled aluminium can will operate a TV set for three hours and is the equivalent to half a can of gasoline. This is not only an awesome environmental conservation effort, but leverages our image as an environmentally sensitive group.

Environment conservation and sustainable development are always on our radar. Social and environmental practices in our group entail the simultaneous creation of economic, environmental, and social value, and taking these practices far beyond compliance. Over the last decade, these measures have been institutionalized. Consequently, these are integrated into our business strategies and in our endeavours to foster inclusive growth as well.

We have purposefully aligned with the best-in-class brand-building/enhancing programmes. These include the setting up of the Aditya Birla India Centre at the London Business School. Its genesis can be traced to the proud Indian who found that though in India excellent management case studies existed, these never made it to the top business schools. To spawn them, our chairman set up this centre with the late Prof. Sumantro Ghoshal as its first director. Likewise, thirteen years ago, to build the Aditya Birla brand at premier institutes, we instituted the Aditya Birla Scholarship Programme at select IIMs, IITs, and BITS, Pilani. Today, with 200 scholars on our roster, the scholarships have become aspirational, and students who are named Aditya Birla scholars say that it is the pull factor in their placements, both in India and globally.

Many case studies on our group have been published. To cite just a few of these in the last one year—*Harvard Business Review* (How Emerging Giants Are Rewriting The Rules of M&A, by Prof. Nirmalya Kumar), in books prescribed for MBA students on the world map—for example, Prof. Bob De Wit and Ron Meyer's book titled *Strategy—Process, Content, Context, an International Perspective, Aditya Birla Group—The Indian Multinational* by Prof. Ashok Som, Associate Dean, ESSEC Business School, Paris. Prof. Pritam Singh and Asha Bhandarker's book titled *In Search of Change Maestros*, a fifty pager on Kumar Mangalam Birla, Prof. Robert H. Rosen's *Just Enough Anxiety—The Hidden Driver of Business Success*, a chapter on Kumar Mangalam Birla.

Through the Aditya Birla Centre for Community Initiatives and Rural Development, our team of 250 people reaches out to 3000 villages, making a qualitative difference to the lives of seven million people, with annual spends that exceed $30 million, running over forty schools and sixteen hospitals. Our focus areas in India are healthcare, education, sustainable livelihood, infrastructure, and espousing social reform. In line with our commitment to sustainable development, we have partnered with the Columbia University in establishing the Columbia Global Centre's Earth Institute in Mumbai. To embed corporate social responsibility (CSR) as a way of life in the organization, we have set up the FICCI–Aditya Birla CSR Centre for Excellence, in Delhi. Likewise, we are engaged in community projects that impact people's lives in Egypt, Asia, North America, and in all places where we have a major presence. However, our companies choose the cause that they wish to identify with, depending on the needs of the local population.

The consistency of our communication has ensured that there is no disconnect between the internal brand enhancing/bonding piece and the external image or messages that we beam. In sum, enhancing the Aditya Birla brand in India and taking it to the world is fixated on three major touch points. The three sides of our brand triangle are fostering a meritocracy based on competency and values that is so enduring to our people within, delivering superior value to our customers, shareholders, and other stakeholders, and transcending the conventional barriers of business to reach out to the underprivileged sections of society in an effort to facilitate inclusive growth.

Today, the group is among India's most respected and admired companies. One believes that monitoring is very vital. After all, what gets measured gets done.

Conclusion

There is reason to cheer as the stakeholders regard Aditya Birla as:

- a global organization (taking India to the world)
- a group that has embraced diversity with a significant absence of monolithic thinking (forty nationalities)
- professionally managed, with an excellent team at the top, led by a dynamic chairman—the best face of the group
- a great employer
- a group with the following most associated values— integrity, trustworthyness, followed by established, global, and future focused
- a group whose products create a bouquet of benefits. They have customized the value chain, escalated innovation, exuded top quality, and delivered a great experience
- a group whose investor relations are a benchmark. The group's pace of growth seems to defy exhaustion. They are making good profits and are extremely focused

And each of these statements is a true reflection of our group's character. In 1995, we reported revenues of $2 billion with ten nationalities and operations in eight countries. In these fifteen years, we have grown fifteen times with revenues nearly $30 billion. Today, our group spans twenty-seven countries, employing people of over forty nationalities, and has bench strength of 1,30,600 committed workforce. Of these, women account for 17 per cent of the managerial and supervisory cadre. We have been voted among the best women-friendly workplaces. Together, all these help us fly our group flag higher and higher.

Though the temptation to wear the cat-that-ate-the-canary smile is lurking, one of the greatest lessons we have learnt in our group is that complacency is death. So collectively, the push to take our Aditya Birla brand to an even higher peak will be more forceful. Encouragingly, the keepers of the flame are everywhere!

Discussion Questions

1. Comment on the adoption of the rising sun as the corporate logo globally.

2. Drawing information from the case and the website of Aditya Birla group—http://www.adityabirla.com/ our_companies/our_companies.htm, comment on how the brand has been able to manage its international operations and grow globally.

3. 'The group has adopted brand standardization strategy while going global'. Do you agree with this statement? Give reasons, why or why not?

Index

Related Titles

SALES AND DISTRIBUTION MANAGEMENT, 2/e

Tapan K. Panda, Great Lakes Institute of Management Studies, Chennai and **Sunil Sahadev,** University of Sheffield, UK

The second edition of Sales and Distribution Management is a comprehensive textbook, which has been updated and enlarged with new chapters. Specially designed to meet the requirements of management students specializing in sales and marketing, it gives a balanced presentation of the concepts of sales and distribution through examples and cases. Readers will find this textbook highly useful for its application of theoretical concepts explained through illustrative corporate examples and cases.

9780198077046 | Paperback | 748 Pages

SERVICES
Marketing, Operations, and Management

Vinnie Jauhari, IIMT, Gurgaon and **Kirti Dutta,** BULMIM, Delhi

Services: Marketing, Operations, and Management explores core concepts of the service industry and uses numerous examples, exhibits, flowcharts, and illustrations to explain them. Key contemporary issues such as impact of technology, managing quality and excellence, ethics in service marketing, and strategies for business growth are explored in detail, as well as overview of emerging service sectors. Management students will find this book highly useful for its explanation of key concepts through industry-related examples. It will also be useful to professionals in service industry due to its practice-oriented approach.

9780195689082 | Paperback | 604 Pages

RETAIL MANAGEMENT, 2/e

Chetan Bajaj, Fellow IIM-B, **Rajnish Tuli,** Millward Brown, and **Nidhi Varma Srivastava,** Millward Brown

The second edition of Retail Management is a comprehensive textbook, which has been extensively updated with new chapters and case studies. Specially designed to meet the requirements of management students specializing in marketing, it presents the key concepts of retail management through examples and cases. Users will find this textbook highly useful for its application of theoretical concepts explained through illustrative examples, relevant cases, clear illustrations, and excellent selection of descriptive photographs.

9780198061151 | Paperback | 800 Pages

MARKETING RESEARCH

Sunanda Easwaran, IBS-Mumbai and **Sharmila J. Singh,** GFK Mode India, Mumbai

Marketing Research is a comprehensive textbook specially designed to meet the needs of management students. It combines the quantitative and qualitative aspects of marketing research, and addresses its utility for both the researcher and the end-user. It provides in-depth coverage of key elements of the subject: its theoretical foundations, techniques of planning and design, research methodology for implementation of quantitative and qualitative techniques, presentation and interpretation of findings through reports, and use of marketing research techniques for developing and evaluating marketing strategies.

9780195676969 | Paperback | 604 Pages

Other Related Titles

- 9780195689099 Joshi: International Business
- 9780195671230 Joshi: International Marketing (with CD)
- 9780195667585 Apte: Services Marketing
- 9780195677942 Ghosh: Industrial Marketing
- 9780198072027 Mallik: Sales Management

- 9780198075943 Sinha ar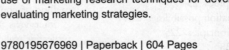g Retailing, 2/e
- 9780198069843 Kulkarni, Jahirabadkar, and Chande: E-business
- 9780198074120 Jethwaney & Jain: Advertising Management 2/e